ISBN 978-0-260-02655-2
PIBN 10923135

THE BABYLONIAN EXPEDITION

OF

THE UNIVERSITY OF PENNSYLVANIA

SERIES A: CUNEIFORM TEXTS

EDITED BY

H. V. HILPRECHT

VOLUME XVII, PART 1

BY

HUGO RADAU

"ECKLEY BRINTON COXE, JUNIOR, FUND"

PHILADELPHIA

Published by the Department of Archaeology, University of Pennsylvania

1908

¶ The Editor determines the material to constitute a volume and reports to the Committee of Publication on the general merits of the manuscript and autograph plates submitted for publication; but the Editor is not responsible for the views expressed by the writer.

LETTERS

TO

CASSITE KINGS

FROM THE

Temple Archives of Nippur

BY

HUGO RADAU

Sixty-eight Plates of Autograph Texts. Twelve Plates of Halftone Reproductions

---

PHILADELPHIA

Published by the Department of Archaeology, University of Pennsylvania

1908

MacCalla & Co. Inc., Printers
C. H. James, Lithographer
Weeks Photo-Engraving Co., Halftones

To

Mrs. Sallie Crozer Hilprecht

My Benefactress

As a very small token of profound and lasting gratitude

PREFACE

About the same time when the children of Israel were invading the land of Canaan preparatory to their final conquest these letters (DUB^{mesh}) were inscribed on clay. They form part of the "Temple Archives" ($DUB\ MU^{mesh}$) of the Cassite period, situated on the west side of the Shatt-en-Nîl. In all probability these Archives were found in one or several buildings (connected with each other), known as the *É.DUB shá É.GAL* and including the Temple Library and the Temple School. The Cassite Kings at this time were the chief administrators of the affairs of the Temple of *Enlil* at Nippur; for they are known by the title *shakkanakku Enlil*, characterizing them as the representatives of Enlil on earth, who had "to put the seal" (*kanâku*) of the god to each and every transaction made by and for the Temple. Nothing could be done without their consent, approval, or authority (seal). While the "Temple Archives" proper give us a picture of **the business methods** of the Temple administration, under the chief supervision of the King, these letters represent **the correspondence about those methods.**

Among them we find complaints from governors about non-delivery or delay in the delivery of goods by the chief bursar of the Temple, medical reports about the sickness of certain ladies connected with the sanctuary, complaints about goods asked for, but not received, accounts of the disposition of taxes gathered, requests for wages, building material, food, clothing, and the like.

The Temple of *Enlil* being a richly endowed institution, royal officers kept watch over its proper administration and welfare and reported about the various affairs of *Enlil's* property to his earthly representative, the King. Thus we find reports about the deplorable condition of canals, about the prospects of the harvests on the fields belonging to the Temple, about building operations with suggestions as to desirable improvements, about certain expeditions undertaken in defence of *Enlil's* earthly possessions, etc.

Though most of these letters are addressed to the "Lord," *i.e.*, the "King" who had his residence at least temporarily in Nippur, some of them may be classified as part of an "official correspondence between Temple or State officers." There are even letters in these archives written by the kings themselves (comp. Nos. 75 and 93).

This collection of official letters from Nippur forms an exact parallel to the letters from the so-called Kuyunjuk collection of Nineveh, which constitutes the remains of the famous library of King *Ashshur-bân-apal* excavated by Layard and Rassam.

The letters here published have been copied during the winter of 1906–07 from the originals to be found in the Babylonian Museum of the University of Pennsylvania. Nos. 33*a*, 59*a*, 60*a*, 73*a* and 95–99 have been added after the plates had been arranged and prepared for the press (November, 1907). With the exception of three (Nos. 33*a*, 84, 85) these letters are mostly fragmentary, badly damaged, and poorly preserved. This being the case, it was my aim to reproduce, as nearly as possible, all the marks and wedges of every sign in question, bearing in mind that a reliable copy *must* and *ought to be* an *exact reproduction* of the "*original*" as it presents itself to the eyes of the copyist, and not of his "thoughts" or of what he "expects" to find in a particular passage. This principle having been strictly adhered to, I came to the result that the following signs are used interchangeably: (1) *di* and *ki*; (2) *lì*, *bi*, *ni*, *ir*, *lit*, *sha*; (3) *ib*, *ur*, *lu*; (4) *ish*, *ma*, *ba*, *zu*, *shag* (*libbu*), *su*; (5) *ku*, *shú*, *lu*; (6) *im*, *aḫ*, *a'*, *mur*; (7) *du*, *ush*, *ta*, *shá*, *ra*; (8) *az*, *ug*; (9) *ad*, *ṣi*, *mir*; (10) *be*, *nu*; (11) *al*, *shil*, etc., etc.

As the texts here submitted have been written by more than fifty scribes, and as each scribe has his own peculiar *ductus*, I tried to imitate that *ductus* in the best manner possible. This is the reason—apart from the copyist's own ability of writing cuneiform signs—for the varied execution of the copy of the letters here published. The copyist, in fact, did not try to give in the following pages an exhibition of his ability in copying inscriptions, but he rested content with a faithful reproduction of *all* the peculiar characteristics of the *ductus* of the several scribes. After the letters had been copied and translated, the copy was once more compared with the originals. In this wise I flatter myself to have obtained an absolutely reliable copy. It is, therefore, the fond hope of the copyist that the prospective decipherer will not commit a mistake like the one the writer of No. 45 complains of when he writes to his "Lord": "I have written concerning 'pots' that they be brought down, but they were 'straw'! What for has my 'Lord' sent this?" The "Lord's" order-filler misread apparently the two signs: ^{mesh} = *KAN.NI*^{mesh} – *diqarâti* = "pots" for ^{mesh} = *IN*^{mesh} = *tibnu*^{mesh} (Hebr. תֶּבֶן) = "straw"!

These letters forming, so to speak, the connecting link between those of the Ḫammurabi and Amarna periods on the one hand and those of the later Assyrian and Babylonian on the other, it is, of course, quite natural to find that they show the several characteristic features of the periods mentioned. Thus the sign *PI* is still used, at least sometimes, for *wi*; a *ṭ* does not yet exist; we have *di-im*, *te-e-ma* and *NE-ma*. The latter ought to be transcribed rather by *de-ma* than by *ṭe-ma*. The *q* begins to make itself felt in quite a good many instances. Yet, wherever *ki* is written for *qi*, I transcribed accordingly.

It will be noticed that I read the name *NIN.IB Errish*(*t*). This reading I am still prepared to maintain, not only on account of the gloss *urash*, but also on account of the identity of ^{ilu}*NIN.IB* and ^{ilu}*Er*(*r*)*ish*, see *The Monist*, Vol. XVII, No. 1 (Jan., 1907), p. 142. The Aramaic transcription of *NIN.IB* is not אנרשת but אנושת, as is now beyond question, it being plainly written in the latter fashion on several unpublished tablets in Constantinople, and also on an ostracon from Nippur preserved in the Babylonian Section of the Museum of the University of Pennsylvania (private communication of Prof. Hilprecht; see also p. 41, note). אנושת apparently does not represent the *pronunciation* (this is *Errish*(*t*)), but an *attribute* of ^{ilu}*NIN.IB* and all those gods who, in the Babylonian ''Trinity in Unity,'' at one time or another, played the rôle of the ''Son.'' It is, therefore, not exclusively confined to ^{ilu}*NIN.IB*, the ''Son'' of ^{ilu}*En-lil*. I propose to read אנושת = *en usâti* = ''*lord of help*,'' an attribute ascribed, among others, also to ^{ilu}*Marduk*, the ''Son'' of ^{ilu}*É.A*; cf. the *nom. propr.* ^{m} ^{ilu}*Marduk-en-usâti*, quoted by Delitzsch, *H. W. B.*, p. 107*b*, under *usâti*. Instead of *usâti* we find, at the time of the Cassites, also the writing *ú-za-ti*, cf. *B. E.*, XIV, 125 : 12, ^{m}*En-ú-za-ti*, a noteworthy peculiarity which shows that *usâti*, *uzâti* has to be connected with the Sumerian *A.ZU* = *âsû* = ''*helper, physician*.'' We know that ^{ilu}*IB* (gloss *urash*) is = ^{ilu}*NIN.IB* (see *Bêl, the Christ*, p. 16, note 8; p. 18, III; p. 19, 2), but *IB* (gloss *urash*) is also = *barû* (II R. 62, 36*a*), and *barû* is = *A.ZU* (Reisner, *Hymnen*, p. 7, 18. 19). From this it follows that *IB* = *A.ZU*, and ^{ilu}*NIN.IB* = ^{ilu}*NIN.A.ZU* (cf. II R. 57, 51*a*,*b*, where the star (*mul*) ^{ilu}*NIN.A.ZU* is identified with ^{ilu}*NIN.IB*). Again, ^{ilu}*IB* is also = ^{ilu}*MASH*, but *mash* changes with *másh*, cf. *mash-pad* = *másh-pad* (*E. B. H.*, p. 256, note 16); *mash-shu-gid* (Cyl. A 20 : 5) = *másh-shu-gid* (Cyl. A 12 : 16, 17), and *másh* is likewise = *barû* = *A.ZU*. I take, therefore, אנושת to stand for אן = *en* = *NIN*, and ושת = *usâti* = *uzâti* (the abstract for the concrete noun) = *A.ZU* = *IB* = *MASH*. In other words, ^{ilu}*IB* or ^{ilu}*MASH* is ''*the helper*,'' ''*the physician*'' (hence the *patron god* of the physicians), and ^{ilu}*NIN.IB* or ^{ilu}*NIN.A.ZU* the ''*lord of help*,'' the ''*helping lord*.'' As such a ''*lord of help*'' he is the veriest ''*Saviour*''—a saviour that saves not only from bodily or(!) spiritual harm (notice that sickness is the result of the evil spirits within a person; if these demons are cast out, the sick person recovers!), but also one who delivers mankind from death, destruction, and the grave. He is the ''merciful one" (*rêmênû*, K 128 = Jensen, *Kosm.*, p. 470), the "merciful god" (*ilu rêmênû*, I R. 17 : 19), the "one who gives life" (*qa-ish TI.LA*, I R. 17 : 19), "who gives the spirit of life" (*qâ'ish napshâti*, Jensen, *l.c.*), "who quickens the dead" (*muballit me[tûti]*, Jensen, *l.c.*), who delivers the dead out of the nether world: "who has been brought down into the nether world, his body thou bringest back again" (*sha ana arallê shûrudu pagarshu tuterra*, *Bêl, the Christ*, p. 45, note 2; cf. ψ xlix. 15, "God will redeem my soul from the power of Sheol"; or ψ xvi. 10, "For thou will not leave my soul to Sheol").

From these considerations it follows that the "Son" of the Nippurian Trinity (*Enlil—NIN.IB—NIN.LIL = Bau*) was the prototype not only of Nin.Girsu in the Girsu Trinity (*Enlil—Nin.Girsu—NIN.LIL = Bau*) or of Marduk in the Eridu Trinity (*É.A—Marduk—Damkina = Sarpanitum*), but even of Christ in the Christian Trinity (Father—Son—Holy Spirit); in each and every case the "Son" was the *Saviour*, the *en usâti*; hence Christ was rightly called the "Jesus" and was greeted, when entering Jerusalem, with joyful "*Hosannahs*," הושיע־נא, "Save (now, O Lord)!"

While writing this Preface, there lies before me a copy of "The so-called Peters-Hilprecht Controversy." Prof. Hilprecht's critics make so much ado about the "probable" place of *provenance* of the so-called *Lushtamar* letter, all of them claiming that if the envelope were opened and the contents read, its place of origin would be settled for all time to come. This very clamor proves better than anything else that those gentlemen never have read a Babylonian letter! To help clear the atmosphere a little in this respect, I may be permitted to say a few words about the place of origin of letters in general.

1. In no letter thus far published is there ever found an absolute *reliable indicium* about its place of origin. The only thing in a letter which might possibly help solve such a question is the so-called *invocation* frequently found after the address. If, *e.g.*, for the protection of his correspondent, a writer invokes certain gods worshipped in a certain city, it is *probable* that that writer hailed, resp. sent, his letter from that city the gods of which he invoked. Cf. here No. 89, where the writer *Pân-AN.GAL-lu-mur* invokes the gods of *Dûr-ilu* for the protection of the addressee; hence the *probability* is that the writer hailed and wrote from *Dûr-ilu*. But this, as I said, is and must remain a *probability only*, for we find in the letters here published another example in which the writer invokes the gods of Nippur. This letter (No. 38) has likewise been found in Nippur. Now it is not at all likely that the writer, when sending his letter to the "Lord" at Nippur, was *himself in Nippur*. If he were, he would most assuredly have appeared before the "Lord" in person, thereby saving himself the trouble of writing a letter, which had to be baked, encased in an envelope,

addressed, sealed and handed over to a messenger in order to be delivered. What then is the inference from this invocation? Does the invocation prove that the letter was sent *from Nippur to Nippur*, where it was found? Such a thought would be simply ridiculous. All we can say is this: the writer of No. 38, because he invokes the gods of Nippur, was in all probability a Nippurian, but was *away* from Nippur when writing that letter. The invocation of that letter, then, does not prove anything at all with regard to the place *whence* that letter has been sent.

2. Prof. Hilprecht has some very good, convincing, and absolutely reliable reasons why he assigns the *Lushtamar* letter to the business or administrative section of the Temple Library of Nippur. We believe his words a thousand times more than those of his accusers, which, at the very best, are merely hearsay. In fact, his critics have absolutely nothing to bring forward in corroboration of their claim that "the *Lushtamar* letter did not come from the ruins of Nippur, but from those of Sippar." In corroboration of this hearsay talk Prof. Hilprecht's critics now point out that the seal impression of the *Lushtamar* letter mentions certain persons who are known from tablets that have been found at Sippar. What is there on the envelope of the *Lushtamar* letter to justify such a strange conclusion? Besides the address "to *Lushtamar* (*a-na Lu-ush-ta-mar*)", I find a seal impression which reads: *Ilu-shú-Ba-ni dam-qar* | *mâr I-bi-*^{ilu}*NIN.SHAḪ* | *ardi* ^{ilu}*NIN.SHAḪ-ge.* The same persons occur again on a tablet published in *B. E.*, VI^1, 50 : 19, 20, which tablet was "probably" excavated in Sippar. The critics draw the conclusion, it seems, that, because the same persons occur on both tablets (the *Lushtamar* letter and *B. E.*, VI^1, 50), and because *B. E.*, VI^1, 50, was "probably" found in Sippar, the *Lushtamar* must have been found in Sippar likewise. But can anyone imagine that *Ilu-shú-Ba-ni*, *a resident of Sippar*, would write to *Lushtamar*, *another resident of Sippar*, which he must have done if the letter had been found at Sippar? If *Lushtamar* had been a resident of Sippar, like *Ilu-shú-Ba-ni*, is it not much more probable that the latter would have gone in person to the former and communicated to him his wishes orally? Instead of this contention being against Prof. Hilprecht, it much rather speaks decidedly for him. We may admit that the *Ilu-shú-Ba-ni* of the *Lushtamar* letter and the *Ilu-shú-Ba-ni* of *B. E.*, VI^1, 50, are both one and the same person; we also may admit that both were residents of Sippar; but from this it by no means follows that the *addressee*, Mr. *Lushtamar*, lived likewise in Sippar. On the contrary, the fact that *Ilu-shú-Ba-ni*, a possible inhabitant of Sippar, did *write* to *Lushtamar* would prove *a priori* that the latter was *not* a resident of Sippar, but was, as Prof. Hilprecht, for reasons given in his "Controversy," quite rightly and correctly claims, a resident of Nippur.

In conclusion, I must apologize to the Editor and the Publication Committee for the length of the Introduction to the letters here published. In view of the extraordinary importance of these letters for the history, religion, language, grammar, and lexicon of the Babylonians, but more especially for a correct understanding of the terms "Temple Archives," "Temple School" and "Temple Library," it was absolutely necessary that the wrong impressions created by those who hold a contrary view should be set aright. If I have done nothing else but created a basis upon which to reconstruct the system of administration, education, and worship of the Babylonians at 1500 B.C., I shall be more than repaid for my labors in connection with this volume.

It only remains to thank here the Provost of the University, Dr. C. C. Harrison, and the Director of the Museum of Science and Art, Mr. S. F. Houston, for their hospitality, kindness, and courtesies shown to me during my sojourn in the Museum. To express my gratefulness to Mr. Eckley Brinton Coxe, Jr., through whose generosity the Museum is enabled to publish the following pages, gives me special pleasure. I am sure I voice the sentiments of all Assyriologists when I say that this noble and unselfish benefactor erects by these publications, the elegance of which is not attained by any other similar works, much less surpassed, an everlasting monument upon which all scholars look with admiration and gratefulness. To my friend and teacher, Prof. Dr. H. V. Hilprecht, who so generously and freely assisted me in words and deeds during the course of the preparation of this volume, whose valuable time, profound scholarship, and learning were at all times most abundantly at my disposal, who not only read the proof-sheets, but who constantly and continually helped me most liberally with his valuable advice, I am especially most grateful. I only hope and pray that the work of the pupil may be worthy of the master. It is a special delight to be able to express publicly my sincere gratitude to Mrs. Sallie Crozer Hilprecht for her most generous benefactions bestowed upon me during the last two years while here in Philadelphia. Were it not for her help I never could have written this book. May she graciously condescend to accept this work as a very small token of my profound and lasting gratitude.

HUGO RADAU.

Philadelphia, Pa., May 1, 1908.

LIST OF ABBREVIATIONS.

A. F. ..Hugo Winckler, *Altorientalische Forschungen.*

A. J. S. L. L. "The American Journal of Semitic Languages and Literatures," edited by R. F. Harper.

A. P. Bruno Meissner, *Beitrage zum Altbabylonischen Privatrecht.*

A. S. K. T Paul Haupt, *Akkadische und Sumerische Keilschrifttexte.*

B. A *Beitrage zur Assyriologie und vergleichenden Semitischen Sprachwissenschaft*, edited by Friedrich Delitzsch and Paul Haupt.

B. E. "The Babylonian Expedition of the University of Pennsylvania," edited by H. V. Hilprecht.

Bel, the Christ Hugo Radau, "Bêl, the Christ of Ancient Times."

C. B. M "Catalogue of the Babylonian Collections in the Archaeological Museum of the University of Pennsylvania," prepared by H. V. Hilprecht.

Creation Story Hugo Radau, "The Creation Story of Genesis I, a Sumerian Theogony and Cosmogony."

C. T. ."Cuneiform Texts from Babylonian Tablets, etc., in the British Museum." Printed by order of the Trustees.

E. A. H. ."The E. A. Hoffman Collection of Babylonian Tablets in the General Theological Seminary, New York City."

E. B. H. Hugo Radau, "Early Babylonian History."

H. .R. F. Harper, "Assyrian and Babylonian Letters belonging to the K Collection of the British Museum."

H. L ..L. W. King, "The Letters and Inscriptions of Hammurabi."

H. W. B. ..Friedrich Delitzsch, *Assyrisches Handworterbuch.*

J. A. O. S. .."Journal of the American Oriental Society."

J. R. A. S. .."Journal of the Royal Asiatic Society."

K. ..Kuyunjuk Collection.

K. B ..*Keilinschriftliche Bibliothek*, edited by E. Schrader.

L. C. L. ..C. H. W. Johns, "Babylonian and Assyrian Laws, Contracts, and Letters."

L. S. S. ..*Leipziger Semitistische Studien*, edited by A. Fischer and H. Zimmern.

O. L. Z. ..*Orientalistische Litteratur-Zeitung*, edited by F. E. Peiser.

P. ..F. E. Peiser, *Urkunden aus der Zeit der dritten Babylonischen Dynastie.*

P. S. B. A. .."Proceedings of the Society of Biblical Archaeology."

R. .."The Cuneiform Inscriptions of Western Asia," edited by Sir H. C. Rawlinson.

S. A. K. I. ..F. Thureau-Dangin, *Die Sumerischen und Akkadischen Konigsinschriften.*

U. A. G. ..Hugo Winckler, *Untersuchungen zur altorientalischen Geschichte.*

Z. A. ..*Zeitschrift fur Assyriologie und verwandte Gebiete*, edited by C. Bezold.

CONTENTS.

TIME AND AGE OF THE LETTERS.

All the tablets here published are *Letters—DUB, dup-pi, dup-pa, IM.* They were excavated in Nippur during the second to fourth expeditions[1] of the University of Pennsylvania (1889 1900), and form part of the so-called *Temple Archives*[2] of Nippur, partly published by Clay, *B. E.*, XIV and XV. The facts that these letters were found, when unpacked by Prof. Hilprecht, intermingled with the tablets of *B. E.*, XIV and XV, which are all dated in the reign of certain *Cassite Kings*, that they are of the same peculiar "color of clay," have the same "form" and "writing" as those of the Temple Archives, would, *a priori*, make it reasonably certain that we have to assign them to the Cassite period. Apart from these *criteria* there are others which prove, beyond a doubt, that the letters here published did, and actually do, belong to the reigns of either one or the other of the following Cassite kings (see Hilprecht, *B. E.*, XX[1], p. 52, note 1):

Kings.	Reigned according to "List of Kings."	Last Year found on Nippur Tablets	About
Burna-Buriash II		25 (or 27[3])	1450–1423 B.C.
....			
Kuri-Galzu[4] II	25	23[5]	1421–1396 B.C.
Nazi-Maruttash (son)	26	24[6]	1396–1370 B.C.
Kadashman-Turgu (son)	17	16[7]	1369–1352 B.C.
Kadashman-Enlil II (son)	[1]1 or [1]2	6[8]	1352–1340 B.C.
Kudur-Enlil (1st(?) son)	6(?) (Notice discrepancy!)	8(!)[9]	1339–1331 B.C.
Shagarakti-Shuriash (2d(?) son)	13	12(!)[10]	1331–1318 B.C.
Kashtiliashu II (son)	8	6[11]	1317–1309[12] B.C.

[1] Cf. Hilprecht, *B. E.*, Series D, Vol. I, pp. 289–568. For the second expedition see also Peters, *Nippur*, Vol. II, p. 188.

[2] "Temple Archives," to mention it here, were called at the time when all these documents were written: *DUB MU*^{mesh}, *DUB shú-ma-(a-)ti*, *DUB.SHA.RA*, *DUB MU.BI.IM*, *DUB GISH*, *DUB za-kar-tum*. For a discussion of these terms see below under "Results," p. 83.

[3] The last year thus far known was the 25th. Cf. *B. E.*, XIV, 9 : 5ff. ^{arhu}*ENGAR.GAB.A ûmu* 10^{kam} *shattu* 25^{kam} *Bur-na-Bu-ri-ia-ásh LUGAL-E*. But Prof. Hilprecht informs me that Burna-Buriash II seems to have ruled

Among these *criteria* and *indicia* may be mentioned (*a*) that the *persons* introduced in these letters are to be found—to a great extent at least—also in the dated documents of the Temple Archives. The following few examples will illustrate it.

^{m}*In-na-an-ni*, who figures so conspicuously in the texts of *B. E.*, XIV, as one who transacts (*i-na qât*) the business of the Temple's storehouses at Nippur and elsewhere[13] during the 18th,[14] 21st,[15] and 23d[16] year of Kuri-Galzu[17] and the 1st[18] and 2d[19]

at least twenty-seven years, according to a fragmentary tablet of the Cassite period recently catalogued by him (No. 12907), which though insufficiently dated: "Shabâtu, 12th day, 27th year," according to internal evidence must be assigned to the reign of Burna-Buriash or Kuri-Galzu, in all probability to the former. After an examination of the personal proper names occurring on this tablet I agree entirely with Prof. Hilprecht's conclusions.

[4] That this Kuri-Galzu has to be identified both with "Kuri-Galzu, the son of Burna-Buriash," and with "Kuri-Galzu *siḫru*, the son of Kadashman-Harbe," will be shown below *sub* "Chronology," pp. 63ff.; hence the "gap" between Burna-Buriash and Kuri-Galzu.

[5] *B. E.*, XIV, 38 : 15f. [^{arhu} .] *ûmu* 16^{kam} *shattu* 23^{kam} ^{ilu}[*Kur*]-*e*-[*Ga*]*l-zu*.

[6] *B. E.*, XIV, 86 : 15f. (Case) ^{arhu}*ASH.A.AN* *ûmu* 17^{kam} *shattu* 21^{kam} *Na-zi-Mu-ru-ut-ta-ásh*.

[7] *B. E.*, XIV (pl. 61), 114*a* (= E. A. H., 179): 51. ^{arhu}*SHEG.GA* *ûmu* 3^{kam} *shattu* 16^{kam} *Ka-dàsh-man-Tur-gu*.

[8] For this ruler see Clay, *B. E.*, XIV, p. 4, and *l.c.*, No. 116 : 8ff ^{arhu}*ASH.A.AN* *shattu* 6^{kam} ^{ilu}*Ka-dàsh-man*-^{ilu}*En-lil*.

[9] This is the last year mentioned in the published texts from the Temple Archives that I can find. Clay, *B. E.*, XIV, pp. 3, 71 (whom Hilprecht, *B. E.*, XX^{1}, p. 52, note 1, follows), gives the year 9 as the last, referring to *l.c.*, No. 124 18f. But here we have clearly the year 8, for we read, ^{arhu}*SHE* *shattu* 8(?)^{kam} ^{ilu}*Ku-dùr-ri*-^{ilu}*En*-[*lil*]. Cf. here *l.c.*, 123 : 21 and *P.* 135 : 22—both of which are likewise dated in the 8th year.

[10] Hilprecht, *B. E.*, XX^{1}, p. 52, note 1, has shown that the tablet *B. E.*, XIV, 139, is not dated from the 22d (Clay, *l.c.*, pp. 3, 72), but from the 2d year; hence the last recorded date is found in *B. E.*, XIV, 138 : 32, ^{arhu}*GAN* *ûmu* 10^{kam} *shattu* 1[2](cf. l. 2)^{kam} *Shá-ga-ra-ak-ti-Shur-ia-ásh* *LUGAL*. Cf. also *P.* 111 : 15 | 131 : 18, and especially 87 : 14ff. [^{arhu}]*ENGAR.GAB.A* *ûmu* 5^{kam} [*shattu*] 12^{kam} [*Shá-gar*]-*ak-ti-Shur-iá-àsh* (= 6) [*LU*]*GAL KI-SHAR-RA* (= *kishshati*).

[11] *B. E.*, XIV, 144 : 9 [*shattu*] 6^{kam} *Kash-til-ia-shú* *LUGAL-E*. For the pronunciation of *Bi* as *Kash* in this name, cf. Thureau-Dangin in *O. L. Z.*, 15th February, 1908, *Sp.* 93.

[12] Or possibly about 1296–1289 B.C. Cf. III *R.* 4, No. 2 (Sennacherib's capture of Babylon, *i.e.*, either the first (702 B.C.) or the second (689 B.C.) took place), "600 years after Tukulti-NIN.IB," who reigned seven years over Babylon, following immediately upon Kashtiliashu.

[13] *E. g.*, *Za-rat-IM*^{ki}, *B. E.*, XV, Nos. 3, 63, 86. *Kâr*-^{ilu}*NIN.IB*^{ki}, *B. E.*, *l.c.*, No. 99. *Du-un-na-a-ḫi*^{ki}, *l.c.*, No. 112. ^{âlu}*Za-rat-Dûr*-^{ilu}*Gu-la*^{ki}, *l.c.*, Nos. 114, 128. ^{alu}*Dûr*-^{ilu}*Marduk*^{ki}, *l.c.*, No. 120. *Kâr-UD.NUN*^{ki}, *l.c.*, Nos. 124, 135. *Bît*-^{m}*É.KUR-MU-MU*, *l.c.*, Nos. 138, 139, etc., etc. See also pp. 81; 85, note 3; 110.

[14] *B. E.*, XIV, 29 : 3; 30 : 3. The tablet, *l.c.*, 23 : 8 (dated in the 13th year of Kuri-Galzu), where it is reported that *KU.MUN* was paid (*nád-nu*) to (or by?) ^{m}*In-na-an-nu*, was not taken into consideration here.

[15] *B. E.*, XIV, 35 : 3.

[16] *B. E.*, XIV, 38 : 10, where it is stated that certain animals, which had been loaned out, are to be returned to (*inamdin ana*) Innanni.

[17] From the 22d year of Kuri-Galzu Innanni shared honors with his successor, ^{m}*Mar-tu-ku*, *B. E.*, XIV, 36 : 3.

[18] *B. E.*, XIV, 41*a* (pl. 56) : 3, cf. l. 12ff.: ^{arhu}*KIN*-^{ilu}*Innanna* *shattu* 1^{kam} ^{ilu}*PI*(= *Na*!)-*zi-Ma-ra-ta-ásh*.

[19] *B. E.*, XIV, 42 : 2, 19ff ^{arhu}*GUD.SI.SÌ*(= *di*) *ûmu* 3^{kam} *shattu* 2^{kam} ^{ilu}*Na-zi-Ma-ru-ut-ta-ásh* *LUGAL-E*.

year of Nazi-Maruttash[1]—*i.e.*, during a period of at least ten years[2]— is represented in our texts as the recipient of four letters,[3] two[4] of which have been addressed to him by ^{m} ^{ilu}*NIN.IB*(resp. ^{ilu}*MASH*)*-TUR.USH-SE-na*.[5] From the contents and the tone of these two letters it is apparent that Innanni was the "chief bursar" of the Temple's storehouses, where nothing could be either received or expended without his knowledge and consent, and that Errish-apal-iddina was likewise a person of no mean rank; for he hires workmen, and dares to command Innanni: "Thou, hurry up, give the seed corn to the city."[6] Apparently then he was at the head of a city. More than this, he even had certain prefects (*ḫazannâti*) under him, for he requests Innanni in another letter: "Thou shalt not accept the sesame of the prefects."[7] This latter passage shows that Errish-apal-iddina, because he had authority over *ḫazannâti*, "city prefects," must have been a "governor," a "*bêl paḫâti*."[8] Comparing these results with the texts of *B. E.*, XIV and XV, we learn that a certain place, called either *Dûr-*^{m} ^{ilu}*NIN.IB-TUR.USH-SE-na*^{ki}[9] or *Bît-*^{m} ^{ilu}*MASH*[10](resp. ^{m} ^{ilu}*NIN.IB*[11])*-TUR.USH-SE-na*^{ki}, flourished as a "barley depot" during the 13th year of Kuri-Galzu[12] and the 19th,[13] 22d,[14] and 24th[15] year of Nazi-Maruttash—*i.e.*, during a period of at least thirty-two years, including

[1] The statement in *B. E.*, XIV, p. 8: "All the tablets in which this name (*i.e.*, *Innannu*) occurs, with the exception of one, which is dated in the reign of Nazi-Maruttash, belong to the reign of Kuri-Galzu," will have to be modified accordingly.

[2] Cf. here also the *Bît-*^{m}*In-na-an-ni* (situated in Nippur, *B. E.*, XV, 115 : 5; 135 : 6) which flourished from at least the 22d year of Kuri-Galzu (*B. E.*, XIV, 36 : 2, 11) to the 15th year of Nazi-Maruttash (*B. E.*, XIV, 65 : 7, 11). Add here to *Bît-Innanni* of *B. E.*, XV, the following references: 66 : 6 | 117 : 2 | 141 : 22 | 155 : 20, 22. A *Mâr-*^{m}*In-na-a[n-ni* is mentioned in the 6th and the 7th year of Shagarakti-Shuriash (*B. E.*, XIV, 132 : 22).

[3] Nos. 83–86.

[4] Nos. 83 and 84.

[5] Possibly to be read *Errish(t)-apal-iddina*. For the possible reading of *NIN.IB* resp. *MASH* as *Errish(t)*, see *The Monist*, XVII (January, 1907), pp. 140ff. Clay reads this name either *NIN.IB-mâr-iddina* (*B. E.*, XIV, p. 49*a*) or *NIN.IB-apal-iddina* (*B. E.*, XV, p. 38*a*). Why this change, considering that in all the passages known to me the writing *TUR.USH* = *apal* is found?

[6] No. 83 : 24 *ù at-ta ḫa-mu-ut-ta al-ka-am-ma SHE.ZER a-na âlu-ki i-din*, see p. 112.

[7] No. 84 : 3, *SHE.GISH.NI shá ḫa-za-an-na-a-ti la ta-ma-ḫa-ar at-ta*, etc., see p. 114.

[8] This follows also from a comparison of, *e.g.*, *B. E.*, XIV, 99*a* (pl. 59 = E. A. H., 195): 4, 7, 16, 26, 29, 41 with *B. E.*, XIV, 168 : 59, 51, 26, and especially l. 40, *i.e.*, in this latter tablet, which is an "inventory of cattle," the "*shá Bît-*^{m} ^{ilu}*NIN.IB-TUR.USH-SE-na*" apparently stands for *pi-ḫat* ^{m} ^{ilu}*NIN.IB-TUR.USH-SE-na*.

[9] *B. E.*, XIV, 18 : 7 (notice that *KI-II* refers back to *Dûr-* of l. 6). In *B. E.*, XIV, pp. 49*a*, 58*b*, this name is read *NIN.IB-mâr-iddina*^{ki} resp. *NIN.IB-mâr-iddina*, but in *l.c.*, p. 58*a*, *Dûr-*^{m} ^{ilu}*NIN.IB-mâr*(read: *apal*)*-iddina*^{ki}.

[10] *B. E.*, XIV, 76 : 2.

[11] *B. E.*, XIV, 79 : 4 | 84 : 2.

[12] *B. E.*, XIV, 18 : 7, 1.

[13] *B. E.*, XIV, 76 : 2, 8.

[14] *B. E.*, XIV, 79 : 4, 11.

[15] *B. E.*, XIV, 84 : 2, 9.

the time during which Innanni was the "chief bursar" at Nippur. Hence Innanni and $^{m\ ilu}$*Irrish-apal-iddina*, the founder, owner, and occupant of *Dûr* (resp. *Bît*)-$^{m\ ilu}$*Irrish-apal-iddina*, were contemporaries.[1]

Again in No. 9 : 21 a certain ^{m}*Bana-a-sha*-^{ilu}*Marduk*, when writing to his 'Lord" (*be-li*), states that he has, in order to corroborate the truthfulness of his communications, "made to be his witnesses" a certain $^{m\ ilu}$*Nergal-Ba-ni*, the prefect (*ḫa-za-na*) of Rakanu, and the prefect (*ḫa-za-an-na*) of Bît-^{m}Ki-din-ni,[2] upon whom his "Lord" may call, if he desires confirmation of the truth. The "prefect" of Bît-Kidinni was, of course, Kidinni.[3] This statement of Banâ-sha-Marduk, no doubt, indicates that he stood in some kind of a relation to the prefect Kidinni. What this relation was we may gather from a tablet,[4] dated in the 20th year of Kuri-Galzu, which reports that Banâ-sha-Marduk received certain cereals[5] "on the authority" or "by order" of[6] ^{m}*Ki-di-nu-û*[7]—the latter apparently being the superior of the former. But we can go a step farther. *B. E.*, XIV, 99*a* (= E. A. H., 195) : 35,[8]

[1] Cf. here also *B. E.*, XV, 124, where a certain ^{m}*Ri-esh-Shamshu(-shu)* or ^{m}*Ri-esh-Shamshi-shu* (this reading preferable to Clay's *Ri-esh-tû-shu* (*B. E.*, XV, p. 40*b*) or *Ri-esh-ûmi-shu* (*Z. A.*, XX (1907), p. 417f.) in view of such names as ^{m}*Ri-esh-na-pa-aḫ-shú*, *B. E.*, XV, 24 : 7, and ^{m}*Ri-esh*-^{ilu}*En-lil*, *l.c.*, 19 : 16) receives from (*ina qât*) Innanni a certain amount of grain as *KU.QAR*-wages, which grain was taken from that belonging to (*ina libbi SHE shá*) $^{m\ ilu}$*MASH-TUR.USH-SE-na*. The tablet is dated in the 22d year (*sc.* doubtless of Kuri-Galzu). In *B. E.*, XV, 136 (dated the 23d year, *sc.* of Kuri-Galzu), Innannu endorses the payment of *GIG* (= *kibâtu*, "flour," Jensen, *K. B.*, VI, p. 485) to certain *pa-te-si* $^{pl.a}$ "by order of" or "in the employ of" —thus receiving the amount specified "on the authority of," *i.e.*, "per" (= *qât*; in this differing from Clay, *B. E.*, XV, pp. 5, 6, who translated *qât* "in the hands of" or "paid to"; *qât* may or may not (as here) be expressed before the second name in "lists of payments") $^{m\ ilu}$*MASH-TUR.USH-SE-na*. These two tablets prove beyond a doubt that Innanni and Errish-apal-iddina were contemporaries during the 22d and 23d year (of Kuri-Galzu).

[2] No. 9 : 21, *a-na shi-bu-ti-ia* $^{m\ ilu}$*Nergal-Ba-ni ḫa-za-na shá* ^{alu}*Ra-ka-nu ù ḫa-za-an-na shá Bît*-^{m}*Ki-din-ni ásh-ta-ka-an*, see p. 106.

[3] Notice that in our letter the prefect of Bît-Kidinni is not mentioned by name, simply because there was no other prefect of the "house of Kidinni" than Kidinni himself—a fact quite well known to the "Lord."

[4] *B. E.*, XIV, 34 : 6.

[5] *ASH.AN.NA* (wheat), *GÙ.GAL* (beans), and *siḫ*(= *ZAG*)-*ḫi-li* (caper, cf. Hilprecht, *B. E.*, Series D, Vol. I, p. 538).

[6] Thus I translate, because the name of Kidinû *follows* that of Banâ-sha-Marduk.

[7] *Kidinni* is a shorter form of *Kidin(n)û*. The latter is, as the long *û* indicates, a hypocoristicon of some such name as *Kidin-NIN.IB*, *-Nergal*, *-Rammân* (cf. No. 33 : 12), *-Sin*, *-Ulmash*, etc. See "List of Names" in *B. E.*, XIV, p 46*b*. Cf. also 18 : 22, ^{m}*Ki-di-ni*; 23 : 23, ^{m}*Ki-din*-^{ilu}*Marduk*, and *B. E.*, IX, p. 61*b*, and *l.c.*, X, p. 53*b*, ^{m}*Ki-din*.

[8] Owing to the fact that the writer was in Europe while reading the proofs of his *E. B. H.* (thus having no access to the E. A. H. Collection), it happened that E. A. H , 195 was erroneously reckoned to the Neo-Babylonian period; it should have been read, *E. B. H.*, p. 328 *sub e*: "The dynasty of the Cassites, 175–195," instead of 194. Clay, *B. E.*, XIV, p. 2, note 3, however, infers from this inaccuracy that the writer did not understand the nature of the tablet in question. Turning to the "Table of Contents" of *B. E.*, XIV, p. 69, No. 99*a*, I find that its author does not give its contents either. I take this opportunity to state what I regard to be the contents of this and two exactly similar tablets (*B. E.*, XIV, 168 and 99), which are interpreted somewhat differently by Dr. Clay, who sees in No. 168 a "record of

informs us that there lived in the 11th year of Kadashman-Turgu (l. 46) a certain ^{m}*Ki-di-nu-ú* who was one of the prefects, *ḫazannâti* (*l.c.*, col. XV : 22), belonging to the *pi-ḫat* of ^{m} ^{ilu}*En-lil-bêl*(= *EN*)*-nishê*^{mesh}*-shu* (l. 41). Now, as ^{m}*Ki-di-nu-ú*

collections" (see *l.c.*, p. 73), while No. 99 in the same volume is pronounced to be a "record of the collection of taxes in animals" (see *l.c.*, p. 69). All three tablets just referred to are *inventories*. Cf., *e.g.*, 99*a* : 46 (and see 99 : 1), *mi-nu LIT.GUDḪI.A ù GANAM.LUḪI.A NIN.AN*^{mesh}, "the *number* of large and small cattle belonging to the *NIN.AN*^{mesh}." The latter were two "beings"; one was called *NIN AN.GAL*, ll. 13, 34 (cf. *B.E.*, XIV, 89 : 1, 9; 104 : 3; 131 : [1], 18; 136 : 16; 138 : 31), and the other *NIN.AN.TUR*, l. 41 (cf. *B. E.*, XIV, 89 : 1, 16; 136 : 29 (!)), and, per analogy, we ought to expect a *NIN.AN.TUR* also in l. 21. What these *NIN.AN*^{mesh} were, cannot be made out as yet. From Letter No. 85 (see p. 115) I would like to infer that Inbi-Airi was such a *NIN.AN* or *qadishtu*. From the arrangement of the tablet in question we might draw the conclusion that the "large cattle" were under the chief supervision of the *kash-shu* (*not* = Cassite) ^{m}*Ki-lam-du*, ll. 1, 2, 14; while the "small cattle" were under that of the *kash-shu* ^{m}*Amel-Ba-nu-ú* (if *kash-shu* were = "Cassite," Amel-Banû would be one with a good Babylonian name), ll. 22, 23, 35 (the traces given in *B. E.*, XIV, are, no doubt, wrong). Each *kash-shu*, it seems, had several (three or more?) *bêl piḫâti* under him. And as, according to our tablet, the three *pi-ḫat* included in the *kash-shu* of Kilamdu are exactly the same as those of the *kash-shu* of Amel-Banû, it is most likely that a *kash-shu* is the *general overseer* of either the *large* or the *small* cattle, *irrespective* of *territory*; in other words, a *kashshu* has the supervision of *all* small or of *all* large cattle of a *NIN.AN* scattered over all the different provinces (*piḫâti*). I propose, therefore, to derive *kashshu* from כשש, "to gather" (Jensen, *K. B.*, VI[1], pp. 322, 562), here in the sense of "one under whose jurisdiction are gathered a number of *bêl piḫâti*," *i.e.*, "governor- or overseer-in-chief." A *bêl piḫâti*, on the other hand, is responsible for the flocks of *both* the *large and small cattle* herded in his territory, which responsibility is always expressed by *qât* = "*per*", see ll. 11 (cf. l. 7); 12 (cf. l. 4); 17, 20 (cf. l. 16); 32 (notice the *ù*(!) and cf. ll. 29 and 26); 42 (cf. l. 11); hence we have to translate, *e.g.*, l. 11, "total 10 (*sc.* oxen of six years) *a-na za-bal KU.QAR* ^{amelu}*RIQ ù KA.ZID.DA qàt* (= *SHÚ*) ^{m} ^{ilu}*Shamash-nâdin-aḫê*^{mesh}," by "(are employed) for the carrying (*zabâl* = inf.; cf. our No. 34 : 40, *i-na* ^{gish}*MAR.GID.DA IN ki-i az-bi-la*, when I was bringing straw in the harvest (lit. "long") wagons, the horses, etc.) of the *KU.QAR*-wages of the vegetable- and grain-gatherers 'per' (*sc.* order, information of) Shamash-nâdin-aḫê (the *bêl pi-ḫat*, l. 7)"; or l. 17, "total 83 cattle, the property (*na-kam-tum*) of Mâr-Idînanni-Shamash, 'per' (order, information of) Enlil-bêl-nishê shu (the *bêl pi-ḫat*, l. 16)." The territory of a *pi-ḫat* was subdivided into two to six (cf. ll. 2, 3 and 35–40), or possibly more, *ḫazannâti*, and each *ḫazannu* or "prefect" had one (cf. ll. 2, 3, etc.), two (cf. ll. 27, 28 and 36, 37) or more *na-gid* or "shepherds" under him. The *nagid*, *ḫazannu*, *bêl piḫâti*, *kashshu* of this tablet correspond exactly to the *nagid*, *nu-banda*(*-gud*), *PA*, *pa-te-si* of the "inventory" lists of the Ur dynasty tablets, as published in *E. B. H.*, pp. 333–361 (for *nu-banda* = *ḫazannu* see, *e.g.*, Meissner, *Ideogramme*, No. 1159). It will be noticed that the cattle introduced by *TA* = *itti* or *EN* = *adi* are *never* counted, hence *TA* = *itti* cannot mean here "together with," nor can *adi* be translated by "in addition to". *TA* = *itti* has to be rendered by "besides," and *EN* = *adi* by "apart from." For *TA* cf. *e.g.*, l. 13, *TA* 15 *ki-is-bu*, *i.e.*, "besides 15 (that were given for a) sacrifice to the dead." For *kisbu* see, besides Zimmern, *Rituall.*, p. 160, 11; Jensen, *K. B.*, VI[1], pp. 446, 517; also *B. E.*, XV, 185, I : 5; 200, I : 6, *ki-si-bu ù ri-im-ku*. For *EN* = *adi* cf. l. 5, *EN* 1 *shul* (not *lam*, as Clay's copy gives, see XIV, 168 : 16, *EN* 5 *shul-ma-ni* and cf., *l.c.*, l. 15, *shul-ma-na-a-tum*; XV, 199 : 21, 22; *shul*(= *DI*)*-ma-nu*)*-ma-nu*, *i.e.*, "apart from one (that was given for a) peace(-offering)." Cf. also l. 18, *EN* 2 *GUD MU*-4 *ù* 1 *LIT shá i-na Kâr-EN.KUR.KUR*^{ki} *bu-uk-ku-ra*, *i.e.*, "apart from two oxen, four years old, and one cow which are being taken care of in Kâr-EN.KUR.KUR." For *bukkura* cf. also XIV, 168 : 55, *shá i-na shattu* 1^{kam} *bu-uq-qu*(!)*-ra*, and *l.c.*, l. 16, *tab-ki-ir-*(XIV, 99*a* : 10, *tab-kir*(!)*-ti*)*tum shá ma-du-tu ú-pa*(!)*-ak-ki-ru-ni*, which shows that we have here a verb *baqâru* = *paqâru* = Hebr. בקר, Piel: "to cleave, discern, to look after a thing"; met with also in *Neb.*, Winckler, I : 18 (quoted by *H. W. B.*, p. 181*b*), where *mu-ba-ak-ki-ir qa-ar-ba-a-tim* should be translated by "who looks after the fields," *i.e.*, "who takes care of them." A *tapqirtu*, accordingly, would be a "flock which requires special treatment," a "special looking after," and XIV, 168 : 16, quoted above, might be translated. "the flock(s) requiring a special looking after of the several shepherds they take care of them." Lastly cf. l. 43: *EN* 20 *zu-bit-ti MU* 11^{kam}, *i.e.*, "apart from 20 (special) 'holdings' of the 11th (the *ḫazânu* and superior of Banâ-sha-Marduk[1]) is only another writing for ^{m}*Ki-din-ni* (the *ḫazânu* of *Bît-*^{m}*Ki-din-ni* and the high and influential witness of Banâ-sha-Marduk, the writer of Letter No. 9), there can be absolutely no reason against our identifying both and establishing the fact that Banâ-sha-Marduk, the writer of No. 9, must have lived between the 20th year of Kuri-Galzu[2] and the 11th of Kadashman-Turgu,[3] or during a space of about forty-three years.

In like manner we might go through the whole "List of personal names" or

year" (cf. l. 32, *si-bi-e-ti* — special holdings of the 10th and the 11th year - here, because *not* introduced by *EN*, they are counted. Cf. also 99 : 65, *GANAM.LU*$^{hi\ a}$ *shá si-bi-ti shá* ^{alu}*Tukul-ti-Be-li*^{ki}, *i.e.*, "small cattle of the special holdings of the city T."). The root of *za-bit-ti* = *si-bi-e-ti* — *si-bi-ti* is צבת, and we have here the same word as *ṣibittu*, which Delitzsch, *H. W. B.*, p. 562*b*, 2, translates by "*Eigentum*." These examples show that the different shepherds herding the cattle of the *NIN.AN*^{mesh} had among their herds very often animals belonging to other people, which animals were designated either by *nakamtu*, "property" (XIV, 99*a* : 17), or by *sibitti*, "special holdings"; cf. here also XIV, 99 : 16, *i-na MU* 11^{kam} ^{ilu}*Ka-dash-man-Tur-gu a-di LIT.GUD*$^{hi\ a}$*-shu i-na* ^{alu}*En-lil*^{ki} *il-ta-an-ma-ar* [follows enumeration], *i.e.*, "in the 11th year of K. there were seen in Nippur in addition to his (*i.e.*, of $^{m\ ilu}$[. . . .], l. 1) cattle also the following." Clay, *B. E.*, XIV, p. 52*b*, also mentions a title or office, *ki-mu*, as occurring after the name *Shamash-nâdin-aḫi* in 99*a* : 11, 32. These two references are an evident mistake, yet *KI MU* does occur in 99*a* : 38 (after $^{m\ ilu}$*Shamash-nâṣir*) and in l. 40 (after $^{m\ ilu}$*Shamash-iqisha*). For still other occurrences of *KI MU* after *proper names* see, *e.g.*, *B.E.*, XV, 132 : 23, ^{m}*Daian-*^{ilu}*Marduk KI MU* ^{m}*EN* (= *Adi* or *Bêl*)*-mu-ti-ilu* (notice that we have two names in *this* line only!); *l.c.*, 174 : 11 (again in this line only two names!); *l.c.*, 96 : 14, ^{m}*Bu-un-na-*^{ilu}*AG KI MU UD.DA-ge*; *B. E.*, XIV, 168 : 25, etc., etc. The meaning of this expression we gather from *B. E.*, XIV, 168 : 31, 3 *LIT.GAL shá i-na DUB.SHA.RA shá shaṭtu* 10^{kam} *MU* (= *shum*) ^{m}*Qu-un-nu-ni shaṭ-ru*, *i.e.*, "3 large cows which are entered (*shaṭru*) in the inventory tablet(s) (which form part of the "Temple Archives") for the year 10 under the name of Qunnuni." *KI.MU*, when standing between two (proper) names, has to be transcribed *ki shum* and must be rendered by "for the name"; hence ^{m}*X na-gid ki shum* ^{m}*Y na-gid* is a "shepherd whose name is entered in the inventory tablet 'for' that of another, the real or original, shepherd who, at the time when the inventory was taken, happened to be away from his flock", in other words, ^{m}*X ki shum* ^{m}*Y* is as much as "X, the substitute for Y." In conclusion I may mention here that several mistakes are to be found in this tablet, as, *e.g.*, col. VII : 8, read "19" instead of "20" (l. 8, cols. I–V only 19 cattle are enumerated; the mistake has probably its origin in l. 8, col. I); col. X : 34 gives as "grand total" 376, but if we add together the totals of col. X, as given in the copy, we receive the sum 386, or 10 too many. These 10 "too many" are found in col. X : 25, where we ought to read, according to the different items of cols. I–IX, 83, instead of 93, as the copy gives it. As the grand total is correctly given as 376, we must suppose that the mistake is not attributable to the original, but to the copyist. These notes, I hope, will convince the reader that we have to see in *B. E.*, XIV, 99*a* (and all similar tablets, called in Vol. XIV "records of the receipt of taxes in animals") an "inventory" of the flocks (including at the same time an inventory of the "butter" (*NI.NUN*, col. VIII, Obv.) and "wool" (*SIG*$^{hi\ a}$, col. XII, Rev.) yielded by them) of the great and small cattle of the *NIN.AN*^{mesh} under the chief supervision of two *kash-shu*. This inventory includes such additional notes as might be found necessary to account for certain "absent" or "present" cattle that originally did, or did not, form a component part of the flocks mentioned. For inventory tablets from the time of the kings of Ur cf. Hilprecht, *B. E.*, Vol. I, part 2, Nos. 124, 126, and my *E. B. H.*, pp. 333–361.

[1] Bâna-sha-Marduk, the contemporary of Amel-Marduk, No. 3 : 16, has probably to be differentiated from this one here. The former lived and flourished during the time of *Shagarakti-Shuriash*.

[2] *B. E.*, XIV, 31 : 6.

[3] *B. E.*, XIV, 99*a* (= *E. A. H.*, 195) : 35.

"scribes"[1] and show that they lived during the reign, or were contemporaries, of one or the other of the above mentioned Cassite kings. Seeing that such an investigation would lead too far here, we reserve it for Series C.

We need not, however, rely entirely upon the "persons" introduced in these documents to establish for our letters a Cassite origin and age. There are other means at our disposal which lead to the same result. Among these might be enumerated:

(*b*) The *Cassite names* of the persons mentioned as, *e.g.*, ^{m}*Gu-za-ar-AN* (= *ilu*?),[2] ^{m}*Si-ri-da-ash*,[3] *Mâr*-^{m}*Û-su(!)-ub-Shi-pak*,[4] *Mâr*-^{m}*Û-da-shá-ásh*,[5] ^{m}*Na-zi*-^{ilu}*En-lil*,[6]

[1] ^{m}*Ardi-GASHAN* (= *Bêlit*), the writer of No. 5, is mentioned in *B. E.*, XIV, 40 : 30 (dated in the 21st year of Kuri-Galzu, l. 23) as *DUB.SAR* or "scribe." Cf. also the *DUB.SAR Erba-Marduk* of *B. E.*, XIV, 127 : 11 (dated "the beginning of the reign of Shagarakti-Shuriash", for the expression cf. *The Monist*, XVII (January, 1907), p. 150), with the writer(s) of Nos. 13, 14 (81?), 82, and see pp. 14, note 7; 117; 121.

[2] No. 87 : 3. Cf. ^{m}*Gu-za-ar-za-ar-Bu-ga-ash*, C. B. M., 3532 : 16 (quoted by Clay, *B. E.*, XV, p. 31*a*, and *l.c.*, p. ix), which, no doubt, is the same as ^{m}*Gu-NI(!)-za-ar-Bu-ga-ash* (thus read by Clay, *B. E.*, XIV, p. 43*b*, and quoted from C. B. M., 3646), seeing that *NI* might be read *zal* = *zar*. The interchange of *l* and *r* in the different languages is too well known as to require further examples. *Gu-zar-zar* resp. *Gu-zal-zar* "might" be an intensive form of *Gu-zar*, which latter we find in our text. If *AN* be read *ilu* we would have here a "mixed" name—partly Cassite, partly Babylonian; for such names cf., *e.g.*, *Kadashman*-^{ilu}*Enlil*, *Kudur*-^{ilu}*Enlil*, *NIM.GI-shar-ili*, etc. In view of such names as Guzarzar-Bugash, Guzalzar-Bagash, we might be justified in reading our name here Guzar-Bugash, thus identifying the Babylonian *AN* with the Cassite *Bugash* and attributing to the latter the rôle played by *AN* in the Babylonian pantheon.

[3] No. 28 : 5 in [*Bît*]-^{m}*Si-ri-da*(or *shá*?)-*ash*. Is this name to be compared with *Si-ri-ia*, *B. E.*, XV, 198 : 30, and *Si-li*-[*ia*; for this emendation cf. Clay, *Z. A.*, XX (1907), p. 417f.], *l.c.*, 88 : 2, with interchange of *l* and *r*?

[4] No. 55 : 2. For the reading *Shi-pak*, instead of *Shi-ḫu*, see *B. E.*, XV, 190, VI : 15, *Me-li-Shi-pa-*[*ak*], and Clay, *l.c.*, p. 3, note 4. Cf. here the names *Ú-zu(!)-ub-Shi-pak*, Scheil, *Textes Élam. Sém.*, I, p. 93, 1, 3; *Ú-zu-ub-Ḫ.A.LA* (*sic*, against Clay, *l.c.*, XIV, p. 54*b*), *B. E.*, XIV, 132 : 27, and *U-zu-ub-SHI-ia-SAḪ*, Clay, *l.c.*, XV, p. 45*b*. For the interchange of *s* and *z* cf., among others, also *za-bit-ti*, *B. E.*, XIV, 99*a* : 30, with *si-bi-ti*, *l.c.*, 99 : 65, and *si-bi-e-ti*, *l.c.*, 99*a* : 32. In view of this interchange we cannot connect *Ú-su-ub* = *U-zu-ub* with עזב and see in our name a formation similar to that of *Nabû-u-za-bu* ("*Nebo ist Entgelt?*"), quoted by Del., *H. W. B.*, p. 35*b*. *Uzub*, *Usub*, no doubt, is a side-form of *u-zi-ib* = *e-ṭe-rum*, Del., *Sprache der Kossaer*, p. 26 : 12. For the interchange of *i* and *u* cf., *e.g.*, *lish-ki(!)-nu*, No. 35 : 33; *li-mi-ish-shi-ru-ni*, 55 : 12, etc. *Ú-su-ub-Shi-pak*, then, is = *Eṭir-Marduk*, *i.e.*, "Protect, oh Marduk!" *Úzub-Ḫ.A.LA* = "Protect my portion" (*sc.* oh god!); *Uzub-SHI-ia-SAḪ* = "Protect my face (= me), oh Shamash," or possibly "the protector of my face is Shamash." See here also the remarks to *NIM.GI*, introduction to No. 33*a*.

[5] Thus to be read according to *B. E.*, XV, 168 : 4, where we have *ash* for *ásh*. According to 55 : 8, 16, 20 this person was the messenger of King Burna-Buriash, see p. 53, note 2.

[6] No. 24 : 25. This half Cassite and half Babylonian name is found again in C. B. M., 3520 : 13 (*B. E.*, XV, p. 38*a*). Whether the element *Na-zi* be the same as *Na-aḫ-zi*, which Clay, *B. E.*, XV, p. 4, note 2, thinks to be possible, cannot be made out as yet. It is, however, a fact that *aḫ* and *a'* very often change in these texts—a phenomenon overlooked by the author of Vols. XIV and XV, as seen from *B. E.*, XV, p. 37, note 1, where we have *Mi-na-a-a'-di-a-na-AN* (= *ilu*) for *Minâ-aḫṭi-ana-ili*. For this interchange of *aḫ* and *a'* cf. *Ki-shá-aḫ-bu-ut* (34 : 1), resp. *Ki-shaḫ-bu-ut* (35 : 1), with *Mar*-^{m}*Ki-shá-a'-bu-ut*, *B. E.*, XV, 188, I : 25 (not registered by Clay), II : 13 (*l.c.*, p. 49*a*, wrongly has *aḫ* for *a'*); ^{alu}*Mâr*-^{m}*Ba-aḫ-lu-ti*, *B. E.*, XV, 159*c* : 5 (the ^{alu}*Ṣiḫru*-^{m}*Ba-aḫ-lu-ti* and all others quoted under ^{alu}*Ṣiḫru* in *B. E.*, XIV, p. 58*b*, and XV, p. 53*b*, have, of course, to be corrected into ^{alu}*Mâr*-; cf. *âlu shá Mâr-Shilibi* in Scheil, *Textes Élam. Sém.*, I, p. 100) with [*Mâr*]-^{m}*Ba-a'-lu-ti*, *B. E.*, XV, 120 : 3. From this we might infer that *Na-aḫ-zi* could also be written *Na-a'-zi* and become *Na-zi*. But the intermediate form *Na-a'-zi* has not yet been found; hence the identification of *Na-aḫ-zi* and *Na-zi* must, at the present, be left open.

ᵐMe-li-Shi-pak,[1] and lastly *ᵐMe-li-ⁱˡᵘShu-qa-mu-na,*[2] who, as regards his name, is a thorough Cassite, but who, as regards his national sentiments, was a good Babylonian citizen, for his son[3] bears the unmistakably Babylonian name *ᵐ ⁱˡᵘPA.KU-SHESH-SE-na = Nusku-aḫ-iddina.*[4]

(*c*) Certain *cities* or *places* peculiar to both, our letters here and the dated tablets of the Cassite kings. Among these may be mentioned *ᵃˡᵘArdi-GASHAN*^{ki} (*= Bêlit*),[5] *Bît-ᵐKi-din-ni,*[6] *BÀR.TUR*^{ki},[7] *ᵃˡᵘDûr-EN.KUR.KUR*^{ki},[8] *Dûr-ⁱˡᵘEn-*

[1] No. 17 : 32. Also mentioned in *B. E.*, XIV, 125 : 8 (13th year of *Ku*[*ri-Galzu*]) and *l.c.*, XV, 190, VI : 15.

[2] No. 59 : 11. In *B. E.*, XV, p. 4, this name is considered to have a Babylonian element. As *Meli* is correctly recognized as a Cassite element, the god Shuqamuna is evidently regarded as a Babylonian divinity. The fact, however, that Shuqamuna was not known in the Babylonian pantheon till the time of the Cassites proves, apart from other considerations, that he must have been introduced by them. For *Shu-* also the writing *Shú-* occurs, see *B. E.*, XIV, 132 : 11; XV, 136 : 10.

[3] On account of *mâr* (not *mârê*^{mesh}), l. 14, I do not hold *ᵐBu-un-na-ⁱˡᵘNIN.IB*, l. 12, to be a son of Meli-Shuqamuna.

[4] No. 59 : 13.

[5] Nos. 13 : 7 | 66 : 24. In 18 : 19 we have *ᵃˡᵘArdi-NIN* (*Bêlit*)^{ki} and in 11 : 20 *ᵃˡᵘArdi-GASHAN*^{ki}. The latter writing is found also in *B. E.*, XIV, 123*a* (= E. A. H., 180) : 5 (8th year of Kudurri-Enlil, l. 13).

[6] Nos. 9 : 23 | 44 : 15. For the *ḫazânu ᵐKi-di-nu-ú = ᵐKi-din-ni* see above, pp. 4ff.

[7] No. 53 : 38, to be read (according to Br. 6900) *Pa-rak ma-ri*^{ki} (so also Clay, *Z. A.*, XX (1907), p. 417f., correcting *B. E.*, XIV, p. 57*b*, *passim*). The *mâri* is, of course, the Nippurian *mâr κατ' ἐξοχήν*, *i.e.*, *ⁱˡᵘNIN.IB*. From *B. E.*, XIV, 133 : 3, 6 we learn that it existed in "the seventh year of Shagarakti-Shuriash," l. 13. Cf. here also the *KAS ᵃˡᵘParak-mâri*^{ki} in *B. E.*, XIV, 107 : 3, and see below, p. 10, note 3.

[8] No. 17 : 18, 26. *EN.KUR.KUR* in our letters is used either of *ⁱˡᵘNIN.IB* or of *ⁱˡᵘEn-lil*, never of Marduk of Babylon, see, *e.g.*, No. 21 : 11, 17, and cf. *ⁿᵃʳᵘNam-ga-ri-shá-EN.KUR.KUR* in No. 59 : 9. For the omission of *ilu* before names of gods cf. among others, also *lu-ma-as-si*, *B. E.*, XV, 163 : 38 (the city mentioned in *B. E.*, XV, 159*c*: 12 has to be read *ᵃˡᵘ ⁱˡᵘEn-lil-IGI.BAR.RA*, *i.e.*, "Enlil looks favorably upon," and not (Clay, *l.c.*, p. 52*a*) *ᵃˡᵘBêl-lim-mas-su*(?)); *Ishtar* (*U.DAR*), *l.c.*, 185 : 36 | 188, I : 13 | V : 15; *Ṣarpanitum*, *l.c.*, 163 : 31; *Sham*(= *U*)-*shi*, *l.c.*, 96 : 10; *Shamshu*(= *UD*)^{shú}, *l.c.*, 167 : 33, 34; *NIN.AZAG.BI*, *l.c.*, 186 : 24; *Sin* (= *XXX*), *l.c.*, 164 : 7 | 166 : 5; *É.A*, *l.c.*, 186 : 6; *En-lil*, *l.c.*, 132 : 16 | 175 : 65 | 154 : 27; *Marduk*, *l.c.*, 96 : 20; *Nusku*, C. B. M., 3472, etc., etc. A *Dûr-EN.KUR.KUR*^{ki} is mentioned in *B. E.*, XIV, 5 : 6 (11th year of Burra-Buriash). Cf. also *ᵃˡᵘDûr-be-el-KUR.KUR* in *B. E.*, XV, 64 : 1 and the *Dûr-EN.KUR.KUR.GAL*, *l.c.*, 159*c* : 10. The correct reading of the different writings would be *ᵃˡᵘDûr-bêl-mâtâti-(rabû)*, "the fortress (wall) of the (great) lord of lands," *i.e.*, of Enlil of Nippur. Now we know from such passages as *B. E.*, XV, 37 : 4, that the temple of Enlil as the *bêl-mâtâti-rabû* is very often referred to simply as *É.AN* = *bît-ili*, *i.e.*, "the house of the god" *par excellence*, and that Enlil himself is very often spoken of as the *AN* or *ilu*, *i.e.*, "the god" (*B. E.*, XIV, 16 : 1, see below, p. 80); hence Enlil, "the great lord of lands," might also be called "the great god of lands." Furthermore, it is well known that *KUR.KUR* = *mâtâti* = lands (= "world," "cosmos") is also = *KALAM* = *mâtâti* = lands (= Babylonian world = Shumer and Akkad), hence the reading *Bît-ⁱˡᵘUN.GAL En-lil*^{ki} defended in *Z. A.*, XX (1907), p. 419, must be abandoned in my judgment. There is no god *UN.GAL*! *B. E.*, XIV, 148 : 15, 18, has to be read *É-AN.KALAM.GAL-EN.LIL*^{ki} = *Bît-Ili-mâtâti-rabû Nippur*^{ki}, *i.e.*, "the temple of the great god of the lands at Nippur," which temple is the *É.KUR* inhabited by *Enlil-NIN.IB-Nusku* or better, which is occupied by the Nippurian *Trinity* in *Unity*: *Enlil* (Father) *NIN.IB* (Son) - *Ninlil* = *Gula* (Mother, resp. wife of the Son), cf. for the latter also *B. E.*, XV, 34 : 2, *Bît-ⁱˡᵘGu-la ù AN.KALAM.GAL-EN.LIL*^{ki}, *i.e.*, "the temple of Gula and *NIN.IB*" (= Enlil; the temple of the god standing for the god's name, cf. *apil-É-shár-ra* = *NIN.IB*). Cf. here also the note on *AN.GAL* = *ⁱˡᵘKA.DI* = *Enlil* farther below, p. 20.

lil$^{hi.a\text{-}mesh\text{-}ki}$,[1] ^{âlu}*Dûr-Ku-ri-Gal-zu*,[2] and lastly ^{mâtu}*A.AB.BA*^{ki}.[3]

[1] No. 39 : 21, or written also *Dûr-*^{ilu}*En-lil*$^{hi.a\text{-}ki}$, No. 3 . 33, 38, 41, which latter is mentioned in *B. E.*, XIV, 5 : 10 (11th year of Burra-Buriash) and *l.c.*, 78 : 4 (22d of Nazi-Maruttash). A ^{âlu}*Dûr-*^{ilu}*En-lil*$^{hi.a\text{-}ki}$ we find in *B. E.*, XIV, 118 : 1, 30 (5th year of Kudur-Enlil), and a ^{âlu}*Dûr-*^{ilu}*En-lil*$^{mesh\text{-}ki}$ in *l.c.*, XIV, 127 : 4 (beginning of the reign of Shagarakti-Shuriash). In this last passage the same city is mentioned in l. 7, where its name is ^{âlu}*Dûr-*^{ilu}*En-lil-li-e*^{ki}—a most interesting writing, showing that even at the time of the Cassite kings ^{ilu}*EN.LIL* was pronounced and read Enlil resp. Ellil, or still better: *Enlilû* with a plural *Enlilê*, the long *û* or *ê* still betraying the fact that we have here a Semiticized Sumerian word. For such formations cf., *e.g.*, ^{gu}*-za* = *kussû* = Hebr. כסא, "throne." Clay's view, *A. J. S. L. L.*, XXIII, pp. 269f., that Enlil was always pronounced Enlil must be modified, as will be shown elsewhere. The name Enlil, signifying originally the chief god of Nippur, was in course of time applied to each and every god that played the same rôle in the religious conception of the Babylonians as did Enlil of Nippur. The same holds good of *NIN.LIL* = *Bêlit*, *É.KUR* – temple, ^{ilu}*Innanna* – Ishtar – goddess, *AN* = *ilu* = god; cf. the German word "Kaiser" = Cæsar, etc. In other words: Enlil, originally the *name* of a god, became later on a *title*, as such signifying "the highest lord," the *bêl* κατ' ἐξοχήν, just as *AN* became later on "*the god par excellence.*" Enlil, when a *name*, is read and pronounced Enlil, resp. Ellil, but when a *title*, it must be pronounced *bêl*. Not only linguistically, however, but also from a religio-historic standpoint is this name and writing important. It shows us that ever since the time of the "kings of Ur and of the four corners of the world," when Enlil of Nippur was referred to as ^{ilu}*En-lil-li En-lil*^{ki}*-a* (*E. B. H.*, p. 272, l. 5) or as *En-lil*^{ki}*-a* ^{ilu}*En-lil-li* (*E. B. H.*, p. 269, note 11; p. 271, l. 5), *i.e.*, "Enlil of the Nippurians" or "the Nippurian Enlil" (for the formation *En-lil*^{ki}*-a* = Nippurian, see *GISH-ḪU*^{ki}*-a* (*E. B. H.*, p. 79, l. 28; p. 81, l. 55) = ^{galu}*GISH.ḪU*^{ki} (*E. B. H.*, p. 76, ll. 5, 8; p. 81, note 1, *et pass.*). Ḫrozny's theory, *Z. A.*, XX (1907), p. 421f., to read *GISH.ḪU* = *Umma* or *Alma* is untenable. From the fact that *ḪU* has the pronunciation *Umma* or *Alma*, it does not yet follow that *GISH.ḪU* has to be read likewise *Umma* or *Alma*), there came to be known in Babylonia a "collection" (*ḫi.a*) of Enlils, among them *Sin* (of Ur), *Dagan* (of Isin), *Shamash* (of Larsa), *Marduk* (of Babylon), *AN-SHAR* = *Ashshur* (of Ashhur), and the Cassite Enlil = *Ḫarbe*, thus demonstrating beyond a shadow of a doubt that Enlil ceased very early to be a *name* and became a *title*. There is no *old* Enlil or *Bêl* as over against a *new* or later *Bêl* (= Marduk), but all gods called Enlil have simply put on the jacket of the chief god of Nippur, *i.e.*, they were identified with him—an observation clearly showing that the "religion" of Nippur formed the *pattern* after which the religion of all other Babylonian cities was formed. Cf. my remarks in *Old Penn*, February 16, 1907, p. 3. This latter statement is not contradicted by *B. E.*, XV, 102 . 13, 14, where we hear of two cities called *Dûr-*^{ilu}*MAR.TU-labiru*(= *SHA*)^{ki} (Clay, *l.c.*, p. 52*b*, *Dûr-Amurru-û*^{ki}) and *KI-II*(= *Dûr-*^{ilu}*MAR.TU*)*-eshshu*(= *BIL*)^{ki} (Clay, *ibid.*, *Dûr-BIL(NE)*^{ki}), for here *labiru*, resp. *eshshu*, does not refer to ^{ilu}*MAR.TU*, but to *Dûr*; *i.e.*, we have here an "old" and a "new" *Dûr-*^{ilu}*Martu*, or two parts (hence no items given for "new" *Dûr-*^{ilu}*Martu*) of one city, cf. the German *Alt-* and *Neu-Stettin*.

[2] Nos. 45 : 23; 57 : 15, 20, or only *Dûr-Ku-ri-Gal-zu*, Nos. 13 : 7; 23 : 29. From No. 13 : 7 it is evident that this city cannot have been too far away from Nippur, it being connected with it by a *ki-sir*(= *BU*)*-ti* or "stone dam," hence the same canal that passed by Nippur must have passed by Dûr-Kuri-Galzu (and ^{âlu}*Ardi-Bêlit*) likewise. The ruins represented at the right of No. I, below No. III (see the Plan of Nuffar in Hilprecht, *B. E.*, Series D, Vol. I, p. 305, and regarded by Hilprecht as covering the ruins of the fortified palace of the *patesis* of Nippur, which, like the palace of Sargon at Khorsabâd, formed a bulwark in the fortification line of Nippur), in all probability represent those of Dûr-Kuri-Galzu. Notice also that the "canal" which starts from the Shatt-en-Nil (for which see No. V), between Nos. I and IV, passes the lower part of the ruins to the right of No. I. The first occurrence of this place is in an omen-tablet (inspection of a liver) from the 11th year of Burra-Buriash, *B. E.*, XIV, 4 : 11, *LU.ARDU*^{mesh} *li-mur-ma a-na Dûr-Ku-ri-[Gal-zu] li-she-bi-l[am]*. This passage is not referred to in *B. E.*, XIV, nor in the corrections, *Z. A.*, XX (1907), p. 417f. It is again mentioned in *B. E.*, XIV, 12 : 42, dated *i-na* ^{arḫu}*KIN-*^{ilu}*Innanna II-tu* (*i.e.*, *shanûtu*) *shá shattu* 1^{kam} *Ku-ri-Gal-zu*. These two passages prove that this place was founded not by *Kuri-Galzu ṣiḫru*, but by the older *Kuri-Galzu*. Notice in this connection that the last quoted tablet gives us the first occurrence of a *second Elul* for the Cassite period, being called there not ^{arḫu}*KIN*(-^{ilu}*Innanna*) *II*^{kam} (*B. E.*, XV, 46 : 4) nor ^{arḫu}*KIN*(-^{ilu}*Innanna*) II$^{kam\ ma}$ (*B. E.*, XV, 46 . 3; 69 : 11; 106 : 5), but ^{arḫu}*KIN-*^{ilu}*Innanna II-tu*. This month had its origin, as we know,

(*d*) Certain *peculiarities* which our letters here have in common not only with

---

at the instigation of Ḫammurabi, see King, *Letters*, No. 14 : 6, where it is called ^{arhu}*KIN-*^{ilu}*Innanna II*$^{kam.ma}$. It was not recognized in *B. E.*, XIV, p. 62, No. 12, where the month is left out.

[3] Nos. 22 : 15(?) | 37 : 10 = $^{m\hat{a}tu}$*Tamtim*, the "sea country." For the close relation between Babylonia and the sea country at the time of the Cassites see Weissbach, *Babyl. Miscellen*, p. 7, where (*B. E.*, 6405) a certain *Û-la-Bu-ri-ia-ash* appears both as "king of $^{m\hat{a}tu}$*A.AB.BA*" and as "son (*TUR*) of *Bur-na-Bu-ra(?)-ri-ia-ash*" (probably the same as Burna-Buriash II, the son of Kuri-Galzu I, see p. 71). (Cf. now also King, *Chronicles concerning Early Babylonian Kings*, and Winckler, *O. L. Z.*, November, 1907, where it is recorded that *Ulam-Bur(i)ash*, the brother of *Kashtiliashu I*, conquers the "sea country," and that *Agum*, the son of *Kashtiliashu I*, "goes out against" the same country and "captures *Dûr-É.A*." For the occurrences of *A.AB.BA* = "sea" or "sea country," see also *B. E.*, XIV, 58 : 50, 53 (13th year of Nazi-Maruttash) | 168 : 18, 22, 23 | XV, 199 : 26, 27, 33, 38, 40, and the *GIR.RI A.AB.BA* in *B. E.*, XIV, 147 (= E. A. H., 182) : 6. In connection with the reading and the signification of the last mentioned expression, Clay, *B. E.*, XIV, p. 3, finds sufficient reason to correct a statement made in *E. B. H.*, p. 329, where the question was asked, "Is this latter (*i.e.*, *GIR.RI A.AB.BA*) to be classed among the kings of this dynasty?" He, although admitting that "it is not impossible that it is a ruler's name," thinks, however, that "the fact that there is no gap in that part of the list of kings which these archives represent, into which it would fit, speaks against it being a ruler's name." However, what is assumed by Prof. Clay to be a fact, can only be regarded as a theory—a theory from which other scholars, the present writer included, beg to differ. No valid reason has as yet been brought forward to show that, *e.g.*, Kuri-Galzu was the *immediate* successor of Burna-Buriash. On the contrary, there exists a great divergence of opinion with regard to the succession of Kuri-Galzu upon the reign of Burna-Buriash. To illustrate this I quote such prominent scholars as Winckler, *Das alte West-Asien*, p. 21; Delitzsch, *Chronologische Tabellen*; Weissbach, *Babyl. Miscellen*, p. 2f.; Hilprecht, *B. E.*, XX[1], p. 52, note 1. The latter, *e.g.*, when speaking of the succession of Kuri-Galzu upon Burna-Buriash's reign, expresses himself (*l.c.*) quite carefully, saying: "Kuri-Galzu, his (*i.e.*, Burna-Buriash's) son and *possibly not his immediate successor*." From this divergence of opinion it will be apparent that it is by no means a "fact" that there is no gap in that part of the list of kings which these archives represent. For a full discussion of the questions here involved see pp. 59ff. Clay, however, is doubtless correct in denying to *GIR.RI A.AB.BA* the title "king," and likewise in seeing in him no "person" at all. I also accept his proposition to read *Gir-ri Tâmtu*, but I am unable to agree with his interpretation of *Girri-Tâmtu* as a "place name," as which we find it (*l.c.*, p. 58*a*) mentioned in the list of "Names of Places." For both his reading and its identification with the name of a "place" he invokes as "conclusive evidence" a passage in *B. E.*, XIV, 131 : 2, "where *Girru* (= *KAS*) *Tam-tim* is written," comparing this with *Girru* (= *KAS*) *Dûr-ilu*^{ki} (*l.c.*, XIV, 161 : 7) and with *Gir*(*sic* Clay)*-ir-ru*, *Mi-iṣ-ru* (*Trans. Dep. of Arch. U. of P.*, Vol. I, Part 3, p. 223f.). On account of the importance of this new interpretation proposed by Prof. Clay, it is necessary to examine that author's "places" mentioned under *Girru*, *B. E.*, XIV, p. 58*a*, a little more carefully. We begin with *B. E.*, XIV, 131, which reads: 3 *qa NI DUG.GA* | *a-na KAS* (= *girru or ḫarrânu*) *Tam-tim* | $^{m\ ilu}$*NIN.IB-DUGUD-SHESH* (*sic* copy; *sc.* ^{mesh})*-shu* | *GAR-nu* | ^{arhu}*SHEG-a-an* | *shattu* 8^{kam} | ^{ilu}*Sha-garak-te-Shur-iâ-a*[*sh*]; *i.e.*, either "3 qa of good oil for the journey to the sea(-country) which N. is making," or, possibly better, "3 qa of good oil which *NIN.IB-kabtu-aḫi-shu* (= N. is the most important one of his brothers) has put up (*GAR-nu* = *shaknu*^{nu} = permansive; cf. in this connection *ma-ḫi-ir* = permansive, as *e.g.*, *B. E.*, XV, 86 : 6) for (*a-na*) the KAS, *i.e.*, the journey (lit. the way) to the sea." Then follows date. ACCORDING TO THIS TRANSLATION THE "PLACE" GIRRU-TAM-TIM RESOLVES ITSELF INTO A "JOURNEY TO THE SEA." *B. E.*, XIV, 161 reads: 17 *qa* 1 *DUG GÙ.ZI.NI GISH.BAR-SHE.BA* | 18 (*qa*) *NI GISH.BAR-5-qa* | 37 *qa SHE.GISH.NI GISH.BAR-SHE.BA* | ^{arhu}*DUL.AZAG* | *ûmu* 26^{kam} | *shattu* 23^{kam} | *KAS* (= *girru*, *ḫarrânu*) *Dûr-ilu*^{ki} | ^{m}*Nûr-*^{ilu}*DIL.BAT IN.SAR*; *i.e.*, "17 qa (in) one vessel, *kâsu* (see Meissner, *Ideogr.*, No. 2048)-oil, GISH.BAR provender, 18 (qa in one vessel) sesame-oil, GISH.BAR-5-qa, 37 qa of sesame, GISH.BAR provender, month Tishri, the 18th, year 23. Journey to Dûr-ilu. Nûr-DIL.BAT has entered" (*sc.* in the "Temple Archives," (cf. *shá i-na DUB.SHA RA … shaṭ-ru*, *B. E.*, XIV, 168 : 34, 43) as having paid out or received). *B. E.*, XIV, 147 (= E. A. H., 182, cf. *E. B. H.*, p. 329) reads: 28 (*gur*) *ZID.DA* | ^{m}*Î-li-ish-man-ni* | ^{arhu}*SHE.KIN.KUD* | *ûmu* 1^{kam} | *shattu* 10^{kam} | *gir-ri A.AB.BA*; *i.e.*, "28 gur of flour Ili-ishmanni (*sc.* has received or put up or given). Adar, the 1st, year 10. Journey

the "Temple Archives," but also with the letters from the Ḫammurabi and the Amarna periods. Among these may be mentioned:

(*a*) The use of *âlu-ki*,[1] or *a-li-ki*,[2] "city," for simple *âlu*.

(*β*) The use of *DISH* before *be-li*[3]—a peculiarity so far met with only in tablets of the Amarna[4] period.

to the sea." There is lastly a text which is of the highest importance in this connection here, but which has not been referred to by Clay, it being quoted by him neither under *Girru* (*B. E.*, XIV, p. 58*a*) nor under ^{alu}*BÀR.TUR*^{ki} (*l.c.*, p. 57*b*). Its importance consists in the fact that there is to be found between *KAS* (= *girru*) and *BÀR.TUR*^{ki} the determinative for "city," *âlu*, thus showing conclusively that *KAS* does NOT belong to *BÀR.TUR*^{ki}; if it did, such a place would have to be written ^{alu}*KAS.BÀR.TUR*^{ki}, and not *KAS* ^{alu}*BÀR.TUR*^{ki}, as we find it here. The text, *B. E.*, XIV, 107, reads: 31 *qa ZID.DA* | 24 (*qa*) *SHE.BAR* | *KAS* (= *girru*, *ḫarrânu*) ^{alu}*BÀR.TUR*^{ki} | 2 *qa SHE.BAR a-na te-e-ni* | *ûmu* 17^{kam} | ^{arḫu}*ENGAR shattu* 14^{kam} | ^{ilu}*Ka-dàsh-man-Tur-gu LUGAL.E*; *i.e.*, "31 qa of flour, 24 qa of barley (for the) journey to Parak-mâri (and) 2 qa of barley for grinding" (*têni* = *ḪAR.ḪAR* = *KIKKA* — *qa-mu-ú* = *GAZ* = *ḫashâlu*, cf. *H. W. B.*, p. 698*b*, and *B. E.*, XIV, 84 : 4 | 91 : 4 | XV, 171 : 11, KU.QAR GAZ ZID.DA). Then follows date. In the above given texts, then, the *KAS Tam-tim*, *KAS Dûr-ilu*^{ki}, *Gir-ri A.AB.BA*, *KAS* ^{alu}*BÀR.TUR*^{ki} are not "places," but "journeys" to *the places* named after *KAS* resp. *Gir-ri*, and the tablets in which these expressions occur do not represent "payments" (Clay, Table of Contents, *B. E.*, XIV, p. 71f.), but are what the Germans would call "*Verproviantirungs-Bescheinigungen*" resp. "*Anweisungen*." As such they are exactly similar to, *e.g.*, that published by Thureau-Dangin, *R. T. Ch.*, No. 351, which reads: "*X. qa zid-gu lugal* | *ud* 3^{kam} *sheg uru* | *X. qa zid KAS*(!)-*shù* | *Gimil-Ì-li lugh* | *ù Ib-ku-shù dumu nu-banda* | *A.AB.BA*(!)-*shù mu-gha-shù gin*(= *DU*)-*na*"; *i.e.*, "so and so many qa of GU-flour, royal quality, for (*a*) three days (stay) in the city, so and so many qa of flour to Gimil-Ili, the sukal, and to Ibkusha, the son of the nu-banda, *for the* journey (*KAS-shù*) to the sea (*A.AB.BA-shù*) which they make (lit. 'go') for the purpose (*shù*) of fishing (*mu-gha*)." Here is *KAS-shù A.AB.BA-shù* exactly the *a-na KAS Tam-tim* of *B. E.*, XIV, 131. A journey to the sea from Nippur demanded on account of its distance and duration some kind of "*Verproviantirung*." This, likewise, is true of a journey to Dûr-ilu on the Elamitic boundary, and if so, then Parak-mâri cannot be sought in the immediate neighborhood of Nippur, but must have been some distance away from the latter place. This note, I trust, will have shown the necessity of removing the *KAS* resp. *Girru-Tamtim* and the *Girru-Dûr-ilu*^{ki} from the list of "places," and of assigning to *Girru-Miṣru*, *i.e.*, "The Miṣru-road" = "road to Miṣru" its proper place among the "highways" of Babylonia.

[1] Cf. Nos. 24 : 22 | 27 : 20 | 28 : 17 | 34 : 39 | 38 : 6 | 52 : 6, 20 | 66 : 14, 27 | 83 : 17, 26. See here also *âlu-ki karû Ash-tab-gan-tug*, *B. E.*, XIV, 23 : 2; *âlu-ki*, *B. E.*, XIV, 5 : 3; *âlu-ki-Kal-bi-ia*, *B. E.*, XV, 66 : 2. Whether *KA A.GUR.DA-âlu-ki*, *B. E.*, XIV, 29 : 2, may be mentioned in this connection, or whether *âlu* be here = *ri* (cf. the god *Za-za-ru* and *Za-za-ri*, *E. B. H.*, p. 53, note 11, 10), *i.e.*, whether we have to read *Pî-nâriri-ki*, must remain, in view of *B. E.*, XIV, 35 : 12, *Pi-i-Na-a-ri*^{ki}, doubtful. For the Amarna period see the passages cited by Bezold, *Oriental Diplomacy*, p. 71; for the Ḫammurabi period cf., *e.g.*, *C. T.*, VI, 27*b* : 17, 24, 30, *âlu-ki*; *C. T.*, IV (Bu. 88-5-12, 689), pl. 45 : 21, *âlu-ki UD.KIB.NUN*^{ki}, and for the time of Naram-Sin, see Scheil, *Textes Élam. Sém.*, II, pp. 3, 13.

[2] No. 29 : 11. This is, however, doubtful, for *a-li-ki* may be taken here also as a first pers. praet. (*sic!*) of לקה and be translated "(as many as) I have taken," see pp. 100, note; 108, note 1.

[3] No. 20 : 1, 8, 9, 11, but in l. 4 it is omitted.

[4] Bezold, *l.c.*, p. XVI, says that *DISH* is found in the Amarna letters of the L. collection before *aiab* "foe," *iashi* "me," *amelu* "man," *ḫazânu* "prefect," *mâru* "son," *ramâni-ia* "myself," and *sharru* "king," but he omits *EN* = *bêlu*. In view of our letter, quoted above, we have to see in places like Amarna, L. 16 : 1, 21 or L. 52 : 1, *pass.*, where the sign for *EN* has the peculiar form of *I-en*, the determinative *DISH* + *EN* and read either ^{m}*EN* = *bêlu* or ^{I}*EN* = *bêlu*. Knudtzon, *Die El-Amarna-Tafeln*, has, quite correctly, recognized this *DISH*.

(γ) The use of *ḫal*,[1] also written *ásh-ásh*, to express the plural.

(*e*) Even *glosses*[2] seem(!) to appear in our letters—an observation showing that we have to do here with an originally *non*-Babylonian people.

[1] No. 33*a* : 3, 21, *âlu*^{ḫal}; *l.c.*, l. 15, *an-nu-ú-tum* (= plural) *âlu*^{ḫal}. Clay, *B. E.*, XIV, p. 58*a* is inclined to regard this in *l.c.*, 166 : 25 (read 21) as a new city, ^{alu}*ḪAL* or *Bârû*, but there *âlu*^{ḫal} is a *plural*, as a comparison with ll. 4, 8, 13, 16, 19 clearly shows. An ^{alu}*ḪAL* (Clay, corrections in *Z. A.*, XX (1907), p. 417f.) does likewise not exist in *B. E.*, XV, 132 : 1, where we are told what amounts of grain were paid out (*nad-nu*) in the cities (*âlu*^{ḫal}) of Ishtar-apal-iddina, who, therefore, must have been a *bêl piḫâti* with several *ḫazannâti* (city prefects) under his command. For other occurrences of *ḫal* = *ásh-ásh* see, *e.g.*, *B. E.*, XIV, 18 : 2, *âlu*$^{\text{ásh.ásh}}$; *B. E.*, XV, 185 I : 6 | 200 I : 7, *É A.N*$^{\text{ash.ásh}}$; *B. E.*, XV, 178 : 3 | 200 IV : 9, *MU*$^{\text{ásh ásh}}$ (Clay's copy gives in the last quoted passage *zîr* for *MU*, but this may be a peculiarity of the scribe). These passages quoted from Vols. XIV and XV for the use of *ḫal* as a plural sign may be compared with King, *Letters*, 39 : 5, *É*$^{\text{ḫi a}}$ *âlu*^{ḫal}, and Bezold, *l.c.*, p. 71, under *âlu*.

[2] While we have in No. 6 : 7 only *ISH*, and in No. 21 : 9 *ip-ru*, we find in No. 53 : 36, [. .] + 10 *gur ISH e-pi-ri*, with which cf. Amarna, L. 16 : 3, *ISH*, *i.e.*, *e-bi-ri*. Is No. 28 : 24, *A mu-ú ma-a'-du ù zi-na-nu it-tal-ku*, to be compared with Amarna, L. 31 : 10, *A*^{mesh}, *i.e.*, *mi-ma*?

II.

LETTERS BETWEEN TEMPLE AND STATE OFFICIALS.

The letters published in this volume may be conveniently subdivided into three classes:

(*a*) Letters of diverse writers addressed *a-na be-lí-ia*, "TO MY LORD," *i.e.*, letters written by various royal and Temple officials and addressed TO THE KING, Nos. 1–74.

(*b*) One[1] letter from a king (*LUGAL*) to Amel-Marduk, or, more specifically, a letter of King Shagarakti-Shuriash to his sheriff-in-chief and attorney of state (*GÛ.EN.NA*), No. 75, see pp. 132ff.

(*c*) Letters of several writers to certain persons named in the address; in other words, letters constituting an official correspondence between officers of the Temple and the State, Nos. 76ff.

For the sake of convenience and in order to show the fundamental difference between the letters of Class (*a*) and those of Class (*c*), as regards their "address" and "greeting," we begin with the letters between Temple and State officials. Among these letters we find:

1. One[2] addressed by a father to his son. Both hold official positions in storehouses (*karû*), but neither the name of the father nor that of the son is given.

2. One[3] written by a certain ^{m} ^{ilu}*A-shur-shum-êṭir*(*KAR*) to the governor[4] ^{m} ^{ilu}*En-lil-*[*bêl*(= *EN*)*-nishê*^{mesh}*-shu*],[5] who flourished at the time of Kadashman-Turgu.

3. Two written during the reign of Burna-Buriash by the celebrated trader in slaves, ^{m} ^{ilu}*En-lil-ki-di-ni*,[6] and addressed

[1] In all probability No 93 is a fragment of a royal letter.

[2] No. 76. For a translation see below, p. 144.

[3] No. 77.

[4] The *bêl piḫâti*; this follows from the greeting in l. 5, *ù a-na pa-ḫa-t*[*i-ka*] *lu-ú shul-mu*.

[5] Thus I propose to read his name, identifying him with the *bêl piḫâti* mentioned in *B. E.*, XIV, 99*a* : 16, 41; cf. *ibid.*, ll. 17, 20, 42 (dated the 11th year of Kadashman-Turgu). He was a contemporary of the *ḫazânu* ^{m}*Ki-di-nu-ú* and of ^{m}*Bana-a-sha-*^{ilu}*Marduk*, the writer of No. 9, see p. 5.

[6] For further details see below, pp. 51ff.

(*a*) To ^{m}*A-ḫu-shi-na.*[1]

(*b*) To ^{m}*Im-gu-ri.*[2]

4. Eight letters, addressed to certain officials, in which the writer calls himself "brother," *aḫu*,[3] of the one to whom he addresses his letters. Among these the following are to be mentioned:

(*a*) One[4] written sometime between the 12th year of Nazi-Maruttash and the 14th year of Kadashman-Turgu and addressed by $^{m\ ilu}$*En-lil-mu-kin-apal* (= *TUR.USH*)[5] to ^{m}*A-mi-[l]i-ia.*[6]

(*b*) Two from ^{m}*Erba-*^{ilu}*Marduk*[7] and addressed

(*α*) To the sheriff-in-chief at the time of Kudurri-Enlil, ^{m}*Aḫu-ú-a-Ba-ni*,[8]

(*β*) To $^{(sal?)}$*Da-ni-ti-ia.*[9]

[1] No. 78. An ^{m}*A-ḫu-shi-na* is mentioned also in *B. E.*, XIV, 25 : 12, 15, 23 (17th year of Kuri-Galzu) and in *l.c.*, 167 : 11, 12 (25th or better 26th year, which can refer only to the reign of Burna-Buriash, because Enlil-kidinni is mentioned in all other tablets as living only under that ruler's reign). From this we may infer that King Burna-Buriash reigned in fact at least twenty-five or twenty-six years. See also p. 1, note 3.

[2] No. 79. This person, although not mentioned in *B. E.*, XIV, XV, has to be identified with ^{m}*Im-gu-rum*, the writer of Nos. 22, 23. See introduction to No. 23 below, p. 94.

[3] This, no doubt, is to be understood *cum grano salis* and parallel to Burna-Buriash's calling himself "thy brother," when writing to the king of Egypt (cf., *e.g.*, *Amarna*, L. 2). That we are in many cases *forbidden* to take the term "brother" literally is shown, *e.g.*, by *C. T.*, XXII, Pl. 3, No. 11, where the writer ^{m}*SHESH*^{mesh}*-MU-*^{ilu}*Marduk* addresses his letter to his "brothers," *SHESH*^{mesh}, among whom is to be found *another* ^{m}*SHESH*^{mesh}*-MU-*^{ilu}*Marduk*. If "brother" were to be taken in its literal sense here, we would have *two brothers of the same name*—a thing impossible even among the Babylonians. *Aḫu* in this connection means probably nothing more than "friend."

[4] No. 80.

[5] Cf. *B. E.*, XIV, 55 : 4 (12th year of Nazi-Maruttash); *l.c.*, 56*a* : 24 (13th year of *ditto*); *l.c.*, 60 : 2 ; 62 : 2 (14th year of *ditto*); *l.c.*, 65 : 12 (15th year of *ditto*); *l.c.*, 99*a* : 20 (11th year of Kadashman-Turgu); *l.c.*, 106 : 2 (14th year of *ditto*).

[6] In this form it is found neither in *B. E.*, XIV, nor XV. Is ^{m}*A-mi-lu* the *ma*(!)*-ḫi-ṣu* (*sic!* not *ZU.ḪI.ṢU*, Clay, *B. E.*, XV, p. 26*b*; cf. *H. W. B.*, p. 400*a*, and Meissner, *A. P.*, p. 115, note 1), *l.c.*, XV, 37 : 15 (13th year of ?) to be compared with *Amili-ia* as "*Kosename*"; cf. the German "*mein Männchen*."

[7] Erba-Marduk, the author of No. 81, hailed either from Larsa or more probably from Sippar, while the writer of No. 82 was, no doubt, a Nippurian, see p. 23. The latter I would identify with the *DUB.SAR* Erba-Marduk of *B. E.*, XIV, 127 : 11 (dated in the beginning of the reign of Shagarakti-Shuriash) and with the writer of Nos. 13, 14. The former, being a contemporary of *Aḫu-ú-Ba-ni*, lived during the time of Kadashman-Enlil (see following note) and Kudur-Enlil. Cf. also *Mâr-Innibi*, 81 : 9, with *Inniba*, *B. E.*, XIV, 56*a* : 20 (13th year of Nazi-Maruttash) and *Ilu-MU.TUK.A-rîmu* (Meissner, *Ideogr.*, No. 3857), 81 : 16, with the person of the same name in *B. E.*, XIV, 116 : 6 (6th year of Kadashman-Enlil) and *l.c.*, 124 : 17 (8th year of Kudurri-Enlil). For possibly still another Erba-Marduk, see introduction to No. 35, p. 121, and cf. p. 107.

[8] No. 81. A son of *Aḫu-ú-a-B[a-ni]*, Nûr-Shuqamuna by name, is mentioned in *B. E.*, XIV, 119 : 32 (5th year of Kudurri-Enlil). The father, then, probably lived during the time of Kadashman-Enlil and possibly was still alive during Kudurri-Enlil's reign.

[9] No. 82. Before *Danitia* there is neither a *DISH* nor a *SAL* to be found. As in the texts of this period *all nom. propr.* have either the "male" or "female" determinative, it is apparent that *Daniti-ia* must be a kind of "*Kose-name*" or possibly one signifying a "profession." Notice in this connection the difference between *TUR.SAL* ^{m}(!)*Mà-*

(*c*) One[1] from ^{m}*Gu-za-ar-AN*[2] to the Temple official ^{m}*In-nu-ú-a.*[3]

(*d*) One[3] from ^{m}*Pân*(= *SHI*)-*AN.GAL-lu-mur*,[4] an inhabitant of *Dûr-ilu*^{ki}, to a high Temple and State officer of Nippur, ^{m}*NIN-nu-ú-a.*[5] This letter, although it had been sent to ^{alu}*UD.KIB.NUN*^{ki}, *i.e.*, to *Sippar*, where ^{m}*NIN-nu-ú-a* happened to be at that time, was found by the Expedition of the University of Pennsylvania at Nippur.

(*e*) One[6] written during the time of Burna-Buriash and addressed by ^{m}*Î-li-ip-pa-ásh-ra*[7] to [^{m}]*Da*(?)-*li-li-sh*[*á*?].[8]

(*f*) One[9] from ^{m} ^{ilu}*Sin*(= *XXX*)-*êrish*(= *ENGAR*)^{ish},[10] a storehouse official,

---

du-du (*B. E.*, XV, 163 : 13), on the one hand, and *TUR.SAL* (^{su}) *ma-an-di-di* (*B. E.*, XV, 155 : 7 | 161 : 4) resp. *TUR shá-an-gi-e* (*B. E.*, XV, 168 : 17) on the other. Cf. also our "Smith" and "smith." Notice further that whenever a *nom. propr* is found without the determinative *DISH* (or *SAL*) it does not signify the name of a person (kings are excepted because they are *gods*!), but a *place* called after that person, see, *e.g.*, ^{ilu}*Shamash*(= *UD*)-*tu-kul-ti* (*sic!* without *âlu*, *DISH*, and *ki*), 16 : 8, 12; ^{ilu}*Gir-ra-ga-mil*, 3 : 13, 17, 20, but also ^{alu} ^{ilu}*Gir-ra-ga-mil*, 3 : 38, 40 + fr. d, resp. ^{alu} ^{ilu}*Gir-ra-ga-mil*, 3 : 31. The name *Daniti-ia* by itself looks like a feminine of *Danâ* (for which cf. *H. W. B.*, p. 223*a*) + *ia*, but if it were a feminine then the *ka-shá* (l. 5) and *ta-ash-pu-ra* = second pers. (l. 10) would be, to say the least, quite strange; we would expect *kashi* resp. *tashpuri*. The name is not to be found in *B. E.*, XIV, XV.

[1] No. 87. [2] For this name see p. 7, n. 2. [3] No. 89. [4] See pp. 19ff.; 25, n. 4; 27, n. 8.

[5] In view of the fact that *NIN* has very often not only the pronunciation *NI* but also that of *IN*, we would be justified in identifying ^{m}*Nin-nu-ú-a* (No. 89) with ^{m}*In-nu-u-a* (No. 87). For *NIN* = *NI* cf., *e.g.*, ^{ilu} (^{ni})*NIN.IM*($^{ma\ ru}$)^{ki}, III R. 68, No. 3, 51, and see II R. 60, 23*a* + 22*b*; ^{ilu}*NIN*(^{ni})-*sa-a*, III R. 69, No. 5, 64; ^{ilu}*NIN*($^{ni\ ga\ re}$). *GA.KAS*, III R. 69, No. 4, 64 (see also ^{ilu}*EN*($^{ga\ re}$). *GA.KAS* in III R. 68, 21*a*); ^{ilu}*NIN.PISH* has the gloss *ni*(= *NIN*) + *ki-li-te* (= *PISH*), III R. 68, No. 3, 16. For *NIN* = *IN* cf., *e.g.*, ^{ilu}(^{in})*NIN ner-gál nin-e-ne-ge* = ^{ilu}*ditto e-tel-lit be-li-e-ti*, A. S. K. T., No. 11, col. III, 61f. (= II R. 18, 63), IV R. 55, 8*b*, with ^{ilu}*NIN ner-gal sag-gig-ga*, IV R. 56, 12*a*; 20*b*. This shows conclusively that *NIN* = *NI* = *IN*, and hence ^{m}*NIN-nu-u-a* "might" be read ^{m}*In-nu-u-a* and be identified with the addressee of No. 87. Neither ^{m}*In-nu-u-a* nor ^{m}*NIN-nu-u-a* are to be found in *B. E.*, XIV, XV. Comparing these two names with such formations as ^{m}*Aḫu-u-a*(-*Ba-ni*, No. 81 : 1), ^{m}*In-na-an-nu-ú-a* (*B. E.*, XV, 37 : 24), it would be better to transcribe ^{m}*In-nu-e-a*, ^{m}*NIN-nu-e-a* and regard the *ea* as the pron. suffix of the first person, "my." In that case these two names would be either "*Kosenamen*" or hypocoristica.

[6] No. 88.

[7] For the writing *NI.NI* = *ì-li*, a plural of majesty signifying always the *highest* god, whether he be Anu, Enlil, Sin, Dagan, Shamash, Marduk, Ashshur, etc., see *The Monist*, XVI (October, 1906), p. 637, and *l.c.*, XVII (January, 1907), p. 145, where it was shown that *NI.NI* may change with *DINGIR.RA*, *AN*, *AN*^{mesh} and *AN.AN*. An ^{m}*Ilu*(= *AN*)-*ip-pa-ásh-ra*, the father of NIN.IB-Ba-ni, is mentioned in *B. E.*, XIV, 2 : 9 (6th year of Burna-Buriash).

[8] The *Da* might possibly be *ik* or *SHESH*, and the *shá ia*. To judge from *ka-shá* (not *kashi*), l. 5, this name is that of a male person. A ^{m}*Da-li-lu*(!)-*shá* (= *male*) occurs in *B. E.*, XV, 156 : 23, but in *l.c.*, XIV, 58 : 7 (13th year of Nazi-Maruttash); XV, 163 : 8 | 188 II : 17 (here *li* = *NI*) that very same name is a *female*. If, after all, this name should have to be read as given above and should prove to be (notwithstanding the *ka-shá* in l. 5) a female, then cf. *B. E.*, XV, 163 : 35, ^{f}*In-na-ni-ia* (not ^{f}*In-na-an-ni-ia* as given by Clay, List of Names, *l.c.*, pp. 34*a*, 48*a*) with ^{m}*In-na-an-nu-ú-a*, *B. E.*, XV, 37 : 24. *Dalili-ia*, considered by itself, might be taken as a hypocoristicon and be translated "my obedience" sc. "is towards that or that god" a name applicable to both male and female persons.

[9] No. 90.

[10] According to *B. E.*, XIV, this person lived during the 24th year of Nazi-Maruttash (*l.c.*, 86 : 14) and the 7th (*l.c.*, 94 : 5), 10th (*l.c.*, 98 : 4), and 11th year of Kadashman-Turgu (*l.c.*, 106 : 12 | 111 : 6). From these passages we learn that he was the son of ^{m}*Nûr*-[. . . .] and the father of *Aḫudutum* and *Nergal-nâdin-aḫê*.

stationed, as it seems, at different points[1] at various times, and addressed, no doubt, to ^{m}*Irîm*(Meissner, *Ideogr.*, No. 3857)-*shu*-^{ilu}*NIN.IB*,[2] the chief bursar at Nippur during the time of Kadashman-Turgu.

(*g*) One[3] written by the royal official (probably *itû*) ^{m}*Il-li-ia*[4] during the reign of Nazi-Maruttash and addressed, as it seems, to the chief bursar of Nippur, *Martuku.*[5]

5. Four[6] letters addressed to ^{m}*In-na-an-ni*,[7] the chief bursar of the Nippurian Temple storehouses during the reign of Kuri-Galzu.

(*a*) Two[8] of these were written by the governor ^{m} ^{ilu}*NIN.IB* (or *MASH*)-*TUR.USH-SE-na.*[7]

(*b*) And two[9] by a lady of high rank, in all probability a *NIN.AN.GAL*[10] or high priestess, ^{f}*In-bi-Ai-ri*[11] by name.

6. One[12] from ^{m} ^{ilu}*D*(*T*)*ar-ḫu-nûr*(= *ṢAB*)-*gab-ba*,[13] a merchant, to ^{m}[*D*]*în* (= [*DI*]-*KUD*)-*li*-[*mur*].[14]

[1] In *B. E.*, XIV, 86 : 3 he appears as a witness at a transaction in the storehouse of *Kâr-Zi-ban*^{ki}; in *l.c.*, 98 : 2 the chief bursar of Nippur, ^{m}*Irîm-shu*-^{ilu}*NIN.IB*, transacts business for (*ki qât*) ^{m} ^{ilu}*Nergal-nâdin-aḫi*^{me}, son of ^{m} ^{ilu}*Sin*(= *XXX*)-*êrish*(^{ish}) at *Kâr* ^{ilu}*Ba-u*^{ki}, in *l.c.*, 106 : 12, he is found among certain witnesses at ^{alu}*Shar-mash*; in 111 : 6 ^{m} ^{ilu}*Nergal-nâdin-aḫi*^{mesh}, son of ^{m} ^{ilu}*Sin-êrish*(^{ish}), receives grain from (*ina qât*) ^{m} ^{ilu}*En-lil-zu-lu-li* and ^{m}*Irim-shu* ^{ilu}*NIN.IB* at the storehouse (*i-na bît karû*) of Nippur; and in our letter he seems to have been connected with ^{alu}*Dûr*-[. . . .], 90 : 5.

[2] Although the name is broken off, yet the circumstances of the time and the contents of the letter justify such an emendation. For this official see also Clay, *B. E.*, XIV, p. 8.

[3] No. 92.

[4] A person with this name occurs *B. E.*, XIV, 48*a* : 7 (6th year of Nazi-Maruttash). That he was a *royal* official I conclude from 92 : 24ff., *ḫa-mu-ut-ta shú-up-ra-am-ma a-na LUGAL lu*(!)-*ta-pu-ush ù nikasi*(= *NI*(*G*).*SHIT*)-*ni it-ti u-ḫa-mi-ish i ni-pu-ush-ma*, and that his position must have been a high one, such as was that of an *itû*, follows from 92 : 9, *ù SHE.BAR ma*-[. . . . . cf. l. 22!] *bêlê* (= *EN*)^{mesh} *pi-ḫa*-[*ti*, cf. l. 20; . . .]*ul i-ma-gu-ru* . . . .

[5] The name is broken off. The contents of the letter and the time when it was written justify this emendation.

[6] Nos. 83–86.

[7] See pp. 3ff.; 110ff.

[8] Nos. 83, 84.

[9] Nos. 85, 86.

[10] Or possibly a *NIN.AN.TUR*. For both of these expressions see pp. 4, note 8; 115.

[11] This "fruit of Ijjar" is not mentioned in *B. E.*, XIV, XV. Because she was writing to Innanni, she must have flourished during the time of Kuri-Galzu. For further details see "Translations," pp. 115f.

[12] No. 91.

[13] The first sign in this name is the last variant given in the "Sign List" of *B. E.*, XIV, No. 28; cf. *B. E.*, XV, 151 : 2, ^{m}*Lu-dar*(!)-*be-li*. For the identity of *Tar-ḫu*, *Tar-ku*, *Tar-gu*, see Hilprecht, *Assyriaca*, p. 119. *Tar-ḫu*, being called here "the light of everything (= the whole of the world)", is as such identified, not only with *Shamash* (cf., *e.g.*, Ranke, *B. E.*, Series D, III, p. 147*a*, *Shamash-nu-ùr-ma-tim*), but also with *Sin* (Ranke, *l.c.*, p. 163*a*, *Sin-nûr-mâti*; see also Clay, *B. E.*, XIV, 19 : 23). ^{ilu}*Sin* (= *XXX*) is according to II R. 48 : 33 = *TUR.KU* (gloss *du-mu-gu*), hence *D*(*T*)*ar-ḫu* = *Sin* = *Tur-k*(*g*)*u*. As regards the linguistic difficulties cf., for the change of *a* and *u* in proximity of an r, Hilprecht, *B. E.*, XX^{1}, p. 17, note 4, and for the change of *k* and *ḫ*, cf. *kammu* and *ḫammu*, Jensen, *K. B.*, VI^{1}, pp. 385, 568. After -*ba* there is broken away a -*ma*.

[14] As the *DI* and *mur* are missing, we possibly might read [^{m}*I-na*]-*ṣil*(= *KUD*)-*li*-[. . . .]. With ^{m}[*D*]*in-li*-[*mur*], *i.e.*, "may *he* see judgment," cf. 27 : 18 ^{m}*Di-in-ili*(= *AN*)-*lu-mur*, "may *I* see the judgment of god." Neither *Tarḫu-nûr-gabba* nor *Din-limur* is mentioned in *B. E.*, XIV, XV.

7. To this class have been added, after the plates and the MS. had been prepared for the press, several fragments, of some of which it may be doubtful whether they belong here or to the letters addressed "to my Lord."[1]

As only one[2] letter from this period has been published so far, it would seem advisable to treat of this class of literature in its general aspects more fully here.

Each and every letter consisted originally—as it does at our present time—of two integral parts: the ENVELOPE and the LETTER proper. None of the ENVELOPES of this class of letters has been preserved to us—an unmistakable sign that all these communications had been received and read by the addressee. From the analogy of other letters known to us and partly preserved in the collections of the University of Pennsylvania, we may, however, conclude that the envelope originally exhibited (*a*) an *address*, reading either (*α*) *a-na* ^{m}*Y.*, *i.e.*, "To ^{m}Y." (here giving the name of the addressee)[3] or (*β*) *dup-pi* ^{m}*X. a-na* ^{m}*Y.*, *i.e.*, "Letter of ^{m}X. (= writer) to ^{m}Y." (= addressee),[4] and (*b*) the *seal*[5] impression of the writer. In no case, however, was a *date* or the *place* of the writer or addressee ever put on the envelope—an omission which seriously hampers us in determining the time when or the place where or to which each letter was written.

The fact that all of these letters have been found at Nippur does not yet justify us in maintaining that they have been originally addressed to that place; for it can be shown that at least one of them, though found in Nippur, was yet sent to Sippar, whence it was brought back to the city of Enlil and deposited there with the rest of the Temple Archives. The purpose of the envelope, then, was to insure (1) privacy, (2) safe delivery to the person named, (3) authenticity.

The contents of the LETTER PROPER divide themselves easily into three parts:

[1] Nos. 93ff.

[2] This is to be found in F. E. Peiser, *Urkunden aus der Zeit der dritten babylonischen Dynastie in Urschrift, Umschrift und Uebersetzung*, Berlin, 1905, under P. 111. Its introduction reads:

A-na ^{m}*A-mur-ri-ia ki-bé-ma* | *[um]-ma* $^{m\ ilu}$*Sin(= XXX)-MU-[SE]*^{ma} *SHESH-ka-ma* | ^{ilu}*Sin* (= *XXX*) *a-ab AN*^{mesh} *kul-lat* | *nap-shá-ti-ka li-iz-zu-ru*, which cannot be rendered with Peiser by "*Sin der Vater der Götter möge all deine Seelen bewahren*," but must be translated by: "Sin and(!) the father of gods may protect all thy souls"; this follows clearly from *li-iz-zu-ru* = plural! Although this letter is very fragmentary, yet this much can be made out with certainty: The boundary stone of a certain piece of property could not be found, and hence its boundaries could not be determined exactly. A certain $^{m\ ilu}$*Sin(= XXX)-tab-ni-uṣur* knew the position of that stone; he, therefore, was asked: *al-ka-ma mi-iṣ-ri-ti kul-li-im ù ku-du-[ur-ru . . . .]*, *i.e.*, "come, show the boundaries and the boundary stone." The rest of the letter is too fragmentary to warrant any translation.

[3] Cf. the celebrated Lushtamar tablet with the address *a-na* ^{m}*Lu-ush-ta-mar* or the letter from the Sargonic period which is written *a-na Lugal-ushumgal*.

[4] Cf. per analogy the address of No. 24, *dup-pi* ^{m}*Kal-[bu] a-na be-lí-shú*.

[5] Traces of a seal impression are still discernible on No. 21. On the Lushtamar and the Sargonic tablets the seal is quite distinct and clear.

(*a*) *address*, (*b*) *greeting*, which is coupled in some instances with an invocation to the "gods" to bless and protect the addressee, (*c*) *subject matter*. With the exception of No. 76, where the subject matter of the communication is introduced quite abruptly by "thus (saith) thy father" (*um-ma a-bi-ka*),[1] the *address* of these letters is clad, in sharp contrast to those published under Nos. 1–74, into one of the following two formulas:

Into (*a*) *a-na*[2] *ᵐY. ki-bé-ma*[3] *um-ma ᵐX.-ma*,[4] *i.e.*, "to Y. speak, thus saith X."[5]

or

Into (*b*) *a-na*[6] *ᵐY.*[7] *ki-bé-ma*[3] *um-ma ᵐX. aḫu*[8]*-ka-ma*[9], *i.e.*, "to Y. speak, thus saith X., thy brother."[10]

In none of these letters, then, does the writer ever call himself "*thy servant*," nor does he ever express the humble petition, "*before the presence of my Lord may I come!*"—an observation which is, as we shall see, of the highest importance for the correct understanding of the nature of the letters here and those of Nos. 1–74.

The *greeting*, whenever it occurs in one of these letters, invariably takes its place after the emphatic *-ma* terminating the address.[11] Its simplest form is *a-na kâsha*[12] *lû*[13] *shulmu*,[14] *i.e.*, "unto thee greeting." If the addressee happens to occupy an especially high position in life, the writer may extend his greeting, as is done in No. 77, even to "the house" and the "domain" of his correspondent: *a-na ka-a-shá*

[1] This peculiar introduction of what the father had to say to his son is, no doubt, due not so much to the parental or any other relation as to the mental strain under which the father labored at the time when writing the letter. The son was negligent in making his report (*di-e-ma*) to the "barley overseer" (*be-el SHE BAR*), who in turn caused the "father" to delay his report to the "Lord" or King. For a translation of this tablet see below, p. 111.

[2] Nos. 77, 78, 79, 83, 84, 85, 86, 91.

[3] Also written *ki-bi-ma*, so in Nos. 77, 81, 82, 88, 91.

[4] This emphatic *-ma* is invariably found at the end of the address, and as such a *-ma* lengthens the preceding syllable, the name of the writer of No 85 cannot be *ᴵIn-bi-Ai-ri-im*, but must be *ᴵIn-bi-Ai-ri*.

[5] This is also the stereotyped formula used by Ḫammurabi when writing to his subjects, such as, *e.g.*, Sin-idinnam. For a justification of the above given translation of this formula see King, *Letters of Ḫammurabi*, Vol. III, p. XXV, note 1, Delitzsch, *B. A.*, Vol. IV, p. 135 below; Nagel, *B. A.*, Vol. IV, pp. 477ff. Knudtzon's translation (*Die El-Amarna-Tafeln*, *pass.*), "*hat gesprochen*," is out of place.

[6] Nos. 80, 81, 82, 87, 88, 89, 90, 92.

[7] In case the writer wishes to express his particular devotion to his correspondent he may add after *a-na ᵐY.* some such words as *shá a-ra-mu-shu*, "whom I love," cf. No. 89.

[8] Written either *SHESH-ka-ma*, Nos. 80, 81, 87, 88, 89, [90], 92, or *a-ḫu-ka-ma*, No. 82.

[9] As *aḫu-ka* is here the attribute to *ᵐX.*, hence an inseparable part of the latter, the emphatic *-ma* naturally takes its place after the attribute.

[10] For the signification of this term see already above, p. 14, note 3.

[11] *I.e.*, after *ᵐX.-ma* or after *aḫu-ka-ma*.

[12] Written either *ka-shá*, Nos. 82, 87, 88, 89 [90, 92], or *ka-a-shá*, Nos. 77, 81.

[13] Written *lu* in Nos. 88, 89, or *lu-ú* in Nos. 77, 81, 82, 87.

[14] *Shul-mu* in Nos. 77, 81, 82, 89 [90], or *shú-ul-mu* in Nos. 87, 88, 92. *DI-mu* has not yet been found.

bî[ti-ka] ù a-na pa-ḫa-t[i-ka] lu-ú shul-mu, i.e., "to thee, thy house, and to thy *paḫât* greeting." In many cases there is coupled with this greeting an *invocation* to the gods of the *writer's* city in the form of a prayer for the well-being and protection of the addressee. These invocations are of the highest importance, both for determining the exact domicile of the writer and for a correct understanding of the religion of the Babylonians. To illustrate this by one example I may be permitted to quote the "invocation" of No. 89 *in extenso*, gathering from it the facts that (1) *Pân-AN.GAL-lu-mur* (*i.e.*, "May I see the face of *AN.GAL*"), the writer, was a resident of *Dûr-ilu*^{ki},[1] whose gods he invokes, and that (2) the "divine court" of *Dûr-ilu*^{ki} was formed after the pattern of the Nippurian court, as such consisting of Father (*AN.GAL*), Son (*TAR*), and Mother (*NIN.LIL*)—three persons, though distinct, yet one: a veritable Trinity in a Unity.[2] It reads (89 : 4f.):

4 *AN.GAL*[3] *ù* ^{ilu}*NIN.LIL* ^{ilu}*TAR ù* ^{ilu}*GU*	*AN.GAL* and *NIN.LIL*, *TAR* and *GU*,

[1] See also 89 : 21, 26.

[2] Cf. *The Monist*, XVII (January, 1907), p. 148, and *Old Penn*, V, No. 21 (February 16, 1907), p. 3, col. III.

[3] That the divinity *AN.GAL* cannot be here = ^{ilu}*A-i* (II *R*. 57, 13*a*), the wife of ^{ilu}*SHAG.ZU* (= Enlil, Sin, Rammân, Shamash, Marduk), a female, but must be a *male*, is apparent from his being coupled with ^{ilu}*NIN.LIL*. *AN.GAL ù* ^{ilu}*NIN.LIL* are male and female, husband and wife. A male *AN.GAL* as god of *Dûr-ilu*^{ki} occurs also in Jensen, *K. B.*, VI, p. 64, 21 (cf. *l.c.*, p. 62, 20, where the verb *i-pu-la* = masc. (not *ta-pu-la*!) refers back to *AN.GAL*). Among the tablets of the Ur dynasty, now being copied and published by Dr. Myhrman, I saw a variant of date No. 12 (*E. B. H.*, p. 255), reading *mu AN.GAL* [*Dur-rab-ilu*^{ki}] *é-a ba-tur*, instead of, as it is commonly found, *mu* ^{ilu}*Ka-di Dûr-rab-ilu*^{ki} *é-a ba-tur*, *i.e.*, "in the year when *AN.GAL* was brought into his temple in *Dûr-rab-ilu*^{ki}," see also Thureau-Dangin, *S. A. K. I.*, p. 229, 7. This proves that *AN.GAL* = ^{ilu}*Ka-di*, and if *AN.GAL* be a *male*, then ^{ilu}*Ka-di* MUST be a *male* likewise. Again, in an inscription translated in *E. B. H.*, p. 255, note 12 (see Thureau-Dangin, *l.c.*, p. 176, 2) *AN-mutabil*, the *shakkanakku* of *Dûr-ilu*^{ki}, calls himself the *mi-gir* ^{ilu}*Ka-di na-ra-am* ^{ilu}*Innanna*, *i.e.*, "the favored one of Kadi, the beloved of Ishtar." Here Kadi is coupled with and in opposition to Ishtar, hence must be a male and the husband of Ishtar (= *NIN.LIL*). Lastly, in II *R*. 57, 54*a* ^{ilu}*Ka-di* is identified with ^{ilu}*Nin-Gir-su* and with ^{ilu}*NIN.IB*, both being *male* divinities and gods of thunder and lightning; hence Thureau-Dangin (*l.c.*, p. 176, 2, and *passim*), Huber (*Die Personennamen in den Keilschrifturkunden aus der Zeit der Könige von Ur und Isin*, *A. B.*, XXI, p. 171, note 11, who thinks that Kadi "*war die Hauptgottin von Dûr-ilu, die Gemahlin des* ^{d}*GAL*") and others, who see in ^{ilu}*Ka-di* a female, are wrong. The pronunciation of the name of this god is neither *Ka-di* nor *Ka-silim* (Huber, *l.c.*,) but ^{ilu}*Gu*(=*KA*)-*sir*(=*DI*=*NU*!); as such he is the same as ^{ilu}*GU.NU-ra* (= *Gu-sir-ra*). For the reasons of this identification see my forthcoming volume on the *Religious Texts of Nippur*. ^{ilu}*NIN.LIL*, here coupled with *AN.GAL*, hence his wife, is, of course, the same who otherwise is known as "the wife of Enlil," and who, as wife of Enlil, is "the mistress of *En-lil*^{ki}," *i.e.*, ^{ilu}*NIN.EN.LIL*^{ki}, II *R*. 59 : 9. But in the passage just quoted she appears not as the wife of Enlil, but as that of ^{ilu}*NIN.IB* or ^{ilu}*MASH*. We have seen above that *AN.GAL* or ^{ilu}*Ka-di* was identified with ^{ilu}*NIN.IB*. From this it follows that Kadi *originally* played the rôle of the "Son" (just as Enlil did in the Trinity. *AN-EN.LIL-AN*!), but was, when he became the chief god of Dûr-ilu, identified also with the Father, *i.e.*, with Enlil, whose wife now becomes also his (*i.e.*, Kadi's) wife. In the rôle of the "Son" we find Kadi also in such proper names as ^{m} ^{ilu}*Ka-di-da-bi-ib* (*bi*, *bu*; *B. E.*, XIV, 14 : 4; XV, 36 : 18, etc.), *i.e.*, "Kadi is speaking," *sc.* through, or by means of, the thunder; ^{m} ^{ilu}*Ka-di-da-bi-En-lil*^{ki} (*B. E.*, XV, 119 : 10. Omitted by Clay. Thus I read on account of the *t* in *bi*), which name might be translated either by "Kadi is the good (= *ṭâbi*, *sc.* child) of Nippur"

(*i.e.*, Enlil; cf. *Marduk apil Eridu*, where Eridu, the city of god É.A, stands for the god himself), or by "Kadi is the *dabi* (= *SHACH* = *ḫumṣiru* = "pig," the emblem of *NIN IB*, see *The Monist*, XVII (January, 1907), p. 143) of Nippur (= Enlil)." Again, if *NIN.LIL*, "the mistress or queen of Nippur," becomes the wife of *AN.GAL*, the highest god of Dûr-ilu, she *ipso facto* acquires also the title "mistress or queen of Dûr-ilu." This now helps us to understand the passage in Meissner, *Bauinschriften Assarhaddon's*, *B. A.*, III, p. 238, 42f. = *l.c.*, p. 297, 12 (K. 2801), together with its parallel text and variants in *l.c.*, p. 307, 31f. (K. 221 + 2669), which has been completely misunderstood by all who took *AN.GAL* resp. Kadi to be a female. The passage reads. *AN.GAL shar-rat Dûr-ilu*^{ki} ^{ilu}*Ṣir* ^{ilu}*Be-lit-balâṭi* (= *TI.LA*) ^{ilu}*Dur*(= *KU*)*-ru-ni-tum* ^{ilu}*SAG* ^{arḫu}*Bu-bi-e ki-rib biti a-na Dûr-ilu*^{ki} *âli-shu-nu ú-tir*. It will be seen that in this passage the gods of Dûr-ilu are not connected by "and," but are simply enumerated in their succession. From what was said above it follows that we have here "three pairs" consisting of *husband* and *wife*; have, therefore, to translate: "*AN.GAL* (and) the queen (= *NIN.LIL* = *bêlit* = *sharrat*) of Dûr-ilu [variant: ^{ilu}*GASHAN* (= *Bêlit*, mistress of) *Di-ri* (= Dûr-ilu)]. *Ṣir* (and) the *Bêlit-balâṭi* (= "mistress of life") [variant: ^{ilu}*EN.TI.LA* = "lord of life"!], *Dûr-ru-ni-tum* (= fem. of ^{ilu}*KU*($^{du-ru-nu}$) V.A, III *R.* 68, 9*a*) (and) *SAG* in the month *Bu-bi-e* into the temple in Dûr-ilu, their city, I brought."

According to the Nippurian pattern we can now establish the following Trinity for Dûr-ilu:

AN.GAL (Father) — *Ṣir* (Son) { *Bêlit-balâṭi* (wife of the Son) / *Bêl-balâṭi* (masc.!) } = { *Sharrat Dûr-ilu* (Mother) / *Bêlit Di-ri* }

which corresponds exactly to that of Nippur, viz.:

EN.LIL (Father) — *NIN.IB* (Son) { *Ba-ú* (*Gula*) (wife of the Son) / *NIN.IB* (masc.!) / *NIN.DIN.DUG.GA* / *NIN.EN.LIL*^{ki} } = *NIN LIL* (Mother)

In the Nippurian pattern *NIN.IB* appears as the *ur-sag*, "chief servant," or *sukkal*, "prime minister, ambassador," or *apil*, "son" of Enlil, and *Ṣir* is called in the Dûr-ilu Trinity the *me-ru*, "son" (or if read *ship-ru*, then = "messenger") of (*shá*) ^{ilu}*Ka-di*, see Scheil, *Textes Élam. Sém.*, I, p. 91, 23 (= Plate 17). *NIN.IB* is the *apil É-shar-ra*, and in V *R.* 52, I : 19, 20 ^{ilu}*Ṣir* is identified with ^{ilu}*She-ra-aḫ* and termed the *ra-bi-iṣ É-shàr-ra*, "the watchman of Esharra," *i.e.*, of the house of the totality, the Universe. *NIN.IB* as ^{ilu}*L* or as ^{ilu}*En-kur-kur* is the same as his father *Enlil*, and in V *R.* 31, 2, Rev. 30, ^{ilu}*Ṣir* is identified with his father ^{ilu}*Ka-di*. *NIN.IB* is both *male* and *female*. As *male* he is the *husband* and called also ^{ilu}*IB*, and as *female* he is the *wife*, then known also as *Ba-ú*, *Gula*, or *NIN.DIN.DUG.GA* = *muballiṭat mîti*, "who restores the dead to life" (see also *The Monist*, XVII (January, 1907), p. 141f.). The wife of *Ṣir* appears here likewise both as a *female* (*Bêlit-balâṭi*, "mistress of life") *and* as a *male* (*Bêl-balâṭi*, "lord of life"); hence she is paralleled exactly by *NIN.DIN.DUG.GA* = *Ba-ú* = *NIN.IB* female and male! From this we may infer (1) that *Ṣir* played the same rôle in Dûr-ilu as did *NIN.IB* in Nippur; (2) that Kadi must have been the "god of Esharra" according to the people of Dûr-ilu, just as Enlil was the "god of Esharra" according to the Nippurians, *i.e.*, Kadi = Enlil, and the wife of Kadi = *NIN.LIL* (cf. here also the name *AN.GAL* = Kadi with *AN.GAL.KALAM.MA*, the name of Enlil of Nippur, *B. E.*, XIV, 148 : 15, 18 | XV, 34 : 2); (3) that the "Son" in each and every case is the same as the "Father," *NIN.IB* = Enlil; *Ṣir* = Kadi; (4) that the "wife of the Son" is = the "Son" (hence male and female): they are "*one* flesh." Again, the "wife of the Son" is also identified with the latter's "Mother": ^{ilu}*NIN.EN.LIL*^{ki} = *Ba-ú* = *NIN.DIN.DUG.GA* is also = ^{ilu}*NIN.LIL*, the *Bêlit* κατ' ἐξοχήν, who otherwise was known also as *Ishtar*. But *Ishtar* is, as is well known, male and female and appears in the inscription of *AN-mutabil* as the wife of Ka-di, while in our letter the wife of *AN.GAL* (= Kadi) is called ^{ilu}*NIN.LIL*; hence *Ishtar* is = ^{ilu}*NIN.LIL* and both are *male* and *female*. (Cf. here also the ^{ilu}*Gá-ra* = *AN* = *Antum* = *NIN.LIL*, the wife of ^{ilu}*É-kur* = *AN* = *Anu* = *Enlil*, hence *Enlil* = *AN* and *NIN.LIL* = *AN*: *both are one—male and female*; see *Bêl, the Christ of Ancient Times*, p. 17). Now if the wife of Kadi = *AN.GAL* be male and female, then the same observation applies, *mutatis mutandis*, also to Kadi, *i.e.*, Kadi, the husband of *NIN.LIL* = *Ishtar* must be also a female; as such a female he appears in II *R.* 57, 18*a* and in Sp. 1, 331 (= *Z. A.*, VI, p. 241) compared with Reisner, *Hymnen*, p. 116, 11. The net result of this last observation is this: (1) the wife of the Son is not only one with the Son, but is also the same as the "Mother"; (2) the Mother being identified with the Father, the Father is thus proven to be *one* with the Mother (or third person) and *one* with the Son (second person); in other words the divine court of each and every city, though consisting of three persons, clearly distinct: the begetter (Father), the conceiver (Mother), the begotten (Son), are yet *one*: clearly and unmistakably a *veritable Trinity in a Unity*.

But how are we to account for ^{ilu}*Dûr-ru-ni-tum* and ^{ilu}*SAG* on the one, and ^{ilu}*TAR* and ^{ilu}*GU* on the other hand?

If ^{ilu}*Dûr-ru-ni-tum* be not only a fem. of ^{ilu}*Du(r)runa*, but also the wife of ^{ilu}*SAG*, as was claimed above, it would follow that ^{ilu}*SAG* is the same as ^{ilu}*Du(r)runa*, the masc. of Durrunitum. From III *R*. 68, 9*a* we learn that ^{ilu}*Du(r)runa* was the *first* (*SAG*) of the *seven* [*gud*?]-*balanga* (or is [*gud*]-*balanga* to be read here = *rabiṣu*?) *AN.NA-ge*, *i.e.*, "tambourines" (= tambourine-beaters, heralds, creatures who proclaim "the glory of God") of *AN.NA*. In Pinches, *J. R. A. S.*, January, 1905, p. 143f. (= 81 8 30, 25), Obv. col. II. 7, 6, ^{ilu}*SAG* is called *SAG.GAR*, *i.e.*, "*Hauptmacher*" = captain, chief (= the *first* (*SAG*), cf. *Du(r)runa*, the *first* of the "seven"!) and is identified with ^{ilu}*MIR*, which latter is according to *l.c.*, ll. 19, 20, not only = ^{ilu}*IM*, "the god of lightning," but also = *En-di-zu-gim* = *GU* (Pinches, *l.c.*, l. 1). In our letter ^{ilu}*GU* is coupled with ^{ilu}*TAR*, who is to be read according to III *R*. 68, No. 2, 53, *ki-tam-ma*, and is called there the *LU GH* or *sukkallu* ^{ilu}*Ka-di-ge*, *i.e.*, "the (chief) messenger of Ka-di." Taking all these passages together we might derive the following results:

1. God *TAR*, the messenger of Kadi, being coupled with *GU*, must be the latter's husband—in other words, *GU* is here a *female*.

2. *GU*, although a female, appears also as a *male*, being identified not only with *MIR* but also with *IM*—both male gods, and gods of thunder and lightning—nay, even with *SAG*.

3. *SAG* being coupled with the female ^{ilu}*Dûr-ru-ni-tum*, and being identified with *MIR*, *IM* and *GU*, must be a *male* and the masc. counterpart of *Dûr-ru-ni-tum*, *i.e.*, he is the same as *Du(r)runa*.

4. *GU*, the wife of *TAR*, is the same as *SAG*, the husband of Durrunitum—*i.e.*, *husband* and *wife* are ONE, hence also *male* and *female*. (Cf. for *TAR* + *GU* also *AN* + *KI* = *shamû* + *irṣitim* = *Anu* + *Antum* = husband and wife = *AN* + *AN* = *AN*, *Bêl*, *the Christ*, etc., p. 20f. Is the ^{ilu}*Tar-qu* an artificial (foreign, Cassite? or Elamitic?) name, consisting originally of ^{ilu}*Tar* and ^{ilu}*GU* = husband and wife = one, ^{ilu}*Tar-qu*?).

5. ^{ilu}*SAG*, because called "*Hauptmacher*" and identified both with the "god of storm and lightning," and with ^{ilu}*Dur(r)una*, the first of the seven heralds of *AN.NA*, must have been the "*Hauptmacher*" or chief, the first of the "seven," which seven can only be the "sevenfold manifestations" of the powers of nature, *i.e.*, of the lightning and storm. The "seven" correspond on the one hand to the "seven sons" of Bau (*Creation Story*, pp. 15 and 23, note 6), and on the other hand to "the seven gifts of the Holy Ghost" or the "seven archangels," or the "seven virgins," the emblem of the church, the sphere of the Holy Ghost, the "bride of the Lamb," "the body (!) of Christ." These "seven" were in the Babylonian religion *always* identified not only with the "Son" whose "servants" (*nu-banda* = *ekdûti* = *ḫazânu*) they were, but also with the "*Mother*," resp. "the wife of the Son" hence *Labartu* (Myhrman, *Z. A.*, XVI, 153 — Weissbach, *Babyl. Miscellen*, p. 42) and *Ishtar* had "seven names" (Reisner, *Hymnen*, p. 109, 57f.), hence also the remarkable name of ^{ilu}(*NIN.LIL* =) *NIN.GAL* in V *R*. 30, 46*a*, where she is called ^{ilu}*Si-VII-bi*, *i.e.*, "the goddess Seven." (Cf. here also the seven names of ^{ilu}*NIN.LIL*, III *R*. 68, 5*c*, *dff*. — III *R*. 67, 20*a*, *bf*., the fourth of which is ^{ilu}*Su-kur-ru*, who is identified in Thureau-Dangin, *R. T. Ch.*, 10 : 3, with *Im-gig-ghu*, a cognomen of ^{ilu}*Nin-Gir-su* = ^{ilu}*NIN.IB*, the god of thunder and lightning. See further the "seven sons" of ^{ilu}*NIN KA.SI* or $^{ilu(si-ri-is)}$*RIQ* (the wife of *Ka-di*), III *R*. 68, No. 1, 26*c*. *fff*.; "the seven sons" of ^{ilu}*Pap-nigin-gar-ra* and ^{ilu}*Nin-pap-nigin-gar-ra* (*i.e.*, of *NIN.IB* and *Gula*) in III *R*. 67, No. 1, 25*c*, *dff*.; the seven sons of ^{ilu}*En-me-shàr-ra*, III *R*. 69, No. 3, 61*a*, *b*, etc., etc.). This name shows clearly that "the seven" were considered to be "one" (notice also that in the religious texts very often the singular is used in connection with the ^{ilu}*VII-bi*)—just as the "sevenfold gift" of the Holy Ghost is the Holy Ghost in her (*ruaḫ* is feminine) completeness, or as the "seven virgins" are "the Church," the "bride of the Lamb." These "seven," when pictorially represented on seal-cylinders, etc., appear as *seven* weapons—six of them are to be found generally on the back of the god or goddess and one (the twin-god = *Shàr-ur* and *Shàr-gaz*, etc.) in his or her hand, or as *seven* curls, braids (Gilgamesh! Samson: in the hair lies the strength!), or as *seven* rays or beams of light, etc., etc. And as these *seven* represent the *fulness* of the power of the divinity, the number *seven* became in course of time the "number of the fulness of the

5 *AN*^{mesh} *a-shib É-DIM.GAL-* KALAM.MA[1]	the gods that inhabit É-DIM.GAL-KALAM.MA,
6 *nap-shá-ti-ka li-iṣ-ṣu-ru*	may protect thy life (lit. souls),
7 *ki-bi-is-ka li-shal-li-mu*	keep thy steps!
8 *libbi*^{bi} *a-na a-ma-ri-ka*	(How) my heart has urged me
9 *iṣ-ṣi-ḫa-an-ni*[2]	to see thee!
10 *man-nu pa-ni-ka ba-nu-ti li-mur*[3]	Whosoever may be permitted to see thy gracious face
11 *ù da-ba-ab*[4] [*ḪI* (– *ṭâb*)^{ab}][5]	and who is of "good words,"
12 *ki*(?)[6]*-na NIN*(?)-[. . . .]	to . . . .

godhead," it became the divine and sacred number *par excellence*. Cf. the *sevenfold* candlestick, the emblem of the fulness of the divinity in the Old Testament. See here my article "The Latest Biblical Archaeology" in the *Homiletic Review*, February, 1908 (written March, 1907), pp. 100ff. To make the certain doubly certain I may mention in this connection that there appears in III *R* 68, 11*a*, as the *third* of the *seven* tambourine(-beaters, heralds, angels) a certain ^{ilu}*Galu-An-na*, to be read in Assyrian ^{ilu}*Amel-ili*, who is in Hebrew none other than the well-known *Gabri-el*, "the man of *El* or *ilu*"—one of the seven archangels, the heralds and proclaimers of the glory of God when he appears under thunder and lightning and through whom he reveals himself! For a full discussion of all questions raised here see my forthcoming volume on the *Religious Texts of the Temple Library of Nippur*. In conclusion I shall give here the two parallel *Trinities* of *Dûr-ilu* as gathered from our letter and from the building inscriptions of Assarhaddon:

AN.GAL (Father) — ^{ilu}*TAR* (Son) — ^{ilu}*GU* (wife of Son) = ^{ilu}*NIN.LIL* (Mother)

{ *AN.GAL*, ^{ilu}*Ka-di* } — ^{ilu}*Ṣir* — { ^{ilu}*Bêlit-*, ^{ilu}*Bêl-* } *balâṭi* = { ^{ilu}*Shar-rat Dûr-ilu*^{ki}, ^{ilu}*Bêlit-Di-ri* }

^{ilu}*SAG* (husband) ^{ilu}*Durrunitum* (wife)
^{ilu}*GI*
^{ilu}*MIR*
^{ilu}*Du(r)runa*
} The first of the *seven* manifestations of the powers of nature (= Son).

[1] If the Trinity of Dûr-ilu be formed after the pattern of the Nippurian, it follows that the temple of that city must bear the same or similar names as that of Nippur. *É DIM.GAL-KALAM.MA* means "The temple (*É*) which is the great (*gal*) firmament (lit. 'band,' *DIM* = *riksu*) of the world (*sc* here the 'Babylonian world' as microcosmos formed after the macrocosmos)." Among the names of Enlil's temple at Nippur we find, *e.g.*, *Dur-an-ki*, *i.e.*, "the firmament (*dur* = *riksu*) of heaven and earth (*i.e.*, the world, the macrocosmos)"; see also *Bêl, the Christ*, etc., p. 21 and notes.

[2] *I*^{2} of צוח. Cf. N. E., 63 : 50, *in-ba na-shi-ma a-na a-ma-ri ṣa-ai-aḫ* and see Jensen, *K. B.*, VI^{1}, pp. 411, 440, 169.

[3] That is, "all who are in thy immediate *entourage*, who have the privilege of appearing before thee, who are thy friends and equals." Cf. here the New Testament phrase, "to see the face of Christ" = "to be like Christ," the highest honor conferred upon Christians

[4] Those "of good words" (lit. "speaking") are the friends outside the immediate environs of a person. All persons, near and far, who are not slanderers may listen.

[5] Supplemented according to 38 : 7f., *ma-an-nu pa-an ba-nu-tum shá be-li-ia li-mur* [*ù*] *man-nu da-ba-ba ḪI-ab* (= *ṭâb*) [*a-na*] *be-li-ia li-il-te-mi um-ma-a a-na be-li-ia-ma*.

[6] According to the passage quoted in the preceding note, we would expect here *a-na aḫi-ia* or better *a-na* ^{m}*NIN-nu-ú-a*. The traces on the tablet are, however, as reproduced. The sign *NIN*(?) looks rather like a *SAL* + *ma* = *mimma*; besides, if *NIN*(?) were the beginning of *NIN-nu-ú-a*, we miss a *DISH* before the *nom. propr.*

13 *lish-te-[me]*	may listen!
14 *um-ma-[a a-na aḫi-ia-ma]*	The following to my brother:

Again, Nos. 81, 82 seemingly appear to have come from the same writer, Erba-Marduk. Yet the fact that the writer of No. 81 invokes "Shamash and Marduk,"[1] while he of No. 82 implores "the significant lord,"[2] speaks, no doubt, in favor of a separation of both writers. I believe, therefore, that the author of No. 81 was an inhabitant of either Larsa or Sippar,[3] and that the writer of No. 82 hailed from Nippur,[4] being at the time when this letter was written away from his seat of residence. To deduce from the invocation in each and every case the exact domicile of the writer is, of course, not possible, because we do not know as yet *all* Babylonian cities with their chief gods. Thus it would, *e.g.*, be useless trying to determine the habitat of the writer of No. 87, who invokes for the protection of the life of his brother "the gods that inhabit the great heavens."[5] An argument *ex silentio* is rather precarious, yet the complete absence of any form of greeting or blessing or endearing term as "brother" in all letters addressed to ^{m}*In-na-an-ni*,[6] the severe and sometimes disagreeable[7] chief bursar of the Temple storehouses at Nippur, is significant.

The *subject matter* of a letter, following, as it does, immediately upon the address, or, if the address be coupled with a greeting[8] resp. an invocation, upon the latter, is

[1] No. 81 : 1, ^{ilu}*UD ù* ^{ilu}*Marduk nap-shá-ti-ka li-iṣ-ṣu-rum*.

[2] No. 82 : 6, *be-li kab-tum [nap-sha]-ti-ka li-iṣ-ṣur*. *Kabtu*, when used figuratively, has the signification "heavy" (*sc.* in *quality*, not quantity), *gewichtig*, *bedeutungsvoll*, significant, weighty, important, foremost, first (= *asharidu*), and when attributed to a *god* makes that god play the rôle of the "Son"; *i.e.*, an *ilu kabtu* is in every case the god of "lightning, thunder, and storm." This title is attributed, among others, to *Nabû* (the preacher, or herald of the Father, IV *R.* 11, No. 3 : 13, 14), *NIN.IB* (cf. the *nom. propr.* $^{m\ ilu}$*NIN.IB-kabtu* (= *DUGUD*)-*aḫê*(!)-*shu*, *B. E.*, XIV, 131 : 3. Only by reading *aḫê* (even if written without *me* or *mesh*) instead of *aḫi* (Clay) does this name give any sense: "*NIN.IB* is the weighty one among his brothers"), *En-lil* (IV *R.* 24, No. 2, 11, 12, 23, 24. Enlil is here not the "god of heaven and earth," but "the lord of the *LIL* or storm"—one of the few passages which betray the fact that Enlil *originally* played the rôle of the "Son," and this he did in the Trinity: *AN* (Father), ^{ilu}*En-lil* (Son), *AN* = ^{ilu}*NIN.LIL* (Mother)).

[3] Seeing that Larsa (*UD.UNUG*^{ki}) is mentioned neither in these letters nor in *B. E.*, XIV, XV, while Sippar (*UD.KIB.NUN*^{ki}) occurs quite frequently (see, *e.g.*, No. 89 : 21, 26, and the *Kâr-UD.KIB.NUN*^{ki}, *B. E.*, XV, 109 : 1), I prefer to regard Sippar as the home of the writer of No. 81.

[4] Where *NIN.IB* was worshiped as the "Son," the *be-li kab-tum*.

[5] No. 87 : 5, *AN*^{mesh} *shá a-si-bu ina sha-me-[e rabûti]*. Thus I propose to read, and by doing so I take the sign looking like *rat* to stand for *sha-me-[e]*. Cf. here an analogous passage in *B. E.*, X, 96 : 5, where Clay, *l.c.*, p. 69*a*, finds a city *Kab-ri(tal)-li-ri-im-me-shi*, but where *me-shi* has to be separated from the name of the city and has to be read *sha ina* (= *me*) *pâni* (= *shi*); see *The Monist*, XVII (January, 1907), p. 151.

[6] Nos. 83–86.

[7] This applies also to Aḫushina (78 : 1), as the expression *li-ti-ga-am at-ta* shows. The slave-dealer Enlil-kidinni was dissatisfied with the actions of Aḫushina.

[8] In 39 : 2 the introductory *um-ma-a a-na be-li-ia-ma* stands, quite strangely, *before* the greeting.

invariably introduced directly, either without[1] or with the help of *um-ma-a*,[2] or *um-ma-a a-na* ^{m}*Y.-ma*.[3] As most of the letters published in this volume do not deal with one subject only, but discuss, on the contrary, very often as many as ten different affairs, it is of the highest importance to be acquainted with certain *particles* and *phrases* that are employed to introduce either (*a*) a completely *new subject matter*, not referred to in a previous communication, or (*b*) the *answer* to a former inquiry or note.

Among the *particles* or *phrases* used by the writer in order to *introduce* his *answer* (*um-ma-a*[4]) to a former note or inquiry may be found the following:

(1) *ásh-shum*[5]; (2) *shá*[6]; (3) *i-na bu-ut*[7]; (4) *shá ta-ash-pu-ra*[8]; (5) *shá x.x. shá*

[1] So among other places also in Nos. 76 : 2 | 78 : 1 | 81 : 3 | 85 : 3. Cf. here for the letters discussed under Chap. III, Nos 3 : 1, 7 : 1 | 8 : 3 | 12 : 1, 21 : 1 | 22 : 5, 23 : 4 | 33 : 7 | 35 : 1 | 37 : 7 | 40 : 3, 49 : 2 | 52 : 5.

[2] Nos 81 : 5 | 83 : 3. This introductory *um-ma-a* is not to be found in Nos. 1–74; cf. the following note.

[3] Nos. 80 : 1 | 82 : 8 | 87 : 7, 92 : 1. To the *um-ma-a a-na* ^{m}*Y.-ma* corresponds in Nos 1–74 an *um-ma-a a-na be-li-ia(-a) ma*, which is most generally found in connection with the address: *ardi-ka* ^{m}*X. a-na di-na-an be-li-ia lul-lik*, where it follows either (*a*) immediately upon *lullik*, so in Nos 1 : 3 | 4 : 4, 21 : 3, 29 : 3, 39 : 2 | 40 : 2, 41 : 2 | [45 : 3], or (*b*) upon the "greeting," as in Nos. 9 : 5 | 11 : 3 | 26 : 3 | 27 : 3 | 31 : 5—but in 39 : 2 it stands *before* the greeting!—or (*c*) upon the "invocation," so in No. 38 : 11. In connection with the address: *a-na be-li-ia ki-bé-ma um-ma* ^{m}*X.-ma ardi-ka-ma a-na di-na-an be-li-ia lul-lik* it is found in three passages only, viz., in Nos. 13 : 4 | 14 : 4 | 17 : 6. In No. 26 : 3 we have wrongly *be-li-ia* for *be-li-ia-ma*.

[4] Sometimes also *um-ma*, instead of *um-ma-a*, is found. Notice here that the *um-ma-a* resp. *um-ma*, in connection with these particles or phrases, may (1) *introduce the answer* to an inquiry (= "I beg to state that"), (2) introduce a *quotation* from a previous communication (= "saying"), (3) may be *left out* altogether. For examples, see under the following notes, *passim*, and cf. below *sub* 11, pp. 26 and 27, note 8.

[5] *I.e.*, "as regards." Cf. 81 : 6f., *ásh-shum mári*^{mesh} *Ni-ib-bu-rum shá GÙ.EN.NA-ka ash-shá-mi-ka im-ta-na-aḫ-ḫa-rum um-ma-a a-na Mar-*^{m}*In-ni-bi a-na di-ni* [. . . .]; *i.e.*, "as regards the Nippurians whom thy (deputy) sheriff has received on thy account (= upon thy command) (*sc.* for the purpose of holding them as prisoners), the following 'To Mâr-Innibi for judgment [they have been brought, or he has brought them].'" Cf. here also Nos. 11 : 4 | 14 : 5 | 23 : 33 | 26 : 8, 12, 17 | 27 : 15 | 28 : 5 | 34 : 19 | 35 : 13, 15, 25, 30 | 57 : 2, 4 | 60 : 8 | 69 : 3.

[6] With the same meaning as *ásh-shum*, *i.e.*, "as regards," Nos. 83 : 8, 15 | 86 : 16 | 87 : 8 (followed by *shá iq-ba-[a]*, cf. p. 25, note 3*b*; p. 26, note 5). See also Nos. 3 : 21, 24 | 17 : 7, 8 | 31 : 11, 15, 25, 27, 34 : 33 | 60 : 9.

[7] With the same or similar meaning as *shá* or *ásh-shum*, see also p. 25, note 4, and cf. 83 : 19 (context mutilated), translation on p. 112. Among the letters addressed to the "Lord" we find it, *e.g.*, in 11 : 7, *i-na bu-ut KU*$^{bi\ a}$ *be-li la i-sa-an-ni-iq-an-ni*, cf. below, p. 109. The *i-na bu-ut di-qa-ra-ti a-na ra-di-i al-ta-[pa]* of 15 : 10 does not belong here; see p. 142.

[8] "With regard to what thou hast written," or "replying to your recent communication," so far not yet found in this class of letters. It corresponds in the letters, Nos. 1–74, to *shá be-li ish-pu-ra*, "with regard to what my Lord has written," which latter may be found either *with*, so in 3 : 29 | 26 : 3, or *without* following *um-ma-a*, cf. 39 : 38, "xx. concerning which my Lord has inquired (*sc.* I beg to say that = *um-ma-a*) *a-na be-li-ia ush-te-bi-la*, 'I have sent (it) to my Lord.'" Cf. here also 62 : 7? *Um-ma-a* in 33*a*: 6 introduces a quotation from a previous communication; the answer to this quotation begins with *um-ma-a a-na be-li-ia-ma*, l. 9; for a translation see p. 137. Cf. here also 31 : 18 and [*i-na-a*]*n-na ki-i shá be-li i-shá-pa-[ra]* in 3 : 60.

ta-ásh-pu-ra[1], or abbreviated, *shá x.x. ta-ásh-pu-ra*[2]; (6) *ásh-shum x.x. shá ta-ash-pu-ra*[3]; (7) *a-na bu-ut x.x. shá ta-ash-pu-ra*[1]; (8) *x.x. shá tash-pu-ra* resp. *taq-ba-a*[5];

[1] "With regard to x.x. concerning whom (which) thou hast written (lit. sent)," see No. 86 : 18f: *shá* ^{m}*E-mi-da-*^{ilu}*Marduk shá ta-ásh-pu-ra ul na-ka-rum shú-ú a-ḫu-ia um-ma a-bi-ta lu shú-pi-is-su at-ta am-mi-ni ki-i ar-di te-te-pu us-su*; *i.e.*, "as regards Emida-Marduk concerning whom thou hast written (*sc.* I beg to state — *um-ma-a*) 'he is not the enemy (evil person), he is my brother,' (therefore), please (*um-ma*) grant him his wish, etc." Notice in this connection that *lu* is connected here with the *Imperative*. Or have we to suppose that *shupissu* is = *shupussu*, Permansive III[2]? Prof. Hilprecht translates differently, regarding the *lu* as a mistake for *ku*(—*ka*), "thy," and taking *abita* in the sense of command, order, edict, in which it generally appears in the letters of the Kuyunjuk Collection: "As regards Emida-Marduk, concerning whom thou hast written: 'he is not the enemy, he is my brother,' (I beg to state) thus: 'make him execute thy order (*abitaku*).'" Cf. in this connection p. 110, note 3.

[2] The *a* in *ra* shows that this is a relative clause, *i.e.*, that a *shá* has to be supplied before *ta-ásh-pu-ra*. (For another similar abbreviation see below, note 3). Cf. 86 : 4, *shá AZAG GI ta-ásh-pu-ra um-ma-a shá mári*^{mesh} *EN.LIL*^{ki} *AZAG GI ḫaṣ*(?)*-ṣu-na*(!) *shú-ú i-na EN LIL*^{ki} ^{amelu}*DAMQAR*^{mesh}, etc.; *i.e.*, "as regards the gold (*ḫuráṣu*) concerning which thou hast written I beg to say (*um-ma-a*, so better than 'saying,' and making what follows a quotation): 'he of the Nippurians who keeps the gold is in Nippur, may the merchants, etc.'" Notice here the form *ḫaṣ-ṣu-na* relative clause as indicated by the *a* of *na*. It must be a Permansive II[1]; but how is the *a* of *ḫaṣ* to be explained? We would expect *ḫuṣ-ṣu-na*. Have we to suppose that *ḫaṣ* had also the value *ḫuṣ*? The forms *ba'i* = *bu'i*, Delitzsch, *Gram.*, p. 270; Jensen, *K. B.*, VI[1], p. 350, or *ba'amma* = *bu'amma*, Jensen, *l.c.*, p. 372, are hardly analogous here, because in these latter forms the *a* is due, no doubt, to the *b*. In view of the imperative *rammik*, *Gr.*, *l.c.*, for *rummik*, we might see in *ḫaṣṣuna* a dialectical *Nebenform* of the Permansive for *ḫuṣṣuna*. Prof. Hilprecht regards *ḫaṣṣuna* as being differentiated from the regular *ḫuṣṣuna*, Perm. II[1], under the influence both of the final "*a*" of this word and of the "*á*" in the preceding *ḫuráṣu*, to facilitate the pronunciation of the two words (containing both *ḫ* and *ṣ*) by avoiding three "*u*" words immediately following each other. Per analogy, we would expect in Nos. 1–74 a phrase like: *shá x.x. shá be-lí ish-pu-ra*, but this is not found in our letters. Instead of it we have, so far, only *ásh-shum x.x. shá be-lí ish-pu-ra*; see the following note.

[3] With the same signification as *shá x.x. shá ta-ásh-pu-ra*, cf. also *shá* and *ásh-shum*. Cf. 82 : 9, *ásh-shum* ^{amelu}*AZAG GIM* (= *kudimmu*) [*shá*] *ta-ash-pu-ra*, context mutilated. This phrase corresponds in Nos. 1–74 to (*a*) *ásh-shum x.x. shá be-lí ish-pur-ra*, so in 11 : 16 | 23 : 19 | 26 : 15, for which see pp. 99, 119. Cf. also 27 : 12, *ásh-shum NI.GISH pish-shat bît be-lí-ia shá be-lí ish-pu-ra* 1 (*gur*) 24 (*qa*) *NI GISH pish-shat shatti* 1^{kam} 1 *qa NI.GISH ul ad-din*, *i.e.*, "as regards the oil, ointment for the house of my 'Lord,' concerning which my 'Lord' has written (*sc.* I beg to state that) 'of the 1 *gur* 24 *qa* of oil, ointment for one year, I have not (yet) given (paid, delivered) a single *qa*.'" Or 27 : 18, *ásh-shum* ^{m}*Di-in-ili-lu-mur shá be-lí ish-pu-ra um-ma-a a-bu-us-su-ú ṣa-ab-ta-ta i-na âlu-ki i-na a-shab be-lí-ia a-na be-lí-ia* [*a*]*k-t*[*a*?]*-be* (or *bi*?)*-ma*; *i.e.*, "as regards *Dîn-ili-lûmur*, concerning whom my 'Lord' has written, saying (= *um-ma-a*, introduces here *quotation* from previous communication, *not* the answer): 'Art thou interceding for him?' (the long *ú* in *a-bu-us-su-ú* indicates a *question*, *Gr.*, p. 215, ;) (*sc.* I beg to say that = *um-ma-a* = answer to inquiry) 'I have spoken in the 'city' (*i.e.*, Nippur) in the presence of my 'Lord' to my 'Lord,' etc.'" See here also 27 : 27 | 57 : 2 | 59 : 16. (*b*) To *ásh-shum x.x. shá be-lí iq-ba-a*, 23 : 11, 21, see pp. 98, 99. (*c*) To *ásh-shum x.x. be-lí ish-pu-ra* (*sc.*, *shá* before *be-lí* and cf. above, note 2), cf 26 : 17 (see p. 119); 28 : 5, *ásh-shum* ^{m}*Iz-gur-*^{ilu}*DIL.BAT shá i-n*[*a Bît*]*-*^{m}*Si-ri-da-ash be-lí* [*ish-pu-r*]*a* [*u*]*m-ma-a IMER KUR.*[*RA*^{mesh}*-ia li-i*]*m-ta-aḫ-ra-ni ù a*[*n-nu-um-ma i*]*q-ta-ba-a um-m*[*a-a IMER*]*.KUR RA*^{mesh} *am-ma-ar-ma mâr ship-ri-ia i-li-ki-ma i-lak*; *i.e.*, "as regards *Izgur-DIL.BAT* (= Ishtar), who is (at the present) in Bît-Siridash, concerning whom my 'Lord' has written, saying (*um-ma-a* = quotation): 'let him receive my horses' (I beg to say, *sc.*, *um-ma-a*): 'Behold he spoke as follows (*um-ma-a*): "I shall (will) examine the horses, but my messenger shall (will) take (them) and go"'" Notice the peculiar form *i-lak* = *illak*! (A reading *i-shet* = "he shall run, *i.e.*, go away, leave instantly with the horses," might also be possible.)

[4] This is used here in apparently the same signification as *shá* resp. *ásh-shum x.x. shá ta-ash-pu-ra*—hence *i-na* or *a-na* (see instantly) *bu-ut* = *shá* resp. *ásh-shum* (cf. p. 24, note 7). See here 89 : 15f.: *a-na b*[*u-u*]*t* [*sc.*, *dîni ameli*]

(9) the "object" concerning which there was a reference in a former letter, and to which now the answer is to be given, is placed at the beginning of the sentence without any introductory particle whatever[6]; (10) *shum-ma ta-sap-pa-ra* or *ta-al-ta-al-ma*[7]; (11) *um-ma* or *um-ma-a*[8]; (12) if more subjects than one are referred to in

---

shá ta-ash-p[u-ra um-ma-a] a mi-li-e K[U.DA] ki il-qu-ú-[ni] il-ta-al-shú-nu-ti ù it-ta-an-na shú-nu-ti, *i.e.*, "replying to your recent communication [concerning the judgment (or fate) of the men] I beg to state the following (*um-ma-a*): 'he has examined the men after they had taken (stolen?) the wheat flour, and (in consequence of this examination: *ù* = result; the *ù may* be translated here also by *but*; cf. for this *ù* between sentences, Jensen, *K. B.*, VI[1], pp. 325, 336, 337, 339, and Johnston, *J. A. O. S.*, XIX, p. 50) acquitted them.'" For I[2] *sha'âlu*, used of judicial cross-examination, see Jensen, *l.c.*, p. 531. *It-ta-an-na-shú-nu-ti* I take as I[2] אנן (from which we have *annu*, "*Zusage*"): *i'-ta-nana, itta-nana, ittanna*; the *a* at the end indicates the third person of a chief sentence. A "possible" derivation from Hebr. ענה, "to answer," which "might" seem to be preferable here on account of the following (l. 21) *um-ma-a* (see p. 27, n. 8), does not fit. Or should we derive it from אנה, *H. W. B.*, p. 98*b* (from which we have *mânû*, "Ruhelager"), and translate "he imprisoned them"? The "he" according to the context must be some unnamed *GÙ.EN.NA*, "sheriff," or possibly a judge or king. Among the letters addressed to the "Lord" we find a similar expression, *e.g.*, in 39 : 4, *i-na bu-ut A.SHAG*^{mesh} *shá Tuk(= KU)-kul-ti-É.KUR*^{ki} *shá b[e-li] ish-pu-ra ik-te-di-i[r-ru?]*; see translation on p. 127.

[5] "(As regards) the x.x. concerning whom (which) thou hast written or spoken" is, after all, only a shorter form of *shá, âsh-shum*, or *i-na (a-na) bu-ut x.x. shá ta-ash-pu-ra*, cf. (5)–(7). Although not to be found in Nos. 76ff., it does occur, *e.g.*, in No. 27 : 35, *ù* ^{amelu}*SHA.KUD.DA* (= *mâkisu*, tax-gatherer) *shá be-lí ish-p[u-ra . . . .]-ma i-la-am-mi-[i]d*, "and as regards the poll-gatherers concerning whom my 'Lord' has written (I beg to state that) 'he . . . . and shall find out.'" No. 31 : 17, *ù SIG SHIG shá be-lí iq-ba-a [ush]-she-bi-la*, "and with regard to the 'good wool' about which my 'Lord' has spoken (*sc.*, in a former letter, I beg to state that) 'I have sent it.'"

[6] This is a still further abbreviation of (8); in other words, it is the same as (5)–(7) with both *shá, âsh-shum, i-na (a-na) bu-ut* and *shá tashpura* (resp. *shá be-lí ishpura*) left out, so that only the *x.x.* = *object* remains. Cf. here 35 : 10, *ù* 70 ^{gish}*PUHADU*^{mesh} *shá be-lí-ia iq-bu-ú*, "and as regards the 70 (gur) of *kasû*-root (see Meissner, *Ideogr.*, No. 3796) belonging to my 'Lord' (*sc.* concerning which my 'Lord' has written, I beg to state that) 'they informed me that, etc.'"; see translation, p. 123. See also 12 : 4, *A.SHAG*^{mesh} *shá be-lí id-di-na* ^{m}*U-bar-ru a-na be-lí-ia iq-bu-ú um-ma-a A.SHAG*^{mesh} *un-di-shi-ir a-na-ku ul ush-shi-ir* "as regards the fields, which my 'Lord' has given and concerning which (*iq-bu-ú* = relative!) Ubarru has reported to my 'Lord' saying: 'he has forsaken (them).' (*sc.* I beg to state that) 'I have not forsaken (them).'" A construction like this elucidates clearly the terseness and businesslike character of these letters.

[7] "(And) when thou writest or askest" is found in the letters addressed to the "Lord" (Nos. 1–74) under the form *shum-ma be-lí i-sap-pa-ra* or *shum-ma be-lí il-ta-al-ma*. For the former see 31 : 9, *shum-ma be-lí i-sap-pa-ra li-sha-nim-ma(?) a-na-ah zi-li-shi-ma*; *i.e.*, "(and) when my 'Lord' writes: 'they (one) may repeat' (*sc.* the treatment formerly applied to the sick person, I must tell my Lord that) 'her side (= Hebr. צלע) is too weak (*sc.* for such a repetition).'" In this connection notice the *shi* after *zi-li* for *shá*, due to assimilation, facilitated by the preceding sibilant and repeatedly known also from the tablets of the Murashû archives. For the latter cf. 56 : 5, *shum-ma be-lí il-ta-al-ma* ^{gish}*U.[HU] + SI shá ru-ku-bi shá be-lí-ia i-pu-shú a-na-ku lu-us-ba-at-ma lu-pu-ush-[ma]*; "when my 'Lord' asks that they make the pole(s or shafts) for the chariot of my 'Lord' (*sc.* may I beg my Lord that) I be permitted to take hold of it (them) and make it (them)?" For ^{gish}*U.HU + SI* cf. *B. E.*, XV, 32 : 1, ^{gish}*ú-hi-nu*; for *HU + SI* see Meissner, *Ideogr.*, No. 1206 = *hinnu*, and for *hinnu*, Del., *H. W. B.*, 284*a*: ^{gish}*HU + SI.MA* = *hi-in(-nu, sic!) e-lip-pi* = "*ein Theil eines Schiffes.*" All of which passages show that *HU + SI* has here the pronunciation *hin* and that ^{gish}*U.HU + SI* has to be read accordingly ^{isu}*ú-hin*. It must be here the "shaft" or "pole" of the wagon and is distinct from the *hin* (not *uhin*!) of a ship. The ^{abnu}*ú-hi-nu* of 91 : 5 was probably a stone of the shape of a "pole," *i.e.*, "finger," and the 2 *ú-hi-in-nu hurâṣi* of Str., IV, 116 . 2 (cf. *l.c.*, 220 : 12, "5 *ú-hi-nu*") are, therefore, "2 gold bars." This would prove that the Babylonians had besides "the money in rings" also that "in bars."

the letters, they are introduced either (*a*) directly or (*b*) by *ù*[9] or (*c*) by *ù* and one of the above given particles or phrases.[10]

Letters *not in answer* to a previous communication are much simpler in form and construction. In these the subject matter is stated either *directly*,[11] or the

[8] Whenever these particles are found they take up either (*a*) the *um-ma* after *ki-bé-ma* or (*b*) the *um-ma a* of the introduction: *um-ma-a a-na* ᵐ*Y.-ma* resp. *um-ma-a a-na be-li-ia-ma* or (*c*) some other *um-ma(-a)* in the text of the letter; they are, therefore, nothing but particles that introduce direct speech by quoting either from a previous communication or by giving the answer to an inquiry or note; see p. 24 notes 2, 4. For *um-ma* 86 : 18ff. is instructive. While l. 19 contains the "answer" (with *um-ma-a* omitted) to the 'Lord's' inquiry concerning Emida-Marduk, we still find another sentence introduced by *um-ma* in l. 20. This *um-ma* must take up a preceding *um-ma(-a)*, to be found either in the text of the letter or in the introduction, seeing that it otherwise stands quite isolated. I think we may translate this *um-ma* by '(seeing that this is so) therefore, please (*um-ma*), grant him his petition (or will), *i.e.*, let him do it (but cf. p. 25, note 1).' For *um-ma-a* cf., *e.g.*, 89 : 21f. *L.c.*, ll. 17f. (see p. 25, n. 4), contain the answer to an inquiry of ᵐ*NIN-nu-ú-a* with regard to the fate (judgment?) of certain men who had taken (stolen?) wheat flour. L. 21f., introduced by *um-ma-a*, which latter takes up the [*um-ma-a*] of l. 14, contains an answer to another inquiry, resp. reprimand, which had been expressed (in a former letter addressed to *Pân-AN.GAL-lûmur*) in probably some such words as "Why hast thou not communicated by a messenger the result of the trial of these men long ere this?" Answer l. 21f., *um-ma-a mâr ship-ri-ia shá a-na* ᵃˡᵘ*EN.LIL*ᵏⁱ *a-na muḫ sharri* (= *LUGAL*) *ash-pu-ru* (erasure) *ki* (erasure) *i-mu-ru-ka-ma-la a-sap-rak-ku iq-ba-a um-ma-a i-na* ᵃˡᵘ*UD.KIB.NUN*ᵏⁱ *shu-ú mâr ship-ri-ia ul ash-pu-rak-ku mâr ship-ri-ia a-na* ᵃˡᵘ*UD.KIB.NUN*ᵏⁱ *al-tap-rak-ku um-ma-a a-na* ᵐ*NIN-nu-u-a-ma de(= NE)-im-ka ù shu-lum-ka shú-up-ra*; *i.e.*, "(But as regards thy reprimand in thy letter of recent date I beg to assure thee of) the following (*um-ma-a*): 'my messenger whom I had sent to Nippur to the king was, when he saw (= would see) thee, to have told everything I had written thee. But he (the messenger, when he had returned to me) said (*um-ma-a*) "he (*i.e.*, ᵐ*NIN-nu-ú-a*) is in Sippar." (This is the reason why) I have not sent my messenger to thee (and why) I have (now) dispatched my messenger to thee at Sippar with the following note (*um-ma-a*): "To ᵐ*NIN-nu-ú-a*. Send thy news and thy greeting (*i.e.*, with this letter, asking for an answer by "return mail")." '" The events discussed in this letter are the following: (*a*) *NIN-nu-ú-a* of Nippur has written to *Pân-AN.GAL-lûmur* of Dûr-ilu concerning the fate of certain men who had taken wheat flour, at the same time reprimanding him for his negligence in not having communicated to him by messenger the outcome of the trial long ere that. (*b*) *Pân-AN.GAL-lûmur*, wishing "to kill two birds with one stone," entrusted the answer to the inquiry and reprimand to his messenger, whom he had to send to the king at Nippur anyhow. (*c*) The messenger found the king at Nippur, but not *NIN-nu-ú-a*, being informed that the latter had left for Sippar, where he could be addressed. (*d*) *Pân-AN.GAL-lûmur*, anxious to avoid receiving a second reprimand and to show his "brother" (l. 3) that his accusation of negligence was unmerited, at the same time wishing to assure him that "he still loves him" (l. 1), and that "he wants to see him personally and explain matters to him" (l. 8f.), dispatches at once, in order not to lose further time, his messenger with this letter to Sippar, asking for a reply. (*e*) This letter was received by *NIN-nu-ú-a* at Sippar, brought back with him to Nippur, deposited by him among the "Temple Archives," where it was excavated by the Babylonian Expedition of the University of Pennsylvania, and carried thence to Philadelphia to the Museum of Science and Art. To the *um-ma(-a)* of these letters corresponds an *um-ma-a a-na be-li-ia-ma* of Nos. 1–74. See 33*a* . 9, 12, 18 compared with l. 5 (see pp. 137f.); 45 . 18 compared with l. [3] (see p. 143); 18 : 26 compared with l. 3.

[9] Cf. *e.g.*, Nos. 11 : 19, 20, 22 | 12 : 14 | 17 : 27 | 24 : 24, 32, 36 | 26 : 20 | 27 : 30, 32 | 28 : 16 | 34 : [16], 17 | 35 : 10, 17, 21 | 37 : 15, 20 | 39 : 7, 12, 17 | 45 : 7, 10 | 48 : 16, 20 | 58 : 7, 12 | 60 : 9, 11 | 66 : 27 | 81 : 15, 18 | 83 : 19, 24, 27 | 84 : 11, 13 | 92 : 9.

[10] *Û shá*, 3 : 40 + tr d. | 27 : 38; *ù x.x. shá be-li ish-pu-ra*, 27 : 27; *ù shá be-li ish-pu-ra*, 31 : 18, etc., etc.

[11] Cf. 76 : 2, *i-din pa-nu-ú-ka*; 78 : 5, *li-ti-qa-am at-ta*; 84 : 4, *la ta-am-ḫa-ar at-ta*; 85 : 4, 9, 11, *i-di-in*; 83 : 3 begins with a question expressing a surprise: *am-mi-ni ash-pu-r[a-ak-ku]*, *la ta-al-li-i-m[a?]*, which is introduced by *um-ma-a*, *c.* p. 111.

writer may use as a kind of introduction some such words or phrases as: *enni*,[1] *eninna*,[2] *inanna*,[3] *anumma*,[4] *be-lî i-di kî*,[5] etc., etc.

[1] No. 10 : 8, [*en?*]-*ni*, "behold."

[2] "(Behold) now." Written either *e-nin*, 34 : 6; or *e-nin-na*, 34 : 11; or *e-ni-en-na*, 20 : 6 | 43 : 11 | 69 : 5. Cf. also the following note.

[3] "Now." Cf. 3 : 19 (cf. with parallel passage in l. 30, where we have *i-na-an-na-a*(!), and see *a-nu-um-ma-a*, note 4). 10 | 21 : 27 | 31 : 35 | 58 : 2 | 3 : 60, [*i-na-a*]*n-na ki-i shá be-lî i-shá-pa-r*[*a*]. See also *ù i-na-an-na*, 11 : 9; [*ù*] *i-na-an-na a-na be-lî-ia al-tap-ra*, 3 : 23; *ù i-na-an-na be-lî il-ti-di*, 21 : 26. Cf. also preceding note.

[4] "Now." See 86 : 8, and cf. *a-nu-um-ma-a*, 24 : 11, with *i-na-an-na-a*, note 3.

[5] "My Lord knows that," 12 : 16 | 13 : 1; *be-lî i-di shá*, 71 : 15; *a-na be-lî-ia al-tap-ra be-lî lu i-di*, 11 : 28.

III.

LETTERS BETWEEN OFFICIALS OF THE TEMPLE OR STATE AND THE KING.

Even a most perfunctory perusal will and must convince the casual reader of the *fundamental difference* in language and address as exhibited in the "letters between Temple and State officials" and those to be discussed here. In the former the writer addresses his correspondent, whose name he always mentions, simply by "thou": "*thou* shalt do this and that," "to *thee* I have sent," "with regard to what *thou* hast written," etc., etc. In the latter the addressee is invariably "*the Lord*," without ever being mentioned by name, and is spoken of as "my Lord": "*may my Lord* do this and that," "to *my Lord* I have sent," "with regard to what *my Lord* has written," "the following to *my Lord*," etc. Surely such a formality must have a historic basis, must have been required by etiquette, must have been rigidly enforced, and must have been absolutely necessary. Considering, furthermore, the fact that the various writers who sent their letters to this "Lord" lived at diverse periods during a space of about 150 years, it at once becomes evident that the term "Lord" here employed cannot have meant a *single person*, but must have been applied to several individuals holding the *office* of "*Lord*." Taking these *a priori* considerations as my guide, I was able to collect and publish in this volume *seventy-eight letters* (Nos. 1–74) addressed to the "Lord"—fifty of them having the address "to my Lord," etc., either completely or partially preserved, while the rest (twenty-eight) refer to the "Lord" in their text.

In the Table of Contents has been given a complete list of all writers addressing their letters to the "Lord"; we may, therefore, dispense with a recitation of their names here, though this would, in many cases at least, help us materially towards a right appreciation of the exact position and relation of the various writers to their "Lord." An investigation of this kind would necessarily lead us far beyond the scope of these introductory remarks here; it must, therefore, be reserved for Series C. All we are concerned with here is to determine, if possible, the meaning of the expression "my Lord," *be-lí* or *EN-li*; and by doing this we will, *ipso facto*, it is hoped, arrive at tangible results which are both absolutely necessary for a correct understanding of the nature of these letters were published, and of the highest importance for determining the exact relation between *Temple* and *State*, or, to express it in more modern phraseology, "between Church and State," as represented by Enlil, the god of Nippur on the one hand, and the Cassite king or kings on the other.

The question, then, has to be asked and answered: Who is the *BE.NI*, *i.e.*, *be-lí*, or "Lord," of these letters?

When trying to answer this question it would seem necessary to discuss *in extenso* here all those passages which may or may not, as the case may be, shed any light upon this term. The most important among these passages are (1) the *address;* (2) the *greeting;* (3) such *incidental references* in the text of the various letters which elucidate the position of the "Lord" in his relation to the writer or the Temple.

All letters to be discussed in this paragraph, like those treated in the previous chapter, were originally enclosed in an *envelope*, which was sealed with the writer's seal and *addressed*, as may be gathered from No. 24,[1] where, fortunately, a portion of the envelope has been preserved, as follows:

dup-pi [m]*X.* (giving here the name of the writer) *a-na be-lí-shú*; *i.e.*, "Letter of X. to his Lord."

The fact that a letter could be addressed to and safely received by a person called simply "Lord" suffices to call our attention to the pre-eminence of the addressee: he must have been a "Lord" *par excellence*, a "Lord" like unto whom there was none other—a person who went and was known throughout the country by the title *be-lí*.

Unfortunately for our investigation, there have not been published among the so-called "Letters of Ḫammurabi"[2] any that are written to King Ḫammurabi himself. If such letters were known to us, it would be a comparatively easy task to ascertain how he as king was addressed by his subjects. And yet, thanks to Ḫammurabi's well-known habit of quoting frequently from his correspondent's letters when answering them, we are able to establish the important fact that Ḫammurabi, though king, was yet addressed by his subjects[3] not as *LUGAL* = *sharru*,

[1] Here we have to read: *dup-pi* [m]*Kal-[bu]*, *a-na be-lí-shú*. [m]*Kal-bu* was the writer, according to *l.c.*, l. 9.

[2] L. W. King, *The Letters and Inscriptions of Ḫammurabi*, Vols. I–III.

[3] In King, *l.c.*, Vol. I, No. 1, ll. 8f., Ḫammurabi quotes from a letter of Sin-idinnam, saying: "And thou (*i.e.*, Sin-idinnam) answeredst: 'Those four temple servants he (*i.e.*, Ibni-[ilu]MAR.TU) caused me to conscribe as *per* his sealed contract, but one of them, a certain Gimillum, I (*i.e.*, Sin-idinnam) sent *a-na ma-ḫar be-lí-ia*, before my Lord (*i.e.*, Ḫammurabi).' This is what thou hast written. Now they have brought before me (*a-na ma-aḫ-ri-ia*) that certain Gimillum whom thou hast sent." Cf. also the quotation from Sin-idinnam's letter, King, *l.c.*, Vol. I, No. 1, l. 13: *be-lí li-ish-pur-am*, "my Lord (*i.e.*, Ḫammurabi) may send," and also that in King, *l.c.*, Vol. I, No. 8, l. 10 (compared with l. 14): *shum-ma be-lí i-qa-ab-bi*, "if my Lord (again Ḫammurabi) thinks." Taribatum speaks to Ḫammurabi, King, *l.c.*, Vol. III, p. 62 (No. 75), l. 5: "the crews of the ships *shá be-lí i-si-ḫa-am*, which my 'Lord' has desired," and [ilu]*EN.ZU-ma-gir* refers to the seal of Ḫammurabi as the *ka-ni-ik be-lí-ia*, "the seal of my 'Lord,'" King, *l.c.*, Vol. I, No. 26, 7.

"King," but as *be-li* or "Lord." It must, however, be conceded here that at the time of the Hammurabi dynasty the title *be-li* was not exclusively used of a king. On the contrary, several letters are known to us, written by persons calling themselves "thy servant" (*ardi-ka*) and addressed to the "Lord," where the title *be-li* expresses nothing but the position of a "higher" with regard to a "lower" person; *i.e.*, where *be-li* indicates simply the rank of the "master" as opposed to that of the "servant" (*ardu*).[1]

Again, when we examine the so-called Tell-Amarna letters (written at about the same time as those published here) with regard to the *usus loquendi* of the title "Lord," we find that both *governors*[2] and *kings*[3] may be designated by it.

The fact, however, that the title "Lord" *might* be and *actually was* used both during the Hammurabi and the Amarna periods as a title of the king is not yet proof sufficient to warrant a conclusion that the *be-li* of our letters designates in each and every case a king likewise. Such a conclusion must, in order to stand the closest scrutiny and severest criticism, be absolutely beyond the pale of skepticism and

[1] Cf., *e.g.*, *C. T.*, II, p. 19 (Bu. 91-5-9, 290), *a-na be-li-ia ki-be-ma um-ma Be-el-shú-nu ardi-ka-ma*. *C. T.*, II, p. 20 (Bu. 91-5-9, 291), *a-na be-li-ia ki-be-ma um-ma ^{ilu}UD-ra-bi-ma* (*sic!* without *ardi-ka-ma*). *C. T.*, II, p. 48 (Bu. 91-5-9, 2185), *a-na be-li-ia ki-be-ma um-ma Ib-ga-tum ardi-ka-ma*. *C. T.*, IV, p. 19 (Bu. 88-5-12, 278), *a-na be-li-ia ki-be-ma um-ma Ardi-^{ilu}Ul-mash-tum-ma* (without *ardi-ka-ma*!). *C. T.*, VI, p. 27 (Bu. 91-5-9, 113), *a-na be-li-ia ki-be-ma um-ma Ta-tu(?)-ur-ma-tum amat(= GIN)-ka-ma*. *C. T.*, VI, p. 32 (Bu. 91-5-9, 585), *a-na be-li-ia ki-be-ma um-ma ^{ilu}EN.ZU-ta-ia-ar-ma* (without *ardi-ka-ma*). Cf. also *C. T.*, IV, p. 1 (Bu. 88-5-12, 5), *ki-ma be-li at-ta ti-du-ú*, with *C. T.*, II, p. 20 (see above), l. 4, *ki-ma be-li i-du-ú*.

[2] Cf., *e.g.*, *Amarna*, B. 219, [*a-na*] ^{amêlu}*GAL* ^{m}*EN-*[*ia ki-be-ma um-ma*] *Ba-PI(= ia)-di ardi-*[*ka-ma*], to which title Winckler, *K. B.*, V, p. xxxiv, note 2, remarks: "*Zu diesem wird hier gerade so gesprochen, wie sonst zu dem König. Man kommt auf die Vermutung, dass der Schreiber gemeint hat den 'grossen König'* (*sharru statt amelu*)." Seeing that we find the same address in B. 146, [*a-na* ^{amêlu}] *GAL EN-ia* [*ki-be-ma um-ma*] *Ḫi-bi-PI(= ia) ardi-ka* (cf. ll. 8, 11; Rev. ll. 7, 8) I do not think that ^{amêlu}*GAL* is here a title of the king, but in all probability that of a high official (governor?) of the king. In *Amarna*, B. 10, Aziri addresses his "father," the governor of Amurru (l. 15, cf. with B. 92 : 1, ^{amêlu} ^{alu}*A-mu-ur-ra*) as follows: *a-na* ^{m}*Du-u-du* ^{m}*EN-ia a-bi-ia um-ma* ^{m}*A-zi-ri mar ka ardi-ka*. Winckler, *A. O. F.*, Vol. II, p. 312 (whom Johns, *L. C. L.*, p. 330, follows) finds in the expression (*a-na*) *a-PI-lim shá* ^{ilu}*Marduk ú-ba-al-la-tu-shú*, *i.e.*, "the man whom Marduk may keep alive" (*V. A. Th.*, 793 = Meissner, *B. A.*, II, p. 579), the title of a (the) king during the Hammurabi dynasty. Though *amelu* is used in the Code of Hammurabi for "nobleman," "one that lives in a palace," I cannot accept this view, simply and solely because we find in the phrase just quoted besides *amelu* (see also *C. T.*, II, p. 29, *C. T.*, IV, p. 21) also *shú-bi-ri-ia* (*C. T.*, IV, p. 12; cf. with this title also our letters No. 52 : 11, *shú-pi-ri-shú-nu*; 21 : 20, *shú-pi-ir-*[. . . .]; Delitzsch, *H. W. B.*, p. 683*b*; Johns, *A. D. D.*, III, p. 327) and *a-bi-ia* (*C. T.*, VI, p. 32).

[3] See here, *e.g.*, the letter of Akizzi addressed to the king of Egypt in the following words (*Amarna*, L. 37), *a-na* ^{m}*Nam-mur-*[*ia*] *mâr* ^{ilu}*UD be-li-ia um-ma* ^{m}[*A-ki-iz*]*-zi* ^{amêlu}*ardi-ka-ma*, and cf. B. 29, *a-na be-li* (*sic!*) *LUGAL* $^{mâtu\ ki}$(?)*Mi-iṣ-ri-e a-bi-ia ki-bé-ma um-ma* ^{m}*Zi-i-*[*ka*]*r mâr LUGAL mâr-ka-ma*; *i.e.*, "to the Lord (*sic!* not 'my Lord,' which had to be *be-li-ia*), the king of the land of the Egyptians, my father, etc.," instead of the more commonly used *a-na LUGAL be-li-ia LUGAL Miṣri* or *a-na LUGAL Miṣri be-li-ia*.

reasonable doubt; in other words, it must be warranted by facts which cannot be controverted.

Somewhat farther we would advance, it seems, if we were to compare the "address" as exhibited in the letters to the "Lord" with that discussed in Chapter II. While the address in the "letters between Temple and State officials" runs simply "To Y. speak, thus saith X.," it reads here either

(*a*) "*To my Lord speak, thus saith* ^{m}X. (= name of writer), *thy servant*," which, with the exception of two letters (Nos. 8 and 46), is invariably followed by what might be called a "*Höflichkeits*"-formula: "*before the presence of my 'Lord' may I come*"[1]: *a-na be-lí-ia*[2] *ki-bé-ma um-ma* ^{m}X. *ardi-ka-ma*[3] *a-na di-na-an*[4] *be-lí-ia lu-ul*(or *lul*)-*li-ik*(or *lik*)[5]; or

(*b*) "Thy servant ^{m}X. (= name of writer). Before the presence of my 'Lord' may I come": *ardi-ka* ^{m}X.-*m*(*a*)[6] *a-na di-na-an be-lí-ia lul-lik*(or *lu-ul-li-ik*).[7]

The difference in the address between the letters written to the "Lord" and those discussed in Chapter II is marked and fundamental and may be briefly summed up as follows:

(1) In the letters spoken of above the writer *never* called himself *ardu* or "servant;" on the contrary, if he wanted to express any relation at all, he did so by applying to himself the term "brother," *aḫu*.

(2) He *never* addressed his correspondent by *be-lí*, "my Lord," but simply mentioned the name of the addressee without any title whatever.

(3) He *never* used the phrase "before the presence of my 'Lord' may I come."

The last mentioned peculiarity is also the distinguishing feature between our letters here and those of the Ḫammurabi period, in which the writers, it is true, called themselves "*ardu*" and their addressee *be-lí*, but in which they never used the "*Höflichkeits*"-formula *a-na di-na-an be-lí-ia lul-lik*. On account of the absence of this phrase the letters of the Ḫammurabi period prove themselves at first sight— without even considering their contents—to be nothing but simple epistles of an inferior (servant) to a superior person (lord).

[1] For a justification of this translation see below, pp. 58, note 2; 104, note 1.

[2] Notice here the difference between the address of the letter proper and that of the envelope. While the former is always addressed "to my (!) Lord," *a-na be-lí-ia*, the envelope has "to his(!) Lord," *a-na be-lí-shú*.

[3] That this emphatic *-ma* indicates the end of the address proper we have seen above, p. 18, notes 4, 9.

[4] So always; a possible *di-na-ni* has not yet been found in these letters.

[5] Nos. 2, 3, 5, 6, 7, 8, 10, 12, 13, 14, 15, 16, 17, 19, 20, 25, 30, 37 [43, 44, 49, 50, 51].

[6] For *-ma* cf. No. 4 : 1 [^{m}]*A-na-ku-rum-ma*; the *-ma* in No. 21 : 1, ^{m}*Ilu-MU.TU.KA-rí-ma*^{ma} (Meissner, *Ideogr.*, No. 3857), may(!) be a phonetic complement to *rímu*; for *m* cf. *Mukallim* (Nos. 31, 32, 33), *Shiriqtum* (No. 38), *Ubarrum* (Nos. 39, 40), etc. This *-ma* or *m* terminates the address proper, see note 3.

[7] Nos. 1, 4, 9, 11, 21, 22, 23, 26, 27, 28 29, 31, 32, 33, 33*a*, 34, 35, 36, 38, 39, 40, 41, 42 [45, 47, 48].

It would seem, then, that a correct interpretation of the words "before the presence of my 'Lord' may I come," as regards their application to persons, might bring us somewhat nearer to a valid understanding of the term "my Lord." Examining all letters so far published with regard to the usage of the phrase *a-na di-na-an be-lí-ia lul-lik*, we find that it may be employed in letters addressed either (*a*) to an official called ^{amelu}*LUGH* = *sukkallu*[1] or (*b*) to the King, *LUGAL* = *sharru*.[2] Now, as the ^{amelu}*sukkallu* as "ambassador" or "chief representative" (for that is the meaning of the term *sukkallu* in those letters) shares the king's honors, we might suppose that the *be-lí* of our letters was such a chief representative of the king or kings of the Cassite dynasty. As representatives of the Cassite kings—especially with regard to the affairs of the Temple, resp. its storehouses—appear, as we learn from *B. E.*, XIV, XV, a certain Innanni, the chief bursar during the time of Kuri-Galzu, and his successors Martuku (time of Kadashman-Turgu), Irîmshu-NIN.IB (time of Kadashman-Turgu and Kadashman-Enlil), etc.[3] That none of the three chief bursars just mentioned can be meant by the *be-lí* here is obvious. Fortunately we possess four letters, addressed to Innanni, which are absolutely void of any of the three fundamental criteria; in them the writers do not call them-

[1] See *e.g.*, *H.*, VII, 748, *ardi-ka* $^{m\ ilu}$*AG-ú-shal-lim* (cf. also below, *H.*, VII, 747, a letter by the same writer addressed to the king) *a-na di-na-an* ^{amelu}*LUGH be-lí-ia lul-lik um-ma-a a-na be-lí-ià-a-ma*. *H.*, VIII, 781, *ardi-ka* $^{m\ ilu}$*Marduk-SHESH-ir a-na di-na-an* ^{amelu}*LUGH be-lí-ià lul-lik* ^{ilu}*A-nim u* ^{ilu}*Ish-tar* [*a*]-*na* ^{amelu}*LUGH be-lí-ià lik-ru-bu um-ma-a a-na* ^{amelu}*LUGH be-lí-ia-a-ma*. *H.*, VIII, 805, *ardi-ka* ^{m}*Mar-duk a-na di-na-an* ^{amelu}[*LUGH be-lí-ia*, cf., l. 5] *lul-lik* ^{ilu}*AG* [*ù* ^{ilu}*Marduk*] *a-na be-lí-ià lik-ru-b*[*u um-ma-a*] *a-na* ^{amelu}*LUGH be-lí-*[*ia-a-ma*]. *H.*, VIII, 841, *ardi-ka* $^{m\ ilu}$*EN-shu-nu a-na di-na-an* ^{amelu}*LUGH be-lí-ia lul-lik* ^{ilu}*Marduk u* ^{ilu}*Ṣar-pa-ni-tum a-na be-lí-ià lik-ru-bu um-ma-a a-na be-lí-ia-a-ma*.

[2] In connection with a modified form of address (*a*)—see p. 32 - we find it, *e.g.*, in *H.*, V, 516, *a-na LUGAL be-lí-ia ardi-ka* $^{m\ ilu}$*EN-SE-na a-na di-na-an LUGAL be-lí-ia lul-lik* ^{ilu}*AG u* ^{ilu}*Marduk a-na LUGAL be-lí-ia lik-ru-bu um-ma-a a-na LUGAL be-lí-ia-a-ma*. *H.*, VIII, 793, *a-na LUGAL be-lí-ia* (= *Ashshur-êtil-ilí*^{mesh}, son of *Ashshur-bân-apal*) *ardi-ka* $^{m\ ilu}$*EN-ib-ni a-na di-na-*[*an*] *LUGAL be-lí-ia lul-lik* ^{ilu}*AG u* ^{ilu}[*Marduk*] *a-na LUGAL be-lí-ia lik-*[*ru-bu*].

In connection with address (*b*)—see p. 32—it occurs, *e.g.*, in *H.*, IV, 422, *ardi-ka* ^{m}*AD-ia-KI-ia a-na di-na-an* ^{sic}*LUGAL.GI.NA* (= *Sharru-ukin*) *be-lí-ià* [*sc.*, *lullik*, left out here] *lu-ú* [*sc.*, *shul-mu*] *a-na* ^{sic}*LUGAL.GI.NA be-lí-ià um-ma-a a-na LUGAL be-lí-ià-a-ma*. *H.*, VI, 512, *ardi-*[*ka* ^{m}*X*. . . . . *a-na di-na-a*]*n* ^{sic}*LUGAL-ú-kin LUGAL SHU* (= *kishshatu*) *be-lí-ia lul-lik* ^{ilu}*AG u* ^{ilu}*Marduk a-na LUGAL lik-ru-bu um-ma-a a-na LUGAL be-lí-ia-a-ma ûmu*^{mu}*-us-su a-na ba-laṭ ZI*^{mesh} (= *napshâti*) *sha LUGAL be-lí-ià* ^{ilu}*EN u* ^{ilu}*AG ú-sal* (= *NI*)*-li*. *H.*, VII, 698, *ardi-ka* $^{m\ ilu}$*EN.BA.SHA a-na di-na-an LUGAL* [*sic! H.*, but nothing is missing] *sha be-lí* (! = the king of the lords) *be-lí-ia lul-lik* ^{ilu}*AG u* ^{ilu}*Marduk a-na LUGAL be-lí-ia lik-ru-bu um-ma-a a-na LUGAL be-lí-ia-a-ma*. *H.*, VII, 721, [*ardi*]*-ka* $^{m\ ilu}$*Marduk-MU-SE-na* [*a*]*-na di-na-an LUGAL be-lí-ia lul-lik um-ma-a a-na LUGAL be-lí-ia-a-ma*. *H.*, VII, 747, 749, *ardi-ka* $^{m\ ilu}$*AG-ú-shal-lim* (749 has $^{m\ ilu}$*AG.DI-im*, cf. also above, *H.*, VII, 748, a letter by the same writer addressed to the ^{amelu}*LUGH*) *a-na di-na-an LUGAL be-lí-ià lul-lik um-ma-a a-na LUGAL be-lí-ià-a-ma*. *H.*, VIII, 803 [*ardi-ka* $^{m\ ilu}$*Mar*]*duk-MU.MU* ^{amelu}*EN.*[*NAM a-na di*]*-na-ni*(!) *LUGAL be-lí-ia* [*lul-lik* ^{ilu}*AG u* ^{ilu}] *Marduk a-na be-lí-ià lik-ru-bu* [*um-ma-a a-na be*]*-lí-ia-a-ma*. *H.*, VIII, 832, 833, 835, 836, 837, *ardi-ka* $^{m\ ilu}$*AG.EN.MU*^{mesh} *a-na di-na-an LUGAL be-lí-ia lul-lik um-ma-a a-na LUGAL be-lí-ia-a-ma*.

[3] Cf. Clay, *B. E.*, XIV, p. 8.

5

selves "thy servant," nor do they beg to be permitted "to come before his presence," nor do they term him "my Lord."

Though we did not yet arrive at a positive result, we may claim at least a negative one, and that is: the *be-lí* of these letters cannot have been a representative of the Cassite king, such as Innanni, the chief bursar of the Temple storehouses at Nippur, was at the time of Kuri-Galzu.

Trying to determine the exact significance of the expression *be-lí*, we get, it would seem, a good deal farther in our investigation if we examine the formula of *greeting*,[1] *a-na . . . . shul-mu*[2] (which here, as in the letters above, is very often coupled with an invocation), and all those *incidental references* in the text of the letters which allude to the personality of the bearer of this title. In doing this we learn that the Lord was in possession of (1) a "house," *bîtu*[3]; (2) a "house and field," *bîtu ù ṣîru*[4]; (3) a "house, city, and field," *bîtu âlu-ki ù ṣîru*[5]; (4) a "field," *eqlu*[6]; (5) a "city and field," *âlu-ki ù ṣîru* (resp. *ṣîru*^{ki})[7]; (6) a "city, field, and house," *âlu-ki ṣîru* (resp. *ṣi-ri*) *ù bîtu*[8]; (7) "large and small cattle," *LIT.GUD*$^{hi.a}$ *ù GA.NA.M.LU*$^{hi.a}$[9]; (8) "young cows and oxen," *lâti bu-ra-ti ù alpê bu-ru-ti*[10]; (9) "harvests of the land and [pastures] of the field," *i-bu-ri shá m[a-ti ù ri-t]i(?) ṣîru*[11]; (10) "canals and ditches," *nâru*[12], *nam-ga(r)-ra*[13]; (11) "messengers," *mâr ship-ri*[14]; (12) "workmen," resp. "soldiers,"

[1] With the exception of No. 39 to be found always after *tullik* and before the introductory *um-ma-a a-na be-lí-ia-ma*. No. 39 has the greeting, quite strangely, after the last mentioned introductory phrase.

[2] Always written either *shú-ul-mu* or *shul-mu*; *DI*(= *shúl*)*-mu* has not yet been found.

[3] Nos. 22 : 4 | 23 : 3 (writer ^{m}*Im-gu-rum*); 35 : 3 (writer ^{m}*Ki-shah-bu-ut*, cf. also note 5): *a-na É be-lí-ia shú-ul-mu*. Cf. also the *bâb shá É be-lí-ia* in 26 : 19 and the *NI.GISH pish-shat É be-lí-ia* in 27 : 12.

[4] No. 11 : 2 (writer ^{m}*Be-la-nu*): *a-na É ù EDIN shá be-lí-ia shul-mu*. For *EDIN* cf. p. 75, note 1.

[5] No. 31 : 2 (writer ^{m}*Ki-shá-ah-bu-ut*, cf. also note 3): *a-na É be-lí-ia âlu-ki ù [EDIN shá be-l]í-ia shú-ul-mu*.

[6] Cf. No. 16 : 5, *A.SHAG-ka*, "thy field," *i.e.*, the Lord's.

[7] No. 9 : 3 (writer ^{m}*Bana-a-sha-*^{ilu}*Marduk*). *a-na âlu-ki ù EDIN shá be-lí-ia shú-ul-mu*. No. 17 : 5 (writer $^{m\ ilu}$*NIN.IB-GA.BU-AN*^{mesh}): *a-na âlu-ki ù EDIN*^{ki} *shá be-lí-ia shu[l-mu]*.

[8] Nos. 26 : 2 | 27 : 2 | 28 : 3 (writer ^{m}*Ku-du-ra-nu*): *a-na âlu-ki EDIN* (26 : 2, *ṣi-ri*) *ù É be-lí-ia shú-ul-mu*.

[9] No. 51 : 4 (name of writer broken away): [*a-na LIT.GUD*$^{hi.a}$ *ù*] *GA.NA.M.LU*$^{hi.a}$ *shá* [*be-lí-ia shul-mu*]. No. 16 : 1 (writer $^{m\ ilu}$*NIN.IB-*[. . .]): *a-na LIT.GUD*$^{hi.a}$ *ù GA.NA.M.LU*$^{hi.a}$ *sh[ú-ul-mu] ù shá be-lí-ia shú-ul-mu*, *i.e.*, "to the large and small cattle, greeting; and to all that belongs to my Lord, greeting!" For *LIT.GUD*$^{hi.a}$ *ù GA.NA.M.LU*$^{hi.a}$ (= *alpê ù ṣênê*) cf. also *B. E.*, XIV, 99 : 1 | 99*a* : 46 | 132 : 1.

[10] No. 10 : 4 (writer [. . . ^{ilu}] *Marduk*): [*a-na LIT*^{mesh} *bu-ra-ti*] *ù GUD*^{mesh} *bu-ru-*[*ti*]. Cf. also No. 60.

[11] No. 25 : 4 (writer ^{m}*UR-*^{ilu}*NIN.DIN.DÙG.GA*): *a-na i-bu-ri shá m[a-ti ù ri-t]i(?) EDIN shú-ul-mu*.

[12] He was at least co-owner, cf. No. 40 : 21 (writer ^{m}*U-bar-rum*): *me-e* ^{nâru}(= *A.GUR*) *Ilu*(= *AN*)*-i-pu-ush ù me-e* ^{nâru}(= *A.GUR*) *Na-la-ah me-e zi-it-ti shá be-lí-ia*, for translation see p. 132. Cf. also the *mâ* (= *A*) *be-lí-ia* in 1 : 11.

[13] No. 10 : 15, *ù shá u a-na pa-an nam-ga-ri shá be-lí-ia a-shi-ib*; *l.c.*, l. 20, *nam-gar-ra shá be-lí-ia li-mash-shi-ir*.

[14] No. 8 : 17 (writer ^{m}*Ba-il-*^{ilu}*Marduk*): *mâr ship-ri shá be-lí-ia*. Cf. [34 : 21] | 53 : 37, *mâr ship-ri-ka*.

ummâni (= *ṢAB*$^{hi\text{-}a}$), *ṣâbê* (= *ṢAB*^{mesh})[1]; (13) "servants," *ardu*[2]; (14) *shattam* and ^{amelu}*PA.ENGAR*[3]; (15) *itû*[4]; (16) "tax-gatherers," *mâkisu*[5]; (17) "sheriffs,"

[1] No. 39 : 17 (writer ^{m}*U-bar-rum*) *ṢAB*$^{hi\text{-}a}$ *shá be-lí-ia*. Cf. 46 : 9, *ṢAB*$^{hi\text{-}a}$-[*ka*] and 58 : 12, *ṢAB*$^{hi\text{-}a}$ *shá be-lí im-ḫu-ru*. From 9 : 17, 100 *ṢAB*$^{hi\text{-}a}$(?) *gi-in-na-tu ki-i ig-nu-nu ṢAB*^{mesh}(?) *shá be-lí-ia ir-ta-pi-is*, it is apparent that there seems to have been a difference between *ṢAB*$^{hi\text{-}a}$ and *ṢAB*^{mesh}; the former are = "men," while the latter are = "soldiers"; for a translation see p. 106. In *B. E.*, XIV, XV, *ṢAB*$^{hi\text{-}a}$ and *ṢAB*^{mesh} are used interchangeably, cf., *e.g.*, *l. c.*, XIV, 56*a* : 26, *PAD* 27 *ṢAB*^{mesh} *shá u ga-ri-e i-pu-shu*, *i. e.*, "food (wages) for 27 'men' who have tilled (made) the fields," and according to *l.c.*, l. 30, the ^{amelu}*RIQ* and *KA.ZID.DA* have *ṢAB*^{mesh}.

[2] This follows not only from the term "servant" which the various writers apply to themselves when writing to their "Lord," but also from the fact that very frequently other persons are referred to in these letters as "thy (*i. e.*, the Lord's) servant," *ardi-ka*. Among the persons thus spoken of as the "Lord's" servant we find, *e.g.*, ^{m}*Erba-*^{ilu}*Marduk*, 27 : 30, 32 | 29 : 4 [5] | 35 : 17 | 65 : 9 (cf. here also ^{m}*Erba-*^{ilu}*Marduk*, the writer of letters Nos. 13, 14, 81, 82); $^{m\ ilu}$*NIN.IB-SHESH-SE-na*, 1 : 16, 17; ^{m}*BA.SHA-*^{ilu}*IM*, 34 : 31, 35; ^{m}*I-na-É.KUR.GAL*, 24 : 32; $^{m\ ilu}$*DIL.BAT-Ba-ni*, 11 : 18, ^{m}*Ku-du-ra-ni*, 35 : 31 (cf. also the writer of Nos. 26, 27, 28); ^{m}*Me-li-Shi-pak*, 17 : 32; ^{m}*Na-aḫ-zi-*[^{ilu}*Marduk*], 42 : 12, 13; ^{m}*SHESH-shú-ásh-ra*, 15 : 7, ^{m}*É.SAG.ÌL-zu-ri-ia* [*ardi-ka*], 9 : 15. Cf. 21 : 27, *II ardi-ka*.

[3] No. 39 : 3 (writer ^{m}*U-bar-rum*); [45 : 4, name of writer broken off]: *a-na SHAG.TAM* (or possibly better *A.SHAG*, cf. 39 : 4) *ù* ^{amelu}*PA.ENGAR shá be-lí-ia shu-ul-mu*. To *SHAG.TAM* (= *UD*) : plural and without *amelu* cf. 35 : 33, *be-lí a-na SHAG.TAM li ish-pu-ra-ma NI.GISH shub(* *RU)-ta lish-ki-nu-*[*ma*], see translation p. 125. See also 21 : 4, *i-tu* ^{amelu}*SHAG.TAM shá a-na shul-mi-shú al-li-ku shá-al-ma shá be-lí-ia ish-ta-la-an-ni* (original gives *ir*), "the *itû* of the *shattam* for whose welfare (interest) I have come, has asked me about the welfare (here = 'news,' as in *de-im ù shu-lum* = 'good news') of my 'Lord' ", 27 : 15, *ásh-shum NI.GISH i-tu-ú SHAG.TAM-mi e-she-ir*, "as regards the oil (*sc.* concerning which my Lord has written, I beg to state that) 'the *itû* of the *shatammi* (so, no doubt, better than: "as regards the oil of the *itû*, the *shattammi*, etc." and this because (1) the letter is addressed to the "Lord"; (2) *shattammi*, terminating in *i*, requires a noun on which it is dependent, (3) if *shattammi* were the subject we would expect a form *esh(i)rû*) is taking care of it,' " 54 : 25, ^{amelu}*SHA*[*G-T*]*AM*. The *SHAG.TAM*, in all passages quoted, being closely connected with the watching, guarding, taking care of (27 : 15) or storing (35 : 33) of the *NI.GISH* or sesame oil, must have been an official in charge of the oil of the Temple or Palace. Delitzsch, *H. W. B.*, p. 696*a*, "*ein Berufsname*"; Meissner-Rost, *B. S. S.*, III, p. 359, and Zimmern, *Rituall.*, p. 93 = *zammêru*, "*Sanger*"; Jensen, *K. B.*, VI¹, pp. 531, 532 = *shaknu*, *qêpu*, "*Statthalter*"; King, *Letters of Ḫammurabi*, III, p. 57 : 3, "overseer of cattle"; Delitzsch, *B. A.*, IV, p. 186, on the basis of *Letters of Ḫammurabi*, 39 : 5, *SHAG.TAM*^{mesh} *shá É*$^{hi\text{-}a}$ *AN*^{hal}*-ka* compared with *l. c.*, 37 : 7 and No. 15 : "*Tempelverwaltung, ein hoheres Tempelverwaltungsamt.*" ^{amelu}*PA.ENGAR* is hardly better than $^{amelu\ gish}$*ENGAR*, seeing that the sign *PA* looks rather like *GISH*. ^{amelu}*PA.ENGAR* = *akil errishi*, *iklari*, "overseer of the farmers or irrigators." If read $^{amelu\ gish}$*ENGAR*, this official would be one who had charge of the "works of irrigation:" ^{amelu}*narṭabi*, see also p. 127, note 2.

[4] ^{m}*Ki-shaḫ-bu-ut*, the writer of No. 35, after having passed through the positions of *na-gid*, *ENGAR*, *RIQ*, calls himself, *l.c.*, l. 25, *a-na-ku i-tu be-lí-ia*. As *itû* he was in charge (of the storehouse affairs) of the city *Dûr-*^{ilu}*PA.KU*^{ki} (see below, p. 120). ^{m}*Kal-bu*, the writer of No. 24, who had been entrusted by royal grant with the administration of the city *Mannu-gir-*^{ilu}*IM*, calls himself, *l.c.*, l. 36, *a-na-ku i-tu* [*be-lí*]*-ia*. In 26 : 17 the *i-tu-ú* ^{m}*Iz-gur-*^{ilu}*NIN.IB* "puts up" *shá-ki-i*: *ásh-shum shu-ki-i shá i-tu-ú* ^{m}*Iz-gur-*^{ilu}*NIN.IB shá-ak-nu-ma be-lí ish-pu-ra a-na bâb shá bît be-lí-ia ul i-la-ak*; for translation see p. 119. Cf. also 21 : 27, *GAL i(?)-tú?* Also other persons had an *itû*. The writer of No. 11, ^{m}*Be-la-nu*, says, *l.c.*, l. 21, *i-tu-ú-a ma-am-ma ia-a'-nu*, and $^{m\ ilu}$*En-lil-ki-di-ni*, the slave dealer, commands ^{m}*A-ḫu-shi-na* (78 : 1): *Mâr-*^{m}*Mu-ra ni i-tu-ú-a li-ti-qa-am at-ta*. In 21 : 4 we have an *i-tu* ^{amelu}*SHAG.TAM*, and in 27 : 15 an *i-tu-ú SHAG.TAM-mi* (see preceding note). Delitzsch, *H. W. B.*, p. 157*a*, gives only "*itû*, ein Berufsname." The root of this word is אתה, "to see", to the same root belongs also another *itû*, "side, boundary." A side of a house (or of a piece of land, etc.) is any of its four extremities which "looks" towards a certain direction, either north, south, east, or west. The extremities of a piece of land which look towards or in the different directions are its *itû*, pl. *itê*, or "boundaries"; hence the person called *itû* is "one who *looks out* towards or in the different directions, or *sides* or *bound-*

GÙ.EN.NA[6]; (18) *na-'i-ri-e na-'i-ra-a-ti SAL E-di-ir-ti ù bîtu*[7]; (19) "cities," *âlu*$^{hal s}$;

aries -may they be those of property or of other business interests—of his master," "one who looks out that the various sides of his master's interests be protected." Such a person who "looks out" for his master's interests (as did Kalbu, after having been entrusted by royal grant with the administration of *Mannu-gir-*^{ilu}*IM*) at the time of Ur-Ninna, king of Shirpurla, was called an *Á.NI.TA* = "one who is at his side." The latter, then, is the exact Sumerian counterpart of the Semitic-Babylonian *itû* = *itu* + *âju* = "one who is at the side of somebody, who guards his interests" (cf. *Nippurû* = *Nippur-âju*, one who lives at, belongs to, Nippur, a Nippurian), "his *administrator*, his *representative*": just as the sides (*itû*) represent a piece of property, guard it against trespassing, so an *itû* represents and guards and looks out for the interests of his master.

[5] No. 27 : 35 (writer ^{m}*Ku-du-ra-nu*): ^{amelu}*SHA*(= *NIG*).*KUD.DA shá be-li ish-pu-[ra]*. For *SHA.KUD.DA* cf., besides the passages quoted in *B. E.*, XIV, XV, also *l.c.*, XIV, 5 : 5 | 18 : 2 | 125 : 14 | XV, 122 : 7 | 131 : 17 | 157 : 25 | 166 : 18, etc.

[6] For this officer see introduction to No. 75, below, pp. 133f.

[7] The passages in which this phrase occurs as part of the greeting are the following. No. 36 : 3 (writer [$^{m\ ilu}$]*IM.LUGAL.AN*^{mesh}) : [*a-na* . . . . *SA*]*L E-di-ir-tim* [*ù É be-li-ia sh*]*a-ul-mu* [. . . . *ma-a'*]*-di-ish shú-ul-mu*; 31 : 3 (writer ^{m}*Mu-kal-lim*): *a-na na-'i-ri-e na-'i-ra-ti ù É be-li-ia shú-ul-mu SAL E-di-ir-tu li-pi-tu an-ni-tum il-ta-pa-as-si*(? or *su*?) *a-na TUR.SAL* ^{m}*Ku-ri-i ù TUR.SAL* ^{m}*Aḫu*(= *SHESH*)*-ut shu-ul-mu shi-ir-shi-na da-ab*; 32 : 1 (writer ^{m}*Mu-k[al-lim]*): [*a-na*] *na-'i-ri-e na-'[i-ra-ti SAL*] *E-di-ir-ti* [*u*] *É be-li-ia shú-u[l-mu]*; 33 : 1 (writer [^{m}*M*]*u-kal-[lim]*): [*a-na*] *na-'i-ri-e na-'i-ra-a-ti* [*SA*]*L E-di-ir-t[i] ù É be-li-ia shú-ul-mu*. *nâ'irê*, *nâ'irati* are participles masc. and fem. plur. of נאר, which Delitzsch, *H. W. B.*, p. 139*b*, translates by "*schreien, brüllen*." Jensen, *K. B.*, VI[1], p. 588, assigns to *nâ'ru* a signification "*klagend*." We have to combine both significations here and translate *nâ'irê*, *nâ'irâti* by "howlers (masc. and fem.) of lamentations" = "lamentation men and women," who began their operations, as is well known, at the time of sickness, death, or funeral of a person. This is apparent also from the texts quoted above, for all of them are nothing but reports of a physician about the progress of the sickness of certain ladies connected, no doubt, with Enlil's sanctuary. Cf., *e.g.*, 31 : 9f., *shum-ma be-li i-sap-pa-ra li-shá-nim-ma a-na-aḫ zi-li-shi*(!)*-ma* (for translation see p. 26, n. 7) *shá TUR.SAL* ^{m}*Mush-ta-li* (cf. 32 : 7) *i-shá-ta-tu ba-al-da shá* (cf. 32 : 13) *pa-na i-gi-en-ni-ḫu i-na-an-na ul i-gi-en-ni-iḫ shá TUR.SAL* ^{m}*Ilu*(= *AN*)*-ip-pa-ásh-ra II i-shá-tu shá uḫ-ḫu-ra-tum shi-i-pa it-ta-di*, etc. For *i-shá-ta-tu*, *II i-shá-tu* cf. *l.c.*, l. 26, *ut-shi-il i-shá-ta-ti* [*shá*(?) *uḫ*]*-ḫu-ra*; l. 28, *i-shá-ta-tu shá ṣi-li* (cf. *zi-li*, l. 10 = Hebr. צלע, "side") *shá uḫ-ḫu-ra*, and 33 : 21, *i-shá-ta-tum*. *Ishâtâtu* (*ti*, *tum*) is either a plural of *ishâtu* = "fire, fever" (for formation cf. Delitzsch, *Gr.*, p. 188), or, less probably, a plural of *ishâtu* (= *eshîtu*?), syn. of *ka-ra-ru-u*, which Delitzsch, *H. W. B.*, p. 143*b* (*sub eshîtu*), translates by "*eversiones*." The *II i-shá-tu* is, no doubt, "the double fever" in the sense of either "intermittent fever" or, more probably, of "chills and fever." *Ba-al-da* = Permansive I[1], third pers. plur. fem. after *ishâtâtu*. For *ganâḫu* cf. the Talmudic lexica *sub* גנח = "to suffer from *angina pectoris*," and for *shîpu nadû*, "to grow, become old," see Jensen, *K. B.*, VI[1], p. 511; here, because used of sickness, it has the meaning "to become chronic." The passage, then, might be translated: "With regard to the daughter of Mushtali (I beg to report that) the fevers are improving; what was suffering before is not suffering any more now. With regard to the daughter of Ilu-ippashra (I beg to report that) the 'double fever' which is remaining (= third pers. sing. fem. Perm. II[1] after *II i-shá-tu* = singl.) has become chronic," *i.e.*, it appears at regular intervals. Cf. also 33 : 7f., *ûmu* 28(?)^{kam} *shá mu-shi ish-te-en a-ka-la it-ti pa-pa-si ú-ul ú-ga-at-ti ba-ra-[a]r-tum ki-i iq-ta-ú um-mu* [*iṣ*]*-ṣa-bat-si*, and *l.c.*, l. 25f., *ûmu* 29^{kam} ^{ilu}*UD na-pa-[ḫi] mâr ship-ri-ia ul-te-ṣa-a ki-i shá be-li iq-ba-a te*(!)*-e-im mu-shi a-lam-ma-ad-[ma*(?) *i-n*]*a* ^{ilu}*UD na-pa-ḫi a-s[há]-ap-p[a-r]a* [*te-e*]*-im su-ma-nu a-[lam-]ma-ad-[ma ù*(?) *a-n*]*a ra-bi-e a-[shá-a]p-pa-ra* [*shá*(?)] *dup-pa a-na* [*muḫ*] *be-li-ia* [*ul-te*]*-bi-la*. With the exception of *ishtên akâla itti papasi* everything is plain. Is this a food prepared with the *papasi*? For *papasu* cf. also *B. E.*, XIV, 163 : 42, *III* ^{dug}*tallu* (= *RI*) *pa-pa-su* ^{ilu}*A.GUR*, which shows that *papasu* was taken from the river, and is probably the "slime" of the river; cf. also Küchler, *Medizin*, p. 128, "*Brei, Schlamm*." Also in *B. E.*, XV, 44 : 23 it is paid, like *MUN*, *GÛ.GAL*, *GÛ.TUR*, *siḫ-ḫi-li*, to certain (work)men; is, therefore, different from *pappasu*, Delitzsch, *H. W. B.*, p. 531*a* (against Clay, *B. E.*, XIV, p. 28, note to No. 8, l. 4). From the above given passage it appears that the *nâ'irê* and *nâ'irâti* began their operations (*ba-ra-ar-tum* =

"guards," *maṣṣartu*[9]; "fortress(es)," *bi-ir-ta*[10]; "chariots," ^{isu}*narkabtu*[11] and *sak-shup-par*[12]; (20) "carriages," *ru-ku-bi*[13]; and last, but not least, (21) "creatures,"

"lamentation"; Del., *H. W. B.*, p. 188*a*, mentions only a *bararum*, syn. *ikkillum*, "*Wehklage*"; see also 17 : 4) while the lady was still under treatment (*ul uṣatti*) and sick. No wonder, then, that she was seized with fever (*ummu*) after those men and women had finished their lamentations. In the closing lines Mukallim reports that he will send out his messenger early at dawn of the 29th day, "as his 'Lord' had commanded," in order to learn through him how the sick person had passed the night (*te-e-im mu-shi*) and how the *su-ma-nu* (= *samânu*, the *u* on account of the *m*, *H. W. B.*, p. 503; Jensen, *K. B.*, VI^{1}, p. 571°) was progressing. Women, by the name *SAL E-di-ir-tum*, are mentioned in *B. E.*, XIV, 10 : 3, 12, 14, 19 (21st year of Kuri-Galzu, ll. 31, 23) and a *TUR.SAL GAB E-di-ir-tum* occurs in *l.c.*, 58 : 12 (13th year of Nazi-Maruttash). As this lady is closely connected with the lamentation men and women, it seems probable to suppose that she was at the head of that profession. What the real meaning of *li-pi-tu an-ni-tum il-ta-pa-as-si* (or *su*? = *il-ta-pa-at-shi* or *-shu*, *i.e.*, √לפת, so, no doubt, better than a "possible" √שבס or שבת) in No. 31 : 5 is, is not clear to me. With *lipit(t)u lapâtu* cf. *Amarna*, B. 6, Rev. 3, 7. 9; B. 218, Rev. 3, 4. It is construed with double accusative, as here, also in IV *R.*, 15*, col. I : 14. 15, *ap-pi u ish-di i-sha-a-ti lu-pu-ut-ma ana marṣi si-bit-ti-shu-nu ai it-ḫu-u*; but neither the signification given by Delitzsch, *H. W. B.*, p. 382*a*, "*umsturzen, anrühren*," nor that by Jensen, *K. B.*, VI^{1}, p. 379, "*berühren, schlagen, werfen*," nor King's (*Letters of Ḫammurabi*, III, p. 279), "to overthrow, to destroy," nor Nagel's (*B. A.*, IV, p. 479), "*zogern, verzogern*," nor even Kuchler's (*Med.*, p. 75), "*stossen, anstossen, beruhren, umstossen, vernichten, antippen*," seem to fit here. Cf. also the *li-bi-it ilim*(= *AN*), "visitation of god," *Ḫam. Code*, XXXVIII, 77, and our letter No. 17 : 9, 14, *a-di shá me-e la-pa-ti*. Also this letter treats of sickness, cf., *e.g.*, l. 18, *ù shá pa-na ma-a'-da i-ni-i'-i-shú i-na-an-na ul i'-i-ish*—an expression exactly parallel to *shá pa-na i-gi-en-ni-ḫu i-na-an-na ul i-gi-en-ni-iḫ* in Nos. 31 : 13 | 32 : 13; hence *eshû* must signify a suffering from a certain malady and not merely a "Verwirren," Kuchler, *Med.*, pp. 137, 138; Delitzsch, *H. W. B.*, p. 143*a*. What sickness this was is indicated in l. 4, *i-na ba-ra-ri* (cf. above *ba-ra-ar-tum*) *ki i'-i-shú*. Another letter that touches upon sickness, to mention it here, is No. 22 : 8 (writer ^{m}*Im-gu-rum*), *di-im mur-ṣi-shá ki ish-a-lu-shi ri-ik-sa ki e-si-ḫu ú-ra-ak-ka-su-shi*. ^{m}*Mu-kal-lim*, the writer of Nos. 31, 32, 33, and possibly of 17, was, no doubt, a physician. And as physicians are always under the patronage of goddess Gula, the *azugallatu rabîtu* or "great physician," the one who *muballiṭat mîti*, "quickens the dead" (*sic*!), I propose to identify our writer with the ^{m}*Mu-kal-lim* mentioned after the *bît* ^{ilu}*Gu-la* in *B. E.*, XIV, 148 : 9 (the 17th year), who lived during the time of Burna-Buriash. As such a physician and priest in the Temple of Gula he had to look after the welfare of the "ladies of the sanctuary," for notice that *Mukallim* sends not only greetings (*shulmu*) and good wishes (*da-ab* = *lû ṭa-ab*, 31 : 8) for the well being (*shi-ir-shi-na*, lit. their flesh, their body) of "the daughter of Kurî" and "the daughter of Aḫuni," who had, no doubt, recovered from their sickness under his care, but he reports also about the sickness of the following *women*. (1) "The daughter of *Mushtali*" (31 : 11 | 32 : 7); (2) "the daughter of *Ilu-ippashra*" (31 : 15); (3) the lady *La-ta* (? or *shá*) (31 : 20), (4) the ^{SAL}*Aḫ-la-mi-ti* (*i.e.*, "the nomad"; 31 : 25 | 32 : 8. Cf. also *B. E.*, XV, 188 V : 11, *SAL Aḫ-la-mi-tum*, and *aḫ-la-mu-ú*, *l.c.*, XIV, 16 : 6; XV, 154 : 26, besides the passages quoted by Clay in *l.c.*, XV, p. 51*a*); and (5) the daughter (*TUR.SAL*) of the lady (*SAL*) *Ush* (or *Ba*)-*ba*-[. . . .] (31 : 27).

[8] No. 33*a* : 3, *a-na âlu*^{ḫal} *maṣṣartu*(-*EN.NU.UN*) *shá be-li-ia shú-ul-[m]u*. For *âlu*^{ḫal} = plural, see p. 12, note 1.

[9] For *EN.NU.UN* = *EN.NUN* — *maṣṣartu* see Delitzsch, *H. W. B.*, p. 478*a*, and cf. *H.*, II, 187, Rev. 5 (a letter of ^{m}*Ishdi*-^{ilu}*PA* to the *mâr sharri be-li-ia*), *shulmu* (= *DI*)^{mu} *a-na EN.NUN*^{mesh} *gab-bu*, "greeting to all the guards," and *H.*, II, 186, Rev. 1 (by the same writer), *EN.NUN shá LUGAL*.

[10] No. 33*a* : 31, 36, *bi-ir-ta shá be-li-ia*.

[11] No. 33*a* : 6, 10, 13, 22, 29, 31, 34, 35. Chariots are also mentioned in *B. E.*, XIV, 124 : 10 | XV, 13 : 2 | 21 : 7; they are to be distinguished from the *ru-ku-bi* and ^{gish}*MAR GID.DA*, see below, note 13.

[12] No. 33*a* : 27f., *um-ma-a a-na be-li-ia-ma be-li a-na sak-shup*(= *RU*)-*par liq-bi-[ma] II* ^{isu}*narkabtu a-na gir-ri shá be-li i-gab-bu-ú lil-li-ik ù a-na-ku lu-uk-ka-li-ma i-na II* ^{isu}*narkabtu bi-ir-ta shá be-li-ia lu-uṣ-ṣur*; for translation see p. 139. In *B. E.*, XV, 154 : 41 (not mentioned by Clay) a *sak*(=*SAG*)-*shup-par LU*[*GAL*] is mentioned, and from *l.c.*, 13 : 5 (not mentioned by Clay) we learn that a certain ^{m}*Er-ba-a-tum*, the [*s*]*a-ak*(*sic*!)-*shup-par*, received (*im-ḫu-ur*) from (*i-na*

NI(G)-GÀL-tum nap-ti. On account of the difficulties that are to be encountered in this expression it is necessary, it would seem, to give the passage in which it occurs in full. It is found in the "greeting" of a letter (No. 38) written by a certain *[m]Shi-ri-iq-tum,* an inhabitant of Nippur (*âlu-ki,* l. 6), whose gods he invokes for the protection of his "Lord." The writer, unfortunately, is not mentioned in any of the tablets published in *B. E.,* XIV, XV. Though a *[m]Shi-riq-[tum]* is to be

---

qit) *[m]Mar-tu-ku,* the chief bursar of the Nippurian Temple storehouses during the reign of Nazi-Maruttash, ½ *ma-na ZAG.SA* (a metal, or a kind of leather?) *a-na ḫa d(t)il* (or *-bit*; *-bat*; *-ziz*) *shá [isu]narkabtu*; *i.e.,* either for the "mounting" (metal) or "covering" (leather) of a chariot. Seeing that a *sak-shup-par* is in each and every case closely connected with "chariots," which he may command when they are sent out on an expedition (see p. 139, ll. 28ff.), we may conclude that a *shup-par* is a "charioteer," and a *sak-shup-par,* a "chief, commander, captain, general of the charioteers." The word *shup-par* has to be derived from שפר, "to govern," from which root, as Jensen, *K. B.,* VI[1], p. 410, has shown, we have also the words *ishpar* (a form like *ikribu, irrishu*) - *eshpar* = (Sum. *ESH.BAR* =) "*Zaum, Zugel,*" *shipru,* "*Zaum, Gebiss*" and *ushpara* — "*Insignie des Königs*" = "*Zaum.*" With *ishpar* Jensen, *l.c.,* quite correctly compares the Syriac אַפְסָרָא = "*Halfter*" (for such changes of radicals cf. *e.g.,* Sum. *SHU.NIR* Assyr. *shurinnu*; Assyr. *laḫru* — Hebr. רחל, etc.) According to this a *shuppar* would be "one who governs, directs the chariots by having hold of the *ishpar, eshpar, ushpar*" — Syr. אַפְסָרָא, or "bridle" of the horses. Delitzsch, *H. W. B.,* p. 685*a,* mentions an officer called *[amelu]shù-UD-SAG,* "Oberst, General." That this cannot be read with Delitzsch, *l.c., shud-shaqû,* but must be transcribed with Winckler, *Forschungen,* I, p. 476, 2 (and before him Guyard, *Notes de lexicographie Assyrienne,* Paris, 1883, § 33) by *shu par-shaq* (or better *saq*) is evident from the passages quoted above. Furthermore, in view of the analogy that exists between *sak-shuppar* and *shuppar-saq* on the one hand and *gal* + *galu* = *lugal* (cf. *gal* + *ushum* = *ushumgal,* etc.) on the other hand, I propose to identify both. As *gal* + *(ga)lu,* "the great one among men" (cf. *GAL.SAG* = *rab-saq* = the great one among the *saq*) becomes the "great man," *κατ' ἐξοχήν, i.e.,* the *lugal* or "king," so *sak-shuppar,* "the chief among the charioteers," becomes the *shuppar-sak, i.e.,* "the charioteer of the chief," and as such the "chief's (*i.e.,* of the kings) foremost charioteer," "the charioteer-in-chief." From this, however, does not yet follow that we have to correct with Hoffman, *Z. A.,* II, p. 54f.; Marti, *Gram. des Bibl. Aram.,* p. 53, the אֲפַרְסְכָיֵא, Ezra 5 : 6 (cf. also Ezra 1 : 9, אֲפַרְסַתְכָיֵא, אֲפָרְסָיֵא) into ספרסכיא in order to make it agree with *shup(p)ar-saq(k).* A change from א into ס is much harder to imagine than a simple aberration of the eye from one ס to another ס, which took place if we suppose that אפרסכיא stood for אפסרסכיא, *i.e.,* אפסר, emphatic אפסרא (which is the Syr.-Aram. word for "*Halfter*" (Jensen), better "bridle," "bridle-holder" = Assyr. *a(i, u)shpar* - the *ushpar* as insignia of the king represents him as one who "holds the bridle" = who "governs" the people) + (א׳)ככ (= *sa-aq(k)*). The אפרסכיא = אפסרסכיא, then, were "the bridle-holders," "governors-in-chief." This also against Hinke, *B. E*, Ser. D, IV, p. 185.

[6] No. 56 : 6, *[gish]U.ḪU + SI* (= *û-ḫin,* "pole, shaft," see p. 26, n. 7) *shá ru-ku-bi shá be-li-ia,* cf. also the *[gish]ḪU + SI. SI shá be-li-ia* in 51 : 18. See in this connection also Friedrich, *O. L. Z.,* August, 1906, 465, on *[isu]ru-uk-bu. Rukubi* are to be distinguished from *[gish]MAR.GID.DA,* which latter signify, at this time, either "harvest wagons" (lit. "long wagons" = *ereqqu,* Meissner, *Ideogr.,* No. 1148, cf. No. 31 : 39, *i-na [gish]MAR.GID.[DA] IN ki-i az-bi-la IMER.KUR.RA[mesh],* etc.; *i.e.,* "while I was fetching the straw in the harvest wagons, the horses, etc.") or "wagon loads," cf. the *[gish]MAR.GID.DA[mesh] te-li-tum* = "the wagon loads of the crop, harvest (sc. of grain)," No. 52 : 35 and *B. E.,* XIV, 118 : 1, 29, 30. In *B. E.,* XV, 91 : 1, 2 (cf. our No. 54 : 7; 52 : 33), the harvest (*te-li-tum*) of the *pa-te-si* is computed according to *[gish]MAR.GID.DA,* "wagon loads." For the various amounts of grain paid as "hire" (*ID*) for "harvest wagons," see, *e.g., B. E.,* XIV, 141 : 6 | XV, 28 : 11 | 101 : 12 | 103 : 10. In *B. E.,* XV, 155 : 36 a certain amount of grain is mentioned as *bi-la-at [gish]MAR.GID.DA*; as this here can mean nothing but "hire for harvest wagons," we have the proof that *ID* = "hire" has to be read *bi-la-at,* from *biltu,* "*Abgabe, Steuer, Tribut*" (*H. W. B.,* p. 232), *and* "hire." Cf. also the *SHE shá [gish]MAR.GID.DA[mesh] napḫar shá a-na âli* (Nippur) *shá-ru-bu, B. E.,* XV, 107 : 6, and see the *[gish]MAR LUGAL* (?!) in *B. E.,* XIV, 124 : 16, and the *[gish]MAR AZAG.UD* in our No. 28 : 16.

found in a letter of ^{m}*Gu-za-ar-AN* to ^{m}*In-nu-ú-a* (87 : 8), we are still unable to assign No. 38 definitely. In all probability *Shiriqtum* lived sometime during the reign of Kuri-Galzu, *i.e.*, somewhere between 1421 1396 B.C. That part of the letter with which we are concerned here reads (38 : 1ff.):

1 *ardi-ka* ^{m}*Shi-ri-iq-tum a-na d*[*i-na-an*]	Thy servant Shiriqtum; before the presence
2 *be-li-ia lu-ú-ul-li-*[*ik*]	of my "Lord" may I come!
3 ^{ilu}*SUGH*[1] *ù shar-rat* ^{ilu}*EN.LIL*[^{ki}]	SUGH and the queen of Nippur

[1] From a religious standpoint this greeting is most important. It teaches us that the Nippurian Trinity Enlil, NIN.IB, Ninlil or Gula (Bau) -was known also as

SUGH (Father) *NIN.IB* (Son) ^{ilu}*NIN.MAGH* (wife of the Son) *shar-rat* ^{ilu}*En-lil*^{ki} (Mother).

Without going into details here (see my forthcoming volume on the *Religious Texts from the Temple Library of Nippur*), I may be permitted to show briefly that the gods mentioned in this letter form indeed a parallel "Trinity in Unity."

^{ilu}*SUGH* (thus the sign has to be read, and not *DAR* (Jensen), see my forthcoming volume) was originally the name of a god playing the rôle of the "Son." This is still evident from II *R.*, 57, Obv., l. 35, *c. d.* where ^{ilu}*SUGH* (with the gloss *Tishhu*) is identified with ^{ilu}*NIN.IB*, who in our letter occupies the position of the "Son." Cf. also ^{ilu}*SUGH EN um-ma-ni*, "the lord of hosts," Zimmern, *Shurpu*, IV, p. 24. 71; ^{ilu}*SUGH* (gloss *sud*) *NIGIN* = *mu-bal-lu-u ai-bi*, "the destroyer of the enemy," K 2107, 19—two attributes of the "Son," who, as the personification of the powers of nature ("the seven," "the Igigi" and "the Anunnaki," etc.), protects the faithful and destroys the wicked. Just as ^{ilu}*NIN.IB* (the Son) was also = ^{ilu}*IB*, and this one = ^{ilu}*É.KUR*, "the god of Ekur," *i.e.*, Enlil (see *Bêl, the Christ*, p. 17), so ^{ilu}*SUGH* (originally the Son) appears in this letter at the head of the Nippurian Trinity is, therefore, here = ^{ilu}*Enlil*, the "Father" or "first person," and as such clearly a *male*. *SUGH* = Enlil, as the highest god of Nippur, is, of course, "the king of Nippur," and his wife would naturally be called "the queen of Nippur," *shar-rat En-lil*^{ki}. The latter is coupled in this invocation with *SUGH*, hence *SUGH* and *shar-rat En-lil*^{ki} are husband and wife. That the "queen of Nippur" was indeed none other but ^{ilu}*NIN.LIL* follows also from other considerations, of which I shall mention only one: *NIN.IB*, "the son of Enlil," is called in *K. B.*, I, p. 175. 18, the *ilitti Ku-tu-shar bêltu*, "the one borne by Kutushar, the mistress (*bêltu* = *NIN*)"; but Kutushar is according to III *R.*, 38, 3*a* = *shar-ra-tu* or "queen." Hence *sharratu* must be the wife of Enlil (= *SUGH*), *i.e.*, she is ^{ilu}*NIN.LIL*, the "queen of Nippur." Furthermore, Enlil, the "Father" or "first person of the Nippurian Trinity," is in every case identified with his wife, the "Mother," or "third person of the Trinity": they are, as "husband and wife," "one flesh." This Unity is still clearly attested to by the inscriptions themselves. Above we saw that *SUGH* or Enlil was a *male* divinity, but ^{ilu}*SUGH* is according to II *R.*, 35, 18*a* the same as "Ishtar of Eridu," generally called *An-nu-ì* (not *ni*)-*tum* or Antum. Antum again is identified with ^{ilu}*Gà-ra*, the wife ^{ilu}*É.kur* = Enlil (see *Bêl, the Christ*, p. 17). The wife of Enlil is called also Ninlil or *sharrat En-lil*^{ki} (our letter), hence ^{ilu}*SUGH* is on the one hand the same as ^{ilu}*Enlil* and on the other = ^{ilu}*Ninlil*, *i.e.*, the "Father" and the "Mother," or the "first" and the "third person" of the Nippurian (and of any other Babylonian) Trinity are *one*, *male* and *female* in one person. What this Unity means we know: it is nothing but the Babylonian prototype of the Greek Οὐρανὸς καὶ Γαῖα, "the heaven and earth" or "the firmament of heaven and earth"; the upper part, "the firmament of heaven," or "heaven" is the husband or "Father," and the lower part, the "firmament of earth" or "earth" is the "Mother": "*Mother earth*." This oneness, this unity, is also expressed in such names of Enlil as ^{ilu}*Dur-an-ki* or ^{ilu}*Dur-an* or *AN*, the Σαυη ὁ κόσμος Βαβυλώνιος (see *Bêl, the Christ*, p. 21).

The "heaven and earth" or cosmos had a son, called ^{ilu}*NIN.IB*. The Babylonian name for cosmos is not only *an-ki*, but also *É.KUR* or *É-shar-ra*, hence NIN.IB is termed the *bu-kur Nu-gim-mut i-lit-ti É.KUR*, *K. B.*, I, p. 52 : 2; the *apil É.KUR*, I R 15, VII : 55; the *bu-kur* ^{ilu}*En-lil bi-nu-ut É-shàr-ra*; I R. 29, 16 (= *K. B.*, I, p. 171 : 15, 16);

4 *nap(sic!)-ti be-li-ia li-iṣ-ṣu-rum* — may protect the life (lit. souls) of my "Lord";

5 ^{ilu}*NIN.IB u* ^{ilu}*NIN.MAGH a-shib* — NIN.IB and NIN.MAGH who inhabit

---

the *dumu-ush* (= *apil*) *É-shàr-ra zi-kir-shu*, Craig, *Rel. Texts*, I, p. 13 : 17; the *apil É-shàr-ra*, IV R. I, 31*a*. Seeing that the "cosmos" is represented by Enlil (= *SUGH*) and Ninlil (= *sharrat Enlil*^{ki}), NIN.IB appears also as the *EN dumu* ^{dingir}*En-lil-lal-ge* = *màr* ^{ilu}*ditto*, Reisner, *Hymnen*, p. 123 : 6f., or as the *L* ^{dingir}*NIN.IB dumu* ^{dingir}*L*, K. 170, Rev. 14, and as the *ilittu Ku-tu-shar* (= *sharratu*, see above) *biltu*, *K. B.*, I, p. 175 : 18. As such a "Son" he is his Father's "voice" (*qulti*, cf. the קוֹל of Jahveh), III *R.* 67, 68*c*, *d*, through whom the Father speaks and reveals himself; he is his "messenger," the *sukkal É.KUR*. V *R.* 51 : 26*a*, whose business it is to enforce and guard the commands of his Father: ^{ilu}*NIN.IB nàṣir* (*SHESH*) *purussê* (*ESH.BAR*) *a-bi* ^{ilu}*En-lil*, II *R.* 57, Obv. 21, 25*c*, *d*. He can do it, for he is the *ur-sag kal-ga*, "the mighty hero" (lit. "head-servant"), "who has no equal" (*gab-ri nu-tug-a*), and he does do it by means of his "seven sons" (cf. ^{ilu}*NIN.IB* = ^{ilu}*Pap-nigin-gar-ra*, II *R.* 57, Rev. 57*b*, who, according to III *R.* 67, No. 1 : 25*c*, *d*ff. (= II R., 55 : 59*a*, *b*), has "*seven*" sons, among whom (l. 35) is to be found a certain ^{ilu}*Ùr-NUN-ta-u[d-du-a]*. The latter appears also among the "*seven*" sons of *Bau* and *Nin-Girsu* (*Creation Story*, p. 23: 6, where *É-nun* must be read, instead of *kalam*)), who are his *TUR.DA* or *ekdûti*, "mighty ones" (German: *Recken*). The chief one (*NU* or *ma-lik*) among these "seven mighty ones," since the time of the kings of Ur, is ^{ilu}*PA.KU* or *Nusku*, while ^{ilu}*NIN.IB* himself is the ^{ilu}*LUGAL.TUR.DA*, "the king of the mighty ones." That these "seven sons" are nothing but the sevenfold manifestations of the powers of nature, *i.e.*, of *NIN.IB*, the god of lightning and storm, has been indicated on p. 21, and will be proved in detail in my forthcoming volume. And as the "seven powers of nature," headed by Nusku, are simply manifestations of the "Son" or NIN.IB, through which he reveals himself, Nusku came to be identified with NIN.IB (see *Bêl, the Christ*, p. 2, note 10, and p. 3, notes 1ff.). NIN.IB, again, was, as "Son," identified with his "Father," Enlil; cf. here the names ^{ilu}*L*, ^{ilu}*EN.KUR.KUR*, ^{ilu}*SUGH*, all of which stand for Enlil and *NIN.IB*; hence the "Father" is = the "Son" and the latter is = Nusku, the (chief of the) *seven powers* of nature: all are *one* and yet *distinct*. In this wise it happened that "the seven" came to stand for the "*fulness of the Babylonian godhead*," just as in the Christian religion the "seven gifts" of the Holy Ghost stand both for the "fulness of the Holy Ghost" and for "the godhead," or as the sevenfold candlestick represented the "fulness of the godhead" in the Old Testament. On account of this symbolic significance, the "seven" was looked upon as the *most sacred* and the *most evil* number, it being both *holy* and *tabû*. So is also the Holy Ghost. He is on the one hand the *most gracious comforter*, and on the other the only being that *does not pardon* a sin committed against him: the sin against the Holy Ghost being unpardonable (see here also my review of Prof. Hilprecht's *B. E.*, XX^{1}, in the *Homiletic Review*, February, 1908, pp. 100ff., which was written, however, in March, 1907).

^{ilu}*NIN.MAGH*, who appears also in III *R.* 68 : 21*g*, *h* (cf. ll. 19, 17) as the *DAM-[BI-SAL]* of ^{ilu}*NIN.IB*, must be here likewise (because coupled with him) the wife of NIN.IB. But in II *R.* 59: 19; III *R.* 68 : 19*g*, *h* (cf. l. 17) there appears as the wife of ^{ilu}*MASH* = ^{ilu}*NIN.IB* the goddess *NIN.EN.LIL*^{ki}, *i.e.*, the "mistress of Nippur," who was, as we saw above, the same as *Ku-tu-shar*, the "queen and mistress of Nippur." Again, in Reisner, *Hymnen*, p. 17, No. 23, Rev. 22, 23, *NIN.MAGH* is called the *AM* (= *ummu*), "mother," of ^{ilu}*IB.A* = ^{ilu}*NIN.IB*. From this it follows that the "wife of the Son" is the same as the "Mother" or the "third person" of the Babylonian Trinity; in other words, the "Son" marries or may marry his own "Mother"! The explanation of this extraordinary phenomenon is simple enough. The "Mother," we saw, was the *earth*, and the "Son" was said to be the *powers of nature*: the wind, rain, storm, lightning, etc. The "Son," although begotten by the "Father" and borne by the "Mother," marries every spring his own "Mother"; *i.e.*, the rains of the spring unite themselves with "Mother" earth, in consequence of which she becomes, after the dead and barren season of the winter, fructified, brings forth new life, quickens the dead (*muballiṭat mîti*): the vegetation *and* the (seven) equinoctial storms (the seven sons). And because the "Son" marries his own "Mother" he now becomes "one flesh with her," hence ^{ilu}*NIN.IB* and ^{ilu}*NIN.MAGH* (*sic*! not *NIN.ENGAR*!?) are identified, are *one*: III *R.* 68 : 18*g*, *h* (cf. ll. 21, 17). Cf. also ^{ilu}*NIN.MAGH* = *Antum*, II. *R.* 51, No. 2, l. 2 (Hommel, *S. L.*, p. 48, 36). *Antum* = ^{ilu}*NIN.IB*, *Bêl, the Christ*, etc., pp. 16, 18. ^{ilu}*NIN.MAGH* is, therefore, a name signifying the "Son," the "wife of the Son," and the "Mother."

In conclusion I may add a few words about the pronunciation of ^{ilu}*NIN.IB*. In my review of Clay's volume

6 *shá âlu-ki NI(G – GAR, sha)-GÀL (= ik)-tum nap(sic!)-ti-ka*	the city (*i.e.*, Nippur) may protect thy creatures (subjects)!
7 *li-iṣ-ṣu-rum ma-an-nu pa-an*[1]	Whosoever
8 *ba-nu-tum shá be-lí-ia li-mur*	may see the gracious face of my "Lord"
9 [*ù?*[2]] *man-nu da-ba-ba ṭâb*(=*ḪI*)^{ab}	[and] whosoever be of "good words"
10 [*a-n*]*a be-lí-ia li-il-te-mi*	may listen to my "Lord"!
11 [*um*]-*ma-a a*-[*na b*]*e-l*[*í-i*]*a*-[*ma*]	The following to my "Lord":

Two peculiarities of this text require some words of explanation. The first is the word *nap-ti* in ll. 4 and 6. According to the greeting of 89 : 6[3] we would expect

entitled *Business Documents of Murashû Sons of Nippur* (= *B. E.*, X) I tried to show (see *The Monist* for January, 1907 (Vol. XVII, No. 1), p. 139) that *NIN.IB* was originally an *Amurritish* god coming from the "westland," where *he had been identified with* ^{ilu}*MAR.TU*, and where he was called *Irrishu*, resp. *Irrishtu*. Three months after my review had appeared, Dr. Clay read a paper before the American Oriental Society, on April 5, 1907, in which he had reached the same conclusion, viz.: *NIN.IB has to be identified with* ^{ilu}*MAR.TU*. Though I naturally was sorry not to find in his treatise any reference to my review, and to learn from p. 2 of the *J. A. O. S.* for 1907 that the reading *Irrish(t)u* was known to him only from "private communication," I still greeted Clay's discovery with rejoicing. Upon the basis of his investigations Clay thought to be justified in rejecting any and all readings of the name אנושת so far proposed. He accordingly proceeded, being encouraged in this by Jensen's reading (*'nwusht* = *namushtu* = *namurtu*), and identified אנושת (thus has to be read, see "Preface") with *En-washtu* = *Enmashtu* = *En-martu*. The objections to such a reading, however, are evident to every Assyriologist: *MAR.TU*, a *Sumerian* ideogram, cannot be treated as an *Assyrian word*, *martu*, to which one applies Semitic-Babylonian phonetic laws (the change of *r* to *sh* before *t*), making *martu mashtu*. Surely, every Assyrian would unhesitatingly translate a word *En-mashtu* (*martu*) by "*the lord of the daughter*" or "*owner of a daughter.*" A Sumerian ideogram *MAR.TU*, signifying "westland," according to Assyro-Babylonian grammar, cannot become a "daughter," or *martu*. The god *MAR.TU* played in the westland the same rôle as did, *e.g.*, Enlil in Nippur, or Sin in Ur, or Marduk in Babylon, *i.e.*, he was the highest god among the Amurrites, hence being identified not only with ^{ilu}*KUR.GAL*, "the god of the great mountain" or "world" (an attribute of Enlil, Sin, Marduk, etc.; this shows that *KUR.GAL* cannot be read in each and every case Amurru, but must be understood quite frequently of Enlil or Anu or Sin or Marduk, cf. ^{ilu}*BE* = *bêl* = *Enlil* and *Ea*), but also with 'Ur = אור (cf. here also *C. T.*, II, 12 (Bu. 88–5–12, 212), l. 30, ^{ilu}*Marduk*(!) *ù* ^{ilu}*En-zu*-^{ilu}*MAR.TU*, *i.e.*, "Marduk and Sin-Amurru"). There were known in Babylonia a "Sin of Ur," a "Sin of Ḫarran," a "Sin of Amurru," a "Sin of Nippur" (cf. here the date of Dungi, *E. B. H.*, p. 256, 15: *mu* ^{dingir}*Uru-ki En-lil*^{ki} *é-a ba-tur*. Of this Nippurian Sin we have quite a number of hymns and prayers in our Museum), and many others. I also beg to differ from Prof. Clay's explanation of the *dingir dingir* in the name *Warad-dingir-dingir-Mar-tu*, found in his paper referred to above (p. 7 of the reprint), in which, upon the suggestion of Prof. Jastrow, he states with regard to *dingir-dingir* that it is a *pluralis majestatis* corresponding to the Hebr. אלהים. That name has to be read *Warad-AN*-^{ilu}*MAR.TU* and shows that *MAR.TU* was identified, as is to be expected, with the highest and oldest Babylonian god *AN*. *AN*-^{ilu}*MAR.TU* is, therefore, parallel to the *AN ṣi-ru-um* ^{ilu}*EN.LIL* (*Code of Ḫammurabi*, I : 1, see *The Monist*, Vol. XVI (October, 1906), p. 634) or to the well-known ^{ilu}*EN.LIL ilî* ^{ilu}*Marduk*. Cf. also for the formation *Warad-AN*-^{ilu}*MAR.TU* names like *Galu*-^{ilu}*Ba-ú-Mar-tu* (or is *Mar-tu* here a title?), Reisner, *Telloh*, 159, VI : 23; *Galu*-^{ilu}*DISH-AN*, Reisner, *l.c.*, 154, III : 4. This last name is especially interesting, showing us that ^{ilu}*DISH* was not only ^{ilu}*É.A* (Br. 10068), but also *AN*; notice also that *DISH* is = 60, which is the number of *AN*, and *AN* is = *ilu*.

[1] For this and the following see above, p. 22.

[2] The traces visible seem to be against such an emendation, but the parallel text, 89 : 11, justifies it, see p. 22.

[3] *AN*^{mesh} *a-shib É.DIM.GAL.KALAM MA nap-shá-ti-ka li-iṣ-ṣu-ru*.

here the word *nap-shá-ti* for *nap-ti*. Should the writer have made twice the same mistake of omitting *shá*, or have we to see in *naptu* a synonym, resp. side form of *napshâti*? As I personally cannot imagine that our writer could be guilty of committing the same error twice in a space of only three lines, I prefer to consider *nap-ti* not as a mistake for *nap-shá-ti*, with the *shá* left out, but as a synonym of *napishtu*, from the root אנף(?), "soul," "life." The second peculiarity is met with in the expression *NI(G).GÀL-tum nap-ti-ka*. If these two words have to be connected, thus taking *NI(G).GÀL-tum* as the *nomen regens* of *nap-ti*, we will have to admit that this is a rather singular *status constructus* relation. We would expect either *NI(G).GÀL-tum shá nap-ti-ka* or *NI(G).GÀL(-ti, -at) nap-ti-ka*. However, such *status constructus* relations may be paralleled, cf. *e.g.*, *ul-tu ûmu*^{mu} (for *ûm*) *ṣa-a-ti*, *Neb.*, V *R.* 64, I : 9; *kîma pûrîm ṣêri, ḫarânam namraṣa*, quoted by Delitzsch, *Gram.*, p. 192, note. If, then, *NI(G).GÀL-tum nap-ti-ka* be *one* expression we may compare with it the well-known *NI(G).ZI.GÀL* = *shiknat napishti* = *NI(G).GÀL-tum* + *ZI* = *shikittum nap-ti* = creatures - an attribute ascribed not only to ^{ilu}*NIN*(var. *SAL*)-*in-si-na*, the *ám kalam-ma ZI.GÀL kalam gim-gim-me*, "the mother of the world, who creates the creatures (*ZI.GÀL* = *NI(G).ZI.GÀL* = *shiknat napishti*) of the world," *E. B. H.*, p. 202, note I, 1, but also to Shamash, the *be-el shik-na-at napishtim*^{tim}, IV *R.* 28, No. 1, 7, 8*b*. This gives us the important result that the writer Shiriqtum ascribes in this passage *divine attributes to his* "Lord," which would be not at all surprising if it can be proved that the "Lord" was in each and every case the "King"; for we know that the Cassite kings of this period, like their Egyptian contemporaries, were *deified*, as is indicated by the sign *ilu*,[1] so very often found before their names. The intended signification of this passage, then, is clearly this: "May *SUGH* and the queen of Nippur protect 'the life of my Lord'," *i.e.*, my Lord himself, "and may *NIN.IB* and *NIN.MAGH* that inhabit the city (*sc.* of Nippur) protect my 'Lord's' creatures"—a prayer for the protection of the "Lord" and his "subjects."[2]

[1] See Clay, List of Names, *B. E.*, XIV, and especially Hilprecht, *B. E.*, Series A, Vol. XX, Part 1, p. 52.

[2] If it were possible to read instead of *ki* (in *âlu-ki*) = *DUL* (cf. Clay, List of Signs, *B. E.*, XIV, No. 136) we might be tempted to transcribe l. 6, *shá* ^{ilu}*DUL.NI(G).GÀL-tum nap-ti-ka*, and translate: "that inhabit the 'mountain of creatures,'" thus taking *DUL.NI(G).GÀL-tum* to be another name for *DUL.AZAG*, "the holy mountain" of the nether world, of which ^{ilu}*NIN.IB* was, as we know, the "king" (*LUGAL*). But this cannot be done, simply because *ki* is absolutely certain. A third explanation might be suggested by taking *NI(G).GÀL-tum nap-ti* (l. 6) as standing in opposition to *nap-ti* = "soul" (l. 1); *SUGH* and the queen of Nippur may protect the "soul" of my Lord, and *NIN.IB* and *NIN.MAGH* may protect "thy body." This would fit very well, for we know that the wife of *NIN.IB* was "the great physician," who cared for the "spiritual" (*napti*) and "bodily welfare" (*NI(G).GÀL-tum napti*) of her people. However, a signification "body" = *NI(G).GÀL-tum napti* is not known to me. Hence the only translation that seems linguistically justified is the one given above. For *ZI.GÀL* cf. also Jensen, *Z. A.*, VIII, p. 221, note 5.

Even though it be admitted that the "Lord" was in possession of all that has been enumerated above, it might still be objected that, *e.g.*, a *sukkallu* or the "*king's representative*" was designated here by the title *be-lì*, and this the more as he "apparently shared honors with his royal masters"; for we saw on p. 33 that certain writers used the phrase "before the presence of my 'Lord' may I come" not only in their letters to the king, but also in those which they addressed to his "representative." Surely such a high officer of the king would naturally have been in possession of cities, guards, houses, lands, wagons, chariots, fields, cattle, and servants. Or it might be said that a *governor*, *bêl paḫâti*, was meant by *be-lì* in our letters; for he as the head of a *government* and the superior of the *ḫazannâti* or *city prefects* had, as a matter of course, under his command cities, chariots, servants, houses, lands, etc., etc., and writers, addressing their letters to such an official, would quite naturally include in their greeting some kind of a wish for the prosperity and the safe-keeping of their "Lord's" possessions.

Fortunately for our investigation here we have a letter, published in this volume, that has been written to a governor. And how does the writer address the governor? By *be-lì* or "Lord"? Does he beg to be permitted to "come before the face" of his Lord? Does he call himself "thy servant"? Nothing of the kind. The writer simply names his addressee by name and extends his greeting to him, his house, and his government. An address in a letter to a governor at this period, then, reads (No. 77 : i ff.):

1 *a-na* $^{m\ ilu}$*En-lil-*⌊*bêl*(= *EN*)*-nishê*^{mesh}*-shu*[1]]	To Enlil-bêl-nishê-shu
2 *ki-bi-*⌊*ma um-ma*⌋	speak, thus saith
3 $^{m\ ilu}$*A-shur-shum-êṭir*(= *KA*[*R*]"*-ma*]	Ashur-shum-êṭir:
4 *a-na ka-a-shá bî*⌊*ti-ka*⌋	to thee, thy house
5 *ù a-na pa-ḫa-t*[*i-ka*]	and thy *government*
6 *lu-ú shul-*[*mu*]	greeting!

Again, in No. 24 Kalbu, the writer, *itû*, "dust and loving servant," after having reported to his "Lord" that a city and its gate had been destroyed, adds in l. 29ff.:

29 *ù Mâr-*^{m}[. . . .]	Also Mâr-[. . . .],
30 *bêl paḫâti* (= *EN.NAM*[2]) *a-na ardi-ka ki-i il-li-ku um-ma-a*	the governor, when he had come to thy servant (*i.e.*, to the writer), said:

[1] For this emendation and for the time when this governor lived (11th year of Kadashman-Turgu) see p. 13, n. 5.

[2] For *EN.NAM* = *bêl paḫâti* see Delitzsch, *H. W. B.*, p. 519*b*.

31 *abulla*(=*K.Ì.GAL*)^{ki} *i-ma-ad-di*[1] *tu-shá-an-na-ma taddan*(= *SE*)-*na*[2]	"They make lamentations on account (of the loss) of the gate. Duplicate (it)."

In this passage the "governor" evidently is quite a different person from the *be-lì* or "Lord"; nay, he, although a *bêl paḫâti*, has to go to the *itû* Kalbu with the request, no doubt, that the latter report the loss of the gate to the "Lord," in order that a new one be made.

That also a "representative" or *sukkallu* of the king cannot be meant by the "Lord" in our letters is evident from a passage of No. 35 : 24ff., which reads:

24 *ù libittu* (= *SHEG*) *ia-a'-nu*	There are also no adobes!
25 *ásh-shum a-na-ku i-tu be-lì-ia*	As regards this that I, the *itû* of my "Lord,"
26 *al-li*(? or *la*?)-*ka a-na* ^{m}*Erba-*^{ilu}*Marduk*	have come (gone up to thee saying): "Send to Erba-Marduk
27 *shú-pu-ur-ma a-na* ^{m}*Ku-du-ra-ni*	that he send to Kudurâni"—
28 [*li*]-*ish-pu-ra-ma sukkalmaḫḫu* (=*PAP.LUGH.*[3]*MAGH*) *li-i*[*q-bi*]	"so may the *sukkalmaḫḫu* (*i.e.*, Erba-Marduk) finally give orders (*sc.* to Kudurâni)
29 *libittu* (= *SHEG*)^{mesh} *li-il-bi-nu*	that adobes be made (lit. that they make adobes)."

A beautiful example of "red tape" for this remote period! The sense of this passage is apparently the following: Kishaḫbut, the writer and *itû* (p. 35, n. 4), living in Dûr-Nusku during the reign of Kadashman-Turgu, had at some previous time gone (up) to his "Lord" with the request that the *sukkalmaḫḫu* (a higher officer than a *sukkal*) Erba-Marduk be instructed to issue orders to Kudurâni (the chief brick-

[1] In view of the fact that *maṭû* = *LAL* (S^{b} 112), which latter in the Temple Archives of this period signifies "a *minus*," "a loss," one might be inclined to translate "the gate is gone." Against this must be said, however, that *bâb-GAL.LA* = *abullu* is feminine, hence we would expect *ta-ma-ad-di*. *I-ma-ad-di* I take, therefore, as a third pers. plur. for *imaṭṭû*. For *i*, instead of *û*, cf. Delitzsch, *Gram.*, p. 252, and for the signification "*klagen, stöhnen u. dergl.*," Jensen, *K. B.*, VI[1], pp. 361, 557: "They (*i.e.*, the inhabitants, or the German indefinite *man*) make lamentations on account of the gate," *i.e.*, "they deplore its loss."

[2] By translating as given above I consider *tushannama tadanna* as a continuation of the "speech" of the governor, and not as a request of the writer. If the latter were to be preferred we should expect a phrase *be-lì lishanna-ma* (= *lushanna-ma*), cf. l. 31, *be-lì a-ma-as li-mur-ma*. *Tushannama tadanna* is a ἓν διὰ δυοῖν = "thou shalt duplicate and give" = "thou shalt give again."

[3] For *PAP.LUGH* = *LUGH* = *sukkallu* cf. III *R.* 67, 55, ^{ilu}*LUGH* = ditto (*i.e.*, ^{ilu}*PAP.LUGH*).

maker) that adobes be made. The writer, after having returned from his "Lord," and having waited for some time to see whether his request had been complied with or not, finds that this had not been done. He, therefore, takes in this letter another opportunity to remind his "Lord" once more of his former request. "May," he says, "the *sukkalmaḫḫu* Erba-Marduk upon thy command now finally issue orders for the making of adobes. This is very urgent, seeing that there are absolutely no adobes at hand" (l. 24). The "red tape" in connection with this order (the *itû* writing to the *be-lì* that he give instructions to the *sukkalmaḫḫu* that this one issue orders to the chief brickmaker that the latter induce his men to make adobes) shows clearly that the *sukkalmaḫḫu* was the inferior of the *be-lì*: he had to receive instructions from his "Lord" before he could issue the necessary orders, and the writer, knowing this, does not write directly to the *sukkalmaḫḫu*, but directs his request to the proper authorities, the *be-lì*. Only by doing this could he (the writer) expect that his wishes were ever conformed with. The *be-lì*, being here the superior of the *sukkalmaḫḫu*, cannot possibly have been a *sukkal*.

There is, however, still another and last possibility to be considered in connection with this title. In Delitzsch, *H. W. B.*, p. 457*a*, we are told that the *manzaz pâni*, *i.e.*, "one who takes his stand before the king,"[1] was the "*Ranghöchster, höchster Würdensträger*" (*sc.* of the king). Is not perhaps this highest of all royal officials intended by *be-lì* in our letters? The answer to this supposition is given by a letter (No. 48 : 27) in which the writer, whose name is unfortunately broken away, assures his "Lord," *be-lì*:[2] *ul mu-shá-ki-lu*[3] *a-na-ku lu man-za-az pa-ni a-na-ku*, *i.e.*, "not a mischief breeder, but a *manzaz pâni* am I." Surely, no *manzaz pâni* could or would ever speak to another *manzaz pâni* in this manner, because (1) there was not or could not have been *another* highest(!) official by this name; (2) even if there were, no official would ever humiliate himself as far as to call his *brother* officer "my Lord," nor would he humbly beg "to be permitted to appear before his equal's face"! Such things might be possible at present, but they are absolutely excluded and wholly unthinkable, nay, absurd for a period to which these letters belong, the time of the Cassite kings, when petty jealousies reigned supreme. If, then, the "Lord" of this *manzaz pâni* could not possibly have been a "brother" officer, but was, as the title indicates, that official's "Lord," then the only conclusion to be

[1] Cf. Scheil, *Textes Élam. Sem.*, I, p. 97 : 13, *ma-an-za-az pâni* (= *SHI*) *LUGAL*.

[2] Cf. 18 : 2, *a-na di-[na-]an be-[l]i-i[a lul-[lik]*, and *l.c.*, ll. 3, 26, *um-ma-a a-na be-li-ia-ma*.

[3] III[1] of *akâlu* = *musha'kilu*, *sc.* *qarsê*, lit. "one that nourishes false accusations." Cf. here also No. 20 : 6, *e-ni-en-na an-nu-tu-ma-a ka-ar-ṣu-ú-a-a shá a-na* ^{dish}*be-li-ia i-ku-lum um-ma-a* ^{dish}*be-li a-na pa-ni-shú ul-te-shi-ba-an-ni*, etc.

arrived at under these circumstances is that the "Lord" of the *manzaz pâni must have been and actually was the* **King.**

We need not, however, content ourselves with emphasizing merely what the "Lord" was not or could not have been. Thanks to the wonderful collection of Babylonian letters preserved in the Museum, of which only a very small part is published here, there are abundant *direct proofs* at hand which, if correctly explained, establish once and for all the truth of the conclusion above arrived at by a process of elimination.

To enumerate all the data which furnish direct proof for our conclusion would lead me far beyond the scope of the present investigation. I must content myself, therefore, with the following:

(*a*) The address as it is found in No. 24 could never have been written to any official, high or low, but the King. It reads (No. 24 : 1ff.):

A-na be-lí-ia:

1 *As-mi lu-ul-li-i*	*zêri*[1] *ishtu*(=*TA*) *shame*(=*AN*)-[*e*]
2 *la ma-ir*[2] *an-ni*	*gù-ra-di li-e-i it-pi-sh*[*i*][3]
3 *nu-ùr aḫê*(=*SHESH*)^{mesh}-*shu*[4]	*PI-in-di-e*[5] *na-ma-a-ri*

[1] In view of such forms as *lu-ú-ul-li-ik*, No. 38 : 2; *li-ish-pu-ú-ra-*[*am-*]*ma*, No. 39 : 23, and many others, one might be inclined to see in this sign a variant of *ik* and read *lu-ul-li-i-ik*, "may I come." But against this is to be said that (1) in all texts of this period only the regular form for *ik*, as given by Clay, Sign List, *B. E.*, XIV, No. 257, is to be found; (2) the *TA-AN* [+ one sign] would be completely left in the air; (3) having examined this sign repeatedly, I am absolutely confident that it is none other but *ZER* = *zêru*, "seed." The *TA-AN* then is easily amended to *ishtu shame-*[*e*]. For an analogous attribute of a Cassite king cf. the inscription of Agum-Kakrime (Jensen, *K. B.*, III[1], p. 134, col. I : 3), where this king calls himself *zêru el-lum shá* ^{ilu}*Shú-qa-ma-nu*, "the pure seed of Shuqamuna." Cf. also in this connection the sign of god, *ilu*, before the names of the Cassite kings of this period.

[2] So rather than *la ba-ir an-ni*, "who does not deny grace." The attribute here ascribed to the "Lord" has its origin in the fact that the writer had to report to his *be-lí* rather sad news, which possibly might be attributed to his (the writer's) negligence, see ll. 11ff.

[3] For *it-pi-shi* see Hilprecht, *B. E.*, XX[1], p. XII, note 7.

[4] In this expression two divine attributes fall together, viz., *nûr mâti* resp. *nûr âli-shú* or *nûr gab-ba*, ascribed especially to *Sin*, *Shamash*, and *D*(*T*)*ar-ḫu* (p. 16, n. 13), and *asharid aḫê-shu*(*sha*), found in connection with *NIN.IB* and *Ishtar*, *i.e.*, with all gods who played the rôle of the "Son" and "his wife."

[5] Delitzsch, *H. W. B.*, p. 532*a*, mentions a word *pindê*, which he takes to be a plural, quoting III *R.* 65, 9*b*, "*wenn ein neugeborenes Kind pi-in-di-e ma-li voll ist von p.*" In our text *PI-in-di-e* is apparently a noun in the genitive (after *ana*, l. 1) and the *regens* of *na-ma-a-ri*. As such a noun it is a *fit'âl* of רדה: *rit-di-e* = *rid-di-e* = *rin-di-e* = *ri-in-di-e*, which latter, when graphically expressed, becomes *PI-in-di-e*. This "Lord," being the "light," *i.e.*, the first and foremost of his brothers, has, of course, the power, authority, and right to "order," "appoint" the *namâri*—a function of the sun in the early morn; he is, therefore, identified here with the moon, who as "Father" asks his "Son" (the sun) to do his bidding: "to lighten the world." Hilprecht takes *PI-in-di-e* as a *fa''al* form: *raddaj* = *vaddê* = *vandê* = *vendê* (*a* with following *n* is often changed to *e* or *i*) = *vindê* = "appointer, commander."

4 *ki-ib*[1] *kab-tu-ti*	*ra-ásh-ba-nu-ú-ti*[2]
5 *e-pi-ir*[3] *um-ma-ni*	*pa-ásh-shur ni-shi*
6 *e-tel ki-na-te-e-shú*[4]	*shá* ^{ilu}*A-nu* ^{ilu}*En-lil u* ^{ilu}*É.A*
7 *ù* ^{ilu}*Be-lit-ì-lì*(=*NI.NI*)[5]	*ki-ib-ti*[1] *du-um-ki*

[1] *Ki-ib, ki-ib-tu* = *qîpu, qiptu*. Delitzsch *H. W. B.*, p. 584*a*, defines a *qîpu* to be one "*der mit etwas betraut ist,*" and of *qiptu* he says, *l.c.*, that it is a "*Darlehen*, spec. *zinsenfreies Darlehen*(?)." On the basis of our passages here it would be better to see in a *qîpu* "one (may he be king, governor or common man) who holds something in trust as a gratuitous gift from a higher person (god or king), for whom he administers, rules, governs it." This "something" thus held, administered, governed is a *kiptu*. What this "something" in each and every case is has to be determined by the context. It may be a city, or money (cf. here the faithful steward of the New Testament who used or administered the *kiptu, i.e.*, the talents gratuitously given him, wisely), or even an empire. As the "Lord" here referred to is the King (see under *b*), the *kiptu* is the "kingship" held in trust by him as a gratuitous gift from the gods of the whole world, for whom he has to administer it in such a way as to tend towards "grace and righteousness," hence *dumki ù mishrê* are objective genitives. To take them as subjective genitives would be senseless, because everything that comes from the gods is in itself gracious and righteous. A king that administers his *kibtu* in such a way is a *shar mi-shá-ri-im*, *Neb. Grot.*, I, 1. For *ki-ib* = *qîpu*, see also 46 . 17, *ki-ib-ka* (*i.e.*, the Lord's) *a-a-um-ma ul i-mu-ur*.

[2] A plural of *rashbânu*, and this a form in *-ân* (which forms adjectives and nouns, Delitzsch, *Gram.*, § 65, p. 175, No. 35) of *rashbu*.

[3] *E-pi-ir . . . . pa-ásh-shur*. The correct explanation of these words depends upon whether we see in them participles or nouns. If *e-pi-ir* be the participle of *epêru*, "*sattigen, versorgen*" (Jensen, *K. B.*, VI[1], pp. 438, 572) we might see in it a translation of the well-known title of, *e.g.*, the kings of Isin, Larsa, Warka, who call themselves in their inscriptions *Ú*.*A* = *êpirum, zâninum* (Delitzsch, *H. W. B.*, p. 115*b*). Cf. for the kings of Isin: Sin-mâgir (Thureau-Dangin, *A. S. K. I.*, p. 204, No. 1, l. 2), Ishme-Dagan (*l.c.*, p. 206, No. 5, l. 2), for the kings of Larsa: Sin-iddinam (*l.c.*, p. 208; No. 5, l. 3; p. 210, l. 8 above; *d*, l. 3), Arad-Sin (*l.c.*, p. 212*b*, l. 5; *c*, l. 7; p. 214*d*, l. 8), Rim-Sin (*l.c.*, p. 216*a*, l. 13; p. 218*c*, l. 10; p. 220, l. 11 above; *f*, l. 11); for the kings of Warka: Sin-gâshid (*l.c.*, p. 222*c*, l. 8). If *êpir* be a participle then *pashshur* must be one likewise, in which case the latter might stand for *pâshur* = *pâshir*, Delitzsch, *H. W. B.*, p. 549*b*: "*Loser, der sich gnadig annimmt, Erbarmer*" (cf. V R. 21, 53*a*, *b*; 65*a*, *b*, *nap-shú-ru* syn. of *re-e-mu*). As, however, a writing *pa-ásh-shur* for *pâshir* would be somewhat strange for this period, it is preferable to take *pa-ásh-shur* in the sense of *pashshûru*, "platter," and then, of course, *e-pi-ir* not as a participle, but, on account of the parallelism, as a *stat. constr.* of *epru* (so also Hilprecht and Hommel in personal communications), "the food of people, the platter (πίναξ) of men," from which, *i.e.*, from whose (the Lord's) grace they all eat. For *epêru* as a divine attribute cf. also the proper names ${}^{m\ ilu}$*En-lil-e-pi-ir*, *B. E.*, XV, 181 : 12; ${}^{m\ ilu}$*En-lil-e-pir* (*sic*! neither *tu*, Clay, *l.c.*, p. 28*b*, nor "perhaps" *tir*, Clay, Corrections(!) in *Z. A.*, XX (1907), p. 417f.), *l.c.*, 37 : 9; ^{m}*XXX-i-pi-ra-an-ni*, *l.c.*, 180 : 17; ^{f}*Bêlit*(= *GASHAN*)*-e-pir-ra-at*, *l.c.*, 155 : 27; ${}^{m\ ilu}$*SHU*[4]*.UD.DA-e-pir(ir)* (*sic*! Clay, *l.c.*, p. 33*b*, wrongly *Ilu-shu-urra-e-pir(ir)*), *l.c.*, 186 : 10. For *SHU*[4]*.UD.DU* cf. the proper name in *R. T. Ch.*, 330, Rev. 2, a name like ^{m}*Mar-duk*. From this it follows that the "Lord" as *e-pi-ir um-ma-ni* has a divine attribute: he was *deified*.

[4] The long *ê* in *ki-na-te-e-shú* is noteworthy. I take *kinâtê* as a plural of *kinâtu*, *H. W. B.*, p. 338*b*. Cf. also *H.* III, 333 : 1, *LUGAL ki-na-a-te*. Besides this plural the *B. E.* publications give us two others: *ki-na-ta-ti*, *B. E.*, IX, 5 : 3 | 22 : 7, and *ki-na-at-ta-ti*, *l.c.*, 45 : 6 | 106 : 5. Hilprecht ascribes the long *ê* to the open syllable under the verse accent.

[5] Notice here the *ù* before Bêlit-ili and the *u* between Enlil and É.A. The first three gods represent the "whole world," the cosmos as it was known since the time of the *Enuma elish* epic, *i.e.*, since the time when Babylonia proper (*Ki-en-gi-ki-BUR.BUR* = Shumer and Akkad = *kalam* = "high and lowland") had extended its confines south over the *low*lands as far as and embracing the Persian Gulf ("the *lower* sea" = *apsu*) and north over the Armenian mountains and the "westland" (notice that these two lands are likewise known as *BUR.BUR* = Akkad = *high*lands) up to and including the Mediterranean Sea ("the *upper* sea"). In this wise it happened that the *kalam* became a *kur-kur* and the ^{dingir}*LUGAL.KALAM.MA* a ^{dingir}*LUGAL.KUR.KUR*; in other words, the microcosmos became a macrocosmos which included the two oceans and was called *É-shàr-ra*, being as such inhabited by Anu (heavenly ocean = upper sea),

8 *ù mi-ish-ri-e*[1] *ish-ru-ku-ú-shú*

9 *be-lì-ia ki-bé-ma um-ma* ^{m}*Kal-bu*[2] *ip-ru*

10 *ù ar-du na-ra-am-ka-ma*[3]

TRANSLATION.

To my "Lord"—

1 Glorious in splendor, Seed out of heaven;

2 Not summoning punishment, Strong, powerful, wise one;

3 Light of his brothers, Ordering the dawn;

4 Ruler of mighty, Terrible lords;

5 Food of the people, Platter of man;

6 Hero of his clan, Whom the triad of gods

7 Together with Bêlit Presented a fief

8 Tending towards grace And righteousness—

9 to my "Lord" speak, thus saith Kalbu, thy dust

10 and thy loving servant:

The attributes here ascribed to the "Lord"—such as "the strong one, the powerful, the wise one," "the ruler of weighty and mighty ones," "hero of his family"; his being identified with the gods, as such being called "seed out of heaven," "light of his brothers," "the orderer of the dawn"; his holding in trust the administration of a "fief tending towards grace and righteousness", which was gratuitously given him by the gods of the whole world and not by any human being, shows absolutely and conclusively that we have here a divinely appointed ruler, who holds his king-

Enlil (*kur-kur* = *kalam*, the *terra firma*, as consisting of the upper (= *BUR.BUR*) and the lower (*ki-en-gi*) firmament), É.A (terrestrial ocean = *apsu* = Persian Gulf), see *Bêl, the Christ*, p. 11, note 3. Bêlit-ili, because identified in the inscriptions with Antum, Ninlil, and Damkina, represents here the feminine principle of the "world," "cosmos," Esharra. What the writer, then, wants to say with these words is this: "the whole world, as represented by its triad of gods, united in bestowing upon the Lord the *ki-ib-ti du-um-ki ù mi-ish-ri-e*"—not a ruler made by man, but a divinely appointed sovereign is the "Lord" of the writer Kalbu.

[1] Though we have forms with *e*, instead of *i*, in the third pers. singl. or plur. (cf. *e-si-ki-ir-ma*, 3 : 18; *e-pi-(it-)te-ma*, 3 : 19, 30, 32; *e-ri-ba-a*, 26 : 13, etc.), yet we never find an *e* used as a phonetic complement in these forms, hence I read here not *e-ish-ru-ku-ú-shú*, but *mi-ish-ri-e*(!) *ish-ru-ku-ú-shú*. *Mi-ish-ri-e* I take as a plural of *mîsharu* = *mishru* (cf. *epiru*, *epru*; *gimiru*, *gimru*; Delitzsch, *Gram.*, p. 105, § 45), "righteousness" (hence not of *meshrû*, "riches," *H. W. B.*, p. 688*a*), and *dumqi*, on account of the parallelism, in the sense of "grace," *H. W. B.*, p. 222*b* (against Jensen, *K. B.*, VI[1], p. 418, "*Schönheit, Gutheit, gute Beschaffenheit*"). The *e* may(!), however, stand for *î* (cf. 92 : 27) = "behold!"

[2] Neither the name of this writer nor that of any other person occurring in this letter (cf. ^{m}*E-tel-bu mâr* ^{m}*Ush-bu-la*, l. 12; ^{m}*I-na-Ê.KUR.GAL*, l. 32; ^{m}*Na-zi-*^{ilu}*En-lil*, l. 25, and the city ^{âlu}*Man-nu-gi-ir-*^{ilu}*IM*, ll. 13, 18) is mentioned in *B. E.*, XIV, XV. See now, however, the *Bît-*^{m}*Ush-bu-la*, *Neb. Nippur*, III, 5 (= Hinke, *B. E.*, Series D, IV, p. 148).

[3] In view of 89 : 1, *shá a-ra-mu-shu*, "whom (the addressee) I (the writer) love," I prefer to translate *ar-du na-ra-am-ka-ma* as given above, and not as "thy beloved servant." It is hardly to be expected that the "Lord" loves the "dust," but the "dust" loves his "Lord," is delighted to come in contact with his Master.

ship by the special favor of, and governs his people for, his gods in order that graciousness, truth, and uprightness may forever reign supreme. As such a divinely appointed ruler, he has, of course, also the bodily welfare of his people at heart—he is both their "food" and their "platter": by him and through him the gods are both the "givers" and the "gift."

(*b*) To make the certain doubly certain we may be permitted to consider briefly another section of this letter. The paragraph, important for our discussion here, reads (24 : 18ff.):

18 *ù ^{alu}Man-nu-gi-ir-^{ilu}IM*[1] *shá LUGAL ra-in ga-[ti]*[2]	Even the city Mannu-gir-Rammân, with which the **King** is entrusting me (*i.e.*, which I hold as fief of the king)
19 *ù be-lí a-na rid-ṣabê* (= *MIR.NIT. TA*[3]) *an-nu-ti id-di-na*[4]	and which my **Lord** has handed over to these conscribers,

[1] A city called after the name of a person. In such cases the *DISH* before the proper name is, if preceded by *âlu*, always omitted, cf. *^{alu}Ardi-GASHAN*, 66 : 21; *^{alu} ^{ilu}Gir-ra-ga-mil*, 3 : 31; *^{alu}Gir-ra-ga-mil*, 3 : 39; or only *^{ilu}Gir-ra-ga-mil*, 3 : 13, 17, 20; *^{ilu}UD-tu-kul-ti*, 16 : 8, 12, but *Bit-^{m}Ki-din-ni*, 9 : 23, so always after *Bit-* in our letters. The name of the person means "who is like Râmman," and corresponds to the Sumerian *A-ba-^{dingir}IM-gim*. The *gi-ir*, therefore, in this name represents the Sumerian *GIM* or the regular Babylonian *kima* (or *ki*). As the *a* in *ana* or *ina* may be omitted and the *n* assimilated to the next consonant, so the *a* of *kima* has been omitted here and the *m* assimilated itself (by first becoming an *n*) to the following r, but this it could do only if *^{ilu}IM* was actually read *^{ilu}Rammân*. This writing, then, proves that *^{ilu}IM* was not read, at the time of the Cassites, *Adad* but *^{ilu}Rammân*. For the change of *k* to *g* cf. *akanna* — *aganna*, p. 53, note 6.

[2] The *ti* which is broken away stood originally on the right edge of the tablet, in the break indicated in the copy. *Ra-in* = *ra-im*, *m* before *q* (even if the *q* belongs to another word, cf. *ana*, *ina*, *kima* above) may become an *n*, Delitzsch, *Gram.*, § 49*a*. For ראם *c. double acc.* see *H. W. B.*, p. 604*a*, 2, "*Jem. mit etwas begnaden, d. h. beschenken*"; here lit.: "with which the king entrusted my hand." It is the *term. technicus* used in the so-called "boundary stones" for a "royal grant," cf. *e.g.* Scheil, *Textes Élam. Sém.*, I, p. 89. Our writer Kalbu, then, has received the city Mannu-gir-Rammân by "royal grant."

[3] *MIR.NIT.TA*. King, *Letters of Ḫammurabi*, III, p. 99, note 5, was the first to recognize that the sign which looks like *ŠI* has to be read *MIR*. It is found with either two (*Letters of Ḫammurabi*, 3 : 7, 11 | 26 : 10, 16 | 36 : 14 | 43 : 4, 7, 19, 23, 27, 29) or three (B[3], 118 (= *C. T.*, VI, 27) : 14) or four (*Letters of Ḫammurabi*, 1 : 19, 22) wedges at the beginning. Delitzsch, *B. A.*, IV, 485, read this sign *BARA* which in our letters looks quite differently, cf. 3 : 13 | 41 . 8 (*BAR* = *parakku shá ḫu-lu-up-pi*) | 66 : 7 (*parakku ^{ilu}En-lil*). Cf. also *Z. A.*, XVIII, 202f. and *l.c.*, p. 393; Harper, *Code of Ḫammurabi*, List of Signs, No. 135. The latter quotation shows that the signs wrongly read *IP.USH* or *ṬU.USH* (*E. B. H.*, p. 423 *passim*) are to be transcribed *MIR.NIT*. Although Delitzsch read wrongly *BARA* for *MIR*, yet he was the first to recognize its true meaning. While King, *l.c.*, translated our signs by "captain of troops," "driver of slaves," and Nagel (*B. A.*, IV, 137) by "*Truppenfuhrer*," Delitzsch rendered it (*l.c.*) by "*Militärbehorde*." The *an-nu-ti* shows that *MIR.NIT.TA* must be *masc. plur.* *TA* apparently contains only the "overhanging" vowel of *USH* = *NIT*. *MIR.NIT.TA* is = *rid-ṣabê* = a composite noun in the plural, in which case only the last noun has the plural form. Harper, *Code of Ḫammurabi*, p. 183, probably gives the best translation of *rid-ṣabê*, rendering it by "recruiting officer; one who impresses men for the corvée." In view of the fact that the phrase of the Ḫammurabi Letters, *ana MIR NIT shaṭâru* resp. *mullû* (Delitzsch, *B. A.*, IV, 487 = *conscribere*), corresponds exactly to our *a-na MIR.NIT.TA nadânu*, I prefer to translate as given above. From this it is evident that Kalbu held the city Mannu-gir-Rammân by "royal grant," subject to military service. All royal "grants" were, therefore, fiefs.

[4] *iddina* = relative after *shá*, l. 18.

20 *i-na la-me-e*[1] *na-di zu-un-na i-na sha-me-e*	is destroyed by inundations: rains out of the heavens
21 *ù mi-la i-na nak-bi*[2] *ki-i i-di-nu*[3] *sha*[4]*-ku*	and floods out of the depths are, when (after) he had handed her over, overflooding her!
22 *âlu-ki shá be-lì i-ri-man-ni i-na la-me-e*	Yes, the city with which my **Lord** has entrusted me is destroyed
23 *na*[5]*-di a-na ba-la-at a-i-ka-a lul-lik*	by inundations! Where shall I go to save my life?

Kalbu, "the dust and loving servant," reports here to his Lord, who is gracious and pardoning, that a great misfortune had overcome the city with which he had been endowed by royal grant: a tremendous flood has destroyed it. As a result of this the writer is in danger of losing his own life, crying, therefore, out in despair: "Where can I possibly go to save myself?" The change of tenses in l. 18 (*ra-in ga-ti*) and l. 22 (*i-ri-man-ni*) pictures quite vividly the progress of the flood. While in l. 18 Kalbu is still the possessor of the city, holding it in trust for his Lord, he has lost it in l. 22, appearing as one that has been holding it.

If we compare in this paragraph the words "the city Mannu-gir-Rammân with which the **KING** is entrusting me" (l. 18) with those of l. 22, "the city with which **my Lord** has entrusted me," we will have to admit that the writer refers in one sentence to the **KING** and in the other to his **LORD** as the one who had given him (the writer) authority over the city. But if we admit this, then we will have to admit also the other, viz., that *the Lord* (**BE=LÌ**) *is the King* (**LUGAL**).

(*c*) And because the "Lord" is the "King," therefore could our writer, in one and the same letter, speak of his master as *be-lì* and as *LUGAL*, when he complained in the closing lines as follows (24 : 36f.):

[1] *La-me-e* is apparently used here in the same sense as *edêlu*, l. 15. Literally translated it means "is cast into encircling." What this encircling was the words that follow tell us: it was an encircling caused by "rain and floods," hence an "inundation, a deluge."

[2] To "rains out of the heavens and floods out of the depths" cf. the parallel expressions of the biblical flood story, הַגֶּשֶׁם מִן־הַשָּׁמַיִם and מַעְיְנֹת תְּהוֹם, Gen. 7 : 11.12 | 8 : 2.

[3] To *i-di-nu*, which refers back to *id-di-na*, l. 19, hence = *id-di-nu*, cf. besides l. 37, *i-di-na-an-ni*, also 83 : 29, *la ta-di-in*; 87 : 17, *shá ta-di-na* and 57 : 18, *kêmu* (= *KU*) *ma-ad-gan* (cf. *B. E.*, XIV, 106*c* : 2; XV, 181 : 1; Delitzsch, *H. W. B.*, p. 136*a*) *shá ta-ta-tu* (root לאה?, Delitzsch, *H. W. B.*, p. 366*a*, Jensen, *K. B.*, VI[1], p. 442. Notice that *lu'tu*, pl. *lu-ta-tu* is a syn of *murṣu* = *GIG.BA*, which latter we find again in *KU.GIG.BA* = *kibâtu* (Jensen, *K. B.*, VI[1], p. 485), hence *lu-ta-tu*, a kind of coarse, dirty flour) *a-na PAD É-AN li-di-nu*. A possible derivation from *dînu* or even *danânu* is out of place here.

[4] This older form of *shá* I found, so far, only here. Cf., however, *B. E.*, XIV, Sign List, No. 272. The permansive expresses here the idea that the overflooding is still going on.

[5] Nothing is missing before *na-di*.

36 *ù a-na-ku i-tu b[e-lì]-ia a-na a-la-a-ki*	And I, the *itû* of my "Lord," though I have written to the "King" concerning my going (away, *i.e.*, leaving)
37 *a-na LUGAL ki-i ash-[pu-r]a LUGAL ul i-di-na-an-ni*	yet the "King" has not given me (an answer or permission to do so[1]).

Kalbu, who was looking out for the interests of his "*Lord*" continually and in all directions (*itû*), feels somewhat slighted that he should be treated by the "*King*" in the way he was. He had, in a previous note dispatched to the King, asked "where to go" (cf. also l. 23), but the King had not advised him what to do, hence his renewed complaint here.

(*d*) At the same result we arrive if we study another letter published under No. 55. Though the beginning[2] and the end of that letter are broken away, yet the passage important for our investigation is, fortunately, preserved and clear. From this epistle we learn that the **King** (*LUGAL*, l. 8), upon the instigation of ^{m} ^{ilu}*En-lil-ki-din-ni*, commanded his messenger *Mâr-*^{m}*Û-da-shá-ásh* to "go and send certain persons" (l. 10f.). But in l. 20 of this very same letter the *royal* messenger refers to his *King's* command by saying (l. 21f.), "when ^{m} ^{ilu}*En-lil-ki-di-ni* had spoken to **my Lord** (*be-lì-ia*), my **Lord** (*be-lì*) sent word to me saying: send the persons, etc." (follow the exact words which the king had spoken to his messenger and which the messenger now quotes, l. 9f.). Here, then, again one and the same person is referred to as both **King** (*LUGAL*) and **Lord** (*be-lì*). But this could be done only if the **Lord** was indeed the **King.** The letter, as far as it concerns us here, reads (55 : 2f.):

2 *Mâr-*^{m}*Û-su-ub-Shi-pak i-di ù lu-ú TUR.TUR*[^{mesh}][3]	Mâr-Usub-Shipak knows. And with regard to the young slaves
3 *shá na-shá-nu*[4] *li-il-ta-a'-a-lu um-ma-a i-na a-[ma-as-su-nu]*	whom we are holding prisoners let them inquire as follows:

[1] Or "adjudged me worthy of an answer," see p. 104, note 5.

[2] On account of the absence of the address it is very doubtful whether this letter belongs to those "addressed to the 'Lord'" or whether it ought to take its place behind No. 75.

[3] *TUR.TUR*^{mesh}, to be read according to l. 5, *ṣi-iḫ-ḫi-ru-ti*, are here "youngsters," "young slaves." Cf., however, *H.*, III, 289, *a-mat LUGAL a-na amelu* ^{mâtu}*Tam-tim-a-a* ^{amelu}*AB.BA*^{mesh} *u TUR*^{mesh}(!) *ardi*^{mesh}*-ià* (see also *H.*, III, 296, 297, V, 518) with *H.*, III, 295, *a-mat LUGAL a-na amelu* ^{mâtu}*Ra-sha-a-a* ^{amelu}*AB.BA*^{mesh} *u ṣiḫ(= NE!)-ru-ú-ti.*

[4] Perm. I[1], first pers. plur. for *nashâ-ni* of נשא; here with the same meaning as, *e.g.*, *Letters of Ḫammurabi*, No. 1 : 23, *ka-an-ki-im shá Ib-ni-*^{ilu}*MAR.TU na-shu-ú*, "the contract which Ibni-Martu holds," *i.e.*, "which he has in his possession, which he keeps"; it being above in opposition to *mushshuru*, "dismiss," ll. 12, 13, requires here some such signification as "to hold as prisoner,"

4 *ma-ti shá-a'-ma-tu-nu*[1] *ù TUR. TUR*^{mesh} *na-shá-nu-ma*[2]	"When are ye finally going to decide their affairs, seeing that we are holding the young ones as prisoners?"
5 *Mâr-*^{m}*Ísh(?)-pi-la-an-du*[3] *ṣi-iḫ-ḫi-ru-ti ki i-ki-ba-na-shi*[4]	After Mâr-Ash(?)pilandu had committed to us the young ones
6 *ki-i ni-il-li-ku a-na* ^{m} ^{ilu}*En-lil-ki-din-ni*	and we had gone we spoke (as commanded) to Enlilkidinni.
7 *ni-iq-ta-bi* ^{m} ^{ilu}*En-lil-ki-din-ni a-na LUGAL*	And after Enlilkidinni had informed the KING,
8 *ki-i iq-bu-ú LUGAL Mâr-*^{m}*Û-da-shá-ásh*	the KING gave orders to Mâr-Udashash
9 *di-ma*[5] *il-ta-ka-an um-ma-a shú-pu-ur-ma*	as follows: "Send
10 ^{amelu}*DAM.QAR*^{mesh} *ù TUR.TUR*^{mesh}	the agents and the young slaves

[1] *Shîmu c. ina*, "to decide," "determine the fate with regard to something," "to give a decision with regard to something," "to decide an affair."

[2] See note 4, page 51.

[3] The reading of this name is not certain. If the *ásh* which is written here strangely at the lower end of *DISH* does not belong to the name we might read *Mâr-*^{m}*Pi-la-an-du*. Also some such readings as *Mâr-*^{m}*Ásh-pi-la-*^{ilu}*DU* or *Mâr-*^{m}*Pi-la-*^{ilu}*DU* might be possible. A reading *Mâr-*^{m}*Na-ásh-la-an-du* (resp. ^{ilu}*DU*) is, however, less probable.

[4] For *qîpu* (here *c. double acc.*), "to entrust something to somebody," see p. 47, note 1.

[5] Jensen, *K. B.*, VI[1], p. 412, doubts whether *shakânu* may be construed with double accusative. Here and p. 125, n. 8, it is. *Dima* (=*ṭêma*) *shakânu c. acc.*, lit. "to make news to somebody," *i.e.*, "to make them known to somebody," "to report," and as it is here the king who "makes these news known to his messenger," it is equivalent to "to order," "to command." It is interesting to observe that the following verbs may be used in connection with *ṭêmu*:

(*a*) *lamâdu*, "to learn news," here only with the first pers. of the verb, hence = "to inform one's self of something." Cf. 57 : 21, *di-im É*[*.AN*] *a-la-ma-ad*, 33 : 28, *te*(!)*-e-im mu-shi a-lam-ma-ad*; 33 : 30, [*te-e*]*-im su-ma-nu a-lam-ma-ad*. See also *C. T.*, VI, 31 : 21, *a-na te-im a-va-tim shá-a-ti la-ma-di-im*.

(*b*) *nadânu*, "to give news," "to inform." Cf. *B. E.*, XIV, 114 : 1, *shá ḪA* (= fish) *LUGAL di-e-mi i-din-*[. . .].

(*c*) *sha'âlu*, "to ask for news about something," "to inquire about it." Cf. 22 : 8, *di-im mur-ṣi-shá ki ish-a-lu-shi*.

(*d*) *shakânu*, "to give news," "to report," "to command," "to order." Cf. 59 : 10, *di-e-ma i-shá-ak-ka-nu*; 67 : 6, *di-ma lu-ush-ku-na*(?); 80 : 13, *di-ma shu-kun-ma*; 92 : 21, 31, *te*(!)*-e-ma shú-kun*; 9 : 16, *shakin* (= *GAR*)^{in} *de*(= *NE*)*-mi* (here not an "officer," but a permansive: "is reporting concerning (*shá*) *Bit-Sin-issaḫra*"). From this it will be evident that an ^{amêlu}*shakin*(*-in*) *ṭêmi* may be (*a*) either a "reporter," who keeps his "superior" informed about the affairs of certain cities or territories, etc., or (*b*) he may be (if he be, *e.g.*, a king, etc.) one that "gives commands" to his inferior. Cf. furthermore 55 : 9, *di-ma il-ta-ka-an*; 55 : 23, [*di-ma i*]*l-ta-ak-na-an-ni*. In view of the two latter phrases we cannot explain 34 : 38, *be-li di-e-ma il-KU*(!)*-na-an-ni* as standing for *beli ṭêma il-qu*(!)*-na-an-ni*—which would be without any sense—but we must, seeing that the sign *KU* has also the value *tuk*(*g*), postulate that value here and read *il-tuk*(!)*-na-an-ni*, or we must suppose that *KU* could be read (besides *tuk*(*g*)) also *tak*(*g*): *il-tak*(=*KU*)*-na-an-ni*. In the latter case we would have here a new value for *KU*, viz., *tak*(*g*).

(*e*) *shapâru*, "to send news." Cf. 53 : 40, *di-im ta-sap-pa-ra-am-ma*; 84 : 11, *di-im ta-ash-pu-ra*; 57 : 17, *di-e-ma li-ish-pu-ra-am-ma*; 76 : 5, *di-e-ma shú-up-ra-am-ma*; 94 : 8, *te*(!)*-ma shú-up-ra*; 89 : 29, *de*(= *NE*)*-im-ka ù shú-lum-ka shú-up-ra*—the latter phrase being used for "a request of a letter in answer to a note sent."

(*f*) *turru*, "to return news," "to advise," "*Bericht erstatten*." Cf. 76 : 9, *di-e-mi a-na be-el lu-te-ir*.

11 *shá* ^{m} ^{ilu}*En-lil-ki-di-ni shú-pu-ur-ma*	of Enlilkidinni send, that
12 *li-mi-ish-shi-ru-ni*[1]	they dismiss them (*i.e.*, set them free)."
13 *mâr ship-ri LUGAL*[2] *a-na mu-ush-shú-ri-ni*[3]	(Now) when the royal messenger had come for the purpose of dismissing
14 *ki-i il-li-ka shú-ú ki ú-ṣi-bi-ta-na-shi*	us (*i.e.*, of securing our release) (then) he, after he had seized us,
15 *a-na mu-uḫ LUGAL ul-te-bi-la-na-shi*	brought us before the KING.
16 *LUGAL a-na Mâr-*^{m}*Û-da-shá-ásh um-ma-a*	Whereupon the KING said to Mâr-Udashash:
17 *shá-al-ma-at*[4] *aq-ta-ba-ak-ku um-ma*	"Have I not sent greetings (*i.e.*, a letter containing greetings) unto thee and commanded thee saying:
18 *ta-al-ta-pa-ar-ma TUR.TUR*^{mesh}	'Thou shalt send that they
19 *shá* ^{m} ^{ilu}*En-lil-ki-din-ni un-di-ish-shi-ru-ni-i*[5]	dismiss the young slaves of Enlilkidinni'?"
20 *Mâr-*^{m}*Û-da-shá-ásh a-ka-an-na-a*[6] *iq-ta-bi*	Mâr-Udashash answered under those circumstances
21 *um-ma-a* ^{m} ^{ilu}*En-lil-ki-di-ni a-na be-li-ia*	as follows: "After Enlilkidinni had spoken to 'MY LORD,'
22 *ki-i iq-bu-ú be-li a-na ia-a-shi*	'MY LORD'
23 [*di-ma i*]*l-ta-ak-na-an-ni um-ma-a*	commanded me saying :
24 [*shú-pu-ur-m*]*a* ^{amelu}*DAM.QAR*^{mesh} *ù TUR.TUR*^{m}[^{esh}][7]	'Send [that they dismiss] the agents and young slaves [of Enlilkidinni], etc.'"

[1] Stands for *lu* + *umashshirû-ni*. *La* + *u-* (if 3 pers.) or *lu* + *i-* = *li, so always!* For the *i* in *mi-ish* = *mash* cf. also *un-di-ish-shi-ru-ni-i*, 55 : 19; *li-ṣi-el-li-lu-ma*, 66 : 22; *e-ki-ir-ri-im-ma*, 23 : 10; *li-ri-id-du*, 60 : 13; *ú-ṣi-bi-ta-na-shi*, 55 : 14; *li-ṣi-bi-tu-shú-nu-ti*, 58 : 11; *i-di-ik-ku-ú*, 40 : 7, etc., hence an emphatic *a* with *i* preceding or following may become an *i*.

[2] The royal messenger here referred to is *Mâr-*^{m} *Û-da-shá-ásh*, l. 8.

[3] Lit. "for our dismissal", the infinitive being treated here as a noun, hence *-ni* for *-na-shi* (ll. 14, 15).

[4] *Shá-al-ma-at* here not a plur. of *shalimtu*, but a permansive = (*lu*) *shalmât*(*a*), "peace (greeting) be unto thee." This would make it appear that the Cassite kings, when writing to their subjects and using any greeting at all, employed the following formula: *shulmu iashi lû shalmâta*, "I am well, mayest thou be well." The later Babylonian resp. Assyrian kings said, as is well known, in its stead, *shulmu iashi libbaka lû ṭâbka* (resp. *libbakunu lû ṭâbkunushi*).

[5] *Undishshirû* = *umdashshirû*. The long *i* in *ni-i* I take as the sign of a question, hence standing for original *u*: *i* instead of *u* on account of the *i* in *ni*.

[6] Cf. here also *a-ka-an-na*, 3 : 35, 37 \| 11 : 4 \| 63 : 2 \| 95 : 8. *B. E.*, XIV, 2 : 13 \| 8 : 10, 13; *a-ka-an-na-ma*, 67 : 7. See also *e-ka-an-na-am*, 52 : 25, on the one and *a-gan-*[*na*], 21 : 9, 11; *a-ga-an-na*, 71 : 9, on the other hand. For the last cf. also Behrens, *L. S. S.*, II[1], p. 2.

[7] To be completed and translated according to ll. 9f.

We need not, however, be satisfied merely with the result that the "Lord" is in each and every case the "King," but we can go a step farther and identify definitely the King of No. 55.

Enlilkidinni,[1] who plays such an important rôle in this letter and who clearly must have been a person of influence and affluence, he being in possession of "young slaves and agents" and having access to the King (who listens to his entreaties and acts accordingly), appears also as the writer of the two letters, Nos. 78, 79, and is as such a contemporary of Usub-Shipak,[2] of Mâr-Udashash,[3] of Aḫushina (78 : 1). The last is mentioned as *patesi* in the 17th year of Kuri-Galzu (*B. E.*, XIV, 25 : 12), receiving *PAD LU.ARDU* in the 26th(!) year (of Burna-Buriash, *B. E.*, XIV, 167: 12, cf. l. 11) and *KU.QAR* *iṣunarkabtu* in the 3d year (of Kuri-Galzu, *B. E.*, XV, 21 : 7), and is found together with a certain Murânu in a tablet from the time of Kuri-Galzu (cf. Innanni, l. 25), *B. E.*, XV, 194 : 7, 8. This Murânu[4] was a son of Meli-Shaḫ and a *patesi*, living during the 18th year of Kuri-Galzu, *B. E.*, XIV, 28 : 5. A "son of Murânu," *Mâr-mMu-ra-ni*, who likewise is a *patesi*, is mentioned not only during the 13th year of Ku[ri-Galzu, *sic*! against Clay], *B. E.*, XIV, 125 : 6, 8, 13, but he appears also in the letter No. 78 : 4 as a contemporary and *itû*(!) of Enlilkidinni. From No. 79 : 1 we learn that Enlilkidinni was a contemporary of Imguri, who again, as writer of Nos. 22, 23, is contemporaneous with Ḫuzalum (22 : 6) and Kidin-Marduk (23 : 23). But Ḫuzalum as well as Kidin-Marduk figure as witnesses in certain business transactions executed between Enlilkidinni and some other parties at the time of Burna-Buriash, more particularly Ḫuzalum[5] is mentioned as witness in the 21st year of Burna Buriash (*B. E.*, XIV, 8 : 30) and Kidin-Marduk[6] in the 19th (or 18th?) year of the same king, *B. E.*, XIV, 7 : 34. Taking all these passages together, there can be absolutely no doubt that the Enli kidinni of Nos. 55, 78, 79 is the same person as the one who appears in the tablets of *B. E.*, XIV, as living during the 3d (*l.c.*, 1 : 6, 30, Clay wrongly 1st) 6th (*l.c.*, 2 : 7, 19, 29), 19th (*l.c.*, 7 : 14, 38) and 21st (*l.c.*, 8 : 22, 25, 33) year of Burna-Buriash. From this it follows that the "Lord" and "King" of No. 55, the contemporary of Enlilkidinni, was none other but *King Burna-Buriash.*

Having established the identity of the King, we can now more specifically determine the occupation of Enlilkidinni. Above we saw that Enlilkidinni was in

[1] Written either *m iluEn-lil-ki-din-ni*, 55 : 6, 7, 19, or *m iluEn-lil-ki-di-ni*, 55 : 11, 21 | 78 : 3 | 79 : 3.

[2] Identical with Uzub-Shipak in Scheil, *Textes Élam. Sém.*, I, p. 93, I : 3 (a kudurru from the time of Kashtiliashu).

[3] The name of this royal messenger is, so far, not mentioned again.

[4] The Murânu of *B. E.*, XIV, 128 : 8, living at the time of Shagarakti-Shuriash (1st year) is another person.

[5] Son of *m iluEn-lil-bêl(= EN)-AN^{mesh}*

[6] The father of *mTa-ki-shum.*

possession of agents (*DAM.QAR*), young slaves (*TUR.TUR*^{mesh} = *ṣi-iḫ-ḫi-ru-ti*) and of an *itû*, "one who looked out for his superior's interests." If we compare this with the tablets of *B. E.*, XIV, we find that Enlilkidinni was the son of ^{m} ^{ilu}*NIN. IB-na-din-SHESH*^{mesh} (*l.c.*, 1 : 6 | 7 : 14, here: *SE-SHESH.SHESH*), living in *Bît-*^{m} ^{ilu}*En-lil-ki-di-ni* (*l.c.*, 2 : 8), where he kept slaves (*NAM.GALU.LÙ* . . . . *ka-lu-ú*, *l.c.*, 2 : 6, 8), whom he bought from (*KI* . . . . *IN.SHI.IN.SHAM*, *l.c.*, 1 : 4, 8 | 7 : 12, 15) other slave-dealers (*DAM.QAR*, *l.c.*, 1 : 4); he had even his own agents (No. 55 : 10, *DAM.QAR*^{mesh}) and representatives (*itû*, Mâr-Murâni by name, No. 78 : 4) who had continually to look out for their employer's interests. Here it is especially interesting to note that one and the same person could be a *pa- e-si* and at the same time also an *itû* for a dealer in slaves, as was the case with Mâr-Murâni. This business must have been quite profitable and must have carried with it a great influence at the King's court, for Enlilkidinni need only appear before King Burna-Buriash, requesting the release of his slaves, and his wishes are instantly complied with. No wonder then that the "house of Enlilkidinni" became rich and powerful, flourishing as late as the time of Rammân-shum-uṣur and Meli-Shipak. The boundary stone, London, 103,[1] the provenance of which is unknown, has been stealthily abstracted (by some workmen employed by the *B. E.* of the University of Pa.?) from the ruins of Nippur. On this stone are mentioned not only the *GÙ.EN.NA* or "sheriff" of Nippur (I: 20, 48, III: 7) and the "*piḫat* of Nippur" (III: 42) —which by themselves would show whence that stone came—but also such names as *Bît-*^{m} ^{ilu}*En-lil-ki-di-ni* (IV : 29, 44; V : 31) and *Aḫu-da-ru-ú*, the "son" (*mâr*,[2] *i.e.*, = "descendant") of ^{m} ^{ilu}*En-lil-ki-di-ni* (IV : 13, 40; V : 1),[3] who was, as we just saw, a rich and influential slave-dealer at Nippur during the time of Burna-Buriash. Cf. furthermore the writer of No. 25: 2, ^{m}*Ur-*^{ilu}*NIN.DIN.DUG.GA*, with the person bearing the same name in London, 103, I : 6; also the ^{ilu}*Parak-mâri*^{ki} (*l. c.*, V, 15, with our No. 53 : 38) and the "canal of *Dûr-*^{ilu}*Enlil*," *Nam-gar-Dûr-*^{ilu}*Enlil*, *l. c.*, III, 23, with

[1] Preserved in the British Museum, No. 103 of the Nimroud Central Salon, and published by Belser, *B. A.*, II, p. 187f. A translation was given by F. E. Peiser in *K. B.*, III[1], p. 154f.

[2] For *mâr* = "descendant," see below, Chapter IV, pp. 64, 65.

[3] The following members of the "House of Enlilkidinni" are known:

^{m} ^{ilu}*NIN.IB-na-din-SHESH*^{mesh} (or *SE-SHESH.SHESH*).
|
^{m} ^{ilu}*En-lil-ki-di-ni*, the founder of the house.
| ? (*mâr* here "descendant.")
^{m}*Aḫu-da-ru-ú* (see *K. B.*, III[1], pp. 158, 160, IV : 12, 45).
|
^{m} ^{ilu}*En-lil-shum-iddina* (= *MU.MU*).

Aḫu-darû lived during the time of *Rammân-shum-uṣur* and *Meli-Shipak*, and *Enlil-shum-iddina* during the latter's reign.

our Nos. 3 : 33, 34, 38, 41 | 39 : 41; *B. E.*, XIV, p. 58*a*; XV, p. 52*a*; X, p. 70*a*. Such identity of names and places cannot be accidental.

(*e*) If now it be admitted, as it undoubtedly must be, that the "Lord" of our letters is always and invariably the "King," then, of course, it is not at all surprising that we should find in this collection epistles written by the King himself. Prof. Hilprecht informs me that he has seen several of them (one of them sent by King Nazi-Maruttash) while examining in Constantinople the tablets of the Nippur find. Fortunately I am in the position to publish at least one[1] of them here. It is a "royal summons" sent by King Burna-Buriash to his sheriff (*GÚ.EN.NA*), *ᵐAmel-ᵈᵘMarduk*, to arrest certain men accused of *lèse majesté*.[2]

(*f*) At last we are in a position to account for the peculiar characteristics of the Amarna Letter, B. 188—characteristics which put this letter into a class all by itself, as such separating it from all the rest of the Amarna Letters, whether they belong to the Berlin or the London collections. The peculiarities of this letter consist in the wording of its "address" and its "greeting," forming, as it were, an exact parallel to the address and the greeting of all of our letters addressed to the "Lord," *be-lí*. Seeing that this letter does form such a striking corroboration of our contention, I shall give it in full, though its lamentable condition would hardly warrant a complete and satisfactory translation. The letter[3] (Amarna, B. 188) reads:

1 *a-na ᵐbe-lí-ia*	To my "Lord"
2 *ki-bé-ma um-ma*	speak, thus
3 *TUR.SAL LUGAL-ma*	saith the princess:
4 *a-na ka-shá ⁱˢᵘnarkabâti*[meshl]*-ka*	Unto thee, thy chariots,
5 [*âlu*ᵏᵃˡ *ù bîti-ka*]	thy cities, and thy house
6 *lu-ú shú-ul-mu*	greeting!
7 *AN*ᵐᵉˢʰ *shá ᵐBur-ra-Bur*(!)*-ia-ásh*	The gods of Burra-Buriash

[1] Another *royal* letter is possibly that published under No. 93.

[2] No. 75. For a translation see below, p. 135.

[3] Since the above has been written there appeared in the *Vorderasiatische Bibliothek* a new translation of the Amarna letters by J. A. Knudtzon. This scholar, when speaking of this letter in the Preface to his translation, says (*Die El-Amarna-Tafeln*, pp. 201.): "*Der erstere* (*i.e.*, No. 12 = B. 188) *stammt nach seiner Schrift wohl am ehesten aus Babylonien, was auch nach dem Ton moglich und nach dem wahrscheinlichen Inhalt von Z. 7 das Nächstliegende ist. . . . . Wenn mit dem, was uber die Herkunft dieses Briefes gesagt ist, ungefahr das Richtige getroffen ist, so ist der "Herr," an den er gerichtet ist, kaum anderswo als in Ægypten zu suchen.*" Knudtzon differs (*l.c.*, p. 98, No. 12) in the following points from the translation (and emendation) as given above: l. 5, [*a*]-*m*[*i*]-*l*[*u-t*]*i* for *âlu*ᵏᵃˡ (but cf. Rev. l. 5); l. 11, *'i*(!)*-ir-ma*, *wandele*; Rev. l. 3, *si-ir-pu* he translates by "*gefarbten Stoff*," but then Rev. ll. 5f. is left in the air. Rev. ll. 7f., *il-ti*(!) *li*(!)*-bi-ka*, 8 *l*[*a*] *ta-*[*d*]*a-*[*b*]*u*[*-u*]*b* —9 *ù ia-a-shi il-ku l*[*a*] *te-te-en-du-ni* which is rendered by "*Mit deinem Herzen wirst* (or *sollst*) *du n*[*ic*]*ht r*[*e*]*d*[*e*]*n . . . ., und mir wirst* (od. *sollst*) *du . . . . n*[*ic*]*ht errichten*."

8 *il-ti-ka li-li-ku*	may go with thee!
9 *shal-mi-ish a-li-ik*	Walk in and out
10 *ù i-na shá-la-me*	in peace!
11 *ti-ir-ma bîti-ka a-mur*	Thy house, I behold,
12 *i-na pa-*[. . . .]	in former times [. . . .]
Reverse:	
1 *a-ka-an-n*[*a*	but now . . . .
2 *um-ma-a ul-tum*^{m}*Gi-*[. . . .	thus: "Since I sent Gi- . . .,
3 *mâr ship-ri-ia ṣi-ir-pa*	my messenger, with a letter
4 *ú-she-bi-la a-na*	containing
5 *âlu*^{hal}*-ka ù bîtim*^{tim}*-ka*	greeting to thy cities
6 *lu-ú* [*shú sic!*]*-ul-mu*	and thy house,
7 *il-ti-*[*nu, sic!*] *i-na bi-ka*	they gave upon thy command
8	. . . .
9 *ù ia-a-shi id ma-la*	and with regard to me remember (know)
10 *te-te-en-da-ni*	all thou hast told me."
11 *ardi-ka* ^{m}*Ki-din-*^{ilu}*IM*	Thy servant is
12 *i-shá-ak-ni*	Kidin-Rammân.
13 *a-na di*(!)*-na-an*	Before the presence
14 *be-li-i*[*a*!] *lu-ul-lik*	of my "Lord" may I come!

The writer of this letter is a "daughter of a king," a "princess." She addressed her epistle to "my Lord." This "Lord," being the "Lord" of a "daughter of a king," cannot be anyone else but a "king." Now I cannot agree with Winckler, *K. B.*, V, p. X, that this letter was addressed to the king of Egypt. On the contrary, the princess, by using a "greeting" and a "phrase" (*ana dinân beli-ia lullik*) so far met with in no other Amarna Letter—a "greeting" and "phrase" paralleled only by our letters here published—shows that she was of *Babylonian origin, i.e.*, she was a Babylonian princess, having been given in marriage to the king of Egypt.[1] We have to see, then, in this letter a "copy"[2] of an original sent to her father, the

[1] From Amarna, London, 1, *e.g.*, we know that a sister of Kadashman-Enlil had been given in marriage by her father, the king of Babylonia, to the Egyptian king. It may not be impossible that this princess is that very same sister about whom Kadashman-Enlil complains in a letter to the king of Egypt that "nobody has ever seen her, whether she is alive or dead," and that this letter is an assurance on her part that she is still well and among the living.

[2] Which happened to be preserved with the other Amarna tablets in the same way as was the "copy" of the letter of *Ni-ib-mu-a-ri-a*, the king of Egypt, to Kadashman-Enlil (Amarna, L. 1). For its being a "copy" speaks also the hastiness and carelessness in which it has been written, cf. *e.g.*, *ul-mu* for *shu-ul mu* (R. 6), *be-li-i* for *be-li-ia* (R. 14), *id* for *i-di* (R. 9), *il-ti* for *il-ti-nu* (Rev. 7). For several other Egyptian copies among the Amarna letters see also Knudtzon, *l. c.*, p. 16.

"Lord" and "King" of Babylonia. This princess, after having communicated her wishes to this "Lord," finds that, according to good woman fashion, a postscript is proper and in order. She forgot to introduce Kidin-Rammân, who, no doubt, brought this letter to the Babylonian king, as "thy servant," assuring in this wise the king that the servant is reliable and may be entrusted with an answer to her letter. Nay, more than this. The princess, finding, after her extended sojourn in the land of the Nile, that she had not employed the correct form of address customary among *Babylonians*[1] when writing to their "Lord" and "King," as we know now, adds another postscript, saying: *a-na di-na-an*[2] *be-lì-ia lul-lik*, "before the presence of my Lord may I come." And by using this phrase as well as the greeting, "to the cities and thy house greeting" (*a-na âlu*^{hal} *ù bîtim*^{tim}*-ka lu-ú shú-ul mu*, Rev. 5f.), the princess proves herself to be a real daughter of the Babylonian king, who, when addressed by his subjects, is always called "**my Lord**," *be-lì*.

[1] When foreigners like, *e.g.*, an Egyptian king write to a Babylonian king they never fail to mention the exact title of the king of Babylonia, calling him invariably *shar* (= *LUGAL*) ^{mâtu}*Ka-ra-*^{ilu}*Du-ni-ia-ash*, Amarna L., 1, *et passim*. For ^{ilu}*Du-ni-ia-ash* see Hüsing, *O. L. Z.*, December, 1906, p. 664, on the one, and M. Streck, *Z. A.*, January, 1908, p. 255f., on the other hand.

[2] For *dinânu* cf. also 24 : 33, *ash-shú di-na-[ni-]ia*, "on *my* account" = *ash-shumi-ia*. Knowing, as we do, that the highest honor conferred upon a servant of the king is to see the king's "face," and remembering that mortal beings always pray for their being permitted "to see the face of such and such a god" (cf. ^{m}*Pân-AN.GAL-lu-mur* and the New Testament promise that the faithful shall see the "face" of Christ, shall see him from "face to face," *i.e.*, shall be admitted into Christ's presence), I translate *dinân* by "presence," though its real signification is "*Selbst, Selbstheit.*" By doing this I am, however, unable to find the difficulty which Behrens, *L. S. S.*, II[1], p. 27, thinks he finds; for it is, of course, self-evident that the writer did not mean to imply in these words that *he* himself may be permitted to appear before the presence of the Lord. All the writer wants to convey through these words is this: may I *by* and *through* the mediation of this letter appear before the Lord; in other words, may the King himself graciously condescend to listen to me by means of this letter when I speak as follows to my Lord (*um-ma-a a-na be-lì-ia-ma*). The writer thus pleads that his letter may not be prevented by the "red tape" surrounding the person of the King from reaching his "Lord" and master. He wants a *personal* interview, he desires that the King himself shall see the letter, and if the writer's wish be granted he, *ipso facto*, is admitted through his epistle to the presence of the King, to the King himself. Nor are the words *mâr shipri-ia ana shulmi sharri sisê u ṣabê altapra*, occurring in *H.*, VII, 721 : 5 (writer ^{m} ^{ilu}*Marduk-MU-SE-na*) and *H.*, VIII, 832 : 5; 833 : 5; 835 : 5; 836 : 5; 837 : 5 (all written by ^{m} ^{ilu}*AG-EN-MU*^{mesh}) to be translated with Behrens, *l.c.*, by "*meinen Boten habe ich mit Gefolge* (*Pferde u. Krieger, d. i. berittene Krieger*?) *zur Begrüssung des Königs geschickt.*" The *sisê u ṣabê* belong, on account of their position, to the king, thus making him a king of "horses" = cavalry (cf. the "horses" = cavalry of the Old Testament, as, *e.g.*, in Deut. 11 : 4: the army of Egypt — their "horses" (= cavalry) and their chariots) and of "men" = infantry—a veritable "war-lord."

IV.

RESULTS.

—

The fact that the *be-li* in all our letters is the *KING* is of the highest importance for a correct understanding of (*a*) *The genealogy of the Cassite kings of this period*; (*b*) *Their seat of residence*, and (*c*) *The nature and purpose of the so-called Temple Archives*.

(*a*) The various investigations conducted by scholars[1] with regard to the genealogy of the kings of this period has, as was to be expected, led to widely divergent results. Without going into any controversy here, I shall confine myself to stating what seems to me the most probable solution of this rather difficult, tangled up, and knotty problem.

From the so-called *Synchronistic History*[2] (= *S. H.*) we learn that at the time of *Ashshur-uballiṭ*, king of Assyria,[3] the Cassites (*ṢAB*^{mesh} *Kash-shi-e*)[4] had revolted and killed ^{m}*Ka-ra-Ḫar-da-ash*, the king of Babylonia,[5] the son (*TUR*) of ^{m}*Mu-bal-li-ta-aṭ*-^{du}*She-ru-ú-a*, a daughter of *Ashshur-uballiṭ*, raising a certain ^{m}*Na-zi-Bu-ga-ash* to the kingship over them.[6] Whereupon *Ashshur-uballiṭ*, to

[1] Cf. *e.g.*, Winckler, *Das alte Westasien*, p. 21f.; Delitzsch, *Chronologische Tabellen* (not accessible to me); Weissbach, *Babylonische Miscellen*, p. 2f.; Clay, *B. E.*, XIV, p. 3 (see p. 10, note 3); Hilprecht, *B. E.*, XX[1], p. 52, note 1; and Thureau-Dangin in *Z. A.*, XXI (1907-1908), p. 176ff., a reprint of which has just reached me. After a lengthy discussion of all historical data furnished, this last scholar established a chronology all his own and confesses: "*Seule la donnée de Nabonide, relative à Shagarakti-Shuriash serait inexplicable: si, en effet, suivant l'hypothèse la plus probable, les 800 ans sont comptés de la fin du règne de Shagarakti-Shuriash à l'avènement de Nabonide, ce chiffre serait trop fort de près d'un siècle (exactement de 90 ans)*. Our scheme given on p. 1 does justice both to Nabonid's statement with regard to Shagarakti-Shuriash (*sc.* that the latter lived 800 years before him, *i.e.*, 539 (end of the reign of Nabonid) + 800 = 1339; above we gave 1331-1318 as the probable time of Shagarakti-Shuriash), and to that of Sennacherib (p. 2, note 12). But, more than this, I believe, with Thureau-Dangin and Ed. Meyer (*Das chronologische System des Berossos* in *Beiträge zur alten Geschichte*, III, pp. 131ff.), that the beginning of the first dynasty of Babylon has to be placed at 2232, and Ḫammurabi, its sixth ruler, accordingly at 2130-2088. Now, if Nabonid informs us that Ḫammurabi lived 700 years before Burna-Buriash (II) (see Bezold, *P. S. B. A.*, Jan., 1889), the latter ruler must be put somewhere between (2130—700 =) 1430 and (2088—700 =) 1388 B.C. On p. 1 we assigned to Burna-Buriash the time between 1450-1423; hence our chronology, given above, comes as near the truth as it is possible at the present.

[2] See Winckler, *U. A. G.*, p. 148 (= *K. B.*, I, p. 194), ll. 8f.

[3] ^{m}*Ashshur-ú-TI.LA MAN* ^{mâtu}*Ashshur*.

[4] Not necessarily "Cassite soldiers," for *ṢAB*^{mesh} at this time is used simply for *ummâni*, "people," changing frequently with *ṢAB*$^{ḫi.a}$, see also p. 35, note 1.

[5] *MAN* ^{mâtu}*Kar-Du-ni-ash*.

[6] *A-na LUGAL-ú-te a-na muḫ-shu-nu ish-shu-ú*.

avenge [^{m}*Ka-r*]*a-In*(!)-*da-ash* (notice this name), went to Babylonia, killed [^{m}*Na*]-*zi-Bu-ga-ash*, made [^{m}*Ku-r*]*i-Gal-zu ṣi-iḫ-ru*, the son (*TUR*) of ^{m}*Bur-na-Bur-ia-ash*, to be king, and put him "upon the throne of his father" (*ina* ^{isch}*GU.ZA AD-shu*).

The questions to be asked and answered in connection with this text are the following:

(1) Why should the *S. H.* say that Ashshur-uballiṭ went out to avenge Kara-Indash? We would expect that the king of Assyria went out to "avenge rather the murdered Babylonian King Kara-Ḫardash." Who is this Kara-Indash, that Ashshur-uballiṭ should display such an interest? In what relation does he stand to the king of Assyria on the one hand and to the murdered king of Babylonia, Kara-Ḫardash, on the other?

(2) What do the words "put him (*i.e.*, Kuri-Galzu *ṣiḫru*) upon the throne of his father" mean? Does "father" refer here to Burna-Buriash or to Kara-Ḫardash? If it refers to the former, then who was Burna-Buriash? In what relation did he stand to Kara-Indash or Kara-Ḫardash or to the Assyrian king that he (the latter) should be so anxious as to secure the Babylonian throne for his (Burna-Buriash's) son, Kuri-Galzu? Why was the son and heir of the murdered Kara-Ḫardash not put upon the throne of Babylon? But if the term "father" refers, as we would expect, to Kara-Ḫardash, thus making Kuri-Galzu *ṣiḫru* the son and successor of his murdered father, then why should Kuri-Galzu be called here (and elsewhere) the "son (TUR) of Burna-Buriash"?

Some of these questions we can answer with the help of *Chronicle P.* (= *Ch. P.*),[1] where we are told that a certain ^{m}*Ka-dàsh-man-Ḫar-be* was the son (*TUR*) of ^{m}*Kar-In*[2]-*da-ash* and of (*sic*! cf., *l.c.*, l. 12) *Muballiṭat-Sherua*,[3] the daughter of *Ashshur-uballiṭ*,[4] king of Assyria; hence Kara-Indash (*S. H.*) = Kar-Indash (*Ch. P.*) was the husband of Ashshur-uballiṭ's daughter, Muballiṭat-Sherua, and the father of Kadashman-Ḫarbe. Ashshur-uballiṭ in avenging Kara-Indash acted, therefore, in the interests of his nearest relations—his daughter and his son-in-law—to preserve the Babylonian throne for the rightful heir. But the rightful heir in this case was the "son of the murdered King Kara-Ḫardash." This would force us to the conclusion that the term "father" of the *S. H.* meant Kara-Ḫardash and not Burna-

[1] So called after its discoverer, Theodore G. Pinches, *J. R. A. S.*, October, 1894, p. 811 (= p. 816), ll. 5f. Cf. also Winckler, *Altorientalische Forschungen*, I *Reihe*, p. 298(= p. 115)f.

[2] This *IN*, according to Knudtzon, *Die El-Amarna-Tafeln*, p. 35, and Delitzsch, *Abh. der sachs. Ges. d. Wiss.*, Vol. XXV, is absolutely certain. So also Ungnad, *O. L. Z.*, Marz, 1908, Sp. 139. Peiser, *ibid.*, p. 140, and Winckler *A. O. F.*, I, pp. 116, 298, read *Ka-ra-Ḫar-da-aš*.

[3] Written ^{f}*Mu-bal-liṭ-at-*^{ilu}*EDIN-u-a*.

[4] Written ^{m}*AN.SHAR-DIN-iṭ*.

Buriash, and that Kara-Ḫardash (*S. H.*) is only another name for Kadashman-Ḫarbe. This is corroborated by the further statement of *Ch. P.* which relates (col. I, 10f.) that the Cassites[1] revolted against and killed *ᵐKa-dàsh-man-Ḫar-be*[2], and raised "to the kingship over them"[3] a certain *ᵐShú-zi-ga-ash*, a Cassite, "the son of a nobody." Whereupon *Ashshur-uballiṭ*, the king of Assyria, went to Babylonia[4] to avenge *ᵐKa-dàsh-man-Ḫar-be*, "the son of his daughter[5]," [killed] *ᵐShu-zi-ga-ash* and put [*ᵐKu-ri-Gal-zu ṣiḫru*, the son (*sic!*) of *ᵐKa*]-*dàsh-man-Ḫar-be*, upon the throne [of his father].[6]

If we were to arrange the genealogies as given by *S. H.* and by *Ch. P.* in parallel columns we would have to do it as follows:

SYNCHRONISTIC HISTORY.		CHRONICLE P.	
BABYLONIA.	ASSYRIA.	BABYLONIA.	ASSYRIA.
Burna-Buriash	*Ashshur-uballiṭ*		*Ashshur-uballiṭ*
Kara-Indash	*Muballiṭat-Sherua*	*Kar-Indash*	*Muballiṭat-Sherua*
Kara-Ḫardash		*Kadashman-Ḫarbe*	
Nazi-Bugash		*Shuzigash*	
Kuri-Galzu ṣiḫru		[*Kuri-Galzu*]	

All scholars have—and, no doubt, correctly—admitted the identity of Nazi-Bugash and Shuzigash[7]; we need, then, not lose any words about this point. But if we do admit their identity we cannot very well deny the other, viz., that Kara-Ḫardash and Kadashman-Ḫarbe are likewise only two different writings of one and the same person. And here it is that I beg to differ from all the other scholars who either take Kara-Ḫardash to be a mistake for Kara-Indash (so Winckler), or who remove him altogether from the list of kings (so Weissbach). What might possibly

[1] Here *nishê (UN)*^{mesh} *Kash-shi*.

[2] Notice that the *shu* in l. 10 refers back to l. 5.

[3] *A-na LUGAL-ú-tu a-na muḫ-shu-nu*.

[4] *^{matu}Kar-^{ilu}Dun-iâ-ash*.

[5] *TUR TUR.SAL-shu* = Muballiṭat-Sherua.

[6] The words in [ ] are broken away, but they have been added here because they are the only rational and logical emendation of the text. See for this emendation also Winckler, *Altorientalische Forschungen*, *l. c.*

[7] Denied now, as I see, among others, also by Knudtzon, *Die El-Amarna-Tafeln*, p. 38. The reasons—if they may be called so—adduced by Knudtzon against the identity of these two persons are not at all convincing, in fact, they are against both the *S. H.* and the *Ch. P.*

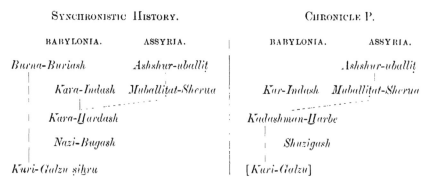

have been the reason of these two seemingly widely divergent readings, Kadashman-Ḫarbe (*Ch. P.*) and Kara-Ḫardash (*S. H.*)?

If I were to put before the various scholars in the realm of Assyriology a combination of signs, such as ^{gish}*KU* ^{ilu}*L*, asking them to transcribe, read, and translate it, what would be the result? One would read it *kakku* ^{ilu}*NIN.IB*, the other *kakku* ^{ilu}*Enlil*, the third *kakku* ^{ilu}*Nin-Girsu*, and translate it "the (a) weapon is (of) *NIN.IB*, or *Enlil*, or *Nin-Girsu*." A fourth, if he suspected a *nomen proprium* in that combination and knew that it was taken from a tablet belonging to the Cassite period and was aware that, at the Cassite period, the names of "cities called after a person" may be written without the determinative *DISH* (cf. ^{ilu}*Gìr-ra-ga-mil*, ^{ilu}*UD-tu-kul-ti*, etc., in "List of Cities"), might read that very same combination *Tukulti-*^{ilu}*Enlil* (*NIN.IB*, *Nin-Girsu*) and think it represents a "city." A fifth, again, would object seriously, pointing out that the "names of the Cassite kings" are likewise very often written without the *DISH* (cf. *e.g.*, Burna-Buriash in *B. E.*, XIV, 1 : 30 | 2 : 29 | 4 : 18, etc., etc.), and read accordingly (translating it back into Cassite) *Kadashman-*^{ilu}*Ḫarbe* (or Enlil, or NIN.IB, or Nin-Girsu). A sixth, lastly, would maintain that Cassite kings were *gods* or were identified with gods, hence a name ^{gish}*KU* ^{ilu}*L* should express the "name" or the "attribute" of a god; he accordingly would see in that combination such an attribute and would read and transcribe it by "weapon of god L," which would be in Cassite—what? And why is there such a difference of opinion among scholars when reading and transcribing personal names? Answer: Any modern Assyriologist has, or he thinks he has, the privilege to transcribe ideographically written names—be they those of persons or of gods—according to his own notions; thus one may see in the name ^{ilu}*SUGH* a *male*, the other takes it to be a *female*, and the third declares both are wrong: ^{ilu}*SUGH* is a "hen(-goddess)". To be sure, all three are *right* and all three are *wrong*. What modern scholars do now, the old scribes did 3,000 years before them. The name *Kadashman-Ḫarbe* means in Cassite "*my support is Ḫarbe*," and *Ḫarbe* translates the Babylonian ^{ilu}*Enlil*. *Kadashman-Ḫarbe*, when written ideographically, may be ^{gish}*KU*-^{ilu}*EN.LIL* (^{ilu}*É.KUR*, ^{ilu}*L*, etc.), but this *might*, *per se*, be translated also by "the (my, a) weapon is (of) Enlil (*É.KUR*, *L*, etc.)." Should the writer of the *S. H.* have mistaken the ^{gish}*KU* = *tukulti*, "support," for ^{gish}*KU* = *kakku*, "weapon," and have it translated back into the Cassite language by *kar(a)*, "weapon"? If we knew the Cassite word for "weapon" it would be a comparatively easy task to ascertain whether this suggestion or supposition might hold, but unfortunately we do not know it—at least I do not; and as long as this word is not known to us just so long the hypothesis will have to stand that the writer of *S. H.* mistook the ^{gish}*KU* =

tukultu = *Kadashman*, "support," thinking it was the same as ^{gish}*KU* = *kakku* = *kar(a)*, "weapon". And if ^{gish}*KU* could have been mistaken for *kar(a)* (instead of *tukulti*), the ideogram expressing *Ḫarbe* = *Enlil* might likewise have been mistranslated by *Ḫardash*. If *Ḫardash* be a composite word consisting of *Ḫard* + *ash* we might compare it with *Bugash* = *Bug-ash*. Should *Ḫard* + *ash* be = 5 (×) 10 = 50 = ^{ilu}*L*, and *Bug* + *ash* = 6 (×) 10 = 60 = *AN* or *ilu* (see p. 7, note 2, under *Guzar-AN*)? If this could be proved then the original ideographic writing of this name might have been ^{gish}*KU*-^{ilu}*L*. : *S. H.* translating it by *Kar(a)-Ḫard* + *ash* = a weapon of (is) ^{ilu}*L* and *Ch. P.* by *Kadashman-Ḫarbe* = my support is Enlil. For ^{ilu}*L* = ^{ilu}*Enlil*, see p. 40, note. (The *ash* in *Ḫard-ash* resp. *Bug-ash* is hardly the same as *iash* = *mâtu* = *KUR*; if it were, *Ḫard-ash* might represent either *É.KUR* or *KUR.GAL*, likewise names of Enlil and AN). If, on the other hand, *Ḫardash* be a simple (not composite) name, it might translate such ideographs as ^{ilu}*NAB* (= *Enlil*, V *R*. 44, 46c), ^{ilu}*AB* (= *Enlil*, III *R*. 67, No. 1, Obv. 11*a*, *b*; cf. l. 20, ^{ilu}*NIN.LIL dam-bi-sal*, *i.e.*, of ^{ilu}*AB* = ^{ilu}*Enlil*; in Weissbach, *Babyl. Miscellen*, p. 7 (*B. E.*, 6,405), l. 8, ^{ilu}*AB* is = *Anu* (*AN*): ^{ilu}*AB*(= *AN*) ^{ilu}*SÀR.SÀR* (= *Enlil*) ^{ilu}*SUR.UD* (= *É.A.*) *ù* ^{ilu}*NIN.MAGH* = fem. principle of the world, cf. No. 24 : 6 (p. 47, n. 5), *Anu*, *Enlil*, *É.A*, *Bêlit-ìlì*), or ^{ilu}*IB* (= *Enlil*, *AN*, *NIN.IB*). At any rate, the circumstance that we are not yet able, owing to our ignorance of the Cassite language, to say definitely which ideographic writing was before the eyes of the compiler of *S. H.* does not preclude the possibility that *Kadashman-Ḫarbe* and *Kara-Ḫardash* are one and the same person. This much we can say, however, that the original ideographic writing consisted of ^{gish}*KU* + a name of a god which could be translated both by *Ḫarbe* and by *Ḫardash*. We must maintain the identity of *Kara-Ḫardash* and *Kadashman-Ḫarbe* till we know that it is wrong and absolutely impossible.

Somewhat more difficult is the task to reconcile the two genealogies of Kuri-Galzu. If we knew nothing about the *S. H.* and had only the *Ch. P.*, in which Burna-Buriash is not mentioned with one syllable, nobody would ever have attempted to amend the broken text of *Ch. P.* differently from what was done above, viz., that Ashshur-uballiṭ went out to avenge Kadashman-Ḫarbe,[1] "the son of his daughter (*i.e.*, his grandson)," who had been killed by the Cassites and whose throne had

[1] Notice here the difference between *S. H.* and *Ch. P.* According to the former Ashshur-uballiṭ went out to avenge his "son-in-law, Kara-Indash"; and according to *Ch. P.* the same king wanted to avenge his "grandson, Kadashman-Ḫarbe." As the latter statement is far more to the point, it shows that the narrative of *Ch. P.* is to be preferred to that of *S. H.* Cf. also the writing Kara-Ḫardash (*S. H.*) with Kadashman-Ḫarbe (*Ch. P.*); the latter, no doubt, represents the better tradition.

been usurped by Shuzigash, in order to regain and preserve, of course, the Babylonian throne for the rightful heir of his grandson. But the rightful heir in this case was none other than the *son of Kadashman-Ḫarbe, Kuri-Galzu,* who naturally must have been still a "little child," a *ṣiḫru*,[1] seeing that his great-grandfather, the Assyrian king Ashshur-uballit, was still living. But if Kuri-Galzu was according to *Ch. P.* the *son* and rightful heir to the throne, it follows that the words of *S. H.*, "put him upon the throne of his *father*," can mean only that Ashshur-uballit put Kuri-Galzu *ṣiḫru* upon the throne of his murdered father, Kara-Ḫardash = Kadashman-Ḫarbe; hence the word "father" in *S. H.* does not refer to Burna-Buriash, as the interpreters want it, but must refer to Kara-Ḫardash. Thus, even according to *S. H.*, Kuri-Galzu *ṣiḫru* may very well, yes, *must* have been the son of Kara-Ḫardash = Kadashman-Ḫarbe. And by being put upon the throne of his murdered father, Kuri-Galzu *ipso facto* was put also upon that of Burna-Buriash, seeing that the son[2] of Burna-Buriash, Kar(a)-Indash, was his (Kuri-Galzu's) grandfather.

But if Kuri-Galzu was the "son of Kara-Ḫardash = Kadashman-Ḫarbe," as has been maintained, then he cannot have been, at the same time, the "son of Burna-Buriash," as *S. H.* informs us. Weissbach, who was the last to discuss the genealogies of this period, failed utterly, simply and solely because he did not recognize the true meaning of "son" (*TUR*) in *Kuri-Galzu TUR Burna-Buriash.* In the Black Obelisk of Shalmanassar II (858–824 B.C.), inscription to pictures II (cf. also III *R.*, 5, No. 6, ll. 25, 26), we are told that Jehu (*ᵐIa-ú-a*) was the "*son*" (*TUR*) of Omri (*ᵐḪu-um-ri-i*). But according to what we know from the Old Testament, Jehu was by no means a son (II Kings 9 : 2), but simply a ruler in "the land of the house" of Omri, being the fourth in the succession of his so-called father. Hence the *TUR* = *mâr*, "son," in *Kuri-Galzu TUR Burna-Buriash* does not necessarily have to signify "son," but may, and here *must*, mean "a later (descendant and) 'ruler of the house' of Burna-Buriash," "one that was of the 'line of reign' of Burna-Buriash." This follows also from the following consideration: from several inscriptions published by Hilprecht[3] we know that Nazi-Maruttash was the

[1] For *ṣiḫru* in this sense cf. also *H.*, III, 289 : 2; 296 : 2; 297 : 3; *H.*, V 518 : 3, *ᵍᵃˡᵘAB.BA*^{mesh} *ù TUR*^{mesh}, which changes in *H.*, III, 295 : 2, with *ᵍᵃˡᵘAB.BA*^{mesh} *u ṣiḫ(=NE)-ru-ú-ti*, thus showing that *ṣiḫru* "young" is in opposition to *AB.BA* = *shêbu*, "old."

[2] It should be noticed, however, that there is, so far, no inscription known which states that Kar(a)-Indash was the "son of Burna-Buriash." The above conclusion is nothing but an inference from *S. H.*'s words: "Kuri-Galzu, son of Burna-Buriash," see below, pp. 65ff.

[3] See, *e.g.*, Hilprecht, *B. E.*, I[1], Nos 53, 55, 56, 58, 78, 75 + 136 + 137 (cf. Zimmern, *Z. A.*, XIII, p. 302); *B. E.*, XIV, 39 : 9.

son of Kuri-Galzu, and from a boundary stone of Nazi-Maruttash[1] we learn that this latter ruler was "the son (*TUR*) of Kuri-Galzu and the *SHAG.BAL.BAL* of Burna-Buriash." Now *SHAG.BAL.BAL* means in each and every case nothing but "one who is of the reign(ing house) of," *libbi palê*. Hence the *mâr* (*TUR*) of the *S. H.*, because it corresponds here to *SHAG.BAL.BAL*, must likewise be taken in the signification of *libbi palê*; in other words, the expression *mâr* (*TUR*) *Burna-Buriash* of *S. H.* designates Kuri-Galzu not as son, but as "one who belonged to the line of rulers of the house of Burna-Buriash." As such he may have been the third, fifth, tenth, or hundredth in the line.[2] Kuri-Galzu *was*, and still *is*, the son of Kadashman-Harbe = Kara-Ḫardash, and this he *was* and *is* not only according to *B. E.*, XIV, 39 : 8f. (*ish-tu Ku-ri-Gal-zu TUR* ^{ilu}*Ka-da-ásh-man-Ḫar-be a-di*

[1] Scheil, *Textes Élam. Sém.*, I, p. 86 (cf. plate 16), col. I, ll. 1–5.

[2] Weissbach, *Babyl. Miscellen*, pp. 2f., by first trying to establish for *SHAG.BAL.BAL* an impossible meaning, "*Enkel*," puts the cart before the horse, and at the end of his investigations has to admit after all that *SHAG.BAL.BAL* in all passages cited by him means either "*Urenkel*," "*fernen Nachkommen*," or "*einen um Jahrhunderte späteren Nachkommen*." This alone ought to have been sufficient to convince Weissbach that *SHAG.BAL.BAL* in IV *R.*^{2}, 38, I, 20–26, could likewise not have the signification "*Enkel*." Not heeding this warning, Weissbach arrived at results which were both impossible and disastrous: he had to maintain *three* Marduk-aplu-iddinas, *three* Kadashman-Ḫarbes, *three* Kuri-Galzus; had to remove Kara-Ḫardash altogether from the list of kings and make Kuri-Galzu *siḫru*, "the son" of Burna-Buriash, the *aḫu abi*, the "brother of the father" of Kadashman-Ḫarbe, *i.e.*, had to make him a brother of Kara-Indash. Such manipulations are altogether too subjective to be taken seriously, and overlook the fact that a person at this time is designated only as "X., the son of Y."; in no case is there ever mentioned a grandfather. "*X. mâr Y. mâr Z.*" means at this time "X., the son of Y., belonging to (the house of) Z"(!) and stamps such a person as being of high, special, influential, or distinguished rank. Hinke's (*B. E.*, Series D., IV, pp. 133, 171) *Nabû-zêr-lishir mâr Itti-Marduk-balâṭu mâr Ardi-É.A*, because parallel to *Shâpiku mâr Itti-Marduk-balâṭu SHAG.BAL.BAL Ardi-É.A*, makes *Ardi-É.A* the founder of the distinguished and celebrated surveyor family of which the two brothers, *Nabû-zêr-lîshir* and *Shâpiku*, were later members (not *necessarily* grandchildren). Again, if *mâr be* = *SHAG.BAL.BAL* = "belonging to the reign(ing house) of," then it is, of course, quite natural that Meli-Shipak should call himself (*B. E.*, 6378 = Weissbach, *l.c.*, p. 2) *mâr Kuri-Galzu*. Why? Because Meli-Shipak was an usurper. But someone might object that in *London*, 103 (Belser, *B. A.*, II, p. 187f. = Peiser, *K. B.*, III^1, p. 160), IV, 31, the immediate predecessor of Meli-Shipak, Rammân-shum-uṣur, is referred to as "thy (*i.e.*, Meli-Shipak's; cf. *l.c.*, l. 17) *father* (*a-bu-ka*)." How can he be a usurper if his *father* occupied the throne before him? Apart from the list of kings, where Me-li-Shi-pak is not designated by *TUR-shu* (*i.e.*, the son of Rammân-shum-uṣur), the fact that a *father*, bearing a Babylonian name (as Rammân-shum-uṣur undoubtedly does), would call his son (Meli-Shipak) by a Cassite name is simply impossible in the history of the Cassites and without any parallel. Only the opposite may be admitted, *i.e.*, a Cassite father may call his son by a Babylonian name, but never would a Babylonian degrade himself so far as to acknowledge his oppressors by naming his son with a name which was despised among them. Meli-Shipak, then, by calling himself *mâr Kuri-Galzu*, lays "rightful" claim to the inheritance of the throne of Babylonia, which he would have as "one belonging to the house" (*mâr*) of Kuri-Galzu. The same desire is evidenced by Meli-Shipak's son, Marduk-aplu-iddina (notice the Cassite father and the Babylonianized son!), who does not call himself (IV *R.*^{2}, 38, I, 20–26 = *K. B.*, III^1, p. 162) grandson of Rammân-shum-uṣur, but "*the son* (*TUR*) *of Me-li-Shi-pa-ak* (cf. also List of Kings: $^{m\ ilu}$*SHU-A-MU TUR-shu*, *i.e.*, son of Meli-Shipak), *the SHAG.BAL.BAL of Kuri-Galzu LUGAL la-a sha-na-an*!" For a later example of *mâr* (resp. *aplu*) = "of the," or "belonging to the, house of," cf. *Rîmût*(-^{ilu}*MASH*) *aplu sha Murâshu*, and see Hilprecht, *B. E.*, IX, p. 15.

^{ilu}*Na-zi-Ma-ru-ut-ta-ásh TUR* ^{ilu}*Ku-ri-Gal-zu*), but also according to *Br. Mus.*, 83–1–18,[1] where he (written here ^{ilu}*Ku-ri-Gal-zu*) calls himself "the mighty king, the king of Babylon, the son (*TUR*) of ^{ilu}*Ka-dásh-man-Ḫar-be*, the king without equal (*LUGAL la shá-na-an*)."[2]

But though it might be admitted, as it must, that Kuri-Galzu, "the son" of Burna-Buriash of *S. H.*, was *de facto* the "son of Kadashman-Ḫarbe (*Ch. P.*) = Kara-Ḫardash", as such belonging to the reigning house of Burna-Buriash (*TUR* = *SHAG.BAL.BAL* = *libbi palê*), we still owe an explanation of the fact that there are *other* tablets in existence in which this self-same Kuri-Galzu is not only called, but even calls himself "son (*TUR*) of Burna-Buriash."[3] The question is this: Why should this self-same Kuri-Galzu (*ṣiḫru*) call himself or be called on the one hand "son of Kadashman-Ḫarbe = Kara-Ḫardash," and on the other "son of Burna-Buriash"? What were the reasons, if any, for this playing hide and seek?

We learned from *S. H.* and *Ch. P.* that the father of Kuri-Galzu, Kadashman-Harbe = Kara-Ḫardash, was killed by his own kinsmen, the Cassites, who had revolted against him, and who went even so far as to put a king of their own choice and liking, viz., Nazi-Bugash = Shuzigash, upon the throne of Babylon. We also heard that Kuri-Galzu did not occupy the throne of his murdered father by the wish and the consent of the Cassites, but, on the contrary, by and through the grace of his great-grandfather (on his mother's side), Ashshur-uballiṭ, who forced him while still a child (*ṣiḫru*) upon the dissatisfied Cassites. Is it not more than natural to suppose that the Cassites would feel rather inimical towards their new king, who was in their eyes nothing but an usurper,[4] occupying the throne of Babylon and swaying the royal scepter over them by the intervention and brutal force of a foreign king so inimical to their own interests? And was it not a wise and diplomatic stroke of

[1] See Winckler, *Z. A.*, II, p. 307f.

[2] This very same attribute is ascribed to Kuri-Galzu also in a boundary stone (IV *R.*^{2}, 38, I, 20–26 = *K. B.*, III^1, p. 162) quoted p. 65, n. 2. Kuri-Galzu, "the son of Kadashman-Ḫarbe," is identical with Kuri-Galzu, the predecessor of Meli-Shipak and Marduk-aplu-iddina (see p. 65, n. 2, end).

[3] See, *e.g.*, A. R. C. 146 (Lehmann, *Z. A.*, V, 417); Hilprecht, *B. E.*, I^1, Nos. 35, 36, 39; *l.c.*, I^2, 133 (see also Zimmern, *Z. A.*, XIII, p. 304); Scheil, *Textes Élam. Sém.*, I, p. 93, col. I, 18.

[4] One of the maxims in Babylonian history is that whenever a ruler or king terms himself "the legitimate" this or that, such a ruler is invariably an usurper. The truth of this maxim is clearly established also in Kuri-Galzu's case. One of his favorite titles is *rîjaum kînum*, "the legitimate shepherd," see Hilprecht, *B. E.*, I^1, Nos. 41 + 46 : 3 (cf. Hilprecht, *l.c.*, p. 32, and Zimmern, *Z. A.*, XIII, p. 304); *l.c.*, I^2, 133 : 5, 6 (Zimmern, *l.c.*). Also Kuri-Galzu's son, Nazi-Maruttash, claims this very same title, Hilprecht, *B. E.*, I^2, Nos. 75 + 136 + 137 (Zimmern, *l.c.*, p. 302): 5. What Kuri-Galzu lacked in favor from his subjects he made up in empty assertions.

policy on Kuri-Galzu's part not to call himself "son of Kadashman-Ḫarbe," thus avoiding to remind continually the enraged Cassites of their revolt and their murder committed? The Cassites hated any and every allegiance with the Assyrians, thrust upon them by the marriage of Kar(a)-Indash to Muballiṭat-sherua, knowing quite well that such a friendship would eventually lead—as it actually did—towards disaster. They preferred to have their country return to the *status quo* it occupied before this infamous intermarriage—to the first years of the reign of Burna-Buriash, "the ancestor" of Kuri-Galzu, when he warned the Egyptians, in a letter addressed to their king *Ni-ip-ḫu-ur-ri-ri-ia* (= Amen-hotep IV; *Amarna*, London, No. 2 : 31f.), not to listen to the machinations of the Assyrians, "my subjects" (*da-gi-il pa-ni-ia*). Kuri-Galzu, knowing this and eager and willing to appease his dissatisfied Cassites, did not—great diplomat and "king without equal" who he was—call himself[1] "son of Kadashman-Ḫarbe," but "descendant (*mâr*) of Burna-Buriash"; thus he maintained on the one hand his "rightful," "legitimate" (*kînum*) succession to the throne, and on the other he avoided to remind the enraged Cassites of their revolt and murder.

From all this it would follow that *Kuri-Galzu ṣiḫru* was *de facto* a "son of Kadashman-Ḫarbe," whom he followed upon the throne of Babylonia, but *de arte diplomatica* a "son of Burna-Buriash"; hence we have to place between the reigns of Burna-Buriash and Kuri-Galzu those of Kar(a)-Indash, Kadashman-Ḫarbe = Kara-Ḫardash, and Nazi-Bugash = Shuzigash.[2]

With the publication of these letters the period just discussed receives some new and additional light. Above we showed that all letters addressed to the "Lord" were intended without any exception for the "king." Who this "king" is or was cannot be said, except it be determined in each particular case from the so-called "internal evidence" as gathered, *e.g.*, from the names of persons occurring in a specific letter, from the circumstances of time and place, etc., etc. We also saw that the letter published under No. 24 was especially instructive in this respect. And this it was not only because of its wonderfully poetic introduction—an introduction such as may be found only in a letter addressed to a king—but also because we learned from it that the writer had been entrusted by a "grant" from his "Lord" and "king" with the supervision (*itû*) and administration of the city Mannu-gir-Rammân.

[1] *I.e.*, at least "not generally."

[2] Hilprecht's statement, *B. E.*, XX[1], p. 52, note 1, "Kuri-Galzu, his (*i.e.*, Burna-Buriash's) son, *but possibly not* his immediate successor," I would like to modify by substituting: "Kuri-Galzu, the son of Kadashman-Ḫarbe, the descendant of Burna-Buriash, the successor of his murdered father." Clay's view (*B. E.*, XIV, p. 9), "there is no gap in that part of the list of kings which these archives represent," differs from what I have above stated, p. 10, n. 3.

Now it happens that the writer of No. 24, Kalbu by name, mentions in the course of his communication, addressed to his Lord and king, the latter's father, ^{m}*Na-zi-*^{ilu}*En-lil*. A *priori* we are justified in assuming that if the "Lord" to whom Kalbu addressed his letter was a "king," the "Lord's" father was in all probability one likewise. If so, we would have to see in ^{m}*Na-zi-*^{ilu}*En-lil* a new and, so far, unknown king of the Cassite period. The question then arises to what time of the known Cassite kings have ^{m}*Na-zi-*^{ilu}*En-lil*, together with his son, the *be-lí* of No. 24, to be referred.

The passage which mentions this new king is unfortunately somewhat mutilated, so that its real sense has to remain, for the present at least, still doubtful. If I understand the paragraph in question correctly, it would seem that Kalbu, after having communicated to his "Lord" the news about the dreadful flood which had overtaken the city Mannu-gir-Rammân and himself, threatening him even with the loss of his own life, complains here that the same flood had destroyed also the "gates," together with the "herds" which were kept in their environs, in consequence of which destruction and loss he is left without any means of subsistence both for himself and for the inhabitants of the city. In fact there is nothing left that could be "taken" or "given." That portion of the letter which mentions the "Lord's" and "king's" father, ^{m}*Na-zi-*^{ilu}*En-lil*, may be transcribed and translated as follows (24 : 24f.):

24 *ù abullu* (= *KÁ.GAL*) *erû* (*URU-DU*)^{mesh}[1] *DA*^{mesh}[2] *u laḫru* (= *GA-NAM*)[3] *shattu-II shá ish-tu b[é]-na-ti*[4]	Also the mighty bronze-gates together with the two-year-old ewes which (were kept there) since the time
25 *shá* ^{m}*NA-zi-*^{ilu}*En-lil a-bi-ka ù adi* (= *EN*) *ûmi*^{mi}	of Nazi-Enlil, thy father, even unto (this) day,

[1] *Abullu erû*^{mesh} is a composite noun in the plural, for the formation of which see Delitzsch, *Gram.*, p. 193, § 73.

[2] *DA* here to be taken probably in the sense of *le'û*, Abel-Winckler, *Keilschrifttexte*, Sign List, No. 221; Meissner, *Ideogramme*, No. 1762.

[3] For *GANAM* = *laḫru*, "ewe," see *E. B. H.*, p. 343, and for *MU-II*, *ibidem*, pp. 369ff.

[4] *Ish-tu b[é]-na-ti* . . . *ù adi* (= *EN*) *ûmi*^{mi}. The *ish-tu bé-na-ti*, standing here in opposition to *adì ûmi*, must signify in this connection some kind of a *terminus a quo*. *Bênâti* is, no doubt, related to *bennu*, which Delitzsch *H. W. B.*, p. 180*b*, translates by "father", cf. also Zimmern, *Shurpu*, p. 54, 35, who renders it by "*Ahnherr.*" If this be true, I would like to see in *bênâti* either a plural of *bênâtu* = (*binnûtu* = *biniûtu* =) *binuttu*, which latter word occurs also in *Amarna*, B. 21 : 22, *már ship-ri-ka i-na bi-nu-ut-ti* [*ki-i*] *il-li-ka*, *i.e.*, "when thy messenger came formerly," or a formation like *gâtu*, *aḫrâti*, *dârâti*, *rupiti*, for which see Delitzsch, *Gram.*, p. 189, and *l.c.*, § 65, No. 37, on p. 177, above. *Bênâti* in our passage refers undoubtedly to the "*times* of the father" of the "Lord," hence must mean something like "time of preceding generation," "the time when one's father was living." The root, then, would be *banû*, from which we have *bânû*, "father, begetter." *Adi ûmi*^{mi} stands here for *adi ûmi an-ni-i*.

26 [*e*]-*ka-ku*[1](?) *ù i-na-an-na be-lì it-ti-* [*di shá*][2]	(the floods) have destroyed. And now my "Lord" knows that
27 [*i*(*l*)-*la*][2]-*ka-an-ni i-na-an-na ki-i i-li-* [*ka-an-n*]*i*[2]	they (the inhabitants of the city) will come to me (*sc.* for pay, l. 29). Now, when they have come (*i.e.*, when they are there),
28 [*ù zu-un-nja*[3] *LU*(?)[mesh][7] *laḫru* (= *GA-NAM*) *shattu-II i-si-ru*[4] *mi-na-a*[?][5]	what shall I take and give (them), seeing that the floods have encircled the flocks and the
29 [*lul*]-*qa-am-ma lu-ud-di-in*[6]	two-year-old ewes?

As the succession of the Cassite kings from Kuri-Galzu *siḫru* down to Kashtiliashu is well known and absolutely controllable both by the publications of the *B. E.* and the "List of Kings," and as Nazi-Enlil cannot have reigned before Burna-Buriash—for no documents of the Cassite period have been found at Nippur which antedate the last-named ruler—it is at once evident that Nazi-Enlil, together with his son, the *be-lì* of No. 24, must have reigned during the time that elapsed between Burna-Buriash and Kuri-Galzu *siḫru*.

We saw that the Cassites revolted during the reign of Kadashman-Ḫarbe = Kara-Ḫardash against their king, killing him, and selecting in his stead a king of their own choice, a certain Nazi-Bugash or Shuzigash. We also heard that Ashsur-

[1] *E-ka-ku.* One might expect *e-ka-lu*, but against this is to be said (1) the *ku*, although somewhat doubtful, cannot be very well *lu*. Having examined the sign repeatedly I am unable to discover even the faintest indication of a middle perpendicular wedge, (2) if this were a form of *akâlu*, one would look for *i-ku-lu* A present tense, *e-ka-lu* = *ik-ka lu*, is senseless here. In view of these difficulties I am inclined to connect this form with *akûkâti*(?), *H. W. B.*, p 53*a*, which Delitzsch, however, leaves untranslated Seeing that *akûkâti* is a syn. of *a-sham-shu-tum* and this = *IM.GHUL.LA* resp. *IM.RI.GHA.MUN* (Del., *l.c.*, p. 146*a*, *Orkan*) I propose to translate *akûkati* by storm-flood (cf. also *RI.GHA.MUN*, an attribute of Rammân, the *bêl abûbu*), used either literally or figuratively. In the latter sense it is used also of "spears," which are "thrown" in such numbers into a city that they practically "pour down upon" or "overflood" a city In this meaning it is to be found in *Sarg Ann* 161, *ana puḫur alânishunu a-ku*(?)*-ka-a-ti ad-di-ma*, "into all their cities I threw a veritable flood (of spears)" The root of *e-ka-ku* would be עקק or עכך, it standing for *i'kakû* = *îkakû*, with *a* in the Preterit The subject of *îkaku* is the *zunnu u mila* in ll. 20, 21 : the floods have overflooded = destroyed.

[2] These emendations are, of course, very doubtful, but they seem to me the most probable ones For *alâku* *e* *ae* , "to go, come to," see besides Delitzsch, *H. W. B.*, p. 66*a*, also Jensen, *K. B.*, VI[1], pp 464, 475. If the emendations be correct, these forms would stand for *i-la*(resp *i-li-*)*-ku-in ni*.

[3] The traces of these signs cannot possibly be amended to *KA.GAL erû*[mesh] *DA*[mesh], l. 21 For *LU* = *UDU* = צאן, see *E. B. H.*, pp 343ff.

[4] *Esêru*, "to encircle," is here parallel to *lamû*, used of "floods", see above, l. 20, *i-na la-me-e na-di*

[5] Hardly anything missing after *mi-na-a*.

[6] For the force of this *εν διὰ δυοιν* cf., *e.g.*, *B. E.*, XIV. 38 . 9, 10, "that and that," [m]*X. i-liq-qu-am-ma a-na* [m]*Y. i-nam-din*, "X. shall take and give to Y.," *i.e.*, "X shall pay back to Y.," and *l.c.*, 111 10, 11, "the grain . . . . at harvest time," *is-si-ra-am-ma i-nam-din-ma*, "he shall put up and give," *i.e.*, "he shall return."

uballit, king of Assyria, eager to secure and preserve the Babylonian throne for his great-grandchild, Kuri-Galzu, went out, killed Nazi-Bugash and put Kuri-Galzu upon the throne. Now it is not at all likely that the Cassites would have acquiesced in such a despotic act of the Assyrian king as to kill the king of their choice and liking; nor is it human nature to suppose that the enraged Cassites would have joyfully received the new child-king by the grace of Ashshur-uballit. On the contrary, they will have endured this insult only as long as they had to; they will have waited eagerly for the first moment, for the first opportunity to strike back and rid themselves of a king who was forced upon them. This opportunity came when Ashshur-uballit died, which he, no doubt, did soon after Kuri-Galzu had been seated upon the throne, seeing that he must have been well advanced in years if he could put a great-grandchild upon the Babylonian throne. With Ashshur-uballit out of the way and Kuri-Galzu still a child, the time was propitious to strike and to strike hard. And the Cassites did strike. The result of this "striking" is embodied in letter No. 24: they put up a king who was a king indeed—a king by *the voice of the people. Et vox populi est vox dei:* he was a divinely appointed ruler, a ruler "whom Anu, Enlil, É.A, and Bêlit-ili themselves had presented with a kingship excelling in grace and righteousness." I see then in the *be-lí* of No. 24 a counter-king of Kuri-Galzu during at least the first years of the latter's reign. But if the *be-lí* was a contemporary of Kuri-Galzu, then the Lord's father, Nazi-Enlil, must have lived at the time of Nazi-Bugash. In view of the fact that both these names begin with *Nazi*, and considering how easy it is to misread and mistranslate the name of a god when ideographically written, I propose to identify both. The *Synchronistic History* is, as we saw above, rather arbitrary in transcribing names expressed by ideographs. Now as ^{ilu}*Enlil* may also be written ^{ilu}*É.KUR*, which latter is according to II *R.* 54, No. 3, 10, identified with *Anum*,[1] and as *Anum* changes with *Bugash* in such proper names as *Gu-zar-AN* and *Gu-za-ar-za-ar-Bugash, Gu-zal-za-ar-Bugash,* it is not unlikely that the name *Nazi-Enlil* was written *Na-zi-*^{ilu}*É-KUR* in the original from which *S. H.* compiled his story. This *Na-zi-*^{ilu}*É.KUR S. H.* read *Nazi-Bugash,*[2] and *Ch. P.* shortened it to *Shuzigash.*

Furthermore, Kalbu, the writer, praises his Lord and king as "light of his brothers," which implies that the *be-lí* had brothers. It happens that there is mentioned in *B. E.*, XIV, 10 : 56, a certain ^{m}*E-mid-a-na-*^{ilu}*Marduk,* who is termed *TUR LUGAL,* "son of the king," and who lived, according to that tablet, in the first year of Kuri-Galzu (l. 1). This Emid-ana-Marduk cannot have been the son

[1] See also my *Bêl, the Christ*, pp. 17, 16.

[2] Thus identifying ^{ilu}*É.KUR* according to II *R.* 54, No. 3, 10 with *AN* (=*Bugash*), instead of ^{ilu}*EN.LIL.* For *AN* as a name of ^{ilu}*Ênlil* see p. 80.

of Kuri-Galzu, because the latter was himself a child, nor can he have been a son of Kadashman-Ḫarbe, *i.e.*, a brother of Kuri-Galzu, because if he were he would have to be a *younger*(!)[1] brother; but a younger brother of a *ṣiḫru*, "a child," would not receive "salary," nor can he have been an Assyrian prince—his name speaks against such a supposition; hence the only conclusion at present possible to reach is that *Emid-ana-*^{ilu}*Marduk* was a son of *Nazi-Bugash* = *Nazi-Enlil* and a brother of the *be-lì* of No. 24.[2]

On the basis of the above-given investigations we are prepared to establish the following succession of the Cassite kings covering both periods, the Amarna and that which follows immediately upon it. During the latter our letters here published have been written.

ASSYRIA.	BABYLONIA.	EGYPT.
	Kara-Indash I	
	(?)	
	Burna-Buriash I	
	(?)	
	Kadashman-Enlil I	*Nimmuria* (= *Amen-hotep III*)
	Kuri-Galzu I; daughter	daughter; *Napḫuria* (= *Amen-hotep IV*)
Ashshur-uballit	*Burna-Buriash II*, "ancestor of *Kuri-Galzu II*" (son ?)	
Muballitat-Sherua	*Kar*(*a*)-*Indash II*; *Ú-la-Bu-ri-ia-ash*,[3] king of ^{mâtu}*A.AB.BA*	
	Kadashman-Ḫarbe = *Kara-Ḫardash*	
	Nazi-Bugash = *Shuzigash*	= ^{m}*Na-zi-*^{ilu}*En-lil*
	Kuri-Galzu II, *ṣiḫru*,[4] "of the house of *Burna-Buriash*"	*be-lì* (No. 24); *Emid-ana-Marduk*
	Nazi-Maruttash (to be followed by the kings as given above, p. 1.)	

[1] For footnotes see page 72.

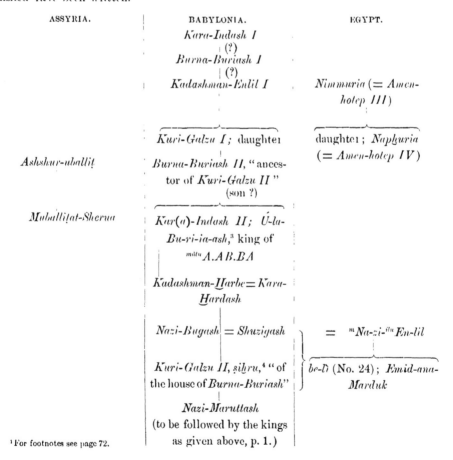

(*b*) The *seat of residence* of the Cassite kings at the time when the letters here published were written.

[1] If he were the *older* brother, he (and not the child Kuri-Galzu) would have been the *rightful* heir to the throne of Babylon.

[2] For a complete rendering of this letter see below under "Translations."

[3] Mentioned in *B. E.*, 6105 (Weissbach, *Babylonische Miscellen*, p. 7), where he is called the "son (*TUR*) *of Burna-Bu-ra(?)-ri-ia-ish*." Cf. now also Thureau-Dangin, *O. L. Z.*, January, 1908, Sp. 31f., who is of different opinion.

[4] Through the kindness of the Editor, Prof. Hilprecht, who gave me special permission (letter of June 22, 1908) to do so, I am enabled to add here a note about the several papers, treating of the same period discussed above, which have appeared since the MS. had been approved and sent to the press. These papers are (*a*) F. E. Peiser, *Chronik P und synchron Geschichte*, *O. L. Z.*, January, 1908, Sp. 7ff., and again, *l.c.*, Sp. 140f.; (*b*) A. Ungnad, *Zur Chronologie der Kassitendynastie*, *l.c.*, Sp. 11f., and *ibidem*, Sp. 139f.; (*c*) J. A. Knudtzon, *Die El-Amarna-Tafeln*, pp. 34ff., especially p. 38 (reached me March, 1908), (*d*) Thureau-Dangin, *Z. A.*, XXI (1907–8), pp. 176ff. (see also above, p. 59, note 1), *O. L. Z.*, January, 1908, Sp. 31f.; *Journal Asiatique*, Janv.-Fév., 1908, pp. 117ff. (received July 1, 1908), and the corrections to the last-named paper, *O. L. Z.*, June, 1908, Sp. 275f. (was not accessible to me till July 11, 1908).

Peiser's and *Knudtzon's* genealogy of the kings of this period is nothing but *Weissbach* re-edited with some slight modifications, hence we need not dwell on their arrangement here. *Ungnad* omits *Burna-Buriash I* (why?) and *Kara-Indash II*. About the latter he remarks (*l.c.*, Sp. 13): "*Ein anderer Karaindaš war wohl der Gemahl der Muballiṭat-Serûa, ist aber selbst kaum König gewesen.*" It is hardly to be expected that the Assyrian king *Ashshur-uballiṭ* with his pronounced intentions towards the Babylonian throne would give in marriage his daughter *Muballiṭat-Sherua* to a Babylonian prince who was not, at some time or another, destined to become the king of Babylonia, nor would he have been so anxious to avenge his "son-in-law" if it had not been for the fact that he wanted to preserve the throne of Babylon for "his own family," *i.e.*, for the descendant of his own daughter. Ungnad's (and Knudtzon's) reading *Kadashman-Ḫarbe* (instead of *Kadashman-Enlil*) is quite arbitrary. Though the Cassite *Ḫarbe* was identified with *Enlil*, from this it does not yet follow that *Enlil* in Cassite names has always to be read *Ḫarbe*. We know that ^{ilu}*Enlil* is = ^{ilu}*Êkur* = *An*, but it would be preposterous to read ^{ilu}*Enlil* = *An*, or *An* = ^{ilu}*Enlil* (see also Thureau-Dangin, *J. A.*, 1908, p. 121, 17). Though Ungnad establishes otherwise the same succession as the one given above, yet I cannot agree with him in details. His argument, *l.c.*, Sp. 12, 2, based upon the expression *ishtu . . . . adi* of *B. E.*, XIV, 39 : 8, to show that *Kuri-Galzu*, the son of *Kadashman-Ḫarbe*, was the same as our *Kuri-Galzu I*, the son of *Kadashman-Enlil I*, contemporaries of *Amen-hotep III*, are contradicted by No. 24 : 24, *ish-tu bé-na-ti shá* ^{m}*Na-zi-*^{ilu}*Enlil a-bi-ka*(!) *ù adi ùmi*, for which see above, p. 68, note 4. Ungnad's statement (*l.c.*, Sp. 12, note 1) that *abbu* (with double *b*) has to be *always* a plural is simply an assertion without any argument. *Abbu*, like *aḫḫu*, is very often nothing but a graphic peculiarity of these times. With regard to the investigations of *Thureau-Dangin* the following. In his latest attempt (*O. L. Z.*, 1908, Sp. 275) this scholar arranges the predecessors of *Kuri-Galzu* (the father of *Nazi-Maruttash*), to whom he assigns the 22d place among the Cassite kings, in the following fashion: (16) *Kara-Indash I*; (17) *Kadashman-Ḫarbe I*, his son, (18) *Kuri-Galzu I*, his son (contemporary of *Amen-hotep III*), (19) *Kadashman-Enlil I*, his son, (20) *Burna-Buriash*, his son (contemporary of *Amen-hotep IV*); (21) *Kara-Indash II*, "*petit-fils(?) de Burna-buriaš*"; (*Nazi-Bugash*, "*usurpateur*"); (22) *Kuri-Galzu*, "*second(?) fils de Burna-buriaš*" and father of *Nazi-Maruttash*. A comparison of this arrangement with the one postulated above will show the following differences: (*a*) *Kadashman-Ḫarbe* = *Kara-Ḫardash* is left out. The reason for this omission is given by Thureau-Dangin, *J. A.*, 1908, p. 127, in the following words: "*Kara-ḫardaš et Kara-indaš mentionnés par l'Histoire synchronique représentent le même personnage* (but why?). *On a supposé que Kara-indaš pourrait être le père de Kara-ḫardaš. Mais le rédacteur n'a pu vouloir dire qu'Ašur-uballiṭ était venu pour venger le père du roi assassiné.*" But this is exactly what he did want to say, see above p. 60. (*b*) With regard to *Kadashman-Ḫarbe* Thureau-Dangin (*O. L. Z.*, 1908, Sp. 275) refers to Knudtzon, *l.c.*, p. 34, note 2, to Ungnad, *O. L. Z.*, 1908, pp. 12, 15, and to his own remarks in *J. A.*, 1908, p. 128, where he says: "*l'introduction de ce personnage a peut-être son explication dans le fait que le rédacteur de la Chronique P aura confondu Kuri-galzu le Jeune, fils de Burna-buriaš, avec Kuri-galzu I*^{er}*, fils de Kadashman-ḫarbe. Il faut sans doute restituer à*

Prof. Winckler, when discussing the Elamitic invasion under *Kitin-ḫutrutash*[1] at the time of ^{m} ^{ilu}*EN.LIL.MU.MU* (*i.e.*, *Enlil-nâdin-shumu*, generally read *Bêl-nâdin-shum*), who is mentioned in the "List of Kings" immediately after *Kashtiliashu II*, says (*Das alte Westasien*, p. 20): "*Unter dem nur* 1½ *Jahre regierenden Bel-nadin-shum I, fällt Kitin-ḫutrutash, König von Elam, in Babylonien ein, verwüstet Dur-ilu . . . . und erobert Nippur, das von den Kassiten Königen bevorzugt und wohl vielfach als Residenz benutzt wurde.*"

Indeed, Nippur has been the favored city of the Cassites since they ascended the throne of Babylon, for already Gandash[2], the first of the Cassite kings, called Nippur "my city";[3] but that it ever had been used as a Cassite residence has, though it was surmised by Winckler, never been proved.

Without going into details here, I am prepared to maintain, upon the basis of the evidence furnished by these letters, that ever since the time of *Burna-Buriash II* till *Kashtiliashu II*, and possibly longer, as the campaign of *Kitin-ḫutrutash* against Nippur would indicate, *Nippur* was, if not *the*, then at least *a royal residence of the Cassite*

l'histoire de Kadashman-ḫarbe, père de Kuri-galzu Ier, le récit de la guerre contre les Sutéens." He accordingly assigns to this *Kadashman-Ḫarbe*, the son of *Kara-Indash* (*Ch. P.*, I, 5f.), place No. 17, and identifies him with *Kadashman-Ḫarbe*, the father of *Kuri-Galzu I* (*B. E.*, XIV, 39 8; Winckler, *Z. A.*, II, p 309). Though the latter identification is undoubtedly correct (see above, p. 64), yet the *Kuri-Galzu*, the son of *Kadashman-Ḫarbe*, is not *Kuri-Galzu I*, but *Kuri-Galzu II*, *ṣiḫru* (see above, p. 61). From this it follows that *Ch. P.* did not only *not* confound *Kuri-Galzu*, the son of *Burna-Buriash*, with *Kuri-Galzu*, the son of *Kadashman-Ḫarbe*, but, on the contrary, knew that both *Kuri-Galzus* were one and the same person For the reason why *Kuri-Galzu ṣiḫru* should have called himself both "son of *Burna-Buriash*" and "son of *Kadashman-Ḫarbe*" see above, p. 66. (*c*) With regard to No. 19 I may be permitted to ask: "On what authority does Thureau-Dangin maintain his statement that *Kadashman-Enlil I* is the son of *Kuri-Galzu I*?" (*d*) *Burna-Buriash*, whom he mentions under No. 20, Thureau-Dangin identifies on the one hand with [. . . .]-*ri-ia-ash*, the son of *Kadashman-Enlil* (Hilprecht, *O. B. I.*, I[1], No. 68), and on the other with the *Burna-Buriash* known from Knudtzon, *l.c.*, 9, 19 (cf. No. 11, Rev. 19), where this ruler calls *Kuri-Galzu* "my father," *a-bi-ia*, maintaining at the same time that the expression "*father*" has to be taken in the sense of "*ancêtre*" (*O. L. Z.*, 1908, Sp. 275). Though it is true that *abu* may, and very often does, mean "ancestor" (Tigl.-Pil. I, col. VIII, 47; Knudtzon, *l.c.*, 16 : 19, compared with *M. D. O. G.*, No. 25, p. 40)—just as *TUR* = *mâru* very often means "*descendant*"—yet Thureau-Dangin still owes the arguments resp. convincing reasons that *abu* of Knudtzon, *l.c.*, 9, 19, *has to* or *must be* taken in the sense of ancestor. Again, the name [. . . .]-*ri-ia-ash* of *O. B. I.*, I[1], No. 68, may be read with Hilprecht, *B. E.*, XX[1], p. 52, note 1, [*Sha-garak-ti-Shu*]-*ri-ia-ash* (the space is large enough for this emendation), see above p. 1. Thirdly, following Thureau-Dangin's methods, we might quite as well maintain that the *dumu-sag* of *O. B. I.*, I[1], No. 68, means "*principal descendant*," thus making *Shagarakti-Shuriash* a "grandson" (instead of a "second? son") of *Kadashman-Enlil*. By the way, on what authority does Thureau-Dangin claim that *Shagarakti-Shuriash* was the son of *Kudur-Enlil*? (*e*) Why does Thureau-Dangin (following Ungnad) omit *Burna-Buriash I*? Does he identify him with *Burna-Buriash*, the son (resp. grandson) of *Kuri-Galzu I* and ancestor (resp. father) of *Kuri-Galzu II*, *ṣiḫru*? What are his arguments for doing so? The result. Thureau-Dangin has failed to bring in any convincing arguments which would force us to modify the above-given arrangement.

[1] See *Ch. P.*, col. IV, 11f.

[2] Written ^{m}*Ga-ad-dáš* (= *UR*).

[3] *Âli-ia Ni-ip-pu* (*sic!*), see Winckler, *U. A. G.*, p. 156, No. 6, l. 11.

kings. This follows (1) from the fact that these letters, having been addressed to the *be-lì*, *i.e.*, to the king, were found in Nippur: letters, if discovered at Nippur and found to be addressed to the king, presuppose that the king must have lived at that place; (2) from internal evidence. (α) *Kishaḫbut*, when answering an inquiry of the king concerning "wool," says, 35 : 13, *ásh-shum SIG*$^{\underline{h}i.a}$ *i-na En-lil*^{ki} *a-na be-lì-ia aq-ta-bi*, *i.e.*, "as regards the wool (I beg to say that) I have spoken about it to my 'Lord' in Nippur." This shows that *Kishaḫbut*, although "out of town" when he wrote his letter, must have been at one time in Nippur, where he reported to his "Lord" about the disposition of the wool; but this he could not do except the king himself was residing in Nippur. Now, as *Kishaḫbut* was a contemporary of *Kadashman-Turgu* (see below, pp. 120ff.), it follows that this king lived in Nippur. (β) *Pân-AN.GAL-lu-mur*, a resident of *Dûr-ilu*, when explaining to *NIN-nu-ú-a* why he had not sent a messenger previously, says, 89 : 21f.: *mâr ship-ri-ia shá a-na* ^{alu}*En-lil*^{ki} *a-na muḫ LUGAL ash-pu-ru ki i-mu-ru-ka ma-la a-sap-rak-ku iq-ba-a*, *i.e.*, "my messenger whom I had sent to Nippur to the king was, when he would see thee, to have told everything I had written thee." Nothing can show more plainly than this passage that the king actually did live and reside in Nippur, where he received not only the reports of his trusted servants,[1] but where he also (γ) gave orders for the disposal of certain goods, see 27 : 29f.: *II biltu shá En-lil*^{ki} *shá be-lì ú-she-bi-la ù XX ma-na shá ardi-ka* ^{m}*Erba-*^{ilu}*Marduk id-di-na ki-i ú-za-i-zu XL ma-na SIG*$^{\underline{h}i.a}$ *ir-te-ḫu-ni-in-ni*; *i.e.*, "(and with regard to) the two talents (of wool) of (= for) Nippur which my 'Lord' has ordered to be brought and the 20 *ma-na* which thy servant Erba-Marduk has paid, (I beg to state that) after they had divided them, they left me (a rest of) only 40 *ma-na*." The "Lord" to whom Kudurâni sends this letter (No. 27) is again Kadashman-Turgu; hence also according to this epistle that king must have resided in Nippur.

The king, however, did not always stay in Nippur, but made, like every good "father of his country," occasional visits to other towns, where he condescended to hear the complaints and grievances of his subjects; of such an incident we read in 23 : 33f.: *ásh-shum* ^{amelu}*USH.BAR*^{mesh} *an-nu-ti shá i-na* ^{alu}*Pa-an-Ba-li*^{ki} *ka-lu-ú i-na Ú-pi-i*^{ki} *a-na be-lì-ia aq-ta-bi ù shá-la-shi-shú a-na mu-uḫ be-lì-ia al-tap-ra be-lì li-ish-pu-ur-ma li-il-qu-ni-ish-shú-nu-ti*, *i.e.*, "as regards these weavers who are being held in Pân-Bali, (I beg to state that) I have not only spoken about them to my 'Lord' in Upî, but I have written three times to my 'Lord.' My 'Lord' may at last send that they take them away (*i.e.*, that they be liberated)." According to

[1] Cf. here also such passages as 27 : 20: *i-na âlu-ki i-na a-shab be-lì-ia a-na be-lì-ia aq-ta-bi-ma*; *i.e.*, "in the city (*i.e.*, Nippur) in the presence of my 'Lord' I have spoken to my 'Lord.'" See also 3 : 22.

this the king was at one time in Upî, where he received the writer [Ingu]rum in audience. The king had promised him to "do something" for the imprisoned weavers, but had, after leaving Upî for Nippur, forgotten all about his promise. The writer was determined that the weavers should be liberated; he had written four times to his Lord, reminding him of his promise, by addressing this (No. 23) and three previous communications to him at Nippur. As Ingurum, the writer, was a contemporary of Burna-Buriash (see below, p. 94), it follows that also Burna-Buriash must have resided in Nippur.

In this connection a passage of *Ch. P.*, col. III, 9, receives a new and welcome light. There it is recorded that Kuri-Galzu, after having conquered the ^{mâtu}*Tam-ti*[*m*, col. II, l. 6], added also Babylon and Borsippa unto his country.[1] How could this be done, seeing that Kuri-Galzu had been seated by Ashshur-uballit upon the throne of Babylon? How could he possibly have added Babylon and Borsippa to his land, if he resided, as "king of Babylon," in Babylon? Surely, if we are able to read between the lines, the succession of events during the reign of Kuri-Galzu must be reconstructed in the following fashion: Ashshur-uballiṭ, after having killed Nazi-Bugash and after having proclaimed his great-grandson king of Babylon, foresaw, no doubt, some such event as was pictured on p. 70, *i.e.*, he feared that the Cassites would arise again and, if possible, get rid of his "child-king." In order, therefore, to insure the safety of Kuri-Galzu he established him, not in Babylon, nor perhaps even in Nippur, but possibly in *Dûr-Kuri-Galzu*—a fortress founded by the older Kuri-Galzu[2] and situated near Nippur. Here he probably lived as long as the *be-li* of No. 24[3] had power enough to maintain his independence. As soon as Kuri-Galzu felt that he was sufficiently strong to cope with his enemies, he went out and conquered them, first of all the Cassite party in allegiance with Nazi-Bugash or his sons, then the sea country, in order to prevent a possible attack from the rear, and last of all Babylon.

As soon as Kuri-Galzu had gotten rid of the *be-li* of No. 24, he established, as is to be expected, his residence in Nippur, where he lived till he had conquered Babylon. After the conquest of Babylon he possibly might have resided also in that city, though there is as yet no proof to that effect.

[1] *Ch. P.*, III, 9, *DIN.TER*^{ki} *u Bàr-sap*^{ki} *muḫ ṣêri*(= *EDIN*)-*ia lu-ù-sha-aṭ-ṭir*; *i.e.*, "Babylon and Borsippa I caused to write (= I had them written, added by means of a treaty after a successful war) to my land (lit. field)." To *EDIN* cf. here the greeting, "to the *field* (*EDIN*), etc., of my 'Lord' greeting," which shows that *EDIN* in the passages given above (p. 31) means the whole territory over which the "Lord" was king.

[2] Cf. *B. E.*, XIV, 4 : 11f., where *Dûr-Kuri-Galzu* is mentioned in the 11th year of Burna-Buriash. See already above, p. 9, note 2.

[3] Who likewise must have resided—for a time at least—in Nippur, or else this letter could not have been excavated there.

As long, then, as we have such indisputable evidence as to the royal residence of the Cassite kings at this period we will have to look upon Nippur as *a*, if not *the*, *residence of all Cassite kings from Burna-Buriash II to Kashtiliashu II*; and if so, we will surely find, at some future time, if the excavations of the University of Pennsylvania are to be continued, as is to be earnestly hoped and desired, a royal palace befitting the glory and splendor of the "king without equal," of Kuri-Galzu *ṣiḫru* and his descendants. Prof. Hilprecht regards the largely unexplored lofty group of mounds forming the eastern corner (cf. the map in Series D, Vol. I, p. 305) of the temple complex as the probable site of the palace of the early patesis of Nippur and also of the Cassite rulers—a palace which, like the Sargon palace at Khorsabâd, at the same time constituted the strongest bastion in the huge outer temple wall.[1]

(*c*) The *nature and purpose of the "Temple Archives,"* including the letters here published, *and their relation to "Royal Archives."*

When I studied Prof. Clay's introduction to *B. E.*, Vol. XIV, purporting to give a general survey of the nature of "Temple Archives," as far as they had been published by him, the questions uppermost in my mind, about which I hoped to receive some information and instruction, were: What are "Temple Archives"? What is their nature and purpose? What do they represent? Clay answers these questions in the following manner (*B. E.*, XIV, p. 5): "With the exception of about fourteen[2] documents these inscriptions (*i.e.*, the 'Temple Archives') are records of the receipt of taxes or rents from outlying districts about Nippur; of commercial transactions conducted with this property; and the payment of salaries of the storehouse officials as well as of the priests, and others in the temple service. In other words, they refer to the handling and disposition of the taxes after they had been collected." If I understand his explanation of the contents of these tablets correctly, I gather that, according to his interpretation, "archives," such as have

[1] Cf. Hilprecht in *B. E.*, Series D, Vol. I, p. 485, and "The So-called Peters-Hilprecht Controversy," p. 254. See also above, p. 9, note 2.

[2] The fourteen documents which form the exception are enumerated, *l.c.*, p. 2, note 1. They are Nos. 1, 2, 7, 8, 11, 39, 40, 41, 119, 123, 127, 128*a*, 129, 135. It will be noticed that, *e.g.*, neither the "inventory" tablets nor the text published in *B. E.*, XIV, 4, are enumerated among these exceptions. I therefore drew the natural inference from the above given enumeration that tablet No. 4 (*B. E.*, XIV) was likewise regarded by the author of the volume as "a record of the handling and the disposition of the taxes," etc., especially as in the "Table of Contents," *l.c.*, p. 61, *sub* 4, not a word was said with regard to the peculiar contents of this tablet. Cf. my statement in *Old Penn*, February 16, 1907, p. 3, col. III, below. However, in a later issue of *Old Penn* (February 23, 1907, p. 8, col. III), my attention was called to a passage occurring in Clay's "*Light on the Old Testament from Babel,*" p. 312, from which I learned with pleasure that the true nature of the text in question was stated there. Cf. now also Jastrow, *Die Rel. Bab.*, p. 277, note 4. As a religious text of a similar type as those known from the Library of Ashurbânapal it is preferable to exclude this tablet No. 4 from our present discussion.

been published by him, are "*records of the handling and the disposition of the taxes from outlying districts about Nippur after they had been collected!*" Clay's reasons for calling these archives *Temple* Archives are the following (*B. E.*, XIV, p. 6). The taxes are *temple* revenues because:

(1) Payments are made out of the *mashsharti shá êkalli* (written *É.GAL*), "temple stipend" (XV, 47); out of the *GISH.BAR.GAL bît-ili*, "full tax of the house of god" (XV, 37); to the *ardu* and *amtu êkalli* (= *É.GAL*), "male and female temple servants" (XV, 152 : 15 and 200, III(!) : 9, 38).

(2) "Priests" (*ishshaku*), "the temple gateman" (*a-bil bâbi bît-a-nu* (*sic*), XV, 93), "the temple shepherd" (*nâqidu shá bîti*, XIV, 132 : 15), "the singer" (*zammêru*, XIV, 6 : 4) are salaried officers.

(3) The property handled is spoken of as the possession of the god, cf. *VI* (*sic*, read *I SHÛ*)[1] *gur she'um GISH.BAR.GAL sha ili* (XIV, 16 : 1), "60 *gur* of grain of the full tax the property of the god."

(4) The temple in these archives is usually called *bîtinu*, "our house," cf. *VI gur LXXXIV qa SHE.BA*(!) *a-mi-lu-ti sha bîti-nu*, "VI *gur* LXXXIV *qa*, wages for the men of our house" (no reference given[2]), or simply *bîtu*, "house," cf. *ipru mârê bîti(-ti)*, "wages for the sons of the house" (XV, 200, I : 38).

With regard to the relation of the Temple to the State, Clay, *l.c.*, p. 6, comes to the following conclusion:

"There is little in the documents (*i.e.*, the Temple Archives) to show that the revenues were collected in the interests of the State, or that the king was a beneficiary, unless perhaps tablet No. 26 : 3 of Vol. XV, which reads: *sha a-na SHE.BA*(!) *Nippur*[ki] *ù Dûr-Ku-ri-Gal-zu*, "which is for the maintenance of Nippur and Dûr-Ku-ri-Gal-zu." This statement is made even in view of the fact (*l.c.*, p. 7) that "amounts are also paid (XIV, 148), *sha si-ri-bi-shu sha sharri, a-na nu-ri sha sharri, a-na sharri*."

It was necessary to state Clay's views about Temple Archives at some length here, because I beg to differ from him upon important points. But before stating my own view with regard to the character and contents of the Temple Archives, it seems desirable to add a few words about two terms often occurring in these texts.

The chief reason why Clay did not recognize the true character and nature of

[1] *SHÛ* is an abbreviation of *shû-shu* — soss — 60, just as *ma* is abbreviated from *ma-na*. For *SHÛ* cf. also *B. E.*, XV, 19 : 20 | 73 : 15 | 149 : 14 | 151 : 45 | 199 : 29, 40, and see the later *KU* = *rubû* or "prince" among the numbers, which shows that *KU* has to be read *shû(shu)*.

[2] But see *B. E.*, XV, 41 : 3.

the "Temple Archives" is to be found in the fact that he failed to see any difference between *É.GAL* = *êkallu* = "palace," *sc.* of the king, and *É-nu*, "our house," "our temple."

É.GAL or *êkallu* in our letters as well as in *B. E.*, Vols. XIV and XV, does not signify the "temple" (Clay, *B. E.*, XIV, p. 6; XV, p. 18, transl. of No. 7, above), but *always* the "*royal palace.*" This follows evidently from *B. E.*, XV, 50– a tablet which I translate and interpret differently than Dr. Clay; see *l.c.*, p. 17, No. 7. On account of its importance I may be permitted to reproduce it here in transcription, adding to it the translation as given by Clay:

1 3 (*GUR*) 90 (Clay wrongly 84) (*qa*) *ASH.AN.NA GISH.BAR.GAL*	3 *gur* 84 *qa* of *ashanna* grain of the full tax,
2 $^{m\ ilu}$*XXX-is-saḫ-ra*	*Sin-issaḫra*
3 ^{abnu}*DUB É.GAL* (= *êkalli*)	(under) the seal of the temple
4 *ú-she-iṣ-ṣa-am-ma*	carried away,
5 *a-na* ^{m}*In-na-an-ni*	and to *Innannu*
6 *i-na-an-din*	he shall pay.
7 ^{arhu}*ASH.A.AN*	(Date.)
8 *shattu* 15^{kam}	
9 3 (*GUR*) 90 (Clay again wrongly 84) (*qa*) $^{m\ ilu}$*XXX*-(^{sic})	3 *gur* 84 *qa* of *ashanna* grain
10 *ASH.AN.NA* (^{sic}) *is-saḫ-ra*	*Sin-issaḫra*
11 *ina SHE.BAR GUR LUGAL*	in the royal seed *gur*
12 *En-lil*^{ki}	of Nippur [small measure.]
13 $^{m\ ilu}$*XXX-is-saḫ-ra*	[Seal of] *Sin-issaḫra*.

Against this translation is to be said: (1) The expression *ina SHE.BAR GUR LUGAL En-lil*^{ki} (ll. 11, 12) can never mean "in the royal seed *gur* of Nippur," but would have to be translated, if *En-lil*^{ki} really does belong to the preceding line, "in (or "according") to the grain-measure of (a) *GUR* of the king of Nippur"; (2) but this translation shows at once that *Enlil*^{ki} cannot belong to *LUGAL*, because, firstly, the Cassite kings, though residing at Nippur, do not take the title "king of Nippur," and secondly, a *royal gur* was everywhere the same, the Nippurian did not differ from that of Babylon or Sippar; (3) the expression ^{abnu}*DUB É.GAL u-she-iṣ-ṣa-am-ma* (ll. 3, 4) can be rendered only "per sealed order (^{abnu}*DUB* = anything that is sealed, "letter," "order," "decree," etc.) of the *É.GAL* (as such to be distinguished from the *DUB É-nu, B. E.*, XV, 36 : 19) he *caused* to go out," or "he caused to carry away." *Sin-*

issaḫra comes to *Innanni*, the chief bursar of the Temple storehouse, with a sealed order of the *É.GAL* calling for 3 *gur* and 90 *qa* of wheat. *Innanni* honors this order at once and gives permission to *Sin-issaḫra* to have it removed, but stipulates that the wheat is to be returned or paid back to him again. Accordingly ll. 1–8 are a "statement" of *Innanni* in the "form of a note of indebtedness" (*Schuldschein*), and as such quite different from a simple "note of indebtedness." (The latter would have to read: *X gur* of wheat *Sin-issaḫra* has per order of the *É.GAL* received (*imḫur*) from (*ina qât*) *Innanni*. *DUB* ^{m} ^{ilu}*XXX-issaḫra*). But any "statement in the form of a note of indebtedness" has, if it is to be valid, to be signed by the debtor. Sin-issaḫra, being the debtor, signs it in the briefest possible way: "3 *gur* 90 *qa* of wheat *Sin-issaḫra* (*sc.* has received) according to the *GUR*(barley)-measure of the king.—Nippur.—Sin-issaḫra." Taking ll. 9ff. in this sense they contain the signature of the debtor in the form of a receipt, which makes the "statement of indebtedness" a regular "note of indebtedness." But, and this is important here, Sin-issaḫra wants grain "per order of the *É.GAL*," and receipts for it as having been given him "according to the *king's*, *i.e.*, the royal *GUR*." This shows quite clearly that in orders for the *É.GAL royal* measures were or had to be used, hence *É.GAL* cannot be the "Temple," but must have been the *palace of the king*. At the same conclusion we arrive when considering sundry other passages. Cf. *e.g.*, *B. E.*, XIV, 167 : 10, where the amount of grain designated as *PAD É.GAL* is differentiated from that intended for the *BÀR* (= *parakku*) ^{ilu}*En-lil* (l. 8), etc., etc. If, then, the *É.GAL* be the "*royal palace*," we have to see in the *karû É.GAL* a "palace or royal storehouse." Such a storehouse is mentioned in the archives and is called *karû ASH.TAB.BA.GAN.TUG*^{ki}.[1] Wheat which was paid at the *karû ASH.TAB.BA.GAN.TUG*^{ki}[2] is called in the closing paragraph (*B. E.*, XV, 38c : 27), *ASH.AN.NA shá i-na maḫ-ri-im im-ḫu-ru a-na ZER É.GAL nadna*^{na}; *i.e.*, "wheat which they (= German "*man*") received formerly and which was given (paid) for (as) seed-corn of the 'palace.'" Again, *B. E.*, XV, 96 is, as Clay correctly recognized (*l.c.*, p. 22), "almost identical" with *B. E.*, XV, 111, which was written two years later. As both tablets are payments of salaries to various officials whose names are identical, or nearly so, in both tablets, and as the one (No. 111) mentions *ASH.TAB.BA.GAN.TUG*^{ki} (l. 24) as the place where the payments to these officials were made, while the other (No. 96 : 1, 25) informs us that it was *Kan-du-ru-*[*ú*^{ki}], we are justified

[1] *B. E.*, XV, 135 : 7, so and so much flour (*ki-mu*), interest (*ḪAR.RA*), *a-na karû É.GAL a-na karû ASH.TAB.BA.GAN.TUG*^{ki} ^{m}*Nu-na-ak-te ish-shi*, "to the palace storehouse, *i.e.*, to the storehouse of (or "called") *ASH.TAB.BA.GAN.TUG Nunakte* took." Cf. here also the *ḫarrân Ásh-ta-ba* in Bu. 91-5-9, 381 (*C. T.*, II, 37), l. 6.

[2] *B. E.*, XV, 38c : 1, *ASH.AN.NA shá i-na karû ASH.TAB.BA.GAN.TUG*^{ki} *GISH.BAR* 5 *qa nadnu*^{nu}.

in identifying both: *ASH.TAB.BA.GAN.TUG*^{ki} is = *Kan-du-ru-*[*ú*^{ki}][1], maintaining at the same time that both were a "*palace storehouse.*"[2] As over against the *É.GAL* or "*palace*" (*sc.* of the king) the "Temple" is called *É.A-nu*, *i.e.*, "House of A-nu," *B. E.*, XV, 93 : 5. Clay, *B. E.*, XIV, p. 6, reads *bît-a-nu*, "our house." But in view of the fact that (*a*) such a monstrous Babylonian form—half Sumerian and half Semitic: *É.A-nu* = *bît-a-nu* = *bîti-nu*— would be, to say the least, very strange for this and later periods;[3] (*b*) that in our letter, No. 35 : 15, *É.A-nu* is followed immediately by *bâb A-n*[*u-um*];[4] (*c*) that the determinative for "god," *ilu*, is very often omitted before the names of gods in these texts, I prefer to read as given above. But in this connection it ought to be remembered that *A-nu* is simply the semiticized Sumerian for *ilu*, signifying in each and every case the *highest god* of a city, whether that god be *AN* or *Enlil* or *Marduk*, or whether the city be *Nippur* or *Babylon* or *Dûr-ilu*, etc. In this way it happened that *Enlil*, the god of Nippur, was simply called *AN* (*B. E.*, XIV, 16 : 1 | 132 : 3, 4, 54; XV, 97 : 3 | 115 : 11 | 143 : 2 | 163 : 28), and the Temple of Enlil at Nippur was termed not only *É.KUR* (*B. E.*, XIV, 148 : 2), but also *É.AN.KALAM.GAL*, "the temple of the great god of the (Babylonian) world" (*B. E.*, XIV, 148 : 15, 18; XV, 34 : 2), or merely *É.AN* (*B. E.*, XIV, 24 : 16; XV, 37 : 1). That this *É.AN* or "*Gotteshaus*" was indeed the temple of Enlil of Nippur is evident from a passage in *B. E.*, XV, 128 : 14, which mentions the *É.AN*(!) *En-lil*^{ki} *shá i-na libbi-nu*, "the house of god (= temple) of Nippur which is in our midst." Of *this* house the Nippurians speak as the *É.AN É-nu*, the "house of god our temple," *B. E.*, XIV, 159 : 2, or simply as *É-nu*, "our temple"; see, among other passages, also *B. E.*, XIV, 148:45, 47; XV, 38 : 2 | 44 : 6 | 71 : 6 | 73 : 10 | 77 : 5 | 79 : 4 | 89 : 3 | 92 : 16 | 127 : 5 | 154 : 21 | 168 : 26. As there was a *DUB É.GAL* (*B. E.*, XV, 50 : 3) so there existed also a *DUB É-nu* (*B. E.*, XV, 36 : 19), as there are mentioned *ardi* resp. *amat É.GAL* (see p. 77) so there occur also *a-mi-lu-ti shá É-nu* (*B. E.*, XV, 41 : 3). All this, then, forces us to separate the *É.GAL* or

[1] Also written *Kan-du-ri-e*^{ki}, see List in *B. E.*, XV. It is also mentioned in our letters 18 : 38, [. .]^{mesh} *shá Kan-du-ri-e* [. . . .] *it-ta-al-ka-ni* [. . . .] *a-na mu-uh-hi be-li-ia* [*ul-te-la*]*-a*. Cf. here also *kadurrû* = *kaddurrû* → *kandurû*, Delitzsch, *H. W. B.*, p. 319*a*, *B. A.*, IV, 485, and Nagel, *l.c.*, p. 182 : (1) *Frohndienst*, (2) *Frohnarbeiter*, *Leibeigener*. The city read by Clay, *B. E.*, XV, p. 53*b*, *She*(?)*-du-ru-ú-er-tu*^{ki} has to be transcribed, of course, *kan-du-ru-ú* ^{âlu}(*UD*)^{ki}.

[2] For other occurrences of *É.GAL* cf., *e.g.*, the *ardi É.GAL* in letter No. 34 : 11 and *B. E.*, XV, 84 : 2 | 152 : 15 | 200 III : 38; V : 6; *amat* (*GIN*) *É-GAL*, *B. E.*, XV, 200 II : 33, 37; III : 2, 9, 21; *libittu*(?) *É.GAL*, letter No. 50 : 11; *shá-lam-ta-shú a-na É-GAL shú-bi-lam*, 59 : 4; *mash-shar-ti shá É.GAL* = "*special fund* (of 10 *GUR*) set aside by the palace for the payment of certain *officers or otherwise*," *B. E.*, XV, 17 : 1. For *mashshârtu* = "special fund," see p. 96, note 4.

[3] Cf. here also the *amelu shá muh É.A-nu*, *i.e.*, "overseer of the house of god," *II.*, VIII, 855 : 1, and see the *EN É* in *B. E.*, XIV, 122 : 1.

[4] And is differentiated from the *É.GAL* which precedes the *É.A-nu*!

"palace" from the *É-nu* resp. *É.AN*, *É.A-nu* or "Temple."[1] If we thus distinguish between *É.GAL* and *É.A-nu*, the tablet published in *B. E.*, XV, 93, becomes of special importance. We learn from it that a certain ^{m}*Amel-Ba-nu-ú*, who is a *a-bil bâbi É.A-nu*, a "doorkeeper of the *Temple*," *i.e.*, a *Temple* official, receives a certain amount of grain in ^{alu}*Kan-du-ri-e*^{ki} from *Innanni*, the chief bursar of the *Temple* storehouses during the time of Kuri-Galzu. But *Kandurê* was, as we saw on p. 80, the same as *ASH.TAB.BA.GAN.TUG*^{ki}, the "Palace storehouse"—hence a *Temple* official is paid out of the *Palace* storehouse, and *Innanni*, the chief bursar of the *Temple* storehouses, appears here also as the chief bursar of the *Palace* storehouse; in other words, *Innanni*, the chief bursar, and *Amel-Banû*, the gatekeeper of the *É.A-nu*, were both *Temple* and *Palace*, *i.e.*, *royal* officials, otherwise *Innanni* could not have exercised authority over the royal storehouse, nor could *Amel-Banû* have been paid out of it. No wonder, then, that *Martuku*, who succeeded *Innanni* in the capacity of chief bursar of the Temple storehouses during the reign of *Nazi-Maruttash*, is called in *B. E.*, XIV, 56 : 9, *a-rad LUGAL*, "servant of the king."

Is it under these conditions to be wondered at that even the king himself—directly or indirectly—should appear as a beneficiary of the revenues of Enlil of Nippur? In proof of our contention that the king actually was such a beneficiary cf. the following expressions, occurring in the "Temple Archives": *bil-la-ti shá LUGAL*, *B. E.*, XIV, 116 : 1; *e-li LUGAL*, *l.c.*, XV, 33, 34; bronze *a-na i-ṭer*(hardly *shul*, *kar*, see p. 88, note 1)-*ti* ^{gish}*MAR LUGAL*, *l.c.*, XIV, 124 : 16; *a-na LUGAL*, *l.c.*, XIV, 148 : (43), 44, 46; *na-gid shá LUGAL*, *l.c.*, XIV, 132 : 17; *sak-shup-par LUGAL*, *l.c.*, XV, 154 : 41; *a-ra-ad shar-ri*, *l.c.*, XV, 199 : 30; *a-rad LUGAL*, *l.c.*, XIV, 56 : 9; ^{amelu}*SAG LUGAL*, *l.c.*, XIV, 132 : 2; *GÙ.EN.NA EN.LIL*[*KI*], *l.c.*, XIV, 136 : 1, etc., etc. Cf. also the facts indicated on p. 79, namely, that a royal measure (*gur LUGAL*) is employed in a *Temple* storehouse, and that *Sin-issaḫra*, though acting as the head of the *Palace* storehouse of *Kandurê* and as such giving grain *a-na É-nu*, *i.e.*, "to our Temple" (*B. E.*, XV, 89 : 3), receives grain "per order of the Palace" (*É.GAL*) from *Innanni*, the bursar-in-chief of the Nippurian Temple storehouses. Cf. also the *ina muḫ LUGAL*, p. 84, note 9.

This result, derived solely from the "Temple Archives" as published by Clay, is more than corroborated by several passages from the letters here published.

[1] See here also the *É*^{ti} = *bîti* in *B. E.*, XV, 200 I . 17, and the *ku-tal É*^{ti}, "the rear palace of the *É*^{ti}," in *l.c.*, XV, 80 : 11 (cf. Letters, No. 23 : 13, *ku-tal*; 23 : 8, *ku-tal-li*, and 60 : 8, *zîr ku-tal*). An *EN É* = *bêl bîti* occurs, *e.g.*, in *B. E.*, XIV, 122 : 4. Whether this *É*^{ti} means "palace," or more probably "temple" cannot be made out as yet with certainty. The *bêl É* is, no doubt, the same as the *amelu shá muḫ É.A-nu*, cf. *H.*, VIII, 855 : 1.

In Chapter III we have shown that all letters addressed to the *be-lì* or "Lord" were intended for the king. Bearing this in mind I included in this collection, for definite reasons, the peculiar tablet published under No. 60. Whosoever merely glanced at the "Temple Archives" known from *B. E.*, XIV, XV, will recognize a similar document in the Obverse of No. 60, while the Reverse apparently is a letter addressed to the "Lord" (*be-lì*) or king, in which an unknown writer begs him to command that, among other things, certain oxen of the *patesi's* be brought down.[1] Now, as the Obverse is a record concerning the receipt of grain (*SHE*) from certain crops (*ḫar-bu*) of the *patesi's*, and as the Reverse contains a letter addressed to the king, the natural inference to be drawn from this letter is that *the king was the person to whom such records had to be sent.* In other words, this tablet proves that *the Temple Archives were records made and kept for the king, as the highest official of the Temple of Enlil at Nippur.* The "*Temple Archives*," therefore, at the same time are *Royal Archives.*

What was the purpose of these archives? *Kishaḫbut*, when answering an inquiry of king *Kadashman-Turgu* whether sesame-oil had been forwarded or not, writes to his "Lord" as follows (35 :30ff.): *ásh-shum shamnu* (= *NI.GISH*) *shá be-lì-ia na-shú-*[*ma?*] *il-ta-na-su a-na* ^{m}*Ku-du-r*[*a-ni*] [*ardi*]*-ka ki-i aq-bu-ú um-ma-a shamnu* (=*NI.GISH*) *i-na qâti-ia* [*i-din*] *be-lì a-na shatammi* (= *SHAG.TAM*) *li-ish-pu-ra-ma shamnu* (= *NI.GISH*) *shub*(= *RU*)*-ta lish-ki-nu-*[*ma*], *i.e.*, "As regards the sesame-oil of my 'Lord' (I beg to report): 'It has been removed' they read, when I spoke to Kudurâni thy servant: 'Give the sesame-oil to me.' My 'Lord' may now send to the *shatammi* that they store up the oil."

The expression *il-ta-na-su* (I³ of שסה) refers here apparently to the action of consulting a tablet recording that such and such an amount of sesame-oil had been removed (*nashi*) by a certain person in the name of the king or "per order of the palace," ^{abnu}*DUB É.GAL*. Everything that was either received from (*shá ina qât . . . . maḫru*) or paid out to (*shá ina libbi shá . . . . ana . . . . nadnu*) or removed (*shá ishtu . . . . nashû*) or taken away from (*shá ishtu . . . . laqû*) or delivered to (*shá ana . . . . shulû*) or taken to (*shá ana . . . . nashû*, resp. *laqû*) the different storehouses or possessions of the Temple under *royal* administration had to be faithfully recorded on *tablets* under the *name* of the donor or recipient, for future reference (as here) or for the examination by the king, resp. his representatives. Hence the Temple Archives primarily are "*Records*" embodying statements about many things in connection with the royal administration of the Temple property;

[1] No. 60 : 9, *ù shá alpi*^{mesh} *shá pa-te-si*^{mesh} . . . . *be-lì li-ish-pu-ra-am-ma li-ri-id-du-*[. . . .].

they are "Administrative Records," more particularly "*Royal Administrative Business Records in connection with the Temple property, resp. its revenues.*" As such they give us an insight into the *methods* employed by the king, resp. his representatives, while administering these revenues.

The action of recording a certain item under the name of a person, city, etc., or names of persons, etc., in the so-called "Temple Archives," is referred to in such expressions as *xx. shá i-na DUB.SHA.RA*[1] . . . *MU* ^{m}*X shaṭ-ru* (*B. E.*, XIV, 168 : 34, 43) or [*xx. shá*] *i-na DUB shá* ^{alu}[2]*Ardi-Bêlit*(= *GASHAN*)^{ki}[3] *shá-aṭ-ru* (*B. E.*, XV, 199 : 37). "*To record,*" then, is *shaṭâru ina*, and "*Temple Archives*" are called *DUB*, resp. *DUB.SHA.RA*. Besides these two there occur still the following names for "Archives," viz., *DUB shú-ma-ti*[4] (thus especially where several items are recorded under various names), or [*DUB*] *shú-ma-a-ti*[5], or *dup-pi shú-ma-ti*[6], or *dup-pi shú-ma-a-ti*,[7] or *DUB MU*^{mesh},[8] or only *MU*^{mesh}[9]; thus apparently designated on account of the expression *MU.BI.IM*[10] = *shumâti*, found so often on tablets of this character. And as we meet instead of *MU.BI.IM* also *GISH*[11] or *za-kar*(!)*-tum*[12] we may not be wrong in saying that "Temple Archives" were termed also *DUB MU.BI.IM*; *DUB GISH*[13]; *DUB za-kar-tum*; *DUB MU.BI.*[14] At the end of each

[1] If the document records that the items are for a certain period, say, *e.g.*, a year, this is entered here, thus *shá shatti x.*^{kam}, *i.e.*, "for the year so and so," cf., *e.g.*, *B.E.*, XIV, 168 : 33.

[2] Or we might transcribe *DUB.SHA.RÍ*(= *uru*).

[3] This shows clearly that *Ardi-Bêlit*, because a tributary storehouse to that of Nippur, had to keep its own records.

[4] *B. E.*, XIV, 168 : 55; XV, 199 : 33, 37, 38, 41.

[5] *B. E.*, XIV, 168 : 22, 58.

[6] *B. E.*, XIV, 99 : 66.

[7] *B. E.*, XIV, 99 : 31.

[8] *B. E.*, XIV, 168 : 17.

[9] ^{I}*In-bi-A-a-ri* writes to the chief bursar *Innanni*, 85 : 8, *SHE.BA MU*^{mesh} *a-na* " ^{ilu}*XXX-is-saḫ-ra i-di-in*, "the wages for those persons (= *MU*^{mesh}) give to *Sin-issaḫra*," *i.e.*, the wages as recorded on the tablet giving the "names" of the persons hand over to *Sin-issaḫra*; so, no doubt, better than *sha'atu*, because in business transactions the amount of wages must always be specified. But the specification was to be found on a *tablet* containing the *MU*^{mesh} = *MU.BI.IM* or "names." See p. 116, note 6.

[10] See *B. E.*, XIV; XV passim. For *MU.BI.IM* we have also *MU.BI*, *e.g.*, *B.E.*, XIV, 51, 1.

[11] *B. E.*, XV, 59 : 2.

[12] *B. E.*, XIV, 89 : 3.

[13] Cf. here also the interesting variant in *B. E.*, XV, 59 : 12, *SHE.ḪAR.RA GISH-rum*(!) which corresponds to *l.c.*, ll. 1, 2, *SHE.ḪAR.RA* . . . . *GISH*, hence *GISH* = *GISH-rum* = *zikarum*^{rum} = *za-kar-tum*.

[14] Cf. here also the *MU.NE.NE* in Cassite Tablets published by F. Peiser, *e.g.*, P. 89 : 15; P. 100 : 6 (l. 5 only, *MU.NE*).

year, *i.e.*, either in the second[1] (so most generally), or the last,[2] or the sixth,[3] in other words, *around the end of the first* resp. *sixth month*, the different heads of the store-houses or of the possessions (*e.g.*, flocks, etc.) of the Temple were required, it seems, to make their yearly[4] reports, *i.e.*, "to draw the balance of accounts" (*epêsh nikasi*,[5] resp. *ri-ḫa-a-nu shá DUB.SHAR*^{meshu}[6]) or "take the inventory" of the stock (*mi-nu shá*)[7] in the presence of (*shá ú-kin-nu*) a *royal*(!) official, either the ^{amelu}*SAG LUGAL*[8] or the *GÙ.EN.NA*, *i.e.*, sheriff,[9] of Nippur, when they (the shepherds or other parties

[1] Cf. *B. E.*, XIV, 57, *SHE GISH.BAR* 6 *ga shá i-na libbi te-li-ti shá shatti* 12^{kam} ^{ilu}*Na-zi-Mu-ru-ut-ta-ásh i-na Za-rat-IM*^{ki} *a-na pa-te-si*^{ki} *nadnu*^{nu}, but dated, l. 35, ^{arḫu}*GUD.SI.SÌ shattu* 13^{kam}. *B. E.*, XV, 23 : 7, *ak-lu ishtu* ^{arḫu}*GUD.SI.SÌ shá shatti* 8^{kam} *adi* ^{arḫu}*GUD.SI.SÌ shá shatti* 9^{kam}. *B. E.*, XV, 25 : 6, *ak-lu GISH.BAR SHE.BA ishtu* ^{arḫu}*GUD(shá)shatti* 9^{kam} *adi* ^{arḫu}*GUD(shá)shatti* 10^{kam}. *B. E.*, XV, 28 : 1, *SHE ASH.AN.NA shatti* 11(!)^{kam}, but dated l. 12, ^{arḫu}*GUD.SI.SÌ shattu* 12^{kam}. See here also *B. E.*, XIV, 133 : 10, *ak-lu* 12 (Clay's copy is wrong and misleading) *arḫu ishtu ûmi* 1^{kam} *shá* ^{arḫu}*GUD.SI.SÌ shá shatti* 6^{kam} *adi ûmi* 30^{kam} *shá* ^{arḫu}*BÀR.ZAG.GAR shatti* 7^{kam}. The *dup-pi ri-ki-ish-ti* (*B. E.*, XIV, 12) was drawn up at the end of the year, *i.e.*, at the time of the *epêsh nikasi*. Here probably belong also tablets like *B. E.*, XIV, 18 : 20 | 52 : 1 | 80*a* : 9; *B. E.*, XV, 112 : 9. In view of these examples it is most likely that also at the time of the kings of Ur the yearly *epêsh nikasi* did not take place in the first (^{ilu}*SHE.ÌL.LA*) but in the *second* (^{ilu}*GAN.MASH*) month—just as at our present times, when the books resp. their accounts are balanced in February. Dr. Myhrman informs me that he has definite proofs which show that not *GAN.MASH* but *SHE.ÌL.LA* was the first month of the year at the time of the kings of Ur. *GAN.MASH* is mentioned so prominently in the tablets of the Ur dynasty because it was, as second month, that of the *epêsh nikasi*. See Dr. Myhrman's forthcoming volume.

[2] *B. E.*, XIV, 58 : 51, so and so much *shá ishtu* ^{arḫu}*BÀR shá shatti* 13^{kam} *adi* ^{arḫu}*SHE.KIN.KUD shá shatti* 13^{kam} . . . . *nadnu*^{nu}. Cf. here tablets like *B. E.*, XIV, 124 : 18; *B. E.*, XV, Nos. 12, 52, 53, 119, 120, 130. In *B. E.*, XIV, 123*a* : 2 the copyist (Clay) must have made some mistakes. While we read *l.c.*, l. 13, *napḫar* 13 *ma-na* 19½ *TU* (sc. *URUDU*) *ZI.GA MU* 8(!)^{kam}, the copy reads in ll. 1, 2, *URUDU ZI.GA* . . . . *ishtu* ^{arḫu}*KIN* (so the traces given) *shá shatti* 7(!)^{kam} *adi* ^{arḫu}*SHE shá shatti* 8^{kam}. According to this the *ZI.GA* would extend over a space of one and a half years—a thing absolutely impossible and against l. 13 where the *ZI.GA* is only for the 8th year; hence read in l. 2, *ishtu* ^{arḫu}*BÀR*(!) *shá shatti* 8(!)^{kam} *adi* ^{arḫu}*SHE shá shatti* 8^{kam}.

[3] *B. E.*, XV, 16 : 10, *ak-lum* . . . . *ishtu* ^{arḫu}*KIN shá shatti* 1^{kam} *adi* ^{arḫu}*KIN shá shatti* 5^{kam}, dated, l. 13, ^{arḫu}*KIN-*^{ilu}*Innanna ûmu* 29^{kam} *shattu* 5^{kam}—hence the *last month excluded*. *B. E.*, XV, 10 : 11, *ishtu* ^{arḫu}*KIN-*^{ilu}*Innanna shá shatti* 1^{kam} *adi* ^{arḫu}*NE.GAR shá shatti* 2^{kam}, *i.e.*, *both months included*.

[4] For half-yearly reports see, *e.g.*, *B. E.*, XIV, 56*a* : 31, *ishtu* ^{arḫu}*DUL.AZAG adi* ^{arḫu}*BÀR.ZAG.GAR*. *B. E.*, XV, 111 : 1, *ishtu* ^{arḫu}*DUL.AZAG shá shatti* 20^{kam} *adi* ^{arḫu}*BÀR.ZAG.GAR shá shatti* 21^{kam}, *i.e.*, the last month excluded, cf. l. 23; so also *l.c.*, 96 : 1. But *B. E.*, XIV, 117 : 1, *ishtu* ^{arḫu}*DUL adi* ^{arḫu}*SHE*, *i.e.*, both included. *B. E.*, XIV, 91*a* : 2, *ishtu* ^{arḫu}*BÀR adi* ^{arḫu}*KIN shá shatti* 3^{kam}, *i.e.*, the *last month included*. For quarterly reports cf. *e.g.*, *B. E.*, XV, 7 : 10, *ishtu* ^{arḫu}*ASH.A.AN adi* ^{arḫu}*GUD.SI.[SÌ]*.

[5] Cf. Letters No. 86 : 28, *ù at-ta* [*NIG*].*SHIT-shú*(?) *e-pu-ush-ma*, 92 : 26, *ù NIG.SHIT-ni it-ti a-ḫa-mi-ish i ni-pu-ush-ma*; *B. E.*, XIV, 99 : 36, *NIG.SHIT ip-shu*; *l.c.*, 140 : 4, *ishtu NIG.SHIT-shú ip-shú*; *l.c.*, 168 : 23; *i-na NIG.SHIT shá shatti* 1^{kam}; *B. E.*, XV, 39 : 16, *i-na NIG.SHIT KU.DA ul id-di-in shú-ú i-pal*.

[6] *B. E.*, XIV, 136 : 1.

[7] *B. E.*, XIV, 99 : 1 | 99*a* : 46 | 132 : 1.

[8] *B. E.*, XIV, 132 : 1, [*mi-nu LIT.GUD*$^{ḫi.a}$] *ù GANAM.LU*$^{ḫi.a}$ *shá i-na shatti* 6^{kam} *Shá-ga-ra-ak-ti-Shur-iá*(= *abnu*)*-ásh* [^{m}*Amel*(?)-^{ilu}] *Marduk* ^{amelu}*SAG.LUGAL ú-kin-nu-ma*. Cf. p. 134.

[9] *B. E.*, XIV, 136 : 1, *ri-ḫa-a-nu shá DUB.SHAR*^{mesh} *shá NIN.AN*^{mesh} *shá* ^{m}*Amel-*^{ilu}*Marduk GÙ.EN.NA En-lí*[*l*^{ki}] *i-na* ^{arḫu} *NE shá shatti* 9^{kam} *Shá-ga-ra-ak-ti-Shur-ia-ásh i-na muḫ LU*[*GAL*] *ú-kin-nu*. For the signification of *GÙ.EN.NA* = sheriff, see "Translations," pp. 133f. Notice the *ina muḫ LUGAL* = "for (in place of) the King."

concerned) had to testify to the truth of their statements[1] before "God" (*AN* = *Enlil!*). This having been done the "records" were sent to "headquarters," *i.e.*, to Nippur. For how could it possibly happen, I ask, that, *e.g.*, a document like that of *B. E.*, XIV, 37, was found in Nippur—a document which records how much grain (*SHE*) was received (*maḫ-rum*) and stored up (*tab-ku*) in the storehouse (*i-na karû*) of *Bu-un-na-*[ilu]*Marduk*[ki] during the 22d year of Kuri-Galzu? Surely, the fact that this document was excavated in Nippur shows that the "head" of the storehouse at *Bunna-Marduk* had to make his report and send it to Nippur. In this connection our letter published under No. 76 is especially interesting. In it the father asks his son, "Send the report to the 'lord of the barley'," *i.e.*, the storehouse official, "in order that I may send my report to the 'Lord (*be-el*)'."[2] No better evidence than the one contained in this letter could be expected to establish our contention that the archives are "administrative records." Or, I ask again, why should *B. E.*, XIV, 65, have been dug up in Nippur, seeing that that tablet states the amount of grain (*SHE*) which *Apil-Rammân* has removed (*ish-sha-a*) by means of ships (*i-na* [gish]*MÀ*) from (*ish-tu*) *Du-un-ni-A-ḫi*[ki]? And again the answer has to be: It is a "record" of the expenditures in connection with the storehouse in *Dunni-Aḫi*[ki] during the first month of the 15th year of *Nazi-Maruttash* which had been forwarded to headquarters. In this wise it happened that we found among these "Temple Archives" so appallingly many documents which apparently came from other places than Nippur.[3] Nippur, therefore, must have been the central "recording office," the *executive department* of the administration of the Temple properties under royal supervision. Such documents, thus forwarded and excavated in Nippur, cannot but be records (yearly, half-yearly, etc., as the case might be) of the receipts, resp. expenditures of grain, etc., in connection with the particular "depot" or "storehouse" from which they come; in other words, they are *business records giving us an insight into the administration of the several "depots" or "storehouses" connected with that of the Nippurian Temple under* the chief *supervision of the Cassite kings;* they are *administrative business records* of the Temple properties, resp. *its revenues*, made and kept for the king.

These administrative records, having arrived at and been received by the executive

[1] More particularly to *three* things. (*a*) *shá pi* (= *KA*) *ki-ni* (= col. I); (*b*) [*shá a-na e-s*]*i-ri nadnu*[nu] (resp. *shá a-na e-si-ri kun-nu*, col. II); (*c*) *ù RI.RI.GA na-gid*[mesh] *a-na pin* (= *SHI*) *AN* (= *ili* = *Enlil*) *ish-pu-ru* (resp. *shá a-na maḫ-ri AN shap-ru*, col. III), *B. E.*, XIV, 132. Notice that amounts of cols. II + III are = col. I!

[2] See below, under "Translations," p. 144.

[3] Cf. here the "List of Places" as given in *B. E.*, XIV, XV, and notice that *Innanni*, the chief bursar of Nippur, had authority not only over the *Nippurian Temple storehouses*, but also over all those mentioned above, Chapter I (p. 2, note 13); yes, even over the *karû É.GAL*, *ASH.TAB.BA.GAN.TUG*, resp. *Kandurê*; see pp. 81, 110.

department in Nippur, had necessarily to have a *place* where they could be deposited for future reference, resp. for inspection by the king or his representatives. This place was the *É* [abnu]*DUB*[1] or also called *É ku-nu-uk-ki*,[2] resp. *É* [abnu]*DUB shá É.GAL*,[3] where they have been excavated by the Babylonian Expeditions of the University of Pennsylvania. And as Hill VI (Hilprecht, *B. E.*, Ser. D, Vol. I, p. 305, Plan of the Ruins of Nuffar) represents the place where all the "Temple Archives", together with the letters here published, have been found, there is nothing which might prevent us from identifying the ruins of Hill VI with the *É* [abnu]*DUB shá É.GAL*, so called *because the É.GAL or "Palace," resp. its occupant, the be-li or king, had to administer the temporal affairs, resp. earthly possessions, of the "Temple of Enlil at Nippur."* This he did either personally or through his trusted servants, the *arad LUGAL* (cf. *Martuku*, the "servant of the king," who is the chief bursar at the time of *Nazi-Maruttash*, *B. E.*, XIV, 56 : 8). Now we also understand the reason why the Cassite kings of this period very often ascribe to themselves the title which precedes all others—even that of "king of Shumer and Akkad," resp. that of "king of the four corners of the world"—the title *GIR.NITA* or *shakkanakku* [ilu]*Enlil*.[4]

[1] *B. E.*, XIV, 101 : 6. Cf. Letter 84 : 7, 10, p. 114.

[2] *B. E.*, XV, 53 : 12. Notice in this connection the *a-na En-lil*[ki] after *É ku-nu-uk-ki*, thus showing that this building was indeed situated in Nippur.

[3] *B. E.*, XIV, 124 : 6.

[4] Cf., *e.g.*, the inscriptions of *Kuri-Galzu* (*ṣiḫru*) in I *R.*, 1, XIV, Nos. 1–3; Winckler, *K. B.*, III[1], p. 154*a*–*c*. For other occurrences of *shakkanakku* see, *e.g.*, Gudea, Cylinder B, VII : 20; VIII : 7; Statue B, IV : 13; *E. B. H.*, p. 255, note 12 (*AN-Mu-ta-bil* the *shakkanakku of Dûr-ilu*[ki]), and Hinke, *B. E.*, Ser. D, Vol. IV, pp. 312*a*, 173. For the reading of the ideogram *GIR.NITA* (not *NER.ARAD*) see Thureau-Dangin, *Z. A.*, XV, p. 46f. With *GIR.NITA* is closely connected the well-known official title *GIR*, so often found in tablets from the second dynasty of Ur. In my *E. B. H.*, p. 424, I said: "The *GIR* seems to have been an officer resembling very much a 'quartermaster.' He had to look after the food of the royal officers as well as that of the priests, and even of the royal flocks." This will now have to be modified. The *GIR* who figures so conspicuously in the Ur tablets was what we might call an "*auditor*," one who had to *approve* the expenditures, resp. receipts, mentioned in those tablets, who had to "O. K." them —put, so to speak, his *seal* to them. Such a function of an "*auditor*" was also exercised by Innanni and his successors as *chief bursars* of the Nippurian Temple storehouses. This is evident not only from the "checkmarks," but also from such tablets as *B. E.*, XV, 1 and 2; *l.c.*, XV, 8 and 9; *l.c.*, 23 and 25. Clay, who translated the first two mentioned, thinks that they were "salary payments," adding, "in this class of tablets the seal impression of another is frequently made upon the document, evidently by an officer who recorded the payment or delivered the goods mentioned" (*B. E.*, XV, p. 19; cf. *B. E.*, XIV, p. 14). This latter explanation contains the reason why Clay misunderstood the character of the tablets just mentioned. The *seal* found on a tablet always proves that the *person* to whom the seal belongs was the *debtor*, was the one who "received" the amount specified in the tablet. Payments of salary at the time of the Cassite kings were well regulated, as is apparent from, *e.g.*, *B. E.*, XIV, 58. If *B. E.*, XV, 1, 2 were, as Clay claims, such payments of salary, there would be, at least in Innanni's case, no regulation whatever; *i.e.*, the so-called salary received by Innanni for the fifth day of the first month (*B. E.*, XV, 2) would be completely out of proportion to that received for the period extending from the first day of the tenth to the fourth day of the first month (*B. E.*, XV, 1). No, not salary payments are those tablets, nor do they indicate that payments had to be or were made to Innanni. They are nothing but *Anweisungen*, or "cheques" or "drafts" on certain storehouses endorsed by the chief bursar; they were "bills" "O. K."-ed by Innanni. When some

From the position the Cassite kings hold in relation to the administration of Enlil's earthly possessions, it is at once evident that *shakkanakku* cannot be derived, with Delitzsch and others who follow him, from "*sha*" + "*kanakku*" and be translated "*Verschliesser, Thürhüter, Vorsteher, Machthaber*" (Deliztsch, *H. W. B.*, p. 338*a*), or "the one of the door" (Jensen, *Z. A.*, VII, p. 174, 1), but that it must be taken as standing for "*sha*" + "*kanâku*" (= *qanâqu*), *i.e.*, "the one who exercises the function of the 'sealing,' one who 'seals,' the man of the 'seal' of Enlil." The Cassite kings of this period, then, are *the authoritative representatives of Enlil*, through whom Enlil, "the king of heaven and earth," exercises his power and his authority, through whom he administers his kingdom, through whom he shepherds and feeds his people—they are "the food of the people, the platter of man."[1] Nothing could be done, nothing could be either removed from or be added to the possessions of Enlil, except the king first gave his authorization (seal); and if the king did, Enlil acted through and by him. The king's approval is Enlil's seal and authority. In this sense the Cassite king, as *shakkanakku* of Enlil, was but the earthly representative of his god—a representative whose business it was to administer and "regulate the tithes of *É.KUR* and Nippur."[2] Now, as the "Temple Archives," *i.e.*, the Archives of the Temple *É.KUR*, the sanctuary of Enlil of Nippur, concern themselves with the administration of Enlil's possessions, and as the king as *shakkanakku* ilu*Enlil* has to seal, to approve them, it follows that these "Temple Archives" are at the same time

governor or other person sent his *mâr shipri* to the chief bursar with the request that certain amounts of grain or certain cattle were to be given to the writer, the chief bursar, after having satisfied himself that the request was justified, sat down, wrote an *Anweisung* to the storehouse, stating what was to be given to the bearer of the draft or *Anweisung* (who in this case was the *mâr shipri*), at the same time "endorsing" it (that it was "O. K.") by putting his name to it. The head of the storehouse, not knowing the *mâr shipri*, thus not being sure that the things asked for would fall into the right hands, asked for identification. The *mâr shipri* identified himself by producing the endorsed or "O. K."-ed draft of the chief bursar. Whereupon he (the *mâr shipri*) received the goods, but had to give up the draft, which now insured the head of the storehouse against any loss or fraud, for he (the head) could cover the expenditure with the certified draft of the chief bursar. These drafts, together with the *DUB MU*mesh to which they belong, were sent to the executive department and, after having been examined, were deposited in the *É* abnu*DUB*. In case where such a draft bears the "*seal*" of a certain person, this seal proves that person, thus represented by it, to be the one who "had actually received" the goods specified in the tablet or draft, and served thus as a safeguard not only for the chief bursar, but also as a means of preventing the head of a storehouse from "cheating"—from saying that certain goods had been delivered to a certain party, while in fact they were not—for the head of a storehouse might possibly imitate an endorsed draft, but he could not very well imitate a "seal impression." Lastly, the "recipient" by putting his seal on the draft could not venture to deny the receipt of the goods, which he otherwise might possibly do by saying that the head of the storehouse had delivered the goods to another party or had forged the "draft." Cf. in this connection the interesting passage in 83 : 35, 36, where Innanni is threatened with an accusation, "thou hast given to *Mâr-Tâdu* (*i.e.*, to another person) an order on my barley." "To give to somebody an order on something" means at this time "*ushshuru a-na* m*X. i-na libbi xx.*"

[1] No. 21 : 5.

[2] *Sa-dar DI.KA* (! = *satuk*) *É.KUR ù EN.LIL*ki, Hinke, *B. E.*, Ser. D, IV, p. 144, II : 3.

Royal Archives; hence the *É* ^{abnu}*DUB* is at the same time an *É* ^{abnu}*DUB shá É.GAL*, because it contained *the official administrative documents of the Temple as approved, sealed by the king.*

Right here some one may object that the *É* ^{abnu}*DUB*, resp. the *É* ^{abnu}*DUB shá É.GAL*, if certain passages of *B. E.*, XIV and XV, and Letter No. 84 are taken into consideration, was used also for "*storehouse*" purposes. Upon closer observation this objection will be found to be of no avail. In *B. E.*, XIV, 104 : 3 we read of a certain amount of butter (*NI.NUN*) belonging to the *NIN.A*[*N*^{mesh}] *shá i-na shatti* 13^{kam} *Ka-dàsh-man-Tur-gu* ^{m}*Irîm-shu-*^{ilu}*NIN.IB im-ḫur-ma a-na É* ^{abnu}*DUB ú-she-ri-bu a-na* 4 ^{karpatu}*SAG*(?) *shá-pi-ik*, "which *Irim-shu-NIN.IB* received in (during) the 13th year of *Kadashman-Turgu* and which he (they?) caused to bring to the *É* ^{abnu}*DUB*, having it put up (or putting it up) in 4 *SAG*-jars." *B. E.*, XIV, 124 : 6f. informs us of two amounts of bronze (*erû*) which ^{m}*Ilu-MU.TUG.A-ri-ma* receives (*ma-ḫi-ir*). The first of these amounts is specified as *shá É* ^{abnu}*DUB shá É.GAL shu-uṣ-ṣi shu-ṣa-a*, *i.e.*, "which the *É* ^{abnu}*DUB shá É.GAL* caused to go (*i.e.*, sent) out," and the other as coming *shá qât* ^{m}*Na-aḫ-zi-*^{ilu}*Marduk*, "per order of *Naḫzi-Marduk*." Both amounts were received *a-na i-ṭer(?)-ti*[1] ^{isu}*MAR LUGAL* "as an indemnity for the royal wagons (chariots)." *B. E.*, XV, 53 : 11f. mentions wheat flour (*ZID.DA ASH.AN.NA*) *shá É ku-nu-uk-ki a-na En-lil*^{ki} *ish*(? or *na*?)*-shú-ú*, "due to (or belonging to) the *É ku-nu-uk-ki* (and which) they brought to Nippur." Finally Letter No. 84 : 5f. contains the following exhortation addressed to Innanni: "*ma-an-nu SHE.GISH.NI li-iṣ-ḫu-tu-ú-ma NI.GISH a-na É* ^{abnu}*DUB li-she-ri-bu ù at-ta SHE.GISH.NI-ka ṣu-ḫu-ut-ma NI.GISH a-na É* ^{abnu}*DUB shú-ri-ib*," *i.e.*, "All who press out sesame must bring oil (in)to the *É* ^{abnu}*DUB*, therefore press out thy sesame and bring the oil (in)to the *É* ^{abnu}*DUB*."[2]

Examining these passages we find that *B. E.*, XV, 53, is an administrative record (having been forwarded to Nippur from *Za-rat-IM*^{ki}), which enumerates the expenditures in wheat made during the course of a year, being therefore dated from the 29th day of the 12th month. At the end of the regular expenditures two additional notes are added, one of which, quoted above, implies that the *É ku-nu-uk-ki* at some previous time must have sent orders to *Zarat-IM*^{ki} that they (= German "*man*") take wheat flour to Nippur. The *É ku-nu-uk-ki* here apparently denotes as much as "the head of the *É ku-nu-uk-ki*," and is as such exactly parallel to our "such and such a *house* has ordered these and those goods." The same is

[1] For *i-ṭer-tum*, "indemnity," see Hilprecht, *B. E.*, IX, 41 : 7, *e-ṭer-ti i-nam-din-u' a-na*, "shall pay an indemnity to."

[2] Cf. here p. 114, notes 3, 4.

true of *B. E.*, XIV, 124, where the *É* [abnu]*DUB shá É.GAL*, *i.e.*, the head of the house mentioned, *shussi shuṣâ* the bronze. These two passages, then, show that *orders were sent out* from the *É* [abnu]*DUB* to certain men or branch storehouses.[1] But this could be done only if the *É* [abnu]*DUB* of Nippur was a building containing the *administrative* and *executive department* of the various branch storehouses connected with the Temple of Nippur. From here orders were sent out for the delivery of goods to this building, and, after having arrived there, they were distributed to wheresoever it was found necessary. It served, therefore, as a kind of a *central clearing house*, which again is paralleled at our present day by the fact that a great business corporation, such as the Temple of Enlil must have been, has likewise a *central clearing house* which is generally connected *with the main office or executive department*. In this sense *B. E.*, XIV, 104, and Letter No. 84 have to be understood. Is it under these circumstances at all surprising that in this central executive office, from which the manifold possessions of the Temple of Enlil were administered, letters should be found which were addressed to the administrator-in-chief, the representative of Enlil, the *be-lí* or king?

We *had* to find such documents in this building, because each and every correspondence carried on about the administration, resp. *methods* in connection *with the administration* of *Enlil's property*, had necessarily to be addressed (*a*) *either to the highest official*, *i.e.*, the *king* as "*shakkanakku of Enlil*," or (*b*) to the king's representative, *i.e.*, his *chief bursar*, etc. And, if so, we *had* to find a correspondence also between "*officials and officials*," *i.e.*, between *officials* outside of Nippur and *the king's representatives* at Nippur. Both classes of correspondence *are* represented: Nos. 1–74 contain letters addressed to the king, and Nos. 76ff. are those addressed to the king's representatives in one capacity or another. With these facts before us, the title of this volume, "*Letters to the Cassite Kings*," is not only justified, but is, in fact, the only proper one.

But the question may be asked, and quite rightly, how have we to account for the fact that letters written by the several kings themselves were recovered from this *É* [abnu]*DUB shá É.GAL*, which was, as has been claimed, the *administrative* department (of the king as highest executive officer) of the Temple of Enlil? Then, again, numerous scientific, historic and religious texts, such as omens, hymns, prayers, incantations, etc., have been found in this "administrative building (resp. buildings connected with each other)." How, I ask, can we account for the presence of *such* texts in the *É* [abnu]*DUB shá É.GAL*? A comprehensive answer to the latter

[1] Resp. that the heads of the storehouses sent their "orders" to the "central" office at Nippur to have them "filled," see No. 15, pp. 142f.

question will be given when the several classes of texts will be published. At the present only this much: At the time of the Cassite kings the *É* [abnu]*DUB shá É.GAL* embraced in its walls the *administrative* resp. *the executive department of the Temple,* by which and through which the *shakkanakku* [ilu]*Enlil,* the king, governed and officially directed both the *temporal* and the *spiritual* affairs of the worshippers of Enlil. In this wise it happened that the *É* [abnu]*DUB shá É.GAL* became the "*Ministerium*" with its different *departments—administrative, religious, educational*—as such containing tablets which are either "administrative records" (Temple Archives) or religious (Temple Library) or educational (Temple Library and Temple School) in character. This I maintain in the face of and notwithstanding the clamor of certain men who, on account of their inability to read and interpret cuneiform inscriptions or who on account of their lack of acumen to discern between the different classes of texts, can, in the ruins of Hill VI[1], not see anything but a "kitchen midden," and in the tablets there excavated, but so much "dried mud," "potsherds," "dead, meaningless, insignificant bricks."

The tablets recovered from the *É* [abnu]*DUB shá É.GAL* form thus an exact parallel to those found in the rightly famous *Library of Ashshur-bân-apal.* To uncover here *all* the various parallels with regard to the several classes of texts would lead me too far, and is, in fact, beyond the scope of these introductory remarks. However, as we are concerned with the "Letters" of the *É* [abnu]*DUB shá É.GAL,* I may be permitted to compare these briefly with those of the K. Collection, *i.e.,* with those letters which form an integral part of the Royal Library of Ashshur-bân-apal.

1. Though we find in *Ashshur-bân-apal's* Library[2] some letters that are addressed to the "prince," *TUR LUGAL,*[3] "princess," *TUR.SAL LUGAL,*[4] or "queen mother," *ÁM LUGAL,*[5] by far the greater number are written to the "KING," *LUGAL.* Of the one hundred and three letters here published seventy-eight[6] are addressed to the *be-li* or *king.*

2. In the Library of *Ashshur-bân-apal, Royal* Library as it undoubtedly was, we also find a correspondence between *officials*; thus we meet with letters addressed

[1] Situated on the west side of the *Shatt-en-Nil;* see Hilprecht, *B. E.,* Ser. D, I, p. 305, Plan of the Ruins of Nuffar.

[2] Here I take into consideration only those letters which are designated as "*K,*" omitting the *D. T.*, *Bu.*, and all other collections.

[3] Cf. K. 641 (H., I, 10); K. 629 (H., I, 65); K. 1101 + K. 1221 (H., II, 152); K. 614 (H., II, 175); K. 589 (H., II, 187); K. 1018 (H., II, 189); K. 1303 (H., V, 500).

[4] K. 476 (H., I, 51).

[5] K. 478 (H., III, 254); K. 825 (H., III, 263); K. 523 (H., III, 324); K. 980 (H., VI, 569).

[6] Nos. 1-74 + 33*a*, 59*a*, 60*a*, 73*a*.

to the (*a*) [amelu]*ENGAR*[1] or *ikkaru*, originally "farmer," here probably a high official; (*b*) [amelu]*[A.B]A KUR*,[2] "secretary of the State"; (*c*) [amelu]*A.BA É.GAL*,[3] "secretary of the Palace"; (*d*) [amelu]*nâgir É.GAL*,[4] "*major domo*"; (*e*) [amelu]*LUGH*[5] or *sukkallu*, "ambassador"; (*f*) [amelu]*ITI*[6] or *abbarakku*; (*g*) [amelu]*GAL.SAG*[7] or *rab-shaq*; (*h*) [amelu]*EN.NAM*[8] or *bêl paḫâti*, "governor"; (*i*) *amelu shá muḫ É A-nu*,[9] "man who is over the house of God," *i.e.*, "the Temple superintendent." In the administrative department of the Temple under the Cassite kings we also have a correspondence between "Temple resp. State officials."[10] If it be objected to my including such letters into a volume ostensibly called "*Letters to the Cassite Kings*," I ask my would-be critics why they do not object to calling the Library of Ashshur-bân-apal a *Royal* Library, seeing that it includes not only a correspondence between "officials and officials" but even such *unmistakably* "*private*[11] documents" as letters from [m] [ilu]*AG-EN-shu-nu* to [m]*Ashshur-mu-dam-me-ik*[12]; from [m]*Um-ma-ni-ià* to [sic]*A-ma-'-gu-nu*,[13] "his brother"[14] (*SHESH-shu*); from [m] [ilu]*Nergal-SHESH-ir* to [m] [ilu]*AG-ú-shal-lim*,[15] "his brother"[14] (*SHESH-shu*); from [m] [ilu]*EN-ú-ḪU* to [m]*Ku-na-a*,[16] "his father"[17] (*AD-shu*); from [m]*MU.GI.NA* to [m] [ilu]*Nergal-SHESH-ir*[18]; from [m]*A-qar-[*[ilu]*EN-lu-mur]* to [m]*EN-ib-ni*[19]; from an unknown writer to [m] [ilu]*PA-IK-shi*,[20] and last, but not least, a letter to [m]*XXX-man-nu-GAR-*[. . .] from [m]*XXX-KAK-[ni?]*,[21] "thy servant" (*ardi-ka*), etc.[22] If it be not objected

[1] K. 568 (H., I, 4); K. 1197 (H., I, 15); K. 1049 (H., I, 38); K. 113 (H. II, 183); K. 112 (H., II 223); K. 13,000 (H., III, 332); K. 88 (H., VIII, 816).

[2] K. 517 (H., I, 62); K. 175 (H., II, 221).

[3] K. 1274 (H., II, 220).

[4] K. 185 (H., I, 112).

[5] K. 1070 (H., I, 70); K. 655 (H., II, 132); K. 986 (H., VIII, 841).

[6] K. 910 (H., II, 145).

[7] K. 597 (H., III, 283).

[8] K. 1376 (H., VIII, 830).

[9] K. 1226 (H., VIII, 855).

[10] Cf. Nos. 76–99.

[11] *Private*(!), because both the writer and the addressee appear in these letters without any titles whatsoever.

[12] K. 1396 (H., II, 185).

[13] K. 831 (H., II, 214).

[14] Cf. above, Part II, p. 14, note 3.

[15] K. 1228 (H., III, 229). Cf. K. 830 below, note 18.

[16] K. 1239 (H., II, 219).

[17] Cf. our Letter No. 76, which is written by a "father" to his "son," p. **144**.

[18] K. 830 (H., V, 527). Cf. K. 1228 above, note 15.

[19] K. 1158 (H., VIII, 854).

[20] K. 578 (H., III, 273).

[21] K. 585 (H., V, 523).

[22] Cf. K. 186 (H., II, 222).

to such apparently "private" letters forming part of a *Royal* Library, it need not worry us to have included in our volume of "*Letters to the Cassite Kings*" twenty-four specimens representing a correspondence between officials and officials.

3. But the most remarkable of all is that there have been found in the Library of Ashshur-bân-apal letters—decrees—written either by himself or by other kings. We have "royal decrees" (*a-mat LUGAL a-na*) to "the Nippurians" (*^{amelu}EN.LI[L^{ki}-a]*)[1]; to "the people of the sea country, old and young, my servants" (*^{amelu} ^{matu}Tam-tim-a-a ^{amelu}AB.BA^{mesh} u TUR^{mesh} ardê^{mesh}-ià*)[2]; to "the Gambulæans" (*^{amelu}Gam-bu-la-a-a*)[3]; to "the Rashaeans, old and young" (*^{amelu} ^{matu}Ra-sha-a-a ^{amelu}AB.BA^{mesh} u ṣiḫ(=NE)-ru-ú-ti*)[4]; to "Shadu and the people of Erech, old and young, my servants" (*^{m}Sha-du' ù ^{amelu}UNUG$^{ki\ mesh}$ ^{amelu}AB.BA^{mesh} u TUR^{mesh} ardê^{mesh}-ià*)[6]; to "*Nabu-* . . . . and the people of Erech, old and young, my servants" (*$^{m\ ilu}$AG-[. .] ù ^{amelu}UNUG$^{ki.mesh}$ ^{amelu}AB.BA^{mesh} ù TUR^{mesh} ardê^{mesh}-ia*)[7]; to *$^{m\ ilu}$EN-ib-ni* (or *KAK*)[8]; to *$^{m\ ilu}$XXX-tab-ni-uṣur* (= *SHESH*)[9]; to *$^{m\ ilu}$AG-ibash(=IK)-shi*[10]; to *^{m}A-shi-pa-a*[11]; to *$^{m\ ilu}$EN-êṭir* (= *SHUR*)[12]; to *$^{m\ ilu}$XV-[nâ'id (= I)]*[13]; to *^{m}Zêru-ú-[a]*[14]; and last, but not least, a royal decree to "the 'Not-Babylonians'" (*a-mat LUGAL a-na la ^{amelu}DIN.TER$^{ki\ mesh}$*)[15]. We furthermore find in this Library royal "orders" (or *decrees*, *a-bít LUGAL a-na*) to "the Babylonians" (*^{amelu}KÁ.DINGIR$^{ki.mesh}$*)[16]; to *$^{m\ ilu}$PA-shar(=MAN)-aḫê(=PAP)^{mesh}-shu*[17]; to the "queen-mother" (*SAL ÁM sharri* (= *MAN*))[18]; to *^{m}Man-nu-ki-^{ilu}IM*[19]; to *^{m}A-shi-pa-a*[20]; to *$^{m\ ilu}$PA-dûr(=BAD)-*

[1] K. 94 (H., III, 287).

[2] K. 313 (H., III, 289).

[3] K. 1051 (H., III, 293).

[4] K. 1139 (H., III, 295).

[5] Cf. K. 5457 (H., VII, 754).

[6] K. 1162 (H., III, 296); cf. 83-1-18, 27 (H., V, 518).

[7] K. 1271 (H., III, 297).

[8] K. 95 (H., III, 288); K. 828 (H., III, 291); K. 938 (H., III, 292). Cf. also 67-4-2, 1 (H., IV, 399), 82-5-22, 97 (H., IV, 400); 83-1-18, 31 (H., IV, 402).

[9] K. 821 (H., III, 290).

[10] K. 1085 (H., III, 294); cf. 82-5-22, 91 (H., V, 517).

[11] K. 1883 (H., III, 298); cf. *a-bít LUGAL a-na ^{m}A-shi-pa-a*, K. 592 (H., III, 305).

[12] K. 13135 (H., III, 299).

[13] K. 13154 (H., III, 300); cf. *a-bít LUGAL a-na $^{m\ ilu}$XV-nâ'id* (= *I*), S. 1942 (H., IV, 417).

[14] 83-1-18, 30 (H., IV, 401).

[15] Bu. 91-5-9, 210 (H., IV, 403). Though numbered "Bu." this tablet undoubtedly belonged originally to the K. Collection.

[16] K. 84 (H., III, 301).

[17] K. 96 (H., III, 302).

[18] K. 486 (H., III, 303).

[19] K. 533 (H., III, 304).

[20] K. 592 (H., III, 305); cf. *a-mat LUGAL a-na ^{m}A-shi-pa-a*, K. 1883 (H., III, 298).

uṣur (= *PAP*)[1]; nay even an "order" of a "princess" to *[I] [ilu]Ashshur-sharrat* (*a-bît TUR.SAL LUGAL a-na SAL [ilu]SHAG*(= *libbu*).*ER-shar-rat*)[2] and a letter of a "prince" (*IM TUR LUGAL*) to the *[amelu]Sha-na-i*[3]. How have we to account for the presence of *royal* letters in a *Royal* Library? Did Ashshur-bân-apal extend his activity in procuring the best and choicest specimens of Babylonian and Assyrian literature as far as to have his scribes copy even royal letters? Or are we to suppose that those *royal* decrees have never been delivered to the various addressees, thus happening to be found in this Library, to which they really do not belong? Or, if they had been delivered, have we to maintain that it was customary to have copies[4] made of letters like these, and have those copies deposited in a Library, so that the king could "keep track" of his various orders and decrees? Or, lastly, did the messengers to whom these decrees had been entrusted go and communicate them to the several addressees and, after having read them to the persons named, bring them back with them and deposit them for future reference in the Royal Library of Ashshur-bân-apal? How, I ask again, could such royal letters possibly be found in a royal library? Whatever reply we may make to these questions, the same with equal force holds good of the royal letters — one or possibly two of which (Nos. 75 and 93) have been published here — to be found among the *administrative records of the Temple under royal supervision.* And as long as there is no objection made to the fact that the *Royal Library* of *Ashshur-bân-apal* may(!), as it actually does, include in its collection of documents both an official *and private* correspondence, just so long will I be justified in maintaining that the letters here published form a part, small and fragmentary though it be, of that collection of tablets now known as "*Temple Archives*," which with the tablets of the *Temple Library* and the *Temple School* constitute the contents of the *É [abnu]DUB shá É.GAL*, or simply *É [abnu]DUB*, the *bît tapshuḫti*,[5] "the place of the appeasing"[6] of Enlil.

[1] K. 622 (H., III, 306).

[2] K. 1619 B (H., III, 308).

[3] R. M. 72 (H., IV, 130), probably belonging to Ashshur-bân-apal's Library.

[4] Cf. here above, Chapter III, for the several copies to be found among the Amarna Letters, see p. 57, note 2.

[5] Cf. K. 11,174 (= *B. A.*, V, p. 631), Rev. ll. 13, 14.

[6] *I.e.*, then as now the favor of a god can be obtained only by contributing freely, in the form of tithes and taxes, towards the maintenance of the worship, ritual, and priesthood of the great Enlil of Nippur. A god can be appeased only by offerings — for the benefit of his (the god's) priests.

V.

TRANSLATION OF SOME SPECIMEN LETTERS.

In order to illustrate more fully the general character of the letters here published I may be permitted to submit a few of them in transcription and translation, adding such critical notes as might be found necessary to elucidate their contents more clearly. While in the autograph plates the letters have been arranged alphabetically according to the names of the writers, I have followed here the, no doubt, more scientific method of giving them in their historical sequence.

I.

No. 23 (= C. B. M. 11,090). (Cf. photographic reproduction, Pl. V, 12, 13.)

Imgurum, a royal official stationed at *Dûr-Kuri-Galzu*, reports to his "Lord," King *Burna-Buriash*, about the affairs in connection with the administration of his office. About 1430 B.C.

The author of this letter, *Imgurum*, has to be identified not only with the writer of No. 22,[1] but also with the addressee ^{m}*Im-gu-ri* of No. 79 : 1, a contemporary of the slave-dealer ^{m} ^{ilu}*En-lil-ki-di-ni*, who flourished, as we saw above (pp. 54ff.), during the time of King *Burna-Buriash*. From this it would follow that *Imgurum* was likewise a contemporary of *Burna-Buriash*. This result is corroborated by the following two considerations: (1) In 22 : 6 *Imgurum* mentions a certain ^{m}*Ḫu-za-lum*, who appears in *B. E.*, XIV, 8 : 30 (dated the 21st year of *Burna-Buriash*) among the witnesses[2] at a legal business transaction executed by ^{m} ^{ilu}*En-lil-ki-di-ni* (ll. 22, 25). (2) ^{m}*Ki-din-*^{ilu}*Marduk*[3] referred to in our letter (l. 23) is mentioned, *B. E.*, XIV, 7 : 34 (dated the 18th, better 19th, year of *Burna-Buriash*), as the father of a certain ^{m}*Ta-ki-shum*, who appears likewise as one of the witnesses at a slave sale executed between the two brothers ^{m} ^{ilu}*NIN.IB-SHESH* and ^{m} ^{ilu}*NIN.IB-MU-MU* (sellers) and ^{m} ^{ilu}*En-lil-ki-di-ni* (buyer). According to l. 29 *Imgurum* was apparently sta-

[1] In both the greeting is the same and in both the writer records about the disposition of adobes, resp. burnt bricks.

[2] Called here ^{m}*Ḫu-za-lum mâr* ^{m} ^{ilu}*En-lil-bêl(= EN)-ilî(= AN)*^{mesh}.

[3] Cf. also the *êlu shá* ^{m}*Ki-din-*^{ilu}*Marduk* in *B. E.*, XIV, 166 : 9.

tioned at *Dûr-Kuri-Galzu*, where he had charge both of certain building operations in connection with its palace or temple (cf. ll. 4–18) and of the weaveries and its personnel.[1] The fact that No. 79 was found in Nippur would show, however, that the writer must have been living, for some time at least, also in Nippur.

The contents of this letter are the following:

(*a*) The disposition of adobes, ll. 4–10.

(*b*) The disposition of burnt bricks, ll. 11–13.

(*c*) Elul is the propitious time for transferring the resting chambers (of the god), ll. 14–18.

(*d*) *Bêl-usâtum* has not yet delivered the bleached wool, ll. 19–20.

(*e*) Accounting of the disposition of wool, ll. 21–28.

(*f*) Complaint, ll. 29–32.

(*g*) Request that certain weavers be finally dismissed out of the prison at *Pân-Bali*, ll. 33–39.

The letter reads:

1 [*ardi-ka* ^{m}*Im-gu*]-*rum a-na di-na-an be-lì-ia*	Thy servant *Ingurum*; before the presence of my "Lord"
2 [*lu-ul*]-*li-ik*	may I come!
3 [*a-na bît be*]-*lì-ia*[2] *shú-ul-mu*	To the house of my "Lord" greeting!
4 [. . .][3] + 6 *M libittu*(= *SHEG-gunû*[4]) *a-di*[5] *ûmi* 4^{kam} *la-ab-na-at*[6]	x + 6000 adobes have been made during four days.
5 [. . . .] *M libittu*(= *SHEG-gunû*) *a-na pi*(?)-*i na-ak-ba-ar*[7]	I caused to fetch y + 1000 adobes to the entrance of the excavation

[1] As *Imgurum* reports (22 : 5) about the condition of ^{f}*Ga-ga-du-ni-tum*, the *zammertu*, who is sick, it would seem that he superintended also the personnel of the Temple or Palace, for a *zammertu* or "songstress" was, no doubt, connected with both the Temple and the Palace.

[2] Emendation according to 22 : 1—hence also our reading of the writer's name, [^{m}*Im-gu*]-*rum*. For this form of greeting see also 35 : 3, p. 121.

[3] The space is too small for *ásh-shum*. Here and in l. 5 a larger number has been broken away.

[4] For *SHEG-gunû* (not given by Clay, List of Signs) cf. Thureau-Dangin, *R. E. C.*, No. 129. Cf. also ll. 5, 11. In 35 : 29 the simple *SHEG* occurs.

[5] "Up to the fourth day," *i.e.*, "during four days," "in the space of four days." Cf. *H.*, IV, 392, Rev. 16, *a-du ûmê*^{mesh} 7, 8, *i-ba-lat*, "he will be well within a space of seven (or) eight days."

[6] For the construction *labnat*, singl. after x + 6000 *libittu*, see Hilprecht, *B. E.*, IX, p. 35, note to No. 6, li. 1, and cf. p. 137, note 3.

[7] Here, of course, not *Grab, Begrabniss*, Delitzsch, *H. W. B.*, p. 580*a*, but "cellar," "excavation." The *pi naqbar* is the "entrance to the cellar," or that place where the cellar empties into the open air or into another room. A "mouth" (*pû*) is ascribed not only to a "cellar," as here, but also to a "canal" (No. 34 : 22; cf. *B. E.*, XIV, 29 : 2, *i-na pî*(=*KA*) *nâri*(=*A.GUR.DA*) *âli-ki*, *i.e.*, "at the mouth of the canal of the city" or "at the mouth of the *Shatt-en-Nîl*, the canal of the city (*sc.* of Nippur) *par excellence*," where the little hamlet, called *Pî-nâri*^{ki}, was situated) and to a *natbaktu*, see 12:9, *i-na pî*(= *KA*) *na-at-ba-ak-ti*, cf. p. 96, note 5.

6 *du-ul-li-ia*[1] *ú-ra-ad-da-ma*[2]	I am working at;
7 *a-di i-na* ^{arhu}*Tashrîtu*(= *DUL. AZAG*) *ush-shi*[3] *a-na-an-du-ú*	and till I shall lay the foundations in the month Tishri,
8 *i-ga-ra shá i-na ku-tal*(= *RI*)-*li*[4] *ad-du-ú-ma*	I shall have torn down the wall which is in the rear (palace).
9 20 *na-at-ba-ku*[5] *uh-hu-ru*[6]	The remaining twenty heaps I shall

[1] For the various significations of *dullu* see, besides Delitzsch, *H. W. B.*, p. 219*b*, also Behrens, *L. S. S.*, II[1], p. 8. Here it is to be taken in the sense of "working at." cf. *II.*, V, 171 : 18, *dul-li shá É.SAG.ÌL*, "the working at Esagil," to be compared with *l.c.*, Rev. 7, which shows that the letter refers to building operations.

[2] *Ú-ra-ad-da-ma*, because construed here with *a-na*, cannot be taken as a II[1] of III ירד, Delitzsch, *H. W. B.*, p. 613*b* (this has *eh*). Jensen, *K. B.*, VI[1], p. 317, has shown that there is only one ירד, although the various significations assigned to this verb by him (*giessen, nachfolgen, hinterhergehen, treiben*) ought to be enlarged so as to include also the meaning *führen* (Behrens, *L. S. S.*, II[1], p. 6, note 2), and "to take," "to fetch," cf. Nagel, *B. A.*, IV, p. 180, and see *Letters of Hammurabi*, No. 78 : 18, *ish te-en ta-ki-il-ka a-na Babili*^{ki} *li-ir-di-a-ásh-shú-nu-ti*, "one of thy trusted servants may bring, take, fetch them to Babylon." The II[1] of ירד is here "causative," *i.e.*, "to cause to bring, fetch." *Uradda* for *uraddi* because it stands in the chief sentence.

[3] *Ushshi a-na-an-du-ú* = *anaddû*, with the signification "to lay the foundations" *sc.* of my *dulli* (l. 6), *i.e.*, of the building I am at present working at. *Addû-ma*, here of the "completed action in the future" = "I shall have torn down" — "I have torn down."

[4] For *ku-tal* see besides Delitzsch, *H. W. B.*, p. 362*a*, also Jensen, *K. B.*, VI[1], p. 464, and below, l. 13, *ku-tal na-ka-si*. In No. 60 : 8 the *zîr ku tal* is mentioned and in *B. E.*, XV, 80 : 11 we are told of the *mash-shar-ra-tum shá i-na ku-tal bîti*^{ti} *tab-ku*, *i.e.*, of the *mashsharrâti* (= pl. of *mashshártu*) which are "poured out," *i.e.*, stored up in the rear of the "house." This latter passage shows that the translation "stipend" for *mashshártu* (Clay, *B. E.*, XIV, p. 30, note below, who follows Delitzsch, *H. W. B.*, p. 433*b*) is out of place here. A "stipend," surely, could not and was not "stored up." *Mashshártu* signifies at this time the "reserve fund," hence it is not only "stored up," but out of it payments are made; cf. *B. E.*, XV, 76 : 2, *SHE... shá i-na libbi mash-shar-ti* ^{arhu}*AB.UD.DU ... nadnu*^{nu}; *l.c.*, XV, 106 : 1, *SHE shá i-na libbi mash-shar-ti i-na* ^{âlu}*Kal-bi-ia*^{ki} *i-na* (= "as") *GISH.BAR.GAL nadnu*^{nu}; *l.c.*, 164 : 1, *SHE... shá i-na libbi mash-shar-tim shá* ^{m}*In-na-an-ni* ^{m}*Ta-ki-shú nadnu*^{nu} (notice here the reserve fund of *Innanni*!). In *B. E.*, XIV, 92 : 2 the *mash-shar-ti shá karû Kâr-Zi-ban*^{ki} is mentioned and in *B. E.*, XV, 47 : 1 we are told that payments were made *i-na libbi* 10 *GUR mash-shar-ti shá É.GAL*, *i.e.*, out of the Palace's reserve fund of 10 *GUR*. *B. E.*, XV, 40 : 5 mentions the total of *SHE nadnu*^{nu} *i-na libbi mash-shar-ti* which *SHE* is according to *l.c.*, l. 1, that *shá i-na karû ÁSH.TAB.[BA.]GAN.TUG*^{ki} *nadnu*^{nu}. From this it follows that the Palace, the several storehouses, officials (like *Innanni*), and even months had each their special "reserve funds." In some passages, as *e.g.*, Str., IV, 371 : 10, *mashshártu* might be translated even by "collateral security." *Mashshártu*, then, is "something that is left over (*mushshuru*) to insure the payments of certain obligations."

[5] *Na-at-ba-ku* here (and in 22 : 15, [*na*]-*at-ba-ki* [*at-t*]*a-ba-ak*) apparently a singl. masc., although after the numeral 20; for construction see p. 95, note 6. Also a *fem.* form of this word is found, see, *e.g.*, 3 : 15, 21, *shá na-at-ba-ak-ti*; 3 : 19, *a-na na-at-ba-ak-ti* (so also *l.c.*, ll. 30, 32); 3 : 20, *mu-ú ul-tu na-at-ba-ak-ti shá* ^{ilu}*Gir-ra-ga-mil* (= a city!) *li-zu-ni*; 68 : 26, *eqlu* (= *A.SHAG*) *shá na-at-ba-ak-ti shá Kâr-*^{ilu}*AG*; cf. also 12 : 6, 10. In 3 : 17, 55 we have *na-at-ba-ak-ta*, and according to 12 : 9, *i-na pî* (= *KA*) *na-at-ba-ak-ti*, it has an "opening," a "mouth," an "access" to which one may come. The plural of *natbaktu* is found in 12 : 1, *x na-at-ba-ka-a-ti*. The root is, of course, *tabâku*, "to pour out"; here, because used of bricks, "to store, pile up." A *natbaku*, *natbaktu* accordingly would be "something that is stored, piled up," a "heap," "pile," comprising a *certain number* of bricks. For *tabâku* in this signification cf. *e.g.*, *B. E.*, XIV, 37 : 2, *SHE mah-rum shá i-na karû... tab-ku*; *B. E.*, XV, 122 : 8, the grain which *a-na libbi SHE.GAL tab-ku*, *i.e.*, "which has been added to the great grain (*das Stamm-, Haupt-korn*)." See also note 4 and cf. *B. E.*, XIV, 144 : 4, 10 *GUR* 1 *PI* (= 36 *qa*) *tu-bu-uk-ku-ú i-na* 1 *GUR* 1 *PI*, *i.e.*, "10 *gur* and 36 *qa* 'stored up' (extra)

10 *e-ki-ir-ri-im-ma*[7] *a-tab-ba-ak*	pile and store up.
11 10 *M agurru*(= *SHEG-gunû AL*[8]) *ameluGUSHUR*(or *ÚR*)*.RA.GAL*^(meshy) *la-ab-na-at*	10,000 burnt bricks of (by?) the *úr-ra-gal* have been made.

—for each *gur* (cf. l. 3) 1 *PI* (or 36 *qa*)." One *gur* of grain stored up at harvest time *lost in volume* during the time of its being stored up, *i.e.*, it dried up, it shrunk hence at the end of, say, one year 1 *gur* of grain would be equal not to 180 *qa* but only to 180 — 36, *i.e.*, to 144 *qa*. The shrinkage of grain at this time, then, was computed at the rate of 1 *PI* or 36 *qa* to 1 *GUR* or 180 *qa*, *i.e.*, at the rate of 1 *to* 5 *qa*. Grain or cereals thus stored up to insure against shrinkage were called *BAL* or *ti-ib-ku* or *tab-ki*, out of which, if not used, payments might be and were made. For (*SHE*) *BAL* cf. *B. E.*, XV, 115 : 1 | 141 : 6 | 94 : 2; for (*SHE*) *tab-ki* see, *e.g.*, *B. E.*, XV, 10 : 7 | 29 : 6 | 115 : 1, 4, and for (*SHE*) *ti-ib-ku*(*-ki*), *B. E.*, XV, 80 : 1 (here it is simply stated that a *tibku* was added to the different items of grain); *B. E.*, XV, 66 : 3 (here we have *GISH.BAR ti-ib-ki* instead of the more commonly used *GISH.BAR tab-ki*, hence *tibki* = *tabki*). How many bricks such a *natbaku* or *natbaktu* comprised, cannot be made out as yet. In view of the fact that the bricks excavated at Nippur, and now preserved in the Babylonian Museum of the University of Pennsylvania, were at all times of a certain "standard size and thickness," and that *tibki* in the historic inscriptions signifies the "height" of a "brick" or "layer of bricks," then a "measure of length" (cf. the German "*so und soviel Backsteinschichten hoch*"), Prof. Hilprecht is inclined to see in a *natbaku* a *quadrangle* or *rectangle* comprising a certain number of *tibki*, hence a "pile which is of a certain height, length and breadth."

[6] Stands either for *shá uḫḫuru*, masc. singl. on account of *natbaku*, or it may be taken as an adjective, Delitzsch, *Gram.*, p. 241*b*. Cf. here 68 : 34, *zêru shá uḫ-ḫu-ru*; 68 : 10, *II ḫar-bi uḫ-ḫu-ru*; 68 : 24, *III* (*gur*) *zêr a-na ma-li-e uḫ-ḫu-ùr*; 31 : 26, *mi-shi-il i-shá-ta-ti* [*shá*(?)*uḫ*]-*ḫu-ra*, *l. c.*, l. 28, *i-shá-ta-tu shá ṣi-li* (= צלין!) *shá uḫ-ḫu-ra*; 37 : 16, *II C SHE GUR shá ùḫ-ḫu-rum*, *l. c.*, ll. 20, 25, *shá-ma-a-ti* *shá ùḫ-ḫu-rum*; 31 : 16, *II i-shá-tu shá uḫ-ḫu-ra-tum*; see also 3 : 5 | 18 : 18 | 33 : 15 | 66 : 10. From these passages it will be evident that *uḫḫuru* has the meaning "that which is left over," "the rest, balance in one's favor, which one either has or which is due him from another." This "rest in one's favor," if ideographically expressed, is called *ÌB-KID* and is to be distinguished from *LÀL.NI*, "the rest, remainder still to be paid, which is against one, one's loss, debt, liability." In other words, in records that are *epish nikasi* (balances of accounts) the items marked *ÌB.KID* represent the "assets," a *plus*, and those called *LÀL.NI* are the "liabilities," a *minus*. For *ÌB.KID* or "assets," "amounts still outstanding in one's favor," cf. especially *B. E.*, XIV, 33 : 2, col. III. Col. I gives the "whole amount due," col. II that "which has been received (*maḫ-rum*)" and col. III the "amount still outstanding (*ÌB KID*)"—hence if we subtract from the "whole amount due" the "item(s) that have been received" we obtain the "*ÌB.KID*," *i.e.*, "which is still due in one's favor, one's assets." For *ÌB.KID* cf. also *B. E.*, XIV, 41*a* : 1 | 92 : 1 | 99 : 49; XV, 68 : 2 | 141 : 8, and for *LÀL.NI* see *B. E.*, XIV, 65 : 27 | 99 : 40, 42 | 136 : 14 | 141 : 8; XV, 78 : 12 | 141 : 25 | 196 : 1 (similar to *B. E.*, XIV, 33 : 2). A synonym, if not a translation, of (*LÀL.NI* or ?) *ÌB.KID* seems to be *ri-ḫa-a-nu*, *B. E.*, XIV, 136 : 1, 4. Ungnad, *O. L. Z.*, 1907, Sp. 141, by reading *TUM.KAD* (resp. *ib-kad*) and translating "rest" is only partially correct.

[7] *E-ki-ir-ri-im-ma*, because parallel to *a-tab-ba-ak*, I propose to derive from קרן, *i.e.*, *ekirrim-ma* stands for original *aqarrin-ma*, hence קרן has a side-form (*iqarrin*), *iqrin* for the usual *iqrun* (Delitzsch, *H. W. B.*, p. 596*b*). The *i* (for *u*) is due to the influence of the *n*, cf. 35 : 33, *shub*(= *RU*)*-ta lish-ki*(!)*-nu* (for *lish-ku-nu*). See p. 125, note 8. For the *i* in *ki-ir*, see already above, p. 53, note 1, and for the *e* (instead of *a*) cf. *uk-te-ir-ri-ib*, 23 : 13; *ik-te-di-ir-*[*ru*], 39 : 6; Delitzsch, *Gram.*, p. 85 and below, p. 119, n. 5. A possible derivation from קרב (= *aqarrib-ma*) is less probable, and a form *ekirrim* = *akarrim* (root כרם, Delitzsch, *H. W. B.*, 351*a*) is against context and parallelism.

[8] Shortened form for *SHEG.AL.GUSHUR.RA* = *agurru*, "burnt bricks." Cf. also 22 : 11, *x M* + 300 *a-gur-ra aṣ-ṣa-ra-ab*, and see following note.

[9] What kind of an office this name represents I do not know. Are we to suppose that the scribe misplaced the *amelu*?. If so, we might read *GUSHUR.RA* (which has to be connected with *SHEG-gunû AL*, cf. note 8) *ameluGAL*^(mesh). Or is it a shortened form of *ameluSHEG.AL.GUSHUR.RA.GAL*^(mesh), "chief brickmakers"—the *SHEG.AL* being omitted either by mistake or to avoid repetition?

12 *ul-tu ûmi* 4^{kam} *agurru* (= *AL-li*)[1] *ab-ta-ta-ar-ma*[2]	After having examined the burnt bricks during (the last) four days,
13 *a-na ku-tal* (= *RI*) *na-ka-si*[3] *uk-te-ir-ri-ib*[4]	I brought them to the rear of the slaughtering house.
14 *ásh-shum bît* ^{isu}*irshê*(= *N.ÀD*)^{mesh}[5] *shá libbi a-su-up-pa-ti*[6]	With regard to the resting chambers which are in the *asuppati*
15 *shá be-lì* ì(= *NI*)-*ṣa-a*[7] *iq-ba-a*	(and) which my "Lord" has commanded to bring out (I beg to state that)
16 *dup-pa ki a-mu-ru i-na* ^{arhu}*Ululu* (= *KIN-*^{ilu}*Innanna*) *a-na* ì(= *NI*)-*ṣi-e*[7] *da-ab*[8]	the month Elul is, as I learned from communications, propitious for bringing them out.
17 *be-lì li-ish-pu-ra-am-ma shum-ma shá* ì(= *NI*)-*ṣi-e*[7]	My "Lord" may send word when I shall
18 *lu-uṣ-ṣi*	bring them out.

[1] *AL-li* = *SHEGAL*, l. 11? But cf. *allu*, Del., *H. W. B.*, p. 70*b*: "*ein Gerat der Ziegelstreicher.*"

[2] *Ab-ta-ta-ar-ma* I propose to take as a præs. I[4] (circumstantial clause) of בור, "to examine," see Meissner, *B. A.*, III, p. 523, and Nagel, *B. A.*, IV, p. 178. By itself a form I[2] of *patâru* (*H. W. B.*, p. 555*a*) or *paṭâru* would likewise be possible, but with what meaning? Cf., however, Delitzsch, *H. W. B.*, p. 522*b*, under *paṭâru* II[2]: *agurri taḫlubtisha up-ta-aṭ-ṭi-ir-ma*, "*war geborsten*," and see p. 122, note 8. Or should we translate after all, "since the fourth day having loosened (departed from, set free) the *allu* (= *term. techn.* for "to stop to make bricks," cf. *mesirra paṭâru* = "*den Gurtel losen*," Jensen, *K. B.*, VI[1], p. 474) I brought," etc.? This latter translation is preferred by Prof. Hilprecht.

[3] With *na-ka-si* cf. ^{amelu}*na-ki-su*, Delitzsch, *H. W. B.*, p. 463*a*.

[4] A II[2] (= causative) of קרב. The common signification of *qarâbu ana*, "to go, march against," is here against the context. For other forms of *qarâbu*, to be met with in these letters, see 26 : 16, *ki-ri-ib*; 3 : 25, *á-ga-ri-bu*; 12 : 16, *ik-te-ri-ib ana*.

[5] For ^{gish}*NÀD* (= *irshu*), as distinguished from *NÀD.KI* (= *maialu*), see Jensen, *K. B.*, VI[1], p. 409, and for *É* ^{gish}*NÀD*, cf., *e.g.*, *H.*, I, 65 : 9, "the bed-chamber of ^{ilu}*AG*." A "bed-chamber," because it can be carried, etc., was, of course, not an *É* or *bîtu*, "house," in its commonly accepted sense. Whose "chamber" is meant here, is not said.

[6] Cf. *bît a-zu-ub-bu bît ka-a-ri*, Str., II, 199 : 1. For the interchange of *s* and *z* cf. on the one hand ^{m}*U*[?]*-su-ub-Shi-pak* (= *Uzub-Shipak*), 55 : 2, and on the other ^{m}*Shá-la-zu-*[*nu*], *B. E.*, XV, 188 V : 18; [^{f}*B*]*e-lì-zu-nu*, *l.c.*, IV : 20; *za-bit-ti*, *B. E.*, XIV, 99*a* : 30, 31, 43, and its plural *zi-ba-a-ti*, *B. E.*, XIV, 121 : 6 | 122 : 6 (standing for *si-bi-ti*, *si-bi-e-ti* = *ṣibittu*, *ṣibtu*, see above, p. 6, note); *qa-az-zu tur-*(Clay's copy gives *tab*)*ra-at*, *B. E.*, XV, 158 : 5, for *qât*(= *SHÚ*)*-su tur-rat*, *B. E.*, XV, 99 : 14 (cf. here also *l.c.*, XV, 39 : 5, *qât* ^{m}*X. tur-rat*; XV, 90 : 45, *shá qa-tum tur-ra-tum*; XV, 6 : 9 | 19 : 12 | 124 : 8, *qa-ta ú-ta-ar*, etc., etc.). I beg to differ from Prof. Clay, who reads *MAR.RAT* (instead of *tur-rat*) and regards this to be a *profession* (see *B. E.*, XIV, p. 57*a*; XV, p. 51*b*). *Qât* resp. *qât-su tur-rat* evidently means "his portion is returned, has been paid."

[7] *Ì-ṣa-a*, *i-ṣi-e* (ll. 16, 17), *i-ṣu-u* (21 : 16) is the infinitive of יצא, cf. *adû* and *idû*, "to know."

[8] For construction and meaning cf., *e.g.*, *H.*, IV, 406 : 16f., *ina muḫ LUniqê*^{mesh} *shá LUGAL be-lì ish-pur-an-ni ina arḫi an-ni-e da-ba a-na e-pa-a-shi*, and *H.*, I, 77, Rev. 3f., *da-a-ba a-na a-la-ki ûmu II*^{kam} *da-a-ba ûmu IV*^{kam} *a-dan-nish da-a-ba*. Any action undertaken by the Babylonians had to be determined by the *barû* priest with regard to its most propitious time.

19	[*ásh*]-*shum ta-bar-ri*[1] *shá be-lí ish-pu-ra*	With regard to the *tabarri*(-wool) concerning which my "Lord" has inquired
20	[*ḫur-ḫ*]*u-ra-ti*[2] *i-na qât* ᵐ*Bêl*(= *EN*)-*ú-sa-tum ul am-ḫu-ur*	(I beg to state that) I have not yet received the bleached(?) wool from *Bêl-usâtum*.
21	[*ásh-shum ḫur*]-*ḫu-ra-tum*[2] *shá a-na ma-an-da-at-ti-ia*[3]	As regards the bleached(?) wool which I have kept
22	[*al*]-*qu-ú*	as my due
23	[*shá be-lí i*]*q-ba-a a-na* ᵐ*Ki-din-*ᵈᵘ*Marduk*	and concerning which my "Lord" has spoken to *Kidin-Marduk*—
24	[*be-lí i-di ki x.*] + 10 *ma-na ta-bar-ri*[1] *an-da-ḫar*	"my 'Lord' knows that I have received only x + 10 *ma-na* of *tabarri*(-wool),
25	[*ina libbi-shú x.*] + 10 *ma-na a-na du-ul-li-ia*	x + 10 *ma-na* of which I have applied as compensation
26	[*al-t*]*a*(?)-*ka-an*[4]	for my work,
27	[*x.*] + 20 *ma-na a-na mu-uḫ be-lí-ia*	and x + 20 *ma-na* I have sent
28	[*ul*]-*te-bi-la*	to my 'Lord.'"
29	[*ḫ*]*ur-ḫu-ra-tum*[2] *i-na Dûr-Ku-ri-Gal-zu*	There is no bleached(?) wool
30	[*shú*(?)]-*ú-bi-'u-ú*[5] *ia-nu*	to be gotten in *Dûr-Kuri-Galzu*.

[1] *Ta-bar-ri*, here without the determinative *SIG* = *shipâti*, is a certain kind of "wool" (Delitzsch, *H. W. B.*, p. 701*a*) or a "garment" (Tallquist, *Sprache*, p. 142). Here, because measured according to *ma-na* (l. 24), it must be "wool," more particularly "dirty(?) wool."

[2] So we have to read according to ll. 29, 31 (not *uḫ-ḫu-ra-tum*). It is here a kind of wool. In Esth., 1 : 6 | 8 : 15, we hear of a certain חור (LXX, *βύσσος*) and in Isa., 19 : 9, of חוֹרָי, in both of which passages the idea of "white" (garments) is predominant. *Ḫurḫuratum* accordingly I propose to explain as "wool that is washed, cleaned, bleached, white" (cf. also Arabic *ḥâra*, *ḥavvara*, "to wash white, bleach"), taking it to be a fem. pl. (*sc. shipâti*) of *ḫurḫuru*, and this a reduplicated form of *ḫur* = חור.

[3] Cf. also 27 : 28, *man-da-at-ta ki-i ú-qa-tu-ú at-ta-din*; 35 : 18, garments which *a-na* ᵃᵐᵉˡᵘ*USH.BAR ù ka-ṣi-ri ki-i man-da-at-ti-shu-nu id-di-nu*; *B. E.*, XV, 200, III : 9, *napḫar* 1 (*gur*) 6 *GIN* (*i.e.*, female servants) *É.GAL a-na man-da-*[*at-ti-shi-na*], all of which passages show that *mandattu* was at this time a certain kind of "stipend," "wages," in the form of "wool," "garments," or "grain," *i.e.*, "food and clothing" for work performed (l. 25).

[4] *Shitkunu c. acc.* and *ana*, "to take something for something," "to make something to be something" (cf. 9 : 21, *a-na shi-bu-ti-ia* ᵐ*X. ù* ᵐ*Y. ásh-ta-ka-an*), here "to apply something as compensation for."

[5] If my emendation be correct—the traces visible speaking decidedly for *shú* (*ku* or *ù* being out of question)—then *shú-ú-bi-'u-ú* may be either (*a*) the infinitive III[1] of ופא, *i.e.*, *shuupu'u* = *shûpu'u* = *shûpû*. But the signification of this verb does not fit into the context. Or, what is more probable, we may consider it (*b*) as an infinitive III[1] of באה, *i.e.*, *shub'uiu* = *shub'û*. If this be true, there remain two peculiarities to be explained, viz.: (1) the long *û* in *shú-ú* and (2) the presence of the *i* in *bi*. For the graphically (not morphologically) long *û* cf. such forms as *lu-ú-ul-li-i*[*k*], 38 : 2, and *li-ish-pu-ú-ra-*[*am*]-*ma*, 39 : 23. With regard to the presence of the *i* in *bi* it should be noticed that we may have in Babylonian, resp. Assyrian, an euphonic *i* or *u after* the *first radical* in all those forms where this

31 [*ḫu*]*r-ḫu-ra-tì*[1] *be-lì li-she-bi-lam-ma*[2]	May my "Lord" send bleached(?) wool!
32 [*d*]*u-ul-li la a-ḫa-ad-dì*[3]	I have no pleasure in my work.
33 *ásh-shum* ^{amelu}*ishparê*(= *ISH. BAR*)^{mesh} *an-nu-ti*	As regards these weavers
34 *shá i-na* ^{alu}*Pa-an-Ba-lì*^{ki}[4] *ka-lu-ú*[5]	who are being held prisoners in *Pân-Bali*
35 *i-na Ú-pi-i*^{ki}[6] *a-na be-lì-ia aq-ta-bi*	(I beg to remind my Lord that) I have spoken to my "Lord" in *Upî* (about them)
36 *ù shá-la-shi-shú a-na mu-uḫ be-lì-ia*	and that I have written three times to my "Lord"
37 *al-tap-ra*	about them:
38 *be-lì li-ish-pu-ur-ma*	my "Lord" may (finally) give orders
39 *li-il-qu-ni-ish-shú-nu-tì*[7]	that they take them away.

II.

No. 55 (= C. B. M. 10,497). (Cf. photographic reproduction, Pl. III, 6, 7.)

Dispute about the exact words of a message sent by King *Burna-Buriash* with regard to the release of young slaves belonging to *Enlil-kidinni*, a slave-dealer. About 1440 B.C.

For introduction, transcription, translation, and notes see above, Chapter III, pp. 51ff.

radical generally is vowelless. With regard to an *euphonic i* after the *first radical* cf. among other forms *li-ki-ri-ku*(= *likrikû*), *H.*, I, 100 : 6; *i-qi-bu-ni*(= *iqbûni*), *H.*, III, 311, R. 8; *li-gi-ru-ru*(= *ligrurû*), *H.*, IV, 387, R. 24; *i-qi-ṭi-bu-ni-shu* (= *iqṭibûnishu*), *H.*, V, 515 : 9; *mu-sha-ki*(?)-*rik*(= *mushakrik*), *H.*, I, 21, R. 1; *ú-she-ḫi-liq*(= *ushehliq*), *H.*, IV, 430 : 7, and possibly *a-li-ki*(= *alqu*? However, *a-li-ki* = city is likewise to be considered), No. 29 : 14. With regard to the euphonic *a* after the originally vowelless first radical the following forms are interesting: *i-su-ḫu-ra*(= *isḫura*), *H.*, V, 515, R. 6; *i-zu-qu-pu*(= *izqupu*), *H.*, IV, 381 : 7; *lu-qu-bu-ki*(= *luqbuki*), *Maqlû*, I : 59. Cf. here also the Hebrew verbs with Chatef vowel under the first radical in the imperfect, Ges.-K., *Gr.*[25], §10, 2, notes *a*, *b*, on p. 49. *Shá-ú-bi-'u-ú*, then, as infinitive III[1] of באה stands for *shub'û*, the *i* being inserted to prevent the assimilation of the guttural to the preceding *b* (*shub'ûu* = *shub'û* = *shubbû*, which latter would be the infinitive II[1] of שׂבא, "to satisfy"). An infinitive III[II] of בוא (*shubu''u* = *shub''u* = *shubi'u*) is less probable. Delitzsch, *H. W. B.*, p. 161*a*, gives only a II[1] of באה with the signification "to seek," "to ask." III[1] would be causative and the sense might be: "there is no bleached wool in D. to make one ask for it," *i.e.*, there is none that one might, could ask for—hence the request of l. 31.

[1] See note 2 on preceding page.

[2] For *lishebilam* = *lushebilam*, see Chapter III, p. 53, note 1.

[3] *I.e.*, "I am disgusted with my job."

[4] "The face of *Bâl*" = an Amurritish name? Probably to be sought in the neighborhood of *Dûr-Kuri-Galzu*.

[5] Cf. *B. E.*, XIV, 2 : 8, five slaves of Enlil-kidini who are *i-na Bît-*^{m} ^{ilu}*En-lil-ki-di-ni ka-lu-ú*; *l.c.*, XV, 152 : 14, the slave . . . *shá i-na* ^{alu}*IM*^{ki} *ka-lu-ú*; *l.c.*, XIV, 135 : 3, *i-na ki-li* . . . . *ik-la-shú-ma*. In 3 : 33, 42 | 15 : 5, 14, *ka-lu-ú* resp. *ka-la-a* signifies the "destruction by water," cf. Delitzsch, *H. W. B.*, p. 329*b* under II כלה: *ka-lu-ú shá me-e*.

[6] Although not registered by Clay, yet a ^{mâtu}*Ú-pi-i* occurs, *e.g.*, in *B. E.*, XIV, 132 : 43, 16, 52.

[7] For ll. 33ff. cf. Chapter IV, p. 71.

III.

No. 24 (= C. B. M. 19,793). (Cf. photographic reproduction, Pls. I, II, 1–5.)

Official report about various occurrences, among which a disastrous flood, under a hitherto unknown Cassite King. About 1430 B.C.

The contents of this letter may be conveniently subdivided into the following parts:

(*a*) *Introduction* and *address*, poetic in its arrangement and conception, ll. 1–10.

(*b*) The *complaint of the tenants of the fields of "The Lord of Lands" about* the actions of *Etelbu mâr* ^{m}*Ush-bu-la*[1] in causing waters to overwhelm their possessions, ll. 11–17.

(*c*) The city *Mannu-gir-Rammân*, which the writer held as fief of the crown, *is deluged* by "rains out of the heavens and floods out of the depths," ll. 18–23.

(*d*) *Gates and cattle are destroyed;* there is nothing left wherewith to keep alive or pay the inhabitants, ll. 24–29.

(*e*) *Report* about the request of the governor *Mâr*-^{m}[. . .] for a new gate, ll. 29–31.

(*f*) *Request* that the King may *look into the affairs of* ^{m}*Ina-É.KUR.GAL*, ll. 32–34.

(*g*) The *writer's urgent request* to the King *to act quickly* and give an immediate answer, ll. 34–37.

For the personality of the *King* and of *his father Nazi*-^{ilu}*Enlil* see above under Chapter IV, pp. 68ff., where also the notes to ll. 24–29 will be found. For the notes to ll. 1–10, ll. 18–23, ll. 29–31, ll. 36–37 see Chapter III, pp. 46ff., 49ff., 43ff., 51. The letter in its completeness reads:

1	*a-na be-lí-ia as-mi lu-ul-li-i zêri*(= *KUL*) *ishtu*(= *TA*) *shame*-[*e*]	To my "Lord"—: Glorious in splendor, Seed out of Heaven;
2	*la ma-ir an-ni gù-ra-di li-e-i it-pi-sh*[*i*]	Not summoning punishment, Strong, powerful, wise one;
3	*nu-ùr aḫê*(= *SHESH*)^{mesh}*-shu PI-in-di-e na-ma-a-ri*	Light of his brothers, Ordering the dawn;
4	*ki-ib kab-tu-ti ra-ásh-ba-nu-ú-ti*	Ruler of mighty and Terrible lords;

[1] Cf. now also the *Bît*-^{m}*Ush-bu-la* in *B. E.*, Series D, IV, p. 118, col. III, 5, where it is reported that it adjoined a district "which had been given to the 'Lord of Lands.'"

5 *e-pi-ir um-ma-ni pa-ásh-shur ni-shi*	Food of the people, Platter of man;
6 *e-tel ki-na-te-e-shú shá* *ilu* *A-nu* *ilu* *En-lil u* *ilu* *É.A*	Hero of his clan, Whom the triad of gods
7 *ù* *ilu* *Be-lit-ì-li* (= *NI.NI*) *ki-ib-ti du-um-ki*	Together with *Bêlit* Presented a fief
8 *ù mi-ish-ri-e ish-ru-ku-ú-shú*	Tending towards grace And righteousness—
9 *be-li-ia ki-bé-ma um-ma* *m* *Kal-bu ip-ru*	to my Lord speak, thus saith *Kalbu*, thy dust
10 *ù ar-du na-ra-am-ka-ma*	and thy loving servant.
11 *an-nu-um-ma-a*[1] *shú-ú ki-i ra-ma-ni a-na*	Behold that one, though I myself have
12 *be-li-ia ap-ki-du-ma* *m* *E-tel-bu mâr* *m* *Ish-bu-la*	recommended him to my Lord, that *Etelbu*, son of *Ushbula*,
13 [ ]*-mat(?)-su ù a-na pa-an* *ilu* *Man-nu-gi-ir-* *ilu* *IM*	has .... his .... even up to the city of *Mannu-gir-Rammân*
14 [ ] *ṣa-ab-ta-ku ash-bu eqlu*(= *A.SHAG*) *shá EN.KUR.KUR*	he has .... which I possess. The tenant of the field of "*The Lord of Lands*"
15 [*um-ma-a a-na* ....]*-mi-ia-ma i-na me-e i-di-la-an-ni*[2]	[came and spoke thus before my .....] "By means of water he has encircled me."
16 [*âlu?*]*ḫal* *shá it-ti-ia lu ash-bu-tu*	The cities which are with me—be they inhabited
17 *lu na-du-tu*[3] *shá EN.KUR.KUR i-na*	or be they doomed—and which belong to

[1] *An-nu-um-ma-a* = *an(n)umma*. Cf. *um-ma-a* = *um-ma* and see also *Ḫammurabi*, 2 : 10; S. 273 : 17; C. T., IV, 27 (B[1] 329) : 10. Jensen, *K. B.*, VI[1], 175, 527, translates *anumma* by "*nun, sofort.*" A translation: "Grace (please grant unto me) if I speak as follows (*um-ma-a*)" is likewise possible. Cf. the dialogue between Abraham and the "angel of the Lord," Gen. 18, 16ff.

[2] *Edêlu ina mê*, not "to shut off from water," but *edêlu*, because a synonym of *sanâqu* = "to shut in" (Jensen, *K. B.*, VI[1], p. 110), has to be translated here "has shut me in, encircled me, enclosed me with or by water." As such it evidently points to the *i-na la-me-e na-di*, l. 20, *e-ka-ku*, l. 26, and *i-si-ru*, l. 28. The tenant or inhabitant (notice the singl. instead of the plural!) of the fields of god *EN.KUR.KUR* (*i.e.*, either *Enlil* or *NIN.IB*; for omission of *ilu* before names of gods see p. 8, n. 8), which were situated in the immediate neighborhood of the city *Mannu-gir-Rammân*, complains of his being encircled by "waters" through the negligence or spite of *Etelbu*, who failed to keep the canals clean. These "waters" became so fierce that even *Mannu-gir-Rammân* was surrounded (*i-na la-me-e na-di*). Added to this "the rains and floods," the city's destruction was complete.

[3] Root *nadû*. The sense is: The complaint is made by all inhabitants—by those who have and those who have not yet suffered from the effects of the inundation. The *shá EN.KUR.KUR* is parallel to that of l. 14—belongs, therefore, to [*âlu?* or *eqlu?*]*ḫal*, l. 16.

pa-an me-e i-ḫa-bu-bu	"*The Lord of Lands*" cry out on account of the waters!
18 *ù* ^{alu}*Man-nu-gi-ir-*^{ilu}*IM shá sharru (= LUGAL) ra-in ga-[ti]*	Even the city *Mannu-gir-Rammân* with which the King is entrusting me
19 *ù be-lí a-na MIR.NIT.TA an-nu-ti id-di-na*	and which my "Lord" has handed over to these conscribers
20 *i-na la-me-e na-di zu-un-na i-na sha-me-e*	is destroyed by inundations: rains out of the heavens
21 *ù mi-la i-na nak-bi ki-i i-di-nu sha-ku*	and floods out of the depths are, when (or after) he (*i.e.*, my Lord) had handed her (the city) over (*sc.* to the conscribers), overflooding her!
22 *âlu-ki shá be-lí i-ri-man-ni i-na la-me-e*	Yes, the city with which my "Lord" has entrusted me is destroyed
23 *na-di a-na ba-la-ad a-i-ka-a lul-lik*	by inundations! Where shall I go to save myself?
24 *ù abullu(= KÁ.GAL) erâ*^{mesh} *DA*^{mesh} *ù laḫru(= GANAM) shattu-II shá ish-tu b[é]-na-ti*	Also the mighty bronze-gates together with the two-year-old ewes which (were kept there) since the time
25 *shá* ^{m}*Na-zi-*^{ilu}*En-lil a-bi-ka ù adi(= EN) ûmi*^{mi}	of *Nazi-Enlil*, thy father, even unto (this) day,
26 *[e]-ka-ku(?) ù i-na-an-na be-lí it-ti-[di shá]*	(the floods) have destroyed! And now my "Lord" knows that
27 *[i(l)-la]-ka-an-ni i-na-an-na ki-i i-li-[ka-an-n]i*	they will come to me; now, when they are there (*i.e.*, have come),
28 *[ù zu-un-n]a LU(?)*^{mesh} *laḫru(= GAN-AM) shattu-II i-si-ru mi-na-a[?]*	what shall I take and give, seeing that the floods have encircled the sheep
29 *[lul]-qa-am-ma lu-ud-di-in ù Mâr-*^{m}*[. . .]*	and the two-year-old ewes? And *Mâr-*^{m}[. . .],
30 *bêl paḫâti(= EN.NAM) a-na ardi-ka ki-i il-li-ku um-ma-a*	the governor, when he had come to thy servant, said:
31 *abulla(= KÁ.GAL)*^{la} *i-ma-ad-di tu-shá-an-na-ma laddan(= SE)-na*	"They make lamentations on account of the gate! Duplicate it!"
32 *ù* ^{m}*I-na-É.KUR.GAL ardi-ka shá a-na be-lí-ia*	And *Ina-É.KUR.GAL*, thy servant, whom I have recommended

33 *ap-ki-du ash-shú*[1] *di-na-[ni-]ia*	to my "Lord"—on my account,
34 *be-lì a-ma-as li-mur-ma a-ḫi-ti-ia*[2]	my "Lord," look into his affairs! If I am to get out
35 *mu-ush-shú-ra-ku*[3] *ḫa-am-dish li-ta-al-lik*[4]	of my predicament then (my Lord) may act (lit. come) quickly.
36 *ù a-na-ku i-tu b[e-lì]-ia a-na a-la-a-ki*[5]	And I, the *itû* of my "Lord," though I have written to the "King"
37 *a-na sharri(= LUGAL) ki-i ash-[pu-ra] sharru(= LUGAL) ul i-di-na-an-ni.*	concerning (my) coming, yet the "King" has not given me (an answer or permission).

IV.

No. 9 (= C. B. M. 11,635).

Banâ-sha-Marduk reports to King *Kuri-Galzu* about the revolt which has broken out in *Bît-^{m} ^{ilu}Sin-issaḫra*. About 1390 B.C.

Above (pp. 4ff.) it has been shown that our writer, *Banâ-sha-Marduk*, lived between the 20th year of *Kuri-Galzu* and the 11th year of *Kadashman-Turgu*, *i.e.*, during a space of about forty-three years. We may assign this letter, therefore, to the time of *Kuri-Galzu*, and this the more because the *Bît-^{m} ^{ilu}Sin-issaḫra*, so named after the head of the royal storehouse (*karû*) *ASH.TAB.BA.GAN.TUG*, situated in *Kandurê^{ki}*, *Sin-issaḫra*, flourished, in all probability, principally during the time of *Kuri-Galzu*.[6] From ll. 19, 20 we may conclude that our writer was a master builder, who, while engaged in building a gate, received news about the revolt in *Bît-^{m} ^{ilu}Sin-issaḫra*, which he, as faithful servant, communicated instantly to his Lord, King *Kuri-Galzu*. Is this revolt connected in one way or another with the uprising of the Cassites under the *be-lì*, the son of *Nazi-^{ilu}Enlil*, mentioned in No. 24?

The contents are the following:

[1] Not *ap-ki-du-ash-shú*, but *ash-shu di-na-[ni]-ia* is to be read. *Ash-shu di-na-ni-ia* again is the same as the well-known *ásh-shum-mi-ia* (27 : 11) = *ana shú-mi-ia* (S. 274 : 17, 4) = *ásh-shú-mi-ia* (C. T., VI, 32 (= B[1] 534) : 4), of the Hammurabi period. From this it follows that *dinânu* = *shumu*, *i.e.*, "all that which expresses the essence of a being," "the being itself" (cf. שם יהוה), or, as Delitzsch, *H. W. B.*, p. 224*b*, gives it, "*das Selbst*," see also p. 58, note 2.

[2] For *aḫîtu sc. shîmtu*, see *H. W. B.*, p. 41*b*.

[3] *I.e.*, "if I am to leave and thus be out of it forever."

[4] Not *lû* + *tallik* but *lâ* + *itallik*, I^{2} *alâku*.

[5] In view of *li-ta-al-lik*, "may act (quickly)!" and *alkam*, "hurry!" etc., we might translate here: "though I have written to my Lord to hasten (*sc.* the reply to my last letter), yet the King has not adjudged me worthy (*sc.* of an answer)." In this case *i-di-na-an-ni* might be derived from דין (= *idîn-anni*), instead of *nadânu*.

[6] See pp. 79, 81, 110, 116.

(*a*) Exhortation to rejoice, ll. 6—?

(*b*) News about the revolt in *Bît-*$^{m\ ilu}$*Sin-issaḫra*, upon information received from ^{m}*É.SAG.IL-zu-ri-ia*, ll. 15–19.

(*c*) The gate is finished, ll. 19, 20.

(*d*) The truth of the communications made in this letter may be verified by calling upon the prefects of *Rakanu* and *Bît-*^{m}*Ki-din-ni*.

1 *ardi-ka* ^{m}*Bana(=KAK)-a-sha-*^{ilu}*Marduk*	Thy servant *Banâ-sha-Marduk*;
2 *a-na di-na-an be-lì-ia lul-lik*	before the presence of my "Lord" may I come!
3 *a-na âlu-ki ù ṣîri* (= *EDIN*) *shá be-lì-ia*	To the city and the fields of my "Lord"
4 *shú-ul-mu*	greeting!
5 *um-ma-a a-na be-lì-ia-ma*	The following to my "Lord":
6 *ad-ru*[1] *shú*[2]*-te-su-uk*	Let the palace rejoice
7 *ù ma*(?)*-ḫi-ṣa*[3] [. . . .]*-ma*	and the soldiers let . . . .
8 *si*(?)*-pi-*[*ri*[4] . . . .]	and the *si-pi-ri* let . . . .
9 *um-m*[*a a-na be-lì-i*]*a-ma*	speaking thus to my "Lord":
10 [. . . .] *shá be-lì*	. . . . which my "Lord"
11 [. . .]	
12 *a-*[. . . .$^{m\ ilu}$*IM-ra*]*-im-zêr*	
. . . . brake	
13 [. . . .] *ú-ba-á*[*sh-shu*?][5]	
14 [. . . .]*-ú-ma ki-ki-i*[6] *ṣi*(? or *ad*?)-[. . .],	. . . .
15 ^{m}*É.SAG.ÌL-zu-ri-ia ar*[*di-ka*]	*É.SAG.ÌL-zuri-ia*, thy servant,

[1] For *adru* cf. Johnson, *J. A. O. S.*, XIX, p. 52, perhaps "enclosure"; Behrens, *L. S. S.*, II[1], p. 47, note 1, "*Palastgemach.*"

[2] So is to be connected, not *ad-ru-shú te-su-uk* (which latter had to be in this case *tesik*). *Shú-te-su-uk*, either infinitive or permansive III[2] of אסק, "to glorify" (Delitzsch's אסך, *H. W. B.*, p. 108*b*, and אסק, *l.c.*, p. 110*b*, belong together).

[3] *Ma*(?)*-ḫi-ṣa* might stand here for *mundaḫḫiṣu*, "soldier."

[4] Cf. with this the ^{amelu}*si-pi-ri*, Delitzsch, *H. W. B.*, p. 509*b*. A reading *e-pi-ri* seems to be against the context.

[5] Very doubtful. Might be II[1] of באה, "to see," or possibly a II[1] of either בוא or בשה.

[6] The context being mutilated, it is difficult to tell whether to connect [. . .]*-ma*^{ki} *ki i-ṣi-*[. . .] or [. . .]*-ma ki-ki-i ṣi*(or *ad*)-[. . .].

16 *shakin*(= *GAR*)^{im}[1] *de*(= *NE*)-*mi shá Bît*-^{m} ^{ilu}*Sin*(= *XXX*)-*is-saḫ-ra*	is reporting about *Bît-Sin-issaḫra* (saying:)
17 *I C ummâni*(= *ṢAB*)$^{hi.a}$[2] *gi-in-na-tá*[3]	"100 men killed, while the
18 *ki-i ig-nu-na ṣâbê*(= *ṢAB*)^{mesh} *shá be-lì-ia*	families were settling down, the soldiers of my Lord."
19 *ir-ta-pi-is*[4] *ù bâba at-ta-di*(?)-*ish*	As regards the gate—I renewed
20 *ib-ta-ta-ak*[5]	it, it is finished.
21 *a-na shi-bu-ti-ia* ^{m} ^{ilu}*Nergal-Ba-ni*	*Nergal-Bâni*,
22 *ḫa-za-na shá* ^{ilu}*Ra-ka-nu*	the prefect of *Rakanu*,
23 *ù ḫa-za-an-na shá Bît*-^{m}*Ki-din-ni*	and the prefect of *Bît-Kidinni* I have
24 *ásh-ta-ka-an*	made to be my witnesses.

V.

No. 29 (= C. B. M. 11,956).

A letter of *Marduk-mushallim*, head of the storehouse at *Dûr-Enlil*, to King *Kuri-Galzu*. About 1400 B.C.

A certain *Marduk-mushallim* endorses in *B. E.*, XIV, 151 : 5, the payment of a specified amount of grain (*SHE*) as *ri-mu-tum* (a kind of wages) to a lady of the *bît a-mi-la-ti* ("house of female (slave)s") and as *SIGISSE.SIGISSE* ("offerings") to ^{ilu}*Sin*. The position[6] which the name of *Marduk-mushallim* occupies on this tablet makes it certain that he was the head of the storehouse at *Dûr*-^{ilu}*En-lil*^{ki}. This tablet is dated simply the "16th year" (l. 7). As only the first four kings (*Burna-Buriash* to *Kadashman-Turgu*) reigned sixteen or more years each, it is reasonably certain that our letter belongs to the earlier Cassite kings known from the Temple Archives. We may, however, go a step farther. The person ^{m}*A-na-tukulti*(= *KU*)-*ilu*(= *AN*)-*ma*, mentioned in ll. 9, 15, I propose to identify with one of the witnesses mentioned

[1] If *shakin dêmi* were here a title, its position would have to be before *ardi-ka*: *shakin dêmi ardi-ka*. I take it, therefore, as a permansive: "is just now (while I am writing this) reporting about (*shá*)." Cf. here also p. 52, note 5*d*. In l. 17, which contains the report, *um-ma-a* has been left out, as is often the case in our letters.

[2] To bring out the difference in writing between *ṢAB*$^{hi.a}$ and *ṢAB*^{mesh} I transcribed as given above. Both (*ṢAB*$^{hi.a}$ and *ṢAB*^{mesh}) signify, however, at this time very often, if not always, simply "men, workmen" (*ummâni*), see p. 35, note 1.

[3] *Gi-in-na-ta ki-i ig-nu-na* = *qinnâta* (fem. plur.) *ki iqnunâ* (3d plur. fem. of קנן) = *qinnâta qinna kî iqnunâ*, *i.e.*, "while the families (employed on the Temple properties) were building a nest," "were settling down." For the signification of *qinnu*, *qinnâti* at this time cf., *e.g.*, *B. E.*, XIV, 126 : 7 | XV, 160 : 29, *qin-ni*; *B. E.*, XIV, 111 : 7, *qin-na-a-ti*.

[4] *Rapâsu* here in the sense of "to kill" (*sha da-a-ki*), Delitzsch, *H. W. B.*, p. 626*a*. The singular being employed, because "objects counted (*ṢAB*$^{hi.a}$ are such objects) are construed as singulars," see p. 95, note 6.

[5] I^{2} of *patâqu* (*H. W. B.*, p. 554*a*; Jensen, *K. B.*, VI^{1}, p. 319) here with passive signification: "it is built, finished."

[6] See also the position of the name of *Innanni* in such tablets of "endorsement," Chapter IV, c, p. 86, note 4.

in a document from the 4th year of *Ku*[1]-[*ri-Gal-zu*], *B. E.*, XIV, 11 : 16. *Erba-Marduk* of l. 4 would, therefore, have to be identified with *Erba-Marduk*, the son of *Sin-nûr-mâti*, *B. E.*, XIV, 19 : 23 (dated in the 13th year of *Kuri-Galzu*). Taking all these facts into consideration I do not hesitate to see in the *be-lì* of l. 2 and in the *LUGAL* of l. 6 King *Kuri-Galzu*, to whom this letter has been addressed. *Marduk-mushallim*, then, was during the reign of *Kuri-Galzu* the head of the storehouse at *Dûr-^{ilu}Enlil^{ki}*, which place must have been situated at a river, resp. canal, deep and safe enough for the *lallû-ships* (*i.e.*, "*Fracht(?)-schiffe*").

The contents of this letter are:

(*a*) The royal provender will be shipped per *lallâ-ships* by the 16th of this month, ll. 4-8.

(*b*) Request that the king send certain men to remove the workmen and clients and to return them to their owner, ll. 9–18.

1 [*ardi-ka* ^{m}]^{ilu}*Marduk-mu-*[*shal-*]*lim*	Thy servant *Marduk-mushallim*;
2 [*a-na di-n*]*a-an be-lì-ia lul-lik*	before the presence of my "Lord" may I come,
3 *um-ma-a a*]*-na be-lì-ia-ma*	speaking thus to my "Lord":
4 [*ásh-shum GAR.LUGAL*[2]] *shá* ^{m}*Erba* (= *SU*)-^{ilu}*Marduk*	As regards [the royal provender] which
5 [*ardi-ka i*]*k-shú-da*	*Erba-Marduk*, thy servant, was to have taken,
6 [*um-ma-a*] *akâli* (= *GAR*) *sharri* (*LUGAL*) *ûmu* 16^{kam}	(I beg to say that) the men shall bring the royal provender
7 *a-na* ^{isu}*mà-là*(= *lal*)*-al-la-a*[3]	upon the *lallâ*-ships
8 *ummâni*(= *ṢAB*)$^{hi a}$ *li-su-ú-ni*	by the 16th (of this month).
9 ^{m}*A-na-tukulti*(= *KU*)*-ilu*(= *AN*)*-ma*	*Ana-tukulti-ilu-ma*
10 *ù* ^{m} ^{ilu}*Sukal*(= *LUGH*)*-she-mi*	and *Sukal-shemi*
11 *ù ummâni*(= *ṢAB*)^{mesh} *shá a-la-ak-shú-nu*[4]	and the men of their company
12 *shú-up-ra-am-ma*	send (give orders)
13 *li-zu-ú-ma lil-li-ku*[5]	that they come,

[1] *Kudur-Enlil* is out of question, because he reigned only six resp. eight years, see p. 1.

[2] Emendation according to l. 6. Very doubtful. Cf., however, the *MA.GAR.RA* of the *Ḫammurabi Letter*, No. 31 : 16, which likewise was put upon the ^{isu}*mà-lal*.

[3] For ^{isu}*mà*(= *elippu*)*-là-al-la-a* see Delitzsch, *H. W. B.*, p. 414*a* (left untranslated) and King, *Letters of Ḫammurabi*, III, p. 7, note 2 (to No. 34 : 10), "processional boat."

[4] Lit., "of their going" (*alâk* – infinitive), "their following."

[5] Lit., "that they may go out and go (come)."

14 *ù ummâni(= ṢAB)*[mesh] *u ki-din-na ma-la shá a-li-ki*[1]	so that *Ana-tukulti-ilu-ma* may return to him
15 [m]*A-na-tukulti(=KU)-ilu(=AN)-ma*	all the men and protégés (clients)
16 *a-na pa-ni-shú li-ter-ra-am-ma*[2]	which I have taken.
17 *ḫa-a]m-di-ish*[3]	Let them do it
18 *lik-sh]ú-da*[4]	quickly.

VI.

No. 14 (= C. B. M. 19,799).

The superintendent of the Temple weaveries reports to King *Kuri-Galzu* about the administration of his office. About 1400 B.C.

As the name of the writer is broken away, it is rather difficult to assign this letter to a definite period. If, however, the emendation of l. 16, *Bît-*[m]*Ki[din-ni]*, be correct, I would refer this letter to the time between the 20th year of *Kuri-Galzu* and the 11th of *Kadashman-Turgu.*[5] Our writer was apparently the royal superintendent of the Temple weaveries. Where these weaveries were situated cannot be made out. Noteworthy in this letter is the statement that one weaver had been a fugitive for one whole year, until he was brought back from the "house of *Kidinni.*" That the Temple employees fled very often from their place of service is well known from the Temple Archives; cf. *e.g.*, Clay, *B. E.*, XIV, p. 34. But that such a fugitive employee, when recaptured, would not be punished is new.[6] Nothing, apparently, is said here of such a punishment of either the fugitive slave or of the man who harbored him, nor is the reward of the two shekels mentioned.

The contents are the following:

(*a*) The . . . . have been put up, ll. 4–7.

(*b*) The King must wait for the garments, ll. 8, 9.

[1] As indicated by the translation, I consider this form to stand for *shá alqu*; cf. p. 100, note. If one prefers he may take it in the sense of "as many as are of (= in) the city (= *áli-ki*)," see p. 11, note 2.

[2] Stands here for *lutêra-ma*, *lu* + *u* of the 3d pers. becomes at this time always *li*. To "whom" shall he return the men? To *Erba-Marduk*?

[3] Cf. here *ḫa-an-di-ish*, 80 : 13 | 93 : 5; *ḫu-am-dish*, 24 : 35, and *ḫa-mu-ut-ta*, 49 : 10 | 51 : 10 | 68 : 12 | 83 : 24 | 92 : 24.

[4] *I.e.*, "May they (*Ana-tukulti-ilu-ma* and the other men, ll. 9f.) come, take the men, and return them to him quickly." *Likshudâ*=*likshudû*, so better than singular : "may he, *i.e.*, *Ana-tukulti-ilu-ma*, do it."

[5] See the remarks to 9 : 21 above, Chapter I (p. 4ff.).

[6] A recaptured slave was put to death at the time of *Ḫammurabi*, *Code*, 8 : 30–36. A man who harbors in his house a fugitive slave was likewise put to death, *Ḫammurabi Code*, 8 : 37–48. To him who captures a fugitive slave are awarded two shekels of money, *Ḫammurabi Code*, 8 : 49–58.

(*c*) The wool just sheared has been removed, ll. 10–12.

(*d*) The fine wool is all gone, l. 12.

(*e*) A fugitive weaver has been recaptured and returned by *Bît-Kidinni*, ll. 13–17.

(*f*) Only one workman bargained for has been received from *Kîsh*,[1] ll. 18–21.

1 [*ardi-ka* ^{m}*X. . . . a-na di-na-an*]	Thy servant X.; before the presence
2 [*be-lì-ia lu-ul*]-*l*[*i-ik*]	of my "Lord" may I come!
3 [*a-na GANAM.LU*] *ù bît* [*be-lì-ia shul-mu*]	To the cattle and the house of my "Lord" greeting!
4 [. . . .] *da*[. . . .]-*ti*	The . . . .
5 [*sh*]*á id-*[*di-*]*nu-ni*	which they (were to) have given,
6 *be-lì li-mu-ùr*	my "Lord" may behold,
7 *id-du-ú-ni* (! sign *bi*)[2]	they have put up.
8 *i-na bu-ut lubushti*(= *KU*)$^{ḫi.a}$	For the garments
9 *be-lì la i-sa-an-ni-iq-an-ni*[3]	do not press me, my "Lord."
10 *shipâtu*(= *SIG*)$^{ḫi.a}$ *shá na-gid*^{mesh}	The wool of the shepherds,
11 *ma-la ba-aq-na*[4]	as much as has been sheared,
12 *it-qu ba-ni-tum*[5] *ia-nu*	they have removed. Good (*sc.* wool) is not here.
13 ^{amelu}*ishparu*(= *USH.BAR*) *ishten*^{en}	One weaver,
14 *shá ul-tu ishten shattu*(= *MU*)	who was a fugitive
15 *ḫa-al-qu*	for one year,
16 *ul-tu Bît-*^{m}*Ki-*[*din-ni*]	they have received
17 *il-te-qu-ni*	from (out of) *Bît-Kidinni*.
18 *ishten*^{en} *amelu li-ib-bu*[6]	Only one of
19 *ummâni*(= *ṢAB*)$^{ḫi.a}$ *ra-ak-su-ú-ti*[7]	the stipulated workmen
20 *ul-tu Kîsh*^{ki}	they have received
21 *il-te-qu-ni*	from *Kîsh*.

[1] For the different cities called *Kîsh*, see Jensen, *Z. A.*, XV, p. 214ff., and Hommel, *Grundriss*[2], pp. 338, 383-390.

[2] For the sign *bi* as variant for *ni, lì*, see "Names of Professions" under *Ḫa-bi*(!)-*gal-ba-ti-i*. A possible derivation from נדב (cf. *nidbû, nindabû*) would be less probable and quite peculiar in formation, (1) because of the long *û* (but cf. p. 129, l. 23), (2) because of the *i* in *bi* (standing for *bû*). The object which was "put up" is unfortunately broken away.

[3] *I.e.*, wait a little longer for them.

[4] For *baqânu* = *baqâmu*, "to cut off," "to shear," see now Hinke, *B. E.*, Series D, IV, pp. 263*a*, 177. Besides the passages quoted there cf. also *B. E.*, XIV, 128 : 1, *SIG*$^{ḫi.a}$ *bu-qu-nu*, and *l.c.*, 42 : 12, *i-ba-qa-nu* (said of *akâlu, shikaru*, and *mi-ri-esh-tum*, hence here at least it cannot mean "to cut off" or "to shear"). See also *a-ba-qa-am-ma*, 2 : 10.

[5] For *ba-ni-tum* (*sc. shipâtu*), fem. of *banû* (syn. of *damqu*), in the sense of "good," "nice," "fine," etc., see Jensen, *K. B.*, VI[1], p. 112.

[6] For *libbû* = *ina libbi shá* cf. Delitzsch, *A. G.*[2], § 108, pp. 226f.

[7] Cf. here the *dup-pi ri-ki-ish*(!)-*ti shá* ^{m}*In-na-an-nu a-na* ^{amelu}*RIQ*^{mesh} *ù KA.ZID.DA ir-ku-su* (*B. E.*, XIV, 42: 1), *i.e.*, "the (tablet of) stipulations upon which I. has agreed with the R. and K."

VII.

No. 83 (C. B. M. 3315). (Cf. photographic reproduction, Pl. XII, 29, 30.)

A letter of complaints, requests, and threats written by the governor *Errish-apal-iddina* to the bursar-in-chief, *Innanni*. Time of *Kuri-Galzu*, about 1400 B.C.

Above, pp. 2ff., it has been shown that *Innanni*, the chief bursar of the Nippurian Temple storehouses, lived and transacted business during a period extending at least from the 18th year of *Kuri-Galzu* to the 2d year of *Nazi-Maruttash*, and that *Errish-apal-iddina*, the governor of *Dûr*(resp. *Bît*)-*Errish-apal-iddina*^{ki}, flourished from the 13th year of *Kuri-Galzu* to the 24th year of *Nazi-Maruttash*. *Innanni*, though frequently mentioned on tablets apparently emanating from the neighboring towns around Nippur, where he was at intervals looking after the interests or possessions of Enlil,[1] was yet a resident of Nippur, cf. *B. E.*, XV, 115 : 5 | 135 : 6, *Bît-*^{m}*In-na-an-nu(ni) Nippur* (= *En-lil*)^{ki}. We also saw that during the reign of *Kuri-Galzu*, *i.e.*, at the time when ^{m}*In-na-an-ni* was bursar-in-chief, ^{m} ^{ilu}*Sin-issaḫra* was the head of the *royal* or Palace storehouse (*karû*), named *ÍSH.TAB.BA.GAN.TUG*^{ki}.[2] But, though the head of that storehouse, he was still subordinate to *Innanni*. This follows not only from No. 85 : 8, 9, where *Innanni* is commanded to give to *Sin-issaḫra* the "wages for certain persons," or from *B. E.*, XV, 50, where he (*Sin-issaḫra*) receives grain from *Innanni* "per order of the Palace," but more particularly from such passages as *B. E.*, XIV, 35 : 3, where it is reported that a certain ^{m} ^{ilu}*PA.KU-ma-lik-AN*^{mesh} receives in ^{ilu}*Karû ÍSH.TAB.BA.GAN.TUG* a certain amount of grain as horse-feed from (*ina qât*) ^{m}*In-na-an-ni*, which shows clearly that *Innanni* must have had and actually did have authority also over the *Palace storehouses*; in other words, *Innanni*, though bursar-in-chief of the Temple storehouses, was *ipso facto* also the chief bursar of the Palace storehouses—he was both a *Temple* and a *royal official*, hence his successor, *Martuku*, is expressly called an *a-rad LUGAL* (*B. E.*, XIV, 56 : 9), a "servant of the king." *Innanni*[3] seems to have been a rather slow and stingy official; the only way to make him live up to his obligations was by threatening him (cf. ll. 12 and 27ff. and 85 : 5).

The contents of this letter are:

(*a*) Complaint over *Innanni's* negligence, ll. 3, 4.

(*b*) Request to urge the workmen not to leave the city, ll. 5-7.

[1] See above, p. 2, note 13.

[2] See Chapter IV, *c*, pp. 79, 81; cf. p. 116.

[3] If the term *aḫu* of No. 86 : 19 is to be taken in its literal sense, *Innanni* would be a brother of ^{m}*E-mi-da-*^{ilu}*Marduk*, *l. c.*, l. 18. See here the interpretation of that passage by Prof. Hilprecht, above, p. 25, note 1, and cf. *Emid-ana-Marduk*, p. 71! Is *Emida* = *Emid* + *ana* (*an* = *am* = *a*)? If so, this would explain the exalted position of Innanni, *i.e.*, Innanni would have been a brother of the *bêlí* of No. 21.

(*c*) Comply with the wishes of the *RIQ* officials, ll. 8, 9.

(*d*) Request coupled with threat, ll. 9–13.

(*e*) Give barley to *Mâr-Tadu*, l. 14.

(*f*) Pay the barley to the *RIQ* of *Shelibi* only in the "presence of the city," ll. 15–18.

(*g*) Thirteen oxen are missing, ll. 19–21.

(*h*) Pay the barley to *Sin-apal-êrish*, ll. 22, 23.

(*i*) Hurry up and pay the seed-corn to "the city," ll. 24–26.

(*k*) Complaint coupled with two threats in the form of accusations, ll. 27–37.

This letter reads:

1 [*a-na* ^m^] *In-na-an-ni ki-bé-ma*	To *Innanni* speak,
2 *um-ma* ^m^ ^ilu^*Errish*(*t*)(= *NIN.IB*)-*apal* (= *TUR.USH*) -*iddina* (= *SE*) ^*r*^[^*a*^-*ma*]	thus saith *Errish-apal-iddina*:
3 *um-ma-a am-mi-ni ash-pu-r*[*a-ak-ku*]	Why have I sent word to thee
4 *la ta-al-li-i-m*[*a*[1]?]	and thou hast not come up?
5 *um-ma-a ummâni*(= *SAB*)^*hi a*^ *an-nu-ti*[?]	Also the following: As regards these men
6 *shá ash-pu-ra-ak-ku tu-sh*[*e-ir-shú*]-*nu-ti-ma*[2]	concerning whom I have sent to thee— "(so) urge them
7 *âlu-ki la mu-ush-shú-u*[*r*]	not to leave the city."
8 *shá* 5 ^*amelu*^*RIQ*^*mesh*^ *shá Nippur* (= *EN.LIL*)^*ki*^ [^*i*^]	As regards the 5 *RIQ* of Nippur—
9 *ku-ri-ib-shú-nu-ti-i-ma*[3] *shá* [*um-mâni*(= *SAB*)^*hi*^]^*a mesh*^	"comply with their wishes!" As regards the workmen—
10 *it-ti Ni-ib-bu-ri-i nam-ṣ*[*a-a*]*r-ta*	"let them, together with the Nippurians,
11 *shú-um-ḫi-ir-shú-nu-ti*	receive the *namṣartu*-vessels.

[1] For the long *i* cf. *ku-ri-ib-shú-nu-ti-i-ma*, l. 9. The traces of -*ma*(?) speak rather for -*ka*. In view of *li-ish-bu-u-ra-am-ma*, 39 : 23, a form *ta-al-li-i-ka* would not be impossible.

[2] *Tu-she-*[*ir-sh*]*ú-nu-ti* is supplied according to l. 36, *tu-she-ir*. Both forms may be taken (*a*) either as a II[1] of ישר (= *tu-iashshir, tu'ashshir, tushshir, tu-she-ir*), "*in den richtigen Zustand versetzen*," Delitzsch, *H. W. B.*, p. 311*a*, or (*b*) they may be (and this is more probable) a II[1] of אשר (= *tu'ashshir*, etc., as above). According to Jensen, *K. B.*, VI[1], p. 409, 410, *ashâru* is a synonym of both *paqâdu* and *sanâqu*. For *sanâqu* in the sense of "to press, to urge," see 14 : 8. Cf. also for אשר Meissner, *Supplem.*, p. 13 (= K. 4587. Obv. 6); Delitzsch, *A. L.*[4]; Zimmern, *K. A. T.*[3], p. 121. The sense apparently is: "urge them by putting them into the right frame of mind." A II[1] of ושר is excluded here.

[3] On account of *shú-um-ḫi-ir-shu-nu-ti*, l. 11, and *tu-ul-te-ḫi-ir-shú-nu-ti*, l. 12, I take this form as a II[1] of כרב, "*Jemandem willfahren*" (not as a II[1] of קרב, "to bring near").

12 *shum-ma an-ni-ta ul tu-ul-te-ḫi-ir-shú-nu-ti*[1]	If this thou doest not grant unto them, (then)
13 *ul at-tu-ú-a SHE.BAR ik-ka-lu*[2]	they shall (no longer) 'eat my "food".'"
14 2 *GUR SHE.BAR a-na Mâr-^ITa-a-du i-di-in*	Give 2 *gur* of barley to *Mâr-Tâdu*.
15 *shá*[3] *^{amelu}RIQ ^{âlu}She-li-bi^{ki}*	As regards the *RIQ* of *Shelibi*—
16 9 *a-mi-lu-us-su a-na pi-i a-mi-lu-t[i-shú]*	"give him the barley for his 9 men upon the demand of his representatives
17 *it-ti*[4] *ash-shá-bi shá âlu-ki*	in the presence of the 'city'."
18 *SHE.BAR id-na-ash-shú-[?]*	
19 *ar-di i-na bu-[ut ....]*	I went down on account of ....
20 *ù alpu shá i-na ^{âlu}[....]*	and the oxen which are in the city of ....
21 13 *alpu ia-a-nu ù* 10 [....] *ia-a-nu*	(and found) that 13 oxen are not there and 10 + x ...... are not there.
22 *SHE.BAR a-na ^{m ilu}Sin(= XXX)-apal(= TUR.USH)-[êrish]*	Measure and pay the barley to *Sin-apal-êrish*
23 *mu-du-ud-ma i-din-ma li-ish-shá-a*	so that he can take it away.
24 *ù at-ta ḫa-mu-ut-ta*	Also hurry up and give
25 *al-ka-am-ma SHE.ZER*	the seed-corn
26 *a-na âlu-ki*[5] *i-din*	to the "city"[5].
27 *ù SHE.BAR* 10 *GUR GISH.BAR GAL shá ^mIb-ni-^{ilu}Marduk*	And as regards the barley, the 10 *gur* *GISH.BAR.GAL*, due to *Ibni-Marduk*—

[1] II[2] of *shaḫâru* = *saḫâru*.

[2] As *SHE.BAR* at this time is the "money" or "wages" in form of "barley" which an employee receives for his services, the phrase "to eat the barley of somebody" clearly means "to be in somebody's employ." According to this *ul at-tu-ú-a SHE.BAR ik-ka-lu* would mean as much as: "my barley, *i.e.*, food they shall no longer eat," "they shall no longer be in my employ," "I will dismiss them." But, and this is important, the threat is directed against *Innanni*. We have here clearly an indication that *Errish-apal-iddina*, the governor, employed these men upon the instigation of *Innanni*, *i.e.*, they were given an office by and through the help of the "political" influence of *Innanni*; and the governor, in order to force *Innanni* to comply with his (the governor's) wishes, threatens him with the dismissal of his (*Innanni's*) protégés. For *SHE.BAR* cf. also p. 113, note 4.

[3] The translation of ll. 15f. depends upon whether we read, l. 18, *id-na-ash-shú* or *id-na-ash-shú-nu*. As there was ample space on the O. of the tablet for the sign *-nu* it would seem strange that the writer, if he wrote *-nu*, should have put it on the R. E. We might translate accordingly: "as regards the *RIQ* ... and his nine men ... so give them (= *idnashshunu, amilûti-shú-nu*)" or "as regards the *RIQ* ... so give him (*idnashshu*) with regard to his nine men (or for his nine men) ... upon the demand of his representatives (*amilûti-shu*)."

[4] The *RIQ* of *Shelibi* must have been a rather untrustworthy official seeing that grain shall be delivered to him in "the presence of the city (*i.e.*, the city's (= *Nippur*) heads)."

[5] The "city" in which *Errish-apal-iddina* was stationed, *i.e.*, "*Bît-Errish-apal-iddina^{ki}*."

28 *na-da-na aq-ba-ak-ku*	"I have told thee to pay it,
29 *am-mi-ni la ta-di-in*	why hast thou not paid it?
30 *shú-ú it-ti-ia te-bi*[1]	He is angry with me.
31 *ul a-shi-im-ma*[2] *it-ti*[3]*-ka*	It will not be my fault, if he does not
32 *ul i-da-bu-ub*	accuse thee, saying:
33 *um-ma-a*[4] *SUM.SAR*[5] *ù SUM.EL. SAR*[6] *KAR*[7]	'No onions and garlic(?)
34 *a-na a-ka-li ia-a-nu*	are there to eat,'
35 *um-ma-a*[8] *a-na Mâr-Ta-a-du*	or: 'thou hast given to *Mâr-Tâdu*
36 *i-na libbi*[9](= *SHAG*) *SHE.BAR at-tu-ú-a tu-she-ir*[10]	an order on my barley.'"
37 *na-ḫa-sa*[11] *aq-ba-ash-shú*	I told him to depart (="to keep quiet"?)

VIII.

No. 84 (= C. B. M. 3258). (Cf. photographic reproduction, Pl. XII, 31, 32.)

Errish-apal-iddina, a governor, writes to *Innanni*, the chief bursar of the Nippurian Temple storehouses, demanding of him to comply with his several wishes. Time of *Kuri-Galzu*, about 1400 B.C.

For general introduction see preceding letter. The contents are the following: (*a*) The sesame of the prefects must not be accepted, ll. 3, 4.

[1] Permansive of תבע.

[2] Lit., "I shall not ordain it; I shall not cause it; it will not be my fault." The sense is: Do not blame me if he (*Ibni-Marduk*) accuses thee (*Innanni*), etc., but I would not be surprised at all if he *does* accuse thee.

[3] *It-ti* here "against"; cf. *dabâb limnûtim dabâbu itti*, No. 75 6, p. 135.

[4] *Um-ma-a* . . . *um-ma-a* introduces the twofold possible accusation with which *Ibni-Marduk* may, and *Errish-apal-iddina* does, threaten *Innanni*, viz., an accusation of *neglect* and one of *fraud*. It seems that *Errish-apal-iddina* had to THREATEN *Innanni* continually in order to make him live up to his agreements (cf. l. 13). The first accusation with which *Errish-apal-iddina* threatens *Innanni* is this: If thou dost not give to *Ibni-Marduk* the *SHE.BAR* he will accuse thee of neglect by saying there are "no onions, etc., to eat!" This shows that *SHUM.SHAR*, etc., belong to, and form part of, *SHE.BAR*; hence "barley" at this time signifies everything that belongs to the sustenance, food, of the people, cf. our "bread." See also p. 112, note 2.

[5] For *SUM.SAR* = *shûmu*, "onions," see *H. W. B.*, p. 647.

[6] *SUM.EL.SAR* probably = "garlic!" Cf. also Meissner, *Ideogramme*, Nos. 2970-2972. Or is *EL* here = *ḪUL*? If so, then cf. *qishshu* = *ḪUL*(= *ú-ku-ush*).*SAR* "cucumber," *H. W. B.*, p. 598*a*.

[7] *KAR* indicates here a certain kind of *SUM.EL.SAR*.

[8] The second accusation with which *Innanni* is threatened by the writer is that *Ibni-Marduk* will say: "Thou hast not only withheld from me what belongs to me, but hast even given an order on *my barley* to *Mâr-Tâdu*, and thus hast cheated me out of my own." Cf. here p. 87, note.

[9] *I.e.*, to take "from" my grain.

[10] See p. 111, note 2.

[11] *Na-ḫa-sa* = infinitive (cf. *niḫêsu*, *H. W. B.*, p. 458*a*, and Jensen, *K. B.*, VI, pp. 388, 496).

(*b*) Bring the oil into "the Tablet house," ll. 5–10.
(*c*) Send the report about the barley, ll. 11, 12.
(*d*) Give three jars of *Lager-beer* to *Ḫashmar*, ll. 13–16.
(*e*) Make the *GAR.RASH KU*, ll. 17–19.

1 *a-na* ^{m}*In-na-an-ni ki-bé-ma*	To *Innanni* speak,
2 *um-ma* ^{m} ^{ilu}*Errish(t)(= MASH)-apal-(TUR.USH)-iddina(= SE)*^{na}*-ma*	thus saith *Errish-apal-iddina*:
3 ^{she}*shamashshammu(= GISH.NI) shá ḫa-za-an-na-a-ti*	The sesame of the prefects
4 *la ta-ma-ḫa-ar*	thou must not accept.
5 *at-ta ma-an-nu*[1] ^{she}*shamashshammu (= GISH.NI)*	All who press out
6 *li-iṣ-ḫu-tu-ú-ma*[2]	the sesame
7 *shamnu(= NI.GISH) a-na É* ^{abnu}*DUB*[3] *li-she-ri-bu*[4]	must bring the oil (in)to the "Tablet house,"
8 *ù at-ta* ^{she}*shamashshammi(= GISH.NI)-ka*	therefore press out thy sesame
9 *ṣu-ḫu-ut-ma shamnu(= NI.GISH)*	and bring the oil (in)to
10 *a-na É* ^{abnu}*DUB shú-ri-ib*	the "Tablet house."
11 *ù di-im SHE.BAR*[5]	Also no report whatever

[1] *Ma-an-nu*, because construed with the plural (*li-iṣ-ḫu-tu-ú-ma, li-she-ri-bu*), has here the signification "all those who."

[2] The root of *li-iṣ-ḫu-tu-ú-ma* has to be, on account of the writing *ṣu-ḫu-ut-ma* (l. 9), צחת. It having here an object, must show an *a* in the present, hence *saḫâtu*, *iṣḫut* (præt.), *iṣaḫat* (præs.), *ṣuḫut* (imperat.). Both Delitzsch, *H. W. B.*, p. 564*b* (wrongly צחר), and Muss-Arnoldt, p. 873, leave this verb untranslated. The action of the *saḫâtu* shall be applied to the ^{she}*GISH.NI*; the result of this is *NI.GISH*, which shall be brought into the *É* ^{abnu}*DUB*. From this it follows that *saḫâtu* means something like "to press," "to squeeze out," by chopping up the ^{she}*GISH.NI* (hence *saḫâtu* parallel to *ṣaḫḫuru*, "*klein machen*," see *H. W. B.*, *l.c.*), and is as such the same as the German "*keltern*." "The oil of the wood," *i.e.*, the *NI.GISH* or *shamnu*, is, therefore, gained by chopping up, pressing, squeezing the ^{she}*GISH.NI* or "sesame leaves (resp. bark)," and is, in fact, nothing but the "oil of the sesame"; hence the *GISH* in *NI.GISH* is the same as the ^{she}*GISH* in ^{she}*GISH.NI*. Now we understand also what a ^{amelu}*NI.SUR* is. From ^{amelu}*GESHTIN.SUR.RA* = *ṣa-ḫi-it ka-ra-ni* = "*Weinkelterer*"(!) we know that *SUR* = *saḫâtu*; hence a ^{amelu}*NI.SUR* is one who presses, squeezes, etc., the *NI*, *i.e.*, the fat (*sc.* out of the milk); in other words he is the "butter-maker"; or if *NI* in *NI.SUR* be the same as the *NI* in *NI.GISH*, he would become the "sesame oil manufacturer."

[3] Cf. pp. 88ff. Whether this *É* ^{abnu}*DUB* refers to that of Nippur or, what is more probable, to that of *Dûr-Errish-apal-iddina*, cannot be made out from this passage.

[4] Ll. 5–7 contain a generally accepted law or custom: It is the rule that .... therefore (*ù* introduces the apodosis) comply thou to this rule: press out, etc.

[5] See introduction to No. 76, p. 143, and cf. pp. 84ff.

12 *mi-im-ma ul ta-ash-pu-ra*	about the barley hast thou sent.
13 *ù* *^{m}Ḫa-ash-mar*	Furthermore as regards *Ḫashmar*
14 *shá ash-pu-rak-ku*	concerning whom I have sent to thee—
15 3[1] *labiru*(= *Ù*[2]) *shikaru*(= *KASH*) *a-na pi-i*[3]	"give (him) upon the demand of his representatives
16 *a-mi-li-e-shú*[4] *i-din*	3 jars of Lager-beer."
17 *ù GAR.RASH KU*[5] *shá a-di*	Also the .... which is for(?) my
18 *li-tu-ú-a*[6]	....
19 *e-pu-ush*	make.

IX.

No. 85 (= C. B. M. 3206).

Inbi-Airi, a lady of high rank, demands of *Innanni*, the chief bursar of the Nippurian Temple storehouses, the payment of barley and wages. Time of *Kuri-Galzu*, about 1400 B.C.

Inbi-Airi, "fruit of Ijjar,"[7] must have been a lady of very high rank, seeing that she dared to write to the bursar-in-chief, *Innanni*, in words which are equal to a peremptory order: "give." It may not be impossible that she was one of the many ladies connected with the Temple, and hence indirectly with the Palace—ladies who are in the "Temple Archives" quite frequently mentioned under the title *NIN. AN^{mesh}*(= *qadishtu*?), but whose *status quo* can, however, not yet be defined more clearly. She, like the governor *Errish-apal-iddina*, experiences the same difficulties in her dealings with *Innanni*, having to warn him "not to act inimically towards her," but to do as told, or else she might lodge a complaint against him with the King! *^{m}Iddina-^{ilu}Nergal* is, no doubt, the same as the one mentioned in *B. E.*, XIV,

[1] *DUK* = *karpatu* is, like *gur*, etc., very often omitted.

[2] The writer had first written *BI* (traces of which are still visible). He erased this and wrote over the partial erasure the sign *Ù* = *labiru*, intending, by doing so, to put special emphasis upon the "old." "Old beer" is, of course, "*Lager-beer*."

[3] Here abbreviated from *a-na pi-i shi-pir-ti*, *i.e.*, "upon the written order of."

[4] *Amelu* used here (as at the time of *Ḫammurabi*) in the sense of "a certain one," *i.e.*, a "representative."

[5] *GAR.RASH KU*. Cf. *B. E.*, XV, 44 : 6, "*x. qa* of flour (*ZID.DA*) as *GAR.RASH* for our house (*É-nu*) *^{m}Be-la-nu* (has given or received?)"; similar is *l.c.*, 156 : 2. In *l.c.*, 79 : 5, we have: *aklum É-nu GAR.RASH ṣil*(= *NUN*)-*li-ḫa*. In *B. E.*, XIV, 117*a* : 3, we hear of 3 *qa SHE GAR.RASH*. These passages show that *KU* is not a part of the ideogram. *KU*, however, cannot be here = *kêmu*, "flour"; if it were, it had to stand *before GAR.RASH*; see p. 123, note 10. Is it possible to take *GAR.RASH KU* here(!) in the sense of *akâli* (*shá*) *ana ḫarrâni* = "*Verproviantirung*," lit. "food for the journey"? The above-quoted passages are, however, against such a translation.

[6] For *li-tu-ú* cf. Delitzsch, *H. W. B.*, p. 386*b*.

[7] For another letter of *Inbi-Airi* see No. 86.

14 : 6[1] (10th year of *Kuri-Galzu*), who appears there as the brother of ^{m}*Nu-ri-e-a*. For *Sin-issaḫra*,[2] the head of the *royal* storehouse, *ÁSH.TAB.BA.GAN.TUG*^{ki}, see pp. 79, 81, 104, 110.

The contents are:

(*a*) Request for payment of barley to

(*α*) *Idin-Nergal*, ll. 3-7, and to

(*β*) ^{f}*Dini*, ll. 10, 11.

(*b*) "The wages for the persons" are to be handed over to *Sin-issaḫra*, ll. 8, 9.

1 *a-na* ^{m}*In-na-an-ni ki-bé-ma*	To *Innanni* speak,
2 *um-ma* ^{f}*In-bi-A-a-ri-im-ma*	thus saith *Inbi-Airi*:
3 3 (*gur*) *SHE.BAR a-na* ^{m}*Idin* (= *SE*)-^{ilu}*Nergal*	Give to *Idin-Nergal*
4 *i-di-in*	3 (*gur*) of barley.
5 *li-mu-ut-ta la te-ip-pu-shá-an-ni-ma*[3]	Do not act inimically towards me,
6 *shá aq-ba-ásh-shú li-ish-am-ma*[4]	but as I have told him let him take
7 *li-il-qa-a*[5]	and carry away.
8 *ipru*(= *SHE.BA*) *MU*^{meshu} *a-na* $^{m\ ilu}$*Sin*(= *XXX*)-*is-saḫ-ra*	The wages (food) for the persons give to *Sin-issaḫra*.
9 *i-di-in*	
10 4 (*gur*) *SHE.BAR a-na* ^{f}*Di-ni mârat* (= *TUR*[7]) ^{m}*Abi*(= *AD*)-*ia*	To *Dini*, the daughter of *Abi-ia*, give
11 *i-di-in.*	4 (*gur*) of barley.

X.

No. 26 (= C. B. M. 19,785).

Kudurâni, the royal superintendent of the Temple storehouse at *Pî-nâri*, reports to King *Kadashman-Turgu* about the administration of certain affairs incumbent on his office. About 1360 B.C.

[1] Notice that this tablet contains in l. 5 the name $^{m\ ilu}$*Sin*(= *XXX*)-*issaḫra*(= *NIGIN*)^{ra}.

[2] Cf. also the *Bît*-$^{m\ ilu}$*Sin-issaḫra* in No. 9 : 16.

[3] Lit., Do not make enmity towards me, but do as told by him.

[4] For *nashû* used in connection with the removal of barley, etc., cf., *e.g.*, *B. E.*, XV, 141 : 11, 16 | 100 : 3 | 55 : 3, etc.

[5] For *laqû*, "to remove barley, etc., from (= *TA* = *ishtu*) a place to (*ana*) another," cf., *e.g.*, *B. E.*, XV, 197 : 5, 7.

[6] In view of the fact that the amount is *invariably stated* and not simply referred to as "*that* (*MU*^{mesh} = *shu'atu*) amount," I see in this *MU*^{mesh} the same expression as that occurring in *DUB MU*^{mesh} = *DUB shumâti*, "Temple record"; in other words, I take *MU*^{mesh} to stand here for *shumâti* = "persons," as mentioned in the "Temple Archives," where they are generally introduced by the expression *MU.BI.IM*. See p. 83, note 9.

[7] *TUR* for *TUR.SAL*; the *SAL* having been omitted here, because the gender was already indicated by the *SAL* which precedes the name *Di-ni*.

The writer of this and the following letters (Nos. 27, 28), ^{m}*Ku-du-ra-nu*, was a contemporary of *Kishahbut*.[1] If so, then *Erba-Marduk* of No. 27 : 27, 30, 32 is, no doubt, identical with the *sukalmahhu* of No. 35 : 28. Taking all other passages into consideration[2] I propose to identify our writer with ^{m}*Ku-du-ra-ni*, the son of ^{m}*U-bar-ri* (see below, p. 126). ^{m}*Ku-du-ra-ni*, being stationed, in the 12th year of *Kadashman-Turgu*, at *Pî-nâri*^{ki} where a certain ^{m}*Ta-ki-shú* receives grain (*SHE*) from him (*ina qât*),[3] must have been at that time the head of the storehouse at *Pî-nâri*^{ki}. In the same capacity he is mentioned among certain storehouse officials or superintendents who paid, in the 13th year of *Kadashman-Turgu*, *SHE HAR.RA* (lit., "interest grain") to the city *Dûr-*^{ilu}*Gu-la*^{ki}.[4] We may, therefore, identify the *be-li* of our letter with King *Kadashman-Turgu* and assign the letter itself to about 1360 B.C.

The contents of this letter are the following:

(*a*) A plan as to how to pay barley to certain officials, ll. 3–8.

(*b*) Concerning fugitives, l. 9.

(*c*) The "stone eyes" will be taken to the gem-cutter's, ll. 12–14.

(*d*) The ploughing has been begun two days ago, ll. 15, 16.

(*e*) The watering tank shall not extend to the King's palace, ll. 17–19.

(*f*) Wells are few in number and pastures do not exist at all, ll. 19, 20.

1 *ardi-ka* ^{m}*Ku-du-ra-nu a-na di-na-an be-li-ia lul-lik*	Thy servant *Kudurânu*; before the presence of my "Lord" may I come!
2 *a-na âlu-ki ṣi-ri*[5] *ù bît be-li-ia shú-ul-mu*	To the city, the field, and the house of my "Lord" greeting!
3 *um-ma-a a-na be-li-ia*[6] *shá be-li ish-pu-ra*	The following to my "Lord": With regard to what my "Lord" has written
4 *um-ma-a SHE.BAR shá* ^{alu}*Ḫi-ba-ri-ti ù* ^{alu}*Kâr-*^{ilu}*Nabû(=AG)*	saying: "The barley of the city of *Ḫibariti* and of *Kâr-Nabû*

[1] See introduction to No. 35, p. 120.

[2] Cf. *e.g.*, ^{m}*Nûr-*^{ilu}*Shamash* (27 : 8, here called *gù-gal-tam*) is mentioned as *pa-te-si* in the 11th year of *Kadashman Turgu* (*B. E.*, XIV, 99*a* : 20). ^{m}*Di-in-ili-lu-mur* (27 : 18) occurs again in the 3d year of *Kadashman-Turgu* (*B. E.*, XIV, 91*a* : 12), etc., etc. Meissner, *G. G. A.*, February, 1908, pp. 130–143, thinks, because ^{m}*Din-ili-lumur* is followed, in the latter passage, by *da-mi-tum* = *tâmitum*, that he must have been a "woman." That *DISH*, instead of *SAL*, *may* be placed before the name of a woman is apparent especially from *B. E.*, XV, 155, 19: "30 *SAL*^{mesh}," among whom (ll. 1–18, 23–31) are to be found *three* (ll. 13, 14, 18) who are determined by *DISH*.

[3] *B. E.*, XIV, 112 : 7.

[4] *B. E.*, XIV, 101 : 14.

[5] In Nos. 27, 28, written likewise by *Kudurânu*, we have *EDIN* for *ṣi-ri*.

[6] Only here without the emphatic *-ma*, see p. 24, note 3.

5 *a-na* ^{amelu}*RIQ*[1] *ù* ^{amelu}*KA.ZID*(= *KU*).*DA*[2] *i-di-in*	give to the *riqqu* and *KA.ZID.DA* officers" —
6 *ki-i shá*[3] ^{alu}*MUM*^{ki}[4]*-ma ga-am-rat* *I C SHE.BAR GISH.BAR.GAL*[5]	"so may my 'Lord,' as soon as the city *MUM-ma* has paid up, (first) set aside (the) 100 (*gur*) of barley, *GISH.BAR.GAL*,
7 *be-li li-mi-da-ma*[6] *a-na* ^{amelu}*RIQ* ^{amelu}*KA.ZID*(= *KU*).*DA*	for the *riqqu* and *KA.ZID.DA* officers,
8 *ù*[7] *SHE.ZER*^{meshu}[8] *lu-ud-di-in*[9] *ásh-shum ummâni*(= *SAB*)$^{hi.a}$ [. . .]	in order that I may be able to pay the seed-corn." As regards the men . . . .
9 *shá hi-il-qu*[10](?) [. . . .]	who have fled(?) . . . .
[. . . . large break . . . .]	. . .
10 [. . . . .]	. . . .
11 *a-na mu-uh be-li-ia* [*ul-te-bi-la*]	"to my 'Lord' I have brought."
12 *ásh-shum* ^{abnu}*SHI*^{mesh}[11] *shá* ^{abnu}[. . . .]	With regard to the "eyes" of . . . stone

[1] Probably the official who gathered the "vegetables" or "green things."

[2] Lit., "the man who has the say (*KA*) over the flour (*ZID.DA*)," as regards its gathering and its disposition.

[3] *Ki-i shá*, *i.e.*, "when it is that," "as soon as."

[4] Written *MUN*, but has to be pronounced here, on account of the phonetic complement *-ma*, *MUM*; cf. *alan* and *alam*, "statue," etc. ^{alu}*MUM*^{ki} may be translated either by "*Wüstenstadt*" or by "flour (cf. p. 123, note 10) city."

[5] Notice that *SHE.BAR GISH.BAR.GAL*, which is "set aside," may be paid out as *SHE.ZER*.

[6] The *a-ma* in *li-mi-da-ma* indicates the chief sentence. *Emêdu c. acc.* and *ana*, "*etwas für jemand festsetzen, bestimmen*," "to set aside."

[7] *Ù consecutivum*.

[8] For *SHE.ZER* = *zêru*, see Meissner, *Ideogr.*, No. 5106.

[9] Ll. 6–8 is quite a strange answer to the inquiry of the "Lord." In fact it is no answer at all, but a *request* on the part of the writer that if he is to pay barley to the *riqqu* and *KA.ZID.DA*, the "Lord" may first of all "set aside" the barley (*i.e.*, give orders that the barley be "set aside")—not that of *Hibariti* and *Kâr-Nabû*, however, but that of ^{alu}*MUM*^{ki}!

[10] The traces speak rather for *ra*, *ta*, *shá*.

[11] ^{abnu}*SHI*^{mesh}, lit. "Augensteine," "pearls(?)." With regard to these "stone eyes of . . . . stone" Prof. Hilprecht writes me under date of July 2, 1908, as follows:

"Among the numerous smaller votive objects left by the Cassite kings in Nippur (cf. Hilprecht, *B. E.*, Series D, Vol. I, pp. 335f.) two classes are especially well represented in the museums of Constantinople and Philadelphia: (1) *Lapis lazuli disks*, known under the name of *ASH-ME* ^{abnu}*uknû* (cf. Hilprecht, *O. B. I*, Nos. 58, 59, 61, and pp. 49ff., and Meissner, *Ideogramme*, No. 28). (2) Little plano-convex round or oval objects in polished agate, resembling eyes. Cf. Hilprecht, *l.c.*, Nos. 29–31, 51, 52, 65, 73, 134, 135, 139. In my 'Description of Objects' I called them simply 'agate cameos.' More exactly they are cut out of two-colored agate in such a manner that the lower white layer represents the white of the eyes, the upper smaller brown layer the pupil. As a rule the pupil alone bears the votive inscription, exceptionally it is engraved on the white layer (73), sometimes cuneiform signs are found on both (135). All the 'agate eyes' so far discovered in Nippur by the four expeditions, especially by the second and third, belong exclusively to the Cassite period. In Babylon similar 'eyes' in agate were found in a jeweler's shop of the Parthian period. From

13 *a-na* ^{m}*I-li-aḫ-ḫi-e-ri-ba*[1] *a-[. . . .*[2]*]-ma*	(I beg to state that) they will be taken (shall take them?)
14 *i-li-ik-qa-a*[3]	to *Ili-aḫḫi-eriba*, the . . . .
15 *ásh-shum shá-ba-shi*[4] *shá be-lí ish-pu-ra*	With regard to the ploughing, concerning which my "Lord" has inquired, (I beg to say that)
16 *ûmu* 2^{kam} *a-na shá-ba-shi e-ki-ri-ib*[5]	I am at the ploughing for the last two days.
17 *ásh-shum shá-ki-i*[6] *shá i-tu-ú* ^{m}*Iz-gur-*^{ilu}*Errish(t)* (= *NIN.IB*)	With regard to the watering tank(?) which the *itû Izgur-Errish*
18 *shá-ak-nu-ma be-lí ish-pu-ra a-na bâbi*	is putting up (and) concerning which my "Lord" has written (I beg to assure my Lord that)
19 *shá bît be-lí-ia ul i-la-ak ku-bur-ra*[7]	it shall not go up (extend to) the gate

the inscriptions on some of them it becomes clear that they also belong to the Cassite period and originally came from Nippur. There are, however, known two identical, beautiful agate eyes (formed of three-colored agate, the lowest light-brown layer serving as a basis for the two upper layers), which date from the time of Nebuchadrezzar II, and according to the story of the Arabs, corroborated by the inscription (running in minute but very clear characters along the outer edge of the pupil), came from the ruins of Babylon. This inscription reads: ^{d}*Nabû-kudurru-uṣur shar Bábili, apil* ^{d}*Nabû-apal-uṣur, ana* ^{d}*Marduk, bíli-shu iqísh(-esh)*, 'N., king of Babylon, son of N., presented it to Marduk, his lord.'

"In view of these characteristic votive objects of the Cassite kings we are scarcely wrong in interpreting 'the stone eyes of . . . . stone' mentioned in the above passage as objects in the shape of eyes cut out of a certain stone, the name of which is unfortunately broken away, but which according to the results of the excavations in all probability was 'agate.'" Cf. in this connection the "eye of God" which sees everything!

[1] In view of *i-li-ik-qa-a* (l. 14) one might be inclined to read here ^{m}*I-li-Aḫ-ḫi e-ri-ba-a[. . .]-ma*, but this would give no satisfactory sense.

[2] We would expect here a "title" or the "name of the profession" of *Ili-aḫḫi-eriba*: "goldsmith," "gem-cutter," etc. The traces, however, do not fit for *zadimmu* or *kudimmu*.

[3] By translating as given above, I take *i-li-ik-qa-a* to be a 3d pers. fem. plur IV[1]: *illiqqâ* = *illaqâ*, referring back to ^{abnu}*SHI*^{mesh}, a *fem. plural* (*abnu* is masc., but more frequently *fem.*). Cf. pp. 131, note, 141, note 2.

[4] The signification of *sha-ba-shi* is very doubtful. I would like to take it as an infinitive of שבש = *sabâsu*, for which see Jensen, *K. B.*, VI[1], pp. 383, 511, who assigns to this verb the significations "*um-, anruhren, dahinsturmen, aufwuhlen*." The last signification is used not only of the "dust," but also of the "ground," *i.e.*, "to plough."

[5] *E ki-ri-ib* = *a-qa-ri-ib*—*e* for *a* on account of the guttural ק, cf. p. 97, n. 7. *Qarâbu c. ana* here "to go at something," just as "a man goes at his enemy."

[6] Reading, form, and signification doubtful. The *shá-ki-i* must be something that is "put up" (*shá-ak-nu*), a kind of building. It must be *long*, for "it shall not go to the house of the Lord." If *shá-ki-i* be a formation like *shugû* (root שגע, *H. W. B.*, p. 640*a*) its root might be either שכה or שקה. Have we to see, therefore, in *shá-ki-i* a side form of *shîqu*, "*Tranke*," Delitzsch, *H. W. B.*, p. 685*b*? *Shuqû* might be a *fu'âl* form.

[7] In view of *shá-ki-i*, "watering tank," I am inclined to see in *ku-bur-ru* the same word as *qubûru*, a synonym of *shuttatu*, which latter Delitzsch, *H. W. B.*, p. 697, translates by "*Loch*," and Jensen, *K. B.*, VI[1], p. 416, by "*Grube*," "*Fallgrube*." Seeing, however, that *shuttatu* is the same as *shá-ut-tu*, and that the latter has the ideograph *u* (*bu-ru*), which also stands for *bûru*, "well," I take *ku-bur-ra* = *qubûru* in the sense of "well."

a-mi-iṣ[1]	of the house of my "Lord." Of wells there are only a few
ù mu-ra-ku[2] *ia-a'-nu-um*	and of pastures there are none.

XI.

No. 35 (= C. B. M. 6057).

Report of the royal superintendent *Kishaḫbut* about his affairs. Time of *Kadashman-Turgu*, about 1355 B.C.

Kishaḫbut,[3] the writer of this and the preceding letter (No. 34), has, if our combinations be correct, gradually worked himself up from a rather lowly position to that of an *itû* (l. 25), an "inspector," of the king. In the 11th year (of *Nazi-Maruttash*)[4] he acted as *na-gid*, "shepherd," for (*ki shum*) ^{m}*Ku-du-ra-ni*.[5] In the 12th year of *Nazi-Maruttash*[6] we find him in *Zarat-IM*^{ki} as one of the *ENGAR*, "farmers," "irrigators," receiving *PAD* or "wages." In the 14th year of the same ruler[7] (month *Tishri*) he is stationed as *riqqu* in *KI*-^{m}*Ga-ir*^{ki}, receiving "*KU.QAR* wages" from *Enlil-mukîn-apal*. Two months later (*Kislev*) we meet him in the same capacity, but in the city *Du-un-ni-a-ḫi*^{ki},[8] receiving some more "*KU.QAR* wages" from *Enlil-mukîn-apal*. In the 15th year of *Nazi-Maruttash*[9] he is still in *Du-un-ni-a-ḫi*^{ki}, where "*KU.QAR* wages" are "furnished" by him to *Apil*-^{ilu}*Rammân* who is to transport them by ship to Nippur. While living in *Kur*(or *Tar*)-*ri-ti*^{ki} he appears, during the 14th and 15th year of *Kadashman-Turgu*[10], again as a "payer of wages." Finally in the 15th year (of *Kadashman-Turgu*[11]) we find him in *Dûr*-^{ilu}*Nusku*^{ki}, apparently as a superintendent (*itû*) of the Temple's storehouse, receiving (*mi-taḫ-ḫu-rum*) grain (*SHE*) from (*i-na qât*) various persons. While in *Dûr*-^{ilu}*Nusku*^{ki}[12] *Kishaḫbut*,

[1] For *amiṣu* = *miṣu*, "to be small, to be few in number (opp. *ma'du*)," see Jensen, *K. B.*, VI¹, p. 543.

[2] As the last paragraph of this letter is apparently concerned with "watering tanks," "wells"—things absolutely necessary for the pasturing of herds I see in *mu-ra-ku* a *maf'al*-form of ירק, *i.e.*, *marraqu* = *mauraqu* = *mûraqu*, "a place of green things," "a pasture."

[3] For the different writings of this name see Chapter I, p. 7, note 6.

[4] *B. E.*, XIV, 168 : 8.

[5] This *Kudurâni* is, no doubt, the same as the one mentioned in our letter, ll. 27, 31, and who appears as the writer of Nos 26–28. For further details see introduction to No. 26, pp. 117f.

[6] *B. E.*, XIV, 57 : 12.

[7] *B. E.*, XIV, 60 : 1.

[8] *B. E.*, XIV, 62 : 17.

[9] *B. E.*, XIV, 65 : 6.

[10] *B. E.*, XIV, 114 : 6.

[11] *B. E.*, XV : 48 : 2. Thus I would supply the date, seeing that *Kishaḫbut* has attained at this time apparently his highest position; this date must, therefore, be the latest.

[12] This city must have had a "palace" (*É.GAL*), an *É A-nu* and a *bâb A-nu-um*, cf. l. 15.

no doubt, wrote the letter translated below. The writer's official life extended, therefore, over a period of thirty-one years (*i.e.*, from the 11th year of *Nazi-Maruttash* to the 15th of *Kadashman-Turgu*), and supposing him to have been twenty years old when first mentioned, he would have been about fifty-one years when he wrote this letter. If our deductions be correct, the *be-li* of l. 1 must have been King *Kadashman-Turgu*.

Erba-Marduk,[1] "the servant" and *sukkalmaḫḫu* of the king (ll. 17, 26), I propose to identify with the one known from *B. E.*, XIV, 19 : 23, as "the son of *Sin-nûr-mâti*."[2] According to this passage *Erba-Marduk* was one of the Temple or Palace servants receiving wages due him for the last six months of the 13th year of *Kuri-Galzu*. Again supposing that *Erba-Marduk* was during the 13th year of *Kuri-Galzu* about twenty years old, he must have been eighty-four years of age in the 15th year of *Kadashman-Turgu*, when he had reached the exalted position of a *sukkalmaḫḫu*. Need we wonder that *Kishaḫbut* should have been somewhat irritated about the slowness of this old and venerable official?[3]

The contents of this letter might be conveniently subdivided into the following parts:

(*a*) Report about a successful completion of building operations, ll. 6–9.

(*b*) Fifty-five out of seventy *gur* of *kasia* due to the King have been sent, ll. 10–12.

(*c*) The disposition of wool has been communicated to the King, while the writer was received, in Nippur, in private audience by his "Lord," ll. 13, 14.

(*d*) Certain buildings (in *Dûr-ilu Nusku^ki*) need "strengthening"(?), ll. 15, 16.

(*e*) The garments have not been paid to the weavers and fullers,[4] ll. 17–19.

(*f*) Digression: Twofold complaint, ll. 20–24.

(*g*) Renewed request that adobes be ordered to be made, ll. 25–29.

(*h*) The sesame oil of the King has been sent, the *shatammu* must now store it, ll. 30–33.

1 *ardi-ka* ^m*Ki-shaḫ-bu-u*[*t*]	Thy servant *Kishaḫbut*;
2 *a-na di-na-an be-li-ia lu*[*l-lik*]	before the presence of my "Lord" may I come!
3 *a-na bît be-li-ia shú-u*[*l-mu*]	To the house of my "Lord" greeting!

[1] Cf. here also above, pp. 7, note 1; 14, note 7; 23, 107.

[2] Clay, *B. E.*, XIV, p. 13*a*, quotes two passages where this *Erba-Marduk* is supposed to have been mentioned, but the second passage (27 : 14) is wrong. Under *Sin-nûr-mâti* only one passage is quoted.

[3] Cf. ll. 25ff., and see already above, Chapter III, pp. 44ff.

[4] Or complaint about *Erba-Marduk* in not sending the garments for the weavers and fullers, see notes to ll. 17f.

4 *ultu*(= *TA*) *ûm*^{um} *ak-shú-d*[*a*][1]	Since the day I began, I have covered
5 *ish-te-en bîta pa-ar-ḫa*[2] *uṣ-ṣa-li-il*[3]	one building with (flower) ornamentations.
6 *ù bîti ru-uk-ki*[4] *shá be-lí i-mu-ru-ma*	And the farther (away) building which my "Lord" has examined
7 *bu-us-su*[5] *na-pa-la*[6] *iq-ba-a*	and whose front side he has commanded to tear down
8 *ki-i a-mu-ru-ma bu-ḫu-ur-shú*[7]	I have, after I had examined it, torn
9 *bu-ud-du-ru*[8] *at-ta-pa-al*[6]	it down to improve its *ensemble*.

[1] Lit., "Since the day when (*sc. shá*, hence the relative *u* in *akshudu*) I went at it," *i.e.*, when I *began* doing it, hence *kashâdu* has here the signification of "to begin, to commence."

[2] *Pa-ar-ḫa*. On account of the *ish-te-en* we cannot connect *Bît-pa-ar-ḫa*, but must take *parḫa* as object to *uṣṣalil*, *i.e.*, *parḫa* must signify something *with which* the *ishten bîta* was "covered." From Exod. 25 : 33; 37 : 20 we learn that a פרח, generally translated by "flower," was an ornament, resp. ornamention, of the "candlestick." There can be no doubt that we have the same word here, but whether the ornaments were in the shape of "flowers" has to remain, at the present, an open question.

[3] II^2 צלל *c. double acc.*, "to cover something with something." Cf. also the II^1 (or II^2?) form in 66 : 22, *É*^{gish}*NAD*^{mesh} *li-ṣi-el-li-lu-ma*. For a different translation of *ṣalâlu* II^1 (a II^2 is not mentioned), see Delitzsch, *H. W. B.*, p. 568*a*, and Jensen, *K. B.*, VI^1, pp. 485, 313.

[4] *Ru-uk-ki* seems to be here in opposition to *ish-te-en*. If so, we might translate *ish-te-en bîta* .... *bîti ru-uk-ki* by "the first (= nearer) house .... the farther (away) house." A place name *Bît-Ruqqi* is out of question.

[5] Either for *pûd-su* (Delitzsch, *H. W. B.*, p. 516*a*, "side"; Jensen, *K. B.*, VI^1, pp. 414, 506, "back"; Kuchler, *Medizin*, "shoulder") or for *pût-su* (Delitzsch, *l.c.*, p. 517*a*, "front"; Jensen, *l.c.*, pp. 506, 525f., 549, 555, "back," "body"). The signification "front side" seems to be here the most appropriate one. Cf. in this connection the strange expression, ^{m}X. (*i.e.*, always the person who puts his seal to the document, the "recipient") *bu-us-su im-ḫa-aṣ-ma im-ḫur* (*e.g.*, *B. E.*, XIV, 11 : 6; 127 : 6; 135 : 6 *et passim*)—no doubt a religious ceremony (cf. the German "*sich bekreuzen*," the Hebrew נִשְׁבַּע, lit. to hit one's self seven times, "*sich besiebenen*"), indicating that the recipient "smote his breast" before he received the things mentioned in the "contract." This "smiting of the breast" on the part of the recipient was a kind of oath, signifying that he (the recipient or debtor) will abide by the terms of the contract. Meissner, *M. V. A. G.*, 1905, p. 308, translates *pût-su maḫâṣu* by "*garantiren*."

[6] *Na-pa-la* .... *at-ta-pa-al*, root נפל = נבל, "to destroy," here "to tear down," cf. Tigl., VI : 28, "the wall .... *a-na na-pa-li aq-ba-shum-ma* I commanded him to tear down." A possible derivation of *at-ta-pa-al* from *apâlu* (for signification see, besides *H. W. B.*, p. 112*b*, also Delitzsch, *B. A.*, IV, p. 81; Nagel, *ibid.*, p. 178; Jensen, *K. B.*, VI^1, p. 369) or from יבל (Jensen, *l.c.*, p. 353) is, on account of *na-pa-la*, out of question here.

[7] Lit., "completeness," "totality," here in the sense of "*ensemble*." Jensen, *K. B.*, VI^1, p. 507, mentions a *buḫru* = *UD* as signifying "*irgend etwas helles*." If we have this *buḫru* here we might translate "in order to improve its light (= *UD* = *buḫru*)."

[8] An infinitive II^2 of בור (cf. the imperative *bu-ut-te-ir*, C. T., IV, 32 (= B^1 598) : 17 and p. 98, note 2) is here, on account of the writing with *d*, excluded. It can, therefore, be only an infinitive II^1 of either פטר or פדר. The signification of פטר does not fit here. Delitzsch, *H. W. B.*, p. 516*a*, mentions a root פדר without giving a translation. Tallquist, *Sprache*, p. 113, following the Hebrew פֶּדֶר, "fat," translated *padâru* by "to be fat." From the context we would expect here some such meaning as "improve." According to this the *alpu* (*immeru*) *tap-di-ru* would be "improved" (in the sense of), "fattened," oxen (or sheep)—oxen that had gone through a special process of "improving" them.

10 *ù* 70[1] ^{isu}*kasû(= PUḪADU)*^{mesh}[2] *shá be-lí-ia*[3]	And with regard to the 70 (*gur*) of my "Lord's" *kasia*—
11 *iq-bu-ú*[4] 55 ^{isu}*kasû(= PUḪADU)*^{mesh}	"they informed (me) that they have paid
12 *ish-shú-ni-ma id-di-nu-ni*[5]	out 55 (*gur*) of *kasia*."
13 *ásh-shum shipâtu(= SIG)*$^{hi.a}$[6] *i-na Nippur(= EN.LIL)*^{ki}[7]	As regards the wool—"in Nippur
14 *a-na be-lí-ia aq-ta-bi*	I have spoken to my 'Lord' about it."
15 *ásh-shum É.GAL É A-nu ù bâb A-n[u-um]*[8]	As regards the palace, the "Temple of God" and the "gate of God"—
16 *ki-i a-ḫa-mi-ish ri-i[t-ta?]*[9]	". . . . one with the other."
17 *ù lubushti(= KU)*$^{hi.a}$[10] *shá ardi-ka* ^{m}*Erba-*^{ilu}*Marduk*	And as regards the garments which thy servant *Erba-Marduk*

[1] The measure *GUR* is (as is often done at this time) left out here; cf. also 37 : 8 and see Tallquist, *Sprache*, p. 21.

[2] For ^{isu}*PUḪADU* or ^{shamm}*PUḪADU.SHAR* or *PUḪADU.SHAR* = *kasû* (*e.g.*, *B. E.*, IX, 29 *et passim*) see now Meissner, *Ideogramme*, No. 3796. Hilprecht in class lectures on *B. E.*, IX, explained it (in 1898) as *κασία*.

[3] A good example showing the difference between *be-lí-ia* and *be-lí*—a difference which is of the highest importance for a correct understanding of many passages in the letters here published. *Be-lí-ia* is always the genitive or dative (used after prepositions or in a *stat. constr.*) and means either "of my Lord" or "to my Lord." *Be-lí*, on the other hand, is either the nominative or vocative and has to be rendered "Lord" or "my Lord." This being true we cannot translate here "the *kasia* wood about which my Lord has spoken" (this had to be ^{isu}*kasû sha be-lí iq-bu-u* or *iq-bu-ú*), but must render as given above. That this difference is rigidly carried through even in the letters of the K. Collection has quite correctly been observed by Behrens, *L. S. S.*, II[1], p. 221.

[4] "They," *i.e.*, the storehouse officials whom I asked about the *kasia*.

[5] Lit., "they have taken (*sc. ishtu kari anni*, *i.e.*, from this storehouse) and they have given," *i.e.*, "55 *gur* have been taken from and have been paid." The payments here referred to were apparently made in installments. The "Lord," however, seems to have received none so far—hence his inquiry and the answer. For a similar *ἓν διὰ δυοῖν* cf. *B. E.*, XV, 159 : 2, *i-na qât* ^{m}*X. maḫ-ru-ma nadnu*^{nu}, *i.e.*, "by X. was paid."

[6] For *SIG* = *shipâtu*, see Zehnpfund, *B. A.*, I, p. 494. Wool is weighed according to *ma-na*, see, *e.g.*, 27 : 31; *B. E.*, XV, 6 : 11 | 11 : 1. For the different kinds of wool at this time cf. *e.g.*, 11 : 10f. | 23 : 19f. | 41 : 12 | 38 : 15f. and *B. E.*, XIV, 94 : 1 | 99*a*, Rev., col. XII, *l.c.*, XV, 11 : 1, etc.

[7] See Chapter IV, p. 74.

[8] Traces of *-um* are clearly visible. See also p. 80.

[9] Emendation doubtful, but probable. *Ritta* = I[1] imperative of רתה, "to fortify, strengthen."

[10] Hardly *KU*, *i.e.*, *ZID* or *ZID.DA* = *qimu* or better *kêmu*, "flour," see, besides Delitzsch, *H. W. B.*, p. 586*b*, also No. 11 : 5. If so, then compare *B. E.*, XV, 181, where the following "kinds of flour" are mentioned: *KU.DA ri-du* (l. 3), cf. *B. E.*, XIV, 117*a* : 6 and our No. 57 : 14 (here without *KU*); *KU ma(!)-at(d)-gan(!)* (l. 4), cf. No. 57 : 18; *B. E.*, XIV, 106*c* : 2; *H. W. B.*, p. 436*a*; *KU pa-ḫi-du* (l. 5), cf. *B. E.*, 117*a* : 2; *KU.GIG* (l. 6). The last is most generally found without the determinative *KU* as, *e.g.*, in *l.c.*, XIV, 18 : 2 | 21 : 2; XV, 10 : 2 | 36 : 3, etc. For *GIG* = *kibâtu*, see Delitzsch, *H. W. B.*, p. 317*a*; Jensen, *K. B.*, VI[1], p. 485f. With *GIG*, resp. *GIG.BA* (= *GIB.BA*?), cf. also *GIG.GIG.BA* in *B. E.*, XV, 46 : 12 | 117 : 1. Hilprecht, class lecture on *B. E.*, IX, read (1898) *GIG.BA* = *gulba* and translated "spelt"; *KU shi-ib-ri* (l. 7), cf. Hebrew שבר; *KU shi-ni-tum* (l. 8), cf. *B. E.*, XIV, 117*a*: 5. Besides these I noted also the following: *KU.MUN*, *B. E.*, XV, 19 : 16 | 164 : 4, 7; XIV, 23 : 1 | 65 : 13; also written *KU.DA. MUN*, *l.c.*, XV, 64 : 7, or only *MUN*, *l.c.*, XV, 16 : 8 | 41 : 20, 22, 35 | 169 : 3 | 181 : 9, which shows that *MUN* at this time was a certain kind of *flour* (not salt); *KU ASH.AN.NA*, *l.c.*, XV, 140 : 1, or only *ASH.AN.NA*, our No. 37: 8;

18 *a-na* ^{amelu}*ishparu*(= *USH.BAR*) *ù ka-ṣi-ri*[1]	was to have given to the weavers and fullers
19 *ki-i man-da-at-ti-shú-nu*[2] *id-di-nu*[3]	as their due (I beg to state that)
20 *a-shar*[4] *ú-kal-lum*[5] *ma-am-ma*[6] *ul im*(?)*-ma-ḫa-ar*	wherever one looks--none has been received:
21 *um-ma-a*[7] ½ *shiqlu*(= *ṬU*)*-ma*[8] *ḫurâṣi* (= *AZAG.GI*)	"not even a half shekel of gold
22 *ul ub-ba-lum*	do they bring."
23 *um-ma-a*[7] *a-na bîti ki-i a-ḫa-mi-*[*ish*]	"(Surely), they are, one with the other, against the 'house' (*sc.* of my 'Lord')."
24 *it*(?)*-ta-shá-ab*[9] *ù libittu*(= *SHEG*)[10] *ia-a'-nu*[11]	There are also no adobes!

KU UD, *l.c.*, XV, 140 : 2; *KU mi-ir qu*, *l.c.*, XV, 140 : 3; XIV, 117*a* : 1; *KU USH*, *l.c.*, XV, 140 : 4; *KU.DA GISH.BAR SHE.BA*, *l.c.*, XV, 140 : 5; *KU ar-ki-i* ("*rückstandiges*(?) *Mehl*"), *l.c.*, XV, 168 : 20; *ki-mu*, *l.c.*, XV, 59 : 20 | 111 : 4, 5 (not to be identified with *ki MU* (= *shum*) between two proper names, for which see p. 6, note); *ki-mu ḪAR.RA*, *l.c.*, XV, 135 : 7. *KU.QAR*, for which see Clay, *B. E.*, XIV, p. 28, note to No. 8 : 4, does probably not belong here. Are also the *ṣi-ḫi-rum*, *SHI GAR.RASH* of *B. E.*, XIV, 117*a*, ll. 1, 3, to be referred to here? With *KU*$^{ḫi.a}$ cf. 109, l. 8.

[1] For *kaṣiru* = *qaṣiru* = "fuller," see Meissner, *M. V. A. G.*, IX (1904), p. 52. [2] See p. 99, n. 3.

[3] The translation of ll. 17–21 depends entirely upon what view one takes with regard to the beginning of the apodosis or answer. Thus *per se* the following translations might be suggested (*a*) "as regards the garments of thy servant—*Erba-Marduk* has given," etc.; (*b*) "as regards the garments of thy servant *Erba-Marduk*—they have given", (*c*) "as regards the garments which thy servant *Erba-Marduk* . . . has given (was to have given)"—answer : l. 20f., *i.e.*, "wherever one looks (where they keep them), none are (have been) received."

[4] For this signification of *a-shar* cf., *e.g.*, C. T., VI, 3 : 12, *a-shar i-qa-ab-bu-ú*, *i.e.*, (I will give it) "wherever he shall say."

[5] *Ú-kal-lum* by itself might be taken either as a II[1] of כול (*i.e.*, *ukâlû-ma*, cf. *ú-ka-a-al*, *Ḫam. L.*, 37 : 6; II[2] *uktali*, Jensen, *K. B.*, VI[1], p. 356), "to lift up" (synonym of *nashû*), used not only of "the head" but also of "the eyes," *i.e.*, "to see"; cf. *kullu shá mimma*(!), II R. 27 : 39, 40*c. f.* Or, if one prefers, he might see in *ukallum* a II[1] of כלה (*i.e.*, *ukallû-ma*) with the signification of "to shut up," "to keep," *c. ina*, "in something," cf. C. T., II, 19 (= B[2] 290) : 1, *ka-li-a-ku*, "I am shut up, kept (in the house of the *abarakku*)"; *B. E.*, XIV, 135 : 3, *i-na ki-li . . . ik-la-shú-ma*. If taken in the latter sense, l. 20 might be translated: "where they keep them (*sc.* the garments) none have been received."

[6] Here "*neuter*" as in S. 273 : 22, *akâla*(= *GAR*) *ma-am-ma a-na a-ka-li-ia*, "something to eat"; *V. A. Th.*, 809 : 8, *a-na ma-am*(?)*-ma*, "for anything," *i.e.*, "at all events," *kaspa shu-bi-lam*. See also Delitzsch, *Gram.*, p. 142.

[7] Introduces here the direct speech of the implied complaint of l. 20.

[8] Stands here for *A.AN*, "viz." For the signification of *A.AN* behind numerals see now Hilprecht, *B. E.*, XX[1], p. 22, note 2, and cf. No. 33*a* : 13, p. 137.

[9] *It-ta-sha-ab*, though parallel to *ub-ba-lum*, is here in the singular on account of the subject "one" implied in *ki-i a-ḫa-mi-ish*. [10] See p. 95, n. 4.

[11] Besides *ia-a'-nu* (so also 11 : 22, 28 | 13 : 15 | 28 : 20 | 87 : 14, 18) there occur the following variants in these letters: *ia-a'-nu-um*, 26 : 20; *ia-a-nu*, 18 : 28 | 66 : 27, 29 | 71 : 16 | 83 : 21; *ia-nu*, 11 : 13 | 23 : 30 | 44 : 11 | 57 : 13, 14 | 81 : 12 | 95 : 14; *ia-a-nu-ma*, 95 : 18; *ia-a-nu-um-mi*, *B. E.*, XIV, 8 : 8. For the *-mi*(= *-mu*, *-ma*) cf. now Hinke, *B. E.*, Series D, IV, p. 282*a*. For this and the following lines cf. pp. 44f.

25 *ásh-shum a-na-ku i-tu*[1] *be-lí-ia*	As regards this that I, the *itû* of my "Lord,"
26 *al-li(?)-ka*[2] *a-na* ^{m}*Erba-*^{ilu}*Marduk*	have come (saying): "Send to *Erba-Marduk*
27 *shú-pu-ur-ma a-na* ^{m}*Ku-du-ra-ni*	that he send to *Kudurâni*"—
28 [*li*]-*ish-pu-ra-ma sukkalmaḫḫu*(= *PAP.LUGH.MAGH*) *li-i*[*q-bi*]	"so may the *sukkalmaḫḫu* (*i.e.*, *Erba-Marduk*) finally give orders
29 *libittu*(= *SHEG*)^{mesh} *li-il-bi-nu*	that adobes be made."
30 *ásh-shum*[3] *shamnu*(= *NI.GISH*)[4] *shá be-lí-ia na-shú-*[*ma?*][5]	As regards the sesame-oil of my "Lord"—"It has been removed" they read
31 *il-ta-na-su a-na* ^{m}*Ku-du-r*[*a-ni*]	when I spoke to *Kudurâni*
32 [*ardi*]-*ka ki-i aq-bu-ú um-ma-a shamnu*(= *NI.GISH*) *i-na qâti-ia* [*i-din*][6]	thy servant: "Give the sesame-oil to me."
33 *be-lí a-na shatammi*(= *SHAG.TAM*)[7] *li-ish-pu-ra-ma shamnu*(= *NI.GISH*) *shub*(= *RU*)*-ta lish-ki-nu-*[*ma*][8]	My "Lord" may now send to the *shatammi* that they store up the oil.

[1] See Chapter III, p. 35, note 4.

[2] The *a* in *al-li-ka* shows that it is dependent upon a suppressed *shá* after *ásh-shum*. And because *allika* is followed by the imperative *shupurma* (l. 27) we have to supply an *ummâ* before *a-na* ^{m}*Er-ba-*^{ilu}*Marduk*, making it a direct speech.

[3] See Chapter IV *c*, p. 82.

[4] From 84 : 6 it is apparent that *NI.GISH*, "the fat of the tree," *i.e.*, *shamnu* or "oil," was obtained by "pressing" (*saḫâtu*) the *SHE.GISH.NI*, *i.e.*, the *shamashshammu* or "*sesame*." *NI.GISH* is, therefore, at this time the "sesame oil." For other occurrences of *NI.GISH* in our letters see 13 : 14 | 21 : 32 | 27 : 12, 13, 15 | 35 : 32, 33, and for *SHE.GISH.NI* cf. 8 : 3 | 65 : 5 | 84 : 3, 5; *B. E.*, XIV, 136 : 1. Cf. p. 111, note 2.

[5] Emendation doubtful, yet probable. For *nashû* in connection with the "removal" of goods "from" or "to" certain places cf. among other passages also *B.E.*, XV, 53 : 12, *ASH.AN.NA* .... *shá É ku-nu-uk-ki a-na EN.LIL*^{ki} *na-shu-u*; *l.c.*, 55 : 3, *KU.DA* .... *shá ishtu shá* (*i.e.*, "which from that of," Clay, *l.c.*, p. 19, No. 14, wrongly "from") ^{alu}*She-li-bi na-sha-a*; *l.c.*, 100 : 1, *SHE sha ishtu EN.LIL*^{ki} *na-sha-a KI-II* (*i.e.*, *SHE shá ishtu*) ^{alu}*Kal-bi-ia* (*sc. na-sha-a*); *l.c.*, 115 : 25, *ASH.AN.NA shib-shum shá* .... *a-na karû ish-shu-ni*; *l.c.*, 181 : 2, *KU.DA* .... *a-na UNUG*^{ki} *ish-shu-ú*, etc., etc. Cf. already p. 116, note 4.

[6] This is, it seems to me, the best emendation according to the traces visible. *I-na qâti-ia i-din*, "give into my hand," is as much as *idinanni*, "give (unto) me."

[7] See Chapter III, p. 35, note 3.

[8] *Shubta shakânu*, *c. acc.*, "to put something on a place," "to make a resting place for something," *i.e.*, "to store it." Here (and p. 52, n. 5) *shakânu* is construed with *double acc.*, the possibility of which appeared to Jensen, *K. B.*, VI[1], p. 112, doubtful. Notice also the vulgar preterit form (*l*)*ish-ki*(!)-*nu* for (*l*)*ish-ku*(!)-*nu*, due, no doubt, to the influence of *n*, aided by the *i* of *lish*; cf. also p. 97, n. 7. If one prefers, he may see in *lishkinu* a III^{II1} of כין, *ushkîn* (cf. *ushmît* of מות) + *lu* = *lishkîn* (for *lushkîn*), taking it as a causative of II[1], for which see Delitzsch, *H. W. B.*, p. 322*a*, "*etwas an einem Ort aufstellen, niederlegen.*"

XII.

No. 39 (= C. B. M. 3661).

Ubarrum, a royal inspector, resp. superintendent, of rivers and canals reports to King *Kudur-Enlil* about the results of his various inspections. About 1335 B.C.

From No. 39 : 21 we learn that the writer of this and the following letter, *Ubarrum*, was in one way or another connected with the city *Dûr-*^{ilu}*Enlil*$^{ki.a\ mesh\ ki}$.[1] This very same city is mentioned, among other places, also in *B. E.*, XIV, 118 : 1[1] (5th year of *Kudur-Enlil*). It happens that this last-named tablet mentions, to a great extent, the same persons which occur again in No. 48.[2] Among the names of No. 48 is to be found also that of ^{m}*U-bar-rum* (48 : 7). From this it would follow that both[3] persons by the name of *Ubarrum*, because closely connected with one and the same city, are in all probability identical. If so, I propose to identify our writer with the father of both *Kudurâni*, *B. E.*, XIV, 112 : 7 (14th year of *Kadashman-Turgu*) and *Zakirum*, *B. E.*, XIV, 114 : 17 (15th year of *Kadashman-Turgu*); in other words, *Ubarrum*, the writer of Nos. 39 and 40, is the father of *Kudurâni*, the writer of Nos. 26[4]–28. *Ubarrum*, accordingly, must have lived at least from the 14th resp. 15th year of *Kadashman-Turgu*[5] (when he appears as the *father* of the two sons just mentioned) till the 5th resp. 8th year of *Kudurri-Enlil* (when he is introduced as contemporary of ^{m}*Na-aḫ-zi-*^{ilu}*Marduk*[6]), *i.e.*, during a space of at least twenty-three years. Supposing him to have been about forty years old when first mentioned, it would follow that he reached an age of at least sixty-three years, and wrote the letters in question sometime during the reign of *Kudur-Enlil, i.e.*, when about sixty years old (5th year of *Kudur-Enlil*). As both letters here published concern themselves with rivers and canals, it is safe to suppose that *Ubarrum* was, at the time of *Kudur-Enlil*, a royal inspector of canals and waterways, about the condition of which he had to and did report to his Lord and King.

[1] Written here *Dûr-*^{ilu}*En-lil*$^{ki.a\ ki}$, see also p. 9, note 1.

[2] Cf. *e.g.*, 48 : 8, ^{m}*Na-aḫ-zi-*^{ilu}*Marduk* = *B. E.*, XIV, 118 : 16, 121 : 11 (8th year of *Kudur-Enlil*); 48 : 11, $^{m\ ilu}$*Ram-mân(= IM)-êrish*^{ish} = *B. E.*, XIV, 118 : 19; 120 : 7 (5th year of *Kudur-Enlil*), 48 : 20, $^{m\ ilu}$*L-GIR-AN*^{mesh} = *B. E.*, XIV, 118 : 12. Cf. also 48 : 22, ^{m}*Bu-na-*^{ilu}*NIN IB* = *B. E.*, XIV, 115 : 3 (here son of ^{m}*In-ni-bi*, 1st year of *Kadashman-Enlil*). In 42 : 5, 7, ^{m}*U-bar-ru* appears as contemporary of ^{m}*Be-la-nu* (l. 17), which latter is likewise mentioned in *B. E.*, XIV, 118 : 21 (5th year of *Kudur-Enlil*) as the son of ^{m}*KUR.GAR.RA*. This last passage is, therefore, against the signification "*eunuch*" which Jensen, *K. B.*, VI[1], pp. 62, 9; 377, assigns to *KUR.GAR.RA* = *kurgarû*.

[3] *I.e.*, our writer of Nos. 39, 40 and that of 48 : 7.

[4] See introduction to No. 26, p. 117.

[5] *B. E.*, XIV, 112 : 7 | 114 : 17.

[6] Cf. No. 48 : 7 with l. 8 and with *B. E.*, XIV, 118 : 16 | 121 : 14.

The contents of this letter are the following:

(*a*) Concerning the fields of *Tukulti-É.KUR*^{ki}, ll. 4–6.

(*b*) Concerning a flooded district, ll. 7–12.

(*c*) Concerning the condition of the fields with crop belonging to *Burrûti*, ll. 12–16.

(*d*) Concerning *Dûr-*^{ilu}*Enlil*$^{ki\text{-}a\text{-}mesh\ ki}$, ll. 17(?)–26.

(*e*) Ll. 27–39, too fragmentary.

This letter may be read and translated:

1 *ardi-ka* ^{m}*U-bar-rum a-na di-na-an be-l[í]-ia lul-lik*]	Thy servant *Ubarrum*; before the presence of my "Lord" may I come,
2 *um-m[a-a] a-na be-[í]-ia-ma*	speaking thus to my "Lord":
3 *a-na eqlî*(=*A.SHAG*?[1]) *ù* ^{amelu}*akil erishê*(*PA*[2](?)*.ENGAR*)*shá be-[í]-ia*	To the field and the chief irrigator of my "Lord"
4 *shú-ul-mu i-na bu-ut*[3] *eqlê*(= *A.SHAG*)^{mesh}	greeting! With regard to the fields
5 *shá Tuk*(= *KU*)*-kul-ti-É.KUR*^{ki}[4] *shá b[e-lí]*	of *Tukulti-É.KUR* concerning which my "Lord" has written (I beg to state
6 *ish-pu-ra ik-te-di-ir-[ru?]*[5]	that) they have established their boundaries.
7 *ù ummâni*(=*SAB*)$^{hi\text{-}a}$ *shá pa-te-si*^{mesh} *ù [la-me-e?]*[6] *me-e*	And as regards the workmen of the *pa-te-si* and the [flood?] of waters
8 *ish-tum*[7] ^{naru}*Tuk*(= *KU*)*-kul-ti-É.KUR*^{ki}	extending from the canal *Tukulti-É.KUR*
9 *a-di ú-ga-ri-e*[8] *shá ta-mi-ir-ti*	to the plains in the neighborhood

[1] Doubtful, supplied according to l. 4. Might be *SHA(G).TAM.*, for which see Chapter III, p. 35, note 3.

[2] The *PA* = *akil* is uncertain. We possibly might have to read $^{amelu\ gish}$*ENGAR*, *i.e.*, "one that tends the watering machine." For ^{gish}*ENGAR*, *i.e.*, *narṭabu*, "*Schöpfwerk*," see Hilprecht, *B. E.*, IX, p. 10, note to l. 2, cf. *Code of Ḫammurabi*, 38 : 11, 14, and above p. 35, note 3. A greeting "to the field and irrigator(s)" would be, it seems, more in accord with the position of *Ubarru*, the royal inspector of canals and waterways.

[3] *I-na bu-ut* = *ina muḫḫi* = *shá* or *áshshum*, see Chapter II, p. 24, note 7.

[4] Cf. here ^{m}*Tukulti*(= *KU*)^{ti}*-É.KUR*, father of ^{m}*Il-li-ia*, *B. E.*, XIV, 18*a*, 7 (6th year of *Na-zi-Ma-ru-ttásh*). As *KU* has also the value *tukulti*, we might transcribe *Tukulti*(= *KU*)$^{kul\ ti}$.

[5] For the double r cf. Behrens, *L. S. S.*, II[1], pp. 47, 1; 29, 4; 35. As I[2] has also passive signification (Delitzsch, *Gram.*, p. 232) we might translate: "their boundaries are established."

[6] So according to No. 24 : 20 (see p. 50, note 1)? An emendation [*la-*]*me-e* or *me-te-iq me-e*, Hinke, *B. E.*, Series D, Vol. IV, p. 146, l. 31, is, according to the traces visible, impossible.

[7] Notice the *m* in *ish-tum* . . . . *a-di*.

[8] For *ugâru*, *i.e.*, "*die zur Stadt gehörigen Ländereien*," see Meissner, *A. P.*, p. 123.

10 *ḫa-am-ri*[1] *shá i-na mi-li ma-ḫa-ri-i*[2]	of the *ḫamri*—the district which during a former flood
11 *mu-ú iṣ-ba-tu-ma ip-ti-nu-ma*[3]	the waters had seized and devoured (I beg to state that)
12 *iz-zi-zu*[4] *iḫ-ta-tu-ni ù ḫar-bu*[5]	they have subdued (*sc.* the [flood] of waters of that district). And with regard to the (field with) crop
13 *shá* ^{m}*Bu-ur-ru-ti shá i-na*	belonging to *Burrûti*, which
14 *ta-mi-ir-ti ḫa-am-ri*	in the inundated district has become free
15 *za-ku*[6] *dù(=dul)-ul-la*[7] *ul i-pu-ush*	(*sc.* from the waters of the flood, I beg to state that) nothing is being (has been) done.
16 *mu-ú ma-ḫa-ru-ú-tum*[8] [. . . . .]	The former waters . . . .
17 *ù ummâni(= ṢAB)*$^{ḫi.a}$ *shá be-li-ia dù(= dul)-ul-la*	And as regards the workmen of my "Lord," (I beg to say that) the work
18–20 [. . . .]	. .
21 [. . . .] *shá Dûr-*^{ilu}*En-lil*$^{ki\ a\text{-}mesh\text{-}ki}$	. . . . of *Dûr-Enlil*.
22 [. . . .]	. . . .

[1] With *ḫa-am-ri*, cf. l. 14; 52 : 19, *zêr*(?) *eqli*(= *A.SHAG*) *ḫa-am-rum*; *B. E.*, XIV, 114 : 13, 14, *Ḫa-am-ri*^{ki}. Delitzsch, *H. W. B.*, p. 283*a*, mentions a *ḫamru* without giving a translation. Küchler, *Medizin*, p. 116, renders *ḫamâru* by "*wallen*." In our passage here *ḫamru* is apparently a kind of *field*, more particularly a field that has been seized and cast into disorder by waters. Prof. Hilprecht (personal communication of July 9, 1908) compares with it, quite correctly, the Hebr. חֹמֶר, Hab. 3 : 15, Ex. 8 : 10, and suggests a translation "*Ueberschwemmungsgebiet*."

[2] *Ma-ḫa-ri-i* (a side form of *maḫrû*) has a plural *ma-ḫa-ru-ú-tum* (l. 16); from this it follows that *mu-ú* (l. 16) must likewise be a plural.

[3] *Ip-ti-nu-ma*, root פתן. The signification "to strengthen, support, protect" (Hilprecht, *B. E.*, IX, p. 53, note ‡), does not fit here, nor does any signification which Delitzsch, *H. W. B.*, p. 553*b*, assigns to it. *Patânu* here is parallel to *ṣabâtu*, and, because it follows the latter, expresses the result of the *ṣabâtu*. Delitzsch, *l.c.*, mentions a *pitnu*, "*Schlinge*," *i.e.*, lit. "a seizer," thus showing again that *patânu* is a synonym of *ṣabâtu*. The waters took (*ṣabâtu*) and seized (*patânu*) the fields during a former flood and, as a result of this, were cast into disorder (cf. Arab. *patana*, *c. i.*, *exciter, séduire*); *pitnat, discorde, sédition, troubles*, etc.). Still better it would be to derive this *patânu*, with Hilprecht, from *patânu* = *akâlu*, "to eat, to devour," Delitzsch, *H. W. B.*, p. 553*b*., hence *patânu*, *iptin*, *ipattan*!

[4] *Iz-zi-zu iḫ-ta-tu-ni* is (like *iṣ-ba-tu-ma ip-ti-nu-ma*) a ἓν διὰ δυοῖν; lit.: "as regards the workmen . . . . they arose, subdued the waters (*sc.* by leading them back into their dams, cf. 10 : 19)." *Iḫ-ta-tu-ni* I take as a I² of חתת, "to subdue," Delitzsch, *H. W. B.*, p. 295*b*.

[5] For *ḫar-bu* see p. 130, note 6.

[6] *Za-ku* I take as a permansive of זכה, "to be or become free of something" (Delitzsch, *H. W. B.*, p. 254*a*). Translate: "with regard to . . . . which (is situated) in . . . . (and which) has become free (*sc.* from the water of the flood)."

[7] For *dulla epêshu* see also Behrens, *L. S. S.*, II[1], p. 8.

[8] Cf. above, note 2.

23 [. . . .] *li-ish-pu-ú-ra-[am-]ma*[1]	. . . . may send
24–26 [. . . .]	. . . .
27 *um-ma-a a-na be-lì-ia i-na* [. . . .]	Also the following to my "Lord": "In . . . .
28–37 [. . . .]	. . . .
38 *shá be-lì ish-pu-ra a-na be-lì-ia*	concerning which my 'Lord' has inquired (I beg
39 *ush-te-bi-la*	to say that) I have sent it to my 'Lord.'"

XIII.

No. 40 (= C. B. M. 5131). (Cf. photographic reproduction, Pl. X, 24, 25.)

Ubarrum, the royal superintendent of rivers and canals, lodges a complaint against the prefect of *Dûr-Sukal-paṭra*^{ki}. Time of *Kudur-Enlil*, about 1335 B.C.

For the general introduction see preceding letter, No. 39.

The contents of this letter, being similar to those of No. 39, may be subdivided into the following parts:

(*a*) Complaint lodged against the prefect of *Dûr-Sukal-paṭra*^{ki} for neglect of a certain canal, ll. 3–20.

The answer to this complaint lodged with King *Kudur-Enlil* by *Ubarru* is, no doubt, contained in No. 42 : 4f.: "As regards the fields, which my 'Lord' has given and concerning which *Ubarru* has reported to my 'Lord' saying: 'he has neglected (lit. forsaken) them,' (*s.c.* I beg to state that) 'I have not neglected (forsaken) them,'" see above, p. 26, note 6. From this it follows that No. 42 is a letter of the "prefect" (*ḫazannu*) of *Dûr-Sukal-paṭra*, addressed to the *be-lì* or King *Kudur-Enlil*, teaching us that the prefect held *Dûr-Sukal-paṭra* as a fief of the crown (*eqlê*^{mesh} *shá be-lì id-di-na*, 42 : 4, cf. below l. 11, *shá i-na libbi*^{bi}*-shú ú-ma-al-lu-ú*), and that royal officers never mention their titles when writing to their "Lord," but have to be content with the attribute "servant," *ardu*.

(*b*) Request that the King issue orders to the sheriff[2] that the waters of the *Ilu-ipush* and *Nalaḫ* canals be led back into their dams, ll. 21–26.

[1] Notice here the long *û* in *bù* and cf., *e.g.*, 21 : 28, *im-qu-ú-tu*; 16 : 12, *i-ra-'u-ú-ub* (or *i-ra-a'-ú-ub*?); 38 : 2, *lu-ú-ul-li-ik*.

[2] The fact that orders shall be given to the "sheriff" shows that the waters of these two canals, in which the King has an interest, had been criminally put to misuse.

1 *ardi-ka* ^{m}*U-bar-rum a-na di-na-an be-li-i*[*a lul-lik*]	Thy servant *Ubarrum*; before the presence of my "Lord" may I come,
2 *um-ma-a a-na be-li-ia-a-ma*	speaking thus to my "Lord":
3 *ḫa-za-an-nu shá Dûr-*^{m}*Sukal*(= *PAP*?)-*pad-ra*^{ki}[1]	The prefect of *Dûr-Sukal-paṭra*
4 *nam-ga-ra*[2] *is-si-*[*ki-*]*ir*[3] *a-di shi-il-ta*[4]	has shut off the canal so that they can irrigate (water) at the most
5 *ta-mi-ra-ti*[5] *shá ḫar-pi*[6] *i-sha-aq-qu-ú*[7]	only two fields with crops,
6 *ù* 20 *ḫar-bu*[8] *shá ub-bu-li*[9]	while there are 20 (fields with) crops which
7 [*ish-shá*(?)]-*ak-nu ù i-di-ik-ku-ú*[10]	are perfectly dry and hence are destroyed.

[1] For formation cf. *Dûr-Kuri-Galzu* and *Dûr-*^{m} ^{ilu}*Errish*(*t*)-*apal-iddina*, *B. E.*, XIV, 18 : 7.

[2] For the various occurrences and writings see under "Names of Rivers and Canals."

[3] *Sakâru* when used of "canals" means "to shut off, stop up, dam" (opp. *pitû*). Cf. *is-ki-ir*, 10 : 9; *e si-ki-ir-ma*, 3 . 18; *is-si-ki-ir*, 31 : 32; *us-si-ki-ir*, 12 : 5. *Issikir* = *itsikir* = *itsakir* (the *i* in the last syllable on account of the r! see p. 97, note 7) = *itsakar*, a I², so far known only from this passage.

[4] *Shi-il-ta* here hardly the same as *shettu* (= *LALSAR*), "field" (Hommel, *S. L.*, p. 76 to S^{c}, 146), but the fem. of *shinâ*, "two"; as such in opposition to "20," l. 6. For the construction cf. *shinâ ûmê* and *shelalti ûmê*, Delitzsch, *Gram.*, p. 333.

[5] *Tamirâti* are the fields situated in the immediate neighborhood and environs of a city, or a flooded, inundated district, cf. No. 39 : 9, 11, pp. 127, 128.

[6] This writing here proves that *ḫar-bu* (l. 6; Delitzsch, *H. W. B.*, p. 289*a*) has to be read *ḫarpu*. Johns, *A. D. D.*, p. 131, assigns to the word *ḫarbûtu* a meaning "waste," or "cropped," that is to say, "stubble" land. Myhrman, *Z. A.*, XVI, p. 176, renders *ḫar-bi* by "*Verwustung*?" In view of the fact that *ḫarbu* has to be read *ḫarpu* and that it renders the Sumerian *EBUR.GID.DA*, "the great (long) harvest," and is the same word as the Hebrew חרף, "harvest," the *ta-mi-ra-ti shá ḫar-pi* must be "fields" that are "*with crops ready to be harvested.*" For *ḫarbu*, cf. 17 : 33 | 11 : 14, 18, 24 | 39 : 12 | 68 : 29; *ḫar-bu* c. numeral, 28 : 21, 22 | 10 : 6 | 60 : 2 | 68 : 5, 6; *ḫar-bi*, 8 : 18; *ḫar-bi* c. numeral, 3: 21, 37 | 34 : 28, 33, 34 | 63 : 10, 11, 15. See also *P.* 96 : 9 and Peiser, *l.c.*, p. 7, note.

[7] *I-sha-aq-qu* may be taken either as 3d pers. plur. masc. præs. I¹: "so that they (= German indefinite 'man') irrigate or can irrigate (= *ein Feld tranken, bewassern*, Delitzsch, *H. W. B.*, p. 685*a*, *b*) only (up to) two fields with crops"; or, which is less probable, *ishaqqû* may be considered a IV¹ = *ishshaqqû*, dependent upon *ḫar-pi*. In this case *ta-mi-ra-ti shá ḫar-pi* would have to be considered as a kind of "composite noun," the gender of which being determined by the word nearest to the verb, *i.e.*, by *ḫar-pi*, a plur. masc. Translate: "so that only two fields with crops are watered."

[8] Objects counted are construed as, and stand in, the singular. Cf. here note 6 and p. 95, note 6.

[9] *Ub-bu li* here not "*Zerstorung durch Insekten*," Jensen, *K. B.*, VI¹, p. 580, but "*ein sehr trocken sein*," *i.e.*, "to be very dry." Lit., "which exist" (IV¹ *shakânu*) as "very dry ones." Or have we to read [*sha*]-*ak-nu* = Perm. I¹, with the same meaning? The size of the break would speak rather for the latter emendation.

[10] The same form occurs again in 66 : 6 (context mutilated). To derive it from דכה (*i.e.*, דקה (!), Delitzsch, *H. W. B.*, p. 216*b*), "to overthrow, cast down, tear down," does not give any sense. We would expect here some such signification as "to perish," but this meaning is not yet established for *daqû*. Delitzsch, *H. W. B.*, p. 52*a*, mentions a root אכה, "*darben, mangeln, etw., entbehren.*" This would fit very well here, but on account of the writing with *d* this root could not be אכה, but had to be אקה, *i.e.*, עקה (related with postbiblical עָקָא, "trouble, distress,"

8 *[be]-lì me-e a-a-ú-ti*[1] *ish-ki-ma*	My "Lord," thus he has watered and
9 *[. . . .]-ú*[2] *nam-gar-ra is-ki-ir*	. . . . the canal he has shut off!
10 *be-lì lish-pu-ra-am-ma ta-mi-ir-ta*	My "Lord" may give orders that he water
11 *shá i-na libbi*^{bi}*-shú ú-ma-al-lu-ú*[3] *lish-ki*	the whole field with which he has been entrusted
12 *ù ub-bu-la li-shá-ak-li-ma'*[4]	and thus put an end to its being dry.
13 *be-lì mi-ig-ra ù e-ri-shá*	My "Lord," may not delight in a favorite
14 *la i-ḫa-ad-di nam-gar-shú mush-shur*[5]	and (or: *i.e.*, in) an irrigator who neglects his canal!
15 *ù shú-ú a-na*[6] *pa-an nam-ga-ri*	Let either the superintendent of the canal
16 *shá be-lì-ia a-shi-ib mu-ú i-na nam-ga-ri-shu*	of my "Lord"—if water be plentiful in his canal—
17 *m[a]-a'-du ù shú-ú a-na pa-an*	or the superintendent of
18 *nam-ga-ri an-ni-i a-shi-ib*	*this* canal (*sc.*, which has been neglected so shamefully by the prefect)

עָקַ, "to embarrass," etc.). I propose, therefore, to take *i-di-iq-qu* as standing for *i'ṭaqqû, iṭṭaqqû, iṭṭeqqû, iṭeqqu, idiqqû*, I[2] of יָקָה, "to be in want." The long *û* at the end is not the plural, but the relative in pause: *iṭṭaqqaju*, after *shá* (l. 6). Hilprecht (letter of July 9, 1908) proposes to derive *idikkû* from *dikû*, postulating the significations: 1, "*stürzen, vernichten, zerstoren*" (transitive); 2, "*umsturzen, umfallen, umkommen*" (intransitive), translating "*und verderben (kommen um)*," and referring this expression to the "*Getreide, das die Kopfe hangen lasst, das umfallt, umknickt.*" However, if one prefers, he may see in *i-di-ik-ku-u* a I[2] or IV[1] (cf. No. 26 : 14, *i-li-ik-qu-a*, see p. 119, note 3) of דכה = דקה with *passive* signification. "and in consequence of which (= *ù consecutivum*) are cast down, destroyed!" The last derivation and translation is possibly better than the one mentioned above ("are in want").

[1] *A-a-u-ti* cannot be here translated by "*wer, welcher*" (*H. W. B.*, p. 17*b*), but must be, on account of its position (after the noun), an *adjective*. *A-a-ú-ti me-e* — "what waters?" *me-e a-a-ú-ti* = "what kind of waters!" *i.e.*, "such waters!" This line, therefore, is a complaint in the form of ridicule and scorn which the writer expresses with regard to the prefect's doings: "My 'Lord!' (or *en-ni* = *en-na*, "behold"?) in such a way, with such waters he has watered the fields!"

[2] Read [*ù shu*]-*u*? For -*ma ù* cf. also p. 138, note 4. Translate: "Thus he has watered seeing that (*ù*) 'that one' (*shú-ú*) has shut off the canal."

[3] Lit., "with which he (*i.e.*, my "Lord") has filled his heart," *i.e.*, "which he has given him." Hence *i-na libbi*^{bi}*-shú* = *ana* (*ina*) *qâti-shú umallû*, "with which he has filled his hand, which he has entrusted to him."

[4] III[1] of כלה, a synonym of סחה, and having the same meaning as *saḫâpu*, "to cover something, to suppress it, to bring to end, to end."

[5] *Mu-ush-shur*, II[1] permansive in circumstantial clause: "leaving," *i.e.*, "who leaves." This explains how the prefect "shut off" (*is-si-ki-ir*, l. 4) the canal: he left it, paid no attention to it, neglected it (Permansive II[1] = duration and intensity!). And by neglecting it, the canal was in course of time filled up with mud. This caused the dryness (*ub-bu-li*, l. 6).

[6] *A-na pa-an* . . . . *a-shi-ib* = *ina pân âshib*, one that dwells, is at the head of something, *i.e.*, a superintendent. Cf. here also 13 : 9, *a-shi-ib pa-ni-shú-nu*. Or is it only "the one who lives near it"?

19 *i-na nam-ga-ri-shú(?)*[1] *me-e lil-ki-ma*[2]	lead (take) waters through (into) his canal
20 *nam-gar-ra shá be-li-ia li-mash-shi-ir*[3]	and (in this case) let alone my "Lord's" canal!
21 *me-e* {nâru}*Ilu-i-pu-ush*	As regards the waters of the *Ilu-ipush*
22 *ù me-e* {nâru}*Na-la-ah*[4]	and the waters of the *Nalah*--
23 *me-e zi-it-ti*[5] *shá be-li-ia*	waters in which my "Lord" has an interest--
24 *be-li a-na GÙ.EN.NA*[6] *shulmu* (=*DI*) *li-iq-bi-ma*[7]	"let my 'Lord' send greeting to the sheriff
25 *a-na ki-sir*(= *BU*)*-ti*[8] *lish-pu-ru-ni-im-ma*[9]	that they lead (the waters) back into the dam
26 *lid-di-nu-ma e-ri-shú la i-ma-ad-di.*[10]	in order that the 'irrigator' do not complain."

XIV.

No. 75 (= C. B. M. 12,582). (Cf. photographic reproduction, Pl. III, 89.)

Royal summons issued by King *Shagarakti-Shuriash* to his sheriff *Amel-Marduk*. About 1325 B.C.

The King as *shakkanakku* {ilu}*Enlil* administered and looked after the Temple property of the god of Nippur, consisting of fields, flocks, taxes, revenues, etc. In the administration of such vast and extended holdings of god Enlil he had to depend, in a large measure at least, upon his officials: shepherds, farmers, collectors of taxes, prefects, governors, etc. It is only natural that such an army of officers, differing

[1] *I.e.*, into the canal of the *hazannu* (l. 3) who had neglected it by forsaking it (l. 14).

[2] *I.e.*, my Lord may command that either he . . . or he lead (take).

[3] Seeing that the *hazannu* has forsaken and neglected his canal, the king shall issue orders to the 'superintendent" (who apparently is a higher official than the "prefect") that the latter lead waters through (into) the neglected canal and in this case do without the waters from the "Lord's" canal.

[4] For the situation of this canal cf. the topographical map of Nippur in *T. D. A.* of *U. of Pa.*, II, p. 223f., and see Clay, *B. E.*, XIV, p. 7, comparing with it what has been said under {nâru}*Nalah* in "Names of Canals and Rivers," below.

[5] See Delitzsch, *H. W. B.*, p. 265*b*; Tallquist, *Sprache*, p. 70, and Meissner, *A. P.*, p. 101.

[6] For this title cf. introduction to No. 75, p. 133.

[7] Lit., "speak greeting."

[8] With *ki-sir-ti*, "stone dam," cf. also 13 : 6.

[9] *Lish-bu-ru-ni-im-ma lid-di-nu-ma*, [illegible]: that they (the men instructed by the sheriff, *i.e.*, the deputy sheriffs) may send or give orders that the waters of the two canals (ll. 21, 22) be given back, returned, led back into their dams.

[10] For *i-ma-ad-di* = *i-ma-at-ti*, root מטה, see Jensen, *K. B.*, VI[1], pp. 364, 557, "*klagen, stöhnen, Wehklage erheben u. dergl.*" and cf. 13 : 18, *ú-ma-da* = *umatta*.

in rank and influence, could not at all times work together in harmony and peacefulness. Then, as now, petty jealousies made themselves felt, which very often took the form of slander. Wheresoever and whensoever opportunity offered itself, one official would accuse the other of all imaginable offenses in the administration of his particular office. The result of such an accusation, which here is indignantly referred to as "*slander*," is this letter.

Ḫanibi, son of *Sâmi*, a shepherd, had complained to the King, his highest superior, of having been slandered by *Errish-nâdin-shum* and others. The nature of this slander is, unfortunately, not to be made out, as the passage in question is very mutilated. It possibly referred to some wrong statements supposedly to have been made by the complainant at the time when the inventory of the flocks was taken. The King, knowing that the affairs of the Temple and State can best be administered only if slanders, wrong accusations, and jealousies give way to peace, quietness, and "brotherly love" among the several officials, dispatches this letter to *Amel-Marduk*, summoning him to produce the orginators of the slanders and bring them before him (the King).

Two things become evident from this letter: (1) Every offense against an official of the Temple or State is a crime against the King—a *lèse majesté*. The King, therefore, appears not only as the person to whom the officials had to and did report their grievances, but he, as good administrator, takes an interest in the happiness and contentment of his subordinates by trying to do justice to both, offender and offended. This he did by inquiring into the *pro* and *con* of the accusations and by passing judgment thereon: the King becomes thus the highest judge, the court of last appeal. (2) *Amel-Marduk*, to whom the royal summons was issued, is evidently an official of the King, whose functions consisted in citing, resp. arresting, and bringing before the King, for purposes of judgment (*dînu*), slanderers or other criminal offenders. From 81 : 6f. we learn that such an official was known by the title *GÙ.EN.NA*, *i.e.*, lit. "strength of the Lord," who may or may not have other *GÙ.EN.NA's*, *i.e.*, deputy sheriffs, under him, for we read, *l.c.*, *ásh-shum mârê*^{mesh} *Ni-ib-bu-rum shá GU.EN.NA-ka ash-shú-mi-ka im-ta-na-aḫ-ḫa-rum um-ma-a a-na Mâr-*^{m}*In-ni-bi a-na di-ni* [. . . .], *i.e.*, "as regards the Nippurians whom thy[1] sheriff has seized (lit. has received) upon thy command (I beg to state) the following: 'To *Mâr-Innibi* for the purpose of judgment [he has taken them[2]].'" *Amel-Marduk*, exercising here the functions of the *GÙ.EN.NA*, has, therefore, to be identified with the *Amel-*^{ilu}*Marduk GÙ.EN.NA En-lil*^{ki}, *B. E.*,

[1] *I.e.*, ^{m}*Aḫu-ú-a-Ba-ni*, the addressee of the letter, who, therefore, must have been a sheriff-in-chief.

[2] See already above, p. 24, note 5.

XIV, 136 : 1. From *B. E.*, XIV, we furthermore learn that *Amel-Marduk* lived during the 5th[1] and 8th[2] year of *Kudur-Enlil*,[3] "the beginning of the reign,"[4] and the 8th,[5] 9th,[6] and 10th[7] year of *Shagarakti-Shuriash*. As sheriff (*GÙ.EN.NA*[8]) he had, of course, a prison (*ki-li*, *B. E.*, XIV, 135 : 3), where such persons as $^{m\ ilu}$*Errish*(*t*)-*nâdin-shum*, the slanderer, were held (*kalû*) for judgment; he had to be present (*ú-kin-nu*) when the several scribes made their final reports (*ri-ḫa-a-nu shá DUB.SHAR*^{mesh} *shá NIN.AN*^{mesh}, *B. E.*, XIV, 136 : 1) or "drew the balance of accounts." In short, wherever and whenever the "affairs (*amâti*) of the King" were in need of the *strong* support of the "arm of the law," the *GÙ.EN.NA* had to give it: he was "the Lord's (*EN-NA*) strength (*GÙ*)," as such acting "for (or in place of) the King," *ina muḫ LUGAL*, p. 84, note 9.

Amel-Marduk seems to have advanced to the office of a *GU.EN.NA* from that of a ^{amelu}*SAG.LUGAL*. In the latter position he is mentioned during the 6th and 7th year of *Shagarakti-Shuriash*. I read therefore, *B. E.*, XIV, 132 : 2, [^{m}*Amel*-^{ilu}]*Marduk* ^{amelu}*SAG.LUGAL*. In his capacity as *SAG.LUGAL* he was present (*ú-kin-nu*) at the taking of the inventory of the flocks (*mi-nu LIT.GUD ù GANAM.LU*). This very same tablet mentions also ^{m}*Ḫa-ni-bi mâr Sa-a-mi* (*l.c.*, l. 12), the *na-gid* or "shepherd," who appears in our letter as the complainant (l. 7). There can, then, be no doubt that the *Amel-Marduk* of our letter has to be identified with the *GÙ.EN.NA* of Nippur, and that the King who addressed this letter to his sheriff was none other than *Shagarakti-Shuriash*. Our letter has, consequently, to be placed at about 1325 B.C. For documents which are clearly official reports (^{abnu}*DUB*) of the sheriff *Amel-Marduk*[9] to his "Lord," *i.e.*, either to King *Kudur-Enlil* or to King *Shagarakti-Shuriash*, see No. 3 (report about the condition of canals, cf. 40 : 24 | 46 : 11); *B. E.*, XIV, 123*a* : 15 (report about the royal(!) *ZI.GA*), and *B. E.*, XIV, 137 (report about the liabilities, *LÀL.NI*, of the prefects, *ḫazannu*). Our letter may be transcribed and translated as follows:

[1] *B. E.*, XIV, 118 : 19.

[2] *L.c.*, 123*a* : 15.

[3] The *Amel*-^{ilu}*Marduk* mentioned in the 13th year of *Ku*[. . . .], *B. E.*, XIV, 125 : 4, belongs to the reign of *Ku*[*ri-Galzu*!]. This against Clay, *l.c.*

[4] *L.c.*, 127 : 3.

[5] *L.c.*, 135 : 3, 15.

[6] *L.c.*, 136 : 1.

[7] *L.c.*, 137 : 27.

[8] For other occurrences see 40 : 21 | 45 : 19 | 46 : 11 | 59 : 5; *B. E.*, XIV, 39 : 1 | 142 : 28; *B. E.*, XV, 191 : 13; Meissner, *Ideogramme*, No. 2050; Hinke, *B. E.*, Series D, IV, p. 261*b*. For the *GÙ.EN.NA* among the gods see my forthcoming volume on "The Religious Texts of the Temple Library."

[9] The *shú-la-âsh-shum* after *Amel-Marduk* in *B. E.*, XV, 171 : 6, which Clay, *l.c.*, p. 26*b*, takes to be a title, is, of course, an Imperat. III[1] of עלה + *shú* + *m*(*a*).

1	*a-na* ^{m}*Amel*-^{ilu}*Marduk ki-bi-ma*	To *Amel-Marduk* speak,
2	*um-ma sharru*(= *LUGAL*)-*ma*	thus saith the King.
3	*um-ma-a a-na* ^{m}*Amel*-^{ilu}*Marduk*	The following to *Amel-Marduk*:
4	^{m} ^{ilu}*Errish*(*t*) (= *NIN.IB*)-*nâdin* (= *SE*)-*shum*(= *MU*)	*Errish-nâdin-shum*,
5	*mâr* ^{m}*Ap-pa*[1]-*na-a*-[*a*?]	son of *Appanâi*,
6	*shá da-ba-ab* [*limnûtim*]	who has slandered
7	*it-ti* ^{m}*Ḫa-ni*-[*bi id-bu-ub*]	*Ḫanibi*;
8	*ù* ^{m}*Dam-qu* [*mâr* . . . .]	and *Damqu*, the son of . . . .
9	[*shá i*]*t-ti* " ^{ilu}*XXX*-[. . . .]	who has slandered *Sin*-. . . .
10	[*da-ba*]-*ab* [*limnûtim idbub*]	
11	*ù* [. . . .]	and . . . .
12	[. . . .] ^{m} ^{ilu}*XXX*-[*êrish*]	. . . . *Sin*-.
13–17	[. . . .]	. .
18	[. . . .] *a bu*(?) *na*(?)	
19	[. . . .]-*di-in*	
20	[. . . .]-*da-ku*	. .
21	[. . . . *be*]-*el da-ba-bi-shú*	. . . . his slanderer
22	*a-na m*[*uḫ*]-*ia*	bring him
23	*shú-bi-la-ash-shú*.	before me!

XV.

No. 33*a* (= C. B. M. 6123). (Cf. photographic reproduction, Pl. IV, 10, 11.)

A general's explanatory letter to the King. About 1400 B.C.

The expressions "guards," "chariots," "fortress," "enemy," "to campaign," "to go on an expedition" (*ana girri alâku* resp. *tebû*), "to plunder," etc., etc., occurring in this letter, show that the writer must have been an officer, more especially a general commanding the chariots (cf. *ash-ba-tu*, l. 22) in his King's army. Unfortunately for our investigation there occurs only *one name* in the whole letter, and this is not mentioned in any of the tablets published in *B. E.*, XIV and XV. We are, therefore, at a loss to state definitely who the King here referred to was. The name of the writer and "general" was ^{m}*NIM.GI-shar*(= *LUGAL*)-*ilî*(= *AN*)^{mesh}, *i.e.*, "*NIM.GI* is the king of the gods"—a formation parallel to *Rammân-shar-ilî*

[1] Or ^{m}*Isin*(= *Ezen*)-*na-a*-[*a*]?

(No. 36 : 1; *B. E.*, XIV, 101 : 5 *et passim*), *Marduk-shar-ilî* (*B. E.*, XIV, 121 : 3), etc. Clay, *B. E.*, XIV, p. 48*b*, mentions a *NIM.GI-ra-bi* (*l.c.*, 142 : 5), and in *B. E.*, XV, p. 38*a*, a *NIM.GI-ra-bu* (*l.c.*, 130 : 3), adding in both cases: "(Cassite)". This addition he, no doubt, made on the strength of Delitzsch, *Die Sprache der Kossäer*, p. 26 : 41, where the Cassite *nim-gi-ra-ab* is explained by the Assyrian *e-ṭe-rum*, "to protect." As, however, *NIM.GI-ra-bi*, resp. *NIM.GI-ra-bu*, corresponds to such names as *Shamash-rabû* (*B. E.*, XV, 183 : 3) or *Ilu-ra-bi* (*B. E.*, XIV, 39 : 7), resp. *Ilu-rabu* (*l.c.*, 106 : 4), we have to understand the so-called Cassite vocabulary *cum grano salis*! *NIM.GI-ra-ab* (*ra-bi, rabû*) *must* be translated by "*NIM.GI* is (the) great one (*sc.* among the gods)." This "great one" was, like *NIN.IB*, a god of lightning, "one who smites the enemies," and also "one who *protects* (*êṭir*) the faithful." In this wise it happened that *NIM.GI-ra-ab* came to be looked upon as the *e-ṭe-rum*, the "protector" *par excellence*. Such an ^{ilu}*E-di-ru* we find among the gods of *É-sag-ìl*, III *R.*, 66, Rev. 13*b*. And as *NIN.IB* was identified with *Enlil*, so *NIM.GI*, resp. *NIM.GI-ra-bi*, was considered to be one with *Ḫar-be* (= *Enlil*); hence the name *NIM.GI-ra-Ḫar-be* (C. B. M. 3446, Clay, *B. E.*, XIV, 48*b*) has to be read *Êṭir*^{ra}*-Ḫarbe*, "a protector is *Ḫarbe*." *NIM.GI* becomes thus the name of a Cassite god who played originally the rôle of the "Son," but who, later on, was identified with the "Father," with *Ḫarbe*.

The several subject matters of this letter are clearly indicated by the stereotyped repetition of the *um-ma-a a-na be-lí-ia-ma* and are the following:

(*a*) *Answer to an inquiry* of the King as to whether the chariots have gone out to the place previously designated, ll. 5–12.

(*b*) The *five old chariots shall go out on the expedition* as commanded, ll. 12–14.

(*c*) Suggestion as to how the *gouvernement* and the fortress may be protected by the cities and by the writer, ll. 15–24.

(*d*) Rectification of the writer's former suggestion as to the use of one chariot, coupled with the request that the King command either the *sak-shup-par* or the writer to go out with two chariots, while other two are to be left behind to guard the fortified camp, ll. 25–37.

The letter reads:

1 *ardi-ka* ^{m}*NIM.GI-shar*(= *LUGAL*)-*ilî*(= *AN*)$^{[mesh]}$	Thy servant *NIM.GI-shar-ili*;
2 *a-na di-na-an be-lí-ia l*[*u-ul-li*]*k*	before the presence of my "Lord" may I come(!)

3 *a-na âlu*^{hal}[1] *maṣṣartu*(= *EN.NU.UN.*[*NA*])[2]	Unto the cities and the guards
4 *shá be-lí-ia shú-ul-*[*m*]*u*	of my "Lord" greeting!
5 *um-ma-a a-na be-lí-ia-ma*	The following to my "Lord":
6 *shá be-lí ish-pu-ra um-ma-a V* ^{isu}*nar-kabti*[3]*-ka*	With regard to what my "Lord" has written, saying:
7 *lu-ú am-ra-ad-ma*[4] *a-shar a-sap-pa-rak-ku*	"Behold I have ordered out thy five chariots; have they started going
8 *tu-ṣi-i-ma*[5] *tal*(= *PI*)*-lak*	to the place I have written thee?"
9 *um-ma-a a-na be-lí-ia-ma*	I beg to state the following to my "Lord":
10 *at-tu-ú-a*[6] *a-na muḫ V* ^{isu}*narkabtu*	"I am there at the head of the five chariots,
11 *shá be-lí i-du-ú a-u i-tu um-ma-a*	as my 'Lord' knows—or has the inspector not informed (my Lord) saying:
12 *i-ba-ásh-shi*[7] *um-ma-a a-na be-lí-ia-ma*	'he is'?" Also the following to my "Lord":
13 *V-ma*[8] ^{isu}*narkabtu labirtu* (= *Ù*)[9] *a-na ṣir-ri shá be-lí*	"The five old chariots shall go to wheresoever my 'Lord'
14 *i-gab-bu-ú il-la-ak*[10]	shall command."

[1] For *ḫal* resp. *ásh-ásh* as plural sign cf. l. 15, *an-nu-ú-tum âlu*^{hal} and see Chapter I, p. 12, note 1.

[2] *EN.NU.UN* = *EN.NU.UN* = *maṣṣartu*, *H. W. B.*, p. 478*a*. See also p. 37, note 9.

[3] Objects counted stand in, and are construed as, singulars—hence *tu-ṣi-i-ma tal-lak*, l. 8—cf. *i-ba-ash-shi*, l. 12; *i-ba-at*, l. 24, and see p. 95, note 6. In l. 34, *II* ^{isu}*narkabtu* are treated, however, as a *masc. singl.*: *lil-li-ik* for *lû tallik*. See also note 10.

[4] Delitzsch, *H. W. B.*, p. 125*b*, mentions a root מרד without giving its signification. According to the context *marâdu* may have some such meaning as "to ask for," "summon," "(to command) to go or bring out" (cf. Arab. *marada*, "*pousser*"), "to be in need of." This passage shows that *marâdu* has an *a* in the Pret. and Pres.: *amrad, amarad.*

[5] By itself this *ἅπαξ λεγόμενον*, expressed in the form of a circumstantial clause (Pret. *plus* Pres., Delitzsch, *Gram.*, § 152, p. 362), might be taken as referring to the writer: "hast thou gone out" (then 2d pers. masc. singl.). In no event, however, can *tu-ṣi-i-ma* be taken in the sense of either "hast thou brought out" (this had to be *tushêṣi*) or "thou (they) shalt (shall) go" (this required a form *tuṣṣi*, cf. l. 26, *uṣ-ṣa-am-ma*).

[6] Literally: "As regards me I have come to the five chariots (and am now with them), as my Lord knows—or has the inspector not (informed my Lord) saying, 'he has come to them' (*sc.* and is now with them)?"

[7] This may be either Pres. of *bashû*, "to be," or Pret. of *bâ'u*, "to come," *plus shi*, referring back to V ^{isu}*narkabtu*.

[8] For this *-ma* cf. 35 : 21, p. 124, note 8.

[9] With *Ù* = *labirtu*, "old," cf. *B. E.*, XIV, 124 : 10, ^{isu}*narkabtu SHU.LGI* on the one hand and *GUD*$^{hi.a}$ *SHU.GI* (*B. E.*, XV, 199 : 12; *E. B. H.*, p. 370, 11) on the other.

[10] By translating as given above, I connect *illak* with *V-ma* ^{isu}*narkabtu*, cf. l. 34 *lil-li-ik*, and see note 3. *Narkabtu*, therefore, is construed in our letter both as *fem.* and as *masc.* If this translation be objected to, we would have to render l. 13: "he shall go with the five chariots," etc., referring the "he" to a person well known to the

15 *an-nu-ú-tum âlu*^{bal} *shá be-lí*[1]	As regards these cities concerning which my "Lord" (has inquired, saying):
16 *i-na mi-ni-i pihâta*[2] (= *NAM*)^{ta}	"With what (how) shall they guard
17 *li-iṣ-ṣu-ru*	the *gouvernement*?"
18 [*um*]-*ma-a a-na be-lí-ia-ma*	I beg to state the following to my "Lord":
19 [*i*]-*na gi-na-a a-na-ku ash-ba-ku-ma*[3]	"I shall be campaigning in the fields
20 *ù*[4] *gi-na-a ir-te-ni-id-du-ma*[5]	while they (are trying to) invade the fields
21 *a-na âlu*^{bal} *shá be-lí shú-ul-m*[*u-shú*]-*ni*	up to the very cities the welfare of which my 'Lord' has at heart.
22 *i-na-an-na V-ma* ^{isu}*narkabtu shá ash-ba-tu-ma*[6]	Now, the five chariots which I have commanded
23 [*b*]*i-ir-ta i-na-aṣ-ṣa-ru*[7] *a-na gir-ri*	must be going out to wheresoever my 'Lord' shall command,
24 *shá be-lí i-gab-bu-ú te-ba-at*	only while they (the cities) guard the fortified camp.

"Lord," concerning whom the writer had received orders to send him out with five old chariots. *Alâku ana girri c. acc.*, "to go (march) with something to," here apparently used of military expeditions. Cf. *tebû ana girri*, l. 24.

[1] Undoubtedly a shortened sentence for *ashshum annûtum âlu*^{bal} *shá belí ishpura umma*. Notice the position of *annûtum*!

[2] *NAM* = *pahâti*, *pihâti* is well known. For *naṣâru c. acc.* and *ina* see p. 139, note 6.

[3] Cf. the later *ki-i i-na* ^{alu}*X. us-ba-ku-ni*. *Ash-ba-ku-ma ù . . . . ir-te-ni-id-du-ma* is, like *i-na-aṣ-ṣa-ru . . . . te-ba-at* (note 7, *q. v.*), a circumstantial clause with a change of subjects. The subject of *ash-ba-ku-ma* is the writer in his capacity as "general" (*i.e.*, his chariots and men) and that of *ir-te-ni-id-du-ma* are the "enemies."

[4] Notice the *-ma ù*! Cf. here "*die Wagen sha râkibushin dîkûma u shina mushshurama râmânushshin ittanallakû*, *deren Wagenlenker gefallen war, während sie selbst verlassen waren und für sich selbst umherfuhren*," quoted by Delitzsch, *Gram.*, p. 364, from Sanh., VI, 9ff.

[5] Jensen, *K. B.*, VI[1], p. 317, has shown (against Delitzsch, *H. W. B.*, p. 612f., who enumerates four roots רדה) that there is only *one* רדה, but the significations which he assigns to this verb (*fliessen*, *nachfolgen*, *hinterhergehen*, *treiben*) do not fit here. Nagel, *B. A.*, IV, p. 480, argued on the basis of *Letters of Hammurabi*, 34 : 7, for a meaning "*holen*, *nehmen*," comparing it with Jud. 14 : 9, "and the honey וַיִּרְדֵּהוּ אֶל־כַּפָּיו he took into his hands." The best translation of I[1] רדה, because construed *c. acc.* and *ana*, would be, it seems to me, "they went (*sc.* to take plunder, cf. also l. 27)," "they invaded," "swept down upon."

[6] For *shabatu* (*ashbat*(!), *ashabat*), "treiben," see Jensen, K. B., VI[1], p. 533. Here, because applied to a "general" in connection with chariots = "to command."

[7] *I-na-aṣ-ṣa-ru . . . . te-ba-at* is a circumstantial clause (Perm. *plus* Pres.), with a change of subjects. The subject of *i-na-aṣ-ṣa-ru* is *âlu*^{bal}, while that of *te-ba-at* is *V-ma* ^{isu}*narkabtu* (cf. note 3). For such constructions see Delitzsch, *Gram.*, § 152, pp. 364, 363 and above, note 3. The suggestion which the writer makes to his King's inquiry is this: "Let me defend the open country with the chariots, while the cities, resp. the inhabitants of the cities, must protect the fortress." To protect the open country chariots are absolutely necessary; with these the general can hurry quickly from place to place and thus drive away the enemy. For the protection of the fortified camp chariots are less needed than men, soldiers, and these the cities shall furnish.

25 *ù it-ti*[1] *a-na tur*(= *KU*)*-ru-ki-ia*[2] ^{amêlu}*nakru*(= *PAP*)	And with regard to the one (chariot with which I was) to smite (the enemy) so that (t)he (enemy)
26 *ul i-ḫad*(= *PA*)*-di*[3] *us-ṣa-am-ma*	may not (again) become fresh, go out, and
27 *i-ḫab-ba-at um-ma-a a-na be-lí-ia-ma*	plunder, the following to my "Lord":
28 *be-lí a-na sak-shup-par*[4] *liq-bi-*[*ma*]	"My 'Lord' may give orders to the *sak-shuppar*
29 *II* ^{iṣu}*narkabtu a-na gir-ri shá be-lí i-gab-bu-ú*	that *he* go with two chariots to wheresoever my 'Lord' shall command,
30 *lil-li-ik ù a-na-ku lu-uk-ka-li-ma*[5]	while *I* may be kept behind (back)
31 *i-na II* ^{iṣu}*narkabtu bi-ir-ta shá be-lí-ia*	and guard with two (other) chariots the fortified camp of my 'Lord';
32 *lu-uṣ-ṣur*[6] *ù a-la-ka*	but if my 'Lord'
33 *be-lí ish-tap-ra-am-ma*	should write, telling *me* to go,
34 *II* ^{iṣu}*narkabtu it-ti-ia lil-li-ik*[7]	then may two chariots accompany me,
35 *ù II* ^{iṣu}*narkabtu li-ik-ka-li-ma*[5]	while *he* may be kept behind with two chariots
36 *bi-ir-ta shá be-lí-i*[*a*]	and guard the fortified camp
37 *li-iṣ-ṣur*[8]	of my 'Lord.'"

[1] *It-ti*, *sc. narkabtu*, is the fem. of *edu*, "one."

[2] Inf. II[1] of תרך. Jensen, *K. B.*, VI[1], pp. 421, 436, 450, 498, *zer-, nieder-schlagen*, Delitzsch, *H. W. B.*, p. 711*a*, *entzweireissen, zersprengen*. *Turruku* is used here apparently in the sense of *maḫâṣu*, both as a means of "defense" and "offense." Lit. translated this line would read: "And with regard to that one (chariot) which was (to serve) for my smiting (*sc.* the enemy)."

[3] A reading *i-pa-di*, from פדה, "to destroy" (cf. *tapdû*, "destruction," Delitzsch, *H. W. B.*, p. 515*b*), though possible, is against the succession of events—we would expect: go out, plunder, destroy! *I-ḫad-di* = *i-ḫaṭ-ṭi* from חטא, "to sin"; and as each and every sin is a "*Vermessenheit (gegen Gott)*," I translated as given above. Prof. Hilprecht suggests a translation, "*möge sich nicht freuen* (*i-ḫad-di* = *i-ḫa-di*, √ חדה)," d. h., "*möge kein Vergnügen daran finden auszurücken*," *in anderen Worten*, "*möge nicht fröhlich darauf losplündern*." (Personal communication of July 9, 1908.)

[4] For the *sak-shup-par* see above, Chapter III, p. 37, note 12.

[5] Notice the difference between *lukkalima*, l. 30 (= 1st person) and *likkalima*, l. 35 (= 3d person). Both forms are IV[1] of כלה, "to be kept back," "to be retained."

[6] *Naṣâru c. acc.* and *ina*, "to protect, guard something with something." Cf. p. 138, note 2.

[7] As *narkabtu* is *fem.* (p. 137, n. 3), we would expect here *lû tallik*, cf., however, *ibid.*, note 10.

[8] The writer apparently has changed his mind since he addressed his last note to the King. He finds that one chariot will not be sufficient to cope effectively with the enemy. Two chariots must be sent against the enemy, while two others are needed to protect the fortified camp. (The *birta* of ll. 31, 36 has, of course, nothing to do with that of l. 23!) He leaves it, however, to the King as to whom to send out or to keep behind with the chariots requested.

XVI.

No. 38 (= C. B. M. 1955) (Cf. photographic reproduction, Pl. VII, 18, 19.)

A letter of *Shiriqtum*, a Nippurian, sent out by his Lord and King to look after the receipts of wool and provender. About 1400 B.C.

This letter has been translated chiefly on account of its manifold peculiarities: (1) ^{ilu}*SUGH*, generally read *Tishhu* and identified either with *NIN.IB* or with *Ishtar*, is here apparently a name for ^{ilu}*En-lil*; (2) the strange form *nap-ti* (ll. 4, 6) for *nap-shá-ti*(?); (3) the unusual *stat. constr.* in *shikittum*(= *NIG.GÀL*)^{tum} *nap-ti-ka* (l. 6); (4) the expression *a-na li-ti* for single *a-na* (ll. 14, 17); (5) the two new words *a-da-tum*^{mesh} and *il-hu-u*; (6) the long *ú* in *lu-ú-ul-li-ik* (l. 2).

Unfortunately there is no other person mentioned in *B. E.*, XIV or XV, known by the name *Shiriqtum*. We are, therefore, at a loss to place this letter historically. This much, however, we may maintain, that our writer was a *Nippurian*, living probably at the time of *Kuri-Galzu* (cf. the invocation and see above, Chapter III, pp. 38ff.), who had been sent out by his "Lord" and King to look after the receipts of wool and provender.

The contents of that part of the letter which is preserved are the following:

(*a*) *A-da-tum*^{mesh} and *ilhu* have been sent, ll. 15-18.

(*b*) 12 *qa* of barley shall be removed, as *per* previous order, ll. 19–21.

1 *ardi-ka* ^{m}*Shi-ri-iq-tum a-na d*[*i-na-an*]	Thy servant *Shiriqtum*; before the presence
2 *be-lí-ia lu-ú-ul-li-*[*ik*][1]	of my "Lord" may I come!
3 ^{ilu}*Tishhu*[2](= *SUGH*) *ù shar-rat* ^{ilu}*Nippur*(= *EN.LIL*)[^{ki}]	*Tishhu* and the *queen of Nippur*
4 *nap-ti be-lí-ia li-iṣ-ṣu-rum*	may protect the life of my "Lord";
5 ^{ilu}*Errish*(*t*)(= *NIN.IB*) *u* ^{ilu}*NIN.MAGH a-shib*	*Errish* and *NIN.MAGH* who inhabit
6 *shá âlu-ki shikittum*(= *NI*(*G*).*GÀL*)^{tum} *nap-ti-ka*	the city (*i.e.*, *Nippur*) may protect thy creatures!
7 *li-iṣ-ṣu-rum ma-an-nu pa-an*	Whosoever
8 *ba-nu-tum shá be-lí-ia li-mur*	may see the gracious face of my "Lord"

[1] Notice here the long *ú*, out of *lû* + *a* (of 1st person), in *lu-u-ul-li-ik*. Though this *ú* may be called a graphically long *ú*, it need not be a *morphologically* long *û* [for *lu-ú-ul-li-ik* may stand for *lû* + *ú-ul-li-ik*, a form well known from the inscriptions, but not yet found in tablets from the Cassite period, Hilprecht]. But then *ú-ul-li-ik* would have to be a II[1], while in this and all other passages it is evidently a I[1]!

[2] For introduction, ll. 3–11, see above, Chapter III, pp. 39ff.

9 *ù(?) man-nu da-ba-ba ṭâb(= ḪI)^{ab}*	and whosoever be of "good words"
10 *[a-na] be-lí-ia li-il-te-mi*	may listen to my "Lord"!
11 *[um-m]a-a a-na be-lí-ia-[ma]*	The following to my "Lord":
[. . . . large break . . . .]	
12	
13 [. . . .]^{mesh} *i-qa-bu-ú*	. . . . they say
14 *a-na li-ti*[1] *be-lí-ia*	to my "Lord"
15 *i-li-qa-a*[2] 2 *MA*[3] *shá a-da-tum*^{mesh}[4]	they (he) will take. Two *mana* of dark-red(?) wool
16 *ù* 2 *il-ḫu-ú*[5]	and two *ilḫû*
17 *a-na li-ti be-lí-ia*	he has sent
18 *il-te-bi-la*	to my "Lord."
19 *ù ṣi-di-tum*[6] *be-lí li-mur*	And as regards the provender, my "Lord" may be assured
20 12 [*SHE*].*BAR i-na-[shú-ú ki]*	that they shall take away the 12 (*qa*) of barley as
21 [*ash-pu?*]-*ra-ka.*[7]	I have written thee(?).

[1] For *litu* cf. King, *Letters of Ḫammurabi*, I, p. XLII; Nagel, *B. A.*, IV, p. 479, and especially Jensen, *K. B.*, VI[1], pp. 337, 403, 466, who quite correctly recognized that *a-na lit* (or, as in our letter, *a-na li-ti*) is as much as *ana*, "*zu hin*."

[2] As the context is mutilated, it is hard to tell whether this is the 3d pers. fem. (or masc.) *plural* (= *iliqâ* = *iliqû* = *ilaqû*; for the vowel *i*, instead of *a*, see also Behrens, *L. S. S.*, II[1], p. 53), or whether this is a *singular*, parallel to *il-te-bi-la* (l. 18), the long *â* at the end indicating the chief sentence. By itself it might be also a 3d pers. plur. (or sing.) preterit (*iliqû* = *ilqû*, see p. 9, note 5), or even a IV[1] = *illiqî(û)*, see above, p. 119, note 3.

[3] *MA* is here an abbreviation of *ma-na* (cf. also *B. E.*, XV, 6 : 11), just as *SHI*[4] is abbreviated from *shú-shi* (*i.e.*, soss), cf. *B. E.*, XV, 199 : 29, 40 | 19 : 20 | 73 : 15 | 151 : 45 | 149 : 14, etc. See p. 77, note 1.

[4] *A-da-tum*^{mesh} must be something that was measured according to *ma-na* —a kind of wool? Strange is here the *shá* between *MA* and *a-da-tum*^{mesh}, seeing that the "object measured" follows almost invariably directly (*i.e.*, without a *shá*) upon the "measure," cf. 23 : 21 | 27 : 31, etc. The *adattu* mentioned in Delitzsch, *H. W. B.*, p. 26*a*, and *l.c.*, p. 31*b*, are out of question here. The former means "*Wohnstatte*," and the latter "*corbeille*," Thureau-Dangin, *Z. A.*, XVII, 196, 1. We may, however, consider it as standing for *adamatum*, *adamtum*, *adantum*, *adattum*, *adatum* (*sc. shipâtu*), *i.e.*, "*dunkelfarbige, dunkelrote, braunrote Wolle*" (cf. II אדם, Delitzsch, *H. W. B.*, p. 26*a*).

[5] If *a-da-tum*^{mesh} be one kind, 2 (*sc. ma-na*) *il-ḫu-ú* might possibly be another kind of wool. The form (*ilḫû*) is, however, against this supposition, for we would expect a formation like *ilḫit* (fem. on account of *shipâtu*) if this existed. Or have we to suppose a reading like: 2 (^{shipatu})*il-ḫu-ú*?

[6] *Ṣi-di-tum*, "provender" (Delitzsch, *H. W. B.*, p. 563*b*: *Reisekost, Proviant*), occurs also in *B. E.*, XV, 143 : 3 | 154 : 15 (Clay's copy gives here *ad*(!)-*di-tum*), and *ṣi-di-su*(= *ṣidît-su*) in *B. E.*, XV, 168 : 30, 33. (Cf. here also the *si*(!)-*si*(!)-*ti* of *B. E.*, XV, 87 : 10?)

[7] Emendation is hardly correct! We would expect *ki (sha) ana be-lí-ia ashpura*.

XVII.

No. 15 (C B M. 11,860).

An unknown writer complains to his "Lord" and King that, though he asked for "pots," "straw" has been sent to him —a mistake showing that even Babylonians could and actually did misread their own signs: IN^{mesh} (= straw) was read instead of $KAN.NI^{mesh}$ (= pots). About 1370 B.C.

More particularly the contents of this letter are the following:

(a) The "good reeds" have been sent to the King, ll. 4–9.

(b) Complaint about the "straw" which has been sent instead of "pots," ll. 10–13.

(c) Request for (a) one talent of copper, ll. 14, 15; (b) for good ḫulup trees, ll. 16, 17.

(d) The affairs of the King are being well looked after by the sheriffs, ll. 18–22.

(e) Communication that the writer had gone to Dûr-Kuri-Galzu for one purpose or another, ll. 23–25.

1 [ardi-ka ᵐX ....]	Thy servant X ....;
2 a-na di-[na-an be-lî-ia]	before the presence of my "Lord"
3 [lu]l-lik u[m-ma-a a-na be-lî-ia-ma]	may I come, speaking thus to my "Lord":
4 [ásh-shum sh]á t[a-ash-pu-ra]	[With regard to thy inquiry(?) ....]
5 [....]-be-(?) ù GI DUG(= UI).GA¹	[whether ....] and the good reeds
6 [....]-a ul-te-b[i-l]a	.... has brought
7 iù [ar]di-ka ᵐAḫu-ra(?)-ásh-shá(?)³	(I beg to state that) thy servant Aḫurashsha
8 GI DUG(= UI).GA a-na be-lî-ia	has brought the good reeds
9 ul-te-bi-la	to my "Lord."
10 ù i-na bu-ut di-qa-ra-ti	Furthermore I wrote that "pots"
11 a-na ra-di-i al-ta-p[ar]	be brought down,
12 ù tibnu(= IN)ᵐᵉˢʰ⁴ be-lî	but they were "straw"!
13 am-mi⁵ an-na-a ú-she-pí-la	What for has my "Lord" sent this?

¹ GI DUG.GA = qanû ṭâbu, good, i e , sound, reeds that are not rotten

² ù introduces here the apodosis.

³ Or ᵐAḫu-shá(?)-ásh(?)-ra(?); both readings are very doubtful.

⁴ The only way to account for such a mistake in sending "straw" instead of "pots" is by supposing that our writer must have used in his former letter the ideogram KAN.NI for diqnâti. The "order-filler" mistook KAN.NI for IN and sent, accordingly, "straw."

⁵ Am-mi = ana-mi = מה : ל. Mi, therefore, is an abbreviation for mînu, "what," Jensen, K. B., VI, p. 472. For another mi = -mu = -ma, see p. 124, note 11.

14 1 *biltu*(= *GUN*) *erû*(= *URUDU*) *be-li*	My "Lord" may send one talent
15 *li-she-bi-lam-ma*	of copper.
16 *si-it ḫu*(?)[1]*-lu-ub da-a-a-bi*[2]	May I bring the rest of the
17 *lu-shal-li-im*[3]	good *ḫulup* trees?
18 *um-ma-a a-na be-li-ia-ma*	Also the following to my "Lord":
19 *a-ma-ti shá GÙ.EN.NA*[4]	"The affairs of the *GÙ.EN.NA*,
20 *ma-la i-ba-ash-shu-ú*	as many as there are,
21 *a-na be-li-ia*	are entrusted safely
22 *pa-aq-da-at*	to my 'Lord.'
23 *a-na* ^al^ *Dûr-Ku-ri-[Gal-zu]*	To *Dûr-Kuri-Galzu*
24 [*at-ta*]*-lak* [. . . .]	I went . . . ."
25 [. . . .]	

XVIII.

No. 76 (= C. B. M. 3660) (Cf. photographic reproduction, Pl. XI, 28.)

A father's peremptory order to his son to send in his report. About 1400 B.C.

From this letter we learn that the "report" (*di-e-ma*, l. 5) took its origin with the "son," who had to send it to the *be-el SHE.BAR* (l. 7). The latter again had to report to the "father," who turned it over to the King (*be-el*).[5] As the report has to be sent by the "son" to the *be-el SHE.BAR*, we may, and this quite rightly, assume that the *di-e-ma* embodied a report about the *receipts*, resp. *expenditures*, of "barley" in connection with a *sub-station* of a *branch* storehouse of the Temple of Enlil, over which the "son" presided.[6] This would give us the following classification of the various storehouses: (*a*) sub-station of a branch storehouse (son); (*b*) branch

[1] The sign *ḫu* looks here like *si* in *si-it*, but a word *si-lu-ub* does not exist; or is *si-lu-ub* = *su-lu-up*, "dates"? As, however, the things here mentioned are apparently building materials (reeds, bronze, *ḫulup* trees), I prefer to read as given above. If *si-lu-ub* = *su-lu-up* be preferred, we might translate: "Shall I bring the rest of the good dates?"

[2] The *bi* has here the appearance of *TUR* resp. *I*. *Daibi* is a *fa''al* form, expressing *quality* or *occupation*. Delitzsch, *Gram.*, p. 168 (§ 65), No. 24. Cf. also the stress laid upon the quality of the *GI*, ll. 5, 8.

[3] On account of the *lu* in *lu-shal-li-im*, this form cannot be the third (which had to be *lishallim*), but must be the first person. But whether it be a I[1] or II[1] is doubtful. I take it to be a II[1], for which see King, *Letters of Ḫammurabi*, III, p. 292.

[4] See introduction to No. 75, p. 133.

[5] It ought to be noticed here that the King, when *addressed* by his subjects, is called *be-li* or *EN-(li)*, but when spoken of to a third person, is referred to as either *LUGAL* or *be-el*.

[6] Cf. here also the request for such a report in No. 84 : 11, see pp. 114, 84ff.

storehouse (*be-el SHE.BAR*); (*c*) main storehouse (father); (*d*) central office at Nippur (King, resp. bursar-in-chief). This letter, then, shows more than anything else that the so-called "Temple Archives" are nothing but *administrative reports* about the receipts, resp. expenditures, of the various branch storehouses of the Temple of Enlil—reports as they had to be made to the earthly representative of the god of Nippur, the King, the *shakkanakku* *ilu Enlil*!

1 *um-ma-a a-bi-ka*	Thus saith thy father:
2 *i-din pa-nu-ú-ka*[1]	"Give,
3 *ul ib-ba-ba-lu*[2]	be good,
4 *ù shum-ma i-na mu-uḫ-ḫi*	and send, as soon as ready,
5 *ti-shú*[3] *di-e-ma*	the report
6 *shú-up-ra-am-ma*	to the
7 *a-na be-el SHE.BAR*[4]	'lord of barley'
8 *di-e-mi a-na be-el*	so that I may send my own
9 (*SHE.BAR erasure*)	
10 *lu-te-ir*	report to the 'Lord' (*i.e.*, the King)."

XIX.

No. 89 (C. B. M. 19,761).

An official of *Dûr-ilu* sends a messenger with a note to the King, then at Nippur. Another note, addressed to *m NIN-nu-ú-a* of Nippur, could not be delivered by the same messenger, because the addressee had gone on business to *Sippar*, fifty miles distant. Whereupon the official of *Dûr-ilu* sent the present explanatory note to Sippar, whence it was brought back by *m NIN-nu-ú-a* to Nippur. About 1350 B.C.

For introduction, transcription, translation, and notes, see above, Chapter II, pp. 19–23; 25, note 4; 27, note 8.

[1] *Pa-nu-ú-ka* might be, *per se*, connected either with *i-din*, "give thy face," *i.e.*, "set thyself about to do something, arouse thyself, be determined," or with *ul ib-ba-ba-lu*

[2] IV[1] of *babâlu*. With the signification here given cf., besides Delitzsch, *H. W. B.*, p. 166*b*, also Jensen, *K. B.*, VI[1], pp. 320, 378, and *B. A.*, III, p. 541, *la bâbil pâni*, "*freundlich, gut*," lit. "one who does not put his face upon, does not turn it towards (something else, *i.e.*, upon or towards evil)"; here "thy face (= plur.) must not be put (*sc.* upon evil)," *i.e.*, "be good," "do not delay." A *bibil-libbi*, accordingly, is something towards which one's heart is turned continually, the fondest thought of one's heart.

[3] שׁי, *i-na mu-uḫ-ḫi* = "to be at a thing," "to be ready."

[4] *SHE.BAR* is here not only the "barley," but everything that goes through the hands of the "lord," as head of a branch storehouse. Cf. also pp. 112, note 2; 113, note 4.

VI.

CONCORDANCE OF PROPER NAMES.

Abbreviations.

addr., addressee; **b.**, brother; **"b.,"** brother (in address); **cf.**, confer; **d.**, daughter; **f.**, father; **f.**, following page; **ff.**, following pages; **l.c.**, *loco citato*; **p.**, page; **pp.**, pages; **q.v.**, *quod vide*; **s.**, son; **si.**, sister; **wr.**, writer.

Determinatives: **ilu**, god; **mesh**, plural; **m.**, masculine; **f.**, feminine; [. .] = text restored; (. . . .) = interpretation of text; **C. B. M.**, refers to the "Catalogue of the Babylonian and General Semitic Section of the Archaeological Museum of the University of Pennsylvania," prepared by Prof. Dr. H. V. Hilprecht. The numbers refer to the cuneiform texts of the autograph plates.

I. Names of Persons.

1. Masculine Names.

^{m}**A**-*a-ri*,[1] 47 : 3.

^{m}*Ab-*[. . .],[2] 69 : 1.

^{m}*Abi*(= *AD*)-*ia*, f. of ^{f}*Di-ni*, 85 : 10.

^{m}*Aḫu*(= *SHESH*)-*ú-a-Ba-ni*, addr., "b." of ^{m}*Erba-*^{ilu}*Marduk* 81 : 1.

^{m}*A-ḫu-Ba-ni*, wr., 2 : 3.

^{m}*Aḫ*(= *SHESH*)-*iddina* (= *SE*)^{na}-^{ilu}*Marduk*, wr., 1 : 1.

^{m}*Aḫu*(= *SHESH*)-*ni*, 31 : 7.

^{m}*Aḫu*(= *SHESH*)-*shá*(?)-*ásh*(?)-*ra*,[3] 45 : 7.

^{m}*A-ḫu-shi-na*, addr., 78 : 1.

^{m}*Ak-ka-du-ú*,[4] 54 : 11.

^{m}*Amel-Ba-ni-i*, 86 : 16.

^{m}*Amel-*^{ilu}*Marduk*,

1. wr., 3 : 2.
2. addr. 75 : 1 3.

^{m}*A-mi-ri-ia*, "b." of $^{m\ ilu}$*En-lil-mu-kin-apal*(= *TUR.USH*), 80 : 1, 5.

[^{m}]*A-na-ku-rum-ma*,[5] wr., 1 : 1.

^{m}*A-na-*^{ilu}*Sin*(= *XXX*)-*tak-la-ku*, 48 : 5.

^{m}*A-na-tukulti* (= *KU*)-*ilu-ma*, 29 : 9, 15.

^{m}*Ap-pa*[6]-*na-a-*[*a*], f. of $^{m\ ilu}$*NIN.IB-nâdin*(= *SE*)-*shum*, 75 : 5.

^{m}*Ap-*[7][. . . .], 69 : 4.

^{m}*Ardi-Bêlit* (= *GASHAN*),[8] wr., 5 : 3.

---

[1] Cf. ^{f}*In-bi-A-a-ri*.

[2] Or $^{m\ ilu}$*En-*?

[3] Or ^{m}*Aḫu-ra*(?)-*ásh-shá*(?).

[4] "The Akkadian!" Cf. ^{amelu}*Ak-ka-di-i* 18 : 25 | 41 : 14.

[5] Cf. *B. E.*, XIV, 11 : 16, or have we to read here ^{m}*A-na-tukulti*(= *KU*)-*ilu-ma*?

[6] Or is *Ap-pa* = *Isin*(= *EZIN*) and *Isin-na-a-a* = "One who is from Isin?" Cf. here the *nom. pr.* quoted under *Ap-pa-ai* in *B. E.*, XIV, p. 40*a* and *l.c.*, XV, p. 27*a*.

[7] See note to ^{m}*Ab-*[. .], above.

[8] Cf. ^{alu}*Ardi-NIN*^{ki} and ^{alu}*Ardi-GASHAN*.

Masculine Names

Ardi(?)-GAB(?)-BA(?)-ma(?) in Bâb-Ardi-GAB.BA-ma (q.v.), 81 : 14.

^{m}Ardi-ia-ú, 48 : 9.

^{m}Ardi-^{ilu}Marduk, wr., 6 : 2.

Ar-rap-ḫa-a-a-[um],[1] 53 : 20, 27, 32.

^{m}Ásh-pi-la-an-du,[2] 55 : 5.

$^{m\ ilu}$A-shur-shum(= MU)-êṭir (= KAR), wr., ["b."] of $^{m\ ilu}$En-lil-[bêl-nishê^{mesh}-shu], 77 : 3.

[^{m}]A-zi-r[u-um], wr., 7 : 2.

^{m}Ba-il-^{ilu}Marduk, wr., 8 : 2.

^{m}Bana(= KAK)-a-sha-^{ilu}Marduk,

1. wr., 9 : 1.
2. 3 : 16.

^{m}Be-la-nu,

1. wr., 11 : 1.
2. 12 : 17.

$^{m\ ilu}$Bêl(= EN)-[. . .],[3] 53 : 16 | 69 : 4.

^{m}Bêl(= EN)-[. . .],[4] 69 : 5.

^{m}Bêl(= EN)-ú-sa-tum, 23 : 20.

^{m}Bu-[. . .],[5] 57 : 1.

^{m}Bu-na-^{ilu}Errish(t) (= NIN.IB), 48 : 22.

^{m}Bu-un-na-^{ilu}Errish(t) (= NIN.IB),[6] 57 : 1 | 59 : 12 | 60 : 6.

^{m}Bur-ru-qi, 50 : 4.

^{m}Bu-ur-ru-ti, 39 : 13.

[^{m}?]Da(?)-li-li-ia, addr., "b." or "si."(?) of ^{m}Î-li-ip-pa-ásh-ra, 88 : 1.

^{m}Dam-qu, 75 : 8.

^{m}Da-an-[. . .],[7] 69 : 3, 6.

$^{m\ ilu}$DAR-ḪU-nâr(= SAB)-gab-ba, wr., 91 : 3.

$^{m\ ilu}$DIL.BAT-Ba-ni, 14 : 18.

^{m}Di-in-ili(= AN)-lu-mur, 27 : 18.

^{m}Dîn(= [DI?]-TAR)-li-[mur?],[8] addr., 91 : 1.

^{m}É.KISH.SHÎR(= NU)-GAL-li-mi-ir, 37 : 18.

^{m}E-mi-da(!)[9]-^{ilu}Marduk, b. (l. 19) of ^{f}In-bi-A-a-ri, 86 : 18.

^{m}EN-, see ^{m}Bêl-.

$^{m\ ilu}$En-[. . . .],[10] 53 : 16 | 69 : 4.

$^{m\ ilu}$En-lil-[bêl(= EN)-nishê^{mesh}-shu],[11] addr., 77 : 1.

$^{m\ ilu}$En-lil-ki-di-ni,

1. wr., 78 : 3 | 79 : 3.
2. 55 : 11, 21. Cf. the following name.

$^{m\ ilu}$En-lil-ki-din-ni, 55 : 6, 7, 19. Cf. the preceding name.

$^{m\ ilu}$En-lil-mu-kin-apal (= TUR.USH), wr., "b." of ^{m}A-mi-li-ia, 80 : 3.

$^{m\ ilu}$En-lil-tu-kul-ti, 15 : 13 | 68 : 20.

^{m}Erba(= SU)-^{ilu}Marduk,

1. wr., "b." of ^{m}Aḫu-ú-a-Ba-ni, 81 : 2.
2. wr., "b." of Da(?)-ni-ti-ia, 82 : 3.
3. 27 : [27], 30, 32 | 29 : 1 | 35 : 17, 26.

^{m}Er-ba-^{ilu}Marduk,

1. wr., 13 : 2.
2. s. of ^{m}Ḫu-up-pi-i, 58 : 5, 7.
3. 65 : 9.

^{m}Er-ba-am-^{ilu}Marduk, wr., 14 : 2.

$^{m\ ilu}$Errish(t)(= NIN.[IB])[12]-[. . .], 52 : 39.

$^{m\ ilu}$Errish(t)(= [$^{m\ ilu}$NIN].IB)-aḫ(= SHESH)-iddina (= SE)^{na}, 1 : 17.

$^{m\ ilu}$Errish(t)(= NIN.IB)-âlik-pâni (= SH[I.DU]), 8 : 25.

$^{m\ ilu}$Errish(t)(= NIN.IB)-apal(= TUR.USH)-iddina (= SE)^{na}, wr., 83 : 2.

---

[1] "The Ar(ra)pachaean." Cf. B. E., XIV, 22 : 15, ^{m}Ar-rap-ḫa-a-a-ú-[um]. In our letter the sign rap looks very much like LUGAL, cf. also Clay, Sign List, B. E., XIV, Nos. 158 and 89. For the interchange of rap and LUGAL cf. ^{dingir}Rap(b)-kam-me-ir and ^{dingir}Lugal-kam-me-ir.

[2] Also the following readings might possibly be suggested: ^{m}Pi-la-an-du, ^{m}Na-ásh-la-an-du, or ^{m}Ásh-pi-la-, resp. ^{m}Pi-la-, resp. ^{m}Na-ásh-la-^{ilu}DU, see Chapter III, p. 52, note 3.

[3] Or $^{m\ ilu}$En-[. . .]?

[4] ^{m}Bêl-[ú-sa-tum]?

[5] Or ^{m}SHE[. . .].

[6] On account of the mâr (not mârê), 59 : 14, I do not consider this person to be a brother of $^{m\ ilu}$PA.KU.SHESH.SE-na and a son of ^{m}Me-li-^{ilu}Shu-qa-mu-na.

[7] Cf. Dannu-Nergal in B. E., XIV, p. 12b.

[8] Or ^{m}[I-na]-ṣil-li-a-[lak], q.v.

[9] See also pp. 25, note 1; 110, note 3.

[10] Or $^{m\ ilu}$Bêl-[. . .]?

[11] According to l. 5 he is a bêl pa-ḫa-ti. A piḫât $^{m\ ilu}$En-lil-bêl-nishê-shu is mentioned in B. E., XIV, 99a : 41.

[12] For the reading of NIN.IB = Errish(t), see The Monist, XVII (January, 1907), p. 140ff. Cf. also "Preface."

Masculine Names

$^{m\ ilu}$*Errish(t)(= MASH)-apal(= TUR.USH)-iddina (= SE)^{na}*, wr., 84 : 2.

$^{m\ ilu}$*Errish(t)(= NIN.IB)-GA.BU-AN^{mesh}*,[1] wr., 17 : 2 | 18 : 1(?).

$^{m\ ilu}$*Errish(t)(= L)-GIR-AN^{mesh}*,[2] 48 : 20.

$^{m\ ilu}$*Errish(t)(= NIN.IB)-nâdin(= SE)-aḫê (SHESH)^{mesh}*, 52 : 13.

$^{m\ ilu}$*Errish(t)(= NIN.IB)-nâdin(= SE)-shum(= MU)*, s. of ^{m}*Ap-pa-na-a [a]*, 75 : 4.

$^{m\ ilu}$*Errish(t)-zêr-ib^{3}-ni*. wr., 15 : 1 | 16 : 2.

^{m}*É.SAG.ÌL-zu-ri-ia*,[4] 9 : 15

^{m}*E-tel-bu*, s. of ^{m}*Ush-bu-la*, 24 : 12.

^{m}*Êṭir(= KAR)-^{ilu}Marduk*, wr., 12 : 2.

$^{(sic)\ ilu}$*Gir-ra-ga-mil*,[5] 3 : 13, 17, 20.

^{m}*Gu-za-ar-AN*,[6] "b." of ^{m}*In-nu-ú-a*, 87 : 3.

^{m}*Ḫa-an-[bu?]*, 68 : 23.

^{m}*Ḫa-ni-[bi]*, 75 : 7.

^{m}*Ḫa-ash-mar*, 81 : 13.

^{m}*Ḫu-[di-ib-ti-i]l*,[7] f. of ^{f}*Ab-b[a-at-t]a-ni-tu*, 78 : 7.

^{m}*Ḫu-na-bi*, 48 : 16.

^{m}*Ḫu-up-pi-i*, f. of ^{m}*Er-ba-^{ilu}Marduk*, 58 : 6.

^{m}*Ḫu-za-lum*, 22 : 6.

^{m}*Ib-ni-^{ilu}KUR*, 3 : 18.

^{m}*Ib-ni-^{ilu}Marduk*,

1. wr., 19 : 1.
2. 81 : 13 | 83 : 27.

^{m}*Idin(= SE)-^{ilu}Errish(t) (= NIN.IB)*, wr., 20 : 3.

^{m}*Idin(= MU) GHE.GAL*,[8] 59a : 11.

^{sic}*Idin-^{ilu}Marduk*,[9] 59 : 18.

^{m}*Idin(SE)-^{ilu}Nergal*,

1. f. of ^{m}*Ki-shá-tum*, 56 : 4.
2. 85 : 3.

^{m}*I-gi-gi*, 4 : 5.

^{m}*I-li-i'-i[a?]*,[10] 21 : 19.

^{m}*I-ṣṣ-aḫ-ḫi^{11}-e-ri-ba*, 26 : 13.

^{m}*Î-li(= NI.NI)-ip-pa-ásh-ra*, wr., "b." of *Da(?)-li-li-ia*, 88 : 3.

^{m}*Ilu(= AN)-ip-pa-ásh-ra*, 31 : 15.

^{m}*Ilu-?-lu-[?]*, 5 : 16.

^{m}*Ilu(= AN)-MU.TUK.A^{12}-rîma^{nu}*,

1. wr., 21 : 1.
2. 81 : 16.

^{m}*Il-li-ia*,[13] addr., 92 : [1], 4, 29.

$^{m\ ilu}$*IM-*, see $^{m\ ilu}$*Rammân-*.

^{m}*Im-gu-ri*, addr., 79 : 1.

^{m}*Im-gu-rum*, wr., 22 : 1 | 23 : 1.[14]

^{m}*I-na-É.KUR.GAL*, 24 : 32.

^{m}*[I-na]-ṣil-ṣṣ-a-[lak]*,[15] addr., 91 : 1.

^{m}*In-na-an-ni*, addr., 83 : 1 | 84 : 1 | 85 : 1 | 86 : 1.

^{m}*In-ni-bi*, 81 : 9.

^{m}*In-nu-u-a*,[16] addr., "b." of ^{m}*Gu-za-ar-AN*, 87 : 1.

^{m}*Iqîsha(= BA-sha)-^{ilu}Rammân (= IM)*, 31 : 35.

---

[1] Probably to be read *Errish-qa-ṣir-ili*, i.e., "Errish is the fuller (*qiṣiru* = *ashlaku*, Meissner, *M. V. A. G.*, IX (1904), p. 52) of the gods." Cf. II R, 57, 35c, d, ^{ilu}*(Ti-ish-ḫu) SUGH* | ditto (= ^{ilu}*NIN.IB*) *sha rum-ku-ti*. See also $^{m\ ilu}$*L-GIR-AN^{mesh}*, 48 : 20.

[2] Probably to be read *Errish-shakkanak-ili*. Cf. here for the present our note to *GIR.NITA* (Chapter IV, p. 86, n. 1) and see my forthcoming volume on the Religious Texts. Clay, *B. E.*, XIV, p. 49a, reads *NIN.IB.KISH* (= *kashkash*)-*ilâni*.

[3] The traces speak rather for *ba*! Cf. ^{ilu}*Zêr-ba-ni-tum*!

[4] An Amurritish name: "*É.* is my rock!"

[5] Here a city named after a person. Cf. $^{alu(ilu)}$*Gir-ra-ga-mil*.

[6] *AN* here in all probability the same as the Cassite *Bugash*, see pp. 7, note 2; 63; 70.

[7] Cf. *B. E.*, XV, p. 32a, *Ḫu-di-ib-til(= BE)-la*, a Mitanni name.

[8] See ^{m}*MU.GHE.GAL*.

[9] Here a city, see under ^{alu}*Idin-^{ilu}Marduk*.

[10] Cf. ^{m}*Il-li-ia*, father of ^{m}*Tukulti(= KU)^{ti}-É.KUR*, *B. E.*, 48a : 7, and see below under ^{m}*Il-ṣṣ-ia*. Or is *i'* = *aḫ*?

[11] Cf. *B. E.*, XIV, 39 : 6, 14, $^{m\ ilu}$*NIN.IB-na-din-aḫ-ḫi*.

[12] Clay, *B. E.*, XIV, p. 45a, reads *MU.TUK.A* = ^{mu}*murashshû*. For the sign *rêmu* see Meissner, *Ideogramme*, No. 3857.

[13] Cf. ^{m}*Il-li-ia*, father of ^{m}*Tukulti(= KU)^{ti}-É.KUR*, *B. E.*, XIV, 48a : 7, and see also ^{m}*I-ṣṣ-i'-i[a]* above.

[14] Or here [^{m}*U-bar*]-*rum*? Cf., however, introduction to No. 23 *sub* "Translations," p. 94.

[15] Or *Dîn-li-[...]*, *q.v.*

[16] Cf. ^{m}*NIN-nu-ú-a* and see Chapter II, p. 15, note 5.

Masculine Names

^{m}*Ir-shá-a*, 1 : 19.
^{m}*Ish-shá-ki*,[1] 54 : 7.
$^{m\ ilu}$*Ishtar-*, see $^{m\ ilu}$*DIL.BAT-*.
^{m}*Iz-qur-^{ilu}Errish(?)* (= *NIN.IB*), *itû*, 26 : 17.
^{m}*Iz-qur-^{ilu}Ishtar* (= *DIL.BAT*), 28 : 5.
^{m}**K***albi*(= *UR*)-^{ilu}*NIN.DIN.DÙG.GA*,[2] wr., 25 : 2.
Kalbi-^{ilu}USH,[3] 37 : 9.
^{m}*Kal-bu*, wr., 24 : 9, 38.
^{m}*Ki-din-*[. . .], 97 : 5.
[^{m}*Ki*]*-di-in*, s. (*TUR.USH*) of [. . .], 1 : 13.
[^{m}]*Ki-di-ni*, s. of [. . .], 18 : 22.
^{m}*Ki-din-ni*, 9 : 23 | 14 : 15.
^{m}*Ki-din-^{ilu}Marduk*, 23 : 23.
^{m}*Ki-din-^{ilu}Rammân*(= *IM*), 33 : 12.
^{m}*Ki-ir-ra-ma*(? *ba*), 21 : 29.
^{m}*Ki-shá-aẖ*[4]*-bu-ut*, wr., 31 : 1.
^{m}*Ki-shaẖ-bu-ut*, wr., 35 : 1.
^{m}*Ki-shá-tum*,[5] s. of ^{m}*Idin-^{ilu}Nergal*, 56 : 4.
^{m}*Ki-ti-i*[*t*?], 28 : 17.
^{m}*Ku-du-ra-nu*,
  1. wr., 26 : 1 | 27 : 1 | 28 : 1.
  2. 35 : 27, 31 (here ^{m}*Ku-du-ra-ni*).
^{m}*KUR.GAL-*[. .], 92 : 16.
Ku-ri-Gal-zu, see ^{alu}*Dûr-Ku-ri-Gal-zu*.
^{m}*Ku-ri-i*, 31 : 7.
^{m}**L***a-ki-pu*, *ardi* *É.GAL*, 31 : 11.
$^{m\ ilu}$*LUGH-*, see $^{m\ ilu}$*Sukal-*.
M*.A.AN.USH*,[6] 37 : 9.
^{sic}*Man-nu-gi-ir*[7]*-^{ilu}Rammân* (= *IM*), 24 : 13, 18.
^{m}*Man-nu-ki-^{ilu}Sukal* (= *LUGH*), s. of [. . .]*-shá*, 18 : 23.
Mâr-^{m}[. . . .], 24 : 29 | 60 : 3, 5.
Mâr-^{m}A-na-^{ilu}Sin(= *XXX*)*-tak-la-ku*, 48 : 5.
Mâr-^{m}Ar-di-Ia-ú, 48 : 9.
Mâr-^{m}Ásh-pi-la-an-du,[8] 55 : 5.
[*Mâr-^{m}*]*Bu-u*[*n-*. . .],[9] 57 : 4 | 60 : 6.
Mâr-^{m}Da-an-[. . .], 69 : 3, 6.
Mâr-^{m}H̱u-na-bi, 48 : 16.
Mâr-^{m}In-ni-bi, 81 : 9.
Mâr[10]*-^{m}Man-nu-ki-^{ilu}Sukal* (= *LUGH*), 18 : 23.
Mâr-^{m}Mu-[. .], 60 : 1.
Mâr-^{m}Mu-ra-ni, *itû*, 78 : 1.
Mâr-$^{m\ ilu}$Sin(= *XXX*)*-mu-ba-liṭ*,[11] 49 : 6.
Mâr-^{m}She[12]*-*[. .], 57 : 4.
Mâr-^{f}Ta-a-du,[13] 83 : 11, 35.
Mâr-^{m}Ú-da-shá-ásh,[14] messenger of King *Burna-Buriash*, 55 : 8, 16, 20.
Mar-^{m}Ú-su-ub-Shi-pak, 55 : 2.
[$^{m\ ilu}$]*Marduk-erba* (= *SU*), 15 : 13
$^{m\ ilu}$*Marduk-i*[15]*-shú*, wr., 50 : 1.
[^{m}]^{ilu}*Marduk-mu-*[*shal-*]*lim*, wr., 29 : 1.
$^{m\ ilu}$*Marduk-nâṣir* (= *SHESH*), 3 : 22, 26 | 15 : 12.
$^{m\ ilu}$*Marduk-ra-im-kit-*[*ti*], wr., 30 : 3.
$^{m\ ilu}$*Marduk-shum*(= *MU*)*-iddina*(= *MU*), ^{amelu}*SAG*, 93 : 7.

---

[1] Notice that we find in this connection generally ^{gish}*MAR.GID.DA shá x* (= numeral) *pa-te-si*^{mesh}. Should we, therefore, read "*m*" = 1 or 60? See under *pa-te-si*^{mesh}.
[2] Cf. Kudurru, London, 103, *passim*, and see p. 55.
[3] Or *M.A.AN.USH*, doubtful whether a nom. pr.; it might be an official's title.
[4] For a writing *a'* instead of *aẖ*, see Chapter I, p. 7, note 6.
[5] Or is this a woman? If so, then cf. p. 117, note 2.
[6] Or *UR*(= *Kalbi*)-^{ilu}*USH*, doubtful whether a nom. pr.; it might be an official's title.
[7] The *gi-ir* for *ki*, *kim*(*a*), *gim* shows that ^{ilu}*IM* was pronounced at this time ^{ilu}*Rammân*, see Chapter III, p. 49, note 1. Here this name is that of a city, see ^{alu}*Gir-ra-ga-mil*.
[8] See under ^{m}*Ásh-pi-la-an-du*.
[9] See under ^{m}*Bu-un-na-^{ilu}Erresh*(?).
[10] Doubtful whether *Mâr-* belongs to the name.
[11] A reading *Mâr-$^{m\ ilu}$Sin-shum*(= *MU*)*-iqîsha*(= *BA-sha*) might also be possible.
[12] Or ^{m}*Bu-*.
[13] Thus I propose to read this name. This, no doubt, is preferable to *Mârat-Ta-a-du*. If the latter reading were adopted the absence of *SAL* would be without parallel, cf. *Mârat*(= *TUR.SAL*)-^{f}(!)*Ba*(? or *Ush*?)*-ba*(? or *ka*?)-[. .], 31 : 27. Here the descent is apparently reckoned through the mother.
[14] Cf. *B. E.*, XV, 168 : 4, ^{m}*Ú-da-shá-ash*(!).
[15] "M. exists." So better than *-ni-shú*?

Masculine Names

^{m}*Me-li-Shi-pak*, 17 : 32.
^{m}*Me-li-^{ilu}Shu-qa-mu-na*, f. of $^{m\ ilu}$*Nusku-aḫ-iddina*, 59 : 11.
^{m}*Mu-[. . .]*, 60 : 1.
^{m}*Mu-kal-lim*, wr., 31 : 1 | 32 : 1 | 33 : 1.
^{m}*Mu-ra-ni*, 78 : 4.
^{m}*MU.GHE.GÁL*,[1] 59a : 14.
^{m}*Mush-ta-li*, 31 : 11 | 32 : 7.
^{m}**Nâdin**(= *MU*)-*nuḫshi* (= *GHE.GÁL*),[2] 59a : 14.
^{m}*Na-aḫ*(or *a'* ?)-*zi-^{ilu}Marduk*, 12 : 12 , 48 : 8.
^{m}*Nannari*(= *SHESH.KI*)^{ri}-^{ilu}*Marduk*, 31 : 11.
^{m}*Na-zi-^{ilu}En-lil*, 21 : 25.
$^{m\ ilu}$*Nergal-Ba-ni*, *ḫa-za-nu shá* ^{alu}*Ra-ka-nu*, 9 : 21.
^{m}*NIM.GI-shar*(= *LUGAL*)-*ili* (= *AN*)^{mesh},[3] 33a : 1.
$^{m\ ilu}$*NIN.IB*-, see $^{m\ ilu}$*Errish(t)*-.
^{m}*NIN-nu-ú-a*,[4] addr., "b." of ^{m}*Pân-AN.GAL-lu-mur*, 89 : 1, [14], 28.
$^{m\ ilu}$*NIN.SHAR-il-la-ti-li-ku-na*, 34 : 12.
^{m}*Nûr*(= *ṢAB*)-^{ilu}*Shamash*(= *UD*),
  1. ^{amelu}*SAG LUGAL*, 1 : 5, [18].
  2. *gú-gal-lum*, 27 : 8.
$^{m\ ilu}$*Nusku*(= *PA.KU*)-*aḫ*(= *SHESH*)-*iddina*(= *SE*)^{na}, s. of ^{m}*Me-li-^{ilu}Shu-qa-mu-na*, 59 : 13.
$^{m\ ilu}$**P**.*A.KU*-, see $^{m\ ilu}$*Nusku*-.
^{m}*Pân*(= *SHI*)-*AN.GAL-lu-mur*, wr., "b." of ^{m}*NIN-nu-ú-a*, 89 : 2.
^{m}*Pi-[. . .]*, wr., 13 : 1.
^{m}*Pi-la-an-du*,[5] 55 : 5.
$^{m\ ilu}$**Rammân**(= *IM*)-*êrish*(= *ENGAR*)^{ish},[6] 48 : 11.
[$^{m\ ilu}$*Rammân*(= *IM*)-*ra*]-*im-zêr*, 9 : 12.
[$^{m\ ilu}$]*Rammân*(= *IM*)-*shar*(= *LUGAL*)-*ili*(= *AN*)^{mesh}, wr., 36 : 1.
$^{m\ ilu}$*Rammân*(= *IM*)-*she-mi*, 59a : 16.
^{m}**Sin**(= *XXX*)-[. . .], 8 : 10 | 66 : 17.
$^{m\ ilu}$*Sin-[. . .]*, 75 : 9, 12.
$^{m\ ilu}$*Sin*(= *XXX*)[7]-*apal*(= *TUR.USH*)-*iddina*(= *SE*)^{na}, 83 : 22.
$^{m\ ilu}$*Sin-êrish*(= *ENGAR*)^{ish}, wr., 90 : 2.
$^{m\ ilu}$*Sin-is-s[aḫ]-ra*, 9 : 16 | 85 : 8.
$^{m\ ilu}$*Sin-ga-mil*, ^{amelu}*MASH*, 72 : 4.
$^{m\ ilu}$*Sin-kara-bi-esh-me*, wr., 37 : 3.
$^{m\ ilu}$*Sin-ma-gir*, 11 : 25 | 59 : 6.
$^{m\ ilu}$*Sin-mu-ba-liṭ*,[8] 49 : 6.
[$^{m\ ilu}$]*Sin-na-din-ap-lim*, 68 : 32.
^{m}*Si-ri-shá*[9]-*ash*, 28 : 5.
^{m}*Sukal*(= *PAP*)-*paṭ-ra*,[10] 10 : 3.
$^{m\ ilu}$*Sukal*(= *LUGH*)-*she-mi*, 29 : 10.
$^{m\ ilu}$*Shamash*(= *UD*)-*sharru* (= *LUGAL*), 11 : 16.
(^{sic}) ^{ilu}*Shamash*(= *UD*)-*tu-kul-ti*,[11] 16 : 8, 12.
^{m}*Shá-mi-la-shá*, ^{amelu}*nangaru*, 59 : 16.
^{m}*SHESH.KI*^{ri}, see ^{m}*Nannari*-.
^{m}*Shi-ri-iq-tum*, wr., 38 : 1.
^{m}*Shi-riq-tim*, 87 : 8.
^{m}**T***ar-ba-zu*, 22 : 13.
$^{m\ ilu}$*TAR-ḪU-nûr*(= *ṢAB*)-*qab-ba*, wr., 91 : 3.
Tukkulti-É.KUR, see under "Places" and "Rivers."
^{m}*Û-ba*[12]-[. . .], 31 : 11.
^{m}*U-bar-rum*,
  1. wr.,[13] 39 : 1 | 40 : 1.
  2. 48 : 7.
^{m}*U-bar-ru*, 12 : 5, 7.
^{m}*Û-da-shá-ásh*,[14] 55 : 8, 16, 20.
^{m}*UR*-, see ^{m}*Kalbi*.
^{ilu}*Ur-ra*-, see ^{ilu}*Gir-ra*-.

[1] Probably to be read either ^{m}*Idin-GHE.GÁL* or ^{m}*Nâdin-nuḫshi*. The latter might be abbreviated from $^{m\ ilu}$*IM* (or *NIN.IB*, etc.)-*nâdin-nuḫshi*.

[2] See ^{m}*MU.GHE.GÁL*.

[3] *NIM.GI* is probably to be read *Êṭir*, see under Translations, pp. 135f.

[4] See also ^{m}*In-nu-ú-a* and cf. Chapter II, p. 15, note 5.

[5] See ^{m}*Ash-pi-la-an-du*.

[6] For the pronunciation of ^{ilu}*IM* = ^{ilu}*Rammân*, cf. *Man-nu-gi-ir-^{ilu}IM*, Chapter III, p. 49, note 1.

[7] So in all names beginning with $^{m\ ilu}$*Sin*-.

[8] Or $^{m\ ilu}$*Sin-shum*(= *MU*)-*iqisha*(= *BA-sha*).

[9] Or *da*?

[10] See also p. 129.

[11] Here the name of a city, cf. ^{ilu}*Gir-ra-ga-mil*.

[12] Or ^{m}*Û-su-[ub-Shi-pak?]*.

[13] Does No. 23 : 1 [^{m}*U-bar*]-*rum* belong here? But see p. 94.

[14] Cf. *B. E.*, XV, 168 : 4, *ash*(!).

Masculine Names

^{m}*Ú-su-ub-Shi-pak*, 55 : 2.
^{m}*Ush-bu-la*, f. ^{m}*E-tel-bu*, 21 : 12.
[^{m}*Ú*]-*she-bu-uṣ*(?)-^{ilu}*En-lil*[1], 18 : 8.
^{m}[. . .]-*ḫu*-[. . .], 72 : 6.
[. . .]-*ik-li-li-ia*,[2] 88 : 1.
^{m}[. . .]-*AN.TIM*, 11 : 19.
^{m}[. . . . .]-*Ishtar*(= *DIL.BAT*), 72 : 5.
[. . .]-^{ilu}*Marduk*, wr., 10 : 2.
[. . .]-*mi-il-kish-sha-ti*(?), 3 : 5.
[. . .]-^{ilu}*NIN.GAL*, 50 : 9.
[. . .]-*shá*, s. of ^{m}*Man-nu-ki-*^{ilu}*Sukal*(= *LUGH*), 18 : 23.
[. . .]-^{ilu}*Shamash*(= *UD*), wr., 41 : 1.
[. . .]-*uṣur*(= *SHESH*), 22 : 17.
See also 43 : 7 ¦ 60 : 10.

2. Feminine Names.

^{f}*A*-[. . .], 78 : 8.
^{f}*Ab-b*[*u-ut-t*]*a-ni-tu*,[3] dr. of ^{m}*Ḫu*-[*di-ib li-i*]*t*, 78 : 6.
^{f}*Ba*(? or *Ush*)-*ba*(? or *ka*?) [. . .], 31, 27.
^{f}*Da-ak-da*, 31 : 11[4] ¦ 41 : 5.
[^{f}?]*Da*(?)-*li-li-ia*,[5] addr., "b." or "si." of ^{m}*Ì-li-ip-pa-ásh-ra*, 88 : 1.
sic *Da-ni-ti-ia*,[6] addr., "si." (or "b."?) of ^{m}*Erba-Marduk*, 82 : 1, 8.
^{f}*Di-ni*,[7] d. of ^{m}*Abi-ia*, 85 : 10.
^{f}*E-di-ir-to*, 31 : 5.
^{f}*E-di-ir-ti*, 32 : 5 ¦ 33 : 5.
[^{f}]*E-di-ir-tum*, 36 : 3.
^{f}*Ga-ga-da-ni-tum*, *zammertu*(= *LUL*), 22 : 5.
[^{f}*I-lu*]*m*(?)-*mu-bal-li-iṭ*,[8] 31 : 23.
^{f}*In-bi-A-a-ri*, wr., si.[9] of ^{m}*E-mi-da-*^{ilu}*Marduk*, 85 : 2, 86 : 3.
^{f}*La-ta*(? or *shá*, *ra*?),[10] 31 : 20.
Mârat(= *TUR.SAL*)[11]-^{m}*A-a-ri*,[12] 17 : 3.
Mârat-^{m}*Aḫu*(= *SHESH*)-*ni*, 31 : 7.
Mârat-^{f}*Ba*(? or *Ush*?)-*ba*(? or *ka*?)-[. . .], 31 : 27.
Mârat-^{m}*Ilu*(= *AN*)-*ip-pa-ásh-ra*, 31 : 15.
Mârat-^{m}*Ki-din*-[. . .], 97 : 5.
Mârat-^{m}*Ku-ri-i*, 31 : 7.
Mârat-^{m}*Mush-ta-li*, 31 : 11 ¦ 32 : 7.
Mârat-*sic*[13]*Ta-a-du*, 83 : 11, 35.
Mârat-^{f}*Ush*(? or *Ba*?)-*ba*(? or *ka*?)-[. . .], 31 : 27.
^{f}*Ri-shá-tum*, 95 : 9.
^{f}*Ta-a-du*[13], 83 : 14, 35.
^{f}*Ush*(? or *Ba*?)-*ba*(? or *ka*?)-[. . .], 31 : 27.

II. Professional and Gentilic Names.

a-bil bâbi, 86 : 24.
aḫ-la-mi-ti,[14] 31 : 25.
[*aḫ*]-*lim-mi-ti*, 32 : 8.
^{amelu}*Ak-ka-di-i*[15], 18 : 25 ¦ 41 : 11.
^{amelu}*aklu*(= *PA*)[16] *ENGAR*, 39 : 3.
a-li-ik pâni(= *SHI*)^{ni}, 37 : 24.

---

[1] *I.e.*, "E. makes to rejoice."

[2] Or [^{m}]*Da-li-li-ia*?

[3] Cf. ^{f}*Ab-bu-ut-ta-ni-tum*, *B. E.*, XV, 185 : 11.

[4] Here the *da* is doubtful; it might be also *ra*, then cf. ^{f}(?)*Da-ak-ra* *TUR.SAL* ^{m} ^{ilu}*AG.DI.TAR*, *B. E.*, XV, 188, IV : 10.

[5] Cf. *TUR.SAL Da-li-lu-shá*, *B. E.*, XIV, 58 : 7. Here probably a "*Kosename*" which the writer applies to his "sister."

[6] A "*Kosename*."

[7] Hypocoristicon for *Di-nu-ili-lu-mur*, cf. *B. E.*, XIV, 58 : 21.

[8] Doubtful whether a *nom. pr.*

[9] But see pp. 25, note 1; 110, note 3.

[10] Might expect ^{f}*La-ta-rak*, but no trace of *rak* is visible.

[11] So also in all following names.

[12] Cf. ^{f}*In-bi-A-a-ri*.

[13] See note to *Mâr*-^{f}*Ta-a-du*.

[14] Cf. *B. E.*, XV, 154 : 26, *aḫ-la-mu-ú* (not registered by Clay).

[15] Cf. ^{m}*Ak-ka-du-ú*, 51 : 11.

[16] Or better ^{gish}*ENGAR*, *i. e.*, *narṭabu*, see pp. 35, note 3; 127, note 2.

Professional and Gentilic Names

amelu (= *GALU*), 14 : 17; *a-PI-lu*, 67 : 7; *a-mi-la*, 66 : 25; *a-mi-li*, 42 : 9 | 72 : 10; *a-mi-li-e*, 89 : 17; *a-mi-lu-ti*, 83 : 16; *a-me-lu-shú*, 92 . 17; *a-mi-li-e-shú*, 84 : 16; *a-mi-lu-us-su*, 83 · 16; *a-PI-lu-us-su-nu*, 51 . 17, 20 | 67 : 13.

ardu,[1] 1 · 1, 16 | 3 : 58 | 14 : 18 | 15 : 10 | 21 : 30, 32 | 27 : 30, 32 | 31 : 34 | 35 . 17, 32 | 41 : 7 | 42 · 13 | 45 7 | 65 : 9 | 67 : 15; *ar-du*, 24 · 10; *ar-di*, 50 6, *ardâni*^{mesh}, 13 : 6; *II ardu*, 21 : 27; *ardi É GAL*, 31 : 11 | 50 : 11.

Ar-rap-ḫa-a-a-um, see " Proper Names."

^{amelu}*AZAG.GIM*, see *kudimmu*.

^{amelu}*bâ'iru* (= *SHU*^{4}*.GHA*),[2] 58 : 3.

^{amelu}*barû*, see ^{amelu}*MÁSH*.

bêl piḫâti[3] (= *EN.NAM*), 24 30 | 41 : 7; *bêlê* (= *EN*)^{mesh} *pi-ḫa-ti*, 92 : 10, 20.

be-el SHE.BAR, 76 : 7.

^{amelu}*DAM.QAR*^{mesh}, 55 : 10, 21 | 86 : 7, 11.

ENGAR see *errishu*.

EN.NAM, see *bêl piḫâti*.

^{amelu}*errishu* (= *ENGAR*)^{mesh}, 11 . 10; ^{amelu}*PA.ENGAR*, 39 : 3. Cf. also *e-ri-shú*, 40 13; *e-ri-shú*, 40 : 26 *et passim*.

GAL see *itû*.

^{amelu}*GAR*, see *shaknu*.

GIR (= *NER*),[4] 22 5.

$^{amelu\ mesh}$*ENGAR* (= *nartabu*), see ^{amelu}*aklu-ENGAR*.

GÛ.EN.NA,[5] 40 : 24 | 45 : 19 | 46 : 11 | 59 : 5 | 81 : 7.

gu-gal-lum, 27 : 8.

^{amelu}*GUSHUR RA.GAL*, see ^{amelu}*ÚR.RA.GAL*.

Ḫa-bi(!)[6]*-gal-ba-ti-i*, 53 : 28; *Ḫa-bi(!)-gal*[7]*-tu-ú*, 53 : 33.

ḫa-za-na, 9 : 22; *ḫa-za-an-na*, 9 : 23 | 72 : 14; *ḫa-za-an-nu*, 40 : 3 | 56 : 3; *ḫa-za-an-na-ti*, 37 : 21; *ḫa-za-an-na-a-ti*, 51 : 14 | 56 : 8 | 84 : 3.

^{m}*Isin-na-a-a*, see " Proper Names " under ^{m}*Ap-pa-na-a-a*.

^{amelu}*ishparu* (= *USH.BAR*), 35 : 18 | 41 : 12, ^{amelu}*USH.BAR*^{mesh}, 23 33.

ishshaku, see *pa-te-si*.

i-tu,[8] 24 : 36 | 33*a* : 11 | 35 . 25, *i-tu* ^{amelu}*SHA(G).TAM*, 21 : 4; *i-tu-ú*, 11 : 21 | 26 · 17 | 34 : 28 | 78 . 4, *i-tu-u SHA(G).TAM-mi*, 27 · 15.

kan-du-ri-e,[9] 18 : 38.

ka-ṣi-ri, 35 : 18.

^{amelu}*KA.ZID* (= *KU*)*.DA*, 26 : 5, 7.

ki-ib,[10] 21 . 4 | 46 : 17.

^{amelu}*kudimmu* (= *AZAG.GIM*), 82 : 9.

Ku-tu-ú-a, 87 : 14.

LUL, see *zammertu*.

ma(?)-ḫi-ṣa, 9 : 7.

^{amelu}*mâkisu* (= *NI(G).KUD.DA*),[11] 27 : 35 | 57 . 7.

man-za-az pa-ni, 48 : 27.

MA.AN.USH (or *NIT*),[12] 37 : 9.

mâr (= *TUR*) *shi-ip-ri*, 4 : 17 | 22 : 17 | 28 · 10 | 33 : 26 | 34 : 21 | 47 : 6 | 53 : 37 | 68 : 37 | 79 · 8 | 89: 21, 25 | 92 . 6; *mâr shi-ip-ri*, 7 : 4 | 13 : 8, 11; *mar ship-ri shá be-li-ia*, 8 : 17; *mâr ship-ri LUGAL*, 55 : 13.

mârê (= *TUR*)^{mesh} *En-lil*^{ki},[13] 86 · 5, 8; *mârê* (= *TUR*)^{mesh} *Ni-ib-bu-rum*, 81 : 6.

mârê (= *TUR*)^{mesh} ^{alu}*Ki*[14]*-im-ma*, 96 · 20, 25.

^{amelu}*MÁSH*, 72 : 4.

---

[1] See also the address of Nos. 1 74 and cf. Chapter III, p. 35, note 2.

[2] Cf. *B. E.*, XV, 162*e* : 14, *napḫar* 11 *SHU*^{4}*.GHA*^{mesh} (omitted by Clay).

[3] Cf. *pa-ḫa-ti-ka*, 77 : 5; *pi-ḫat*, 3 : 41.

[4] Doubtful; it may be *LUL* = *zammertu*, *q.v.*

[5] See introduction to No. 75 under "Translations," p. 133.

[6] So clearly here. At this time the *bi* and *NI* = *lí* are very often written alike, cf. *e g.*, 44 : 6, *id-du-ú-ni* (! = *-bi*!); 9 : 23. *Bit-*^{m}*Ki-din-ni* (!, the sign looks like *bi*!). See *B. E.*, XV, 171 : 17, 175 : 15, *UR.PA.NI* (so Clay, *Z.A.*, XX (1907), p. 417f.).*BI*, which, when compared with *l.c.*, 84 · 5, *UR-ḫaṭ* (= *PA*)*-te-ia*, has to be read (against Clay, *l.c.*, p. 15*b*) *Kalbi* (= *UR*)*-ḫaṭṭi* (= *PA*)*-i-lí* (= *BI* = *NI*). *Ḫa-bi* (! = *NI* = *lí*)*-gal-ba-tu-ú* is, of course, the same as the *Ḫa-li* (sic!, not *bi*)*-gal-ba-tu-ú* of Scheil, *Textes Élam. Sém.*, I, pl. 20 (opp. p. 96), 2.

[7] *Ba* omitted by scribe. Cf. *B. E.*, XIV, 164 · 2, *Ḫa-bi(!)-gal-ba-tu-ú* (not registered by Clay).

[8] Is *i-tú*(?), 53 : 12; *GAL i-tu*(?), 21 : 27, to be conferred here? Cf. here p. 35, note 4.

[9] Cf. ^{alu}*Kandurê* in *B. E.*, XIV, XV, and see Chapter IV, pp. 79ff.

[10] See p. 17, note 1.

[11] See p. 36, note 5.

[12] Doubtful; might be a *nom pr.*: *UR-*^{ilu}*USH*.

[13] See also *Ni-ib-bu-ri-i*.

[14] Or $^{alu-ki}$*IM-ma*.

Professional and Gentilic Names

MIR.NIT.TA, see *ridu*.

^{amelu}*MU*, see *nuḫatimmu*.

na-'i-ri-e,[1] 31 : 3 | 32 : 4 | 33 : 4; *na-'i-ra-ti*, 31 : 3 | 32 : 4; *na-'i-ra-a-ti*, 33 : 4.

na-gid, 68 : 8, *na-gid*^{mesh}, 11 : 9.

^{amelu}*nakru*(= *PAP*), 33*a* : 25; *na-ka-rum*, 86 : 19.

^{amelu}*nangaru*, 59 : 16.

Ni-ib-bu-ri-i, 18 : 21 | 83 : 10; *mârê*(= *TUR*)^{mesh} *Ni-ib-bu-rum*, 84 : 6; *mârê*(= *TUR*)^{mesh} *En-lil*^{ki}, 86 : 5, 8.

^{amelu}*NI(G).KUD.DA*, see *mâkisu*.

[*NU*] *GISH.SHAR*^{mesh}, 12 : 21.

^{amelu}*nuḫatimmu*(= *MU*)^{mesh}, 21 : 23.

^{amelu}*PA*, see *aklu*.

paḫâti, *piḫâti*, see *bêl*.

pa-te-si^{mesh},[2] 3 : 22, 24 | 8 : 18, 22 | 17 : 20 | 18 : 34 | 39 : 7 | 48 : 4 | 60 : 9 | 68 : 11; *pa-te-si*$^{hi.a}$, 68 : 5.

qiṣiru, see *kaṣiru*.

qi-pu, see *ki-ib*.

rê'û(= *SÎB*)^{mesh}, 17 : 27.

ri-du, 16 : 7(?),[3] *rid ṣabe*(= *MIR.NIT.TA*), 24 : 19.

^{amelu}*RIQ*, 26 : 5, 7 | 83 : 15; ^{amelu}*RIQ*^{mesh}, 83 : 8.

^{amelu}*SAG*, 93 : 7, ^{amelu}*SAG LUGAL*, 1 : 5 | 13 : 5, 17.

^{amelu}*sak*(= *SAG*)-*shap-par*,[4] 33*a* : 28.

^{amelu}*sasînu*, 81 : 18.

SÎB, see *rê'û*.

si(? or *ṣ*?)-*pi*-[*ri*], 9 : 8.

su-ma-ak TI,[5] 37 : 22.

Ṣ.ÂB, see *ummâni*.

ṣi-iḫ-ḫi-ru-ti,[6] 55 : 5; *TUR.TUR*^{mesh}, 55 : 2, 4, 10, 18, 24.

shá dul-la ú-she-ip-pi-shum,[7] 13 : 6.

^{amelu}*SHA.KUD.DA*, see *mâkisu*.

shakin(= *GAR*)^{in}[8] *dê*(= *NE*)-*mi*, 9 : 16.

^{amelu}*shakni*(= *GAR*)^{ni}, 28 : 18, *shá-ak-na*, 65 : 4.

shá-pi-ir, 21 : 20.

^{amelu}*SHAR*(? or *RA*?).*KU*,[9] 50 : 15.

sharru(= *LUGAL*), 5 : 22 | 24 : 18, 37 | 29 : 6 | 55 : 15, 16 | 59*a* : 3, 5 | 89 : 22 | 92 : 7, 25; *um-ma LUGAL-ma*, 75 : 2; *mâr ship-ri LUGAL*, 55 : 13; ^{amelu}*SAG LUGAL*, 1 : 5 | 13 : 5, 17.

sha-tam[10] (= *SHA(G).TAM*), 35 : 33 | 39 : 3(?); ^{amelu}*SHA(G).TAM*, 21 : 4 | 51 : 25; *i-tu-ú SHA(G).TAM-mi*, 27 : 15.

^{amelu}*SHÚ.GHA*, see *bâ'iru*.

TUR.TUR^{mesh}, see *ṣi-iḫ-ḫi-ru-ti*.

UD.DI.TA,[11] 37 : 10.

ummâni(= *ṢAB*)^{mesh},[12] 3 : 53 | 8 : 6 | 9 : 18 | 11 : 19, 22, 27 | 12 : 11, 19 | 13 : 14 | 29 : 11, 1[?] | 66 : 14, 22, 26 | 68 : 39 | 93 : 6; *ṢAB*$^{hi.a}$, 9 : 17 | 26 : 8 | 29 : 8 | 31 : 12 | 39 : 7, 17 | 41 : 18 | 46 : 9 | 58 : 12 | 62 : 4 | 67 : 8; *ṢAB*$^{hi.a\ mesh}$, 83 : 9; *ṢAB-ni*, 6 : 8.

^{amelu}*Ú.R.RA.GAL*^{meshu}, 23 : 11.

^{amelu}*USH.BAR*, see ^{amelu}*ishparu*.

^{amelu}*ZADIM*, see ^{amelu}*sasînu*.

zammertu(= *LUL*),[14] 22 : 5.

---

[1] See Chapter III, p. 36, note 7.

[2] See also ^{m}*Ish-shá-ki*.

[3] Cf., however, pp. 123, note 10, and 49, note 3.

[4] See Chapter III, p. 37, note 12.

[5] For this *TI* cf. also *B. E.*, XV, 95 : 3, *dam-qár TI*, read by Clay, *l.c.*, p. 51*b*, *NIN.LIL-ti*.

[6] See p. 51, note 3.

[7] Here the same as the *mushêpishu* of the Ḫam. Letters.

[8] Here, however, a permansive.

[9] Or *LU* = *dub*?

[10] See p. 35, note 3.

[11] Doubtful whether an official. Cf. here the *ud-di-tá* = *KI*, K. 2875, 27, 28 (= *B. A.*, V, p. 533); hence not the title of an official, but a part (the lower?) of ^{mâtu}*Tâmtim*?

[12] See p. 35, note 1.

[13] See p. 97, note 9.

[14] Doubtful, might be *GIR*(= *NER*).

III. Names of Places.

^{mâtu}*A.AB.BA*^{ki}, see ^{mâtu}*Tâmtim*.

^{mâtu}*A-ga-a-dè*(= *NE*), 28 : 21; *A-ga-dè*(= *NE*)^{ki}, 27 : 23.

^{âlu}*A-ma*(or *ba*?)-*la*^{ki}, 96 : 1, 11, 21, 28; cf. l. 7, ^{âlu}*A-ma*^{ki}![1]

^{âlu}*Ardi-Bêlit*(= *GASHAN*),[2] 13 : 7; 66 : 24; ^{âlu}*Ardi-GASHAN*^{ki}, 11 : 20; ^{âlu}*Ardi-NIN*^{ki}, 18 : 19.

ma-at Ásh-shur, 20 : 18.

^{âlu}*Bâb-ili*(= *KÁ.DINGIR.RA*), 60a : 6 | 95 : 3; *KÁ.DINGIR.RA*^{ki}, 62 : 7 | 71 : 8.

^{âlu}*Balâṭi*(= *TI*)^{ki}(?).[3] 65 : 19.

BÀR.TUR^{ki}, see *Parak-mâri*^{ki}.

Bît-^{m}*Ki-din-ni*, 9 : 23 | 11 : 15.

Bît-$^{m\ ilu}$*Sin*(= *XXX*)-*is-saḫ-ra*, 9 : 16.

Bît-$^{m\ ilu}$*Sin*(= *XXX*)-*ma-gir*, 11 : 25 | 59 : 6.

Bît-^{m}*Si-ri-shá*[4]-*ash*, 28 : 5.

Dêr (= *Dûr-ilu*)^{ki}, 5 : 6.

^{âlu}*Dilmun*(= *DIL.BAT*)^{ki},[5] 67 : 5

^{âlu}*DUL-shá-is*(?)-*si-la-aḫ-shu-ri-ia*, 59a : 11.

^{âlu}*Dûr-*[. . .], 90 : 5.

^{âlu}*Dûr-bêl*(= *EN*)-*mâtâti*(= *KUR.KUR*), 17 : 18, 26.

Dû[*r-*^{ilu}*En-lil*]$^{ki\ a}$, 3 : 31; *Dûr-*^{ilu}*En-lil*$^{ki.a\text{-}ki}$, 3 : 33, 38, 41; *Dûr-*^{ilu}*En-lil*$^{ki.a\text{-}mesh\text{-}ki}$, 39 : 21.

Dûr-ilu^{ki}, see *Dêr*^{ki}.

Dûr-Ishtar(= *U.DAR*)-*ṣîrat*(= *MAGH*), 68 : 28.

Dûr-Ku-ri-Gal-zu,[6] 13 : 7 | 23 : 29 | 59a : 4, ^{âlu}*Dûr-Ku-ri-Gal-zu*, 45 : 23 | 57 : 15, 20.

Dûr-^{ilu}*Nusku*(= *PA.KU*), 3 : 40.

Dûr-^{m}*Sukal*(= *PAP*)-*paṭ-ra*^{ki}, 40 : 3.

Dûr-U.DAR.MAGH, see *Dûr-Ishtar-ṣîrat*.

É-, see *Bît-*.

E-ka-la-ti^{ki}, 1 : 18.

^{âlu}*E-mu-ga-at-*^{ilu}*Marduk*,[7] 66 : 3 | 67 : 3.

$^{âlu\text{-}ki}$[8] ^{ilu}*En-ki-SAḪ*, 73a : 15.

En-lil^{ki}, see *Nippur*^{ki}.

^{âlu}*GAL-IM-*[. . .], 65 : 22.

$^{âlu\ ilu}$*Gir-ra-ga-mil*, 3 : 31; ^{âlu}*Gir-ra-ga-mil*, 3 : 39 | 3 : 40, 73; ^{ilu}*Gir-ra-ga-mil*,[9] 3 : 13, 17, 20.

^{âlu}*Ḫi-ba-ri-ti*, 26 : 4 | 27 : 36 | 31 : 33, 37 | 65 : 2.

^{âlu}*Idin*(= *SE*)-^{ilu}*Marduk*, 59 : 18.

$^{âlu\text{-}ki}$*IM-ma*, see ^{âlu}*Ki-im-ma*.

^{âlu}*Kar-*^{ilu}*Nabû*(= *AG*), 26 : 4; *Kâr-*^{ilu}*AG*, 68 : 26, 30, 36.

Kâr-^{ilu}*NIN.LIL*, see *Nam-gar-Kar-*^{ilu}*NIN.LIL*.

^{âlu}*Ki-im-ma*,[10] 96 : 20, 25.

Kish^{ki}, 44 : 19.

^{âlu}*Lu-*[. . .], 51 : 5.

^{âlu}*Lu-ub-di-shá*^{ki}, 99 : 6.

^{âlu}*Man-nu-gi-ir-*^{ilu}*Rammân*(= *IM*),[11] 24 : 13, 18.

^{âlu}*MASH-IM*^{ki},[12] 27 : 5.

^{âlu}*MUM*(= *MUN*),[13] 14 : 13; ^{âlu}*MUM*^{ki}, 27 : 5,[14] 33 | 41 : 15; ^{âlu}*MUM*^{ki}-*ma*, 26 : 6.

Nina^{ki},[15] 17 : 24.

---

[1] Here the *la* is, no doubt, left out by the scribe.

[2] Cf. ^{m}*Ardi-Bêlit*.

[3] Identical with the city *TE*, *E. B. H.*, p. 95, note 1?

[4] Or *da*.

[5] Hardly *âlu*$^{ush.ush}$.

[6] See p. 9, note 2.

[7] Cf. here the *E-mu-qat*(= *SHÚ*)-^{ilu}*En-lil*^{ki} in *B. E.*, XIV, 18 : 4 | 31 : 11, which Clay, *l.c.*, p. 58, reads erroneously *E-mu-shu-Bêl*^{ki}, registering the second passage quoted under ^{âlu}*Nippuru*^{ki}!

[8] For *âlu-ki* see Chapter I, p. 11, note 1.

[9] Cf. ^{ilu}*Shamash-tu-kul-ti*.

[10] Or $^{âlu\text{-}ki}$*IM-ma*.

[11] See p. 49, note 1.

[12] Or ^{âlu}*MUM*, *q. v.*?

[13] For this city cf. *e.g.*, *B. E.*, XIV, 167 : 29 (omitted by Clay), and above, p. 118, note 4.

[14] This is doubtful. Here a reading ^{âlu}*MASH.IM*^{ki} is likewise possible. As, however, this city occurs in a letter of *Kudurânu*, who was closely connected with the ^{âlu}*MUM*^{ki}, I prefer to read as indicated.

[15] Or *Uruk*^{ki}?

Names of Places

^{ālu}Nippur(= EN.LIL)^{ki}, 38 : 3 | 89 : 21 ; EN.LIL^{ki}, 11 : 19 | 13 : 6 | 18 : 20 | 27 : 29 | 35 : 13 | 58 : 4 | 83 : 8 | 86 : 7 | 95 : 17. Cf. shar-rat ^{ālu}EN.LIL^{ki}, 38 : 3; mârê^{mesh} EN-LIL^{ki}, see "Professional and Gentilic Names."
^{ālu}Pa-an-Ba-li^{ki}, 23 : 31.
Pa-lak^{ki},[1] 6 : 5.
^{ālu}Pa-lu^{ki}, 18 : 31.
Parak(= BÀR)-mâri^{ki},[2] 53 : 38.
^{ālu}Pi-[. . .],[3] 72 : 14.
^{ālu}Ra-ka-nu,[4] 9 : 22.
^{ālu}SAL.TUK^{ki}(?), 96 : 11.
^{ālu}Sippar(= UD.KIB.NUN)^{ki}, 89 : 24, 26.
^{ilu}Shamash(= UD)-tu-kul-ti,[5] 16 : 8, 12.
^{ālu}She-li-bi^{ki}, 83 : 15.
^{ālu}Shi-i-tu-na(!)-[li^{ki}], 27 : 1.
^{ālu}Shi-i-tú-na-li,[6] 28 : 22.
^{mātu}Tâmtim(= A.AB.BA)^{ki},[7] 22 : 15 | 37 : 10.
^{ālu}Ta-ri-ba-a-tum, 66 : 23.
^{ālu}TI^{ki}(?), see ^{ālu}Balâṭi^{ki}.
Tuk(= KU)-kul-ti-É.KUR^{ki},[8] 39 : 5.
^{ālu}UD.KIB.NUN^{ki}, see ^{ālu}Sippar.
UNUG^{ki}, see Uruk^{ki}.
Ú-pi-i^{ki},[9] 23 : 35; Ú-pi-i, 1 : 6, ^{ālu}Ú-p[i-i], 65 : 4.
^{ālu}Ûr-ra-ga-mil, see ^{ālu}Gir-ra-ga-mil.
Uruk$^{10 ki}$, 17 : 21.
Uruk^{ki}-labiru^{ki},[11] 34 : 29, 32.
^{ālu}Za-[. . .], 50 : 9.
^{ālu}[. . .], 72 : 11.
[. . .]-bil^{ki},[11] 18 : 14.
[. . .]-di^{ki}, 18 : 11, 13, 15.

IV. Names of Gates.

abulla(= KÁ.GAL)^{la}, 24 : 31; KÁ.GAL, 66 : 21.
abullu(= KÁ.GAL) erû(= URUDU)^{mesh} DA^{mesh}, 21 : 21.
bâbu(= KÁ),[12] 9 : 19.
bâb(= KÁ) A-nu, 27 : 43; bâb A-nu-um, 35 : 15.
bâb(= KÁ) Ardi(?)-GAB(?) BA(?)-ma(?),[13] 81 : 14.
bâb(= KÁ) Nam-ga-ra-Bêl(= BE), 27 : 33.
bâb shá bît(= É) be-li-ia, 26 : 18.

V. Names of Houses and Temiles.

É, see introduction to Nos. 1-74, pass. and Chapter III, p. 34.
É^{mesh}, 31 : 36 | 37 : 23 | 66 : 27, 28.
É.AN,[14] 57 : 19, 21 | 93 : 6; É-A-nu, 35 : 15.
bît be-li-ia, 26 : 19 | 27 : 12 | 50 : 3.
bît sharri(= LUGAL), 59a : 3.
É.DIM.GAL.KALAM.MA,[15] 89 : 5.
É ^{abnu}DUB,[16] 81 : 7, 10.

[1] Cf. B. E., XV, 128 : 3, ^{ālu}Pa-la-ak^{ki}; thus to be read instead of ^{ālu}Pa-ra-ash(?), Clay, l.c., p. 53a?

[2] For pronunciation see Br., List, No. 6900.

[3] Cf. Pi-i-na-a-ri, B. E., XIV, p. 58b.

[4] Or Ra-ka-be?

[5] Cf. ^{ilu}Gir-ra-ga-mil.

[6] Cf. the preceding name. Both are, no doubt, identical.

[7] See p. 10, note 3.

[8] Cf. ^{nāru}Tuk-kul-ti-É.KUR^{ki}, 39 : 8.

[9] Cf. ^{mātu}Ú-pi-i in B. E., XIV, 132 : 43, 46, 52 (not registered by Clay).

[10] Or Nina^{ki}?

[11] Cf. B. E., XV, 102 : 13, Dûr-^{ilu}MAR.TU-Ù(= labiru)^{ki} and l.c., l. 11, KI-II(= Dûr-^{ilu}MAR.TU)-BIL(= eshshu)^{ki}. This passage, then, would testify to the existence, at the time of the Cassite kings, of an "Old" and a "New Erech or Warka."

[12] Cf. a-bil bâbi(= KÁ).

[13] Or bâb Ardi-Tab-tu-ma?

[14] See pp. 80f.

[15] See p. 22, note 1.

See Chapter IV, pp. 86ff.

Names of Houses and Temples

É-^{ilu}EN.ZU-[?], 53 : 22.

É.GAL,[1] 34 : 11 | 35 : 15 | 50 : 11 | 59 : 4.

bît-ilu, see *É.AN*.

bît-^{isu}irshu(= *NAD*), 66 : 21 : *bît ^{isu}irshê*(*NAD*)^{mesh}, 23 : 14 | 66 : 22.

É.KISH.SHÌR(= *NU*)*.GAL*, see Masculine Names.

É.KUR^{mesh}, 66 : 23 ; *É.KUR*, see *Tuk-kul-ti-É.KUR^{ki}* and *^{nâru}Tuk-kul-ti-É.KUR^{ki}*.

É.KUR.GAL, see *^{m}I-na-É.KUR.GAL*.

É.LUGAL, see *bît sharri*.

É-^{ilu}MAR.TU, 73*a* : 3.

É-^{ilu}Nergal(?), 54 : 20.

É.SAG.ÌL, see Masculine Names.

É-SAL.AZAG, 91 : 7.

É-^{ilu}Sin-, see *É-^{ilu}EN.ZU-*.

ku-tal-li, 23 : 8; *ku-tal na-ka-si*, 23 : 13.

parakku(= *BAR*) *^{ilu}En-lil*, 66 : 7 | 70 : 1.

VI. Names of Rivers and Canals.

nâru(= *A.GUR*), 3 : 1, 7 | 18 : 31 | 46 : 4 | 48 : 28.

$^{nâru\ ilu}$Bêlit, see *$^{nâru\ ilu}$NIN.LIL*.

^{nâru}Da-li-ta-ma-na-[.], 6 : 4.

^{nâru}Diglat(= *MASH.TIK.QAR*), 34 : 26.

^{nâru}Diglat(= *M*[*ASH.TI*]*K.QAR*)*-ilu*(= *AN*)*-Nippur* (=*EN.LIL*)^{ki},[2] 3 : 18.

^{nâru}E-tel-bi-[?], 3 : 8 | 66 : 6, 12.

^{nâru}Gam[3]-mar-GAL, 3 : 9.

^{nâru}Idiglat, see *^{nâru}Diglat*.

^{nâru}Ilu(= *AN*)*-i-pu-ush*, 40 : 21.

^{nâru}MASH.TIK.QAR, see *^{nâru}Diglat*.

^{nâru}Na-la-aḫ,[4] 40 : 22.

nam-ga-ra, 40 : 4 | 66 : 15; *nam-ga-ri*, 40 : 15, 16, 18, 19; *nam-gar*(= *sha*), 40 : 14 | 68 : 22; *nam-gar-ra*, 40 : 9, 20; *nam-kar*, 3 : 16; *nam-qar*, 66 : 8.

Nam-gar(=*kar*)*-Dûr*(?)*-^{ilu}En-lil*, 3 : 6[5] | 71 : 15.

Nam-ga-ra-Bêl(= *BE*), 27 : 33; *Nam-qar[6]-Bêl*(= *BE*), 66 : 12.

Nam-gar-Kâr-^{ilu}NIN.LIL, 68 : 22.

^{nâru}Nam-ga-ri-shá-bêl(= *EN*)*-mâtâti* (= *KUR.KUR*), 59 : 9.

nam-kar, *nam-qar*, see *nam-ga-ra*.

^{nâru}Nannar(= *SHESH.KI*)*-gù-gal*, 3 : 14.

$^{nâru\ ilu}$NIN.LIL, 67 : 2.

^{nâru}Pat-ti[7]-^{ilu}En-lil, 28 : 11.

^{nâru}SHESH.KI-gù-gal, see *^{nâru}Nannar-gù-gal*.

^{nâru}Tuk(= *KU*)*-kul-ti-É.KUR^{ki}*,[8] 39 : 8.

VII. Names of Gods.

A-a-ri: *^{m}A-a-ri*; *^{f}In-bi-*.

^{ilu}AG, see *^{ilu}Nabû*.

Aḫu: *^{m}A-ḫu-*; *^{m}A-ḫu-ú-a-*.

^{ilu}AMAR.UD, see *^{ilu}Marduk*.

AN: *AN.RA*, see *DINGIR.RA*; *^{m}AN-*, see *^{m}Ilu-*; *^{nâru}AN-i-pu-ush*; *^{m}Gu-za-ar-*; *^{m}Di-in-AN-lu-mur*; *Dûr-ilu^{ki}*; *^{m}A-na-tukulti-AN-ma*; *^{nâru}Diglat-AN-En-lil^{ki}*; *É-*.

AN^{mesh}: *$^{m\ ilu}$Errish*(*t*)*-GA.BU-*; *$^{m\ ilu}$Errish*(*t*)(=*L*)*-GIR-*; *$^{m\ ilu}$Rammân-shar-*; *^{m}NIM.GI-shar-*.

AN.GAL,[9] 89 : 4; *^{m}Pân-AN.GAL-lu-mur*.

AN.RA, see *DINGIR.RA*.

---

[1] See pp. 78f.

[2] Hence "the Tigris of Nippur" is = "the Tigris of the god(!) of Nippur," in other words, "the god of Nippur" is = "Nippur." Cf. here also *É.AN*(= *ilu*)*-Nippur*(= *EN.LIL*)^{ki}, *B. E.*, XV, 128 : 14, and see p. 80.

[3] Or *Kud*?

[4] Clay, *B. E.*, XIV, p. 7, says that the *me-e ^{nâru}Na-la-aḫ* occur also on *C. B. M.* 3527; but this apparently is a mistake, as the tablet referred to has been published by Clay in *B. E.*, XIV, 149 (see *l.c.*, p. 72). Read *l.c.*, *C. B. M.* 5134, instead of *C. B. M.* 3527.

[5] Here *dûr* looks like *si-ib*, while in 71 : 15 it has the appearance of *si* + *sal*(= *ib*?).

[6] Cf. also 66 : 8.

[7] See Delitzsch, *H. W. B.*, p. 555*a*.

[8] Cf. *Tuk*(= *KU*)*-kul-ti-É.KUR^{ki}*, 39 : 5.

[9] Chief god of *Dûr-ilu^{ki}*; see Chapter II, p. 19, note 3, and cf. *^{ilu}KA.DI*.

Names of Gods

AN-TIM, 11 : 19.

^{ilu}*A-nu*, 21 : 6; *A-nu*, *É*-, *bâb*-; *A-nu-um*, *bâb*-.

^{ilu}*A-shur*: $^{m\ ilu}$*A-shur*-; *ma-at Ásh-shur*.

Ba-li: ^{ilu}*Pa-un*-

Ba-ni: ^{m}*A-ḫ-u-a*-, ^{m}*A-ḫu*-, $^{m\ ilu}$*DIL.BAT*-, $^{m\ ilu}$*Nergal*-; *Ba-nt-i*: ^{m}*Amel*-; *Bana-a*: ^{m}*Bana-a*-.

BE. *Nam-ga-ra-BE*(=*bêl*).

Bêl, see *BE*; *EN*.

Bêl mâtâti, see *EN.KUR.KUR*.

Bêlit, see *GASHAN*; *NIN*; ^{ilu}*NIN.LIL*.

^{ilu}*Be-lit-ì-li*(= *NI.NI*).[1] 21 : 7.

^{ilu}*DAR.ḪU*: $^{m\ ilu}$*DAR.ḪU*-.

^{ilu}*DIL.BAT*, 72 : 5; $^{m\ ilu}$*DIL.BAT*-. ^{m}*Iz-gur*-, ^{alu}*Dilmun*.

DINGIR.RA: *Bâb*(= *KÁ*)-*ili*(*DINGIR.RA*)^{ki}.

^{ilu}*DU*(?), see note to ^{m}*Ásh-pi-la-an-du*.

^{ilu}*É.A*, 21 : 6. See also ^{ilu}*EN.KI*.

É.KISH.SHÌR(= *NU*).*GAL*: ^{m}*É.KISH.SHÌR.GAL*-.

É.KUR: *Tuk-kul-ti-É.KUR*^{ki}, ^{nâru}*Tuk-kul-ti-É.KUR*^{ki}, see also under "Names of Houses and Temples."

É.KUR.GAL: ^{m}*I-na*-.

EN: ^{m}*EN*-; $^{m\ ilu}$*En-lil-EN-nishi*^{mesh}-*shu*.

^{ilu}*En*; $^{m\ ilu}$*En*-.

^{ilu}*EN.KI*: $^{alu.ki\ ilu}$*EN.KI.SAḪ*. See also ^{ilu}*É.A*.

EN.KUR.KUR,[2] 21 : 11, 17; ^{nâru}*Nam-ga-ri-shá*-; ^{alu}*Dur*-.

^{ilu}*En-lil*. 18 : 8 | 24 : 6 | 66 : 6 | 71 : 15; $^{m\ ilu}$*En-li*-; ^{m}*Na-zi*-; *parakku*; ^{nâru}*Pat-ti*-; *Nam-gar-Dûr*-; ^{ilu}*En-lil*$^{ki.a}$: *Dûr*-; ^{ilu}*En-lil*$^{ki.a\text{-}mesh}$: *Dûr*-; ^{ilu}*En-lil*^{ki}, see *AN*.

^{ilu}*Errish*(*t*);[3] $^{m\ ilu}$*Errish*(*t*)-; ^{m}*Bu-na*-, ^{m}*Bu-un-na*-, ^{m}*Idin*-, ^{m}*Iz-gur*-.

^{ilu}*EN.ZU*: *É*-. See also ^{ilu}*Sin*(= *XXX*); *Nannar*.

É.SAG.ÌL: ^{m}*É.SAG.ÌL*-.

Eṭir, see *NIM.GI*.

GAB(?)-*BA*(?)-*ma*(?); *bâb Ardi*-.

Gal-zu: *Dûr-Ku-ri*-.

GASHAN:[4] ^{m}*Ardi*-, ^{âlu}*Ardi*-.

^{ilu}*Gir-ra*, *Gir-ra*: ^{âlu} (^{ilu})*Gir-ra-ga-mil*.

^{ilu}*GU*,[5] 89 : 1.

^{ilu}*Gú-sir* see ^{ilu}*KA.DI*.

GHE-GAL: ^{m}*Ma*-.

Ia-ú [if indeed name of a god and not the hypocorist ending *ia* + nominative ending *u* frequently attached to names without regard to their last element]: ^{m}*Ardi*-.

I-gi-gi: ^{m}*I-gi-gi*.

Ì-li(= *NI.NI*):[6] ^{m}*Ì-li*-, ^{ilu}*Be-lit*-; cf. ^{m}*I-li*-, ^{m}*Il-li*-.

Ilu, see *AN*; ^{m}*Ilu*-, ^{f}*I-lum*-, *Bâb*-, *Dûr*-, ^{nâru}*Ilu-i-pu-ush*.

^{ilu}*IM*, see ^{ilu}*Rammân*.

^{ilu}*Ishtar*, see ^{ilu}*DIL.BAT*; *U.DAR*.

^{ilu}*Ishtar*(= *RI*)-*A-ga-di*(= *NE*)^{ki}, 27 : 23.

^{ilu}*KA.DI*,[7] 5 : 6, 21.

^{ilu}*KUR*: ^{m}*Ib-ni*-.

KUR.GAL: ^{m}*KUR.GAL*-.

Ku-ri: *Dûr-Ku-ri-Gal-zu*; ^{m}*Ku-ri-a*.

La-ta-rak: ^{f}*La-ta-rak*(?).

^{ilu}*LUGH*: $^{m\ ilu}$*LUGH*(= *Sukal*)-, ^{m}*Man-nu-ki*-.

^{ilu}*Marduk*(= *AMAR.UD*), 10 : 2 | 81 : 4; $^{m\ ilu}$*Marduk*-, ^{m}*Aḫ-iddina*-, ^{m}*Amel*-, ^{m}*Ardi*-, ^{m}*Ba-il*-, ^{m}*Bana-a-sha*-, ^{m}*E-mt-da*-, ^{âlu}*E-mu-ga-at*-, ^{m}*Erba*-, ^{m}*Er-ba-am*-, ^{m}*Êṭir*-, ^{m}*Ib-ni*-, ^{âlu}*Idin*-, ^{m}*Ki-din*-, ^{m}*Na-aḫ-zi*-, ^{m}*Nannari*-.

^{ilu}*MAR.TU*: *É*-.

^{ilu}*MASH*, see ^{ilu}*Errish*(*t*)-.

^{ilu}*Nabû*(= *AG*), 7 : 7, 18; ^{âlu}*Kâr*-, *Kâr*-.

Nannari(=*SHESH.KI*)^{ri}: ^{m}*Nannari*-^{ilu}*Marduk*; ^{nâru}*Nannar*(= *SHESH.KI*)-*gù-gal*. See also ^{ilu}*EN.ZU*; ^{ilu}*Sin*(= *XXX*).

^{ilu}*Nergal*: $^{m\ ilu}$*Nergal*-, *É*-, ^{m}*Idin*-.

NIM.GI [if name of a god]: ^{m}*NIM.GI-shar-ilî*.

NI.NI, see *ìli*.

^{ilu}*NINNÛ*(= *L*), see $^{m\ ilu}$*Errish*(*t*)-.

NIN: ^{âlu}*Ardi-NIN*^{ki}, see also *Bêlit*, *GASHAN*, ^{ilu}*NIN.LIL*, ^{ilu}*NIN*-[. . .], 3 : 62.

^{ilu}*NIN.DIN.DÙG.GA*: ^{m}*Kalbi*-

---

[1] See p. 47, note 5.

[2] See p. 8, note 8.

[3] For this pronunciation of ^{ilu}*NIN.IB*, ^{ilu}*IB*, ^{ilu}*MASH*, ^{ilu}*L*, etc., see *The Monist*, XVII (January, 1907), p. 140ff, and cf. "Preface".

[4] Cf. ^{âlu}*Ardi-NIN*^{ki}.

[5] Wife of ^{ilu}*TAR*; see Chapter II, p. 21.

[6] For this element in proper names see *The Monist*, XVII (January, 1907), p. 144c.

[7] Is to be pronounced ^{ilu}*Gú-sir*; see Chapter II, p. 19, note 3. He was the chief god of *Dûr-ilu*^{ki}, a *male* and also called *AN.GAL*.

Names of Gods

^{ilu}*NIN*(?).*GAL*, 50 : 9.

^{ilu}*NIN.IB*: $^{m\ ilu}$*Errish(t)*-, ^{m}*Bu-na*-, ^{m}*Bu-un-na*-, ^{m}*Idin*-, ^{m}*Iz-gur*-.

^{ilu}*NIN.LIL*,[1] 89 : 4; *Nam-gar-Kár*-, $^{nâru\ ilu}$*NIN.LIL*.

^{ilu}*NIN MAGH*,[2] 38 : 5.

^{ilu}*NIN.SHAR*: $^{m\ ilu}$*NIN.SHAR*-.

^{ilu}*Nusku*(= *PA.KU*):[2] $^{m\ ilu}$*Nusku*-, *Dûr*-.

^{ilu}*PA.KU*, see ^{ilu}*Nusku*

PAP, see ^{m}*Sukal*(= *PAP*)-, *Dûr*-^{m}*PAP*-.

^{ilu}*Rammân*(= *IM*). $^{m\ ilu}$*Rammân*-, ^{m}*Iqisha*(= *BA-sha*)-, ^{m}*Ki-din*-, ^{ilu}*Man-nu-gi-ir*-,[3] ^{ilu}*MASH.IM*^{ki}(?).

^{ilu}*RI*, see ^{ilu}*Ishtar*.

SAḪ: $^{âlu\text{-}ki\ ilu}$*EN.KI-SAḪ*.

^{ilu}*Sin*(= *XXX*). $^{m\ ilu}$*Sin*-, ^{m}*A-na*-^{ilu}*XXX-tak-la-ku*, *É*-$^{m\ ilu}$*XXX*-. See also ^{ilu}*EN.ZU*; *Nannar*.

^{ilu}*SUGH*, see ^{ilu}*Tishḫu*.

^{ilu}*Sukal*: $^{m\ ilu}$*Sukal*-. see also ^{ilu}*LUGH*; *PAP*.

^{ilu}*Shamash*(= *UD*), 33: 25, 29 | 41 : 1 | 81 : 4; $^{m\ ilu}$*Shamash*-, ^{m}*Nûr*-.

Shar-rat-^{ilu}*Nippur*(= *EN.LIL*)^{ki},[1] 38 : 3.

SHESH.KI, see *Nannar*.

Shi-pak(= *ḫu*): ^{m}*Ú-su-ub*-, ^{m}*Me-li*-.

^{ilu}*Shu-qa-mu-na*: ^{m}*Me-li*-.

^{ilu}*TAR*,[4] 89 : 4.

^{ilu}*TAR.ḪU*, see ^{ilu}*DAR.ḪU*.

^{ilu}*Tishḫu*(= *SUGH*),[1] 38 : 3.

^{ilu}*UD*, see ^{ilu}*Shamash*.

U.DAR(= *Ishtar*): *Dûr-U.DAR-ṣirat*(= *MAGH*), 68 : 28.

^{ilu}*ÙR.RA*, see ^{ilu}*Gir-ra*.

^{ilu}*USH*: ^{sic}*Kalbi*-^{ilu}*USH*(?).

---

[1] See Chapter III, p. 39, note 1.

[2] See Chapter III, p. 40, note.

[3] For this *gi-ir*, which proves that ^{ilu}*IM* was pronounced ^{ilu}*Rammân*, see Chapter III, p. 49, note 1.

[4] Husband of ^{ilu}*GU*; see Chapter II, p. 21.

VII.

DESCRIPTION OF TABLETS.

Abbreviations.

c., *circa*; **C. B. M.**, Catalogue of the Babylonian Museum, University of Pennsylvania, prepared by the Editor, Prof. Dr. H. V. Hilprecht; **cf.**, confer; **Exp.**, Expedition; **f.**, following page; **ff.**, following pages; **fragm.**, fragment(ary); **inscr.**, inscription; **L. E.**, Left Edge; **li.**, line(s); **Lo. E.**, Lower Edge; **No(s).**, Numbers; **O.**, Obverse; **p.**, page; **pp.**, pages; **R.**, Reverse; **R. E.**, Right Edge; **U. E.**, Upper Edge; **Vol.**, Volume.

Measurements are given in centimetres, width × length (height) × thickness. Whenever the tablet (or fragment) varies in size, the largest measurement is given. The Roman numbers under "description" indicate the several expeditions: I = first; II = second; III = third; IV = fourth expedition.

A. Autograph Reproductions.

Text.	Plate.	To	From	Age.	C. B. M.	Description.
1	1	"My Lord" (*a-na be-li-ia*)	^{m}*Iḫ-iddina*^{na}-^{ilu}*Marduk.*	*Kuri-Galzu,* about 1420 B.C.	11716	Baked. Light brown. Left part of R. and right lower corner broken off. 4 × 5.8 × 2. Inscr. 11 (O.) + 12 (R.) = 23 li. II.
2	1	"	^{m}*A-ḫu-Ba-ni.*	*Kuri-Galzu,* about 1400 B.C.	10930	Baked. Ruled. Light brown with occasional dark spots. Left part and lower half of tablet broken off. 4.5 × 4.5 × 2.6. Inscr. 7 (O.) + 4 (R.) = 11 li. III.
3	2, 3	"	^{m}*Amel-*^{ilu}*Marduk.*	*Shagarakti-Shuriash,* about 1325 B.C.	11426	Baked. Ruled. Light brown. Cracked. Crumbling. Several fragments glued together. Insertion of fragments *a* and *b* on place indicated very doubtful. 14 × 8.4 × 3.2. Inscr. 29 (O.) + 32 (R.) + 3 (U. E.) + 2 (L. E.) + 4 (fragm. *c*) + 4 (fragm. *d*) = 74 li. II.
4	4	"	^{m}*A-na-ku-rum-ma.*	About 1400 B.C.	3660	Unbaked. Light brown. Lower part of tablet broken off. 4.5 × 6.5 × 2. Inscr. 9 (O.)

Text.	Plate.	To	From	Age.	C.B.M.	Description.
						+ 8 (R.) + 2 (U. E.) + 3 (L. E.) = 22 li. II.
5	5	"My Lord" (*a-na be-li-ia*)	^{m}*Ardi-Bêlit.*	*Kuri-Galzu,* about 1400 B.C.	11149	Baked. Dark brown. Cracked. Right lower corner of O. broken off. Lower part of R. not inscribed. 5.5 × 10 × 2.8. Inscr. 16 (O.) + 7 (R.) = 23 li. I (stray tablet found out of place).
6	6	"	^{m}*Ardi-*^{ilu}*Marduk.*	*Kuri-Galzu,* about 1400 B.C.	12559	Unbaked. Light brown. Ruled. Beginning and end of lines crumbled away. Lower part broken away. R. razed off. 7.5 × 8 × 2.7. Inscr. 9 li. II.
7	6	"	[^{m}*A*]-*zi-r*[*u-um*].	About 1350 B.C.	3787	Unbaked. Dark brown. Cracked. Crumbling. Right side and lower part of tablet broken away. 4 × 7.5 × 3. Inscr. 11 (O.) + 9 (R.) = 20 li. II.
8	7	"	^{m}*Ba-il-*^{ilu}*Ma*[*rduk*].	*Nazi-Maruttash,* about 1370 B.C.	10816	Unbaked. Dark brown. Cracked. Glued together. Fragment. Upper left corner of larger tablet. 4.3 × 8.2 × 4. Inscr. 14 (O.) + 14 (R.) = 28 li. III.
9	8	"	^{m}*Bana-a-sha-*^{ilu}*Marduk.*	*Kuri-Galzu,* about 1390 B.C.	11635	Unbaked. Dark brown. Lower part broken off. 5 × 6 × 2. Inscr. 12 (O.) + 12 (R.) = 24 li. II(?). Translation, pp. 104ff.
10	8	"	[. . . . ^{ilu}]*Marduk.*	*Kuri-Galzu,* about 1390 B.C.	3837	Unbaked. Light brown. Ruled. Left half and lower part of tablet broken away. Remainder of R. not inscribed. 5.2 × 4.5 × 3. Inscr. 7 (O.) + 2 (R.) = 9 li. III.
11	9	"	^{m}*Be-la-nu.*	*Kudur-Enlil,* about 1335 B.C.	19781	Unbaked. Light brown, R. darker. O. crumbling and greatly obliterated. 4.8 × 7.3 × 2.2. Inscr. 14 (O.) + 2 (Lo. E.) + 14 (R.) + 1 (U. E.) = 31 li. IV.
12	10	"	^{m}*Eṭir-*^{ilu}*Marduk.*	About 1350 B.C.	11929	Baked. Light brown. Ruled. Beginning of lines on O. broken away. 4.5 × 7 ×

Text.	Plate.	To	From	Age.	C.B.M.	Description.
						2. Inscr. 11 (O.) + 11 (R.) = 22 li. II.
13	11	"My Lord" (*a-na be-li-ia*)	^{m}*Er-ba* ^{ilu}*Marduk.*	*Shagarakti-Shuriash,* about 1325 B.C.	10804	Unbaked. Light brown. Cracked. O. and R. dotted with dark spots. Lower part of tablet broken away. Lower part of R. not inscribed. 5 × 5.2 × 3. Inscr. 11 (O.) + 7 (R.) = 18 li. III.
14	11	"	^{m}*Er-ba-am-*^{ilu}*Marduk.*	*Shagarakti-Shuriash,* about 1325 B.C.	11637	Baked. Dark brown. Lower half of tablet broken away. 4.5 × 3.8 × 2. Inscr. 9 (O.) + 8 (R.) + 3 (U. E.) + 1 (L. E.) = 21 li. II.
15	12	"	${}^{m\ ilu}$*Errish(t)-[zêr-ib-]ni.*	*Burna-Buriash,* about 1430 B.C.	10571	Baked. Light brown. Crumbling. Cracked. Beginning of lines and lower part of tablet broken away. 6 × 4.5 × 2.5. Inscr. 8 (O.) + 8 (R.) + 3 (U. E.) = 19 li. III.
16	12	"	${}^{m\ ilu}$*Errish(t)-[zêr-ib-ni].*	*Burna-Buriash.* about 1430 B.C.	10951	Unbaked. Dark. Ruled. Badly effaced. Upper right and lower left corners broken away. Only upper part of R. inscribed. 5.8 × 9.5 × 2.5. Inscr. 15 (O.) + 3 (R.) = 18 li. II.
17	13	"	${}^{m\ ilu}$*Errish(t)-GA.BU-ilî*^{mesh}.	About 1350 B.C.	19780	Baked. Light brown. Very small script. The end of nearly all lines is broken away. Lower part of R. not inscribed. 4.3 × 6.7 × 2. Inscr. 20 (O.) + 2 (Lo. E.) + 14 (R.) = 36 li. IV.
18	14	"	[. . . .]-*ilî*^{mesh}.	About 1350 B.C.	3655	Baked. Light brown. Most of O. and left part of R. broken away. 6 × 11.5 × 2.8. Inscr. 15 (O.) + 25 (R.) + 1 (U. E.) = 41 li. II.
19	14	"	^{m}*Ib-ni-*^{ilu}*Marduk.*	*Kudur-Enlil,* about 1335 B.C.	19787	Unbaked. Light brown. Ruled. O. crumbling. Lower part of tablet broken away. Only upper part of R. inscribed. 4.3 × 6.8 × 2. Inscr. 12 (O.) + 1 (R.) = 13 li. IV.

Text.	Plate.	To	From	Age.	C.B.M.	Description.
20	15	"My Lord" (*a-na be-li-ia*)	^{m}*Idin-*^{ilu}*Errish*(?).	*Nazi-Maruttash*, about 1375 B.C.	19798	Unbaked. Light. Lower part of tablet broken away. R. mostly crumbled off. 5.8 × 6.3 × 2.4. Inscr. 13 (O.) + 13 (R.) + 3 (U. E.) = 29 li. IV.
21	16	"	^{m}*Ilu-MU.TUK.A-rima*^{ma}.	*Kadashman-Enlil*, about 1345 B.C.	10806	Unbaked. Light brown. Lower right part of tablet broken off. 5.3 × 8.4 × 2.3. Inscr. 14 (O.) + 16 (R.) + 1 (U. E.) + 2 (L. E.) = 33 li. III.
22	16	"	^{m}*Im-gu-rum*.	*Burna-Buriash*, about 1430 B.C.	11101	Baked. Dark brown. Ruled. Lower left corner broken away. Lower part of R. not inscribed. 5.5 × 7.5 × 2. Inscr. 14 (O.) + 4 (R.) = 18 li. II.
23	17	"	[^{m}*Im-gu*]*-rum*.	*Burna-Buriash*, about 1430 B.C.	11090	Baked. Light brown. Ruled. Upper and lower left corners broken away. Beginning of lines on R. mutilated. Lower half of R. not inscribed. 7 × 11 × 2.5. Inscr. 24 (O.) + 15 (R.) = 39 li. II. Translation, pp. 94ff.
24	18	"	^{m}*Kal-bu*.	*Kuri-Galzu*, about 1430 B.C.	19793	Baked. Light. Glued together. Part of case with address. Faint traces of seal-impression on case or envelope visible. Case glued together. Lower part of R. not inscribed. 7 × 10 × 2½. Inscr. 19 (O.) + 4 (Lo. E.) + 14 (R.) + 2 (Case) = 39 li. IV. Translation, pp. 101ff.
25	19	"	^{m}*Kalbi-*^{ilu}*NIN.DIN. DÙG.GA*.	*Kashtiliashu*, about 1309 B.C.	11096	Unbaked. Light brown. Left part and lower half of tablet broken away. Cracked. Glued together. R. crumbling and greatly mutilated. 6.2 × 5 × 2.5. Inscr. 8 (O.) + 4 (R.) + 4 (U. E.) = 16 li. II.
26	19	"	^{m}*Ku-du-ra-nu*.	*Kadashman-Turgu*, about 1360 B.C.	19785	Baked. Dark brown. Lower half of tablet broken away. 6.2 × 6 × 2.6. Inscr. 9 (O.)

Text.	Plate.	To	From	Age.	C.B.M.	Description.
						+ 11 (R.) = 20 li. IV. Translation, pp. 116ff.
27	20	"My Lord" (*a-na be-li-ia*)	^{m}*Ku-du-ra-nu.*	*Kadashman-Turgu,* about 1360 B.C.	12633	Baked. Dark. Glued together. Upper and lower right corners broken away. 6.5 × 10.5 × 2.5. Inscr. 20 (O.) + 1 (Lo. E.) + 20 (R.) = 41 li. II.
28	21	"	^{m}*Ku-du-ra-nu.*	*Kadashman-Turgu,* about 1360 B.C.	10983	Baked. Light brown. Lower part of tablet broken away. Part of O. razed off. 4.6 × 7 × 2. Inscr. 13 (O.) + 13 (R.) + 1 (U. E.) + 2 (L. E.) = 29 li. I (stray tablet found out of place).
29	22	"	${}^{m\ ilu}$*Marduk-mu-[shal-]lim.*	*Kuri-Galzu,* about 1400 B.C.	11956	Unbaked. Light brown. Upper left corner broken away. 4 × 5 × 2. Inscr. 9 (O.) + 1 (Lo. E.) + 8 (R.) = 18 li. II. Translation, pp. 106ff.
30	22	"	${}^{m\ ilu}$*Marduk-ra-im-kit-[ti].*	About 1350 B.C.	10629	Baked. Dark. Ruled. Crumbling. Lower part, end of lines, and R. broken away. 4.6 × 5 × 2.4. Inscr. 6 li. III.
31	23	"	^{m}*Mu-kal-lim.*	*Burna-Buriash,* about 1430 B.C.	11098	Unbaked. Light brown. Ruled. Crumbling. Cracked. O. partly covered with silica. R. upper left and lower right corners crumbled away. 6.8 × 12.4 × 3. Inscr. 19 (O.) + 21 (R.) + 1 (U. E.) = 41 li. II.
32	24	"	^{m}*Mu-ka[l-lim].*	*Burna-Buriash,* about 1430 B.C.	11497	Baked. Light brown. Ruled. Beginning and end of lines on O., lower part of tablet and nearly the whole of R. broken away. Lower part of R. not inscribed. 5.5 × 9.3 × 2.7. Inscr. 14 (O.) + 7 (R.) = 21 li. II.
33	25	"	[^{m}*M*]*u-kal-[lim].*	*Burna-Buriash,* about 1430 B.C.	10514	Unbaked. Light brown, R. darker. Crumbling. Cracked. Greatly mutilated. Lower part of tablet broken away. Line at end of inscription. 6 × 9 × 3. Inscr. 18 (O.) + 15 (R.) = 33 li. III.

TEXT.	PLATE.	TO	FROM	AGE.	C.B.M.	DESCRIPTION.
33a	26	"My Lord" (*a-na be-li-ia*)	^{m}*NIM.GI-shar-ili*^{mesh}.	About 1400 B.C.	6123	Unbaked. Light brown. Occasional dark spots on O and R. Cracked. Signs on some places chipped off, otherwise well preserved. 5 × 7.2 × 2.2. Inscr. 17 (O.) + 18 (R.) + 2 (U. E.) = 37 li. III. Translation, pp. 135ff.
34	27	"	^{m}*Ki-shá-ah-bu-ut.*	*Kadashman-Turgu*, about 1355 B.C.	6058	Baked. Dark. Upper right and lower left corner broken away. 5.2 × 9.5 × 2.3. Inscr. 21 (O.) + 21 (R.) + 3 (U. E.) + 1 (L. E.) = 46 li. II.
35	28	"	^{m}*Ki-shah-bu-ut.*	*Kadashman-Turgu*, about 1355 B.C.	6057	Baked. Light brown. Upper right corner chipped off. On R. occasional dark spots. 4.8 × 7.3 × 2.2. Inscr. 13 (O.) + 1 (Lo. E.) + 15 (R.) + 2 (U. E.) + 2 (L. E.) = 33 li. II. Translation, pp. 120ff.
36	29	"	[$^{m\ ilu}$]*Rammân-shar-ili*^{mesh}.	*Kadashman-Turgu*, about 1350 B.C.	10600	Unbaked. Light brown. Only upper right corner of O. preserved, rest broken away. On R. is only a part of sign *e*(?) visible. 3 × 3.3 × 2. Inscr. 6 li. III.
37	29	"	^{m}*Sin-kara-bi-esh-me.*	*Burna-Buriash*, about 1430 B.C.	19783	Baked. Dark brown. Ruled. R. cracked and lower right corner chipped off. Lower part of R. not inscribed. 5.5 × 9.5 × 3. Inscr. 16 (O.) + 10 (R.) = 26 li. IV.
38	30	"	^{m}*Shi-ri-iq-tum.*	*Kuri-Galzu*, about 1400 B.C.	10955	Baked. Light brown. Lower part and right upper corner of tablet broken away. 6 × 6 × 2.5. Inscr. 11 (O.) + 9 (R.) + 1 (U. E.) = 21 li. II. Translation, pp. 140ff.
39	31	"	^{m}*U-bar-rum.*	*Kudur-Enlil*, about 1335 B.C.	3661	Unbaked. Light brown. Crumbling. Greatly mutilated. R. almost entirely crumbled away. 5 × 8.4 × 2.3. Inscr. 17 (O.) + 19 (R.) + 3 (U. E.) = 39 li. II. Translation, pp. 126ff.

Text.	Plate.	To	From	Age.	C.B.M.	Description.
40	32	"My Lord" (*a-na be-li-ia*)	ᵐ*U-bar-rum.*	*Kudur-Enlil,* about 1335 B.C.	5134	Baked. Dark. Cracked. Glued together. Lower half of R. not inscribed. 5.5 × 9.3 × 2.5. Inscr. 17 (O.) + 1 (Lo. E.) + 8 (R.) = 26 li. III. Translation, pp. 129ff.
41	32	"	[*Nûr?*]-*ilu* *Shamash.*	*Kadashman-Turgu,* about 1350 B.C.	11787	Baked. Dark brown. Cracked. Crumbling. Left part and lower half of tablet broken away. Glued together. 5.2 × 5 × 2.5. Inscr. 11 (O.) + 12 (R.) + 3 (U. E.) = 26 li. II.
42	33	"	*ḫazannu* of *Dûr-Sukal-paṭra,* cf. p. 129.	*Kudur-Enlil,* about 1335 B.C.	11498	Unbaked. Light brown. Lower half of tablet broken away. First line and some signs of R. chipped off. 5 × 6 × 2.5. Inscr. 10 (O.) + 11 (R.) + 2 (U. E.) + 3 (L. E.) = 26 li. II.
43	34	"	ᵐ*Pi*(?)-	About 1350 B.C.	19779	Unbaked. Light brown, O. has large black spot. Crumbling. End of lines on O. covered with silica. Lower part of R. not inscribed. Line at end of R. 5 × 7.2 × 2.3. Inscr. 13 (O.) + 4 (R.) = 17 li. IV.
44	34	"		*Kuri-Galzu,* about 1400 B.C.	19799	Unbaked. Dark brown. Ruled. Crumbling. Cracked. Upper part broken away. Lower part of R. not inscribed. 5.7 × 9.3 × 2.4. Inscr. 11 (O.) + 6 (R.) = 20 li. IV. Translation, pp. 108ff.
45	35	"		About 1370 B.C.	11860	Unbaked. Light brown. Crumbling. Cracked. Upper part of tablet broken away. 4.5 × 7 × 2. Inscr. 12 (O.) + 12 (R.) = 24 li. II. Translation, pp. 112ff.
46	36	"		About 1350 B.C.	10952	Unbaked. Grayish brown. O. has occasional black spots. End of first two lines on O. broken off. 4.3 × 5.7 × 2. Inscr. 9 (O.) + 9 (R.) = 18 li. II.
47	37	"		*Nazi-Maruttash,* about 1360 B.C.	10781	Unbaked. Light brown. Cracked. Glued together.

Text.	Plate.	To	From	Age.	C.B.M.	Description.
						Upper part of tablet broken away. Line after inscription on Lo. E. 5.7 × 7.4 × 2.3. Inscr. 12 (O.) + 11 (R.) = 23 li. III.
48	38	"My Lord" (*a-na be-li-ia*)		*Kudur-Enlil*, about 1335 B.C.	11893	Unbaked. Light brown. First two lines broken away. Cracked. Right upper corner of R. chipped off. 4.5 × 5.8 × 2. Inscr. 15 (O.) + 15 (R.) = 30 li. II
49	38	"		*Nazi-Maruttash*, about 1380 B.C.	10913	Unbaked. Light brown. Cracked. Upper and lower part of tablet broken away. Lower part of R. not inscribed. Line at end of inscription. 4.5 × 4.8 × 2.5. Inscr. 8 (O.) + 3 (R.) = 11 li. III.
50	39	"		*Kuri-Galzu*, about 1400 B.C.	3662	Baked. O. dark, R. light brown. Left and right side and lower part of tablet broken away. Line after O. l. 12 and at end of inscription. Greatly mutilated. Lower part of R. not inscribed. 6.2 × 8.5 × 2.5. Inscr. 13 (O.) + 5 (R.) = 18 li. II.
51	39	"		About 1350 B.C.	10510	Unbaked. Light brown. Ruled. Crumbling. End of all lines broken away. 4.5 × 8 × 2.5. Inscr. 12 (O.) + 9 (R.) = 21 li. III.
52	40	"		*Burna-Buriash*, about 1430 B.C.	10504	Unbaked. Light. Cracked. Upper part broken away. Script almost obliterated. 5 × 9 × 2.5. Inscr. 18 (O.) + 22 (R.) + 1 (U. E.) = 41 li. III.
53	41	"		*Shagarakti-Shuriash*, about 1320 B.C.	11504	Unbaked. Light brown. Crumbling. Glued together. Line at end of inscription. End of lines and beginning of O. broken away. Greatly mutilated. 6.2 × 9.6 × 2.7. Inscr. 22 (O.) + 19 (R.) = 41 li. II.

Text.	Plate.	To	From	Age.	C.B.M.	Description.
54	12	"My Lord" (*a-na be-li ia*)		About 1350 B.C.	11654	Unbaked. O. light, R. dark. Upper part, left side, and lower half of tablet broken away. R. covered with silica. 5 × 5.5 × 2.6. Inscr. 14 (O.) + 12 (R.) = 26 li. II.
55	12	" (?)		*Burna-Buriash*, about 1440 B.C.	10497	Unbaked. Light. Upper half broken away. 7.8 × 5.9 × 3. Inscr. 10 (O.) + 2 (Lo. E.) + 12 (R.) = 24 li. III. Translation, pp. 51ff.
56	13	"		*Kuri-Galzu*, about 1400 B.C.	10822	Unbaked. Light brown. Ruled. Cracked. Crumbling. Upper half broken away. 7 × 5 × 2.5. Inscr. 7 (O.) + 7 (R.) = 14 li. III.
57	43	"		About 1350 B.C.	3668	Unbaked. Dark brown, R. dark. Upper part and left lower corner broken away. 5.4 × 5.3 × 2.5. Inscr. 11 (O.) + 11 (R.) = 22 li. II.
58	44	"		*Shagarakti-Shuriash*, about 1320 B.C.	19800	Unbaked. Dark brown. Ruled. Cracked. Upper and lower part as well as whole of O. broken away. End of lines missing. 5.5 × 8 × 2.5. Inscr. 13 li. IV.
59	14	"		*Kadashman-Enlil*, about 1310 B.C.	11703	Baked. Dark brown. O. completely crumbled away. R. covered with silica. 5.5 × 9.3 × 2.4. Inscr. 3 (Lo. E.) + 16 (R.) = 19 li. II.
59*a*	45	"		*Burna-Buriash*, about 1430 B.C.	10919	Unbaked. Light brown. Cracked. Greatly mutilated. Upper part broken away. 5.3 × 3.8 × 2.3. Inscr. 6 (O.) + 3 (Lo. E.) + 8 (R.) = 17 li. III.
60	45	"		About 1350 B.C.	10914	Baked. Light brown. Ruled. Lower part and end of li. broken away. Temple Record with postscript in form of letter, cf. No. 61. 8 × 3 × 2.5. Inscr. 6 (O.) + 5

Text.	Plate.	To	From	Age.	C.B.M.	Description.
						(R.) + 2 (U. E.) = 13 li. III.
60a	46	"My Lord"(?) (*a-na be-li-ia*)	[. . . .]-*im*.	About 1350 B.C.	3694	Baked. Light brown. Left side and upper part of R. broken away. Line after O. l. 1. Cloth impression on right lower corner of O.—hence strictly speaking no letter(?). 5 × 7 × 2. Inscr. 10 (O.) + 2 (Lo. E.) + 10 (R.) = 22 li. II.
61	46	"			12634	Baked. Brown. O. and upper part of R. broken away. Postscript, cf. No. 60. Lower part of R. not inscribed. 7 × 13 × 2.7. Inscr. 8 li. II.
62	47	"			10878	Baked. Light brown. Fragm. (right lower middle part) of larger tablet. 5.2 × 6 × 4.2. Inscr. 12 (O.) + 8 (R.) = 20 li. III.
63	47	"			10931	Unbaked. Brown. Fragm. of larger tablet. Dark. Ruled. R. completely broken away. 5.5 × 3.7 × 1.5. Inscr. 7 li. III.
64	47	"			10935	Unbaked. Light brown. Crumbling. R. broken away. Fragm. of larger tablet. 3.5 × 4.7 × 1.8. Inscr. 10 li. III.
65	47	"		*Shagarakti-Shuriash*, about 1320 B.C.	10954	Baked. Dark brown on O., light brown on R. Upper and lower part of tablet broken away. End of lines missing. Crumbling and greatly mutilated. 6 × 6.5 × 2.7. Inscr. 14 (O.) + 11 (R.) = 25 li. II.
66	48	"		*Kudur-Enlil*, about 1339 B.C.	11926	Unbaked. Dark brown. Upper and lower part of tablet broken away. End of lines missing. Part of larger tablet. Cf. No. 70. 8.5 × 8 × 3. Inscr. 15 (O.) + 17 (R.) = 32 li. II.
67	49	"			11999	Unbaked. Fragm. (lower right part) of larger tablet.

Text.	Plate.	To	From	Age.	C.B.M.	Description.
						O. dark, R. light brown. R. badly mutilated. 8 × 8.5 × 4. Inscr. 17 (O.) + 13 (R.) = 30 li. II.
68	50	"My Lord" (*a-na be-li-ia*)		*Kudur-Enlil*, about 1339 B.C.	11946	Unbaked. O. dark, R. light brown. Upper, lower, and right part of tablet broken away. Inscription on L. E. in two columns. Cf. No. 69. 8 × 8.5 × 4. Inscr. 17 (O.) + 14 (R.) + 9 (L. E.) = 40 li. II.
69	51	"			10621	Unbaked. Light brown. Fragm. (left lower part) of larger tablet. R. completely broken away. Cf. No. 68. 4 × 4.6 × 2.2. Inscr. 9 (O.) + 1 (L. E.) = 10 li. III.
70	51	"		About 1339 B.C.	3836	Unbaked. Fragm. of larger tablet. Light brown. Cf. No. 66. 4 × 4 × 3.8. Inscr. 5 + 6 = 11 li. III.
71	51	"			10392	Unbaked. Light brown. Fragm. (right lower part) of larger tablet. Ruled. 4.5 × 5.5 × 3.8. Inscr. 10 (O.) + 8 (R.) = 18 li. III.
72	52	"			10924	Unbaked. Light brown. Crumbling. Occasional dark spots on O. and R. Upper part and end of lines broken away. 4.8 × 5.5 × 2.2. Inscr. 9 (O.) + 10 (R.) = 19 li. III.
73	52	"			10658	Unbaked. Light brown. Crumbling. Fragm. of larger tablet. Only on one side is the inscription preserved. 3.8 × 6.5 × 3.2. Inscr. 14 li. III.
73*a*	53	"			10938	Unbaked. Light brown. Cracked. Fragm. (upper middle part) of larger tablet. Greatly mutilated. 3.8 × 5 × 2.3. Inscr. 8 (O.) + 10 (R.) + 2 (U. E.) = 20 li. III.
74	53	"			10853	Unbaked. Dark brown.

TEXT.	PLATE.	TO	FROM	AGE.	C.B.M.	DESCRIPTION.
						Fragm. (middle part) of tablet. Only one side preserved. 5.5 × 6.8 × 2.4. Inscr. 14 li. III.
75	51	*m Amel-ilu Marduk.*	"The King" (*LUGAL*) (cf. No. 93).	*Shagarakti-Shuriash,* about 1325 B.C.	12582	Unbaked. Light brown. End of lines and lower part of tablet broken away. R. almost completely crumbled off. 3.9 × 4.8 × 1.7. Inscr. 10 (O.) + 10 (R.) + 3 (U. E.) = 23 li. III. Translation, pp. 132ff.
76	55	"Son"	"Father."	About 1400 B.C.	3660	Unbaked. Light brown. Cracked. Covered with black spots. Line after O. l. 1. R. has only one line of inscription, rest not inscribed. 5 × 7.5 × 2.3. Inscr. 9 (O.) + 1 (R.) = 10 li. II. Translation, pp. 113f.
77	55	*m ilu En-lil-[bel-nishi meshu-shu].*	*m ilu A-shur-shum-itir.*	*Kadashman-Turgu,* about 1360 B.C.	10575	Unbaked. Dark brown. Cracked. Crumbling. Right side and lower part of tablet broken away. 4.8 × 6.8 × 2.2. Inscr. 10 li. III.
78	56	*m A-hu-shi-na.*	*m ilu En-lil-ki-di-ni.*	*Burna-Buriash,* about 1430 B.C.	10774	Unbaked. Light brown. Lower part of tablet broken away. Only upper part of R. is inscribed. 4.7 × 6.5 × 2.4. Inscr. 10 (O.) + 3 (R.) = 13 li. III.
79	56	*m Im-gu-ri.*	*m ilu En-lil-ki-di-[ni].*	*Burna-Buriash,* about 1430 B.C.	11931	Baked. Brown. Left side broken away. Badly mutilated. Crumbling. Lower part of R. not inscribed. 4 × 6.8 × 2.5. Inscr. 9 (O.) + 4 (R.) = 13 li. II.
80	57	*m A-mi-li-ia.*	*m ilu En-lil-mu-kin-apal.*	*Nazi-Maruttash,* about 1350 B.C.	6056	Unbaked. Light brown. Lower half of tablet broken away. Right upper corner of O. was pressed downward while tablet was still soft. 4 × 4 × 2. Inscr. 8 (O.) + 7 (R.) + 2 (U. E.) = 17 li. II.
81	57	*m Ahu-ú-a-Ba-ni.*	*m Erba-ilu Marduk.*	*Kadashman-Enlil,* about 1335 B.C.	3692	Baked. O. light brown, R. darker. Occasional black spots. Lower part of tablet

Text.	Plate.	To	From	Age.	C.B.M.	Description.
						broken away. 4.5 × 5 × 2.3. Inscr. 10 (O.) + 10 (R.) = 20 li. II.
82	57	*Da-ni-ti-ia.*	^{m}*Erba-*^{ilu}*Marduk*	*Shagarakti-Shuriash,* about 1325 B.C.	11852	Unbaked. Dark brown. Greatly mutilated. O. left lower corner broken away. R. completely crumbled off. 3.7 × 5.1 × 1.7. Inscr. 10 li. II.
83	58	^{m}*In-na-an-ni.*	$^{m\ ilu}$*Erish(t)(=NIN. IB)-apal-iddina*^{na}.	*Kuri-Galzu,* about 1400 B.C.	3315	Baked. Light brown. Occasional black spots on O. Part of right side of O. and upper right corner of R. chipped off. Otherwise well preserved. Line after l. 2 and at end of O. 5.5 × 9.5 × 2.2. Inscr. 18 (O.) + 19 (R.) − 37 li. II. Translation, pp. 110ff.
84	59	^{m}*In-na-an-ni.*	$^{m\ ilu}$*Errish(t)(−MASH)-apal-iddina*^{na}.	*Kuri-Galzu,* about 1400 B.C.	3258	Baked. Light brown. Perfect. Line after O. l. 10. Lower part of R. not inscribed. 4.8 × 9 × 2.3. Inscr. 14 (O.) + 5 (R.) = 19 li. II. Translation, pp. 113ff.
85	59	^{m}*In-na-an-ni.*	^{f}*In-bi-Ai-ri.*	*Kuri-Galzu,* about 1400 B.C.	3206	Baked. Light brown. R. covered with silica. Lower half of R. not inscribed. 5.5 × 4.3 × 2. Inscr. 7 (O.) + 4 (R.) = 11 li. II. Translation, pp. 115ff.
86	60	^{m}*In-na-an-ni.*	^{f}*In-bi-Ai-ri.*	*Kuri-Galzu,* about 1400 B.C.	3675	Baked. Light brown. Lower part of tablet broken away. 4.8 × 5.8 × 2.3. Inscr. 13 (O.) + 11 (R.) + 3 (U. E.) + 1 (L. E.) = 31 li. II.
87	61	^{m}*In-nu-ú-a.*	^{m}*Gu-za-ar-AN.*	About 1350 B.C.	3663	Unbaked. O. light brown. R. darker. Occasional black spots. Lower part of tablet broken away. 5.5 × 6 × 2. Inscr. 11 (O.) + 9 (R.) + 3 (U. E.) + 2 (L. E.) = 25 li. II.
88	62	[^{f}?]*Da(?)-li-li-ia.*	^{m}*Ì-li-ip-pa-ásh-ra.*	*Burna-Buriash,* about 1430 B.C.	3834	Baked. Light brown. Greatly effaced. Lower part of tablet broken away. R. blank. 4 × 4 × 2.2. Inscr. 8 li. III.

Text.	Plate.	To	From	Age.	C.B.M.	Description.
89	62	^{m}*NIN-nu-ú-a.*	^{m}*Pân-AN.GAL-lu-mur.*	About 1350 B.C.	19764	Baked. Dark brown. Right lower corner broken away. 4 × 6.3 × 1.7. Inscr. 14 (O.) + 14 (R.) + 2 (U. E.) = 30 li. IV. Translation, pp. 19ff.; 25, note 1; 27, note 8.
90	63		$^{m\ ilu}$*Sin-êrish*^{ish}.	*Kadashman-Turgu,* about 1350 B.C.	10936	Baked. Dark. Fragm. (left upper part) of tablet. 4 × 5 × 2.3. Inscr. 7 (O.) + 7 (R.) = 11 li. III.
91	63	[^{m}*I-na*]-*ṣil-li-a*-[*lak*].	$^{m\ ilu}$*DAR.ḪU-nâr-gab-ba.*	About 1350 B.C.	19796	Baked. Light brown. 3 lines on tablet. Beginning of first section broken away. O. l. 5 is continued over the whole of R. Lower part of R. not inscribed. 5 × 5 × 2. Inscr. 10 (O.) + 2 (Lo. E.) + 3 (R.) = 15 li. IV.
92	64	^{m}*Il-li-ia.*		*Nazi-Maruttash,* 1390 B.C	19784	Baked. Light brown. Lower right part of tablet broken away. 4.5 × 7.5 × 2. Inscr. 14 (O.) + 2 (Lo. E.) + 15 (R.) + 3 (U. E.) = 34 li. IV.
93	65		"The King"(?) (cf. No. 75).	About 1400 B.C.	3671	Unbaked. Fragm. (lower right part) of tablet. Crumbling. Cracked. Badly mutilated. Other side of tablet completely effaced. 4.5 × 5.3 × 2. Inscr. 8 li. II.
94	65			About 1350 B.C.	3665	Unbaked. Light brown. Crumbling. Line at end of O. and R. Upper part of tablet broken away. O. completely effaced. Lower part of R. not inscribed. 5.8 × 8.8 × 2.3. Inscr. 3 (O.) + 5 (R.) = 8 li. II.
95	66				3671	Baked. O. light brown, R. dark. Large black spot on R. Ruled. Crumbling. Upper part of tablet broken away. 5.2 × 5 × 2. Inscr. 6 (O.) + 10 (R.) + 2 (L. E.) = 18 li. II.
96	67				10775	Unbaked. O. very light, R.

Text.	Plate.	To	From	Age.	C.B.M.	Description.
						darker. Cracked. Crumbling. Fragm. (middle part) of larger tablet. 6.8 × 9.5 × 3. Inscr. 15 (O.) + 14 (R.) = 29 li. III.
97	68			*Kadashman-Turgu*, about 1360 B.C.	10922	Unbaked. Dark brown. Ruled. Upper part and right side of tablet broken away. Last line and all of other side not inscribed. 3.8 × 5.5 × 2.7. Inscr. 7 li. III.
98	68			About 1350 B.C.	10895	Unbaked. Fragm. of larger tablet. Dark brown. Ruled. Crumbling. R. completely broken away. 6.3 × 5.8 × 1.5. Inscr. 8 li. III.
99	68				10915	Unbaked. Brown. Fragm. (middle part) of larger tablet. The other side of tablet completely crumbled away. Cracked. 5.4 × 6 × 2. Inscr. 10 li. III.

B. Photographic (Half-tone) Reproductions.

Text.	Plate.		C. B. M.	Description.
1, 2	I	O. and R. of a letter from *Kalbu* to the "Lord." Cf. Translation on pp. 101ff.	19793	Cf. description of text No. 24.
3, 4, 5	II	Part of envelope, R. E. and Lo. E. of a letter from *Kalbu* to the "Lord." Cf. Translation on pp. 101ff.	19793	Cf. description of text No. 24.
6, 7	III	O. and R. of a letter referring to *Enlil-kidinni*. For Translation cf. Chapter III, pp. 51ff.	10497	Cf. description of text No. 55.
8, 9	III	O. and R. of a royal letter to *Amel-Marduk*. Cf. Translation on pp. 132ff.	12582	Cf. description of text No. 75.
10, 11	IV	O. and R. of a letter from *NIM.GI-shar-ili* to the "Lord." Cf. Translation on pp. 135ff.	6123	Cf. description of text No. 33*a*.
12, 13	V	O. and R. of a letter from [*Im-gu*]-*rum* to the "Lord." Cf. Translation on pp. 94ff.	11090	Cf. description of text No. 23.
14, 15	VI	O. and R. of a letter from *Mukallim* to the "Lord." Cf. Chapter III, p. 36, note 7.	11098	Cf. description of text No. 31.
16, 17	VII	O. and R. of a letter from *Mukallim* to the "Lord." Cf. Chapter III, p. 36, note 7.	10511	Cf. description of text No. 33.
18, 19	VII	O. and R. of a letter from *Shiriqtim* to the "Lord." Cf. Translation on pp. 110ff.	10955	Cf. description of text No. 38.
20	VIII	O. of a letter from *Amel-Marduk* to the "Lord."	11126	Cf. description of text No. 3.
21	IX	R. of a letter from *Amel-Marduk* to the "Lord."	11126	Cf. description of text No. 3.

Text.	Plate.		C. B. M.	Description.
22, 23	X	O. and R. of a letter from *Sin-karabi-eshme* to the "Lord."	19783	Cf. description of text No. 37.
24, 25	X	O. and R. of a letter from *Ubarrum* to the "Lord." Cf. Translation on pp. 129ff.	5134	Cf. description of text No. 40.
26	XI	R. of a letter showing the fragmentary condition of the collection.	10504	Cf. description of text No. 52.
27	XI	O. of a letter from *Imgurum* to the "Lord."	11101	Cf. description of text No. 22.
28	XI	O. of a letter from a "father" to his "son." Cf. Translation on pp. 143ff.	3660	Cf. description of text No. 76.
29, 30	XII	O. and R. of a letter from *Errish(?)-apal-iddina* to *Innanni*. Cf. Translation on pp. 110ff.	3315	Cf. description of text No. 83.
31, 32	XII	O. and R. of a letter from *Errish(?)-apal-iddina* to *Innanni*. Cf. Translation on pp. 113ff.	3258	Cf. description of text No. 84.

C. Numbers of the Catalogue of the Babylonian Museum (Preiared by Prof. Dr. H. V. Hilprecht).

C. B. M.	Text.	Plate.	C. B. M.	Text.	Plate.	C. B. M.	Text.	Plate.
3000			**10000**			10930	2	1
3206	85	59	10392	71	51	10931	63	47
3258	84	59	10497	55	42	10935	64	47
3315	83	58	10504	52	40	10936	90	63
3655	18	14	10510	51	39	10938	73*a*	53
3660	76	55	10514	33	25	10951	16	12
3661	39	31	10571	15	12	10952	46	36
3662	50	39	10575	77	55	10954	65	47
3663	87	61	10600	36	29	10955	38	30
3665	94	65	10621	69	51	10983	28	21
3668	57	43	10629	30	22	**11000**		
3669	4	4	10658	73	52	11090	23	17
3671	95	66	10774	78	56	11096	25	19
3674	93	65	10775	96	67	11098	31	23
3675	86	60	10781	47	37	11101	22	16
3692	81	57	10801	13	11	11119	5	5
3694	60*a*	46	10806	21	16	11126	3	2, 3
3787	7	6	10816	8	7	11497	32	24
3834	88	62	10822	56	43	11498	42	33
3836	70	51	10853	74	53	11501	53	41
3837	10	8	10878	62	47	11635	9	8
5000			10895	98	68	11637	14	11
5134	40	32	10913	49	38	11654	54	42
6000			10914	60	45	11703	59	44
6056	80	57	10915	99	68	11716	1	1
6057	35	28	10919	59*a*	45	11787	41	32
6058	34	27	10922	97	68	11852	82	57
6123	33*a*	26	10924	72	52	11860	45	35

C. B. M.	Text.	Plate.	C. B. M.	Text.	Plate.	C. B. M.	Text.	Plate.
11893	48	38	12582	75	54	19784	92	64
11926	66	48	12633	27	20	19785	26	19
11929	12	10	12634	61	46	19787	19	14
11931	79	56	**19000**			19793	24	18
11946	68	50	19761	89	62	19796	91	63
11956	29	22	19779	43	34	19798	20	15
11999	67	49	19780	17	13	19799	44	31
12000			19781	11	9	19800	58	44
12559	6	6	19783	37	29			

CUNEIFORM TEXTS

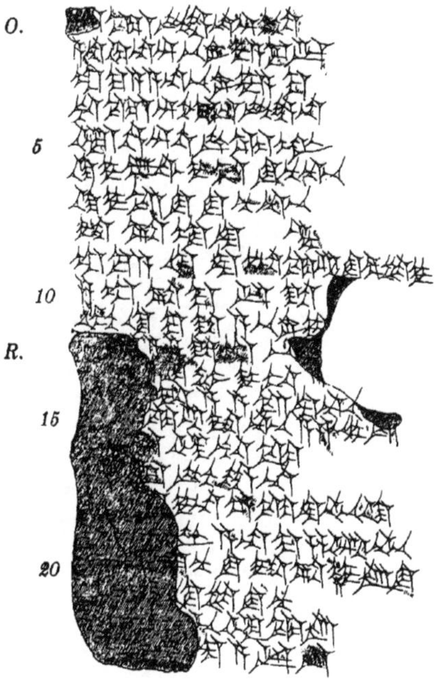

2

Obverse.

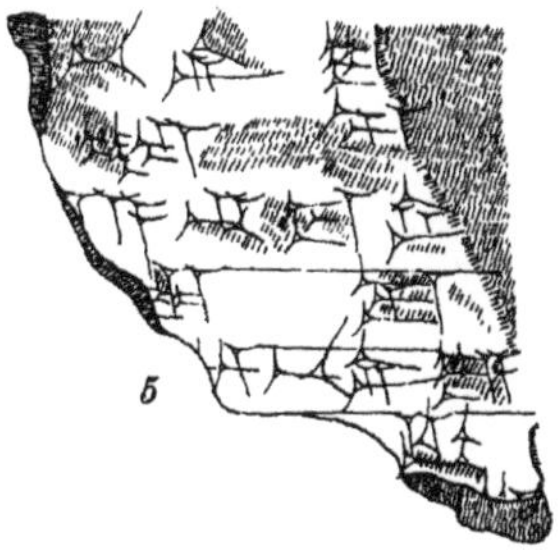

Reverse.

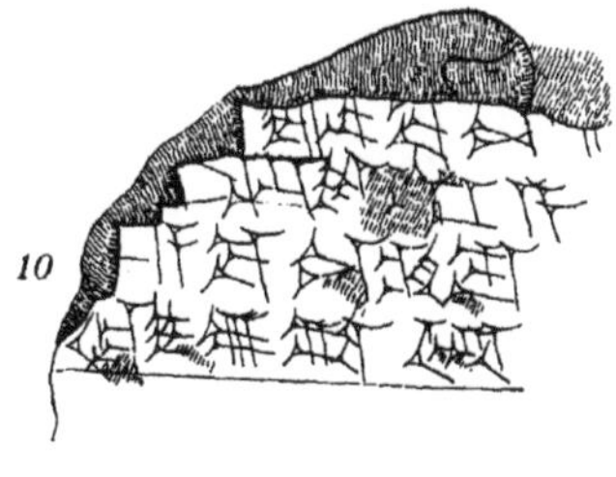

3

Obverse.

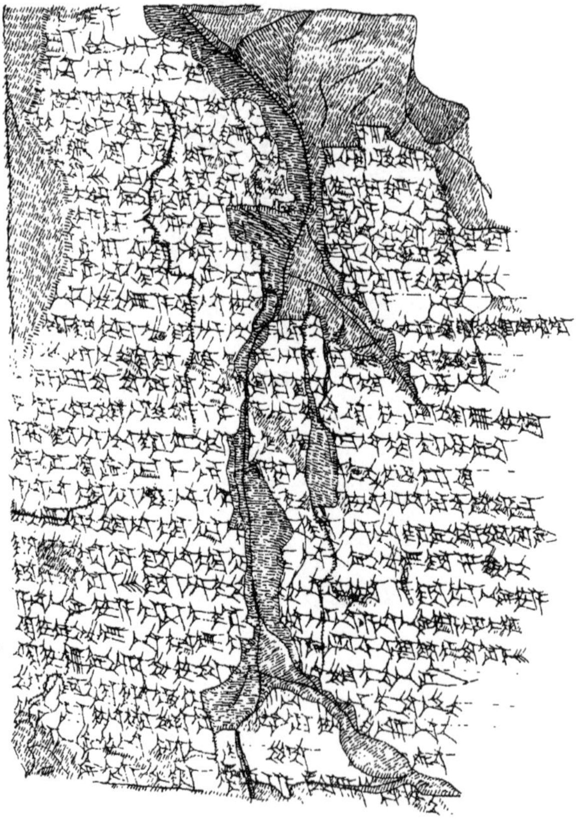

3

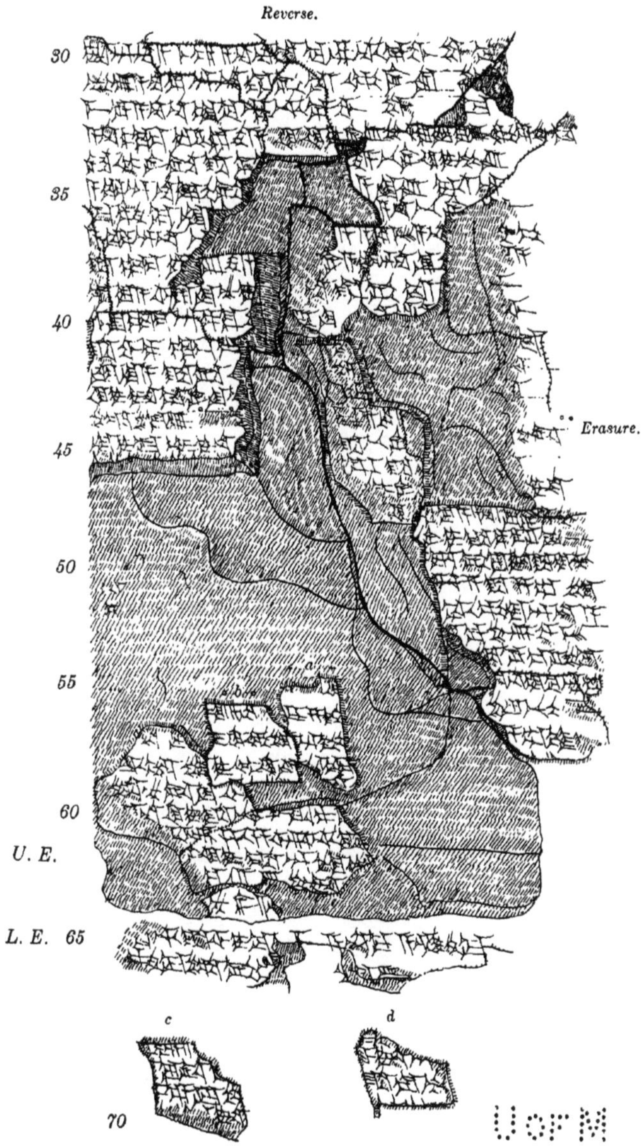

4

Obverse.

Reverse.

U. E.

L. E.

5

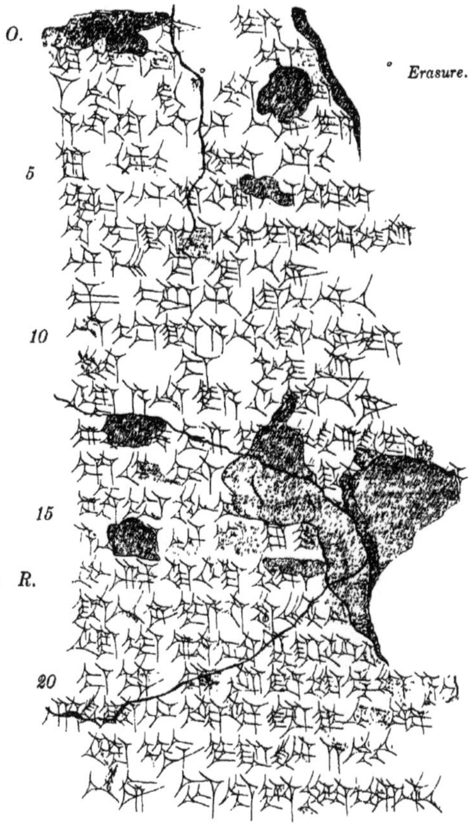

6

7

Obverse. *Reverse.*

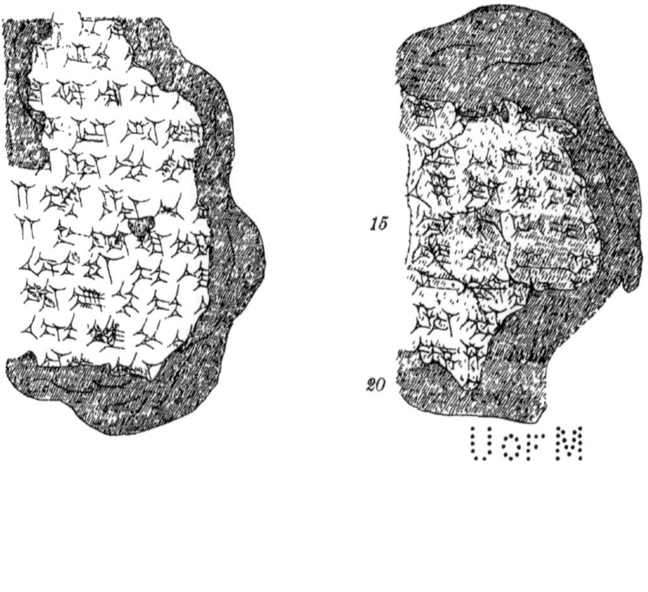

8

Obverse.

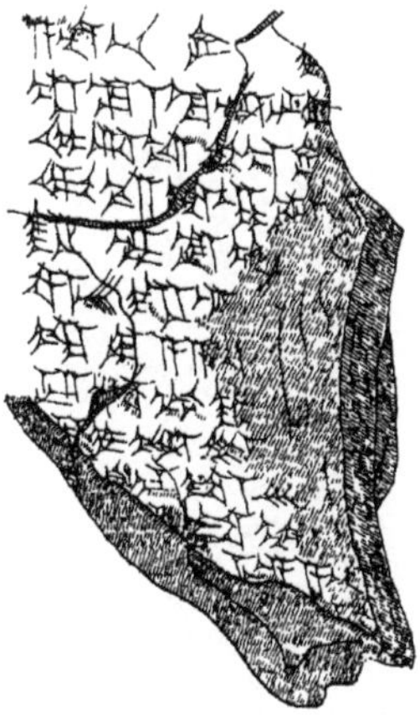

Reverse.

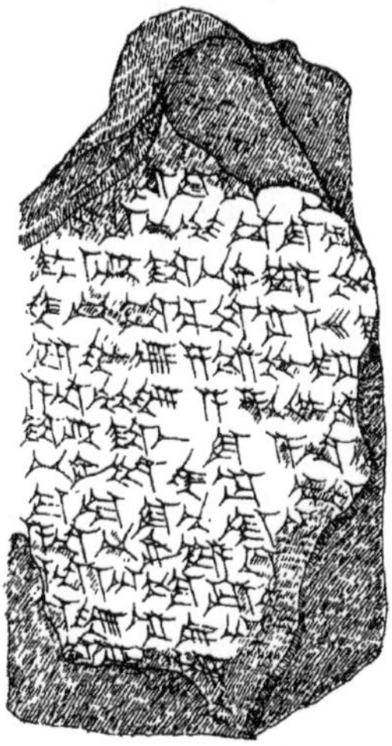

9

Obverse.

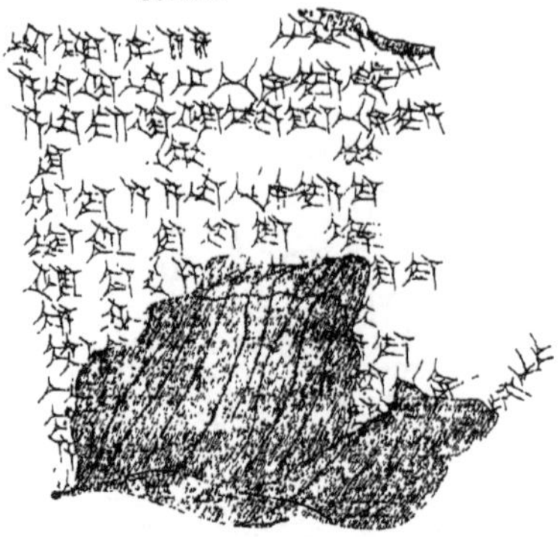

Reverse.

10

Obverse.

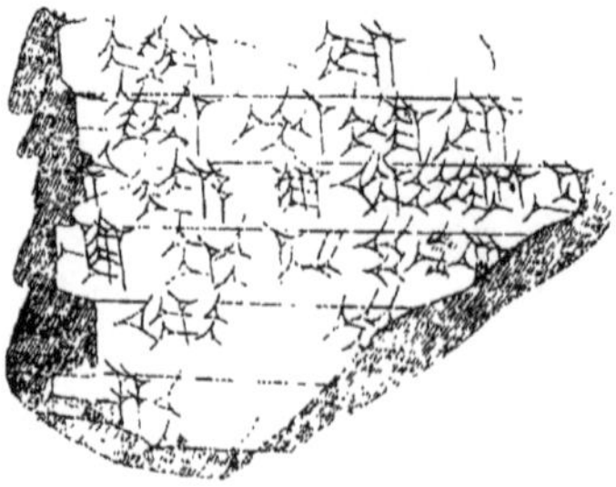

Reverse.

11

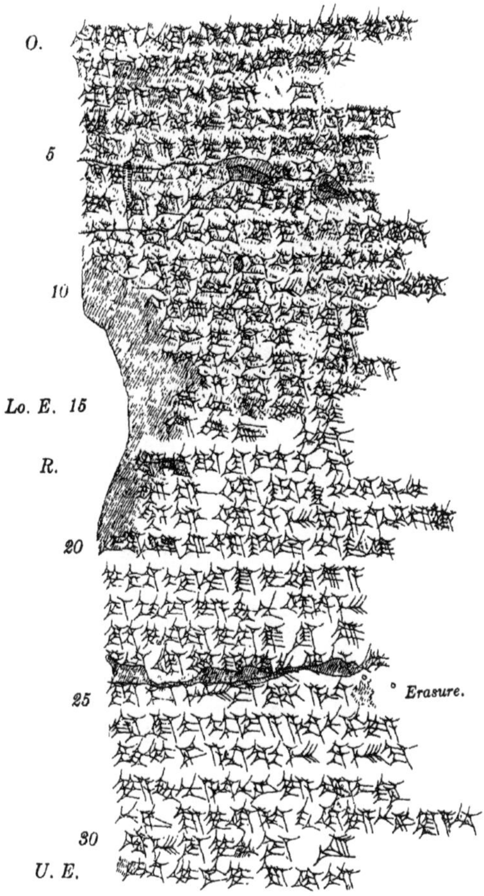

12

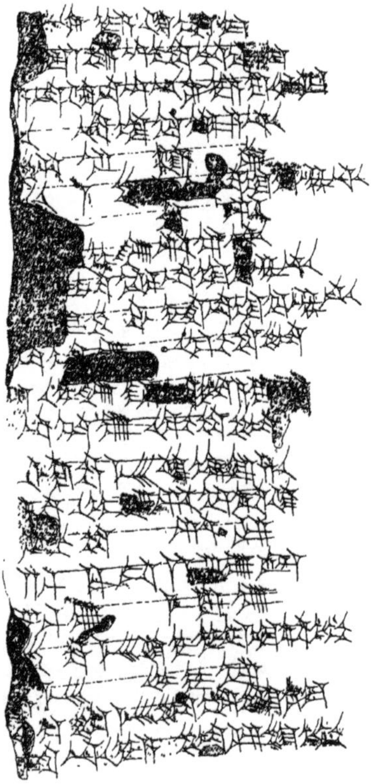

13

Obverse.

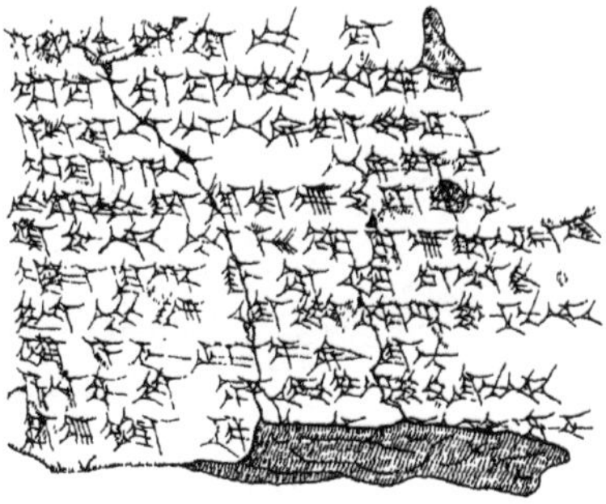

Reverse.

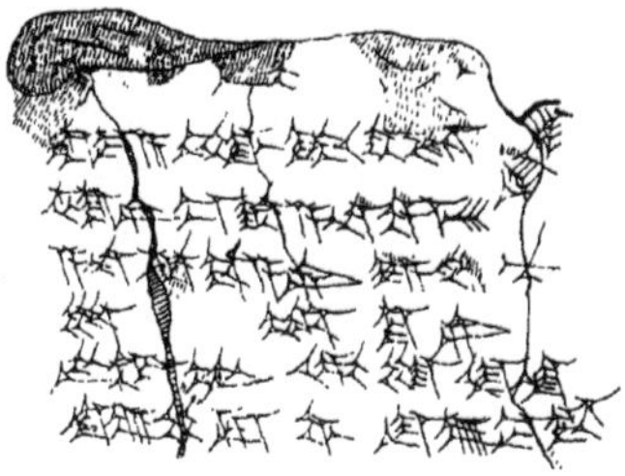

14

Obverse.

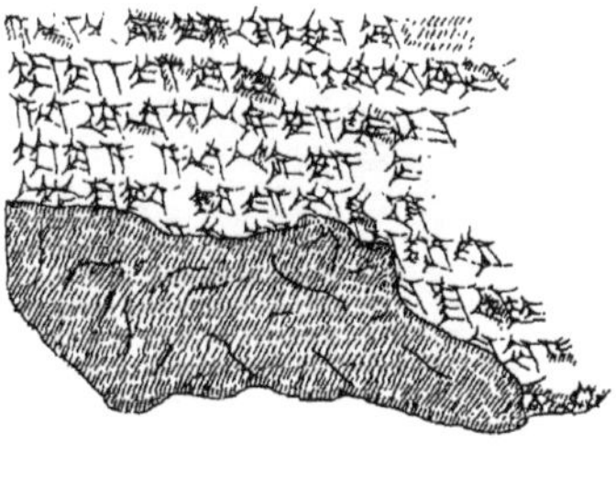

Reverse.

U. E.

L. E.

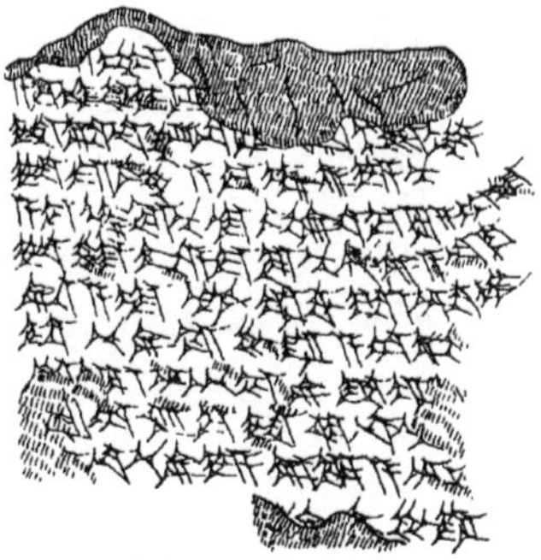

15

Obverse.

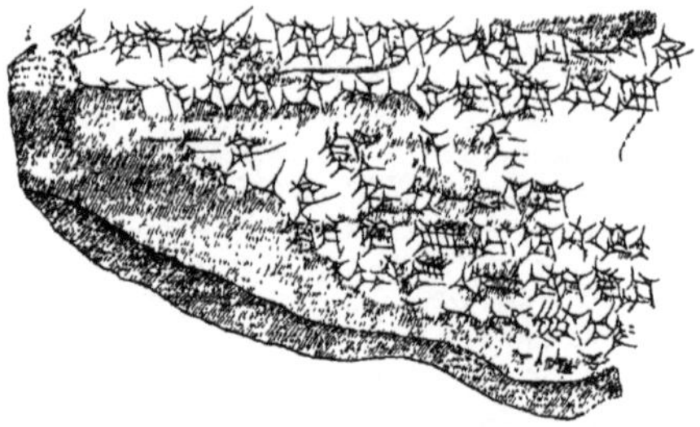

Reverse.

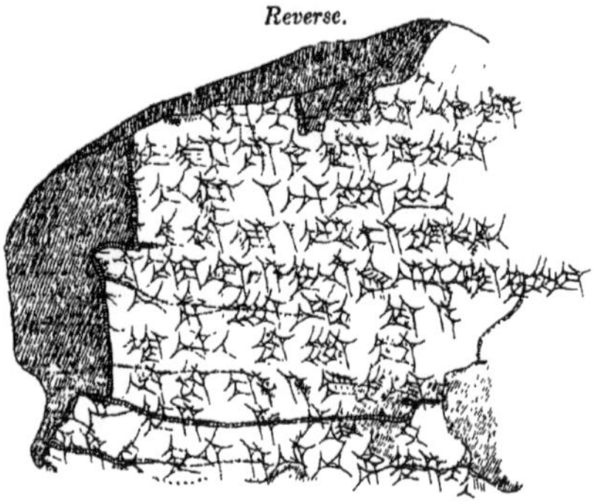

U. E.

16

Obverse.

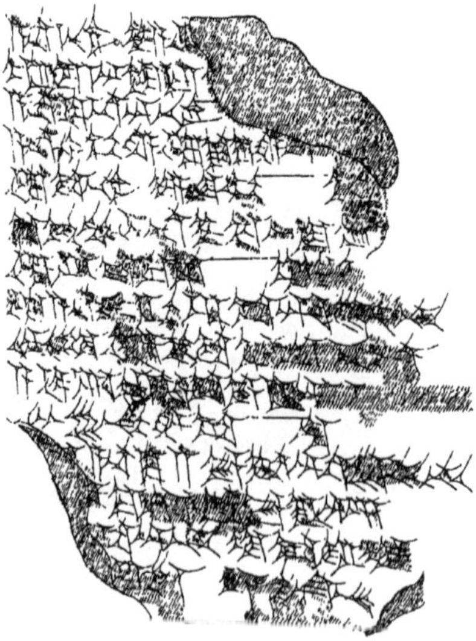

Reverse.

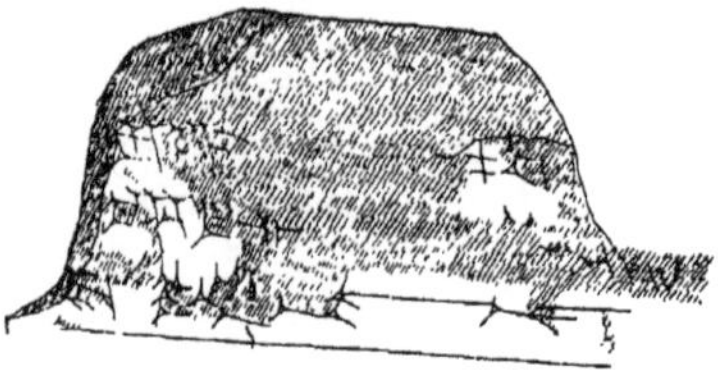

17

O.

Lo. E.

R.

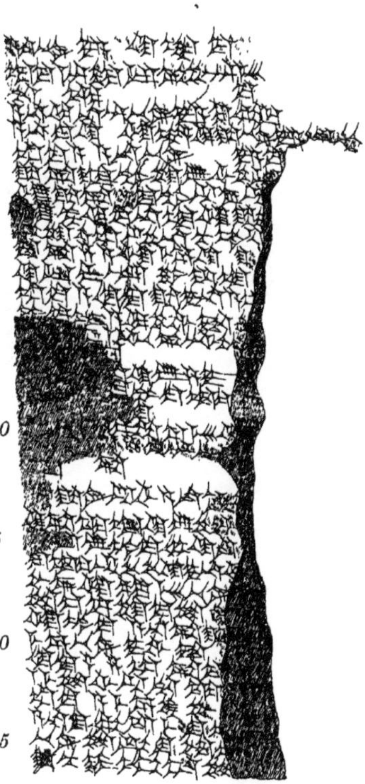

18

Obverse.

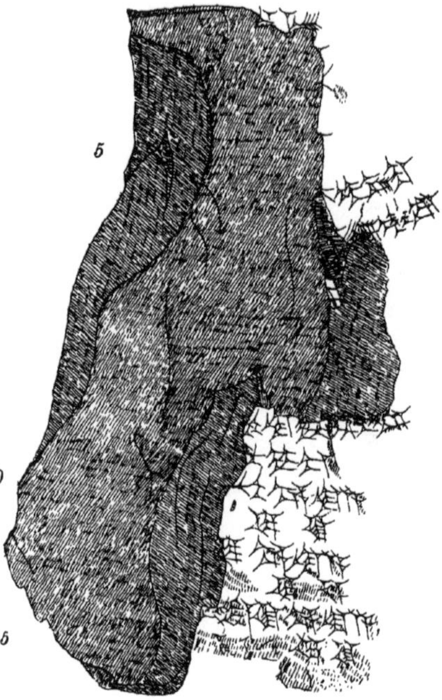

Reverse.

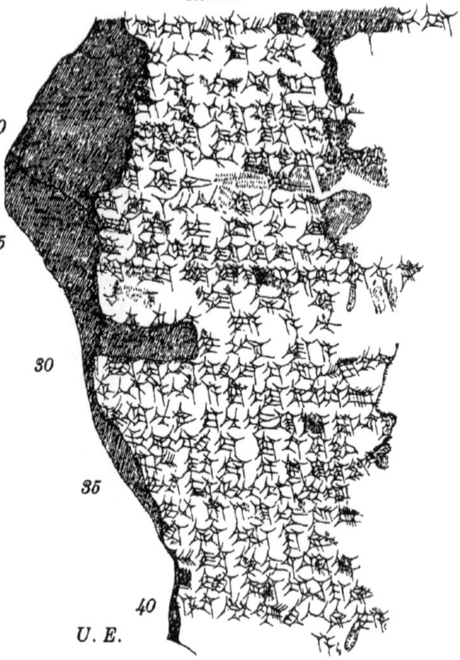

19

Obverse.

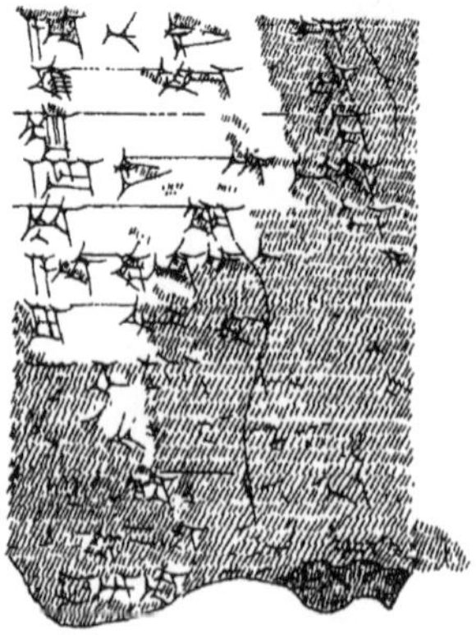

Reverse.

20

Obverse.

Reverse.

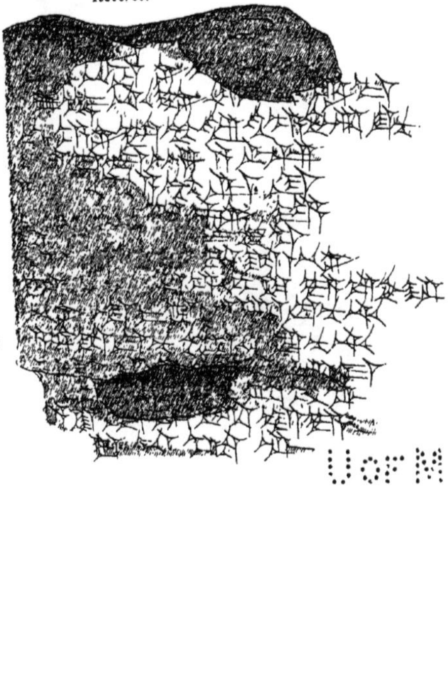

U. E.

21

O.

R.

U. E.

L. E.

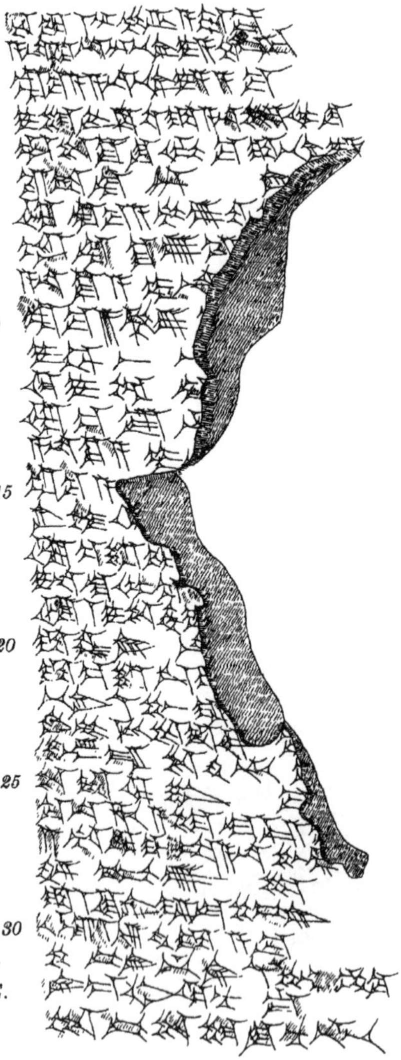

22

O.

R.

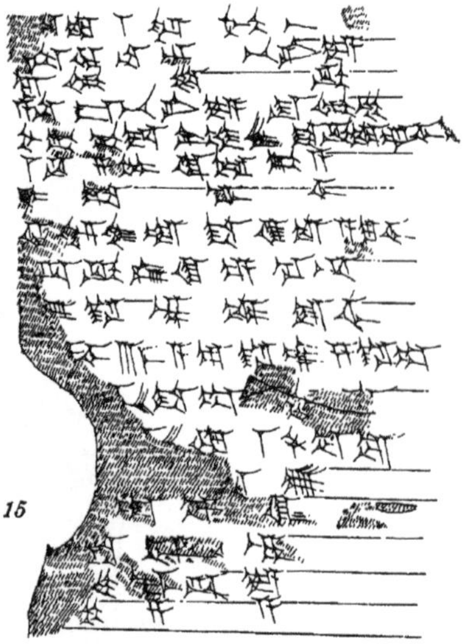

23

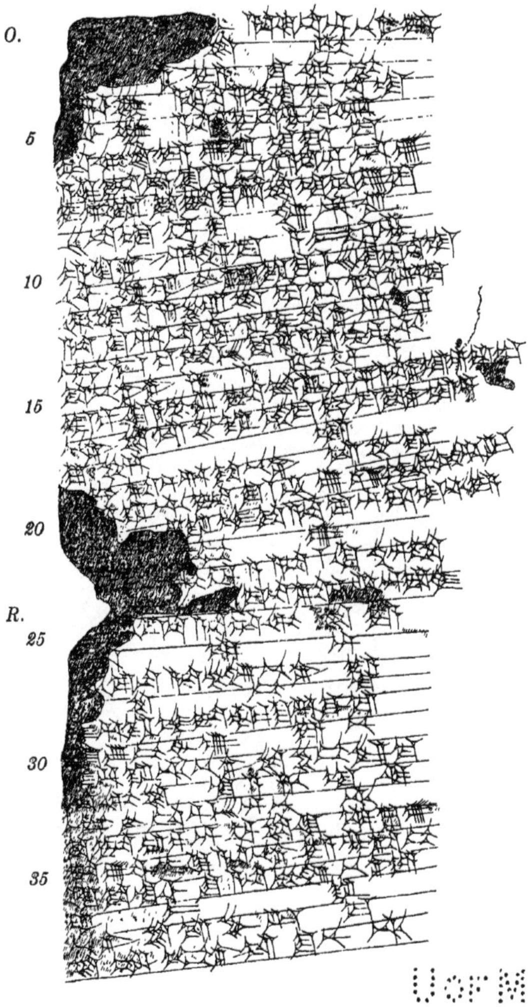

O.

Lo. E.

R.

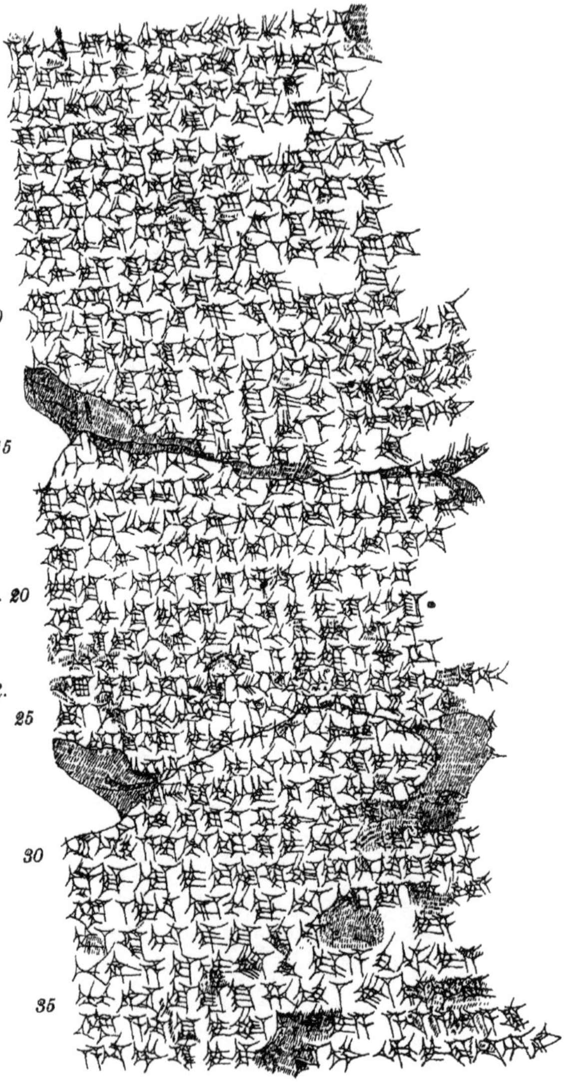

Case.

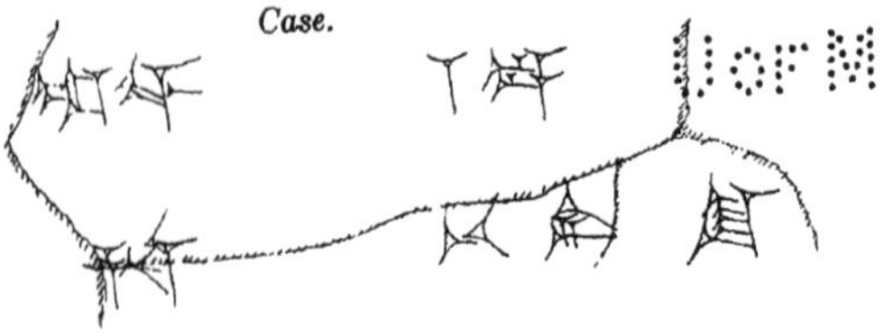

25

Obverse.

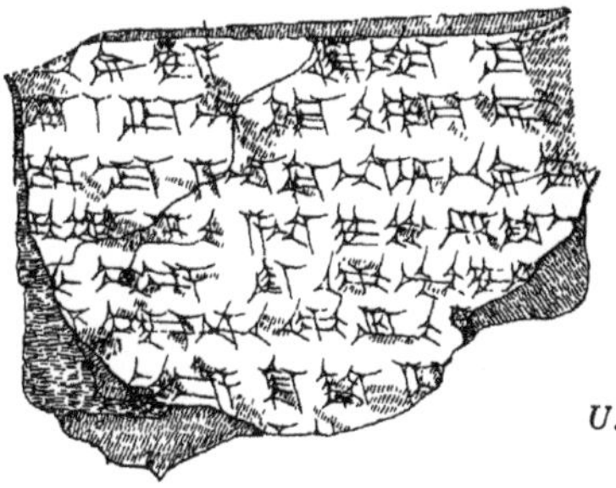

Reverse.

U. E.

° Erasure.

26

Obverse.

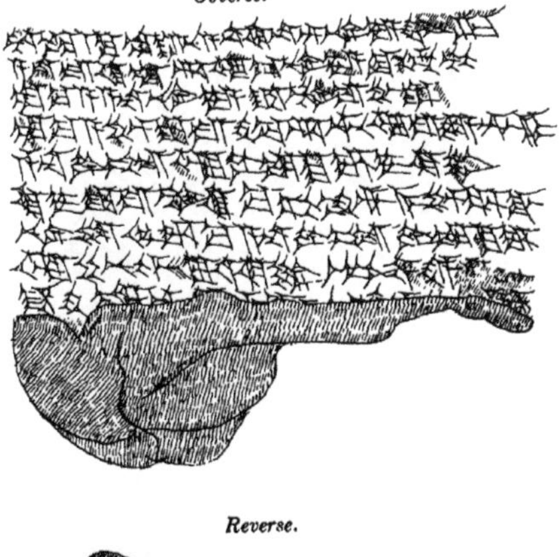

Reverse.

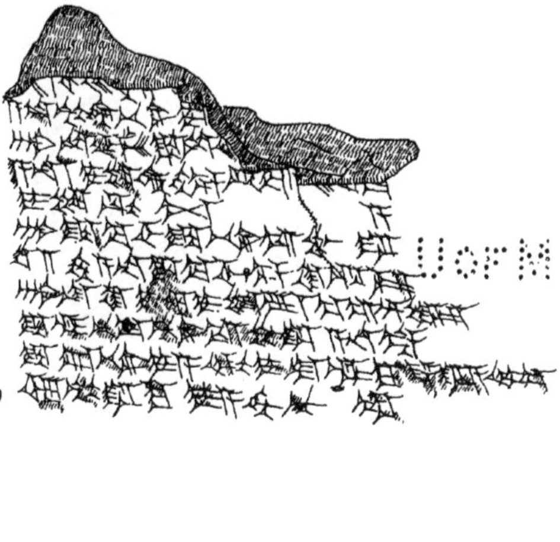

Pl. 20

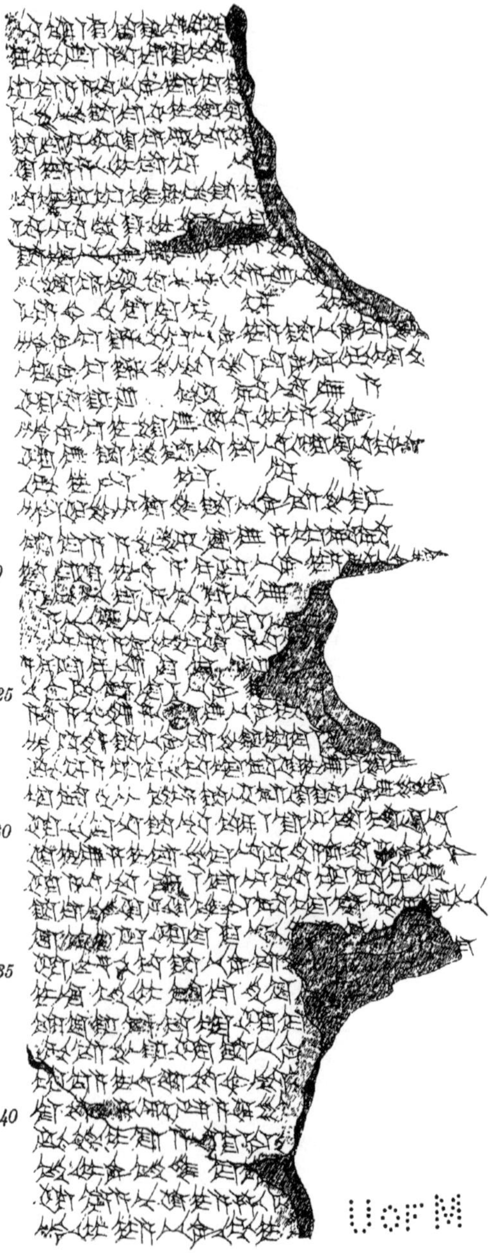

28

Obverse.

Reverse.

Erasure.

U. E.

L. E.

29

O.

Lo. E.

R.

30

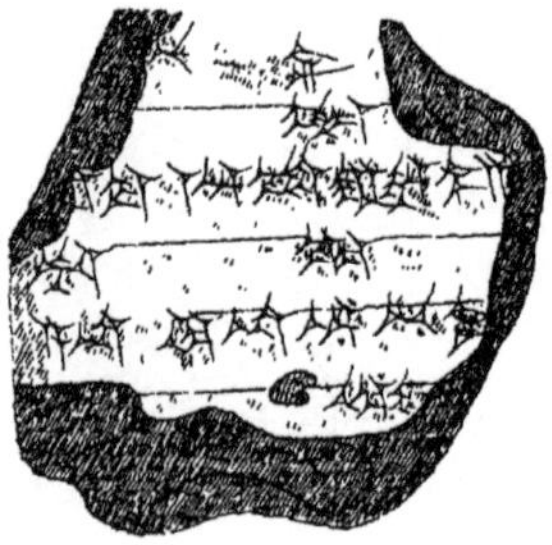

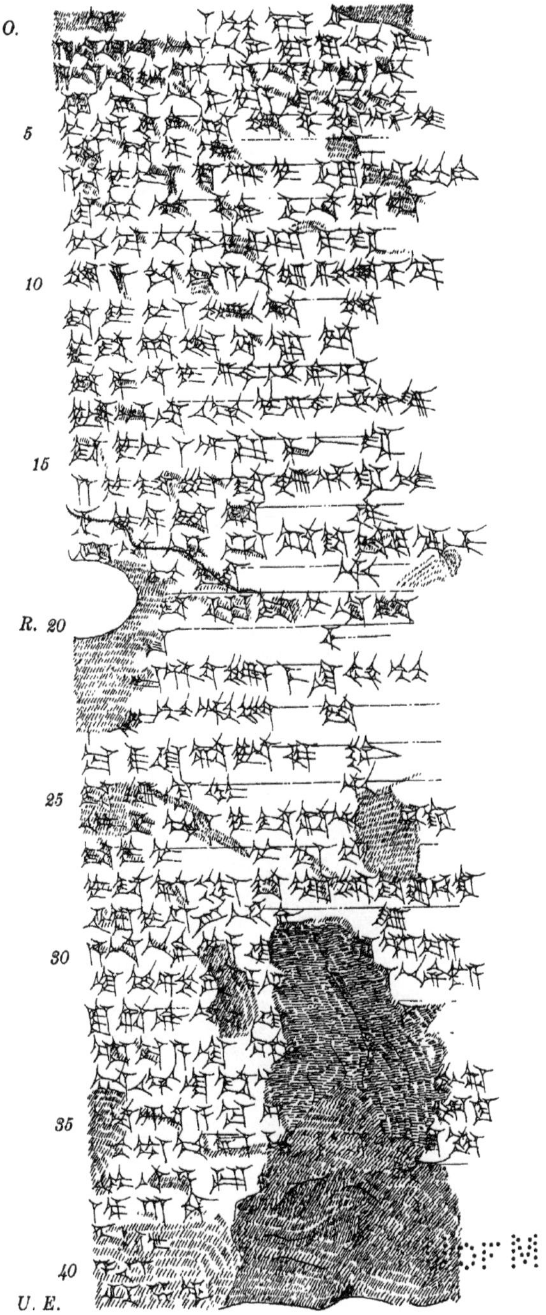
O.
R.
U. E.
DFM

32

Obverse.

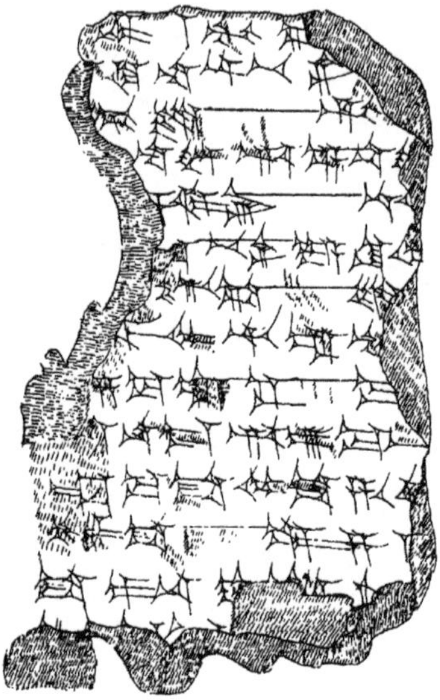

Reverse.

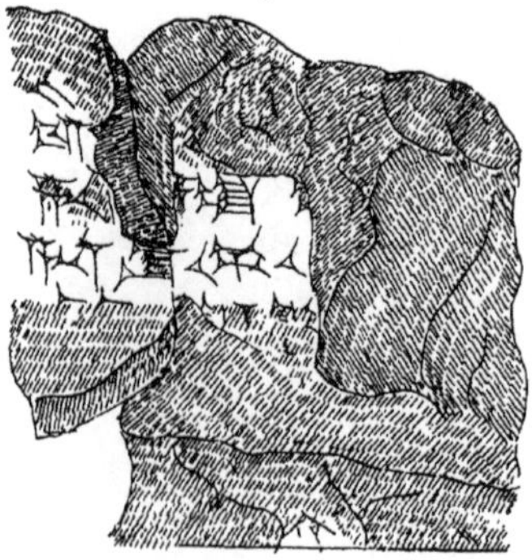

Obverse.

Reverse.

33 a.

O.

R.

U. E.

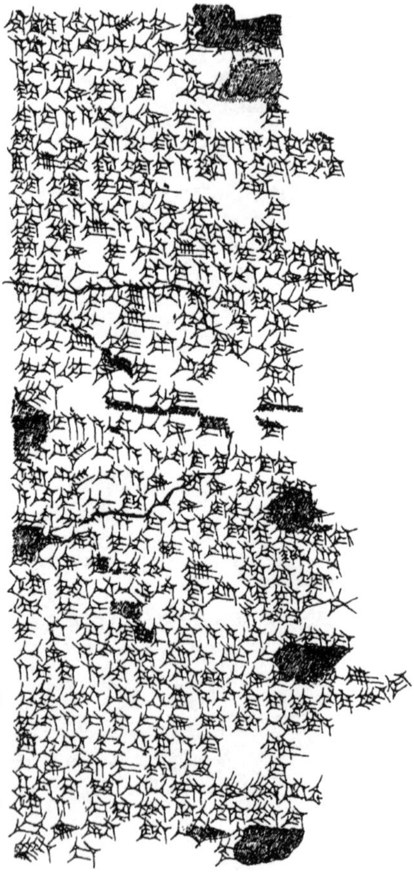

34

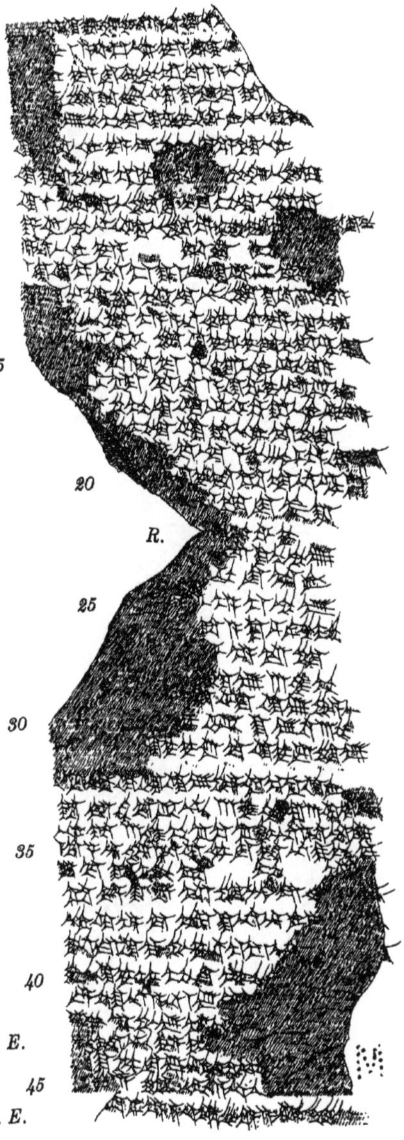

35

O.

Lo. E.

R.

U. E.

L. E.

36

37

O.

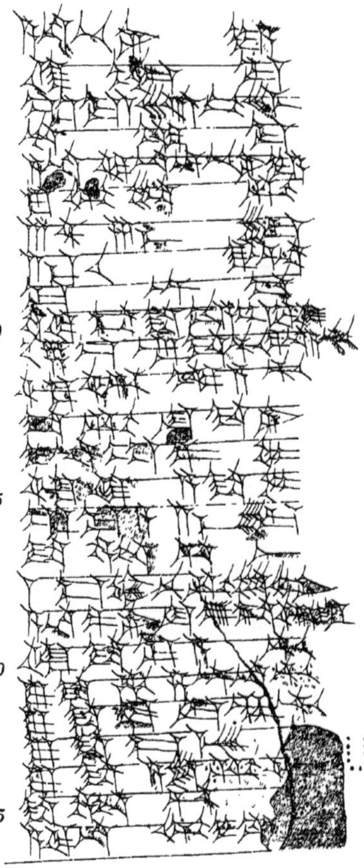

R.

38

Obverse.

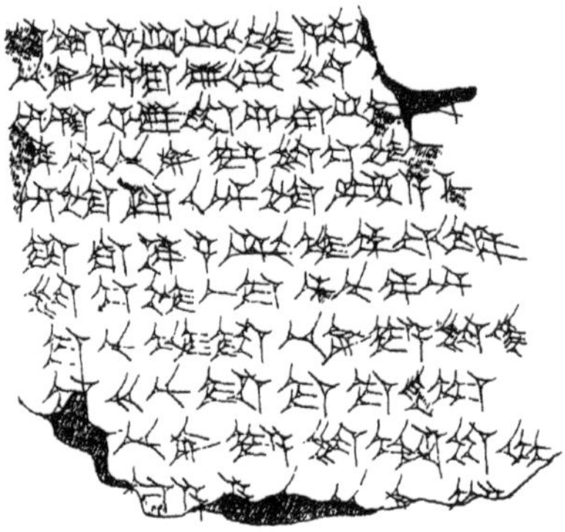

Reverse.

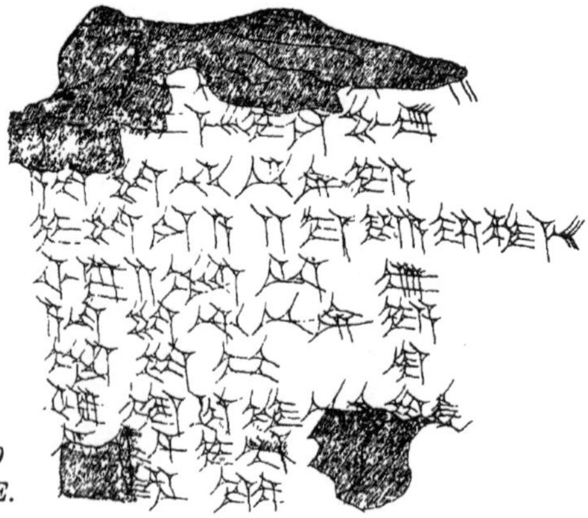

U. E.

O.

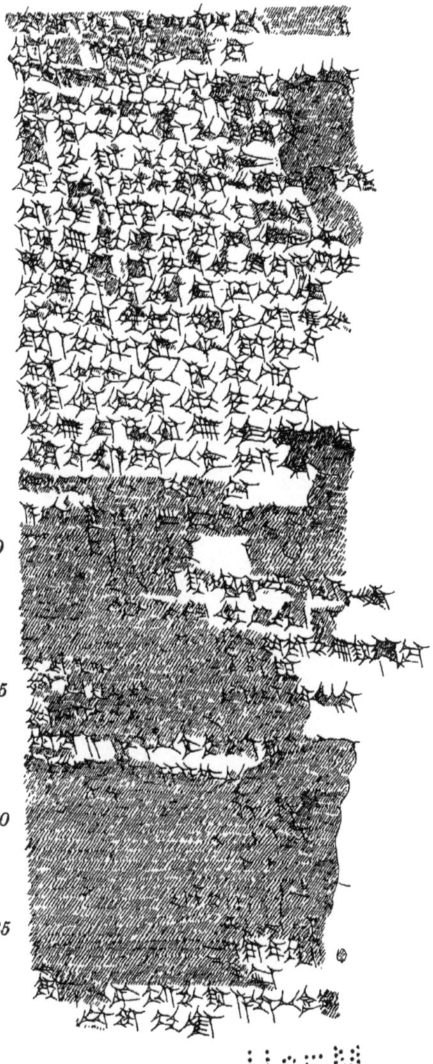

R.

U. E.

40

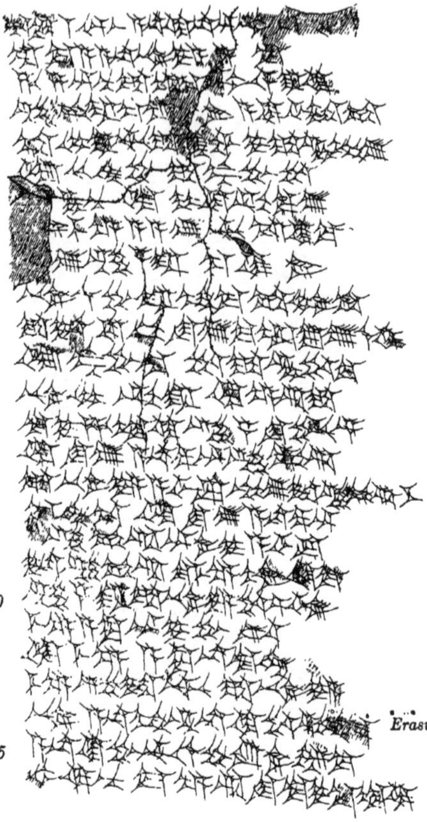

41

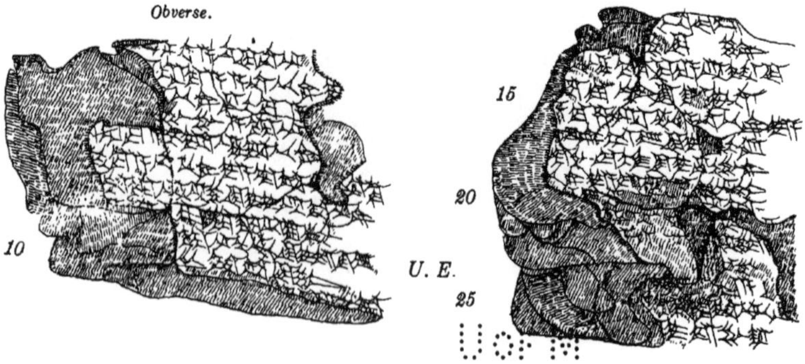

42

Obverse.

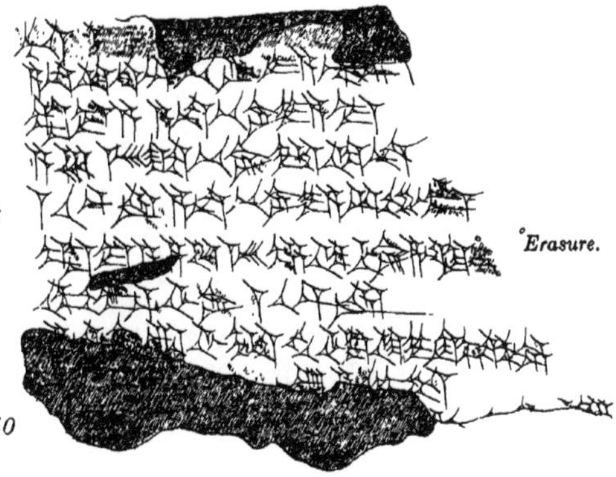

Reverse.

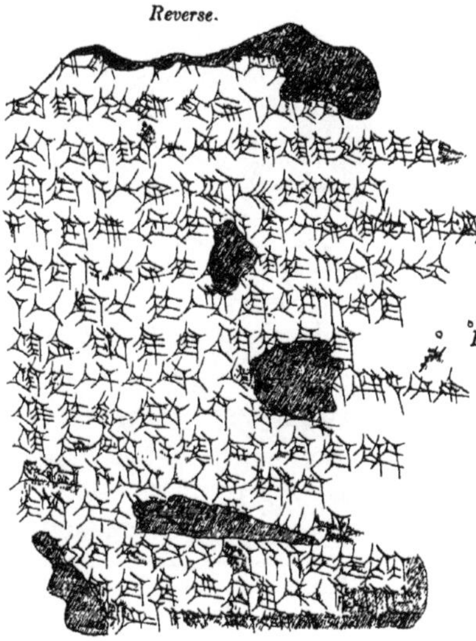

43

44

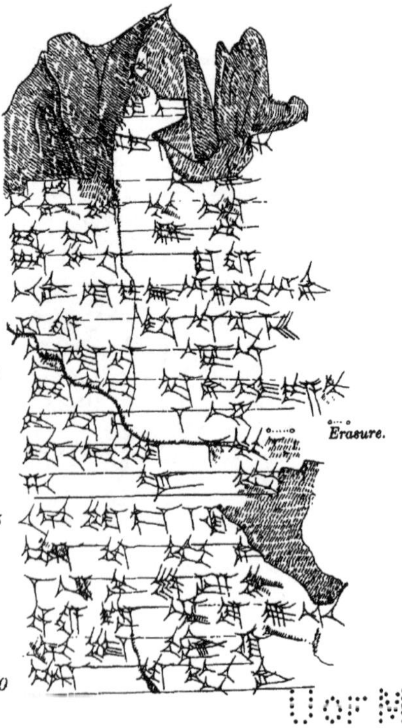

45

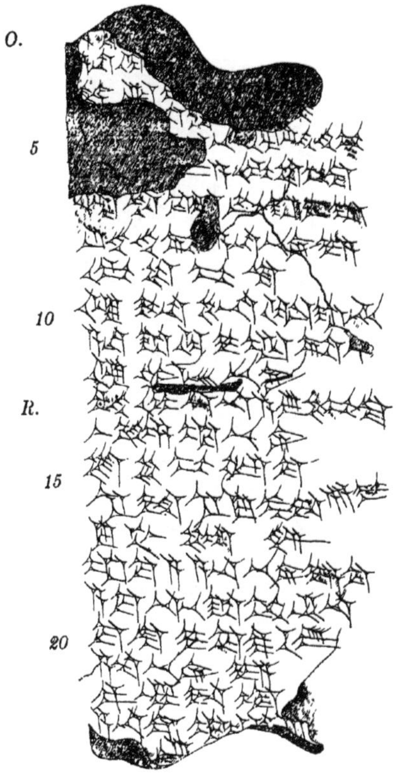

46

O.

R.

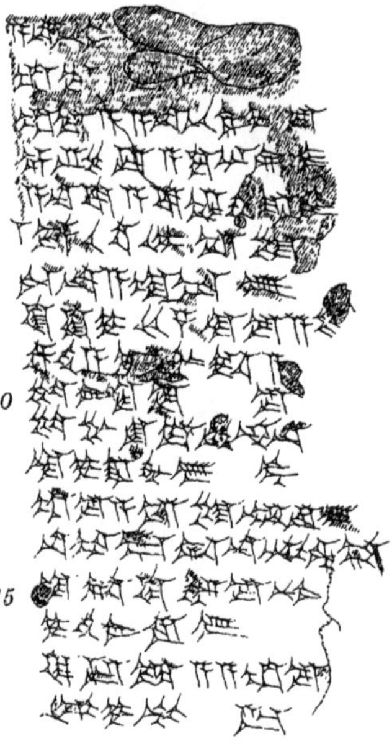

47

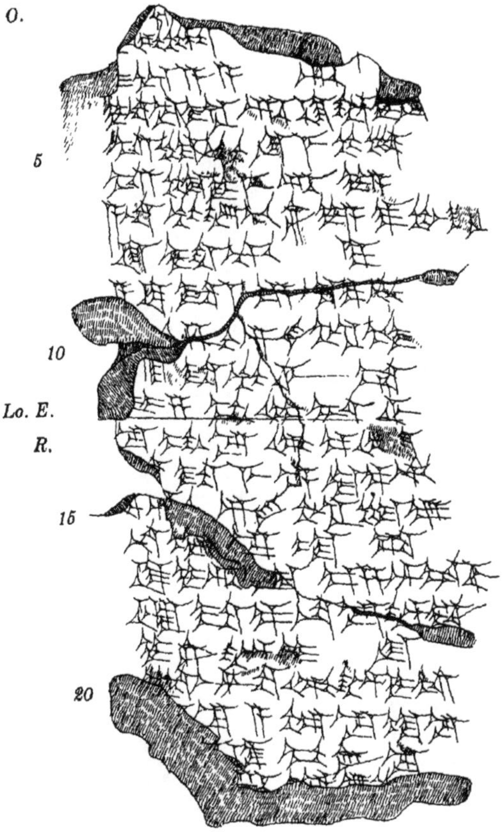

48

O.

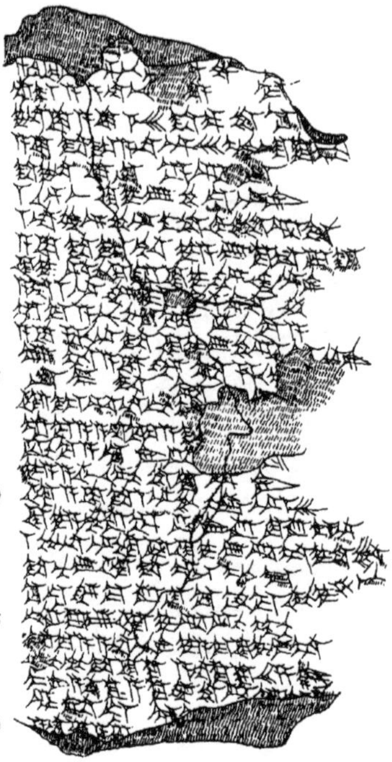

R.

49

Obverse.

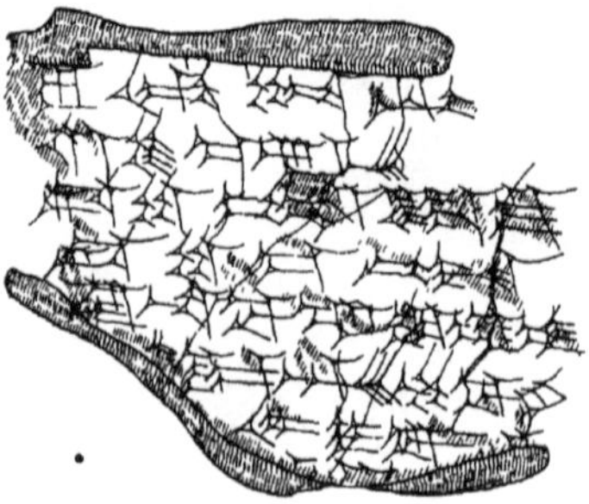

Reverse.

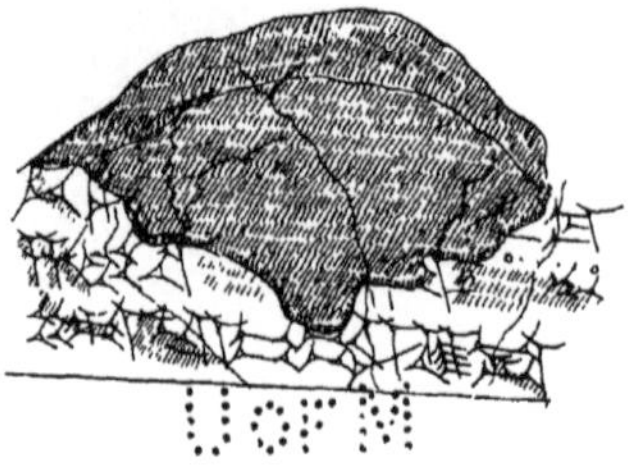

Erasure.

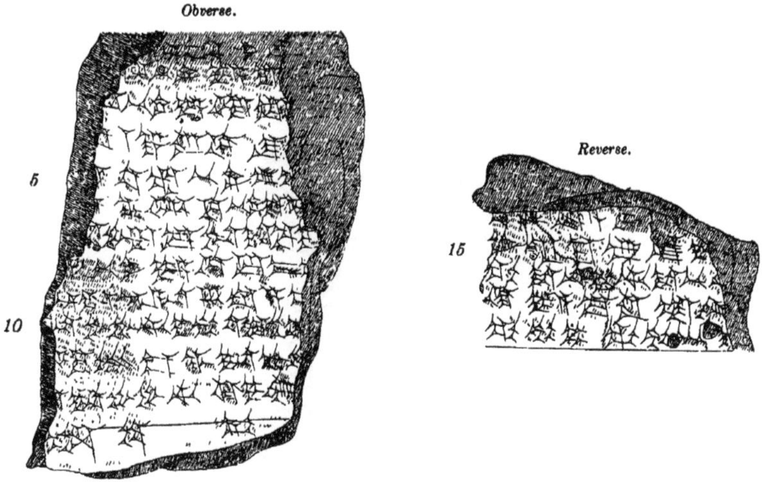

51

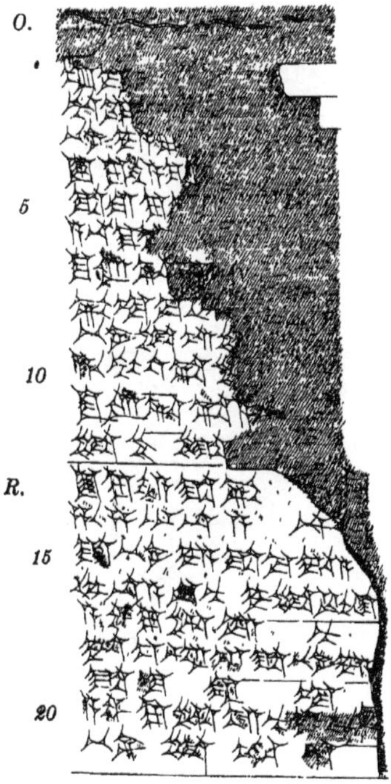

O.

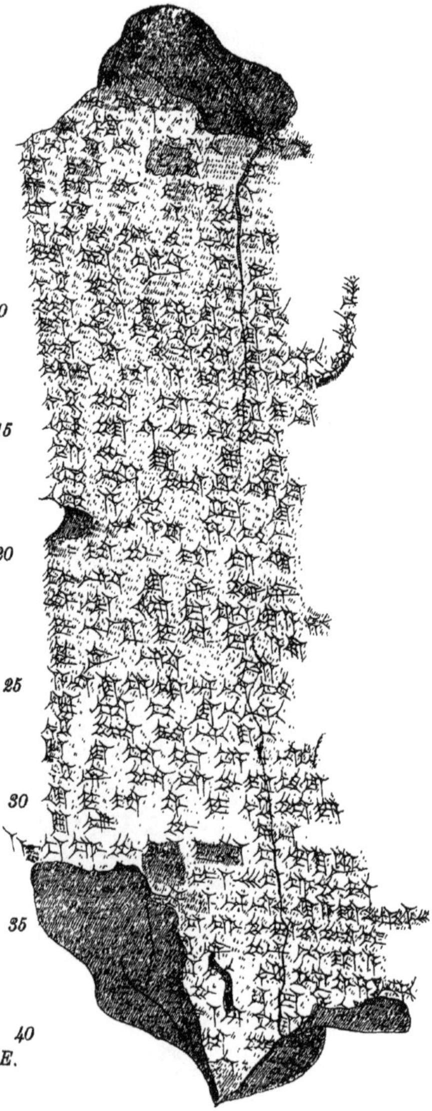

R.

U. E.

Obverse.

Reverse.

54

Obverse.

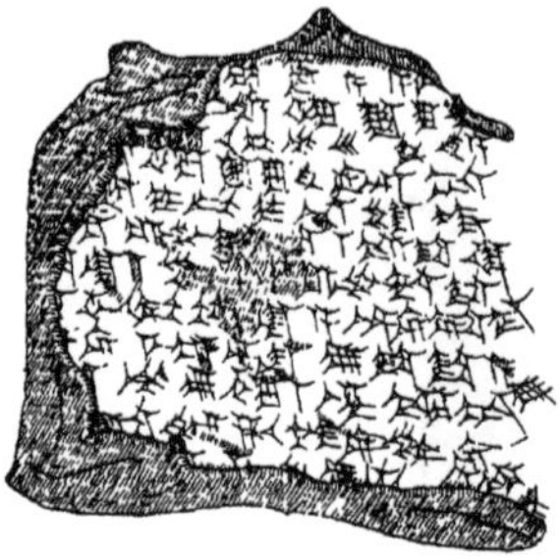

Reverse.

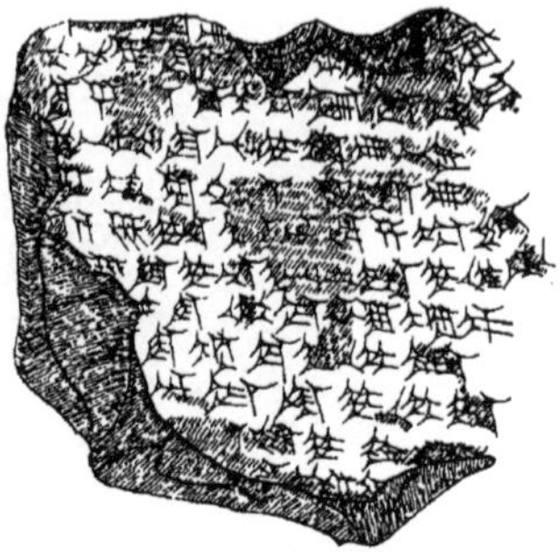

55

O.

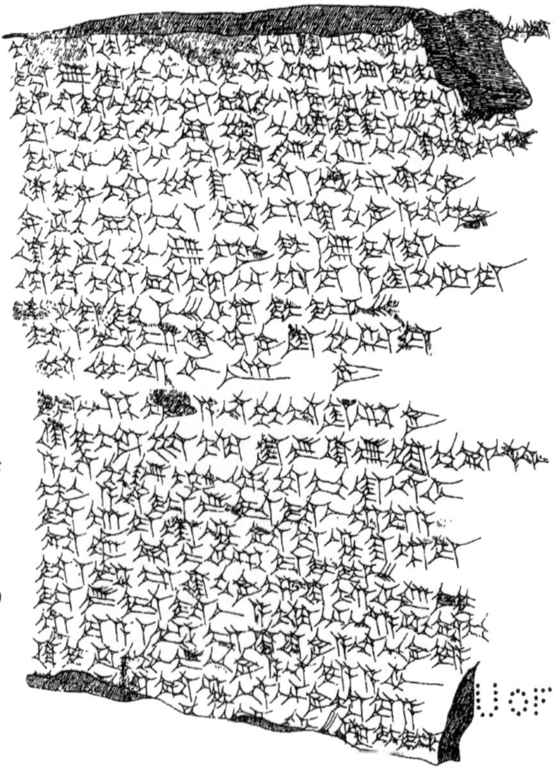

Lo. E.

R.

56

O.

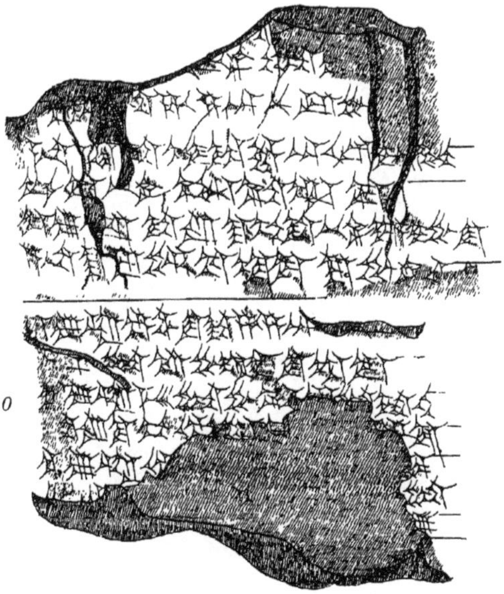

R.

57

Obverse.

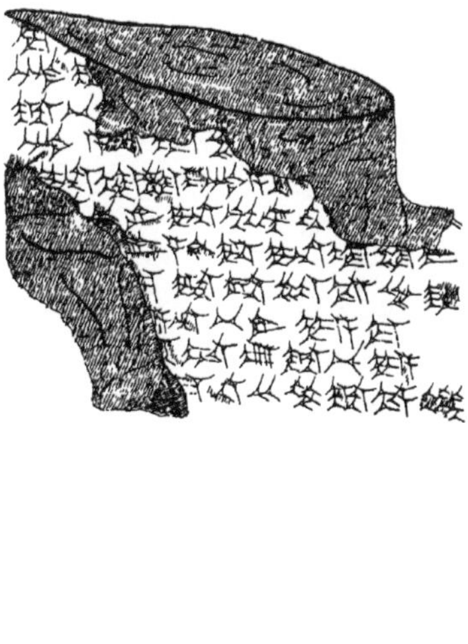

Reverse.

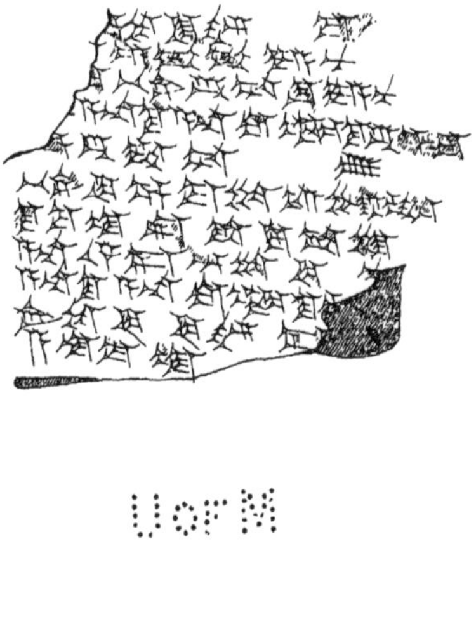

58

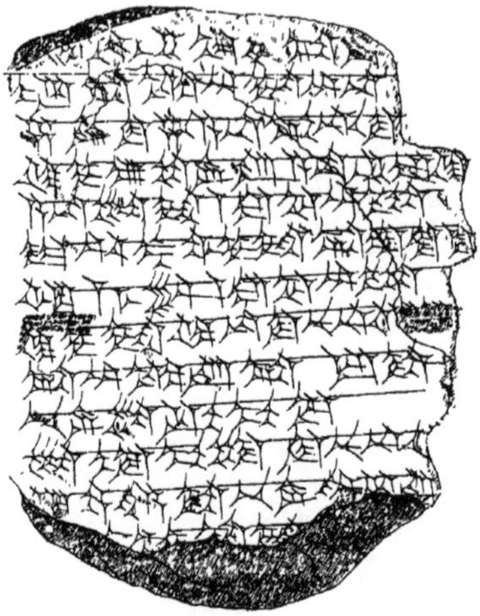

59

Lo. E.

R.

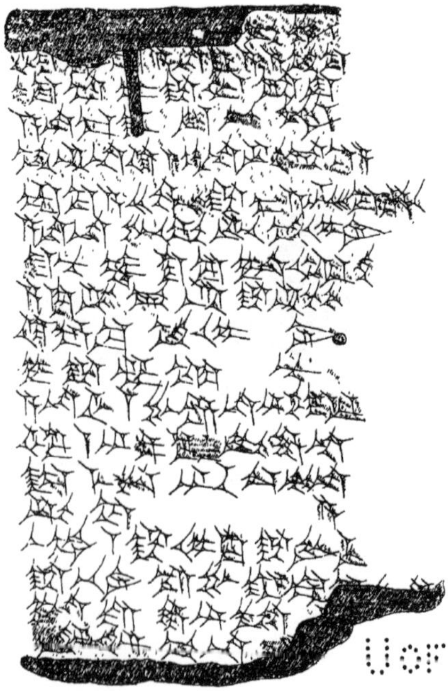

59 a.

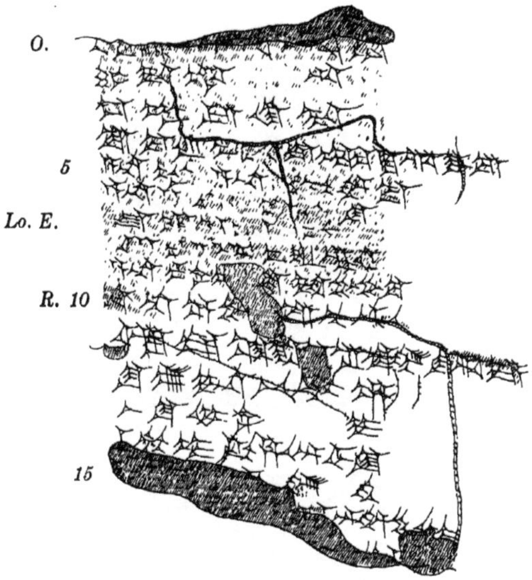

60

Obverse.

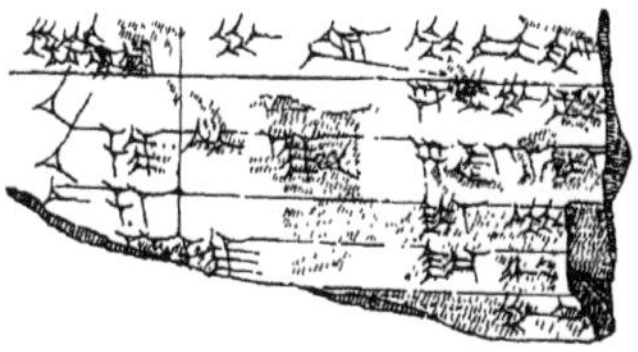

Reverse.

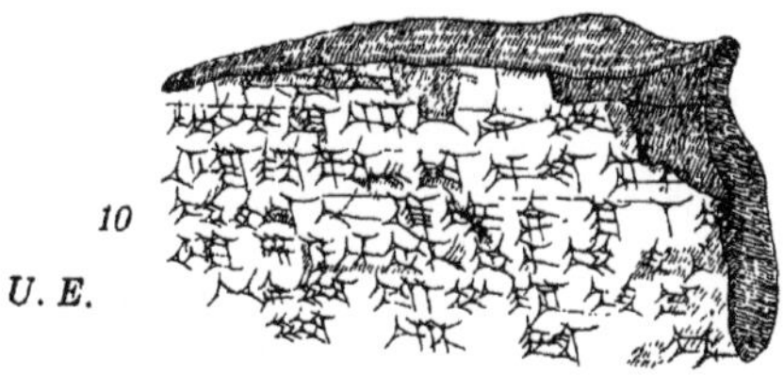

60 a.

Lo. E.

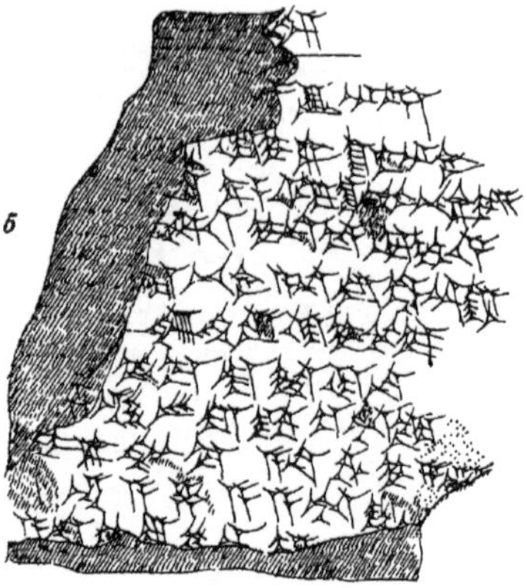

Reverse.

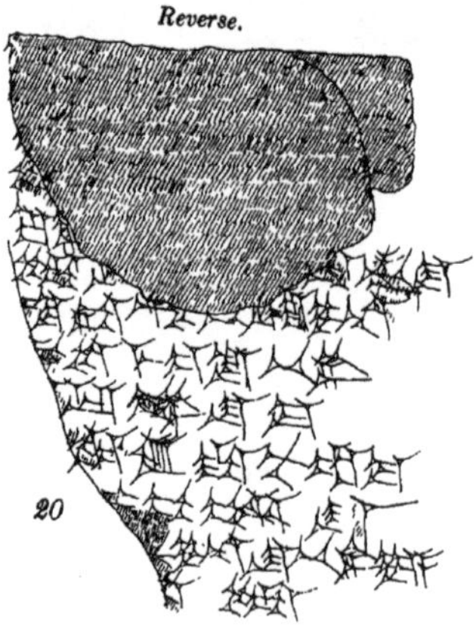

61

Reverse.

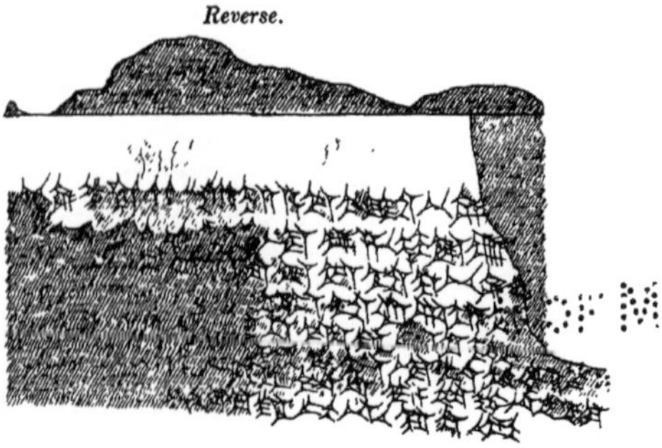

62

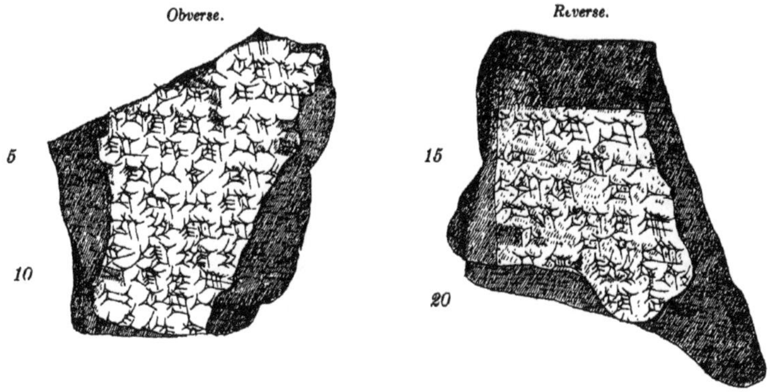

63

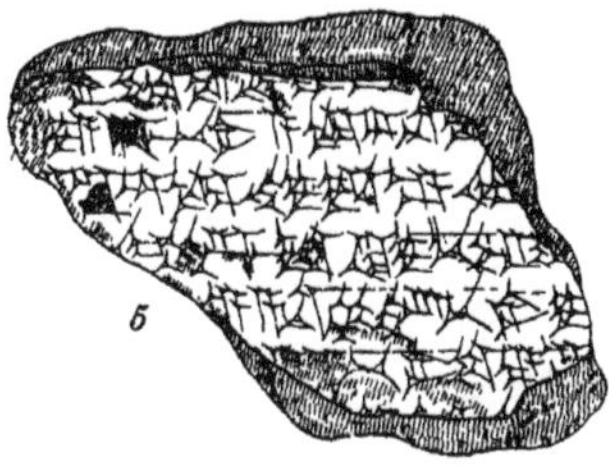

64

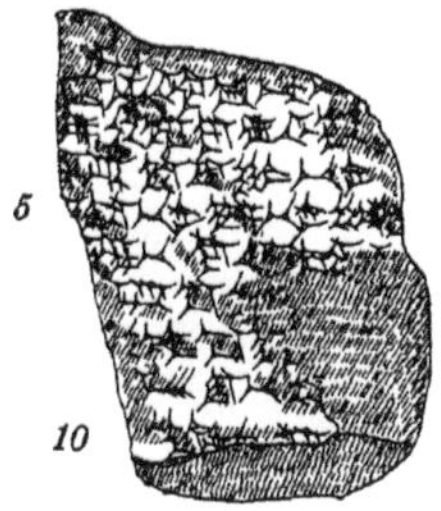

65

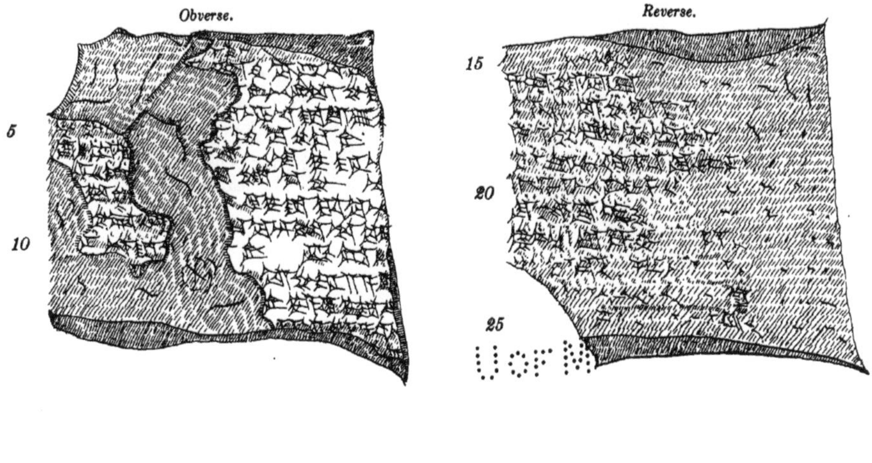

66

Obverse.

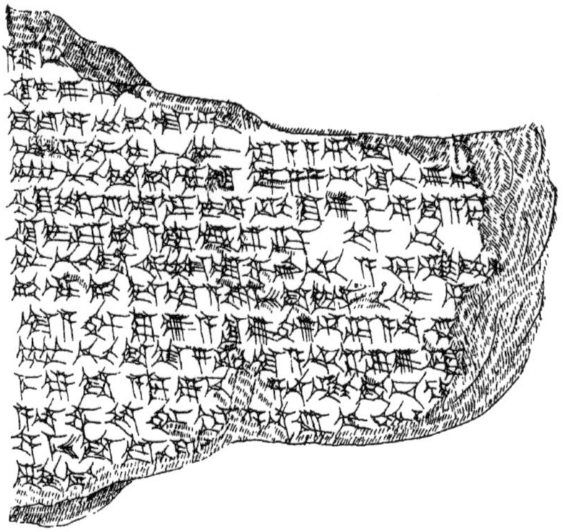

°.. ° Erasure.

Reverse.

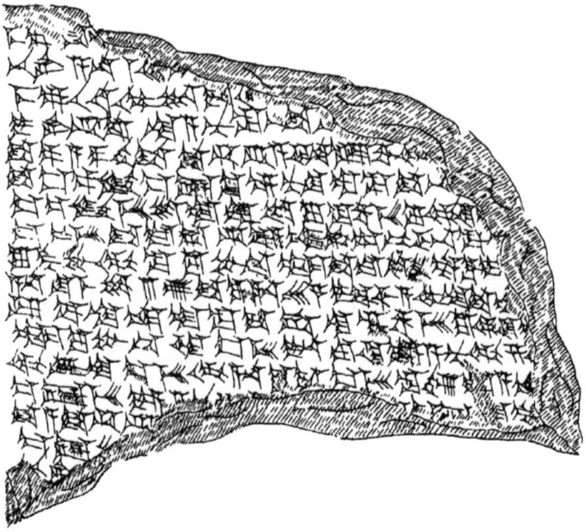

67

Obverse.

Reverse.

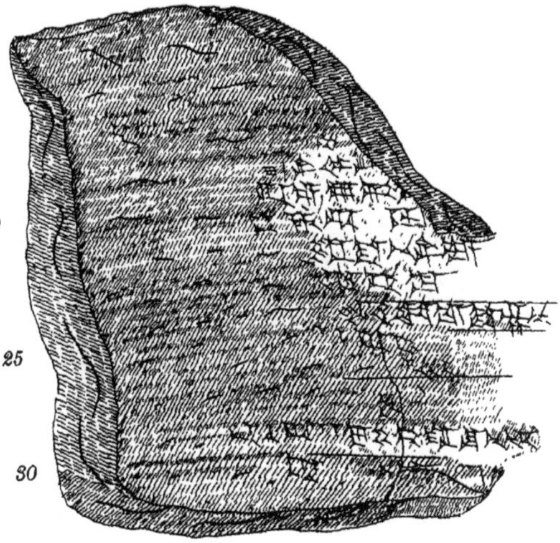

68

Obverse.

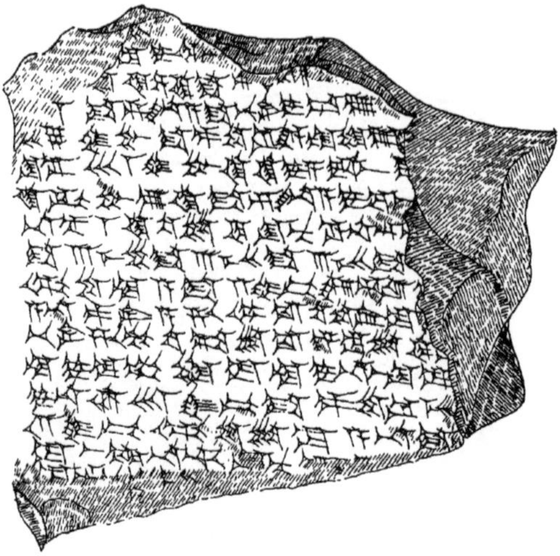

Reverse.

L. E.

69

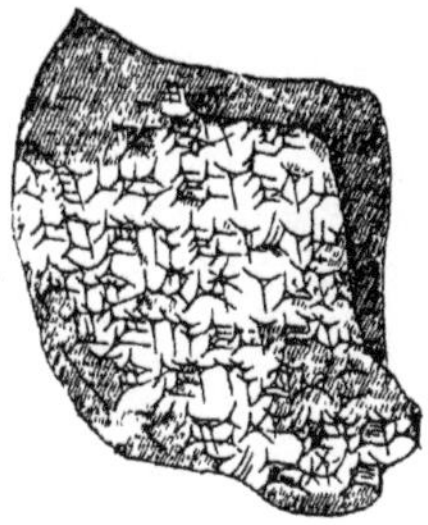

L. E.

70

Obverse.

Reverse.

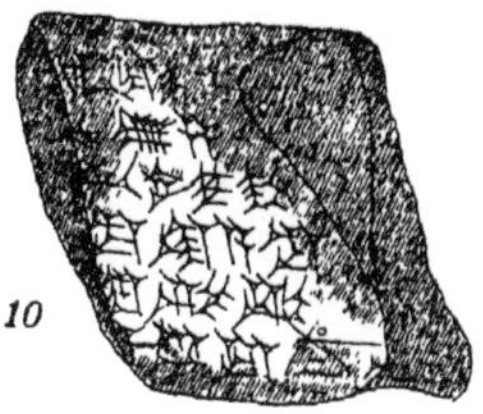

°*Erasure.*

71

Obverse.

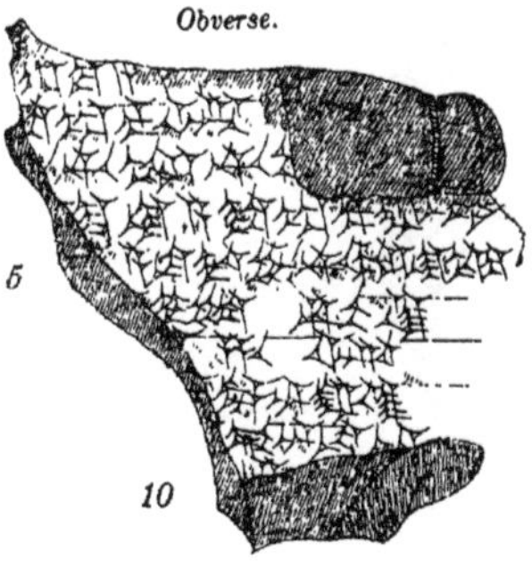

Reverse.

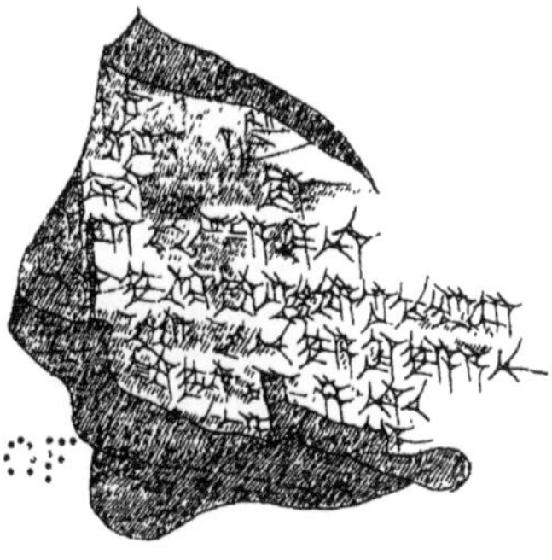

72

73

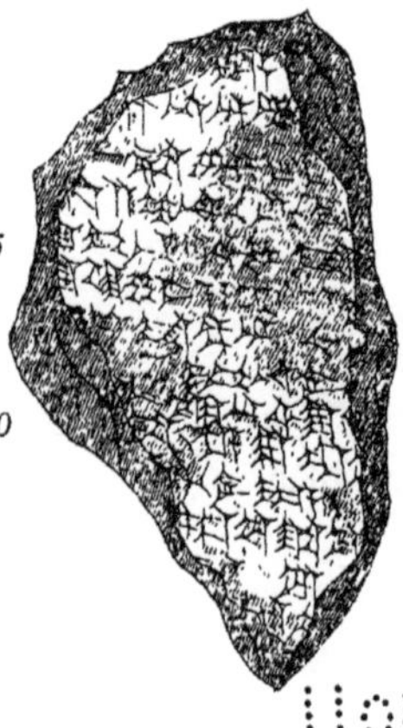

73a.

Obverse.

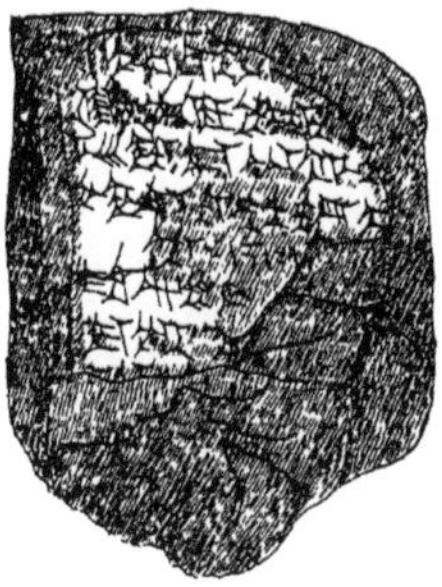

Reverse.

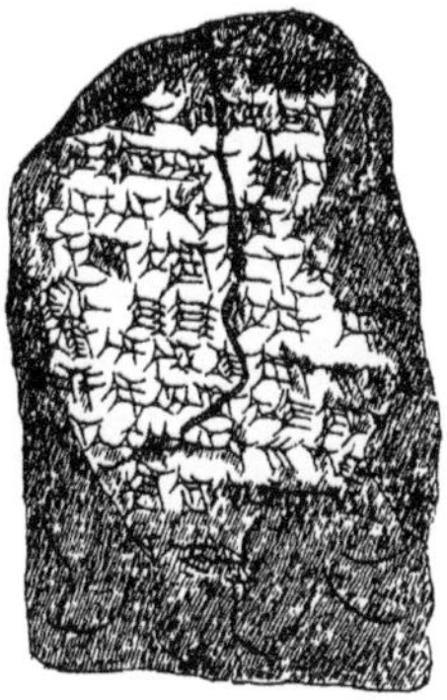

U. E.

74

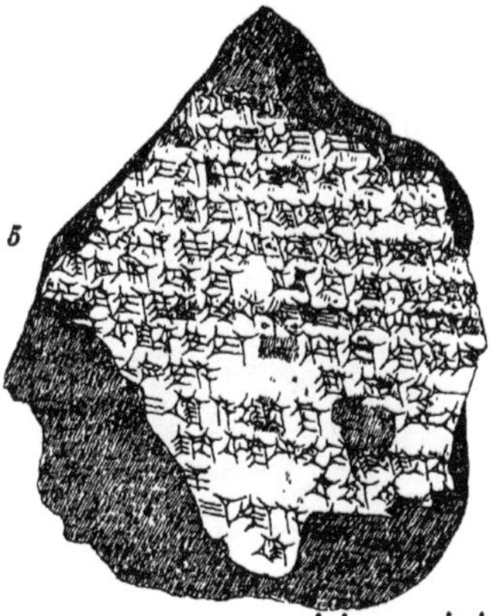

Erasure.

75

Obverse.

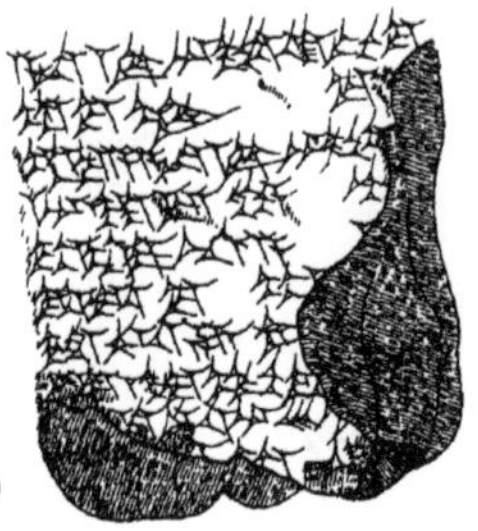

Reverse.

U. E.

76

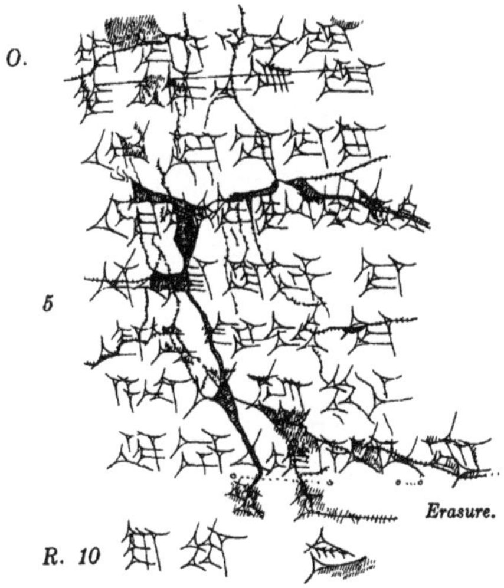

77

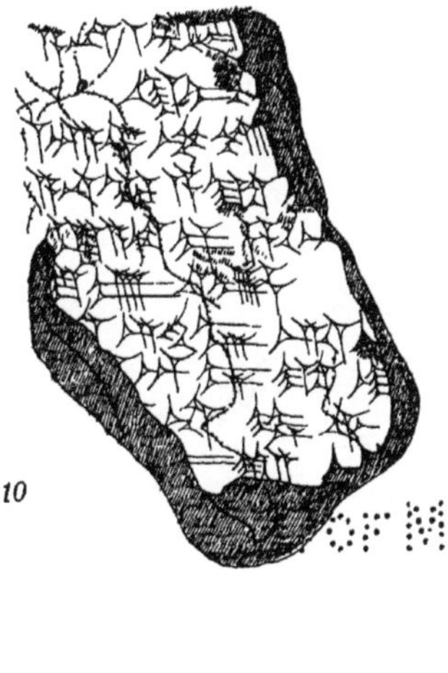

78

Obverse.

Reverse.

79

Obverse.

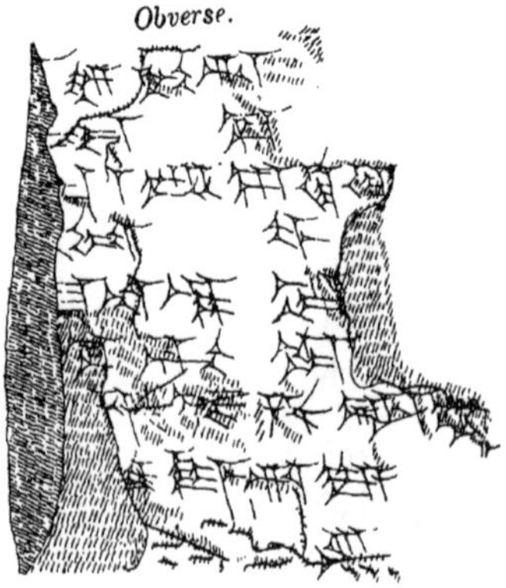

Reverse.

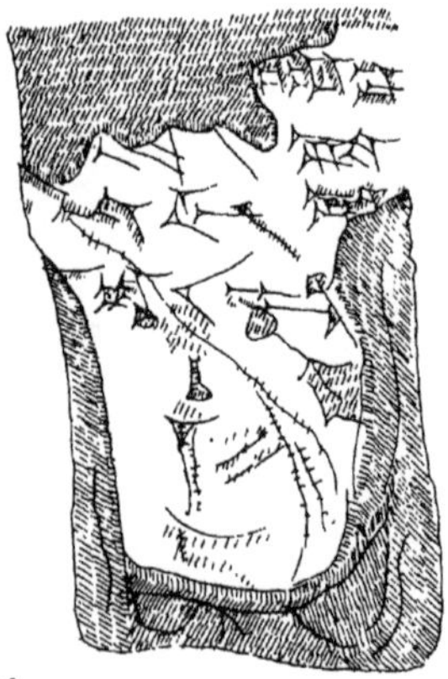

80

Obverse.

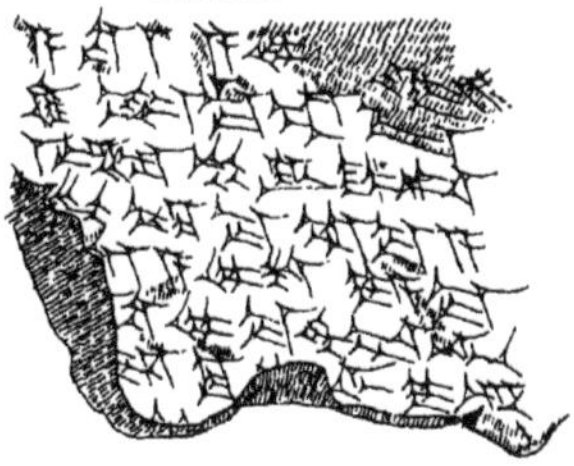

Reverse.

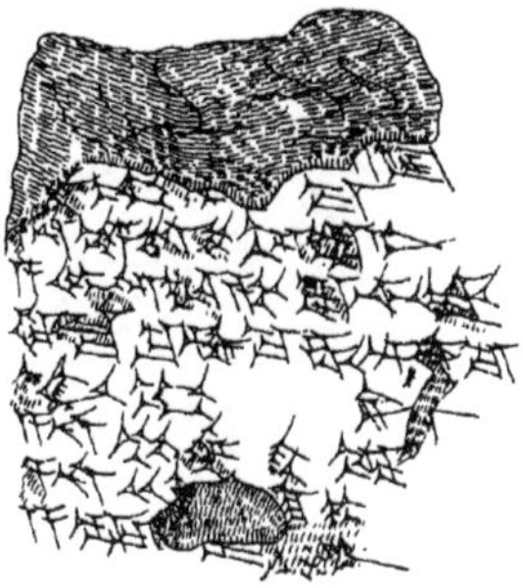

81

Obverse.

Reverse.

82

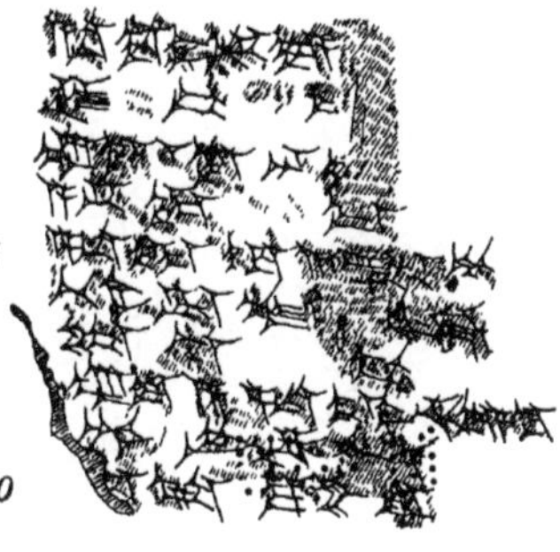

83

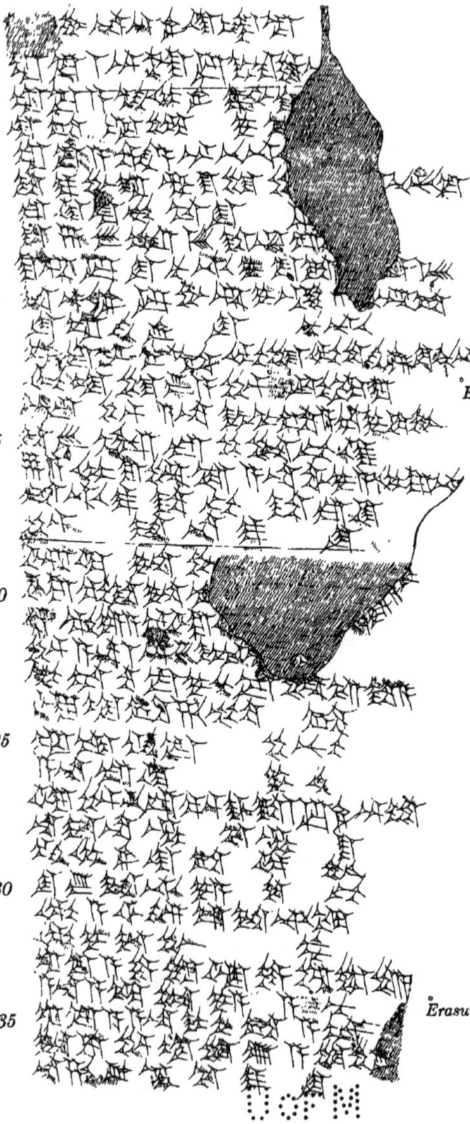

84

O.

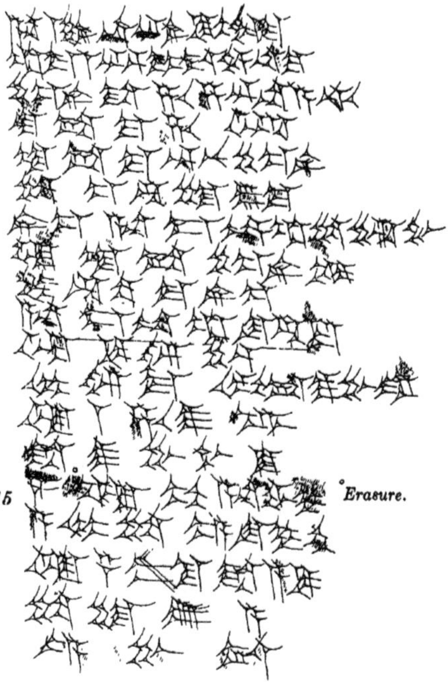

R.

°Erasure.

85

O.

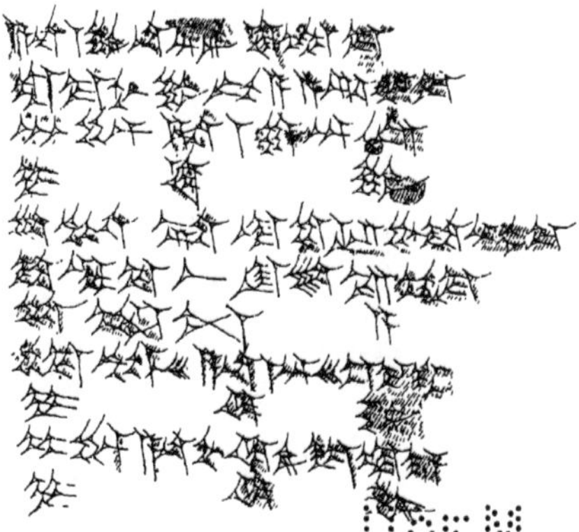

R.

86

Obverse.

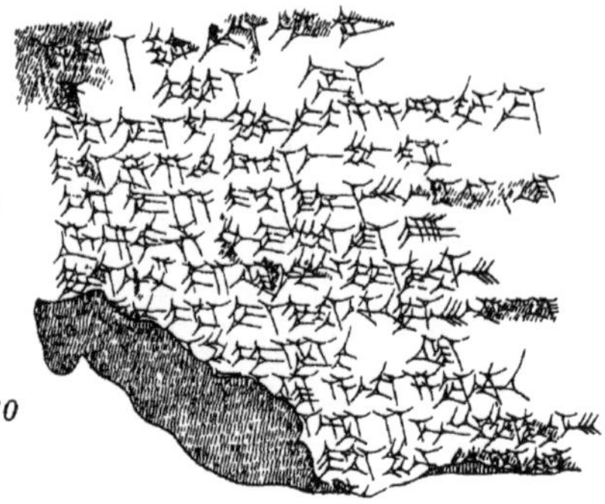

Reverse.

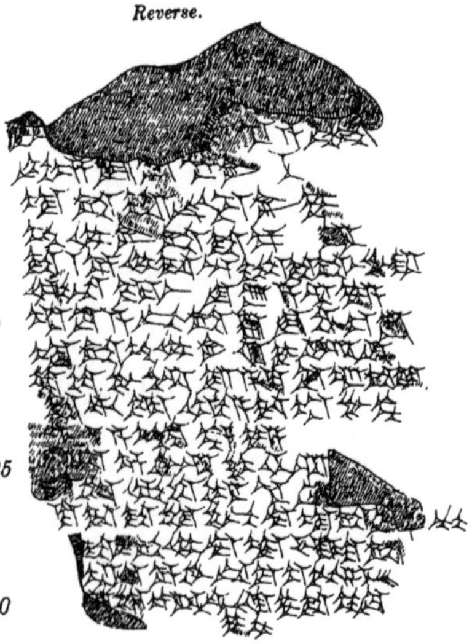

87

Obverse.

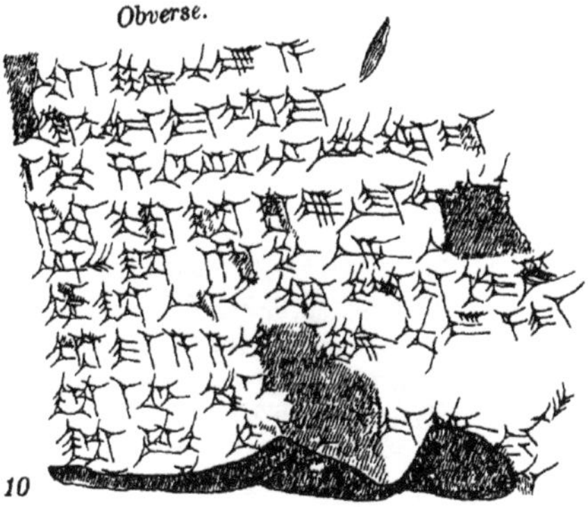

Reverse.

U. E.

L. E.

88

89

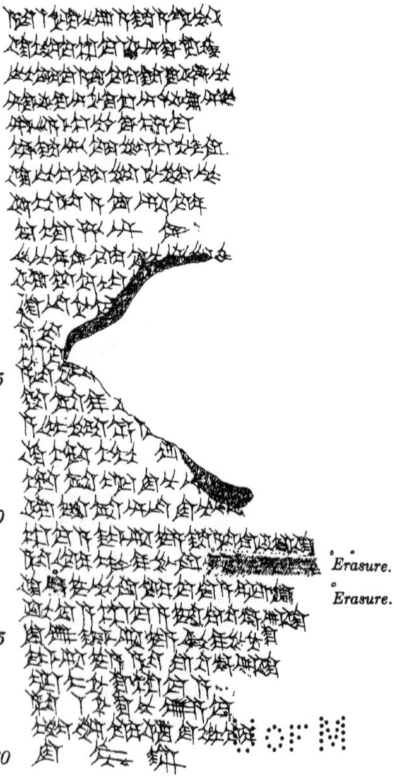

90

Obverse. Reverse.

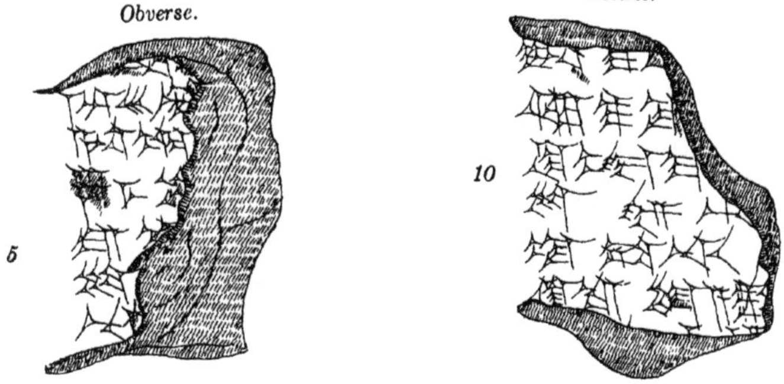

91

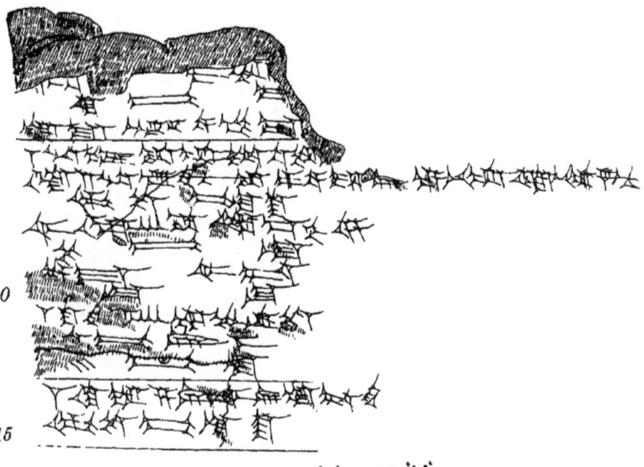

92

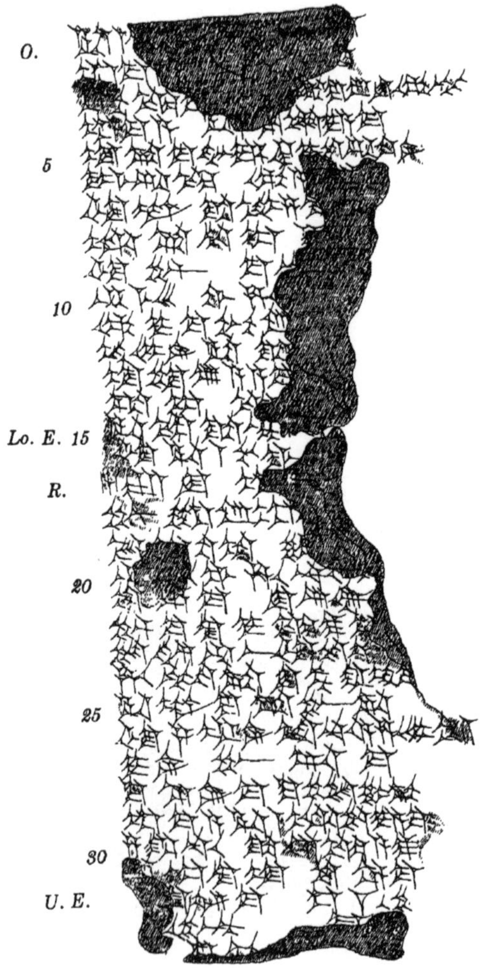

93

94

O.

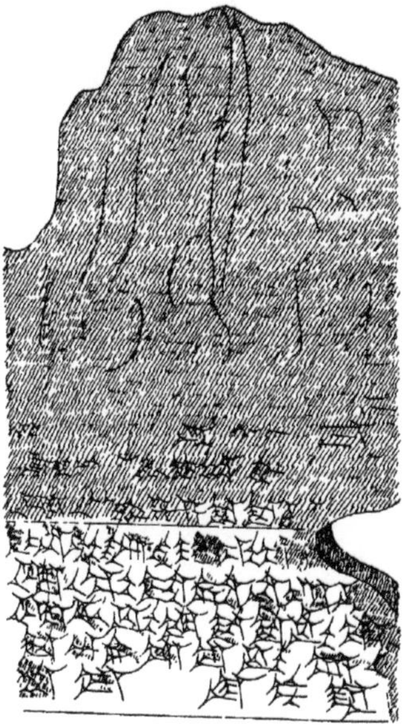

R.

95

O.

R.

L. E.

Obverse.

Reverse.

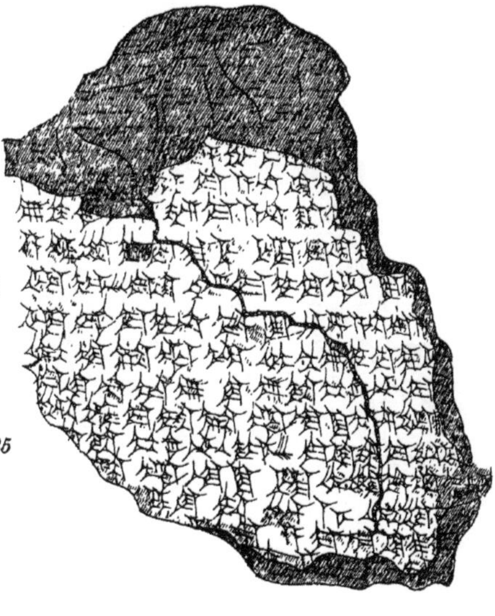

97

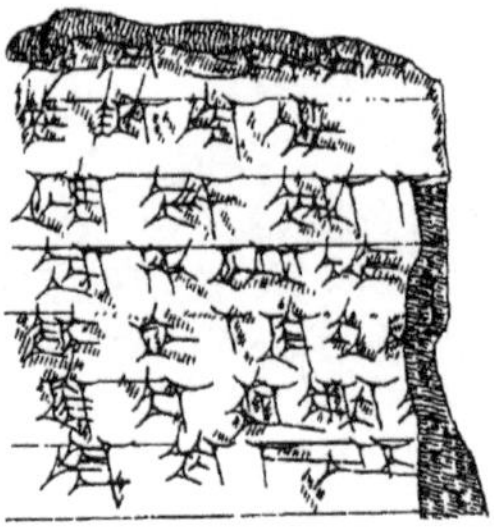

98

99

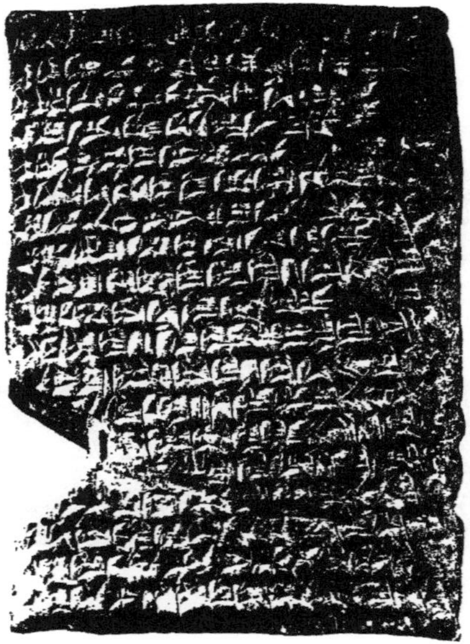

1

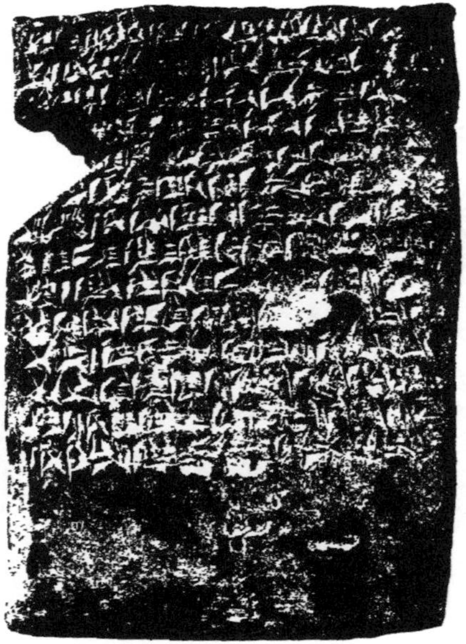

2

OBVERSE AND REVERSE OF No. 24

KALBU REPORTS TO THE KING ABOUT A DISASTROUS FLOOD. ABOUT 1430 B.C

3

4

5

3. ENVELOPE 4. RIGHT EDGE 5. LOWER EDGE OF No. 24

KALBU REPORTS TO THE KING ABOUT A DISASTROUS FLOOD, ABOUT 1430 B.C.

6

7

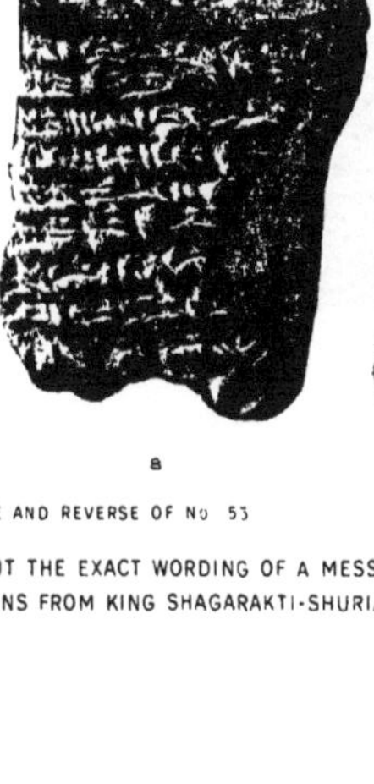

8

9

6 7 OBVERSE AND REVERSE OF No 53

8 9 OBVERSE AND REVERSE OF No 75

6-7 DISPUTE ABOUT THE EXACT WORDING OF A MESSAGE FROM KING BURNA-BURIASH, ABOUT 1440 B C

8-9 ROYAL SUMMONS FROM KING SHAGARAKTI-SHURIASH TO HIS SHERIFF AMEL-MARDUK ABOUT 1325 B C

10

11

OBVERSE AND REVERSE OF No 33A

A GENERAL'S EXPLANATORY LETTER TO THE KING, ABOUT 1400 B.C.

12

13

OBVERSE AND REVERSE OF No. 23

REPORT OF IMGURUM TO KING BURNA-BURIASH ABOUT AFFAIRS IN CONNECTION WITH THE ADMINISTRATION OF HIS OFFICE.
ABOUT 1430 B.C.

14

15

OBVERSE AND REVERSE OF No. 31

A PHYSICIAN'S REPORT TO THE KING ABOUT THE CONDITION OF SICK TEMPLE WOMEN, ABOUT 1430 B.C.

16-17 OBVERSE AND REVERSE OF No 33

18-19 OBVERSE AND REVERSE OF No 38

16-17. A PHYSICIAN'S REPORT TO THE KING ABOUT THE RELAPSE OF A SICK TEMPLE WOMAN. ABOUT 1430 B.C.
18-19. REPORT TO THE KING ABOUT THE RECEIPT OF WOOL AND PROVENDER. ABOUT 1400 B.C.

20

OBVERSE OF No 3

A SHERIFF'S REPORT TO KING SHAGARAKTI-SHURIASH ABOUT THE CONDITION OF CERTAIN CANALS.
ABOUT 1325 B.C.

REVERSE OF No 3

A SHERIFF'S REPORT TO KING SHAGARAKTI-SHURIASH ABOUT THE CONDITION OF CERTAIN CANALS, ABOUT 1325 B.C.

22

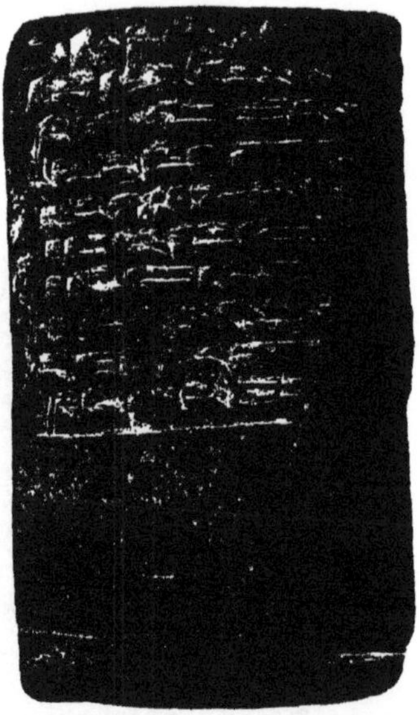

23

24

25

22-23 OBVERSE AND REVERSE OF NO 37

24-25 OBVERSE AND REVERSE OF NO 40

22-23 REPORT TO THE KING ABOUT THE PAYMENT OF GRAIN AND WHEAT. ABOUT 1430 B C

24-25 THE SUPERINTENDENT OF RIVERS AND CANALS COMPLAINS TO KING KUDUR-ENLIL ABOUT THE PREFECT OF DÛR-SUKAL-PATRA. ABOUT 1335 B C

26

27

28

26 REVERSE OF No 52 27 OBVERSE OF No. 22 28 OBVERSE OF No 76

26. REPORT TO THE KING ABOUT THE NON-ARRIVAL OF A CERTAIN SLAVE, ABOUT 1430 B.C.
27. REPORT TO THE KING ABOUT THE ILLNESS OF A WOMAN AND THE MAKING OF BRICKS, ABOUT 1430 B C.
28. A FATHER'S PEREMPTORY ORDER TO HIS SON ABOUT 1400 B C

29

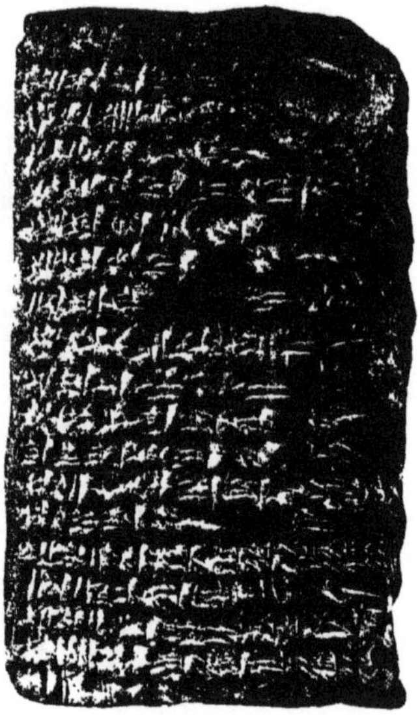

30

31

32

29-30 OBVERSE AND REVERSE OF No 83

31-32 OBVERSE AND REVERSE OF No 8[illegible]

29-32 TWO LETTERS OF COMPLAINTS, REQUESTS, AND THREATS ADDRESSED BY A GOVERNOR TO THE BURSAR-IN-CHIEF, ABOUT 1400 B C

THE BABYLONIAN EXPEDITION

OF

THE UNIVERSITY OF PENNSYLVANIA

EDITED BY

H. V. Hilprecht.

The following volumes have been published or are in press:

Series A, Cuneiform Texts:

Vol. I: Old Babylonian Inscriptions, chiefly from Nippur, by H. V. Hilprecht.
Part 1, 1893, $5.00 (only a few copies left)
Part 2, 1896, $5.00.

Vol. VI: Babylonian Legal and Business Documents from the Time of the First Dynasty of Babylon.
Part 1, chiefly from *Sippar*, by H. Ranke, 1906, $6.00.
Part 2, chiefly from *Nippur*, by Arno Poebel (in press).

Vol. VIII: Legal and Commercial Transactions, dated in the Assyrian, Neo-Babylonian and Persian Periods
Part 1, chiefly from Nippur, by A. T. Clay, 1908, $6.00.

Vol. IX: Business Documents of Murashû Sons of Nippur, dated in the Reign of Artaxerxes I, by H. V. Hilprecht and A. T. Clay, 1898, $6.00.

Vol. X: Business Documents of Murashû Sons of Nippur, dated in the Reign of Darius II, by A. T. Clay, 1904, $6.00.

Vol. XIV: Documents from the Temple Archives of Nippur, dated in the Reigns of Cassite Rulers, with complete dates, by A. T. Clay, 1906, $6.00.

Vol. XV: Documents from the Temple Archives of Nippur, dated in the Reigns of Cassite Rulers, with incomplete dates, by A. T. Clay, 1906, $6.00.

Vol. XVII: Letters to Cassite Kings from the Temple Archives of Nippur.
Part I, by Hugo Radau 1908, $6.00.

Vol. XIX: Model Texts and Exercises from the Temple School of Nippur.
Part I, by H. V. Hilprecht (in press).

Vol. XX: Mathematical, Metrological and Chronological Texts from the Temple Library of Nippur.
Part I, by H. V. Hilprecht, 1906, $5.00.

Series D, Researches and Treatises:

Vol. I: The Excavations in Assyria and Babylonia (with 120 illustrations and 2 maps), by H. V. Hilprecht, 7th edition, 1904, $2.50.

NOTE: Entirely revised German and French editions are in the course of preparation. The first part of the German edition (*bis zum Auftreten De Sarzecs*) appeared in December, 1904 (J. C. Hinrichs, Leipzig; A. J. Holman & Co., Philadelphia, Pa., sole agents for America), Price *4 Mark* in paper covers, *5 Mark* in cloth. The second part is in press.

Vol. III: Early Babylonian Personal Names from the published Tablets of the so-called Hammurabi Dynasty, by H. Ranke, 1905, $2.00.

Vol. IV: A New Boundary Stone of Nebuchadrezzar I from Nippur (with 16 halftone illustrations and 36 drawings), by William J. Hinke, 1907, $3.50.

(OTHER VOLUMES WILL BE ANNOUNCED LATER.)

All orders for these books to be addressed to

THE MUSEUM OF ARCHAEOLOGY,

University of Pennsylvania,

PHILADELPHIA, PA.

SOLE AGENT FOR EUROPE:

Rudolf Merkel, Erlangen, Germany.

THE BABYLONIAN EXPEDITION

OF

THE UNIVERSITY OF PENNSYLVANIA

SERIES A: CUNEIFORM TEXTS

EDITED BY

H. V. HILPRECHT

VOLUME XVII, PART 1

LETTERS TO CASSITE KINGS

FROM THE

TEMPLE ARCHIVES OF NIPPUR

BY

HUGO RADAU

"ECKLEY BRINTON COXE, JUNIOR, FUND"

PHILADELPHIA

Published by the Department of Archaeology, University of Pennsylvania

1908

Lightning Source UK Ltd.
Milton Keynes UK
UKHW020809270219
338009UK00008B/1415/P

9 780260 02655